D1060766

Spirit for Greatness:

Spiritual Dimensions of Organizations and Their Leadership

C. Stephen Byrum, Ph.D.
and
Leland Kaiser, Ph.D.

Tapestry Press, Ltd.
Littleton, Massachusetts 01460

Copyright © 2004 by C. Stephen Byrum and Leland Kaiser.
All rights reserved.

Printed in the United States of America.

ISBN 1-56888-922-4

For Phyllis

With love,
Steve

■ ■ ■

For Betty

With love,
Leland

CONTENTS

FOREWORD

In the early 1990s, Dan Wilford—then the president and CEO of Memorial Hermann Healthcare System in Houston—was flying with his wife, Anne, to yet another leadership development seminar. Dan had always been curious about and energetically involved with a variety of the most well-known leadership programs held throughout the United States. He believed—and was supported in this belief by his board—that continued programs of growth and development for leaders were a source of important new energy for an organization. As he was reviewing the pre-seminar materials for this particular meeting, he commented to his wife that he felt Memorial Hermann could develop its own programs that would be as unique and credible as the program he was attending. Maybe even better.

Dan had become convinced that a number of the programs that had gained significant attention and, in fact, had done a lot of good during the 1970s and 1980s were becoming dated, filled with clichés and buzz words, and not really having the impact he felt was needed. Was there a "next level" of leadership development that could build on the successes of the programs that had come about in the second half of the twentieth century? Was there a "new model" that could renew enthusiasm about leadership and bring new meaning to people in leadership positions? Anne agreed with him and encouraged his questions.

It was not long until Dan's ever-curious mind and strong intent were beginning to formulate the concept of "Spiritual Leadership." Although he was a very committed person in terms of his own church and religious experiences, he was not interested in creating a program that was *religious* in nature. Such an approach had too many limitations, and could even divide people along religious lines. He was interested in the *spiritual*, and he believed that he was considering something much deeper than religion, something that might move to the special "core" of human life where human beings held much more in common than all that might separate them. He believed deeply in the "spirit" of organizations, the "spirit" of teams, and the "spirit" of unique individuals. It was this reality that he wanted to explore and better understand. It was his conviction that once this reality was better understood that it could be incorporated into organizational leadership and personal development in ways that could be transforming in their impact.

In 1996, Dan called together a group of trusted friends and organizational consultants that had worked with his organizations over the years. This group included: Leland Kaiser, Steve Byrum, Michael Annison, John Maurer, Gus Blackshear, Doug Hodo, and Martin Nicholas. The representation of this group involved a prominent healthcare futurist, organizational consultants, the managing partner of a major Houston law firm, a university president, and a minister. As the concept was discussed, the group had an enthusiastic response.

At subsequent meetings of this steering group, the seed idea of a "Spiritual Leadership Institute" was beginning to grow. Plans for an initial curriculum were constructed and Memorial Hermann, along with invited leaders in healthcare from other parts of the country, committed its executive leadership to be the inaugural group to go through the program.

The first official meetings of the Institute began in 1997 and became the occasion for both highly enthusiastic responses from participants and initial revisions and refinements. Word of mouth brought an immediate waiting list situation, and several other Institute programs were started immediately. Soon, the entire leadership of the Memorial Hermann system had been exposed to the Institute programming and were intent on their managers and supervisors having the same experience. Evaluations were more positive than could ever have been dreamed.

Activities of the Institute continued across the next few years, typically engaging four groups of management staff per year. These meetings were spread out over several months, giving participants the opportunity for directed reading and project work between sessions. Programming has continued to be expanded and now reaches all levels of organizations and not simply management and executive leadership. While the Institute was born in a healthcare setting, it is finding application in every sort of organizational setting.

The material found in this book is an interesting compilation that rises from several sources. There are examples of readings that have been used with participants from the very onset of Institute activities. These have "stood the test of time," and have seemed to be particularly valuable to those who have been involved in Institute sessions. Other material is brand new and will even give alumni of the Institute new ideas to extend their learning.

The outline of this volume is fairly simple. The major sections are written by Steve Byrum. The "Interludes" are the unmistakable work of Leland Kaiser. The material is placed in a format that follows the Institute's emphasis on the major focal points of Vision, Ethics, Trust, and Spirituality. These focal points were established by the executive leadership of Memorial Hermann Healthcare System as *the* major guiding values of their organization. While they are critical to Memorial Hermann, they are applicable to any organization.

As Jim Collins expresses in his powerful book, *Good to Great*, it is not easy to help an already good organization become a great organization. In a similar sense, it is not always easy to help strong people become even stronger. The Spiritual Leadership Institute wants to help fulfill both of these ambitions. The Institute has always been about leadership, and it is also about individual growth and development. The Institute wants to operate out of the context of what it understands as the "core spiritual impulse." This impulse and catalyst, simply stated, is the intent and desire—made manifest in real actions—*to make better*. We hope that this volume, in its many organizational and individual applications, will contribute to that outcome.

In constructing this foreword, we want to express a broad range of appreciation to all of those within Memorial Hermann Healthcare System who have helped create, clarify, and sustain the vision of the Institute. Without the formative inspiration of Dan Wilford, the Institute would not have become a reality. Without the continued vision, support, and direction of his successor, Dan Wolterman, the potential of the Institute could not be realized. The wonderful faculty who have given so generously of their time and talent have been the underlying substance of the Institute for almost a decade. The board of the Institute continues to grow in its contribution and influence. For all of these individuals and the now thousands of participants, we express our deepest gratitude. May you be blessed in your lives. Your lives have certainly blessed—and continue to bless—others.

C. Stephen Byrum, Ph.D., SLI Dean
Leland R. Kaiser, Ph.D.
Houston, Texas
Fall, 2004

SECTION ONE:
ETHICS

1. ETHICS: A BASIC INTRODUCTION

WHAT IS ETHICS?

In the late 1960s and early 1970s, the Public Broadcasting System made its debut on the American airways. Its initial programming was new and innovative, winning awards and accolades from both audiences and critics around the world. One of PBS's early creations was a series entitled "The Great American Dream Machine." By more modern standards, this series had an MTV air about it. It was modern in every way, with bright colors, new music, and the latest, most contemporary themes. Seldom did young college students at that time miss "Dream Machine;" it was as popular in its time as "Saturday Night Live" is today.

Like most of the mass media in the late 1960s and early 1970s, "Dream Machine" spent a great deal of time exploring the idea of love. The whole mentality of that period of American history was epitomized by the Dionne Warwick lyrics: "What the world needs now is love sweet love; it's the only thing that there's just too little of." The Beatles said it best: "All you need is love . . . love . . . love is all you need."

"Dream Machine," in one of its most famous programs approached the theme of love in a cartoon format. In the first frame, accompanied by a background of dark colors and solemn music, there is a question mark figure with downcast eyes wandering in a desert. This question mark "man" symbolized a lot of people of that period who were wandering around, not being very successful in finding answers to the questions of their lives. The world, like the question mark man's desert, held few guide posts or directional signs.

In the next frame, the question mark man approaches a box that has the word "soap" written on the side of it, representing the proverbial soapbox of politicians. Another figure is standing on the box shouting at the top of his voice. The question mark man listens. Perhaps there is some answer here. Then, there appears above the politician's head flags which represent the various political ideologies found in the world today: the Stars and Stripes of the United States, the Union Jack of England, the Hammer and Sickle of the Soviet Union, and flags of Israel, Japan, France, and China. After a while, the question mark man bows his head a little lower and walks away. Nothing in the political statements he has been offered brings meaning, satisfaction, or happiness to his life. He is back to the desert to wander some more.

There then follows a next frame in which a character on a different kind of platform is speaking. From this character's dress and the shape of his platform, it is clear that the question mark man is approaching the pulpit of a religious speaker. This time, as the religious speaker shouts his ideas, the different symbols of the great religions of the world appear in the cartoon: the crucifix of Christianity, the Star of David of Judaism, the lotus flower of Buddhism, and the Yin-Yang symbol of Confucianism. After listening closely, the background music becoming more downbeat, and the question mark man heads back to search in the desert. Nothing of the religious statements has moved his life in the direction of greater happiness.

The situation of the question mark man seems totally desolate. Then, in the next frame, another question mark figure can be seen in the back corner of the desert; another searcher is out looking for happiness and meaning. The two figures begin to move toward each other. There is a moment of recognition; the music goes upbeat, and the two question marks converge. They make a large, red heart—a universal symbol of love. The heart pulsates with eager happiness. The scene fades. The question mark characters undoubtedly live happily ever after.

In some respects, life tried to be this simple in the heart of the "hippie movement," during the "Age of Aquarius." Love was the theme. If a person could find love, and if people could simply love everyone else, life would be totally wonderful.

Often, when people try to define ethics, they do so by talking about love. To be ethical means to love. If we are ethical people, we simply love others. Love should be extended to business, economics, industry, and politics.

These nice-sounding platitudes are basically "warm and cuddly." They sound good and are easy enough to affirm. Who wouldn't believe in love? Love is almost like hotdogs, apple pie, the flag, and motherhood. Who wouldn't be for love?

It takes very little genius, however, to realize that real life does not operate in terms of platitudes. It is one thing to talk about love and know all the nostalgic songs about love; it is quite another to really think that it is the motivating force at the core of much of life as it is presently lived. In fact, maybe it is too easy to say all the right things, sing all the right things, and then somehow take for granted that all that is being talked and sung about will just magically happen. Real life simply doesn't work this way. Love is a wonderful ideal, and the world needs wonderful ideals, but ethics is not pulsating valentines—ethics is not love.

The writings of an American thinker named Reinhold Niebuhr gained a great deal of attention in the decades since World War II. Niebuhr believed that there was a lot of sincere talking about love, but little careful thinking about the phenomenon. In Niebuhr's thinking, love was possible but only between individuals in carefully defined situations. A husband might be able to legitimately love his wife, a daughter her mother, or parents their children, but to talk about love in groups for Niebuhr was highly unlikely.

He might entertain the notion that a teacher could really love her students or a doctor her patients, but such circumstances were highly random and unusual. In general, the social dynamics of a teacher/student or doctor/patient relationship was not the stuff of love. It would be difficult to expect the person who waits on you in a restaurant or does a brake job on your car to relate to you on the basis of love. It would be equally difficult to imagine that union and company management representatives would negotiate a labor contract on the basis of love. It may sound good to idealize that such an event would be possible, but the likelihood of love in labor contract negotiations seems a little far-fetched.

So, Niebuhr believes that the primary focus of ethics should be justice. In fact, as far as he is concerned, it is impossible—even in the closest human relationships—for love to occur unless it has been preceded by justice. In other words, a husband cannot say that he loves his wife unless he has been just with his wife. In like manner, parents cannot say that they love their children unless they first are just with their children.

But, what would it mean to be "just" with a wife or "just" with children? By extension, what would it mean to be "just" with an employee, an employer, or a co-worker? Obviously, in every situation, "justice" would probably mean something different. To be ethical might mean not to come to some agreed-upon definition of justice but to take the time to wander about—to think about or struggle with—what being just with another person in a particular situation might mean. In most instances, people would not expect love from others, but it might not be too much to expect—even to demand—justice. It may even be possible for a group of people—industrial producers, healthcare specialists, or engineers—to establish a dialogue which might lead to statements about what would constitute just behavior in various aspects of their professions.

Another thinker, Bernard Kucheman, believes that Niebuhr's idea is an improvement but that the concept of "justice" can easily become a vague platitude as well. Kucheman wants to talk about a "generalization principle" or "principle of fairness." Following Niebuhr's lead, Kucheman believes that it is impossible to elevate the discussion of human interaction to the place of justice unless first there has been a basic and simple discussion of what constitutes fairness in a particular situation.

Kucheman then outlines very specifically exactly what would constitute "fairness." There are two basic guidelines:

(1) If something is right for one person, it must be right for all relatively similar persons in all relatively similar situations.
(2) Are we willing to have others apply to us the rules which we wish to apply to them?

The first fairness principle has to do with equal access. This principle relates to all kinds of questions of separation and discrimination. There can be no ethics if decisions are made on the basis of "external accidents" like the color of a person's skin or a person's gender. To follow the idea of equal access, there is the assumption on a basic, human level that all people are equal. Many, many questions in business and professional arenas are equal access questions.

The second fairness principle takes on the form of the "Golden Rule," an ethical principle that appears in one format or another in almost every culture. Its universal appeal does not diminish its accuracy. If, in fact, people did to others what they desired to be done to them, the world would be radically transformed. What Kucheman adds is the emphasis on making rules that apply to others that you would not want applied to you. Since rules of one sort or another are regularly made in all sorts of pragmatic life situations, Kucheman's refinement of the "Golden Rule" could have wide application.

In any case, Kucheman is not afraid to use the word "wrong." Something is "wrong" if there is some action or treatment that selectively relates to different people in different ways. By these standards, for example, it would be unethical for a rich person's son to be moved ahead of a poor person's son on a waiting list for organ transplants simply because the rich person has more "connections."

Something is "wrong" if norms are applied by a person that would not be acceptable to that person if they were applied to him. Would it be "fair" for a job foreman to arbitrarily expose workers under his control to highly dangerous working conditions that he is unwilling to expose himself—or some of his favorites—to?

Tom Chamberlain, the editor of the outdoor section of *The Chattanooga Times*, describes how a person should embark upon an outing in the woods, especially that person who has been to the woods time and time again but has not found or seen anything of interest:

> Inside, you should wait a moment to let your eyes adjust to the lesser light. It is not hard to see in the forest, but it is important to change your perspective. Life exists up close. If you are wandering with a purpose, then you may miss a lot while looking for specifics. The best times in the woods are aimless, when surprises can be paused for. Seldom will the forest fail to put on a show for those who learn to watch, and especially for those who learn to listen.

> Even when you walk, you must move in a series of pauses. At each hesitation, look around and soak up the distinctive landmarks of that particular spot. Look for signs of the things that have occurred in this place.

> Remember that the normal inhabitants of this area move in stops and starts. Follow their example. A whitetail can walk right past you in the woods and never be noticed. Move slowly and quietly. There is a lot to see in the forest. You will get more out of it than you put in, a lot.

Notice Chamberlain's emphasis—pauses, hesitations, stops and starts—on moving slowly. Clearly, he places an emphasis on the important, decisive reality of time that is taken for CONSIDERATION. The word "consideration" is an interesting word in and of itself. Its ancient root is "sider," which means "star," and refers to the ancient astronomers and astrologers who patiently and painstakingly studied that star for clues about the mysteries of the universe. Thus, "con-sider-ation" means "with the wisdom that comes only from time and contemplation."

In the end, to be ethical may simply mean to take time to give consideration—to take time to carefully and painstakingly weigh and evaluate how one should act in a given situation. Maybe the most valuable possession that anyone has is time; and, to give time may be the most significant concession, attention, or even gift that one person can give another.

Niebuhr is right: love is too much to expect in most of the normal social dynamics that surround human life, especially in group situations that relate to business and work. It may also be impossible to define either justice or fairness in ways that will fit every situation or in ways that everyone will agree on. However, it may be possible to be the kind of person who will stop and pause to give consideration to the dynamics that surround a particular situation. It may be possible to give time to struggle with issues of justice and fairness. The person who does this, at least, has taken a first step on the way to being an ethical person.

ETHICS AS "DEPUTYSHIP"

Dietrich Bonhoeffer came of age in the early part of the twentieth century in Germany at about the same time that Adolph Hitler came of age. While Hitler was becoming a political power in Western Europe, Bonhoeffer was becoming a well-known minister, teacher, and theologian. It would be hard to imagine two people who could be any more on opposite ends of the spectrum. Bonhoeffer vehemently opposed everything that Adolph Hitler stood for.

In the late 1930s, Bonhoeffer began to speak out against Hitler's abuse of power. This caused him some degree of professional harassment, as the Nazis were able to control both university and church appointments. Bonhoeffer was undeterred in his opposition. Several of his friends in the United States believed that he was placing his life in danger and made arrangements for Bonhoeffer to come to a teaching position where he could be safe and comfortable. He refused, believing that his obligation was to his own country and his own people.

There ultimately came a time when Hitler's horror was so great that a group of citizens and army officers created an assassination plot. Bonhoeffer participated in this action, but the plot failed, and Hitler was even more filled with hate and vengeance for the highly-honored teacher. A death sentence was placed on Bonhoeffer, and he was eventually captured and put in prison.

He was such a good man that even his captors could not bring themselves to carry out the death sentence. Defying Hitler, one prison warden and then another would simply "lose" Bonhoeffer and pass him off to some other prison. Only in the last moments of the war did a sweep by the Nazi secret police find Dietrich Bonhoeffer and put him to death. He is now looked upon as one of the most stalwart examples of ethics in the history of human existence.

1. Ethics: A Basic Introduction

While he was in prison, Bonhoeffer was able to write, and his prison writings have become classics of ethical theory. Here was a man who laid his life on the line for what he thought was good and right, even though he knew that he was probably about to die. His ideas about ethics are simple, direct, and compelling in ways still powerful in modern times. His central ethical concept is known as "Deputyship."

What exactly is a deputy? Maybe a common example of a deputy would help. Most people think of "Deputy Dog," a cartoon character famous in the early 1980s. Some are old enough to recall the television western "Gunsmoke" and the deputies Festus Hagen and Chester. Another example that almost everyone knows is the character "Barney Fife" of the "Andy Griffith Show."

Imagine that word reaches Sheriff Andy Taylor that there is trouble somewhere on the back edge of his jurisdiction. He is preparing to go and deal with the situation when Aunt Bea comes running into his office to explain that Opie is again in some kind of trouble at school. Andy must take care of Opie's situation, so he sends Barney to take care of the "official business" that has occurred.

When Barney Fife arrives at the trouble spot and begins to deal with the situation, is he acting only as Barney Fife? The answer is, of course, no. Barney is acting as Barney Fife, but he is also acting ON BEHALF of Andy Taylor. This is the definition of a "deputy;" someone who acts ON BEHALF of someone else.

With this definition in mind, Bonhoeffer believed that our lives are caught up in a network of deputyship relationships. Whether we like it or not, want to deny it or not, our lives are interrelated. No one lives in a vacuum. Martin Luther King, Jr. referred to this phenomenon as the "network of humanity." Life is like a spider's web and is, perhaps, even as fragile as a spider's web. If any part of the web is hurt, the effectiveness and beauty of the entire web is diminished.

Some deputyship relationships are altogether obvious. A parent acts on behalf of a child. An elected official supposedly is deputized by an electorate to act on its behalf. In fact, a person who is driving a car along a highway is in a deputyship relationship with all of the other people who are out there on that same highway. If a person acts without responsibility to this deputyship relationship, danger and chaos can easily occur.

By extension, think about the engineer who takes responsibility for a bridge inspection, a businessman who runs a lawnmower repair service or a chimney cleaning service, or a nurse who dispenses medication to a hall full of patients.

In every instance, there is deputyship, people acting on behalf of other people. To think that such social dynamics can be avoided is ridiculous; there is no way to avoid deputyship.

In the ancient Biblical world, one of the most important ideas that people lived their lives by was the idea of "righteousness." This term has lost a lot of its power as it has been reduced to just one more religious cliché. However, if a close study of the word is undertaken, it does have a couple of rather deep meanings.

Two elements rise to prominence in the Hebrew concept of "righteousness." First, there is REALIZATION. Everything begins with realization. A tree may be about to fall on you and crush you while you sit relaxing in your back yard. You will not even begin to move unless you first REALIZE that the tree is falling. There is no action without realization.

As regards ethics—or "righteousness"—realization means the understanding that we are all in this together. "This" is the world. Our lives are interconnected, which is an indisputable fact of existence. To the extent that this realization is denied, there is the likelihood of unethical activity.

There must, however, be more than realization; there must also be ACTION TO ENHANCE that which grows out of realization. We basically come to the world and find it a certain way. We can then choose to try and leave the world better in some way than we have found it—ENHANCE the world—or we can act as if we have no responsibility whatsoever to contribute in any positive manner. The person who chooses to ACT TO ENHANCE is the ethical person.

Emphasizing the TWO dimensions of ethics noted here is of high importance. It is important to have realizations, but realizations are fundamentally mental events. In some respects, as important as consideration is to ethics, consideration is also a mental event. "Ethics" is only completed in acts. There must be both realizations and action to enhance.

It would be possible for a person to be an expert in good parenting—write books and give lectures about good parenting and show up on all the talk shows as the authority on good parenting—and still, in spite of all this, go home and abuse children. It is possible to "talk" a good game but not "walk" a good game. In ethics, the "walk" must match the "talk." A breakdown between what is thought and said, on the one hand, and what is done, on the other, is known as hypocrisy. Hypocrisy is not just a "church word;" it can extend to all sorts of secular settings.

It is not clear how a sense of deputyship can be promoted. Perhaps it can be mandated by rules and regulations, like those standards of quality care or quality circle processes that have made their way into many business and professions. To have a leader/employer/"boss" in a work setting that gives an example of deputyship, without question, creates an important, positive influence. Some might even feel that the sensitivities that lead to active deputyship are in-born traits of character.

In the end, however, we are creatures of choice. If we do not live by choice, we become little more than puppets on a string being controlled by random forces of society. Most people would be offended to be thought of as no more than puppets. Part of our entire self-concept, particularly as Americans, is that we are free people who can create our lives by choice. Therefore, we can consciously choose to live lives in such a way that life is enhanced and made better.

Ethics may be to some extent a matter of character, environmental conditioning, or the randomness of coincidence and opportunity. But more than all of these, ethics is ultimately a matter of choice.

TWO TYPES OF ETHICS

In the history of the study of ethics, two types of ethics have been designated. These are deontological ethics and teleological ethics. Deontological means "rule-oriented," and teleological means "end-oriented."

In deontological ethics, a person comes into a situation with a set of concrete rules, principles, or ideals that are arbitrary and unchanging. The situation takes second place to the rules and is bent in terms of the rules. Sometimes this position is known as "ethical absolutism." The rules are absolute—nothing about the situation will cause the rules to be altered in any way.

For example, imagine that my brother comes to my house with a young woman named Mary Lou, who he introduces as his fiancé. In his introduction, he says, "I want you to meet Mary Lou. She has just agreed to marry me. Don't you think she's beautiful?" Let's imagine, however, that I observe that Mary Lou is one of the ugliest people I have ever seen. What am I to do?

If I am a deontological ethicist, an ethical absolutist, I have a rule, for example, "Thou shalt not lie." The situation my brother has presented to me is of no consideration; I must simply keep the rules. I can only "tell the truth," state that the girl is totally ugly, and let the cards fall where they may.

Immanuel Kant, the famous German philosopher, held firmly to deontological ethics. He believed that people had a duty to tell the truth and that, in the end, if truth was always literally told, life would work out better in the end. Kant said, for example, that someone might come to your house, tell you that a murderer was chasing him, and ask you for a place to hide. After you had hidden the man, Kant continued, if the murderer were to come asking whether he might be hiding in your house, that you were compelled to tell him that you were hiding the man. While I guess I can appreciate Kant's obsession with truth telling, I'm sure I wouldn't want to hide in his house!

On the other hand, if I am a teleological ethicist, or an ethical relativist, then I do not go into a situation with a hardcore set of rules that are totally binding. Instead, I go into a situation, try to struggle and consider the unique demands it places on me, and act in the best way I can to make the overall situation better in some way. The situation compels me to act with responsibility and care.

Returning to my brother's situation, I may need to consider a few unique realities of this particular situation. Beauty is in the eye of the beholder; the girl may in fact be beautiful to my brother. In addition, he will have to look at her every morning. It may be more humane to "bend the rules" than to hurt the girl's feelings, make my brother mad, or create a disruption in our relationship. If I really am adamant about disliking her looks, I can always say that she looks interesting and tell him in private later how I really feel.

If I decide to take this latter course, then I choose to tell what is literally a lie. From a teleological position, what I have done is responsible and permissible. From the deontological position, I am simply a liar.

The teleological position is called "situational ethics." A person takes each situation on its own merit, weighs it carefully, and then decides what is the most humane thing to do. In teleological ethics, the individual uniqueness of a situation reigns. In a sense, Dietrich Bonhoeffer was a teleological ethicist—a Christian minister deciding to participate in a plot to assassinate Adolph Hitler. The rule "Thou shalt not kill" is set aside because of the terrible tyranny of Hitler, which, in this particular situation, Bonhoeffer decides is a worse evil than the act of murder.

There is a substantial amount of risk involved in teleological living. After all, to be teleological usually involves taking the rules into one's own hands, even breaking the rules. There is an opening of one's self to criticism and even punishment.

A second risk involved with the teleological is that it opens the door to the possibility of becoming the kind of person who does anything and then tries to justify it in terms of the "ends justifies the means." Suddenly, if someone is not careful, a total value relativism can be present in which anything goes. Great self-honesty must prevail, or integrity and character can be quickly jeopardized.

The Danish philosopher, Søren Kierkegaard, advanced the idea of the "teleological suspension of the ethical." He meant by this that there are times when the demands of a situation are such that the normal ethical thing to do must be suspended in order to bring about a higher good. For example, a diabetic may lose both legs to a terrible disease. When those legs are removed, there is a human tragedy. In most instances, the loss of limbs is terrible on any measure. However, in this particular situation, the removing of the legs—the normally bad thing to do—allows for life to continue. So, in the particular situation, the removal of the legs is actually a good thing to do.

Recently, a woman who had been a nurse for nearly thirty years was fired from her job. She is an excellent nurse who has won much recognition for quality work; she has played a key role in saving innumerable lives. Yet, she broke a rule. She was working with a graduate student nurse, teaching her how to do a particular injection. She closely monitored the student nurse's every move in preparing the needle for the injection herself. She was meticulously walking the student through the process.

However, just as the student was flawlessly performing the process under close supervision, an adversary of the older nurse happened to walk into the room. She reported to her supervisor the rule that had been broken. On paper, student nurses are not allowed to give that type of injection. The fact that there is a time-honored tradition of passing on techniques on an apprenticeship basis in nursing did not matter. The nurse was fired.

Was the firing justified? Had she simply broken a rule, or was there a justification in what she had done? Perhaps there should be consideration given to the fact that had something gone wrong, the hospital the nurses worked for could have been severely sued. What if you had to make a decision about this matter?

In fact, we experience situations in which the deontological and the teleological come into play every day that we live. We move back and forth between ethical absolutism and ethical relativism on most of the issues that face our lives constantly. There is probably no job in which the question of bending rules does not arise on a regular basis.

By thinking through the concepts of the deontological and teleological, people become more responsible decision makers. If there is a central core to "consideration," it is undoubtedly the weighing of deontological and teleological elements in the decisions that confront us. To some extent, it is the struggle of consideration itself—rather than the outcome of any particular choice—that gives credibility to all that we do as human beings.

ETHICS AS A FUNCTION OF REWARD AND PUNISHMENT

Once when my children were both young, I came home after a day of teaching classes to find my young son anxiously waiting for me on the stairs inside our front door. The first words out of his mouth as I came in the door were, "Hey, Dad. Gimme five dollars!" Curious about this request, I asked why this money should be handed over. "It's easy," my son replied, "I've been good to Meredith [his sister] all day."

My son looked as if he expected me to immediately go digging for my wallet. Instead, I thought for a moment and then responded to him, "Son, don't you understand? Goodness is its own reward." With a look of disappointment and disgust on his face, my son turned back up the stairs, threw his arms up in the air in frustration, and shouted at his mother, "Mom, he's at it again!" I'm not sure he fully understood the philosophical response I was making to his need for five dollars.

In fact, I did want my son to learn something of the idea that an act that is a "good" act is good without regard for any system of punishment or reward that the action is caught up in. If it was the "right thing" for him to be good to his sister, he should have done the right thing neither as a basis for gaining rewards—the five dollars—nor as a basis for avoiding punishment—the negative reinforcement his parents would have provided had he been "mean" to his sister or done the "wrong thing."

If something is good or right, it is good or right in-and-of-itself. The whole idea of rewards and punishments is secondary.

All of this high-flown idealism may be true in a perfect world, but—for better and for worse—in the world, as it presently exists, there is tremendous emphasis on rewards and punishments. People are often willing to invest major energy, time, and effort only if there is the likelihood of a profitable payback. That profit may be in power, fame, attention, or money, but there is usually some kind of gain to be had, or the investment will not be made. If there is no gain to attain, then there is probably no pain to avoid, or motivation is generally absent.

The modern thinker Ayn Rand, who wrote such popular books in philosophy as *The Fountainhead* and *Atlas Shrugged,* was convinced that life was basically a process of negotiation. Let's imagine in addition to my early work as a teacher that I also make money by building hang-gliders. In my class are three students who have attracted my attention. Mary is very outspoken in class one day about how she thinks that hang-gliding is stupid. She will not be caught dead getting close to a hang-gliding event. I record this statement in my memory because it runs counter to my own feelings and, more importantly, my own second source of income.

Jim, another student, disagrees with Mary. He has tried hang-gliding, loves it, and has saved money—nearly $2000—to invest in a beginner level hang-glider of his own. He is shopping around right now. I certainly record this, as it just so happens that I am nearly finished with a $2000 model that I would love to sell.

Then, a third student, Judy, really gets my attention. She talks for five minutes against Mary's negative feelings. Judy has been hang-gliding for a decade, competes professionally all across the country, and is ready to buy a top-of-the-line, $9000 glider as soon as possible. I just happen to have one of those that I will make a profit of $4000 on. In the back of my mind as she talks, I can see a down payment on a new car dancing in my head.

For Ayn Rand, these three people have different value in terms of potential reward for me. Mary has little value because she is not a potential consumer of what I produce. Jim has some value since he is a potential customer or buyer. I may make sure that he makes good grades in the class. I may overlook a missed homework assignment. I may send him a card at Christmas.

But Judy! As far as I'm concerned, she won't even have to come to class. I'll go ahead and put an "A" in my grade book for her. She is a really strong consumer. I'll send her cards, boxes of cheeses, maybe even a ham or turkey at Christmas. She has great value for me, so I will really treat her in a good, ethical way.

Rand poses the opposite circumstance. Imagine that in addition to being a teacher, I love to eat choice grade, expensive filet mignon steaks. One of my students works at a quick-stop grocery and gas shop that only has meat in cans. This student is not a very strong potential producer of what I want to consume and, therefore, has little worth. How I treat this student is beside the point.

A second student works for a major grocery chain that on random occasions has the type of meat that I want to buy. I am inclined to give this student a little more attention and favors as far as class work and grades are concerned.

Then, a third student works at a specialty meat market that keeps the highest grades of steak for its best customers. It follows that I highly value this student; he produces what I want to consume. My favor will show up in grades or all manner of perks, with the hope that he will reward me with a good deal on meat.

So, life is a process of reward and punishment. Value is added or lost on the basis of production and consumption. Ayn Rand says that smart people figure out some way to make themselves marketable and then negotiate in search of a highest bidder. To approach life from any other perspective is simply naïve. To make judgments on the basis of some idealized code of ethics is for people who just want to hand out engraved invitations to be taken advantage of.

As callous as this phenomenon seems, it appears constantly in business and professional settings. "Goodness" and "rightness" are measured almost solely in terms of what I can gain for myself. There is always someone who is using the majority of personal energy to massage and manipulate the system. Work places are surrounded by "yes" people intent on kissing up to the organization to advance themselves and their projects. Sometimes people on upper echelons in an organization cater to these kinds of people because of the way they increase ego and a sense of power. There is no telling how much manpower is wasted in the games people play around business and professional settings.

What can be done about all this? Real progress would be a steep, uphill climb, but any progress would be helpful. Perhaps, the place to start is with a reexamination of the reward/punishment scheme that is at the core of the workplace. There is a great need to disassociate a person from the idea of "what that person can do for ME." Anyone can be of value, can have good ideas, and can be worthy of respect. As long as I only notice what will give me a personal advantage, I will miss out on a great deal.

In addition, if there is some action that has value, it has value in-and-of-itself, not because it is the idea of the boss' daughter or the person most likely to become the next Chairman of the Board. If there is some task I need to perform, I need to do that task to the best of my ability for my own sake and the sake of the task, not because someone else might notice what has been done. I must first try to satisfy my own standards of quality before I get caught up in a games-playing process, which is only impressing someone who might reward me.

Another expression of this reward/punishment dynamic is seen in the way that people behave based on whether they are being watched or might get caught. Sometimes effort to avoid punishment is greater than the effort actually used in performing assigned tasks.

I once worked in an industrial setting where four separate units were under the supervision of one foreman. The four work areas were about one hundred to two hundred yards apart, and this particular foreman spent a great deal of time moving from one work area to the other. Soon after I came on as a new employee, a utility laborer, I was assigned the task of being a "lookout." I later learned that each area had its own "lookout." We were stationed at strategic points that gave us an overview of our entire work area. We were to look for the movements of the foreman or other supervisory personnel. An expensive portable phone system was utilized so that the foreman's whereabouts in the work area was always known. This allowed for plenty of time for sleep, card playing, idle chatter, and almost anything but work. It would have been amazing how much work could have been accomplished if as much energy was given to production as was given to *avoiding* production.

Plato once told a story about a character names Gyges, a shepherd working for the king of Lydia. After a great storm and earthquake, Gyges climbed into a large chasm that had been created in the earth, and he found a gold ring. When he touched the ring in a certain way, he became invisible.

This strange circumstance raised an interesting question for Plato. What would a truly just person do with this power? Would it become too much of a temptation? Could you resist making your way to some famous model's dressing room or to a bank vault holding millions of dollars? I am reminded of the often-repeated maxim of an old Sunday School teacher who told my young friends and me when we were children, "Character is what you are in the dark when no one is looking." If we are compelled to do what is right even when no one is looking, we have integrity. If the only reason we do something right is to receive a reward, escape punishment, or because we are being watched, our personal integrity is questionable at best. This idea of doing what is right for its own sake is important on every level of a business of profession, but it is particularly significant for these people who are in higher positions of authority and leadership. These kinds of people clearly establish a moral tone in a work environment.

I once worked for a man who was resolutely married, had a whole house full of children, and championed publicly the religious traditions of the "Bible Belt." He was also carrying on a torrid, almost blatantly open affair with a woman in his working environment. Everyone basically knew what was going on.

It was interesting to watch people's reactions to these events. Of course, there was a great deal of behind-the-scenes gossip. But, more importantly, there was a noticeable diminishing of work performance across the entire workplace. People were coming in late and leaving early, not to mention the growing numbers of longer and longer breaks. Assignments were not being followed promptly. There was even a rash of falsification of travel vouchers and even some degree of theft.

When middle managers began to deal with these negative performance factors, they were quickly greeted with the idea that if the boss could bend the rules, they could as well. The moral tone of the entire workplace had been compromised. It is true that this boss' "wrong" behavior should have had no bearing on how others performed their work, especially if they were involved with doing good or right for its own sake. It may be unrealistic, however, to think that for many people, the exact response that I have described will take place a great deal of the time.

Without doubt, one of the most important responsibilities for those in any place of leadership or supervision in a workplace is the establishment of a strong moral tone. If the right kind of moral tone is not established from the top down, a workplace can quickly become an arena of moral chaos.

This is not to say that everything that can be said about rewards and punishments is negative. There is an appropriate place for the positive reinforcement of rewards for work that is well done and for the negative reinforcement prompted by willfully inadequate performance. The key point—and this is a basic element of the "ethical" as it makes its way into professional conduct—is that the distribution of rewards and punishments must be as equitable as they possibly can be.

Nothing moves outside of the "ethical" in a professional setting much more than favoritism. In addition, there is nothing much more productive of negative morale and decreased productivity than favoritism. The stereotypical good-ole-boy "buddy system" is about as unethical as slavery. Both depend on defining people's "places" by means other than objective merit. If the new employee's first question, "Does the boss have favorites?" is answered in the affirmative, then there is an immediate "hollowness" at the core of the system that person is leading.

In conclusion, I almost feel the need for a disclaimer at the end of this section. There has been no attempt to create a Sunday School lesson here. Nor do I want to take an overly pious tone. None of us are saints, and I'll bet that you haven't seen too many halos lately glowing on top of your friends' and colleagues' heads. We are all human beings, with our own odd collection of strengths and weaknesses.

But, somehow, it does seem important to think about life being more than a game played out between the side markers of reward and punishment. Hopefully, it is still true that the best rewards are more internal than external. Is there any substitute for the feeling you have rise within yourself that you have done a good job, that you have done right, or that you have integrity and credibility in terms of your own character?

2. ETHICS AND ACCOUNTABILITY

A SIMPLE INTRODUCTION

On the most basic level of life and work, to be *ethical* is to be accountable. To be accountable is to be responsible. Ethics can be a system of beliefs, rational constructs, dogmas, and doctrines. This is its systemic, abstract level. Ethics must, however, if it is consummated in authenticity, involve actions. This is its extrinsic, performance level. At its best, these actions will be accomplished with a high sense of humanity, decency, even care and love. When this humanity and decency prevails, an intrinsic, personal and relational level is achieved. The great mandate of the ethical teacher, Jesus of Nazareth, was: "whatever you *do* unto the least of these. . . ." He also said, "I have given you an example, now go and *do* as I have *done*."

In the "final judgment" accounts described in the apocalyptic book, *Revelation*, the basis for entry into the eternal Kingdom of God is fairly simply stated: "And I saw the dead, great and small, standing before the throne, and books were opened. Also another book was opened, which is the book of life. And the dead were judged by what was written in the books, by what they had *done*" (20:12RSV). The issue is so important that it is repeated: "And the sea gave up the dead in it, Death and Hades gave up the dead in them, and all were judged by what they had *done*" (20:13 RSV).

Ethics, essentially, is accountability and responsibility for what we *do*. Systemically, we must be clear about *why* we do what we do. Extrinsically, we must move beyond the conceptual, abstract *why* to a committed focus on the actual *what*—the tasks, processes, and actions of our lives, making sure that we perform with skill, artistry, and competence. Intrinsically, we must always examine the *how* of what we do in order to assure that the highest potential for human life is secured, respected, and maintained.

THE "VALUE STRUCTURE" OF ACCOUNTABILITY

I am taking my cues at this point from Robert S. Hartman. In his seminal book, *The Structure of Value*, he wanted to create an "axiology," a *science* of value. To do this, he took his own inspiration from the great astronomer and father figure of modern science, Galileo. Galileo becomes decisive for Hartman because of the new way that he began to look at life. Galileo, like millions of people before him, observed motion. He could have done this in numerous, anecdotal instances: the motion of a sailing ship moving through a body of water; the motion of a horse-drawn cart moving along a street; the motion of a ball thrown by one child to another; or—again, in an anecdotal, singular instance—the motion of a runner in an athletic competition. Galileo, like millions of people before him, could be *descriptive* of these various forms of motion: how the ship looked sleek as it raced behind the wind; how the cart plodded across stones in the street at a tired pace; how the child's pitch of the ball was swift and accurate; how the athlete had broken from a pack of runners and won the race.

Descriptions are fine, but they are only anecdotal; not the stuff of *science*. For Hartman, what Galileo does that is epic and life changing in the end, is the way that he recognizes a *relationship* that is common to all motion. The *relationship* is the space (S) traversed by the movement divided by the time (T) elapsed during the traversal. Galileo then creates an axiom, a formula, that captures what Hartman called the "entire phenomenal field" of motion: $M = S/T$. Now, we have the rudiments of a science. Now, we have something that can be measured. Hartman's "structure of value" approaches the entire concept of "goodness" from this scientific perspective. I have done the same in my major Hartman "assignment," *The Value Structure of Theology*. I have also written extensively about a "Value Structure of Work" in which the primary relationship is the combination of skill set competencies and good judgment. Any work is accomplished through the combination of these two elements. We usually can measure skill set competency. The Hartman Value Profile allows us to measure good judgment.

Now, I am interested in describing a "Value Structure of Accountability." The structural parts of work—competency and judgment—would always apply to accountability because accountability will always be expressed through some sort of accomplishment/work. In other words, to be ethically accountable would always involve the assessment and enhancement/improvement of skill set competencies and the assessment and enhancement/improvement of judgment. This much is axiomatic, but it is also indispensable and should never be overlooked.

The "Value Structure of Accountability" would also include the common, relational factors of skills, talents, gifts and opportunity. Accountability would involve, in this *formula*, the relationship between—on the one hand—skills, talents, competencies, and gifts, and—on the other hand—situational opportunity. I must have skills, or it makes little difference what opportunity presents itself. I would, for example, be of little help to the Los Angeles Lakers in a basketball game. I might have the opportunity—part of the formula—but not have the talent. In a contrasting sense, I may be a trained parachutist—like my friend Chuck Matherson who was an airborne ranger in Vietnam—yet never have an occasion when I actually jump from a plane. Chuck had every talent and skill, with jump wings to prove it, but in four years in Vietnam never, even one time, had the opportunity to employ those skills. In neither of the above-described instances is ethical accountability a real issue; the *formula* cannot come into play with only one side of the relationship represented.

Let's imagine, however, like a group of my friends from Harlingen, Texas, who work for a hospital system there and were traveling to Houston to attend one of the Spiritual Leadership conferences that we do there, that we are moving along an interstate highway and suddenly come upon a wreck. We have certain choices that suddenly appear. We could be in a great hurry, not want to be late, and keep moving toward our destination. We could slow down, gawk a bit at the unfolding tragedy, feel some degree of sympathy for the people involved, and continue our journey. Of course, we could stop and try to help. In the example of my friends, who just happened to be dedicated nurses and EMTs, nothing else mattered in that moment—including a flaming gasoline truck—but to accept the situation that presented itself and begin to use their talents to rescue and save lives. They were heroic, not simply because they helped, but because they fulfilled the *formula* for ethical accountability; they used their considerable talents to meet the needs of the situation. When situation/opportunity and talent/skill/gift meet, the issue of ethical accountability peaks at its strongest.

In the Jewish *Torah* (and the Old Testament of the Bible), there is the dominant concept of *righteousness* (the Hebrew word is *hesed*). To be a righteous person is to fulfill the ideal of what a person ought to be in the eyes of God. For Robert Hartman, to be a righteous person would be to be *good* person. Although the ancient Hebrews were anything but "scientific," the explanation of the word—and the concept attached to it—has a relational quality not unlike what Galileo saw in the phenomenon of motion.

The first dimension of righteousness is *recognition*. It is impossible, obviously, to respond if there has not been recognition. Understood here, recognition is awareness, consciousness, attention, notice. There may be something of an ethical accountability at this point—that will be explored in more detail below—since noticing and paying attention is at least partially an activity that is the result of choice and self-discipline. An outfielder in a baseball game whose attention has drifted off to kids playing with a balloon in the stands and, because of this, misses catching a ball that should have been an easy out, is certainly not being ethically accountable to his profession or to his team. Therefore, in the Hebrew understanding of righteousness, there is the active discipline and intent of trying to be aware of what is taking place in your environment.

However, it is not enough for the ancient Hebrew just to be aware. The second dimension of righteousness is *activity to make better*, activity to improve, activity to help. So, there is a *relationship* here: recognition of need; and, activity—out of talent—to make better. Righteousness is, therefore, a synonym for ethical accountability on the highest levels of intent and activity that can be embraced by human beings. This kind of righteousness is a truer "test of faith" than even the greatest assent and agreement with some dogma or doctrine. It is this very idea that Jesus encapsulates in his story of the "Good Samaritan."

STAGES OF ETHICAL ACCOUNTABILITY

I have been fascinated across my career to study the movements of human consciousness. Notice that I have not said human *thinking*, and thus made the limiting, Cartesian mistake of believing that *thinking* is the highest power of human beings. I repeat: I am not interesting in studying the complexities of human thinking. *Thinking* is not the highest order activity of human being. There is a complex evolution in human consciousness that leads from awareness to action. Consciousness, especially as it moves through various manifestations of judgment toward action reveal the highest order activities we are capable of as humans—our best, the fulfillment of our goodness. In the stages of this evolution, various kinds of ethical accountability can be seen.

(Please note that in the part of the overall discussion that will immediately follow that I am taking liberties with language, spelling, and common usage. If you will look beyond these "liberties" that are being taken, I believe there is constructed here a useful lens through which life can be helpfully ordered.)

The first movement of human consciousness can be called "in-tension." By this, I mean the sense—or recognition/noticing—of some sort of internal tension that captures our attention. There are many examples: the sudden awareness of a baby crying somewhere in the night, the sound of a cat meowing that has gotten accidentally locked outside, the "cold chill" of fear that raises consciousness that there is something dangerous and threatening in your immediate environment, the unmistakable feeling that a child needs to talk about something important. The list goes on endlessly. Constantly—as was said in the movie "Star Wars"—we can become aware that there is a "disturbance in the field." A baseball player senses that a batter is about to bunt or that a runner is about to try to steal a base. A musician senses that the conductor is going to slow the tempo to give more meaning to a phrase in the music being played. Sometimes, in situations like this, we will even find ourselves thinking or saying—after the fact: "I knew that was going to happen. I knew you were going to do that."

Ethical accountability, on the level of consciousness relating to "in-tension," means paying attention, respecting intuitions and "gut instincts," and consciously disciplining ourselves to notice more. In work environments, ethical accountability on this level may mean not allowing ourselves or the people who work for us to become so utterly consumed by busy-ness that there is little likelihood of noticing that which is more subtle. Ethical accountability may also mean having a sufficient degree of rest and relaxation that the energy required for noticing—experiencing "in-tension"—is not completely used up.

The second movement of human consciousness is "in-tention." Here, we move beyond mere noticing to the level of beginning to assembly intent to do something about that which we have noticed. Some people might think that just noticing is accomplishing something, and it is. However, not much is being accomplished in mere noticing. If we do not go beyond the first movement, there has not been much ethical accountability.

With the formation of intent, we may begin to feel some surge of emotion: "This is not right!," "Something must be done!," "There has to be a response!" This emotion, as we move toward in-tention, is a strengthening of the intensity of in-tension. This surge can be experienced as excitement, and people of high in-tention generate excitement almost like the excitement of atomic particles in a chemical reaction.

Ethical accountability on this level may mean becoming troubled about some injustice, getting upset with some immoral activity, or generating some degree of determination to feel that it is important to respond and do something about a situation that is negative or not what it should be. I am even convinced that we can create productive intent around realities that we do not necessarily like. For example, by father was a demanding perfectionist when it came to yard work. I seldom agreed with all of the effort required to meet his expectations, could see many easier and faster way to complete those tasks, and chafed under his demands. However, when the rigorous work was done and I looked at the finished product, I—very begrudgingly—had to admit that it really did look good and he knew what he was talking about. The "vengeance" with which I approached the task, under what felt like pure duress, may have essentially constituted a kind of positive intent.

To be unethically non-accountable on this level might be to simply stay emotionally neutral, create a "don't give a damn" attitude, or simply become passively dismissive—stuff, for want of a better word, happens. At the moment we begin to feel "it doesn't matter," we are on the brink of ethical quandary and accountability malaise; we begin to de-construct our highest potential.

We must be very careful on this second level, however, for sometimes people can become emotionally indignant about some situation, generate a powerful amount of emotional energy, and then feel that they have actually done something by way of response to a negative situation. If all that we do is to generate emotion—or maybe even the very best of intentions, we have not really done much at all. The second dimension must be a "staging area" for the third dimension, or ethical accountability has been left behind, waiting and wanting. Talking about some negative reality or complaining about it is not an adequate response.

The third movement of human consciousness is "ex-tention." Here, there is movement beyond in-tension and in-tention to actually doing, *extending* in-tension and in-tention into real actions. This third movement is the critical moment in ethical accountability. Here, "talking the talk" becomes "walking the walk" to use an old cliché. Without "ex-tention"/extending, true ethical accountability is stillborn. It was a good idea, but nothing was actually *done*.

The final movement of human consciousness is "ex-tension" or external tension, the sense of self-actualization and self-transcendence described by Abraham Maslow at the top of his hierarchy of need. A simpler way to describe "ex-tension" is "the thrill of victory." "Satisfaction" with a job well done, or the feeling of "fulfillment" that comes when parts assemble themselves into larger, more synergistic wholes are, at least, near descriptions of what is experienced when this final movement takes place. Ethical accountability, on this level, may involve allowing yourself to enjoy and appreciate all that has taken place in the three previous movements. Some people do not take time to stop and contemplate what has taken place or stop to celebrate, and thus miss out on enthusiasms and momentums that can become positive reinforcement for further accomplishments. Leaders must be certain that they create "cultures of compliment" and not "cultures of criticism." Overbearing criticism brings a stumbling block into most circumstances that negatively impacts all kinds of accountability. With an emphasis on compliment, we create a "meritocracy;" with criticism, we create a "mediocracy."

A concrete example of these movements can be found in the life of a man by the name of Jack McConnell. McConnell is a medical doctor who gained great fame and fortune by doing research that led to the invention of Tylenol. After his retirement, he moved to what he describes as an exclusive, gated community at Hilton Head in South Carolina. In this environment, he experienced a lifestyle—albeit well-deserved lifestyle—reserved for only the economically elite.

One day as he was driving through his neighborhood, McConnell took note of the number of Mexican-Americans who worked in the area where he lived as maids, housekeepers, and people who worked for lawn care companies. It occurred to him that he and his contemporaries had all sorts of advantages that these people—whose work in many ways made their lives possible—did not come close to experiencing. Foremost in his mind were healthcare advantages.

What McConnell "took note of" and what "occurred to him" constituted an "in-tension," this "inner tension" that has been described as the first movement of human consciousness. He pays attention ("at-tension") to this experience that, on this level, represented ethical accountability.

However, McConnell does not stop at this point. The "in-tension" gathers and intensifies. It begins to manifest itself as an emotional/energy surge expressed in words such as "this is not right," "something has to be done," and—most importantly—"what must I do?" The transition from the emotional surge to the personal question is a high moment in the formation of intent. Now, McConnell begins to feel a high sense of accountability that rises from the combining of talent/skill/gift and opportunity/situation.

It would be very easy for the movements of consciousness to stop at this point, even for McConnell to feel that he had done something. He had taken note of a problem, had felt that it was something bad that needed to be addressed, and had felt some sense of indignation. For many people, this would constitute "mission accomplished," or they would feel that someone else needed to do something about the issue. They might complain to a neighbor or write their congressman.

Instead, McConnell begins to work with his community peers—physicians, hospital administrators, nurses, corporate executives, and business leaders—to develop plans for a free clinic that would bring accessible healthcare to anyone in need. He pushed beyond ideas to get volunteers to both work in the clinic and raise money to support its efforts. Soon, a brick and mortar structure rose from the ground, and—by the time its doors opened—it was fully staffed by all sorts of volunteers. Now, anyone who lived and worked on Hilton Head had healthcare regardless of social and economic standing. "In-tension" and "intention" had become "extention."

McConnell has now lived to see not only this dream fulfilled, but also the Hilton Head clinic has become the paradigm for an entire movement that has extended healthcare to similar situations throughout the United States. His work is honored and esteemed. The "extention" gains increasing energy every day. McConnell and all those associated with him can feel a great sense of "extension" that creates new energy for even larger accomplishments.

A similar illustration of the point being made here can be found in the life of Robert Moffat. Moffat was a young man living in England in the late 1800s. He was searching for something to do with his life when he was invited to hear a speech by the famous missionary/explorer, David Livingston. In Livingston's speech, which Moffatt had not found overly stimulating and a bit longwinded, there had been one phrase that totally captured his attention. In the words of this discussion, this phrase created "in-tension."

Livingston talked about getting up early in the morning in Africa and looking into the far distance to the plains north of where he worked in the central regions of Africa. Livingston said: "To the north in the mists of the morning sun, I see the smoke of a thousand villages untouched by the outside world." Moffatt said that he replayed this phrase in his life a thousand times. In other words, "in-tension" was mounting toward intent.

Then, Moffatt described an interesting transition that took place in his life. Instead of visualizing the villages of Africa being described by Livingston, there was suddenly a question rising in his mind: "What can I do for Africa?" Once, just as with McConnell, the personal question comes into view, the stage is set for the movement to "extention." Moffatt became one of the most dedicated and remarkable missionaries of the age. It was the fulfillment, actualization, and transcendence—the "ex-tension"—of his life.

THE DECISIVE ROLE OF WILL

The above "stages" or "dimensions" of human consciousness and the way they relate to ethical accountability can be "charted" in a more visual manner. Here, we will see various levels or degree or intensity of consciousness. I like the image of a numbered dial on the front of a stove. On the lower numbers, the heat produced by the burner is minimal. As the numbers on the dial move to higher levels, the degree of heat—"excitement" of energy within the burner coils—increases. At the same time in this part of the discussion, a crucial element not emphasized in the preceding comments can be explored more adequately.

Level 1—Awareness/consciousness/noticing/attentiveness to

Level 2—Comprehension/deciding to commit greater attention to

Level 3—Consideration/weighing/evaluation/critical judgment

Level 4—Deciding, choosing, opting

Level 5—Will

Level 6—Action/Actual *doing*

Will is always a critical element in ethical accountability. Will rises from an intensity of commitment and dedication. Will is pushed forward by discipline. Will involves passion, determination, and tenacity. Will is a watershed in the movement to action. Will allows intent to be extended into real actions.

At times, the intensity of will can be raised by group consciousness, what we see our peers doing, and the inspiration of others. At other times, will can be installed in a group by the "follow me" intensity of a true leader. We see the will of someone else, and our will increases. On the other hand, there are plenty of times when we have only ourselves to depend on, and will has to be generated from within regardless of what others may or may not do. There may simply be times when will is generated by a clear sense of what is "the right thing to do." Here, ethical accountability is at its height, like Martin Luther standing—his life at stake in the most literal way—before the dominant powers of his age and saying "Here I stand, I can do nothing else, God help me."

In response to the question of why people "turn out" to be who they are, many discussions will turn to genetics. There is accuracy in this position. I look in a mirror and see the skin coloring of my mother and the body shape of my father. What I have inherited from them is very clear. I might wish that I had my father's coloring and my mother's body shape. At least, I would be a thin person. But, we are what we are in terms of inheritance.

Others will give emphasis to "nurture" that comes from environmental causes. There is little doubt that this position holds some important degree of truth. I was born and raised in East Tennessee. Had I been born in East Berlin and been raised in the 1950s and 1960s, I would have to be different than I am today. What if I had been born in East Pakistan—now Bangladesh? Environment has a causative power that cannot be doubted.

However, by the time a person comes to be an older teenager, a twenty-something, or surely—even with protracted adolescence—into the thirties, the major element in determining who he/she is will be *choice*. I would like to think, to the degree that I am an authentic person, that I am more today who I am based on my *choices* than anything that has to do with heredity and environment. I hope I have overcome and improved upon many of these elements. I am sure that it makes no sense to blame my parents or my upbringing for negatives that I have had plenty of time to overcome or compensate for by choice.

Thus, the component of *will* carries a high priority in any outcomes. I can, of course, be a weak-willed person or surrender my will to that of others. In most cases, these options are not invariably determined aspects of my life. They are, rather, forms of *choice*. On the highest levels of accountability and ethics, I am distinctly responsible for the degree of *will* that I bring to bear on any situation. (I am not absolutely sure about what I am saying at this point. I am very much aware of the interferences that can occur with forms of psychological dysfunction or the way, under certain aberrant circumstances, that *will* can be broken by abuse and others forms of victimization. Outside of these kinds of exceptional circumstances, what I am saying seems to match up creditably with experience.)

"DERAILERS" OF ETHICAL ACCOUNTABILITY

There can be substantial "in-tension" and intent that can serve as a powerful staging ground for actual accomplishment. However, on both personal and corporate levels, there can be equally powerful obstacles—"derailers"— that get in the way of and throw the movement toward action off track. At least, a few of these "derailers" can be described. There are certainly more than are described here. The point is that even the most highly admired and desired ethical accountability can be offset or hindered by these "derailers." Noting prominent ones may help forewarn and better prepare people for facing and overcoming the negative detractors from ethical accountability.

1. Lack of a clear vision—When the overall operating vision of an organization lacks clarity, even the most ethical intent can be derailed. It is the responsibility of leadership in an organization to make sure that vision is clear and, therefore, that it is easier for people within the organization to practice ethical accountability. When vision is accompanied by a sense of purpose and the belief that what is being done has a high level of importance, ethical accountability is more easily achieved. Lack of clarity from the top usually means confusion about "ends," what is being accomplished and why. Confusion about "ends" often results in confusion about "means," how something is being accomplished. Lines that define ethics and that define accountability can be blurred in this circumstance. The ancient text reads: "Where there is no vision, the people perish." Literally, the text means: "Where there is no strong word of direction, people run about in disorganized chaos."

2. Lack of integration—An organization is integrated when the parts fit in an aligned manner into a meaningful whole. When the "parts" do not fit and no one seems to be able to achieve this "fit," it is difficult to know how to be accountable. This "derailer" is often present when "plates are too full," and organizations—or individuals—are trying to do too much. In this situation, that may be full of wonderful intention, nothing is done as well as it could be. The precedent is established for "getting by," rather than for excellence of skills and competency. Once this precedent is established, high accountability holds a secondary importance; the *amount* of what is done takes priority over the *quality* of accomplishment.

3. Spreading an organization too thin—Integration can also be disrupted by trying to accomplish too much with too few people. A standard strategy for diminishing costs is to cut the number of employees. Often this is done by attrition that takes place in a position followed by the decision not to fill that position, but spread the work of the position to other people. This strategy can continue to the point that very accountable people have too much to be responsible for. I may be part of a baseball infield, the shortstop, and the second baseman may retire. It is going to be very difficult for me to play both shortstop and second base, even though the financial savings to the team gained by not replacing the player at second base could be substantial. This difficulty of having too much ground to cover will prevail in spite of my talent

and degree of dedication. What would never, ever be done to a baseball team should not so easily be done in work settings.

4. Excuse making—All too often, organizations—the world—makes it easy to pursue agendas of excuse making. Leadership decisions provide a bold target for excuse making. In this situation, personal standards of excellence must be the measure of accountability, not negative circumstances that exist in a workplace, community, or life in general. Surrendering personal standards, even when organizations are not clearly focused or integrated, will make situations worse not better. Such surrendering of personal standards cannot be justified and creates the very antithesis of ethical accountability. In fact, there is an entire "psychology" of complaint and excuse making. Research demonstrates that 85% of all excuse making is totally ineffectual and leads to no positive end. Approximately 10% is positive as a form of "venting," "getting things off one's chest." Only about 5% of complaining and excuse making is justifiable and makes any positive contribution to life circumstances.

5. External standards for performance—One of the most powerful derailers of ethical accountability takes place when a person uses the inadequacies, lack of competency, or even ethical lapses of other people to justify their own less-than-adequate performance. How easy it may be for me to "coast" at half-speed when my half-speed in getting more accomplished than someone else who is not being ethically accountable in some way. I must—if I am truly accountable—have as my standard my own "best." I must live up to what I am capable of doing, not what I do compared to someone whose accountability is taken with far less seriousness. Even when that person exhibiting less accountability may be recognized or rewarded by some incompetent system of assessment or some incompetent leader, I must still live up to my own highest potential if ethical accountability is to prevail.

6. Lack of flexibility or "nimbleness"—The speed of every kind of change in our modern civilization is astounding. We might want life to slow down or provide us with more constants, but the likelihood of that happening is not very great. It may not even be desirable. Some people will—understandably— resist change, maybe just to stand the chance to stay "ahead of the game" a bit. However, ethical accountability in the kind of world we have created usually means accepting change, dealing with change, and probably even being something of a catalyst for change. To a certain extent, if I am ethically accountable, I will strive to be flexible and nimble. In fact, in working with organizations across this country, "nimbleness" is looked upon as one of the most

desired *values* needed and respected in modern business and industry. James Springfield, the young CEO of Valley Baptist Healthcare System in Harlingen, Texas, and the 2004 American College of Healthcare Executives "Young CEO of the Year Award," says that leaders must—at one and the same time—(A) accomplish tasks and (B) create options. A key issue for Springfield is to be ready when these options begin to appear, and—for him—they may all begin to occur at the same time!

7. Mere verbal responses—We are highly verbal people. We have developed language skills that are amazing. The kinds of communication that are available to us today on a regular basis were unknown on the literary levels of most previous generations. Unfortunately, this great accomplishment can also be a real deterrent to ethical accountability. We can become very skilled in merely talking about negative issues that need to be fixed *and* very positive issues that have the potential of being actually accomplished. Our problem, of course, is that so often we do not get beyond talking. Talking can involve every expression from complaining about what needs to be done to promising what will be done. However, if we only "talk a good game," we have not even begun to be ethically accountable. Authentic accountability always stretches beyond mere conversation. We must be careful with a "Jerry Springfield" mentality where we talk incessantly, rant, rave, and even fight, but never really work our way through to making better. A consulting peer says: "If grandma is in the middle of the living room, drunk and incontinent, talking about it does little good."

8. A quick retreat to attitudes and language of blame and fault—An easy "inventory" can be taken to measure the degree to which this particular "derailer" is present in an organization or in a person's individual life. All that is necessary is to notice—and perhaps keep track of—how quickly a person goes to blame or fault language, how often the words *blame* and *fault* are actually used. Some people beat a quick retreat to these words—and the attitudes that surround these words—before any analysis or explanation of events is ever studied or investigated.

9. The Grass Is Greener Mentality—I have a print hanging in one of my offices that shows a beautiful, grassy hillside. The grass is green and lush across the hill. There must have been wonderful fertilizer and a great deal of good rain. The hillside is bisected by two fencerows that have divided the field into four segments that are basically, exactly alike. In the print, there is an old cow confined in each of the four segments. The cows have their heads

stuck just as far into the neighboring segment as they can. They epitomize the feeling that the grass is somehow greener somewhere else. This mentality destroys accountability and creates a special kind of excuse. In most instances, ethical accountability dictates that we make the most of where we are as opposed to becoming fascinated—and distracted—by what the "grass" may be like somewhere else.

CONCLUSION

One of the most profound discussions of the kind of ethical accountability that is being described here is the ancient "Parable of the Talents." The implications for this classic teaching for modern life in general and organizational life in particular is astounding. If we understood this ancient teaching and advanced it into our individual and corporate value systems, the concept of ethical accountability could not help but be much, much clearer.

In the ancient story, a person of importance leaves his home country for some sort of journey that will keep him away for some period of time. He calls in three of his "direct reports" and gives them money ("talents" in the ancient Hebrew currency). One receives five talents, a second receives three, and the third gets one. They are charged by their "CEO" to do something productive with that money. When he returns, he warns, they will be evaluated in terms of their accountability.

The first worker finds a way to take his five talents and double them. The second person does the same. The number of original talents given or the level of productivity is not the issue. These two workers are extolled and further rewarded because they have taken the initiative to try, to strive, to make every effort to create improvements.

The third worker—and, again, it does not matter where he starts or what he starts with—takes his talent and hides it. He reasons, as he makes excuses to the returning "CEO," that he knew his master was an exacting judge of work who had high expectations. He was so afraid of displeasing him, of losing the one talent, that he did nothing to improve his situation. He only sought to protect the status quo of what was originally there. The owner is deeply angry and disappointed. The man who hides the talent has it taken from him and given to the first man.

Most executives—in fact, the best—that I know are exactly like the owner in the old story. They do not expect everyone to be a five-talent person. They do, however, expect everyone to try to succeed, to expend every effort at succeeding, and push the envelope of dedicating energy to making better. If a person tries and fails, that failure can be overcome. Not to try cannot be overcome. There is room for the person who tries and fails; there is no room for the person who does not try. Trying, giving all effort, stretching to accomplish, expending energy of effort and creativity—all of these kinds of activities are seen as ethical accountability.

Ethical accountability in the modern world, and especially in the modern workplace, requires risk taking. This is not meant to mean moral risk taking, but the kind of risk taking that puts five talents at risk in order to double the achievement. In most instances, risk taking is not something radical and dangerous for most people, but rather a decision not to expend huge amounts of needless energy in preserving comfort zones. If most people expended as much energy trying to achieve new levels of creative accomplishment as they do sustaining comfort zones, most workplaces would be transformed in a positive way.

Maybe the one-talent person is afraid to make decisions. Not to decide is a monumental derailer of ethical accountability. In the movement of human consciousness described above, the moment of decision is the critical moment that drives life toward action. Avoidance of decisions, fear that some decision will "get you in trouble," or the continual strategy of passing decisions off to others, is a major example of how ethical accountability goes unfulfilled. When decisions are not made—or consciously avoided—what might have been realized or accomplished never sees the light of day.

Maybe the one-talent person is simply crippled by tentativeness. Maybe he simply continues to be tentative, even thinking that he will eventually get some activity underway, until his day of accountability arrives. Then, it is too late. Being tentative can be a form of self-destruction. In athletics, more injuries take place when players are being tentative than when they are being aggressive. When ethical accountability becomes tentative, it always becomes less.

Please take note at this point that little or nothing is being said throughout this presentation about ethical accountability in terms of moral astuteness or general human decency. Conversations in these areas should go without saying. The one-talent man may have been a paragon of moral virtue. What is being discussed here is an aggressive, pro-active accountability in which people are known by what they take the initiative to do rather than what they do not do, even if that is very admirable. I have not succeeded in being ethically accountable simply because I have not robbed a bank or harmed someone in some malicious way. Immoral or criminal activities are obviously wrong and represent a total shirking of ethical accountability. But, simply because we have never been arrested, convicted of a crime, or "caught with our hands in the cookie jar" in some way does not mean that we have been ethically responsible. This discussion is not about what we avoiding doing that would have been morally wrong, but about what we need to do to be ethically accountable.

In conclusion, I recently read an article in the somewhat prestigious *Journal of Personality* that captured my attention. The article was reporting on a survey that was done on happy marriages. The point of the survey was to attempt to determine the one, primary ingredient that makes a successful marriage. Some people might think that common interests, being friends, or high moral faithfulness might be the key element. In the research done in the survey, there was a very different answer. The most successful marriages and sustainable relationships were, primarily, because of the presence of *low expectation*. The old cliché comes to mind: "Blessed is he who expects nothing; he will not be disappointed."

In recent studies completed at UCLA, college students coming of age in the twenty-first century seem different from college students of the 1960s. In 1960, fully 85% of all college students surveyed said that "developing a meaningful philosophy of life" was either essential or very important in the work they would do in college. By 2003, only 39% gave the same answers. By contrast, in 1960, 40% of students surveyed indicated that "being well-off financially" was essential or very important. By 2003, this number had increased to 78%. There is clearly a change in priorities being reflected in these responses, and some might even say "low aim." By any measure, "aim" has certainly changed.

I know a person who plays golf by these same standards—if the word *standard* could ever be used. He goes out to the golf course hoping to break a score of 100, a fairly mediocre score. If he happens to shoot 99, he goes away happy. If he shoots 120—which is more likely—he reasons that this was about what he expected. I am convinced that the entire attitude almost assures that a 120 will be the result. In regard to marriage, I wonder how "successful" is being defined. If longevity is the measure, maybe low expectation is a fine ambition and measure. If intensity, depth, sophistication, and beauty are the measures, low expectation will never deliver.

The most decisive and authentic leaders, almost without expectation, are people of high expectation both for themselves and the people around them.

The best coaches I have ever seen are high expectation in their demands on their players. The best personal relationships that I have ever seen are high expectation. The entire concept of ethical accountability is very high expectation. To me, low expectation means the promotion of floundering, mediocrity, and minimal satisfaction and fulfillment. Potential cannot be achieved, even marginally, when low expectation prevails. If the survey is right, I'm not sure I want to be a player in that kind of marriage. If ethical accountability fails to be a primary part of a leader's high expectation, I'm not sure I want to work for that person.

I love the famous lines from Alfred, Lord Tennyson's wonderful poem *Ulysses.* In the poem, the great old warrior, Ulysses, is moving toward the end of his days. His time of adventure and journey are over, but he spends a great deal of time at the docks with the ships and sailors recalling the past while still not being oblivious to what he can still do and what he might yet do in his life. I am convinced that having something of Ulysses' *will* as described by Tennyson would not only become a fitting standard for a person's life—a life of high expectation—but also ensure that ethical accountability was a regular part of a person's day-to-day living.

Tho' much is taken, much abides
Tho' we are not today that strength that in old days
Moved earth and heaven,
That which we are, we are.
One equal temper of heroic hearts,
Made weak by time and fate, but strong in will
To strive, to seek, to find, and not to yield.

Ethical accountability is striving, seeking, finding, and a decisive will for that which is best that refuses to yield. Failure is not sin. Low aim is. If the word *sin* literally means "missing the mark," it makes a great deal more sense to aim high. At least by aiming high, the target—even the center of the target—stands a chance of being hit. It we aim low, there is no chance of hitting the target at all. Low aim is the greatest impediment to ethical accountability experienced in most individuals' lives and in the lives of most organizations. There may be justification for even failure, but there is no justification for not trying, not aiming high.

2. *Ethics and Accountability*

We must remember: in this one, short life that we have the opportunity to live, we do not embrace life as people with a temporary lease. We are owners! While we are here, this life is ours. We are accountable, and at the core of this accountability is the demand to be ethical.

3. CIRCLES OF FIDELITY

INTRODUCTION

Gabriel Marcel was a French philosopher who was born in 1889. He was raised in a remarkably cultured family environment that produced in him a highly idealistic, privileged view of the world. This sophisticated optimism came to a screeching halt when he joined the Red Cross during World War I. His Red Cross assignment to find missing soldiers brought him face to face with gruesome scenes of tragedy, horror, and the worst instances of man's inhumanity to man. His life was forever changed.

Marcel returned from the war with his easy idealism basically destroyed and lost. He rejected abstract philosophy in favor of an emphasis on searching for moral truths that would promote harmony and community between people. In one of his most famous quotes, he said: "Philosophy begins, not with *I am*, but *we are*." He spent the remainder of his life advancing ideas that would help people relate to each other better. The understanding and building of relationships—the "we are"—became the critical issue in human experience that must be struggled with and fought for in families, communities, and in the world of business. In fact, since so much actual waking time in life is spent in work involvements, the building of relationships with a business environment surfaces a key need for life in general.

The core reality of any human group interaction, from families to business, for Marcel was trust, and trust is seen as a by-product of fidelity. Without faithfulness—fidelity—trust will not exist, and to the degree that trust is abused, group existence is handicapped or even destroyed. The basic, foundational dimension of relational existence, from marriages to work units in business, is the ability to trust, to be faithful with other people with whom you are grouped.

It may sound as if Marcel is simply being a nice man who advocates a policy of everyone being totally truthful with each other so that fidelity and trust will prevail, and then everyone will live happily ever after without problems. Such a conclusion would merit little consideration and bring only the least impact upon most real life settings. Marcel's critical assessment of fidelity adds an intriguing insight to the study of human dynamics not seen in many similar discussions.

3. Circles of Fidelity

He believed in the integral power of honesty and truth-telling. Being less than honest, especially in situations of turf protecting conflict avoidance is always seen as a confounding negative. However, great care must be taken in understanding that *not everyone is owed honesty.* There are situations in which a person may not necessarily have a right to that which some individual may honestly know. In such a situation, withholding honesty may not be the same as telling a lie. He describes "circles of fidelity" that can be visually conceived as a target-like collection of concentric circles:

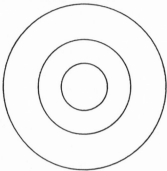

You owe fidelity to those people within your "circle of fidelity," but not to those outside of the circle. For example, I certainly have a total obligation of fidelity and truth-telling to my mate. My mate would inhabit the most inner circle. What my mate and I know about is not the prerogative of those with whom I share outer circles. Not to tell someone on an outer circle something that is inner circle private is not a lie; the people in the outer circle simply do not have a right to inner circle knowledge. In fact, to share inner circle information with outer circle people constitutes an act of infidelity and trust breaking toward that inner circle.

In business and industry, there are many examples that appear on an almost daily basis that reflect Marcel's ideas. People who buy a particular product—a car, for example—are automatically on an inner circle with all those who have produced the car or its parts. They are privileged to any information about performance problems or safety defects. Not to share this knowledge is to break trust, to lie. On the other hand, the general work population may not have a right to information and decisions shared in management meetings. One of the worst mistakes a manager or supervisor can make is to move information shared on an inner circle of fidelity to an outer circle. Some managers will do this to secure an image of power with their direct reports. Others see access to privileged information as a symbol of status. Others simply cannot keep a confidence, and the inner circle information becomes like money in a pocket that must be spent. Soon, a rumor mill of misinformation will spread through a workplace. Productivity, morale, and service are often immediately compromised and victimized.

Executive levels of management must teach and insist on "circles of fidelity." Specific conversations must be held and commitments given to "circles of fidelity." Upper and middle levels of management must be held accountable for upholding and protecting these circles. There are times when a manager or supervisor will be asked questions, and they must answer: "I'm sorry, it is inappropriate for me to share that information." Line of trust must be held and not compromised. To enter a management or supervisory team is to enter a "circle of fidelity." The management team is a special community, and maintaining that community depends on trust. A management team that insists on an inner framework of faithfulness will enhance the power of its leadership. Managers need to explicitly generate dialogues in which the obligation to a "circle of fidelity" is specifically articulated and ownership of that obligation acutely anticipated. Work teams fail or succeed to the degree that "circles of fidelity" are carefully explained, understood, and protected.

When there are periods of downsizing, reorganization, and reengineering that take place in a work environment—and such dynamics of change seem almost constant—"circles of fidelity" will also undergo corresponding change. The group that a person has an inner circle relationship with today may not be the same circle for which inner circle fidelity is demanded tomorrow. Many managers make the mistake of trying to maintain old circles after they have become members of new circles. The demand to eliminate, or at least lessen significantly, the old circle fidelity and embrace fully the new circle fidelity is, of course, difficult. There is the demand of delicate balancing, careful decision-making, and a keen awareness of where institutional and organizational fidelity lies *today*. In one form or another, however, the demand for careful decision-making may have always been the primary attribute of the successful manager and leader in the workplace.

There is no suggestion here that a "circle of fidelity" should be used to protect a lie or conceal information that would be immorally hurtful of people. The first object of fidelity at its most basic level is to not do harm immorally. When an organization is insisting on fidelity to an inner circle, it does so only under the regulation of the rule of basic human morality. When morality that is intentionally being covered by deception prevails, there is a larger loyalty to "truth" that must be followed. In this case, and in this case alone, fidelity must be broken with an inner circle even at the great risk of being ostracized or fired. Such examples as the "whistle blowers" at Enron or the "Pentagon Papers" events that disclosed the dishonesty surrounding the War in Vietnam make heroes of those who resist an immoral system protecting itself by lies and deception. Insider trading, for example, is a perfect instance in which inner circle information can be misused in a way that is destructive of basic public morality. There are stern laws, and rightfully so, that try to prevent "circles of fidelity" from becoming abusive and destructive.

In a similar sense, the presentation is not trying to say that relationships that have been established on one circle should cease to exist when the circle changes. That is not the point at all. The point is simply that when the circle changes that there is a change in the flow of information that becomes new and must be respected in new ways. Old relationships professionally, not personally, change when professional circles change; to try to maintain the same professional relationships across the lines of new circles that have evolved is all but impossible and not particularly desirable.

With these disclaimers in place, and particularly the idea that public morality involves a level of fidelity that all organizational structures must respect, specific work groups need to discuss in detail—as a high-priority dialogue—exactly what "circles of fidelity" mean to their ideal functioning. Everyone in the group needs to know exactly what fidelity means in their circle. When this concept is left without specific discussion, a lack of clarity can prevail that can "come back to bite" work groups in the most surprising ways. In what will follow now, there is an attempt to outline something of the basics for the kind of specific discussion and concrete dialogue that is being advanced as highly necessary.

A MUTUALITY OF ACCOUNTABILITY

Fidelity will, minimally, involve a mutuality of accountability. Within a relationship, for that relationship to function at its highest, participants must hold each other to be accountable for keeping commitments, sharing workloads, being active participants in group decisions, and telling other participants the best that is known, felt, and believed. Holding another person accountable to a group does not have to be a belligerent act; in fact, it assuredly should *not* be belligerent. Nor should holding a colleague accountable be demeaning, embarrassing, humiliating, or sarcastic. Mature, adult human beings must work in some atmosphere of objectivity and factuality in which emotional extremes are consciously harnessed. Until the ability to have mature, mutual accountability is experienced and sustained, the concept of a team, quality circle, or partnership is in name only.

Who better to hold me accountable than a true peer? Who better to challenge my assumptions, decisions, and long-range designs than someone with whom I share the deepest level of vested interest in *our* organization? Who better to tell the king he is wearing no clothes than those commissioned to be his closest advisors? Who better to hold me accountable for not telling all that I think and feel than that group most likely to be hurt by my closed-mouth conflict avoidance? Creating comfort zones where people "look the other way" or expend great energy in covering each others' backsides is not fidelity; it is, rather, the extension and group reinforcement of dishonesty.

When a group comes to the point of mature, mutual accountability without carrying emotional baggage into future interactions, there is a true team made up of emotionally strong players who are, indeed, most concerned with the *team* functioning on its highest level of efficiency *and* integrity. When grudges and revenge scenarios dominate, only the barest lip service is being done to the concept of a team. True fidelity cannot tolerate grudges and revenge.

A powerfully difficult mandate is being delivered at this point. The kind of mature, mutual accountability being described here has to be a constant in a relationship. To practice this accountability "part time" when it is convenient, or when it does not get "too close to my own skin" will never be sufficient. Just the slightest inconsistency in this accountability—just the slightest "favoritism" in this accountability—and it will be fairly well compromised beyond recognition. To think about sustaining the kind of accountability being described here as *fidelity* requires the highest of leadership ability.

A COMMITMENT TO AUTHENTIC LISTENING

Fidelity requires, not a passing, but an active and conscious commitment to authentic listening. Most people recognize that poor communication is the largest obstacle to true partnerships/relationships/teams; at least, poor communication reigns as the number one negative item of assessment in most workplace evaluations. Most people are also quick to realize that authentic listening is much more critical to the communications process than the most articulate speaking. However, authentic listening still seldom occurs because listening is not conceived as a *conscious commitment that directly expresses fidelity.*

Within a highly functioning circle of fidelity, individuals consciously practice a bringing of total focus of concentration to what is being said by another member of the circle. Every attempt is made to break habits of interruption and the completing of another person's thoughts, but even more especially the habit of beginning to formulate a mental response while another person is still speaking. The most *faithful* listener even learns to incorporate a "thinking space" or "space of contemplation" between what is said by someone else and the response that is given to that statement. To see such "contemplation" as a form of responsibility and *fidelity* is a true mark of leadership.

What is being described here is not simply a leadership development concept, but a practiced *art* as the great golfer who is dedicated to hitting thousands of balls on a practice range or putting green. The decision is made by the authentic listener to consciously focus on listening in a way that the other person feels the highest levels of respect for who he/she is or what is being said. The decision is made to "bracket out" one's own thinking processes until *after* speaking is completed by the other person. The guiding design and plan is: listen, consider, speak—listen, consider, speak—listen, consider, speak.

The problem sometimes with "group think" is a process of "listenSPEAK"— a garbled, intellectually awkward process of overlapping non-hearing in which efficient communication is compromised and the results of that poverty stricken communication become random, faulty, and dangerously inexact. People go away from such non-communication believing that they know what someone else has concluded or what a group has reached as consensus without any accurate knowledge of what has really been said. Sixteen persons in a room for three hours, and sixteen "takes" on what is said in the room are carried into the larger workplace. In a true circle of fidelity, there is *distinct* listening, *distinct* consideration, and then—and only then—*distinct* speaking. All else can become only a very thinly veiled exercise of the ego and boardroom gamesmanship.

We create lofty, conceptual ideas of what it means to love someone, to be just with someone, or to respect someone. Often, lofty ideas become only the occasion for parroted clichés. Real fidelity may more readily be expressed in the consciously disciplined acts of basic listening, a kind of "ultimate simple" that is a foundation point for any effective relationship in either work or a person's larger, personal life.

A wonderful incentive for authentic, distinct listening can be found in the words of Alice Ward Jones: "A really good idea is just a midwife to an even better one." There is, of course, the disclaimer—if the "really good idea" is actually heard! So, the true "midwife" of the kind of good ideas that bring an endeavor to a next level of success may simply be authentic, distinct listening. When we see this kind of listening as an aspect of *fidelity*, our entire approach to other people takes on a new—dare we say—*character*.

FAITHFULNESS TO GENUINE CONSENSUS

In a true circle of fidelity, the consensus conclusion reached within the group—as long as public morality is upheld—becomes *my* conclusion outside of the group. Here stands the action from which the circle cannot deviate and the basic operating reality that gives the circles its validity and credibility. If a consensus has been forged through struggle and with attention to public morality that I cannot live with, then I have not been forceful enough, convincing enough, or factual enough during the consensus building process. If a circumstance exists in the power structure of the circle in which I have not been permitted or allowed to be convincing enough, then fidelity has been broken with the true nature of the circle on some other level. Consensus would then be an inappropriate word for describing what has come out of what—in reality— is *not* a true group or team. When any dictatorial voice prevails, the entire concept of consensus is invalidated, and to say—as window dressing—that a consensus has been achieved is a lie. However, it must be admitted that there are numerous precedents for dictatorial voices prevailing only because other voices have chosen to take a path of least resistance, conflict avoidance, or caved in to intimidation. We might lose a paycheck for resisting such dictatorial intimidation, but we will not lose dignity—we will not lose our "souls."

In a genuine consensus building process, everyone who participates is given the fullest opportunity to convince the group of his/her feelings and information. The person giving the information defines whether a full opportunity has been granted by the leader or the group. No one in the circle is obligated to agree, but everyone is obligated to give a full hearing. Once a person agrees that he/she has been fully heard—ask them!—there is an obligation formed to support the group, even if there is not full, 100% individual agreement with the final outcome. The only other option, if a person feels strongly enough, is to withdraw from the group entirely. Most of the time,

3. Circles of Fidelity

a more realistic view would be that there will be times of full agreement, other times in which your opinion is more dominant or better represented in the consensus, and yet other times in which your opinion is less dominant or less well-represented in the consensus.

I am also not talking about a group relationship in which a person, whose ideas have not "won the day," goes away with such negative body language that everyone knows he is at odds with his/her group as obviously as if he/she took out a billboard or climbed up on a stump and made a speech. I once knew a middle level executive who would go away from meeting in disagreement, not expressing that disagreement in explicit detail, but singing "Some gotta' win, some gotta' lose; Good Time Charlie's got the blues." It was a signal to his subordinates that he did not agree; even more that it was not *his* decision and *he* was not to blame. There is no *fidelity* in such strategies.

Fidelity, as in this illustration, is most often, and most harmfully, broken with the circle when the consensus does not represent an individual's opinion, and yet that same individual comes out of the group reporting: "I disagreed," "I held out for you guys, but. . . .," "It wasn't my fault," "You should have seen what *they* have come up with now," or "Don't blame me." Sometimes the dissenting voice is bold and belligerent, begging the question of why such boldness did not show up in the consensus building process. Sometimes the dissenting voice is clandestine and insidious, currying favor with some group outside the circle who do not agree with the consensus the circle has reached. In either situation, the "rules" have been broken and a penalty flag should be thrown.

How a consensus decision is supported by the individuals involved in the consensus building process needs to become the test of whether those individuals should be allowed to continue to participate in that particular group. A person who leaves the room supporting the consensus and then opposes that consensus as his/her decision outside of that room simply should not be allowed to continue as part of that group in the future. Circles of fidelity only function efficiently and effectively when the consensus decision becomes my own decision. The old Nuremberg justification of "just following orders" will seldom stand in the light of day.

THE ISSUE OF LIKING THOSE WITHIN OUR CIRCLES

Fidelity does not necessitate liking. Too much emphasis is placed on liking. Respectful cooperation *and* the need for divergence of attitude and perspective are much more important to a successful work unit—to any relationship. In fact, seldom is it possible to find another person who is either liked all of the time or disliked all of the time. Even in the closest, most fulfilling friendships and deepest personal relationships, liking is not a constant. Liking usually ebbs and flows, and the most successful relationships recognize this reality, accept it, and strive to keep it from becoming any more than a momentary deterrent to larger goals. Liking/not liking often takes the form of favoritism—advancing or withholding attention, access, privilege, and reward—one of the most crippling obstacles in the workplace. Attention can be diverted from individuals who could be making strong contributions to the organizations. The very person who may not be particularly liked at some point can hold the information and expertise that might make for a powerful partner in accomplishing significant tasks.

Few people are strong enough in their own personalities and character to explore with someone else the phenomenon of not liking. This weakness, that only lengthens and exacerbates the potential negatives in any relationship, may rise from the fact that what we do not like in others is often exactly what we most fear in ourselves. To avoid exploring a circumstance of not liking a colleague may parallel a denial about some reality in our own existence as a person. Not liking another person then usually takes the non-constructive and even destructive form of telling others—usually in the group that needs to be able to work together—about the not liking. While these other group members may agree or commiserate, the core of the negative situation is not touched and usually demands a passage of awkward and unproductive time to gain even nominal resolution. Let's talk about what we need to *do* together, not whether we like each other. Conversations about liking/not liking are by their very nature divisive and "de-construct" group potential.

Where there is true fidelity—and emotionally strong personalities—there is a direct admission of the not liking, the affirmation that not liking is a fact of life, the accurate conclusion that most not liking is temporary and situational, and a determined effort to explore, without accusation or blame, the real root of not liking. Obviously, a difficult course is being suggested here, but most not liking is usually tremendously vague or, at least, not as substantial as it may first appear. What we usually claim to first not like is often only a surface reality that masks the true source of trouble. If what we do not like is obvious, we can correct it and move on. However, when emotionally strong personalities—or brave ones—explore as adults the not liking that is taking place in their relationship, the circle of fidelity is almost always enhanced. Often, discoveries and appreciation of others that could never be imagined takes place. Inevitably, for all involved in the exploration of a not liking process, self-growth and personal maturity are a welcome and dependable consequence.

Clearly, an exploration of not liking needs to occur with discretion. Private discussions are always better than public ones. A sensitivity to stress-induced tiredness that makes everyone subject to bad judgment, extreme posturing, and "saying the wrong thing" in anger need to be given careful attention. Some previous agreement that anyone in the exploration can call a "time out" or retreat should be inserted as a factor of control. The role of a facilitator or mediator can be very helpful. Everyone in a not liking exploration must be committed to struggling to preserve his/her own human dignity and that of all others involved.

In a true circle of fidelity, the ability to say, "I don't like" must be zealously maintained. Every opportunity to say "I don't like you" is appropriate if that statement is attached to a deliberative, mature not liking exploration. If not liking can occur—and it will inevitably occur—in those circumstances where groups are created by leaders intent upon surrounding themselves by totally similar voices who establish a pseudo comfort zone of mutual admiration and apparent sameness, a not liking that seldom surfaces or is effectively explored, how much more not liking will be a natural consequence of groups whose dynamism, ultimate security, and integrity come from a wise and indispensable globalization of difference and divergence. In a powerful circle of fidelity, not liking is an inevitable fact that is explored with dignity. As this inevitability is explored, a peculiar, even surprising, bonding process occurs that characterizes the most highly productive teams/relationships that can be found.

Archie Bunker, Edith, Gloria, and Michael/"Meathead" of the famed television series "All in the Family" are the paradigms, not "Father Knows Best" or "The Donna Reed Show." Perhaps every work team should find an exemplar in the classic Lee Marvin movie, "The Dirty Dozen," or the Gregory Peck epic, "The Guns of Navarone." Not liking prevails in profound ways in both of these stories, but never is it allowed to compromise goals and objectives. The not liking is confronted by emotionally strong personalities, and powerful teams capable of accomplishing the longest of odds evolve. In the end, the uniqueness of individual personality is not compromised and even sacrificial relationships—even authentic friendships—are established. That which at the beginning seems most unlikely becomes stunningly effective. These paradigms far outstrip the typical mastering of corporate games of smoke, mirrors, deceptions, and facades that dominate so many work cultures.

A HIERARCHY OF RELATIONSHIPS

The following section—one of the most important and descriptive of the entire presentation—is the direct result of the influence of Dan Wilford. The hierarchical breakdown below is Wilford's, and was part of a presentation that he made many times to his leadership team and general employees while he was President and CEO of the Memorial Hermann Healthcare System in Houston, Texas. Wilford had as much to say about the role of strong and healthy relationships forming the base of a successful organization as anyone I have ever heard. He advances these concepts now as Chairman of the Board of the Spiritual Leadership Institute.

While reaffirming the belief that building relationships is the primary determining factor in the success of an organization—as fully important as intelligence, energy, and commitment—there can be the further clarification that relationships occur across a spectrum of rational possibilities. Within authentic circles of fidelity, there are hierarchies of relationships. The following distribution of possibilities presents itself as eight levels ranked in three key plateaus. The eight levels being described constitutes eight different types of relationship qualifiers. At any one time, a level can be operative for an extended period of time; perhaps, the relationship may never change. At other times, levels can move in and out of themselves with some degree of fluidity.

- Unfamiliar
- Familiar
- Knowledgeable
- Confidence
- Trust
- Admiration
- Love
- Worship

The final three levels probably have little to do with business organizations, and tend to apply more readily to personal and spiritual relationships. When these three final levels become confused with those more appropriate to working environments, chaos can reign. Think, for example, of the calamity that can occur in a workplace when feelings of love become attached to fellow workers in an inappropriate manner. To "worship" someone in a work environment, in a similar sense, is chaotic as there is a tendency to absolutize, to lose objectivity, to become unable to serve with perspective and honesty. Admiration may occasionally occur in a work relationship as a peaking of the movement through the first five levels over extended periods of time.

On the other hand, an organization that disregards the importance of understanding the first three levels is likely to fail or, at least, confound its fullest potential. The first three levels, especially the movement beyond lack of knowledge and unfamiliarity to familiarity and knowledgeability, is a necessity. Decisions between groups or among individuals, motivation and commitment, the very striving for excellence and quality that so many organizations take as statements of faith, are impossible without knowledge-allowing contact. There is no substitute for direct contact that gives personal knowledge, even of the outer circles of the organizational structure. Where people's names are known and family information is expressed as concern or congratulations, familiarity does not breed contempt; it rather generates a feeling of being important, belonging, and being a part of something larger than you while still acknowledging that you are an indispensable, essential element in that larger whole. There cannot be a second plateau—the middle three elements of the relational hierarchy—without significant attention being given to the movements of the first plateau.

The middle plateau levels of confidence, respect, and trust are the focal areas of the most highly effective organizations. The embracing and strategic sustaining of these three levels is infinitely more important than mere liking. In many instance, liking is actually a presumptuous conclusion about a person that rises from weak first impressions on the level of the "Unfamiliar." Only liking that is a by-product of the upper half of the hierarchy will ultimately have authenticity.

By observing interactions within the circle of fidelity that exist along this relational hierarchy, articulate understandings of and objectives for workplace dynamics can be given. For example, I may become involved with someone because I think I *admire* him or her—a jump to a level six involvement. Later, I may find that fidelity has been broken in some way by this person. The person, previously encountered on level six, now plunges into the arena of level one, the "Unfamiliar." I may even say, "I really don't know you." If we are to have a relationship, we may have to start all over again, building a new base of familiarity and knowledge. We may finally be able to get into legitimate confidence and trust again. I may even come to respect the person again. The deeper the "plunges" caused by infidelity, the less the likelihood of recovery or the movement to the higher plateau.

In another scenario, I may have some degree of respect for a person simply because the person is another human being. However, since that respect has not started out in a process of working through the first plateau, it is a shallow respect. It is nothing like the kind of respect gained through a process of lived, experienced familiarity.

What Wilford says in these explanations reminds me of the insights of the great theologian and philosopher, Reinhold Niebuhr. Niebuhr believed that it might be wonderful to say, "I just love everyone; I just love my fellow man." However, the likelihood of this kind of "love" having much substance was very slim. Such statements were mostly clichés and platitudes. For him, love— as with Wilford's third relationship plateau—could occur in only select moments between a small circle of the closest intimates. What needed to occur first was justice, perhaps a "middle plateau" reality. It was impossible for there to be love if there was not first justice. Back off from this perspective one step, and it becomes impossible to be just if there cannot first be an initial plateau of basic human decency and fairness. The idea of Marcel's "circles" supplemented by Wilford's "relational levels" creates a powerful dynamic for articulating the options and possibilities available in human existence on all levels including the world of business.

A CONCLUSION CONCERNING GOALS

Most organizations have goals—financial goals, productivity goals, safety goals, and on and on. All of these are necessary to an organization's overall success. However, there must also be specific *relational* goals and performance measures/expectations related to these relational goals. A group within an organization, or the organizations as a whole, might legitimately pursue the goal of moving through the first six levels of the relational hierarchy. There might accompany this goal setting the degree to which work teams, quality circles, or partnerships of associates are actually *Circles of Fidelity*. Attention to the degree that work groups fulfill the characteristics of these potential circles will make those groups operationally stronger and the work they do more meaningful for the people involved. Operational strength and meaningful work experiences ultimately depend on the conscious and strategic development of relationships more than any other driving force. The key is to make this driving force conscious and not accidental, regular and not random, strategic and not serendipitous. The great philosopher, Robert S. Hartman, said that the higher that a person climbs in an organization, and especially as management approaches *leadership*, the more the relational—the intrinsic—dominates what should be important. And, to the extent that fidelity becomes more of an operative reality in the world of work, perhaps it will become more of a reality in the world of the personal.

4. THE FUNDAMENTAL ETHICAL ACTION: CREATING A GOOD PLACE

INTRODUCTION

After all is said and done, if ethics is understood as accountability and accountability is understood as *doing*, then creation in one form or another must take place. This creation may be a better process, a better relationship, or a better plan—a better anything. The basic spiritual movement is to make better, so creating in a primary outcome of ethics. Leland Kaiser teaches at the "Source" of the universe there are two, complementary "forces" of existence that manifest themselves: benevolence and creativity. This is the "stuff" of God. It is also the "stuff" of living if anyone has intent to be godly. As human beings, we are called upon to create and to be benevolent. We are called to make better. Therefore, if we are ethical, we will become involved—with the talents, skills, and gifts at our disposal—in creating good places.

This short tract represents a synthesis of ideas sparked by the insights of two men whom I consider great thinkers and men of great character. Robert S. Hartman was my mentor and teacher from 1971–1973 at the University of Tennessee in Knoxville, where I was involved in work that led to both a Masters of Art and a Doctorate of Philosophy in axiology, the study of values. Hartman was convinced that the deepest levels of insight into human existence, both individually and corporately, could be gained through a scientific investigation of the valuing processes by which human beings make decisions, determine the direction of actions, and establish identity. Most of my own work across over thirty years has involved teaching and writing about Hartman's concepts and exploring ways that these concepts can be applied to education, religion, personal counseling environments, and consultant work that has taken me into business, industrial, and institutional arenas. I have always held the strong conviction that philosophy that cannot have a direct impact on people's lives—cannot speak to the "marketplace"—lacks credibility and power.

Leland Kaiser is usually presented to the audiences he speaks to across the United States as a "health futurist." He has focused a great deal of the attention of his brilliant career on understanding healthcare in the latter part of the twentieth century and helping healthcare institutions and professionals construct strategic agendas for the twenty-first century. Kaiser is one of the most provocative and original thinkers I have known. It has been my distinct pleasure to work with him on a regular basis as a part of the faculty of the Spiritual Leadership Institute initiated by Dan S. Wilford, former CEO of the Memorial-Hermann Healthcare System in Houston, Texas. Leaders from healthcare and other organizational environments attend sessions of the Institute to explore ways that organizational management can move to new levels of quality and excellence.

These ideas on goodness are inspired by Robert Hartman. The skeletal foundation of the different characteristics of a good place are derived from a speech given in the early 1990s by Leland Kaiser. With his kind permission, I have built on and developed this skeletal foundation in this tract.

The material, which follows, is intended for a broad variety of environments and applications. A home can be a good place. Any work setting can be a good place. Without question, some retreat where people find rest, solace, or even inspiration can be a good place. The possibilities are endless. The need for good places is profound. Maslow was absolutely correct in his assessment of understanding human beings in terms of needs, and his "hierarchy" that moves from safety needs to relational needs to needs for self actualization has influenced two generations and continues to stand the test of time. It is possible to accept Maslow and then overlay his hierarchy with a context that extends his thinking. The two, dominant parameters of human existence are time and space. We live and move and have our being in a time/space continuum. Therefore, we stand in great need of good times and good spaces. Bring these concepts together and add Kaiser's ideas about our capacity as humans to design our environments, and it becomes possible to focus on the idea of creating, by design, good places. A good place would impact, in various ways, every level of Maslow's hierarchy: a good place is safe, a good place meets relational needs, a good place provides a platform for self actualization and transcendence.

The purpose of the tract is to initiate internal dialogue—thinking and evaluation—and external dialogue—conversation—that may lead to a raised consciousness about the places we inhabit as human beings. In the context of these internal and external dialogues, the places we inhabit can become better, and the lives and work done in these places can be distinctly enhanced. By placing this material in the hands of workers across a work environment, the synergy of thought and action that becomes possible is vast. That workers might take the ideas home or into other arenas of their personal lives extends the possibility of enrichment that cannot help but have a positive impact on the workplace and the society at large.

Leland Kaiser's key concept in terms of good places is the word habitat. Perhaps following the concept of "habitat for humanity" active in our culture today, it becomes possible to consciously create habitats that are conducive to productivity, efficiency, creative innovation, and meaningful work for laborers. Perhaps one of the most significant responsibilities for any person in management is the creation of environments in which meaningful and productive labor can occur. In this regard, a habitat is not something that randomly happens to us by accident, but something that consciously happens because of us by design.

THE IDEA OF GOODNESS

The terms *good* and *goodness* are distinctly vague, used without clarity, and ultimately trivialized into cliché. In a room full of fifty people, given the opportunity to define the terms, there would be as many different definitions as people. It becomes impossible, therefore, to talk about a good place without having to first define with clarity and succinctness exactly what the words *good* or *goodness* mean.

Here, the work of Robert Hartman becomes profound. At the core of Hartman's axiology, science of value, is a lifelong search for a definition of good. Without a workable definition, an axiomatic statement, this "science" is defeated before it gets out of the starting block.

Hartman believed that goodness was a property of a concept, and not a property of an object. This beginning statement sounds difficult enough, but in fact makes perfect sense. First, consider properties of objects. The object car has properties that would include tires, steering wheels, engines, windows, and brakes. You could not find good or goodness on a car as an object. (Someone might scrawl the word good in dust accumulated on a car's surface, but this written word would not be a property of the object car.)

In a similar sense, properties of the object tree would include bark, limbs, trunk, fruit, and leaves. You could not find good or goodness on a tree in the same sense as you might find an apple or an orange. Apples and oranges are properties of objects; goodness is not. Finally, consider a human being. Properties of the object person would include hands, hair, feet, legs, but not good or goodness. (Yes, someone could tattoo the word good on his body, but the presence of this decoration certainly does not become part of the normally understood object person, nor does the presence of the word make a person a good person.)

Once it is understood that goodness is not the property of an object, attention can be turned to attempting to grasp the idea that goodness is the property of a concept. What, however, is a concept? I would define concept as a nexus, a collection, of ideas or impressions that surround an experience. For example, I have the concept—for want of a better word—"car-ness." Stick with this strange language for a moment; it will all make sense as you think about it. My concept "car-ness" is the result of all of the car experiences I have had in my life; all of the cars I have seen, read about, owned, ridden in, worked on, looked at pictures of. This concept is similar to, but certainly not exactly the same as, anyone else's car concept, since my experiences with cars is not the same as anyone else's. Most all of our concepts end up being pretty unique and personal because our totality of experiences is unique and personal. But, I do indeed have in an accumulated—and accumulating—"file" in my mind the concept "car-ness."

In a similar sense, all of my tree experiences have resulted in another "file," the concept—again, for want of a better word—"tree-ness." Then, following the line of examples I am using here, I certainly have the concept "person-ness," one of the most important of all concepts to me—one of my thickest "files," since I am a person and relationships with persons have been of such high importance in my life as a person. For most people, their "person file" would be the most complex "file" in their conceptual base.

After it is clear that our minds are filled with all sorts of concepts, then it is possible to hear Hartman's key statement that "goodness is concept fulfillment." By this he means that when some individual instance of some reality, a particular tree for example, fulfills our unique, personal concept of "tree-ness," when in terms of our concept an individual tree is what a tree should be as determined by our concept, we then *endow* that tree with the quality goodness. When a particular tree fulfills our concept of what a tree should be, we say that it is a good tree. (Some degree of concept fulfillment is not so personal, but is supplied by the norms and standards of a culture. In other words, there would be some degree of cultural understanding about what makes a good tree in the most general terms. This cultural understanding is likely to be of influence, though not exhaustively so, on any of our individual concepts.)

Follow the logic of this presentation. A person brings in a car for inspection. The car is a twenty-foot long, gold Cadillac with a built in television, stereo, bar, and bed, and the car used to belong to Elvis! The person who brings the car in professes, "This is a good car!" What the person is saying, of course, is simply that this particular car fulfills his concept of what a car ought to be, and as token of this fulfillment he feels comfortable in assigning the term *good* to the car. Goodness becomes, therefore, a property of a concept.

Very clearly, some other person may immediately say, "No, this is a bad car. It is decadent and, besides, only gets four miles to a gallon of gas." This second person may present a five-foot long, original Honda Civic that has no added decoration or amenity, but gets fifty miles to a gallon of gas. With conviction, the person might assert, "Now, here is a really good car. Obviously, the Honda Civic fulfills the concept for this second person of what a car should be, and the word *good* becomes perfectly appropriate. (On the mere, cultural level, both cars may be good in the sense that they can provide transportation from one point to another.)

Of course, no two concepts of goodness are likely to be the same. In an ideal world, tolerance of differing concepts is promoted. Conversation and accommodation, that leads to some kind of healthy consensus or synthesis of differing concepts often, makes for a productive society. Unbending decrees about what is good or bad have little credibility or efficiency and have lead to destruction and dehumanization. There is no libertine sense of "anything goes" being implied here, but tolerant conversations and dialogues by generous, clear thinking people can result in concepts of goodness that enhance and advance individual concepts. Such is the beauty of intelligent interchange in a democratic society.

Moving away from political implication and grounding the basic concept, consider the tree again. For me, a good tree is a huge, powerful Tennessee tulip poplar. If you knew much about my background you would know why I make this statement so unabashedly. In the yard where I grew up, there was such a tree. In fact, it was the oldest, largest tree in our county. School students from elementary to college age were brought on field trips to see and study this tree every year. It was a landmark in our community, and certainly conveyed a sense of status for me. My brothers and I camped out under the tree, climbed in its high branches, and swung on ropes that reached into its dark, aromatic thickness. It was part of our lives. Personal emotion, history and legacy, heightened our concept and gave it more intensity.

My wife, on the other hand, would not come close to assigning, endowing tulip poplars with the word *good*. Without hesitation, she would immediately think of a beautiful, waxy green, southern magnolia as a good tree. Sometimes I will come into our house to find it filled with the rich smells of magnolia blossoms surreptitiously collected from magnolia trees around our town. She has planted a magnolia in every yard we have lived in during our married life. Once I drove with her deep into central Georgia to a town named Newnan for a magnolia tour. How she delighted in the quantity and quality of magnolias that graced the town! The magnolia certainly fulfills her concept of what a tree should be; it is a good tree.

All of us have friends that we find occasion to introduce to other friends. It would not be uncommon to say, for example, "I would like for you to meet Chuck Matherson; he is a really good person." Of course, this statement is a value judgment made on a highly personal level. Someone else who knows my friend, Chuck, might not make the same judgment. I might need to clarify in more discursive and distinctive terms what I mean by good as it relates specifically to Chuck—he is honest, a great father and husband, a patriot of the highest order, and he loves his mother. On the other hand, what I basically mean by good person is that Chuck fulfills my concept of what a person ought to be. My endowing him with this term says a great deal about Chuck; my statement— any time we assign the word *good*—also says a great deal about us as individuals.

Hartman's idea has both logic and a real "ring of truth." When we feel moved to use the word *good* in its full distinctiveness, we are describing the phenomenon of concept fulfillment. At one and the same time, the process is both rationally sensible and emotionally meaningful in a uniquely personal manner. In fact, an axiological dimension, which is at the core of our existence as human beings, supersedes basic rationality and emotionality; the assignment of goodness epitomizes our ability to make value judgments and captivates us with the experiential realization that something or someone has "added value" for us as individuals.

Therefore, a good place would be a place that fulfills my concept of what a place should be. In a good place, I experientially realize that which has added value for me. I am captivated by a good place, it has meaning for me, and I may even love it. Only a collection of our most intense words allows us to use language to point to a reality that unquestionably touches our lives in a way that any and all words are ultimately inadequate to describe rationally and capture emotionally. A home could be a good place. So could a church, a retreat in nature—mountain tops and ocean shores often qualify for many people, and, for me at least, a beautiful golf course. What about a workplace? Is it possible that where we work could be a good place? Using the language of the former CEO of Coca-Cola, Doug Ivester, the very thought of a workplace as a good place may be a "stretch target." And yet, with all the time we spend in workplaces, that they are good should represent a profound need and challenge. If there is a connection between a fulfilling and meaningful workplace and effective productivity, creating a good workplace might be economically very advantageous.

A final clarification can be both interesting and helpful: concepts can be either rich or lean, or stand somewhere on a spectrum between these basic parameters. For example, would I have the richest car concept or would Richard Petty, Dale Earnhart, Jr., or Jeff Gordon? You would expect that my concept would not compete with these three NASCAR greats; their car experiences would be vastly more involved than my own. In a similar sense, I would expect that having been raised in the foothills of the Appalachian Mountains that my tree concept would be significantly richer than someone raised on the treeless glacier fields of the North Pole. Then, as stated earlier, it would be generally true that our person/people concept is the richest concept we have, since we are persons and spend high energy involved in people relationships. Various forms of human dysfunctionality may, it follows, be the result of lean—underdeveloped, immature—person/people concepts. It is impossible to authentically appreciate, tolerate, like, or especially impossible to move in the direction of fairness, justice, or love, without having come to a degree of richness in one's person/people concept.

I have always felt that most of the problems we confront in human society, whether these problems are manifested in personal, community, work place, or family inadequacies and weaknesses, are the result of a conceptual base that is too lean. The task of growth and development, the infrastructure of hope and promise, is the enrichment of conceptual bases. A good parent enriches the conceptual base of a child; a good educational system does the same. A good leader in a work environment enriches the conceptual base of the workers in that environment; to enrich conceptual bases may be the highest calling of a true leader. Concepts are always enriched by open conversation and dialogue, so close-minded territoriality and ego-weak, tunnel vision is sure to result in lean concepts and diminished promise. Those now often clichéd and trivialized, management "power words" of the second half of the twentieth century, *quality* and *excellence*, are almost always the outcome of enriched conceptual bases.

When leanness of conceptual bases prevails, the Peter Principle triumphs, and lethargy, apathy, mediocrity, and incompetence take center stage.

Now, it becomes possible to move to the insights of Leland Kaiser. Kaiser articulates for me many of the key attributes of a good place. To follow the language being used here, he enriches my concept of what a place should be. Kaiser's outline, which becomes a cue for my extended explanations, includes the following assertion: a good place

- compensates
- potentiates
- facilitates
- provides opportunity
- rewards.

I will add to this list my additional beliefs that a good place has beauty, a good place has simplicity, and a good place has power.

A GOOD PLACE COMPENSATES

When I was thirteen years old, my mother died from cancer. Without question, this tragic event left a profound vacuum and sense of loss in the life of my entire family and my life personally. At first there was a sense of having "no place to turn" for the kind of help, the powerful sustenance and nurture, that only a mother can provide. With great, good fortune my older brother and an aunt reached out to me in ways that were remarkable and even sacrificial. Of course, they did not fully replace my mother—no one could do that, but what they did do rescued and established my life on tracks that have a powerful impact on all that has taken place for me since that time. They were not able to keep a deeply negative situation from taking place, nor could they cover every base of need that arose in my life; but they were strong, assertive forces of compensation that created a life-enhancing counterpoint to the events of loss that had taken place.

In the work that I have done with groups in a variety of workplace environments, there are indications of powerful stressors that the Hartman Value Profile is able to measure. The Profile is refined enough to also distinguish between stressors that are a part of the work environment itself—there are certainly plenty of these—and stressors that are a part of people's personal lives that are brought along with them into the workplace.

Interestingly enough, the Profile tends to indicate that the majority of stressors come with the people from their personal lives into their working environment.

For example, the Profile has one, key index which measures the adequacy of a person's self regard—the capacity that a person has to take care of self or to feel that the self has reason to be cared for in positive ways. Many, many people who take the Profile in the workplace demonstrate the capacity to take care of roles, responsibilities, and obligations in the public sector in a substantially successful manner. Yet, these same people demonstrate a marked negative movement in their ability to leave room to take care of themselves. This lack of adequacy of self regard cannot help but be like a ticking time bomb, ready to explode with all kinds of negative implications for the work environment.

As a counterpoint, I have spent years with people in counseling situations who have struggled successfully to improve on and enhance their capacity for self regard and self care. Without exception, when these waters are successfully navigated, there is what I call a "reverse wave" effect in which a new kind of energy is distributed from that person who has developed more adequacy in self regard. New energy is usually translated into new determination and new direction. Work habits, work commitment, and work morale is distinctively experienced in a more positive manner. This "energy" even carries over to fellow workers and clients being served. When adequacy of self-regard improves, the impact on the workplace is often profound.

Yet, in spite of what would appear to be a fairly easy set of implications to see—improvement of self regard leading to a better energy which is brought to work—many employers insists that worker self regard is simply not part of employer or institutional responsibility. Lip service to employee needs, often in the form of extremely limited and ineffectual employee assistance programs, is the limit of most employer and institutional concern. Expression of sorrow, after the fact of the most negative personal dilemmas, leaves an empty, hollow feeling on the part of employees and some measurable loss of productivity, efficiency, or effectiveness for the organization.

The most significant organizations and leaders within those organizations pay substantial attention to the need to be a force of compensation for employees. Actions of compensation are not seen as "favors" done for the employee, but basic responsibilities to be discharged by the organization and its leadership. Nor is compensation understood only in economic terms. To use Hartman's terms, compensation packages have extrinsic, utilitarian and instrumental value; people have intrinsic, personalistic value. To take that which is intrinsic—people—and think of it only in extrinsic terms—dollar amounts in a benefit plan—is ultimately an action of dis-valuation. Part of a whole, new management philosophy is to be specifically aware of employee needs, and to specifically take action to meet these needs. There is a distinct need to compensate for the negativities that people find in their personal lives. To do so builds a level of trust, commitment, and dedication to workplace goals and objectives that has powerful, positive implications for all that goes on in the workplace. Loyalty and dedication to workplace goals will never have a positive stimulus like strategic objectives designed to meet worker needs.

I remember several years ago having involvement with a church that had a tremendously able minister. Almost out of the clear blue sky, without any warning, the minister's wife filed divorce papers. Not only was the man totally devastated in every personal way imaginable, but a series of events began to unfold that led to the loss of his pulpit and, essentially, the end of a tremendously successful career. The church leadership felt it could not have a minister with this sort of stigma. No efforts were made to help what was in fact simply a young couple having problems. Ironically, their primary problem was the time he was giving to his work. Sixty-five nights prior to the day the papers were served, he had been away from home—doing church business, helping church members, attending church meetings. Instead of having a process set up to help people in this kind of situation, the church simply asked for his resignation. An exceptionally gifted minister was lost, a family was broken.

How much better it would have been for everyone involved in the church if some sort of conscious strategy to understand and prevent negative impact on families had been available. How much better it would have been if there had been specific resources and agendas in place to respond to such circumstances if they took place. To believe that all of these human tragedies were only the problem for those immediately involved was shortsighted and destructive, certainly inconsistent with the avowed ideals of the organization involved. Interestingly enough, that particular organization probably never has done as well or had such a commanding "spirit" as when that minister was at the helm of leadership. By turning its back and a "blind eye" on these very specific, human needs, the organization effectively turned its back on its own best future and its most fundamentally stated ideals. The organization's failure to compensate for its workers and their needs created a negative dynamic that has plagued that organization to this day.

Can a work organization rescue all of its employees? Absolutely not. Can a work organization solve all of its employees' problems? Absolutely not. Is there an unlimited, economic surplus that can allow money to be thrown at every employee difficulty that manifests itself? Absolutely not.

Yet, the inability to solve all problems absolutely and perfectly should not be a deterrent to attempting to solve problems and offer assistance within the limits of reasonable logic and common sense. Conscious strategies of assessment and inquiry will result in the recognition of problems and deficiencies. Conscious strategies of response to these problems will heighten credibility and commitment, and—sometimes when people are especially fortunate—even help enhance and remediate negative situations.

I was part of a "sales call" presentation in which an organization was trying to convince a key executive to support and literally "buy into" a product that might be of benefit to his company and other companies he worked with. The key executive obviously had other concerns on this mind and begin to speak, with deep emotion, about a grandson he was trying to help. The man making the call with me was responsible for building a whole line of business for the university he worked for. How intriguing it was that this man simply set the whole agenda of sales aside and began to focus total attention on the executive's grandson. It was no ploy on his part, but a genuine response to a genuine need. Before the conversation was over, specific strategies of help for the boy were developed and clear agendas created. Nothing more was said about the product being sold. There was a need, at that moment, for compensation. Economics ceased to be of any consideration.

As a result of these responses, a young boy was helped, and a grandfather was made to feel that he had been a prime mover in that process. Weeks later, a "sale" followed, and that grandfather/key executive has advanced the agendas of the university and its representatives beyond any original expectations. However, the "sale" was not the key; the grandson was the key. All else become a matter of course, which unveiled itself. Think about how this entire process would have been different if the person calling on the executive had only had a "sale" in mind. Think about how the entire process would never have realized its fullest potential if a movement to compensate had not taken place. Think about the credibility that this representative of this university gained for himself and for his institution that was exceedingly more valuable than what might result from a "sales call." To say that movements of compensation open the door to powerful results, often beyond any conceived strategy, is a great understatement.

Key leaders in organizations need to have specific discussions directed pointedly at the degree of compensation that the organization can bring to bear on the needs of its workforce. Here compensation distinctly goes beyond economics and touches the personal lives of people involved in the work environment. Yes, there will be some price tag associated with the type of compensation being described here. In addition, there will be times in which this attitude toward and practice of compensation will be taken advantage of. Yet, in the end, a good place cannot be created without compensation. The benefits and long-range rewards will greatly exceed the immediate costs. The positive attitude toward people will create a totally new attitude by workers to the workplace, and by workers toward the organization and leadership, that directs their daily activity. Finally, in fact, by the creation of conscious strategies of compensation, the "walk" of the workplace's stated visions and ideals may match its "talk."

A GOOD PLACE POTENTIATES

The word *potentiates* gives my spell checker fits; it insists that the word does not exist. Most common dictionaries of the English language follow suit. Anecdotes can help guide the way toward an understanding of the word maybe better than definitions.

When Robert Kennedy campaigned for the Presidency in 1968, he repeated over and again a phrase that became the focal point of the idealistic vision he held for the United States. This phrase so captured the essence of Kennedy's unique life that his brother, Edward Kennedy, used it as the central feature of Robert's eulogy, that his brother delivered following Robert's tragic assassination. Kennedy had professed with great passion: "Some men see things as they are and ask why?; I see things as they can be and ask why not?" Kennedy was one of those unique figures who appear too seldom on the world stage who see the potential which exists in people, institutions, and circumstances, and who find a way of triumphing over obstacles of every variety and, by the force of their personality and charismatic will, transform that which is actual into that which is possible. Robert Kennedy knew how to *potentiate;* he was a *potentiator.*

Somewhere along the way I remember hearing a management consultant talking about strategies of management that move organizations in new directions. Suddenly, in the midst of a great deal of cliché that was about to put me to sleep, he started talking about what he called "learned ignorance." The phrase was new to me and seemed in contradiction with itself. My attention was peaked. "Learned ignorance" was, for him, the ability to consciously and strategically stop focusing on the past successes, traditions, and history of an organization in order to give full focus and concentration to how an organization might deal with present tense realities and, even more, how an organization might move into a new future. His accurate insight was that most organizations spend too much time obsessed with some combination of past failures and successes.

This is not to say that learning from failures and successes is not important. In addition, some understanding of the roots manifested in legacy and tradition is beneficial. But, all too often, a tendency triumphs, that gets caught up in status quo thinking and establishment strategies that sustain the past. To be an organization that potentiates always involves a stern discipline that projects into the future rather than rests in the past and all of its accomplishments. There is a scriptural injunction which insists on the efficiency and effectiveness of "putting your hand to the plow and not looking back." All too often, individuals and organizations become compelled with where they have been, not where they are going. To *potentiate* means, in many respects, to have a "learned ignorance" about even the successes of the past.

Even the very best and brightest organizations can move in this direction. In late 1997, a merger took place between the Memorial Healthcare System and Hermann Hospital in Houston, Texas. Both organizations had strong and distinguished pasts. Because the Memorial CEO became the key leader of the new organization, the key Memorial leadership certainly had a distinct advantage in the processes that took place as the merger developed. Conversation and dialogue was often hurt by a phrase that had become central to the brilliant successes of the Memorial experience of the past decade. Suggestions and possible new agendas were presented, typically from the Hermann side of the merger process, that were resisted or rejected by people from the Memorial side saying, "That is not the Memorial way."

Now, look closely at this expression. On the Memorial side, the idea of a "Memorial Way" had almost sacred status, and rightfully so. The concept of a "Memorial Way" designated excellence and class of the highest order and epitomized reputation and character. For those on the Hermann side, however, the phrase signaled almost immediate resistance. They may have wanted to talk about an equally dynamic "Hermann Way." Something of the kind of impasse, albeit a fully predictable impasse that threatens any merger situation, was at hand. In order to move to a new level, it became important to call a moratorium on the phrase, to understand that in the new dynamic that the old phrase had been buried with full and appropriate dignity. Now, the understanding is clear as this merger progresses in significantly positive directions that emphasis must be given to creating a new identity, a "Memorial-Hermann Way" that will find its own uniqueness, integrity, and power. The potential, which exists for the future, finds priority over all of the successes of the past. There is little room for sacred cows in an organization that potentiates; there is a straining toward what might be, not a desperate clutching to what once was. An organization that *potentiates* lives toward the future.

In the work that I have done with the Hartman Value Profile, there is a type of person (Stage/Type 12 in the Hartman interpretations) whose primary characteristic and strength that is brought to an organization is the capacity to recognize and develop potential in people and situations. It is remarkable to watch this person operate in the workplace. You can almost sense the "eye" of a Type 12 person observing surroundings, digesting options, and moving circumstances toward a higher level of fulfillment. In particular, it is intriguing to watch a Type 12 person explore and motivate the potential that resides in human beings. Often the persons being motivated and drawn into a level of higher potential does not even see the potential that exists in their lives. Almost a "magic" of motivation and even inspiration occurs that involves teaching, coaching, encouraging, and stretching. The meaningfulness and even happiness that then occurs in retrospect can be startling. The person or circumstance is potentiated.

When I was a freshman in high school, the football team from our school was typically among the best in the State of Tennessee. In this year, however, we had struggled. Because of the political circumstances involving the loss of an almost legendary coach, only nineteen boys had come out for the team. By the time we came down toward the end of the season, our best lineman had sustained a crippling knee injury and our best running back was in knee braces. We struggled through a season filled with more losses than the team had experienced in years. Things were so desperate that there were even times when a lowly freshman got to play.

Our last game of the season was always against archrival Bradley County, a school in the early 1960s with the most brilliant concentration of athletic teams in the history of high school sports in our state. Bradley County was undefeated and ultimately sent athletes to major colleges across the nation. Yet, on November 6, 1960—a date that still fills my mind—we defeated Bradley County 20–6. As I continue to reflect on what took place that created this astounding victory, what sticks in my mind the most is what the coaches did with us in the week preceding the game. Somehow, and I'm not sure there is any "rational" explanation, these coaches convinced us that we were as good as any team in the world. I almost believe that had we been playing the Volunteers of the University of Tennessee or even the Green Bay Packers that we still could have competed. When we walked on that field that night, there was absolutely no question in my mind that we would win. I remember that feeling as distinctly as if it were yesterday!

Somehow there was a vision of our potential that these coaches saw. Maybe they had analyzed game films and seen possibilities that no other team had seen. As I recall it, however, we added no new plays and had numerous discussions about "getting back to the fundamentals." I believe that there was "something" within us—maybe a modern management consultant would talk of synergy—that was successfully actualized. Whatever the case, we played with a fluid smoothness and tenacious determination that made you feel that you were in some other "zone"—for want of a better word. In perhaps a very crude, although perhaps very sophisticated, way—language begins to fail us once again—this whole event embodied potentiation. What was felt was very real and remains distinct; what was understood is still as much of a mystery today as it was almost forty years ago. Maybe, when potentiation occurs, this is always the case. What if potentiation could become a learned skill? What if, as the Profile suggests, it were possible to actually pick out people who had particular capacities for potentiation?

I once heard a story about a rail-riding hobo, a character prolific and even idolized in my youth, who had ridden trains all of the nation in search of a uniquely special place. He had seen the name of this almost mythic place emblazoned in the writing on the side of boxcars and tank cars he had seen daily across the course of his travels. He talked endlessly of this unique place as if it were a sort of Holy Grail. The place he talked and dreamed of was named "Capa-city." Its name was on everything; how special it must have been! Of course, the hobo was mistaken. There was no special place; the writing on the side of the train cars merely referred to the capacity of bulk of liquid that the train car was designed to carry. There is, however, an insight here: we all have a certain "Capa-city," an epitome of our abilities that we can perhaps possess; we all have a capacity. In a truly good place, there is the recognition and realization of this capacity. This capacity is potentiated.

A GOOD PLACE FACILITATES

The third of Leland Kaiser's aspects of a good place—those realities that fulfill his concept of what a good place should be—lays claim to the idea that a good place facilitates. Of his five key aspects, this one has personally created the largest problems for me. That I have evolved to embrace what I believe Kaiser is saying represents personal growth and development that has come later in life.

I was raised to embrace and give emphasis to the phenomenon of presentation. My role models were often great teachers who had something vital to say in their teaching, were always superbly prepared, and had a special talent for taking complex ideas and making them understandable to broad audiences. As I began my own teaching, counseling, and consulting activities, I spent inordinate amounts of time making sure that my presentations were well-prepared, well-rehearsed, and well-presented. There were always compliments about the quality of the end product—the presentation—so continued reinforcement of this mode of communication gave it even more emphasis.

Psychologically, I guess that I knew that somehow there was a "hiding" to some extent behind the presentation approach. Certainly, I asked for questions, but most of the questions were concerning whether my statements had been understood. I continually told students that part of their test grades would rise from their own processing and assimilating of my information as it compared to their own experiences, but—honestly—I spent most of my grading attention looking for repetitions—of what they said that I had said. The content reigned supreme. In non-academic presentations, I often promised time for question-and-answer sessions, but more times than not my presentation concluded in sync with the end of my allotted time. I was the type of counselor who talked too much and probably diminished the client's talking time. There is little, spontaneous and immediate dialogue between book writers and their readers, so only an occasional letter from some reader provided arms-length dialogue in that context.

In addition, I basically despised—the word is carefully chosen—those times when I would get trapped into "brainstorming sessions." I hated that lackluster scribe who wrote on flipcharts and taped pages of newscript to the wall. Process planning meetings were a waste of time. "Cut to the chase," I cried out. "Just tell me what you think," I protested as one "facilitator" after another trended their way into management meetings and administrative conferences.

Three experiences began to challenge my predispositions and raise, I hope, my work to a new level. First, I began to study the career of the noted philosopher, Ludwig Wittgenstein; I might not always be able to fathom his philosophy, but I could learn from his life. What I learned was startling in a way. Of course, Wittgenstein taught in fairly classical ways; he probably had to. But, as he matured in his career and was more able to determine the mode of his scholarly existence, the more he stopped making presentations. Instead, students would simply show up at his classroom/office/study at the appointed time for their classes. Wittgenstein was there, but there were no lecture notes, syllabi, book reports, or tests. There was simply Wittgenstein. He engaged the students in conversations, conversations about whatever he was thinking about or working on at that time. The students were free to contribute whatever was on their minds. They simply got Wittgenstein. The example was taken up, as a personal challenge, in at least part of my classes. The lecture was put aside. The podium was pushed off to the side. We simply talked. I was often uncomfortable, but could not mistake the unplanned synergy and insight that rose for both students and teacher. There was distinctly learning/teaching, but the mode of encounter took on a completely different texture. For someone who had taught the Socratic method for a quarter century, the irony of what I was experiencing—and liking—was mesmerizing.

I also began to come in contact with colleagues in my consulting rounds who had a deep appreciation for the process of open dialogue, and who were really gifted at making the process work. In the hands of an artist at establishing conversation and advancing dialogue, mere "brainstorming" was quickly transcended. There occurred what the great German existentialists had called *Begegnung*—a "meeting" or "encounter" in which a gestalt event took place that went beyond the sum of what the individual participants brought to the event.

Finally, I began to be asked—as a natural extension of the general consulting work that I was doing—to facilitate everything from large group, strategic planning sessions to conversations between employees or employee groups who had gotten at odds with each other and needed mediation and reconciliation. Some of the most positive—though demanding and even frightening—experiences of meaningfulness and personal authenticity that I have experienced in my working career took place in the midst of these facilitation assignments. While I certainly have not stopped presenting and still see the great value of a well-constructed and well-delivered presentation, the value of facilitation has dramatically asserted itself.

In a good place, the conscious strategy of facilitation is always near at hand. A personal relationship cannot experience its full potential if there is not open and honest conversation. In a family, every member must feel a sense of parity; when a family member speaks, all of the other family members must dignify what is said by listening, seeking clarity, and struggling with what is said. No business or professional setting gains the clarity of expression and flow of vital information necessary for success without a free flow of conversation throughout the organization. When turf management takes the form of withholding information or management dictatorship thwarts conversation by intimidation or half-veiled forms of punishment, the overall effectiveness of an organization is diminished exponentially. When fear of conflict moves people in an organization toward half-truths and avoidance, the promise of the organization is shackled.

The great Desert Storm leader, General Norman Schwartzkof, is reported to have had one, standing rule among his direct reports, a standing rule which he expected to be carried down through his entire command: everyone was expected to tell what they knew, say what they thought, stand up for what they believed. Officers who tried to "play games" with Schwartzkof, say what they thought he wanted to hear, or downplay bad news with sugar-coated window dressing were quickly on their way to another command or a lesser rank. The great general facilitated by the very force of his personality. The input of frontline soldiers was unrelentingly important to Schwartzkof, and he sought the counsel of sergeants and privates as quickly as majors and colonels. This kind of "pursued frankness" is rare in any arena; it becomes a powerful example for anyone who would dare desire to lead others.

Perhaps a few, concrete suggestions might be important for any group hoping to move in the direction of more positive facilitation. This list is certainly not exhaustive, but it is a good starting point. Here, therefore, are actual steps, which can be taken to create a good place in this one regard.

1. Offer a series of seminar/training sessions on conflict understanding and management. Notice that I did not say conflict elimination. Conflict will never be eliminated in a real-life environment. In fact, conflict may be a primary stimulus to progress, growth, and new levels of synthesis.

2. Start offering praise and publicly stated appreciation for those who will actually say what they really think and feel. Promotions and high performance ratings for the kind of behavior being advanced here can also be strong incentive. Do not, on the other hand, tolerate half-truths and corporate gamesmanship.

3. Be extremely sensitive to the way negative or critical information is received. Any person in a leadership position who responds with temper, intimidation, or defensive anger can be certain that the next time out there will be at least one person—and probably several—who will simply be silent. That kind of silence is never "golden" and literally mutes vital conversation and dialogue.

4. Arrange for a biographical film of Schwartkopf to be shown at a staff meeting or distribute copies of his book. Put yourself as a leader in the position of teacher in a way that the concepts of this chapter are shared and given strong emphasis.

5. Include persons in the overall decision-making processes who are not regular members of the executive staff. If you make them feel welcome and secure enough to talk, maybe the executive staff will feel more comfortable about speaking up or, at least, get to see some positive, conversational behaviors.

6. Experiment with using the services of a professional facilitator. Some familiarity with management leadership or your particular arena of operation will probably help. With individuals, small groups, or families, a primary role of a good counselor should be to facilitate conversation. By using a professional facilitator in a corporate setting, a CEO or manager/supervisor can take on the posture of being part of the group. Just this change of meeting proximity can be refreshing and liberating for all involved.

7. Create specific times of reflection and assessment when group members can focus attention on how well conversation and dialogue is really occurring. Have the group discuss the degree to which beneficial facilitating is taking place. This type of conscious debriefing should accompany any key decisions or the carrying out of any critical agendas. It should also address

the process of conversation and dialogue itself. And, above all, remember that no decision is made or agenda carried out without conversation. Facilitation, therefore, has no substitute.

The idyllic flower children of the 1960s "Counter Culture" had a special word, which has always captivated my attention and made me wish for its presence—*serendipity*. Our closest, common synonym may be the word *surprise*. In a serendipitous moment, something takes place that was not anticipated and we are surprised, our attention is captured; we may even be startled. When human beings come together and really engage in honest conversation, serendipity is on its launching pad. When people decide, are empowered and encouraged, or simply find the courage to begin to really talk, an event of power, clarity, insight, and creative invention is about to take place. A good place is seldom an accident; the possibility of serendipity may lie in direct proportion to the action of facilitation.

A GOOD PLACE GIVES OPPORTUNITY

People have crossed oceans, continents, and great vacuums of outer space in the name of opportunity. Work and even sacrifice has often been a small price when opportunity seemed to be in the wings of our lives. There must be something special built into our brains that signals the greatest of effort just when the possibility of opportunity is mentioned. We have a response that would make Pavlov's dog look like a total amateur. The ideal of the communities and societies we have formed in the twentieth century and are now forming in the twenty-first century is that we are able to freely create and reap the rewards of belonging to nations where opportunity, like liberty itself, is a privilege and entitlement. Assured success is not an entitlement, but opportunity should be.

In order for a workplace to be a good place, opportunity must be present. At first glance, this means opportunity for advancement and promotion. Of course, this is true. Nothing is more stimulating and motivating in a workplace than to see effort and accomplishment noticed and responded to in positive ways. Few people enter a workplace intent on remaining in the same position or job that brought them there. We approach work in general with the idea that we will have a chance to climb some sort of "ladder" of success; in fact, success is probably defined in large part by the chance to move up that ladder. Again, the ideal is not entitlement, but opportunity.

On a basic level, opportunity means that there are no intrinsic dimensions of a system that prohibits movement; there are no "glass ceilings." A workplace that prohibits opportunity because of race, sex, or age cannot be a good place. It is impossible to have a truly good place if a political system is in place that advances because of kinship, social connection, or personal fiat, rather than by demonstrable merit and objectively measured performance. A certain by-product of a workplace that encourages the type of opportunity being described here will be divergence and globalization, the eradication of tunnel vision and corporate provincialism. A "level playing field" brings a dramatic synergy to a working environment that contributes exponentially to all of the calculated opportunities that are put in place by wise management practices and judicious business decisions.

There must also be the opportunity to grow in ways other than basic advancement and promotion; in particular, there must be measures of growth in addition to basic monetary increases. Growth is an intrinsic good, an event and activity that is good in and of itself and good in almost all situations. Conscientious people—people of character, integrity, and credibility—have growth as a prime-moving facet of their lives across the entirety of their lives. I heard an extremely authentic person, for whom I have deepest regard, once say, "On the morning of the day I die as a very old man nearing 100, I hope that I experience something new, learning something new, have some thought that I have never exactly had before." This person is intent on forever growing, and his life continues to be dynamic and influential in spite of his years.

My father exemplified this whole spirit of growth in a conversation I observed when he was approaching ninety-two years of age. A friend and I were on business, traveling through the town where my father lived. He insisted that we go out of our way a bit to visit my father; he had heard countless stories about my father, and wanted to meet him for himself. As with most conversations with my father, our visit turned into a couple of entertaining hours. I had heard many of the stories repeatedly, but there was always some added twist or nuance that had not come up before.

Finally, as we stood to leave, my friend said to my father: "When I meet someone of your age, I always like to ask them what was the biggest day of their life, the day that stands forever in their minds as the greatest day of all." My father was stumped for a moment, which was unusual in itself. You could see a brightness in his eyes as he contemplated the question and then came to an answer that was exactly right for him. "Mr. Varnell," he responded to my friend, half his age, "I don't think that my biggest day, my greatest day, has occurred yet." This from a man who had lived more than nine decades! Opportunity and growth were still an active part of his imagination and an active part of his daily life. In the moments before a stroke silenced his life, he was "pontificating" to someone who was visiting him in the hospital about some insight he had just had that morning about how some hospital process could be done more efficiently.

A great deal of opportunity for growth can be identified with education. In a good place, a conscious strategy of continuous education is critical. I emphasize conscious strategy, since a great deal of education in the workplace is randomized and haphazard. With a conscious strategy, specific assessment of specific needs is given priority, learning goals are established that have direct implication for the worker in the workplace, and education is coordinated across work teams and entire work units. Just going off to a conference somewhere becomes a strategy whose time is well past.

In addition to work-related educational needs, which have a direct impact on increasing skills that will make a person more productive and skilled in the workplace, in a good place there is parallel attention to what I call "IDPs," Individual Development Plans. These plans may very well compliment what takes place in the skill sets of a workplace, but in most instances they will be of a more personal nature. In discussions with managers or supervisors, attention will certainly be given to at least an annual review of goals and objectives and performance standards and how these have been met. New standards will likely be established for the coming evaluation period. Then, parallel significance will be given to the employee's IDP. The employee will be responsible for presenting the plan, and how aspects of the plan will be accomplished. The organization then makes itself responsible for helping in the completion of the plan. This may mean some degree of funding or provision for time. By affirming individual development, there is no question that a "payback" in dedication and commitment to the workplace will occur. The happier or more fulfilled—growing and developing—employee will be a stronger influence and contributor to all that takes place in the work environment. In fact, if research is reviewed on why employees stay longer in an organization and feel a sense of commitment to that organization, there is always evidence of conscious attention that is given on the part of the organization to the personal growth and development of its employees.

Finally, and perhaps surprisingly, a good place gives the opportunity to fail. A tremendous amount has been written about stellar organizations that have given emphasis to risk taking. The concept is solid, and unless people work in an environment that allows them to push the horizons of possibilities, the full potential of those people and the work they do will seldom be realized. John Scully, who once ran the highly creative Apple Computer Company, believed that employees who did not fail at least twenty per cent of the time were probably going to become more of an obstacle to a company than an invigorating stimulus.

However, as much as the idea of promoting risk-taking finds its way into the corporate-speak of most organizations, it is still more window dressing than reality. People in high corporate places of supposed leadership pay lip service to the concept more than make it a standard operating procedure. Often the concept is fine until someone does indeed fail; then they are asked to leave or penalized in some way. Failure is often fine if it is not costly, or if it does not make upper levels of the organizational chain of command look bad in some way.

One of the most memorable and remarkable moments I have ever experienced came years ago in a locker room before an important football game. This particular game came halfway through a rather mediocre season that was at a crossroads. We were playing a top-ranked team, and the odds were that we would end that evening with what would have been a devastating loss. The locker room was filled with a tremendous flow of emotion that was palpable in the strong sense of that word.

The coach gave an impassioned pre-game speech with tears flowing from his eyes. This unusual emotion cascaded into all of our lives. We knelt together to pray, and this time it was not a perfunctory reciting of the Lord's Prayer; to the best of whatever religious ability we had, we really prayed. As the prayer ended and we were all huddled together, the coach spoke through more tears: "You young men have a great opportunity tonight. I can't play. The game will be your role. I will help all I can, but the opportunity is yours." He turned and pointed at the door of the locker room and completed his oration: "If I had to run through that door tonight to get to play, then the door would be coming down!"

My eyes caught the eyes of our star offensive end. He had one of the weirdest looks on his face I have ever seen. It was almost as if all of the emotional flow had wound him up into a deep trance. As soon as the words were uttered by the coach about the door—almost in slow motion—my friend began to put on his helmet and fasten his chinstrap. He then turned, without hesitation, and proceeded to attempt to run through the door.

Had he tried this two weeks before, he probably would have succeeded. The locker room and its door had been pretty decrepit. But a near break-in had required a new steel door. When my teammate hit the door, now almost at full speed, he simply melted off of it like a character in a cartoon. He knocked himself out cold and lay there right in the middle of the floor.

I will never forget what that coach did. He moved over to the boy, bent down next to him on the floor, cradled him in his arms, got him to "come to," and helped him up and out the door and onto the playing field. In that moment, any of us would have died for this man. In fact, we did go out that night and win a football game—against all odds. The coach had motivated the young man to attempt to run through the steel door, and the young player had absolutely failed. In the coach's response, he simply picked him back up and got him on his way. This model becomes profound for the corporate environment. A good place gives opportunity to fail, to try, to take chances— and in the process, gives opportunity to fail. Then, if failure occurs, there is the need to pick up, steady, and set people on a new course, a course toward success.

A GOOD PLACE REWARDS

The last characteristic of a good place, which fulfills the concept for Leland Kaiser, is the reality of rewards. How interesting that Kaiser did not put rewards in the first position of priority; many people, if you listen to their most heartfelt discussion, certainly would. Sometimes it seems that all people want to talk about is rewards, and this is usually interpreted in terms of money, pure and simple.

I will never forget two soon-to-be freshman girls showing up in my office before the fall semester started at my college. I was to be their "advisor." One of the girls, with the obvious dominance of the two personalities, cut to the chase: "Do you have the list?", she asked, hardly giving time for introductions or pleasantries. Knowing full well what she was talking about, I still replied: "What list?" She then continued: "Oh, you know, that list they—whoever "they" might be—that tells what the good paying jobs are going to be." There are, in fact, such lists and—for better or worse—such a list had become a standard part of our advisor packages that we were given each fall in our orientation for the new school year.

The girls surveyed the list like it was a map to hidden treasure—which it assuredly was not! Finally, one said to the other: "Look here. Dental hygienist. A one-year program. Starting pay of $17,500.00. What a great chance to meet unmarried dentists! What do you think?" The other girl replied, "Sounds fine to me. Sign us up." A "career" decision, the choosing of a life direction, setting a course for the future? Who knows what to call this sort of decision. All that mattered, in this instance, was the short length of time that would be spent in school and what must have sounded like a grand starting salary. The emphasis was totally on rewards.

Robert Hartman would call this sort of reward an extrinsic or instrumental reward. It serves an immediate purpose, which if these students ran true to course, meant enough money to go in together and rent an apartment, and maybe enough to get saddled with a protracted set of car payments.

On a more significant level, Hartman would then talk about intrinsic rewards. It is the very nature of the intrinsic not to be logically explained or demonstrably measured. This inability is, however, not seen as a negative. On the level of the intrinsic, the rewards are highly personal, highly individualized, and typically result in such realities as meaningfulness, joy, passion, and excitement. School teaching, for example, has never been an activity to be pursued for economic reasons. Fresh out of college in 1976 with a new Ph.D. in hand, I went to work for $11,500 a year. But, the thrill of finally being in that college classroom—a "professor" no less—was the fulfillment of a lifetime. I was getting to do exactly what I had dreamed of doing. In spite of more than a small degree of economic hardship, I could not have been happier with my job.

Interesting enough, after twenty-five years, the economic rewards became much, much more than substantial. Benefit programs had improved and, accompanied by tenure, there was a very secure future. In other words, there were extrinsic rewards, and all of the comfort and predictability that went with them. I left teaching and moved in the direction of a consulting career. Somehow, the teaching had lost its intrinsic quality; not the wonderful students, whom I indeed miss, but the overall teaching experience. I feel quite fortunate now that what I am doing in the challenges of the consulting work that I am pursuing brings the same kind of challenge and excitement—the intrinsic rewards—that I first experienced in the college classroom. To discover at mid-life work that brings you back to the eagerness of that first, full-time—past the doctorate—work is a rare pleasure for which I have a deep sense of gratitude. When challenge, excitement, pleasure, and gratitude become something of the parameters of a person's life experience, the intrinsic has triumphed.

In a good place, there is significance to both extrinsic and intrinsic rewards. In the world we live in today, both are necessities that cannot be diminished. Karl Marx was making a very strong point when he insisted that without some degree of economic freedom, the possibilities of any, real freedom are greatly lessened. A good place goes to great lengths to make sure that the basic economic needs of its workers are met. To do less, makes talking about the intrinsic little more than clichéd window dressing.

Marx was very precise in understanding that both capital and labor are required to produce products, services, and profit. When this occurs, those who have labored have a right to their fair share in the profit that is made. This does not mean that everyone in the producing process with be paid equally, but there will be some measure of relative parity that keeps anyone from being economically abused. Slavery was one type of abuse; the factory system of Marx's world was as well.

Here's what I have in mind: I have a wonderful aunt who worked across most of her life for Sears. She was in ladies ready-to-wear and was a wonderful sales person. She was given the opportunity to invest her bonuses and commissions in Sears stock as a part of a profit-sharing process that the company instituted in the 1950s. It was her choice, but the company provided the option. Across the years, my aunt's stock split several times and became quite valuable. Now, does this mean that she lived in the same kind of house as the President of Sears? Probably not. Does this mean that she drove the same kind of car as the Chairperson of the Sears board? I would not imagine. However, each month she goes to her mailbox and gets her prized Sears check that not only supplements her social security, but allows her options and possibilities that give her freedom and dignity of a sort that her forbears could not have imagined—especially for a woman without any advanced education. In this sense, Sears became a good place for my aunt. A good place rewards extrinsically.

There are many organizations today that feel that once the extrinsic rewards are covered that their obligation to the employee's reward potential is complete. In the more imaginative and even humane work environments, there is a desire to move beyond the extrinsic and approach the intrinsic. This is difficult to do and requires effort and character on the part of organizations.

In order to fulfill something of the intrinsic reward, the working staff in the organization has to be asked in a conscious and strategic manner what it is that they might want or might want to do in order to have/experience what might personally be considered an intrinsic reward.

For years, I made sure that when there was a special occasion in my marriage that a gift of some sort was provided. This was really an important feature of a relationship and, most of the time, my gifts were chosen with both time and effort. After several years, I began to be stumped by this gift-giving process. I frustrated myself with an inability to keep coming up with encore gifts that were somehow bigger or better than whatever the previous gift had been. At one point, I did something that—at the time—seemed really strange. I told my wife that I wanted to accompany her as the gift was bought, that I wanted to actually do the exchange that paid for the gift, but that I wanted her to pick out what she wanted.

I was amazed! She entered into that process with an enthusiasm I'm not sure I had seen in the gift-giving activities that had taken place. She seemed more excited about what she "received" under these new circumstances. If anything, she seemed more grateful to me, although I was certainly doing much less in this new arrangement. Maybe what was more important than anything else was that I was making a concerted effort to determine what was important to her! The process that surrounded these activities and the gifts that were procured were intrinsic.

Could a business replicate something of this attitude and process? I hear my friend Dan Wilford, then President and CEO of the Memorial-Hermann Healthcare System in Houston, probing the idea of what I called in the previous chapter the wonderful and wise insight of "IDPs"—Individual Development Plans. You can tell by now that I am sold on this concept and feel it has remarkable potential. At first, Dan was not sure, but he was always smart enough to inquire. His inquiries convinced him. Here was an initiative that employees responded to remarkably. He saw a direct relationship between advancing this employee emphasis and the vital commitment that employees were bringing to his organization.

An employee would continue, in an IDP process, to participate in a formal performance evaluation process, much like the performance evaluation processes that have been a part of MBO programs for years. The formal process would not be diminished in any way whatsoever.

The performance evaluation process usually takes on the character of the work organization approaching the employee with goals, objectives, and expectations. This is, of course, totally appropriate. With this task accomplished, attention would then turn to the IDP, in which the employee would approach the organization with some sort of plan for personal growth and development, personal improvement. Not only is this perceived as humane, but—without question—such a process should result in a more committed and more dedicated employee who has greater loyalty to the goals of the organization. The organization is demonstrating that it has greater loyalty to the employee. A creative "win-win" is established that has all kinds of potentially positive ramifications.

A climate is established that may result in intrinsic rewards for both the individual worker and the organization. An IDP is not a "wish list," but rather an agreement, which is to be taken seriously, and for which the employee is accepting accountability for fulfilling. The IDP will likely cost the organization something in either time, money, or both. An organization's foundation might, for example, come to understand that foundation funds that have been given to worthwhile community efforts can be shared internally with company employees in ways that increase morale and better the lives of people whose lives are, in fact, given to advance the goals of the organization. There may be many funding options.

How can an organization know if it doesn't ask? What might happen in an organization that discovered something of the intrinsic? The possibilities are almost endless. In a good place, organizational leadership asks! Then, agendas are created in concert with employees that provide the intrinsic reward. Sometimes, the intrinsic reward may not even cost a dime, may not require any formal process; sometimes the intrinsic occurs when there is recognition for a job well done, especially that kind of recognition that comes in saying, "Thank you." Sometimes intrinsic reward takes the form of a pat on the back, congratulations, basic notice from one human being to the next. A good place rewards!

A GOOD PLACE IS BEAUTIFUL

At this point, I am moving beyond the ideas contributed by Leland Kaiser. His insights are a wonderful beginning. I am now stimulated to believe that there are a couple of additional characteristics of good places—following the inspiration of Kaiser—that can be added to our list.

I once had the opportunity to work with a large NICU unit (Neonatal Intensive Care Unit) with a staff of 140 people serving approximately 40 seriously needy infants. A NICU unit is a remarkable place to observe, and this unit did a significant job of saving babies who, only a few years ago, would have had little or no chance at life. The unit did have its problems. There was a strong hierarchy that existed between the various "levels" of workers in the unit and no small measure of territoriality. In my experience, there were a large number of very fine people on every "level," so it was even more disturbing when they did not get along as well as they might. Often "not getting along" was raised to the level of strong conflict and antagonist.

One morning I was working on the unit, doing rounds, trying to gain an insight into the working dynamics by watching the interactions that were occurring as infants were checked for the day. On this particular day, there had already been a small degree of conflict and predictions of more; I was back in a corner, somewhat removed from the people doing the round, focusing on the pad I was taking notes on. I want to emphasize that my attention was pretty strongly riveted on the writing I was doing.

The next moment that unveiled itself, and what I will write about it, seems both strange and out of character to me. However, I would be less than honest if I did not describe precisely what took place. Suddenly, "something came over me." The only analogies I can give—and I have thought about this carefully— is the experience of being out in a large field on a hot day, and a puffy, white cloud drifts over, bringing a moment of shade and coolness. Being in a room where someone comes in with too much perfume on , and driving through an area of the countryside when leaves are being burned in the fall would be similar experiences. These are very real phenomena, and what I experienced in the corner of that NICU was very real in the same sense.

The experience that was impinging upon me from outside of me—that is, the experience that was simply not in any way the creation of my own mind— was so real that I stopped my writing and looked up see what was going on. My eyes were drawn—it was actually more like some kind of "magnetic force field" that was attracting me, pulling my attention toward it—to the small isolet across from me where a very, very sick newborn had been placed. Around the isolete were eight people—a doctor, two nurse practitioners, two nurses, a respiratory therapist, two interns, and a social worker.

These eight people were talking to each other, simply talking to each other. The conversation bounced around from one person to the next in a kind of natural fluidity; all of the tones were direct, hushed, serious, and professional. It did not matter, in that moment, who was on what "level," who made how much money, who had what degrees, what designating initials were on the individual name tag. All that mattered in that moment was a very sick, little baby and what could be done to give that baby a chance to live.

The only response that I had—that welled up within me—was *this is beautiful!* Maybe there are other words that would work just as well, but what fixes itself in my mind is *beautiful!* Now, for some readers I may begin to sound very strange; for others, I may not sound strange at all. This beauty had a real power that reached out and "touched" me. In fact, I think it was "touching" everyone around that isolet with its sick child. They exuded a calmness and control that was striking. Their focus seemed profound. They were at their very best in my opinion at that moment. I am even convinced that the feeling—or whatever it was in that room—was reaching out to that little baby in a way that it contributed positively to that little baby's health. I am convinced that the power of that "beauty" which rose out of the special relationship that existed in that room at that moment had a healing effect and impact.

When I talk to healthcare professionals that I meet in hospitals across the country, people on every level of treatment and care that hospitals provide, they show absolutely no surprise at what I am describing when I talk about this event. These seasoned professionals, with all of the competence and intelligence that modern scientific reasoning can provide, have not even the slightest argument about my conclusions. They often express an interest in my reticence. They claim to see this kind of beauty-become-healing-power all of the time. For many, to be in a place where something like this can occur, even on a regular basis, is part of what draws and compels them to move in the direction of healthcare to begin with. Herein, they often say, is the reward for treacherous hours, high tension, time away from family, and the tensions that so often surround their work.

In a good place, there is a powerful presence of this beautiful. The ancient Greeks had an interesting word for what I am trying to describe here; they spoke about *kalokagathia,* which basically translated means "the good and the beautiful." I am convinced that what they meant by this construction was that at times something becomes so good, it so dramatically fulfills the concept of what something ought to be, that "something" begins to emanate from it. This "something" that emanates, is given off by, rises out of—the language we use is suddenly inadequate to the phenomenon we are trying to describe—this good in its highest manifestation is the beautiful. This beautiful is—maybe *has* is not the right word here—power. That power can "come over us," attract out attention, still and quiet us, give us a stronger degree of concentrated focus, transcend the pettiness that afflicts our relationships, and even have a healing impact. In the moment I have just described, the baby was not the only person in that room who experienced "healing." Don't we experience something of this same experience and its effect upon us when we see a beautiful sunset, when we embrace a broad vista of landscape from a high mountain top, when we are in the presence of great art, when we see a beautiful tree or flower, when we hit a beautiful golf shot or see a beautiful play in a football game or a beautiful play on a theater stage, or when we are around people who—for whatever reason— are "beautiful people" to us.

I try to teach and expose my business clients to what I call "The Executive Walk." Instead of conducting all of our seminars and training sessions, especially when key decisions are being made, in a boardroom, I ask them to try an "off sight" at some place that is more natural than man-made. A state or national park is a perfect place. We spend the day walking around, moving in and out of different pairings informally, sitting on big rocks or soft meadows soaking in sun, watching whatever animals might be nearby. We make sure that we address any "business" that needs to be taken care of. We do not worry about what time it is, and all cell phones and beepers are left back at the office.

The innovation and creativity of the decision-making process that takes place in this setting is always—without exception—vastly beyond what takes place in the office environment. It never fails! The beauty of nature works its "magic," and people are better at what they do than they normally are. Sometimes, when a workable alternative to some problem simply will not seem to come, I ask people to walk off by themselves—be careful not to get lost!—sit alone for a while, and simply see what happens. I watch as people throw stones in a creek, draw designs in the dirt, get caught up in a mother bird feeding its babies, or watch cattle graze in a field. When they come back, usually more relaxed than I ever seem them in their workplace, they usually come back with interesting solutions. The beautiful can also provoke the good— bringing out the best in people—in a kind of "reverse *kalokagathia.*"

I have seen this same phenomenon unveil itself at marriage retreat weekends. Sometimes I fear that people will think I am a lazy consultant. Oh, I make a requisite number of presentations and try not to shortchange people on "information" that they can take back home. But, I have clearly discovered that when I send couples off to take a walk with each other, to look for beautiful leaves or rocks they can bring back to share with the group, or take pictures with a Polaroid camera which they will share with the group, that the couples retreat rises to a level of positive intensity and insight not found in the most brilliant lecture. Just having people walk down a country lane, holding hands, not saying anything, or sit—back to back—on a hilltop and talk, creates a level of communication that has gotten lost at home and, often, a greatly needed healing that is remarkable. The exposure to beauty helps reestablish a sense of the goodness in the relationship that has been missed, overlooked, and somehow lost, maybe for years.

In the late 1880s, the philosopher Friedrich Nietzsche moved to Turin in northern Italy. Nietzsche had been experiencing yet another onslaught of the illnesses that would eventually result in his death. Several, key relationships were in a less-than-ideal state, and he was in great need of an environment in which expression on the level he desired could finds its way back into his writings. He knew that at Turin he was likely to find the catalyst he was searching for that might create personal transformation. At Turin, Nietzsche encountered the beautiful.

In this instance, beauty was made manifest in nature, the grand mountains and running waters, the wooded forests and rolling, high mountain meadows. He would immerse himself in all of this, and let it do its magic. Three times a day, Nietzsche would venture out into the northern Italian countryside on long walks. When he returned, he wrote, and in this process created the great literature and philosophy that became the crowning achievements of his life. He became a "partner" in the pursuit of beauty typified in the lives of other great, creative artists: Thoreau at Walden, Wordsworth as he walked the expanse of Great Britain and Western Europe, Heidegger along the mountain paths of Germany, and Van Gogh in southern France.

Nietzsche admired the ancient Greeks, especially those of the Dionysian persuasion who placed great emphasis on festivals, celebrations, and play. They found in these events, for Nietzsche, the embodiment of beauty; in fact, their constructions had the beautiful as a distinct end in mind. In his classic work, *The Birth of Tragedy*, Nietzsche had become convinced that the beautiful was pursued as a "craving" because of the continuous sense of the possibility of lack, deprivation, and pain that haunted human existence on this earth. The beautiful was both an antidote and a force of compensation.

Unfortunately, for most human beings, this profound reality was usually sought in desperation, after the fact, rather than consciously created before the fact as a kind of prophylactic against the ravages of life that might—or were likely—to come.

In a good place—which Turin distinctly was for Nietzsche—this awareness of negative possibilities generates a distinct need for the conscious creation of realities that will offset the force of the variety of deprivations, pains, and "lackings" that are an inevitable ingredient of most human life in every setting from the home to the workplace. Nietzsche's statement, and my agreement with it, are by no means sentiments of negativism or cynicism about life. On the contrary, life is simply what it is and as it is. Our task is to respond to it in all of its factual actuality. When we create good places, we cease to be willing to passively wait for whatever might come next.

In concluding this section, my thoughts focus on the work of the great German philosophy, Hans-Georg Gadamer. In a classic essay entitled "The Relevance of the Beautiful," Gadamer defers to Plato's definition of beauty: "that which shines forth most clearly and draws us to itself, as the very visibility of the ideal." Here, the ideal stops being a purely conceptual, mental reality and becomes "absolute visibility." This is what took place with me in that NICU unit I described earlier. The "ideal" that these workers on this unit achieved did, to use Plato's words "shine forth most clearly," and I was absolutely "drawn" to it. For at least a moment, as the life of the small baby took charge of that moment, the "ideal" that these workers achieved gained "absolute visibility." The beautiful, the good, *kalokagathia*, were profoundly present. At least for a moment, these workers created a good place. Their challenge, of course: how to create this good place, rather than have it occur almost by accident—not because of them, I am afraid, but in spite of them.

Gadamer goes on to say: "In the beautiful . . . we experience the convincing illumination of truth and harmony." That is precisely what I experienced, as relational harmony that stood beyond territorial turfs gave way to the "truth" of that baby really being all that was important in that moment. When such truth and harmony occurs, and when we experience the convincing illumination, Gadamer says that we will stand back, be moved by the moment, and feel the need to respond: "This is true!" Now, we add the final strand to our three-fold cord: beauty, goodness, and now truth. Of course, he is not talking about any kind of rational, propositional, or scientifically demonstrable truth—what John Hospers called "truth about;" he is describing a higher truth that is undeniably felt, a truth which Hopers called "truth to," a pointing truth that captures and directs our attention to our highest capacities and the highest potentialities of the circumstances we inhabit.

This, of most significance, Gadamer insists that the beautiful he is describing has little to do with the netherworld of airy, esoteric philosophy conceptualized by Plato. In words of very highest importance for our discussion:

> On the contrary, we learn that however unexpected our encounter with beauty may be, it gives us an assurance that the truth does not lie far off and inaccessible to us, but can be encountered in the disorder of reality with all its imperfections, evils, errors, extremes, and fateful confusions.

This dramatic statement means that the beautiful that—to use Gadamer's words—"arrests" us and "compels" us is available to us in the midst of the most ordinary circumstances, even NICU units. In other words, any place can become a good place. There is no need to wait for eternal, heavenly afterlives, or Platonic worlds of pure form. In most respects, we need to learn the constituent elements of a good place and work to consciously and strategically create what it is that we want and what it is that will transform our daily lives.

A GOOD PLACE HAS SIMPLICITY

One of the classic philosophical traditions to rise out of ancient Greece, that has come down with high credibility across the ages is Epicureanism. The great teacher, Epicurus, was concerned about how human beings could find happiness. That, in itself, signals a high benchmark in the evolution of human civilization; the very idea that people could come to the point of speculating about happiness in a world in which life had so often been victimized by fiat and realities beyond human control is remarkable. These ancient Greek, perhaps going back to Aristotle's *Nicomachean Ethics*, actually believed they could create a place in which happiness might be a possibility.

Epicurus is best known for having said that happiness was an exponent of pleasure, and occurs in direct proportion to the amount of pleasure that a person had in life. This position has been grossly misunderstood by most people, and has been turned into a near hedonism. Satiate yourself to the excess, do anything that is fun to the extreme, fill every solitary moment with frivolity, and you will be happy. In most urban communities there is usually an "Epicurean Restaurant," and in most instances its menu is filled with extremely rich foods that are probably more than most people need in their basic diets. After a trip to the Epicurean Restaurant, if you follow this logic, the next step is the nearest orgy. At this point, a person is an "Epicure," a person who pursues pleasure, and is now in line for some large measure of happiness.

Of course, the real teachings of Epicurus did not move in this direction. He was all for pleasure, no doubt, but the pleasure he saw—with exceptional insight and wisdom—was a pleasure borne of simplicity. In most instances, pleasure was a consequence of the diminishing of complexity. If there was even an Epicurean "strategy," it would involve lessening as much complexity as possible and pursuing a life of simplicity. In a classic example, attributed in many traditions by Epicurus, he idealized a loaf of bread, a bottle of wine, a piece of cheese, a beautiful location, and the presence of someone he distinctly cared to be with. On most days, Epicurus' vision sounds tremendously inviting.

Our world, and especially the modern American expression of it, seems hell-bent on finding new ways to add complexity. In doing so, we see stress-related illness and every kind of social excess imaginable skyrocket into larger control of our lives. We yearn for an occasional day off with nothing to do, but find—even in our most relentless planning—that such experiences are almost impossible to achieve. We wish for one more day in the week or one more hour in the day, fully cognizant of the fact that were such time to become available, it would only be used to catch up. We freely recognize, but find no small measure of fear in the fact, that any projections into the future do not involve a less complicated life.

The typical workplace only exacerbates our problems. Organizations have learned that a major, controllable expense—or, at least, a major, controllable expense that requires less creativity in impacting—relates to people. If you can lower the number of people working in an environment, you can save dramatically on personnel costs and all of the benefit packages that are added on. Once this process takes place, it then becomes necessary to add more work to the presently existing workforce. Since the options for this group is either more work or head for the door, and since the grass is not necessarily greener at the next company down the street, most workers simply "deal with it" and are made to feel that they should be happy just to have a job at all. Not only are people asked time and again to embrace more and more work, they are also expected to show no displeasure about the process. To show displeasure becomes a sure sign of "bad attitude" or "poor morale," a clear negative in any performance evaluation processes. I see many, many people in the current workplace who have evolved to the position that they are easily doing the work of 1 3/4 to 2 1/2 people. The hours on the job are endless, but the bills, ambitions, and necessities at home are even more. We become the most overworked people who have lived on this earth, and pleasure seems often a fleeting ghost of some sophomoric wish left over from a distant past.

What have we done to ourselves? What have we done with time? I am convinced in our modern world that we have created at least three types of time, most of which was unknown to the ancient world, even the world of our most immediate ancestors. The first type of time is acquiring time, the time spent acquiring the things which we possess. I can recall being raised in a small town in East Tennessee in the late 1940s and early 1950s. Ours was a very typical family: father who worked, mother who was at home, and four boys. Every Saturday, in a basic routine of our lives, we went to town. On a Saturday morning, my father visited the local hardware store where he would buy whatever supplies he needed to take care of our home and yard. My mother would walk across the town square where there was a "dry goods" store where any clothing that was needed was purchased. There was not a lot of clothes to be bought; a couple of pairs of blue jeans would last the entire school year. You did not dare wear the knees out; if you did, you then wore awful looking, ironed-on knee patches. In the summer, the school jeans were cut off and became shorts. She would then go to the local grocery store where all of our food needs for the coming week would be taken care of. With only the rarest exception, this Saturday morning took care of all of our material and food needs for the entire week.

We have created an entirely different world. Recently, I was looking for a new suit. This required trips to two local malls, two specialty stores, and most of a day of "shopping." Still, I had no suit. A trip to Atlanta, two and one-half hours on the road, and a tremendous amount of traffic frustration were then required before just the right suit was found. Maybe we have too many choices, but by the time the suit, a matching shirt and tie, and—in this instance—a new pair shoes were acquired, a phenomenal amount of time and energy had been spent. Never in all of my youth did anyone to my knowledge in my whole, immediate family ever travel to Atlanta to acquire anything. If you couldn't get it on Saturday morning "in town" or you couldn't order it from the Sears & Roebuck catalog, you probably concluded that you did not need it. If most of us kept track of the acquiring time we spent in any given month, we would be amazed.

The next type of time we have created is maintaining time, the time we spend maintaining the things we have acquired. The lives we have created and the things we have surrounded ourselves with are a lot like modern airline travel. When everything works like it is supposed to, air travel is wonderful. However, once mechanical, weather, or scheduling problems begin to set in, major trauma and powerful inconvenience—not to mention no small measure of what is now call "air rage"—begins to set in. In like manner, as long as all of the things we have work as they are supposed to, life runs fairly smoothly, but let things begin to break down or tear up, and life rages at all new levels of complexity. Try to get anything fixed. See how long it takes to get a plumber, a tree removal service, a car worked on. Expense notwithstanding, we know that finding someone, getting them to look at a problem, getting them back to work on the problem, getting them back again to work on something that didn't exactly get fixed the first time becomes a nightmare.

Then, imagine that we are going to "beat the system" and fix something ourselves. Recently, the water pump went out on my car. I called to several garages to get a price on getting the device repaired; every quote was ridiculous, and no one could even get to me for a week. Of course, to drive a car without a functioning water pump is distinctly a bad idea. In near rebellion at the "system" that presented itself to me, I told my wife that I would do it myself.

On the next Saturday morning, I went to work. It was no simple task. I had to remove part of the grill structure of the car and loosen the radiator so that I could take the fan assembly off to even get to the pump. After about two or three hours, I was finally back to the water pump itself, only to discover that a tool was required that I did not have. After cleaning up and making a trip to two auto parts stores and one hardware store, I found that this particular tool was a special order item and might require a week to get in the store. I gave up, now had to call a wrecker to tow my car to the garage, and still had to wait a week for the exorbitantly expensive job to be completed. There was no price tag for the accompanying frustration that mounted throughout the entire experience. While it is a wonderful feeling to fix something for yourself, the potential for doing this seems to become smaller all of the time.

We encourage a "throw away" culture of disposability that has no small implication for our human lives because it is easier to throw something away and get something new than it is to fix it. In my study is a small, wooden bookcase that my father built years ago. I can remember when that bookcase was the desk that my brother and I studied at in grammar and high school.

4. The Fundamental Ethical Action: Creating a Good Place

Before its life as a desk, that collection of wood had been our dinner table. My father never threw anything away; he was into "recycling" before anyone had ever heard of recycling. How out of place he would be in my world. We may take short jabs at maintaining, but realize the futility of our attempts and go back to the original starting point—acquiring time—and start all over again. Then, with each repetition, we add to the complication; the VCR we have today has too many "bells and whistles," and I dreaded our children going back to college—I couldn't program it or stop the flashing, red lights when our power went off.

Finally, there is paying-for time, the time we spend paying for the things we have acquired and must maintain. We have moved from one person working to "support" a family to two. Beyond this, many families exhibit the typical pattern of either or both parents taking on extra work to provide for additional financial options. I often, for example, see nurses who work a regular weekly shift at their "main" hospital, take whatever overtime is available, and then work a couple of more days PRN at some other hospital. Without exception, when explanations about the amount of work that is being done are given, the need to "make ends meet" always prevails.

The complexity of things that surround our lives becomes amazing by almost any standard. We have multiple vehicles, expensive recreational toys, and wardrobes for every occasion, multi-thousand square foot homes, exotic vacations, and we have not even begun to take care of educational needs that can be vast. In short, all that we have to pay for is mind numbing. Add to all this, the ease of securing indebtedness—especially with credit cards—and the intense "holes" that people dig themselves into are immense. In almost thirty years of a professional counseling practice, almost every marriage problem that came into my office was either caused by or exacerbated by financial issues.

Looking at these three types of time that consume our lives, there seems only one clear solution: we must diminish the number of things that the potential quality and beauty of our existence is choking on. Of course, the solution is much easier to advance conceptually than it is to follow in reality, especially when so much of our self-image and self-esteem seems to be caught up in "right accumulation." Not only must we have the requisite number and selection of things, we must also have all the right labels attached to those things; often, we pay more for the label than we do for the object itself. Yet, we place such tremendous value on affirmation and acceptance from peers and colleagues, that having a myriad of right things takes on the character of becoming our entree, our "ticket" almost, into life itself. As long as this consciousness rules, as long as the advertising media convinces us that its products are necessities rather than luxuries, our acquiring, maintaining, and paying for times will only increase. How ironic that so little time is left for "enjoying time," "relaxing time," or "nothing-ing time." Those days when we could lay down on a green-carpeted lawn and imagine a universe of diverse shapes in the summer clouds that passed overhead seem so very far away.

Not long ago, I had a car which needed to spend the day at the Sears Service Center a few miles from my college. I arranged with a colleague to meet me there in the morning and give me a ride to school, but he would not be able to take me back that afternoon. No problem, I assured him; there would be plenty of opportunities to find rides across the day. However, no such ride presented itself. Still, no problem. I would simply walk out to the entranceway of our college, head toward the main highway, and some student or staff member would recognize me and give me a ride. To make a very long story short, I got to walk the five or so miles to Sears that afternoon.

What amazed me was all that I saw along the way. There were whole buildings, striking views and beautiful vistas, and wonderful birds and animals all along the way that I had never seen before. All of this was in spite of the fact that in my movements back and forth to work and home, that I had driven this particular stretch of highway hundreds, even thousands, of times. When I was forced to slow down, to walk, a whole new world became apparent, unveiled itself. In the speed of my normal day-to-day existence, a great deal had been lost in the "blurr." It is difficult not to wonder what all is lost in the "blurr" of the kind of lives we have created. Without question, health and a sense of well-being gets lost, significant others and children get lost, and maybe any kind of opportunity to have a deep, interpersonal dialogue of self-understanding or maybe an extra-personal dialogue with that which we might call "God" vanishes away as well. Then, we get old and wonder—often with deep grief—why we did what we did to ourselves.

I have become convinced that it is fairly easy to build Babel Towers of complexity. This complexity is then neither easy to manage nor easy to pay for. The more difficult task is to simplify, simplify, simplify. In general, we are just purely making life too hard. While the likelihood of many of us becoming like Thoreau at Walden is not realistically very great—we sometimes claim small Waldens in small pieces, what he did there is still a moving paradigm. These concluding words—written by Thoreau—raise an appealing, high standard for all of us:

> I went to the woods
> Because I wanted to live
> More deliberately;
> To front only the essential facts of life
> And see if I could not learn what it had to teach.
> And not, when I came to die
> Discover that I had not lived.

A GOOD PLACE HAS POWER

When all of the criteria outlined to this point are met, there is a tangible result that can be felt, that has a distinct impact on people: a good place manifests power. Without question, the history of human beings on this planet, especially in the "modern age," has been a story about the pursuit, implementation, holding, and defending of power that has been gained. From one epoch of history to the next, evolutions of power have created the veritable benchmarks by which life has been monitored. Whether it is a new ruler who has come to reign, a baseball player who is challenging a homerun record, or the output of a technological device, the focus on power is central to the world we have created.

Most power is extrinsic; that is, most power that impacts our lives today is external, something that can be measured, and usually is measured by the number of soldiers in your army, warheads in your arsenal, or aircraft carriers in your fleet armada. At other times, this extrinsic power can be measured in a won-lost body count which proves who is winning a war, the Dow Jones average, or a nation's Gross National Product. Power like this is usually translated into control and dominance, the ability to make individuals or whole groups of individuals align with your beliefs, priorities, or designs; "to align," of course, usually really means surrender to some other individual or corporate will.

It is much more difficult to talk about intrinsic power. Words almost always become inadequate to the task, so describing experiences in which intrinsic power has been felt may be the best that can be done. I had the opportunity in the late 1970s to see Richard Burton in New York City's Lincoln Center as King Arthur in "Camelot." When Burton came on stage, it was like a "spell" was somehow cast on the audience. It became as quiet as a profound religious experience or awe. Throughout the evening Burton created an experience that was remarkable; for that moment he was Arthur, and the audience was transported into a mythic realm that was as magical as Merlin.

One night along the banks of the Tennessee River at Chattanooga, in an annual festival we call Riverbend, my wife and I sat on a quilt only yards away from Ray Charles as he sat at the piano and sang into the night. The stars filled the sky, the cool breezes rising from the water chased any hint of a hot summer day away, and Charles made a crowd of 100,000 feel like a small family being entertained in his own backyard. When he sang "Georgia On My Mind," all of us were ready to stay the night, just as long as he sang.

In a similar experience, although the medium was totally different, I sat in Neyland Stadium in the middle 1960s and watch my beloved Tennessee Volunteers go into the third quarter ahead of the Crimson Tide of Alabama. Joe Namath was Alabama's quarterback, but he had been injured and was unable to play in the game. That notwithstanding, the very thought of a victory against Alabama in those days produced feelings that a veritable miracle was about to take place. Somewhere in the midst of the third quarter, Alabama's coach, Paul "Bear" Bryant walked over to the sideline bench and began to talk to Namath. In a moment, Joe was up throwing along the sideline, and when Alabama got the ball back on offense, Namath came into the game. I'm not sure I have ever experienced what happened next. It was—again—like a magic "spell" came over the entire stadium as Namath marched his team back and forth, up and down the field, for one score and then another. From the very moment he walked on the field, there was no question what the outcome of the game would be. For all practical purposes, the game was over from that point on, and everyone in the stadium knew it.

In each of these instances, there was an intrinsic power that rose from these people's individual lives in these specific situations that had an unquestionable impact on the circumstances they were part of. In each instance, and I hate to say this about the Tennessee-Alabama football game, something beautiful took place. In each instance, the individual performers were operating on the highest level of the "good"—they fulfilled the concept of what they were to be and what they were to do in that particular situation. There was the experience of the phenomenon of power.

To move to a more philosophical explanation, the best description of this kind of power that I have ever seen comes from the ancient Greeks where the term *dunamis* rose to the level of a key concept; our modern term dynamo is directly derived from the old Greek term at this point. The first philosophers intimated that there were three levels of human accomplishment:

- "ability," which is basic potentiality
- "capacity," which is potentiality that is realized to some extent
- "might," which is potentiality that is realized to its highest order possible.

In this configuration, a person could have "ability," but that ability not be manifested or realized. This would be like having certain talents and not using them. On a second, more normative level, a person could express ability and therefore be manifesting "capacity." Capacity, depending on the situation, could range from incompetence to high competence; by any measure, however, to express some degree of "capacity" is better than having all of the "ability" in the world, all of the potential in the world, and never manifesting it. In the illustrations I have used above, each of these three person were, at the very minimum, exercising "capacity" on a high level.

The ancient Greeks believed, however, that here was a degree of manifested capacity that was on such a high level of competence that it was simply not a difference in degree along the spectrum that is being described, but almost a difference in kind. When the "bar was raised" to a next echelon on "capacity," there was "might." Here, to use Hartman's term, was the active fulfillment of the concept. In all likelihood, both the good and the beautiful occur. "Might" is a primary Greek term for power at its highest manifestation and fullest result. The great Greek heroes were called *oi dunamenoi*, "The Mighty Ones." These "heroes" manifested competence to the very hilt; they were the very opposite of incompetence and mediocrity.

The great scholar of antiquity, Walter Grundmann, was convinced that *dunamis* as the ancient Greeks used it was used "with specific reference to the subjective spiritual or moral attitude which either makes able or not." At the core of the action of the "hero," the "Mighty One," was will. This "subjective spiritual" and "moral attitude" created—for want of a better word—will power, the core reality at the center of accomplishment. We are very close at this point to Nietzsche's "will to power," a central concept that in most readings is totally misunderstood as a triumph of expansionistic, territorial, dominating extrinsic power. What Nietzsche actually was describing at the heart of his writing was an intrinsic power that rose from within a person as an act of triumphant will to live, to shape and create life, to overcome adversity, to deal with pain and conflict, and to manifest self in all of its uniqueness. Nietzsche continued the theme of "The Mighty Ones," describing what he called an Ubermensch/Overman/Superman.

The ancient Pythagoreans described *dunamis* as a three-fold reality: (1) a mysterious cosmic principle; (2) which can be fitted with effective force—that is, that can make itself manifest in real life; and, (3) then become a dynamic magnitude that fashions all things. In his dialogue, *The Sophist*, Plato was even convinced that *dunamis* was the very "mark/definition of being" itself; if there was "power," there was life at its very best—the fulfillment of the epitome of goodness.

In the Old Testament, there is a clear personification—in a personal God who is active in real history—of this Greek "cosmic principle." Look, for example, at two verses from the book of Exodus (15:6 and 13): "Thy right hand, O Lord, is become glorious in power. . . . With thy hand thou hast led the people, which thou hast redeemed. . . . Thou hast guided them in thy strength unto thy holy habitation." There is a distinct correlation between "hand of God," "power of God," and "will of God." This correlation becomes very important to the understanding that "will" cannot solely be a mental phenomenon; what may have some beginning in a "mental will" must be consummated in bodily effort—by "hand" as it were—or there is no real power. Too often, in the world we inhabit, saying the right words becomes a substitute for doing the right tasks; the ancient world would never call this power.

The New Testament adds its own, unique touches to the evolution of this concept of power. Jesus comes to represent the "Mighty One of Mighty Ones," and in the writings of Paul (Romans 1:4), Jesus is "declared to be the Son of God in power." He applies the concept elsewhere: "The Kingdom of God does not consist in talk but in power" (I Corinthians 4:20), a thought that has full consistency with the ancient Greek designations. In Acts 1:8, Paul's compatriot, Luke, attributes to Jesus a statement that stirs tremendous curiosity: "You [that is, followers, believers, disciples] will receive power after the Holy Spirit is come upon you." In Matthew's Gospel (11:20ff), the miracles of Jesus are referred to as *dunameis*, "actions of power."

CONCLUSION

At the end of the journey of this discussion, one question rises: is it possible for organizations to create power? Is it possible to have power-full organizations that make an impact on the environments they are part of? Even more, is it possible to find/have/develop individuals in organizations who can manifest power in their leadership? Certainly, these kinds of leaders would be "heroes," "Mighty Ones," even "spiritual" leaders.

The old philosopher, Nietzsche, expert in all that we have noted in passing about ancient Greeks and biblical traditions—the roots of western civilization—believed it all was a matter of will. So, do we have enough will to create a good place, a place that has beauty, a place that has power? Wishing and willing are not the same reality, so feeling like the ideas are basically positive ideas, agreeing with the ideas, and wishing that something of the constituent element of a good place could be found will simply never be enough. Wishing does not make it so. Then, can will be more than an accidental, random, spasmodic moment? Can will be sustained over those long periods necessary for real and lasting change and transformation? The questions we raise are heady questions? Any answers will require courage, character, and tenacity. The creation of a good place would be worth the greatest effort.

"The will can tend to whatever the reason can apprehend as good."

—Thomas Aquinas

5. CREATING A GOOD PLACE: SURVEY

INTRODUCTION

1. "Goodness" is not the *property of a concept,* but *the property of an object.*

2. "Goodness" is concept fulfillment. That is, something is "good" to the extent that it fulfills our concept of what it ought to be, should be, or could be in terms of fulfilling its potential.

3. Concepts are either "lean" or "rich."

4. A primary responsibility of leaders is to establish for the people they are leading the "richest" concept possible.

5. A leader cannot establish a "rich" concept unless he/she has a "rich" concept personally.

6. A truly significant question for anyone in a leadership position is, "How *good* do you want to be?"

7. This question has three levels that build on each other:

    (A)   How *good* do you want your organization to be?
    (B)   How *good* you want your leadership team to be?
    (C)   How *good* do you want to be?

8. This question can be answered on a "virtual," "conceptual" level, or it can be answered on a "real," "actual" level.

9. On the "real," "actual" level, the question must be rephrased and become, "What are you *willing* to do to be as *good* as you want to be?" *Willing*, as it is used here, means determined will or will power. *Willing* is not measured by what's okay with you if someone else makes

the effort and decisions; *willing* is measured by what's okay if *you* have to do the hardest work and make the hardest decisions.

10. An accompanying question relates to practical application: "What obstacles are standing in your way personally, standing in the way of your leadership team, and standing in the way of your organization in general?

11. Robert Yates is one of the best-known personalities in the world of NASCAR racing. Yates is not a racing star. He is an engine builder. He is an artist with a race car engine as much as Michelangelo was an artist with marble. He and his company have built engines for some of the greatest racers and cars ever built.

    Recently, a new racing team came to Yates and asked what it would cost for him to build their team an engine than could be used in their newest car. Yates responded—and for those who know Robert Yates, they know he was not kidding: "How fast do you want to go?!"

    The profound question facing most people in leadership positions in an organization—on both a team and a person level—is very similar: "How *good* do you want to be?"

12. Your organization and your team cannot go any "faster"—cannot win any more races, to follow the metaphor—than your personal, team, and organizational *concept*—rich concept—of how *good* you want to be and how *willing* you are to fulfill this concept of "rich goodness." Maybe, at the end of the day, this "rich goodness" is indeed greatness. Maybe, at the end of the day, "rich goodness" is excellence.

THE QUESTIONS

1. How *good* do you want your organization to be?

2. Is your leadership team good enough to inspire and direct your organization to the level you have described in Question #1? If "yes," why? If "no," why?

3. What obstacles stand in the way of you personally to lead and accomplish the goals noted in Question #1?

4. What obstacles stand in the way of your leadership team to lead and accomplish the goals noted in Question #1?

5. What obstacles stand in the way of your organization to accomplish the goals noted in Question #1?

6. How do you rate your own *willingness*, will, and will power?

7. How do you rate the *willingness*, will, and will power of your leadership team?

8. How do you rate the *willingness*, will, and will power of your organization in general?

9. What is most important for you **to do next** to begin to accomplish the goals defined here?

10. What is most important for your leadership team **to do next** to accomplish the goals defined here?

INTERLUDE I

WALKING THE SPIRITUAL PATH

PREFACE

What does it mean to walk the spiritual path? We will attempt to answer this important question. To gain the most from this series, please read the material, ponder it, and then answer the attached discussion questions.

If any of the ideas in this series help your clarify your journey, I will be pleased. After all, we are fellow travelers on a shared journey through the universe. Travel well.

Blessings!

Lee Kaiser

Interlude I

WALKING THE SPIRITUAL PATH 1

I am often asked—is it possible to be both an effective manager and a devoted spiritual practitioner? If so, how can lofty spiritual values best be integrated into the exigencies of management practice? How can you become a spiritual leader?

This series constitutes my answer to this important question. In short, you become a spiritual leader by learning to walk the spiritual path.

People often confuse the terms religious and spiritual. As I use the terms— religion refers to a body of doctrine or a specific set of beliefs—spirituality refers to a relationship you have with something larger than yourself. The good of another person, organization, community, nation or world is a spiritual concern. We live in a relationship universe. To be in a conscious loving relationship with something larger than yourself is to be spiritual. For me, the ultimate expression of spirituality is to be in a loving relationship with God. You may be religious and not spiritual, spiritual and not religious, neither or both. In my case, I attempt to be both spiritual and religious.

One other world of explanation is in order. In all religions there is an inner path and an outer path. The inner path is the path of the mystic. I walk that path. The outer path is the path of membership and participation in a formal church organization. Again, I also walk that path and hold formal church office.

It has been my joy over the years to explore the further dimensions of human consciousness and spirituality. I will report to you my findings.

This series is neither exhaustive nor completely inclusive. You may not have experienced everything I discuss. On the other hand, you may have experienced many things I do not mention. If so, feel free to add your ideas. First and foremost, the spiritual path is a shared voyage.

In our new century, the spiritual dimension will become the most important dimension in business. Managers will become spiritual voyagers setting sail in an ocean of creative possibilities. The goal of this series is to provide for you a spiritual platform useful in management. Spirituality is something you must possess internally. You cannot learn it from a book or buy it in a store. Hopefully, this series will assist you in your search.

WALKING THE SPIRITUAL PATH 2

It is a path of eternal unfoldment.

The spiritual path is a path of eternal unfoldment. It has no end. It is an eternal journey. Each step leads to the next step.

Unfoldment is another term for evolution. You keep evolving into higher stages of soul fulfillment. Each stage poses a hurdle or barrier to your current stage of existence. To move beyond this barrier you must overcome existing limitations and gain greater mastery. Each stage ends when you have passed the initiation connected with that stage. You are a running summary of all of your experiences to date.

Stages require varying lengths of time for successful completion. A difficult stage could take most of your lifetime.

You may gain mastery over an easier stage in a few years, months, weeks, or even days. What is a difficult stage for one person may be easy for another. We are all at different stages in our unfoldment. However, it is safe to say we are all stuck where we are.

To get unstuck requires cognitive, affective, and behavioral changes. We must know better, feel better and act better. To accomplish these necessary changes, we must fail, get back up on our feet, and try again. We overcome by overcoming. There is no easy way. Consciousness is purchased through our experience. There are no shortcuts. In the long run this is a better way. We understand where we are, how we got there, and how to assist others in overcoming a similar barrier. Our greatest struggle in the short run may become our greatest strength in the long run and a pivot point for our ministry to other souls.

Eventually we view all people upon our path as fellow travelers. We have empathy for those who fail and admiration for those who succeed. We love both equally. Both are our teachers. When every person is your teacher, you hold everyone in high regard. Always ask, "What can I learn from this person?" Ask, "How is this lesson connected with my stuckness?"

Every experience becomes grist for your mill of consciousness. Some experiences you will like more than others. The experiences you like least may become your greatest teachers. Try to avoid making premature judgments. Accept what comes and learn from it.

What you can become you already are in the dimension above time, space, and limited condition. Take heart. You have already won in the creationless realms of the Infinite. With patience, you will transform the finite into its infinite expression. It is an eternal journey.

Discussion Question: How would you describe your current stage of spiritual unfoldment?

WALKING THE SPIRITUAL PATH 3

It begins before birth and continues after death.

The spiritual path begins before birth and continues after death. It begins when the Spirit descends, touches matter and creates a human soul. It continues after death as the Spirit returns to its Source (God). Depending upon your theology you may view the journey of the soul in different ways.

The soul (archetype) is an individualized expression of Divinity. It contains a birthright of latent talents and abilities. It is also set upon a path of personal discovery and unfoldment. As the soul unfolds it begins to serve other orders of creation as well as humankind. God delegates to soul all that the soul can comprehend and manifest. This obviously becomes greater over time. As the soul matures it becomes more potent and can serve in more powerful ways the purpose and plan of the Source.

The body, emotions, and mind are at first largely disconnected from the soul. The soul exists in a very subtle realm and must be contacted by the mind and emotions. This requires a process of inner alignment. When the mind and emotions desire such a contact, they send a signal and the soul descends into the lower realms. The first soul contact produces an Epiphany or peak experience. The mind and emotions taste the higher power and a great desire is created to incorporate more soul. Once the heavenly manna is experienced, the life is transformed and set upon a new course. Eventually, even the physical body will begin to reflect the attributes of the soul.

The future will bring us soul-based healthcare. Clients will be taught the skills necessary to contact and embody their spiritual blueprint. Child resource centers and centers for creative sage-ing will explore the outer limits of human potentiation. With soul, mind, emotions, and body alignment, much disease will be designed out of the human population. People will live longer and better. The contemporary movement to integrate complementary and alternative medicine with allopathic medicine is one movement in this direction. The healthier communities movement is another expression of this new frontier of human evolution. Quantum physics will provide the synthesis of science and spirituality needed to move the medical profession out of its current preoccupation with the bodies of patients.

Your current life, then, should be seen in the context of an eternal journey into your soul and ultimately back to the Source. You should be involved in a process of soul discovery and a process of using your soul properties in the service of humankind. You are a vital part of All That Is and you have a song to sing that can be sung by no other. Do not get mired in the materialism of our current age. A new day is dawning.

Discussion Question: What form might soul-based healthcare take in your institution?

WALKING THE SPIRITUAL PATH 4

It is revealed to you from a point beyond time and space.

When you begin walking the spiritual path, you are not alone. Your soul will communicate with you at regular intervals. Since the soul is inspired by Spirit, which is beyond time and space, many revelations will come to you which cannot be explained in terms of logic or reason.

The challenge faced by the spiritual traveler is to build a bridge between the mind and the soul that permits regular downloading of soul information into the conscious mind. The soul operates at frequencies that are out of range of the ordinary mind. The regular practice of meditation, prayer, and inspirational reading helps tune the mind to soul frequencies. Over time an alignment occurs and the mind can reach up to the soul as the soul reaches down to the mind. Under favorable conditions contact occurs.

The unconscious mind acts as a valve allowing only a certain amount of soul downflow. One of the jobs of the unconscious mind is to keep the conscious mind (ego) from being swamped by ego alien material. Too much of a download and a psychotic break could result. It is necessary to convince the unconscious mind that the conscious mind is ready for regular soul contact. This is accomplished through progress on the spiritual path. Eventually, the soul will become the center of the life and both the conscious and unconscious minds will become its servants. This development is what is known as enlightenment or atonement. It is a life work.

Soul contact can vary from a slight intuition, to full color visions, to out of the body journeys. It all depends upon what needs to be communicated and what the person is up to. You will recall that John the Revelator was caught up into the third heaven. This was an out of the body journey. Usually soul contact is not that dramatic. The soul usually communicates with gentle urges and quiet advisings. We need to listen carefully to hear. To listen carefully, the mind must be quiet and under control of the higher senses.

When a revelation occurs it may download at a tremendous speed. The soul rhythms are much faster than mind rhythms. In a few seconds enough material can be downloaded to keep the mind busy with months of translation. You know something went by your consciousness and you have a pregnant feeling, but it will take time to process the material.

Until the conscious mind is ready for soul contact, contact is often made in dreams. Dreams protect the ego from the full impact of the realizations. Dream material can be assimilated slowly into consciousness. Pay attention to your dreams!

Discussion Question: Can you identify a time when you experienced soul contact?

WALKING THE SPIRITUAL PATH 5

The Spirit is one aspect of God shining through you. It is reflected in your path.

The Spirit that activates you is one aspect of God shining into matter. When it reflects into matter, matter receives its impress and forms soul. Soul in turn manifests itself through four vehicles: the physical, emotional, mental and spiritual. The vehicles in turn express themselves in the world and the world reflects the quality of energy coming through the four vehicles. In this manner the environment reflects the energies of the souls that inhabit it.

A person is said to be ensouled to the degree that the soul faithfully reflects and conducts the Spirit. Since the ego (located primarily in the mental vehicle) can remain unaware of soul, the residing soul may have little or no effect on the person's ego or conscious mind.

Atonement or alignment means that Spirit, soul, spiritual vehicle, mental vehicle, emotional vehicle, and physical vehicle are centered with respect to one another. Energy passes easily from one to the other. Any difficulty in any vehicle disrupts the flow of energy and impairs the ability of the soul to express itself in the world.

Ideally, your life path is a reflection of the properties of your soul. You should be doing who you are. This permits a free flow of soul energy into the world. This energy constellates reality events and generates synergy, serendipity, and synchronicity. Gradually the world then begins to reflect all the properties of Spirit that flows through all of the souls. In the best of all worlds the infinite properties of Spirit are manifested throughout all creation. This is heaven on earth or the Garden of Eden.

Now you understand why I say the two major dimensions of future healthcare are potentiation and habitat redesign. Potentiation is the realization of soul potential in each of the four vehicles. Habitat redesign is the creation of environments that invoke and permit the great diversity of soul expressions. In the best of all worlds, soul and environment are mirror images. They have a reciprocal relationship. Each stimulates the other.

If environmental qualities do not match soul qualities, a mismatch occurs and the person is at odds with his environment. This leads to dissatisfaction and retarded growth.

Interlude I

The creation of healthier communities is a good example of habitat redesign. The formation of wellness centers, child resource centers, and sage-ing centers are good examples of potentiation.

Discussion Question: Are you currently doing who you are?

WALKING THE SPIRITUAL PATH 6

Spirit touches matter.

At the level of Spirit all is clear and beautiful, but Spirit touches matter—the infirmities of the flesh. Spirit is unsullied, but must be capable of shining through matter.

A human being stands at the midpoint between Spirit and matter. He has his head in the clouds and his feet on the earth. He must incarnate Spirit and permit it to flow through him into matter. This requires a surrender to Spirit and a capacity to translate the high vibrations of Spirit into the much lower vibrations of physical matter.

The evolution of the earth depends upon greater magnitudes of Spirit finding expression through matter. This spiritualizes matter and permits it to assume higher forms. Since human beings are the highest life form on the earth, the earth depends upon a select group of men and women to become world servers laboring on the frontier of human evolution. These world servers do not come from any single religious or spiritual tradition. They are not appointed or predestined. They have simply agreed, each one separately, to serve in this capacity. This agreement is at the soul level and may or may not be known by the conscious mind. There are conscious agents of evolution and unconscious agents of evolution. The unconscious agent will feel an inner compulsion to serve others. Her life will be guided and opportunities will open that could not have been created by her, working alone. In fact, she does not work alone. Unseen agents work with her from higher dimensions of the universe.

At some point, all unconscious agents become conscious of their chosen role and function in the unfoldment of the Planet Earth. This occurs in an initiation where the "eyes are opened." The initiation may occur in the dream state or in the fully conscious state. From that point on, life has a conscious direction.

Often it is the mentor who triggers the initiation. The mentor always offers the possibility through his/her morphogenic field. The protégé must achieve a certain degree of maturity before the influence of the field is effective. The mentor always speeds up the rate of the protégé's growth by providing the appropriate energy environment.

Incarnating Spirit is not an easy matter. What you understand in your meditation or lucid dream state (where you contact Spirit) may not seem so clear when you are fully awake. The densities are entirely different. The skill is being able to take an image and hold it while adding density to the image.

Interlude I

You are clothing the image in matter. You will never get a perfect fit. You do the best you can. It is never possible to get a perfect reflection from the higher dimensions to the lower dimensions. Each dimension has its own vibration, rhythm, and quality. When in a dimension, all is clear. When changing dimensions some of the clarity is lost. You see this clearly in NDEs (near death states) where the person is exposed to a higher dimension and seldom wants to return to this one. Things get better as you ascend dimensions.

Discussion Question: Who is your mentor? Whom do you mentor?

WALKING THE SPIRITUAL PATH 7

You must find your internal strengths and weaknesses. They will be reflected in events you will meet on your spiritual path.

Walking the spiritual path is an experience in growing self-awareness. What you meet in external life circumstances is always a reflection of your inner state of spiritual maturity. Opportunities will open for you to exercise your strengths and circumstances will develop that force you to face your spiritual weaknesses. The inner world and the outer world are always correlated. If a lesson can be learned in the inner world of awareness, it does not have to be projected into third dimensional reality as an external learning experience.

We always have the option of learning the easy way. However, sometimes we cannot do it and therefore we then have to learn the lesson a harder way in a sequence of life events. If we get it in the first life event, the lesson is learned and we pass on to other lessons. If we miss the lesson in that event, it will come again and again, each time gathering force, until we can no longer ignore it or fail it.

Therefore, in each life circumstance, you should ask, "What am I to learn here?" Always seek the lesson. It may be hard for you to admit the inner weakness the lesson highlights. If it were easy to understand, you would have gained the insight long ago through inner awareness alone.

A lesson that is easy for one person may be difficult for another individual. We often underestimate the difficulty of the lesson for the person experiencing it. We often say, "Why doesn't he just stop drinking?" or "Why is gambling such a problem for her?" As you struggle with your own weaknesses, you gain a real empathy for the struggles of other travelers on the path.

Our inner strengths also attract external circumstances. We thus have an opportunity to serve others and also strengthen our talents in the process. The more you use your gifts to help others, the stronger they become. Finally, you will do with almost no effort what is impossible for many others to accomplish even with great effort. You have gained mastery in that area. Of course the goal is symmetrical development with mastery in all areas. That goal takes a lot of living and lots of mistakes in the process of gaining such mastery.

Once a lesson is learned the trying circumstances depart. You will then wonder why it took you so long to master the weakness. Be of good cheer! This is the same process we all go through in our voyage throughout eternity. You do not have to make all the mistakes yourself. You can learn through the lives of others. It is good to study exemplary lives and learn by inspiration rather than perspiration.

Discussion Question: Give an example of how one of your soul qualities has attracted a life circumstance.

WALKING THE SPIRITUAL PATH 8

Parts of the path are revealed through meditation and prayer. Other parts are learned only through experience.

Walking the path with excellence requires spiritual direction. Where does such direction come from? Meditation and prayer are important sources of direction. They permit the soul to impact the ego and download material from the Spirit.

Some things, however, can only be learned through personal experience in high density, third dimensional space. The Planet Earth is a great classroom. The third dimension has enough density that things can exist without you having to pay attention to them. In the dreamband, for instance, if a thing is out of mind, it is out of existence. In that dimension it is difficult to learn because nothing ever stays fixed in time and space long enough for you to learn from it. You may have noticed in a dream that it is hard to find your way back to where you were just a few minutes previously. The reason for this is simple. For a few minutes, your mind was off the previous environment and it simply disappeared. When you think about it again, it reappears, but not exactly. So you become lost and disoriented. You do not have this problem in third dimensional reality. When you return home from work, your kitchen is still there and in the same way as you left it earlier in the morning.

In walking the spiritual path you move through a variety of life experiences. Many of these experiences are drawn to you since they offer opportunities to overcome weaknesses and enhance your strengths. At first these experiences may seem to be simply coincidental. Later you will realize they were necessary to teach you what you needed to learn.

You are a running adding machine total of your life experiences. A change of experience is a change of consciousness. You incorporate all that you have experienced. All experience is gained in spaces. A design for space is a design for consciousness. At some point on the spiritual path, you will begin to plan your new life experiences. You will plan these experiences on the basis of their ability to add the qualities of consciousness you most desire. Many of these experiences will be in third dimensional reality, but not all of them. We are multidimensional creatures living in a multidimensional universe. We can learn some things at each level of density. Our most difficult learnings will usually be in third dimensional reality where time, space, and condition are slowed down sufficiently for us to comprehend essential relationships.

Discussion Question: How have you designed healing spaces in your organization?

WALKING THE SPIRITUAL PATH 9

You don't always do it right the first time. We must celebrate our failures on the path and learn from them.

We may view the earth as a giant classroom. We are here to learn. We learn by making mistakes. If we had nothing to learn here, we would not be on earth but would be living in a higher dimension.

A mistake is a venture in learning. We are gaining an understanding of how the world works and our relationship to it. The consequences of a mistake concentrate the attention and give us insight into the law of cause and effect. We gain mastery slowly in the earth school.

Insight and understanding must be earned. They cannot be bequeathed to us by a higher being. You cannot pray for any ability. You can only pray for the opportunity to develop that ability in the school of hard knocks. However, once learned, the insight is yours. No one can take it from you.

We are born with a desire to reach out and discover the universe. Psychologists call this the exploratory drive. As long as that drive is strong in us, we are fully alive. It is the nature of a person to incorporate everything in his/her environment. We grow through contacting new opportunities for experience and then incorporating that substance into ourselves. We begin in the third dimension and then graduate into higher dimensions and alternative realities.

Our quest is an eternal quest. We will always seek to learn and then become. Because our universe is a relationship universe, we can form a relationship with any part of it. You can form a relationship with a distant star or with a single cell in your body. It is all a question of the scope and scale of your consciousness.

As we expand our consciousness, we graduate from gross mistakes to more subtle ones. We first learn to control our behavior, then our feelings, then our thoughts, and at last our soul aspirations. The Master Jesus taught that to hate a person is equivalent to killing him. Our legal system is based on physical considerations only. The moral system of the universe is far more comprehensive. Thought control is subtler than simple control of body actions. Soul control is more difficult than thought control. More subtle thoughts and feelings actually have more power for good and evil than more dense physical acts.

Interlude I

When you make a mistake, as you surely will, do not glory in it, but instead celebrate the opportunity to gain mastery. Say, "Thank you universe for the privilege of learning in the one of the greatest schools in the universe."

Discussion Question: Name one of your greatest "mistakes" which has proven to be a treasured learning experience.

WALKING THE SPIRITUAL PATH 10

You can pursue false paths—the byways of life.

Walking the spiritual path requires avoidance of false paths and futile byways. This requires a highly developed sense of discrimination, i.e., being able to discern the false from the true.

Everything in the third dimension is cast in the light of glamour. Materialism, greed, error, and high-density thinking veil it. It is easy to be led astray by the false light of glamour. To minimize this error daily contact with the soul is required. The soul light pierces the negative light of glamour and shows things for what they are, not what they appear to be. Behind the bright lights of the casinos in Las Vegas, Nevada is a realm of poverty, crime and wretchedness, yet tourists pour in by the thousands attracted to the bright lights. Like moths attracted to a naked flame they place themselves on a slippery slope of descent. Behind fame and fortune on Wall Street and Hollywood are misery and loneliness.

Our planet is a schoolhouse. We are here to learn the lessons of the third dimension. We are representatives of Spirit. We are the bridge between Spirit and high-density matter. We are the incarnation of higher possibilities unless we become mired in the heaviness of our world. The third dimension is meant to be an earthy reflection of the celestial spheres. The purpose of the multiverse is to reflect the possibilities of God throughout all of creation in all worlds and in all dimensions. Our world and dimension are dark and heavy compared to others. Here things move slowly and only with great effort. Here every thought becomes a thing. We learn from its thingness. In other dimensions and on other worlds, reality is more ephemeral. Nothing stays in place very long and subjectivity reigns supreme.

We all have ego glitches. These glitches attract matching circumstances that provide opportunities for learning and mastery. If instead, we indulge our weaknesses they enslave us and eventually become our master. Since we have animal bodies and live in a materialistic culture the temptations for soul transgression are many. Everyday we need to review our soul assignments by answering the following questions:

Who am I? Where did I come from? What am I doing here? And where am I going? Additional questions for review might be:

Interlude I

What is God's purpose and plan on this earth? How do my present or contemplated actions conform to God's purpose and plan? What role does my organization play in making the world a better place?

By rising above the clamor of our ego we see as our soul sees. Then we can be assured that are feet are on the right path.

Discussion Question: Where is glamour most evident in your self and in your organization?

WALKING THE SPIRITUAL PATH 11

Look back and tell me a story of where you have been.

You are a total of all that you have experienced. You are the result of where you have been and what you have done. Your life is a continuing myth and you are the mythmaker.

Walking the spiritual path requires a sense of personal history. You need to experience a continuity of consciousness: past, present, and future. Since consciousness is modified by remembered experience or imagined experience, aim to expand your awareness by remembering your past and visioning your future. Learn to control your experiences and you will control your destiny.

Search back and remember where you picked up some of your present characteristics. You carry a genetic memory from all those who preceded you in your genetic lineage. You carry a prenatal memory from the moment of conception and during the stay in your mother's womb. You carry a memory from your experiences in other dimensions, including the dream band. You can also tap into the memory of the planet of which you are a part. These many sources of memories are often the basis of what people call experiences of other lives.

Of course you are also greatly affected by the characteristics of your archetype (soul). These traits were not earned but bestowed upon you by grace. You will not remember having learned them since they were given to you in partially developed form. However, each archetypal quality can be further developed through further effort.

The events you have experienced will have the meanings you assign to them. This is why I say, "Tell me a story of where you have been." The meaning is in the experiencer, not the experience. A bad experience may have a long-term beneficial effect in your overall development. In fact, each time your awareness expands you will reinterpret past life events.

All history is subjective. All history is personal. All history is constantly being reevaluated in the light of present awareness. This is the primary reason that enlightened souls have very little negative criticism of their past. They understand that "all things work together for good to those who love the Lord." Without each event in your past, you could not be the person you are now.

We live lives of synchronicity where each thing we need arrives just in time. Finally, we learn to trust the universe. As we trust, fear disappears. We learn to trust the process of our unfoldment on this planet. Someday we will tell our story with great love and appreciation for what seemed at the time to be good or bad. Our life drama is like a patchwork quilt, sewn together with loving hands, each piece fitted to the other.

Discussion Question: Describe how you are a mythmaker for your organization.

WALKING THE SPIRITUAL PATH 12

Look now and tell me what you are.

Our sense of personal identity grows as we progress on the spiritual path. At first we tend to accept other people's definition of us. Our self concept becomes the mirror image of the concept others have of us, particularly family members. Later teachers and peers will add to our self image. Of course the culture, and historical age also add components of our sense of self. Interestingly, all of this has almost no relationship to who we really are. Our ego is the result of largely chance happenings, most importantly, the time and circumstances of our birth.

Many people never move beyond this circumstantial definition of self. Others, however, may have a life changing series of events that break through the cultural hypnosis and establish soul contact. Often these events arrive in the form of personal crises. When the ego no longer has a good explanation for what is happening, an opening is created for soul downflow. Only one such crisis can ignite a passion for explanation and meaning.

Once the soul journey has begun there is no turning back. No longer will the usual distractions of the world suffice. "Who am I" is the ultimate motivational question. Most often the person seeks answers in the great books of the world or in the search for a personal mentor. In Western culture it is only natural to look outside for answers. Of course the answers cannot be found there. The answer can only come from an internal search back to the source of your identity, your soul.

Meditation is the ultimate path for soul discovery. When the body, emotions, and mind are quiet, the soul can descend through the dimensions of consciousness and impress the ego. With the first soul contact a powerful energy is experienced by the ego. Usually the ego responds with fear. It does not understand what is overshadowing its usual dominance of the person. With patience and practice, however, the ego learns to accept the soul and eventually becomes its obedient vehicle in the lower worlds.

Since the soul is multidimensional, it cannot reveal itself in all its fullness. It can only download the amount of light and energy the lower vehicles (body, emotions, and mind) can tolerate. In this sense, the ego is the limiter of the soul. With expansion of the vehicles, more soul can flow. Therefore the person feels a tremendous expansiveness and an intuition of the soul depths that lie beyond. The ego is now confronting the soundless sound and the dark light of the Void.

Interlude I

This exposure is breathtaking and fixes the feet of the disciple on the endless path of unfoldment. So the question is, "Tell me what you are?"

Discussion Question: How are you different from what many people think you are?

WALKING THE SPIRITUAL PATH 13

What are the current unresolved issues in your life?

We all have unresolved issues in our lives. Earth is a schoolhouse and we are students. Our challenge is mastery of the 3rd dimension on Planet Earth.

Some unresolved issues we are born with. They come through genetic transmission, our connection to the planetary thought stream, qualities of our archetype, and from other sources. Other issues develop as we live and learn, make mistakes, and try to avoid obvious glitches.

We all face the usual challenges of living in a material body which harbors an Infinite Spirit. This produces a natural tension between Spirit and matter. Our body/mind vehicle is the meeting place for resolving this tension through creation of new spiritualized forms. We must acknowledge both the dense physical energies and the subtle spiritual energies and integrate them in our unified instrument.

Unsolved issues manifest in the physical, emotional, mental and spiritual domains. For instance sexual problems have a physical stimulation component, a relationship component, a thought form component, and a spiritual polarity component. In solving sexual difficulties the problem must be overcome at all four levels. If a person does not understand spiritual polarity, harbors highly sexualized thought forms, or has experienced warped interpersonal relationships with other family members—these problems will manifest on the physical level as unregulated physical sexual conduct.

Overcoming a sexual addiction may start at conscious restraint on the physical level, working slowly toward the new spiritual understandings required to transform the problem into a nonproblem. It often happens the other way around, of course, as it does in A.A. with a chemical addiction that is overcome through invoking a higher power.

In a food addiction, bad foods will still look good to you for some time even after you have chosen to leave them alone. This is an indication that the unresolved problem still exists even though it no longer manifests at the physical level.

It is often easier to control your behavior than it is to control your mind. Jesus made reference to this when he talked about looking on a woman with lustful thoughts (of course it can be the other way around) being in the same category as physical adultery. Although Jesus did not make mention of it, changing spiritual awareness is even more difficult than controlling your mind.

Interlude I

On the spiritual path, in general, the more subtle the level, the greater the difficulty in attaining mastery. In meditation, for instance, you may be able to make your body assume the right posture but find your emotions or mind out of control. Having achieved emotional control and then mental control, you will experience the challenge of learning to navigate in the realm of Spirit.

Discussion Question: List a couple of unresolved issues in your life.

WALKING THE SPIRITUAL PATH 14

Look ahead and tell me where you are going.

A sense of destination is a requirement for walking the spiritual path. The spiritual pilgrim must be able to look ahead and know where he is going. This sense of destination may be a well-delineated vision or only a vague sense of direction but it provides an orientation for the pilgrim's life. The closer he returns to the Source, the clearer his vision. At first there is only a vague intuition. Later there is a clear vision. Still later on the path, the pilgrim enters an alternative reality. He becomes a dweller in two worlds.

As the spiritual senses develop, it becomes easier to look ahead on the path. Precognition develops and the pilgrim begins to perceive alternative realities. He will sense the most probable reality and the more preferable realities that can be invoked by an act of will followed by appropriate action. Looking ahead is not a matter of perceiving a fixed fate. It is rather a capacity to perceive the dynamic flux of the universe and its inherent capacity to assume multiple forms that can be invoked by the will and action of spiritual agents.

When you perceive the possibility of multiple realities you can act as a co-creator. The future then becomes a willed reality rather than an accidental turn of events. Walking the spiritual path is a dynamic co-creative effort in partnership with the Source. God, the Source, will manifest in all possible worlds and in all possible ways. By working through created agents, the Source explores its depth and infinite range of possibilities.

All worlds in all universes are particular instances of the Source's creative will to manifestation. As created beings become qualified to participate, they join the Source in this joyful exploration. So the pilgrim journeys not toward a fixed future reality (static idea of heaven), but toward a range of creative possibilities that become available through the pilgrim's expansion of consciousness.

It takes a quantum leap of consciousness to move beyond a fatalistic conception of the environment to a design strategy for the environment. American society is now participating in this leap. In the new millennium, we will assume the status of designers of our reality and inventors of our future.

As I have said before, America will become the first nation in the recorded history of our planet to develop self-conscious design capacity. We will discover that the external world is simply a reflection of our internal states of consciousness. By changing our collective mind, we will change our world. By changing our future we will alter our present and revise our past.

Discussion Question: Briefly describe your future vision for yourself and your organization.

WALKING THE SPIRITUAL PATH 15

What is yet to come?

One who walks the spiritual path lives in the past, present, and future. She remembers what has been, knows what is, and imagines what can be. She also knows that by changing the future she can alter her present and reshape her past. However, the greatest power application is the future. It presents the largest arena of possibilities. There are an infinite number of possible futures. By comparison there are only a finite number of ways the present can be reorganized and the past reinterpreted.

With expansion of your consciousness there are more degrees of freedom in creating your future. You are less shaped by the past or conditioned by the present. However, it is important to understand you are not a totally free agent in the universe. Certain events that occur in your life are determined by larger patterns of causation at regional, planetary, galactic, and universe levels. You cannot change these. However, within these larger patterns are many degrees of freedom that you can realize through acts of insight, will, and appropriate efforts.

Any created being has limited free choice. However, these limits are very large and most people have little idea of the freedom they possess to rearrange life events. We are born with the environment shaping us. As we grow in consciousness we develop an increasing capacity to reshape the environment.

The universe is radically open to rearrangement. It may be viewed as a set of building blocks waiting upon the builder who will provide shape and purpose. Consciousness is that builder.

Walking the spiritual path gives increasing insight and power as consciousness first shaped by outside forces becomes a shaping force in and of itself. Design is the Divine science. We should view our lives as a design project and ultimately our jobs, communities, and planet. Highly evolved civilizations live on designer planets.

As we enter the twenty-first century we will begin to design our future as well as our society. Many of our social pathologies will be designed out rather than treated. We are destined to become architects of our external spaces. To do this we must become masters of our internal spaces. The design of consciousness and the design of a planet are one and the same thing. America will become a designer society. Healthcare will play a leadership role in this design effort. America will become a spiritual nation and will evolve from a materialistic society to a spiritual society. This will not occur overnight, but for those who have eyes to see, the handwriting is already on the wall.

Discussion Question: How is your organization playing a lead role in the effort to design a healthier America?

WALKING THE SPIRITUAL PATH 16

Remember where the road divided in the past and the pathway you took.

Walking the spiritual path entails remembering yourself, your past, and the paths you have chosen. We come to many bifurcations or dividing of the ways. Choices have to be made. Each choice creates a different future. Our lives are running stories that always have multiple endings. We gain wisdom by remembering past choices and understanding how those choices have affected us in the present and will likely affect us in the future.

We master our destiny by making right choices. Sowing and reaping is a basic law of the universe (often called cause and effect or karma). Each thought, feeling, and action goes out into the world. Each disturbs the equilibrium of the world in some way. Each requires a balance factor from the sender. Our good actions return with interest as do our foolish ones.

Yet, we should not be too hard on ourselves. We learn by making mistakes and then rectifying future action based on our learning. Intelligent mistakes create a possibility for better decisions. All actions should be conscious and with full intent. You cannot learn from unconscious thoughts, feelings, or actions. Sometimes our ego tries to kid us by drifting into something with less than full intent. That way we can "benefit" from the action, feeling, or thought without taking responsibility for it. Such kidding ourselves is like quicksand. We sink deeper and deeper.

If you are about to engage in a foolish action (often called sin in the Bible) do it with full intent and be willing to pay the price as a balance factor. This works the same way on the positive side of the ledger. Do a wise act and be willing to accept the benefit that accrues to you.

When facing the dividing of the ways, be as conscious as possible. Examine all possible responses you could make and their likely consequences. Learn to operate the law of the universe in your favor.

In our pathway of evolution the early dividings are rather obvious and simple. As we continue to unfold, the dividings get more subtle. The more difficult dividings require more spiritual reflection. In the vocabulary of the aspirant this is often called discrimination, or the testing of the spirits. Discrimination grows with practice. When the tests of sexuality, power, pride, wealth, popularity etc. are passed with success, more difficult choices will follow.

We should be able to look back on our past and see evidence of our growth, i.e., wisdom in making choices.

Discussion Question: Describe a "dividing of the way" in your life.

WALKING THE SPIRITUAL PATH 17

Remember the mentors you met along the way.

None of us do it alone. We are dependent upon others and others are dependent upon us. We mentor others and we are mentored. We live in an interdependent universe. Nothing stands alone. Everything is connected to everything. Change one thing and you change everything.

It is good to remember your past and recall your many mentors and the lessons they taught. Perhaps your parents were in this category. Parents are usually our earliest teachers. Even people coming from troubled childhoods can usually point to some parental help they enjoyed along the way. Sometimes the parental experiences seemed very negative at the time. However, even in these instances redeeming qualities can often be found. To vow to be unlike your parents may provide a lifetime motivation that is absent from more peaceful families.

What it boils down to is the realization that you are who you are because of all the experiences you have encountered. Take any of these experiences away and you would be a very different person. This realization does not excuse abuses you may have suffered or the people who inflicted them upon you, but these very abuses may have prepared you for your current lifework and ministry.

It is seldom that you will have the same mentor for a lifetime. A mentor can only give you what they have to teach because of who they are. When you have learned these lessons, you graduate to another mentor and a different set of lessons. Do not despair. As a mentor you will also have a series of students. Good mentoring never creates dependency. The object of all mentoring is soul growth.

Just as you have learned to be a good mentor, so you will have to learn to be a good mentee. Any mentor can teach only what you are open to learning. It is important to have a respectful attitude toward your mentors and to appreciate that human beings are not perfect. Mentors too make mistakes and are also on the path of learning and further unfoldment.

So, look back and remember from whence you have come. Remember your teachers—what you learned and refused to learn. Accept that your mentees will do likewise when they reconsider you.

You may even want to touch in now and then to a past teacher. We live in a timeless universe. When you remember, in a sense you return to the past and your mentor is again with you. You may even want to give your mentor another "thanks," particularly if you forget to do so the last time around. And what do you hear? Yes, that sound ringing through the corridors of time was "you are welcome."

Discussion Question: What new spiritual ideas are you open to? What is on the leading edge of your thinking?

WALKING THE SPIRITUAL PATH 18

Call upon your angel mentor (major advisor).

We can enjoy both human and non-human mentors. Our major mentor in the spiritual dimension often goes by the name of our inner guide or guardian angel. The function of this mentor is to guide us on our pathway of spiritual unfoldment. Our angel can connect us with other angels and other inner plane beings as well as work in our behalf with the Godhead itself.

In deep states of prayer and meditation you may suddenly become aware of your guide. You will feel this being as a presence that is attending to your every thought, feeling, and action. There is a subtle energy chord that connects you to your angel. Your angel can increase or greatly decrease the connectivity of this chord depending upon how you are functioning. If you choose to engage in lower life, this creates pain for your angel and he/she will decrease the connectivity in order not to be swamped by your low vibrations. As your energy fields increase in frequency, your angel increases the connectivity and enjoys a closer communion with you.

If the chord is closely connected your angel can overshadow you and work through you. This is not channeling. Your guide inputs information directly into your brain/mind circuits. Your voice, consciousness, and manner will not change. You simply have access to a new sensory/motor channel for as long as your guide keeps it open. During a period of overshadowing you will able to operate at a much higher psychospiritual level than usual. Your mental processes are greatly accelerated. You can feel the high frequency spiritual energies course through your being.

Often we are not very good company for our angel. The angel has to keep at a safe distance through the energy chord. If we want to enjoy continuous guidance, then we must change the way we live. Ask yourself, "Are you fit for the company of your angel?" Any negative thoughts create an uncomfortable tug on the chord. Positive thoughts, particularly those of love and compassion, create a positive tug. Rest assured, when you are doing good work you have the company of inner plane beings.

Your angel and you are matched from the same basic spiritual archetype. Although the angel is working from higher octaves of the archetype, there is a resonance with the lower levels where you are hanging out. If you could function at the higher octaves, you would be in continuous communication with your spiritual mentor. At some point in your personal evolution that becomes your strong desire. At that point you begin making the inner changes necessary to raise your basic spiritual frequencies. Your angel can help you in this regard, but not until you have reached a point of will and action that makes a better connection a high priority for both of you.

Discussion Question: Have you ever sensed the personal presence of a heavenly being?

WALKING THE SPIRITUAL PATH 19

Who are you helping (mentoring)?

As you serve, you are served. As you mentor, you are mentored. The law of the universe is loving service to others. To continue upon the path of progression, we must assist others in their journeys.

Higher life forms release the potential in lower life forms.

God utilizes the principle of maximum downward delegation. You are expected to serve according to your capacity to serve. What you cannot do will be done by others. What you can do, but refuse to do, generates your personal karma.

So, who are you mentoring? Who is your mentor? These are questions we must answer at all points along our path. Mentors find you. You must find those who need mentoring.

Go out and look!

Healthcare must develop an outreach mentality. We must go out and serve people where they live, work, play and pray. It is not about them coming to us, but about us going to them.

A covenant relationship or holy trust exists between the mentor and mentee. It is a contract of mutual expectation and accountability. A mentee can only be helped if he/she wishes to be helped and puts forth good faith efforts in that direction. The relationship between ourselves and our teachers is not one way. They teach. We struggle. They share their consciousness. We must develop our consciousness. Free will is sovereign on our planet. We cannot be helped in spite of ourselves.

You cannot walk the spiritual path alone. To attempt such is to be tempted by the dark forces. Self focus results in self aggrandizement. The forces of light constitute a loving, sharing community.

When we arrive at a loving, sharing community in healthcare, much will be accomplished that now remains beyond our reach. We will experience a surplus of resources.

We are at the breakpoint ready to experience a quantum leap in consciousness. No solution to our healthcare problems is coming from the government. No solution is coming from the marketplace. The solution is empowered communities acting in their own behalf.

We need hundreds of community volunteers acting as mentors to needy families, neighborhoods, and communities. Only a change of mind will change our world. Each healthcare professional on the path of personal discovery is a potential mentor for those who are seeking. As mentors we must reach out and help those who depend upon grace and mercy. If we cannot do that, we should expect the worst and will certainly experience it.

Discussion Question: What special programs does your organization offer to accelerate the spiritual unfoldment of your employees?

WALKING THE SPIRITUAL PATH 20

Progress on the path means increasing love, insight and power.

Spirituality does not exist in a vacuum. With an increase in spirituality comes increased love, insight, and power. These three qualities must coexist in a balanced relationship. Love connects us to God. With that connection comes insight. With insight into the universe we can wield more power to accomplish the purposes of God on this planet.

Walking the spiritual path is a daily activity. Our growth needs continuous stimulation, not binge periods of frantic activity. Our capacity increases through regular use. That means some time must be set aside each day for spiritual meditation and growth. If you are a morning person, use the morning. If you are an evening person, use the evening.

It is important to be in a spiritual frame of mind before going to sleep at night. Our growth in consciousness as we sleep is made possible by an enabling mindset. Place your consciousness upon God as you disconnect from your daily concerns and cares. Heavenly beings can then help you experience and grow. Depending upon your level of consciousness you may or may not remember these nighttime sojourns.

Our goal is to become servers of the Divine plan on all levels of consciousness. It is pointless to try to become a nighttime learner if you pass up all the opportunities during the daytime. The night is an extension of our daily concerns and activities.

Insight comes about as a result of our reading, meditating, and acting. It can also happen when a Being from the spiritual dimension implants the material directly into our consciousness. Our memory banks are open to our Guardians. When we are given material, our responsibility is to use the insights to help others upon their paths of discovery. Each unit of our awareness which is put into motion grows and expands in scope and intensity. We grow through service.

Many saints are primarily upon the path of love. Many scholars are upon the path of knowledge. Other workers in God's kingdom are following the path of action. Of course, we must embody all three paths, but we usually favor one over the other two. By working with other people following different paths we experience the true of joy of partnering and group creation.

Interlude I

Which path is your choice at this point in your life? How do you practice it each day? How have you helped others walking this same path? How do you work with others following the other two paths?

Discussion Question: Do you practice regular meditation and spiritual reflection?

WALKING THE SPIRITUAL PATH 21

You attract circumstances (stage set).

Like attracts like. Cause and effect are two ends of the same rope. What goes around comes around. Cast your bread upon the waters and in many days it will return. Whatever ye sow, that shall ye also reap. All of these sayings are restatements of the divine law of retribution or karma.

It is the law of karma that assures us we can become masters of our own destiny. Consciousness is a potent shaping force in the universe. We write the story line. The universe supplies the stage set.

In synchronicity we see this pairing of events. Synchronicity is noncausal correlation. The head of a coin does not create the tail of a coin, but they always appear together. In the same manner your psyche and your environment mirror one another. Change your mind and your world changes. Examine your life circumstances and you can diagnose the condition of your soul. You always have at hand the materials you need for your soul expression at that point in your evolutionary unfoldment.

The mind by nature is creative. It can reshape the body or the larger environment. When a group of people generate a collective thought form, it can change weather patterns, precipitate an earthquake or bring needed rain to a parched earth. The earth is alive and everything in it. At a quantum level we interact with many large electromagnetic patterns. This makes us custodians of the earth. We can think our planet into sickness or health.

We are a microsystem living in a macrosystem. As above, so below. All levels are interactive. The play calls for a particular stage set and a particular stage set calls for the matching play. By watching the stage set change we can predict changes about to occur in the play. By examining changes in mass consciousness we can predict changes that are about to occur in the world.

Ask and it shall be given. Knock and ye shall receive. The world is a plenum and will provide anything we demand for our personal and organizational drama.

In healthcare we never have a lack of resources, only a shortage of consciousness. By changing our minds we can move from scarcity to abundance.

Interlude I

Examination of the mass media reveals our collective thought forms and the changes about to occur in our world. Everything needful always happens together. We get what we need and what we deserve. Scary, isn't it? Reassuring, isn't it?

Discussion Question: Give examples of synchronicity in your life.

WALKING THE SPIRITUAL PATH 22

You are the author of your book—know the beginning and ending of chapters.

Your life may be viewed as a book. You are the author. What chapter are you currently writing (what is your age)? What is the title of this year's chapter (major themes)? How many chapters are there in your book? List the table of contents by chapter headings. What are the major themes throughout the chapters? What is you favorite chapter (thus far)? What could I learn from reading your book? Are there any dangling threads in some of the chapters that need to be better integrated? Write some alternative endings for your book. This exercise is a major consciousness raising activity. It will give you some new perspectives and empower you to write better chapters for the remainder of your book.

It is important for you to know when it is time to finish a chapter in your book of life. You should not doddle along when everything that can be accomplished has been accomplished. It is easy to become too attached to your old comfort zones and fear growth and change. Just as in a real book, when this happens, boredom is the result both for the writer and the reader. And remember, when you finish an old chapter, you can begin a new one. Each chapter leads to the ones that will follow.

If you get stuck somewhere, the best thing to do is end that chapter and begin a new one. When you finish a chapter, it should be with no regrets. Honor your experience whatever it has been and honor the people that created it, whether you liked them or not. Previous chapters have brought you to where you are now. At some point in the expansion of your consciousness you will be able to look back and understand the need for everything that happened to you. In times of seeming adversity you grow in ways that are invisible to you, yet prepare the way for your life that is to follow. Your soul exists outside 3rd dimensional time and has an uncanny ability to know what you need and create it. If we are open to soul guidance and trust the process, we will be led in an unfaltering manner. But, we must remain open and trusting.

Accept what happens. Bless it. Move on. This is the pathway of progress for the spiritual pilgrim. Control your fear and your desire. They both foreclose better options waiting for you in future chapters. What looks like chaos in your life is often a large emergent pattern that you do not yet recognize. From chaos or the Void comes all creation. Often the old must be destroyed to make room for the new. Your evolution is a dynamic foreword moving process. Go with it, in good times and bad, and you will reap a golden reward.

Discussion Question: What are the major themes in the book of your life?

WALKING THE SPIRITUAL PATH 23

Consider the intertwining of life paths (family).

We never walk alone. We always have both visible and invisible companions. Our life paths intertwine and branch. We separate and rejoin. We end old relationships and begin new ones. We live in a relationship universe where we have the potential to come into relationship with anything, anywhere, anytime. We are unlimited. We just don't know it yet.

The highest laws of the universe are love and service. They also represent the highest laws of the spiritual manager. We are mentors and students. We serve and are served. All higher life forms are obligated to lower life forms in the pursuit of mutual unfoldment.

We are, where we are, to learn what we need to know. We are with those who can best help us take the next needed steps. Every person is your teacher and you teach all those who know you. There is a time and a place for everything. Do not despise your life situation or any person in it. All is needful. You will incorporate your total life experience. You are a running adding machine total. Take in everything that contributes to your life. Love and accept. That which you call blessed may lead to your undoing. That which you call a curse may lead you to life more abundant. Until you see clearly you will not be able to tell a curse from a blessing. Bless where you are, doing what you are doing, knowing those you know. Learn all you can and prepare to move on to greater relationships.

Walking the spiritual path is an adventure in becoming more inclusive in your experiences and resulting insights. As you gain more experience you will become less judgmental and more understanding. A funding shortfall may present an unparalleled opportunity to discover new resources that can now be tapped in your altered state of consciousness. It usually takes a challenge for us to change our minds. The challenge may originally be misidentified as an adversity when in fact it is an open gateway beckoning for our passage and initiation into larger being.

Walking the spiritual path is always full of surprises. About the time we think we have it all figured out, a new contingency appears and we are once more on the fast learning curve.

Interlude I

Chaos is the ultimate learning opportunity. It presents us with new possibilities to be and do. Welcome chaos as a friend and ally. It will take you places you could never go without it.

Discussion Question: What keeps you in your current life situation—what do you most need to learn?

WALKING THE SPIRITUAL PATH 24

Visioning is a powerful way of navigating the path.

We can most efficiently create our next step on the spiritual path by visioning it. We are co-creators with God. If we are in touch with our inner guidance we sense what is needed and begin to imagine its future form. This imagination is creative and will constellate the reality events necessary for us to fill out our holographic imagery. The world we experience is a reflection of the images in our mind. If we have no personal or organizational visions we are simply buffeted about by life events. We move forward slowly, if at all, and largely by default.

Our visions grow and develop as they encounter third dimensional reality. For this reason, we must engage in a constant process of revisioning. We keep getting a clearer and clearer view of our destination as we keep trying to get there. Our first visions may only set a new direction for our efforts. As we learn, subsequent visions will begin to fill in the missing details. Unless you are highly precognitive, you will not see the whole thing in its completed form, the first time you look. You will have fuzzy images but will feel the new energies being invoked by the process of exploration. Because of the heavy density of the third dimension, it always distorts and perturbs the purity of the vision as it exists in the higher dimensions of consciousness. Our skill in working third dimensional matter will determine how much of the vision we can bring through in this dimension. This is why it is so important for the one who is walking the spiritual path to stay grounded and gain expertise in the political, economic, social, and organizational rhythms of consensual reality. Unless you want to live in a cave and make little difference in this world or the world to come, you must learn to work with different densities. As a human being you must have your head in the clouds and your feet on the ground. The Spirit searches the earth for such people who can act as conduits for the Spirit. It pours through individuals, groups, and organizations that have opened themselves to this possibility.

When the Spirit pours into this dimension it creates a "node." This node generates a "sound" in the spiritual dimensions. This sound beckons people, resources and events that will assemble to permit the new creation to take place. Recently I observed with a client that the cast was assembling itself for his new "play." The CEO through his visioning had created a node and was becoming the point of manifestation for his vision to become a third dimensional reality. Some of the new cast members, interestingly enough, did not know why they were there. They simply felt the call and were responding. Indeed this is powerful stuff. Will you volunteer yourself to create a node?

Discussion Question: How can your organization become a "node?"

Clues to your path appear in your dreams.

Your Higher Self attempts to communicate with you in many ways. Through daily events, chance happenings, and body sensations, messages filter into your consciousness. They may or may not be decoded by your ego. One of the most frequent channels of communication utilized by your Higher Self is dreaming. Each night you change your focus of consciousness and enter the dream state. In the dream state you interact with images and symbols of your own making. You occupy an internal world where the usual constraints of the third dimension are lacking.

There are many different types of dreams. Some are a rehash of the days events. Some are simple wish fulfillment. Others are worries that take form and pursue you. However, certain dreams have a different quality. They are more vivid, colorful and have a sense of urgency about them. You do not forget these dreams. They stand out from the background of usual dreaming. These dreams are messages from your Higher Self. They are lucid, well organized and plausible. They convict you with their sincerity. You remember them for days, weeks or years. You may not understand their meaning, but you know their importance for your life.

By meditating upon the meaning of these dreams, a contact can often be established with the Higher Self. Those who seek, find. The clues come in many different ways. A melody floats through your head. You hear a chance remark and recognize its deeper significance. You seeming by chance pick up a book or see something on TV that carries a thread of the answer. By tuning in to the fringes of your conscious mind you see the outline of an answer forming in the shadows.

Later in your practice of dream communication, you will become a lucid dreamer. Here you will know you are dreaming while you are dreaming. When you attain lucidity say, "Take me to where I need to be, to learn what I need to know." Suddenly the dream landscape will be swept away and you will be projected into a higher dimension of consciousness where your Higher Self can appear in a less veiled form.

Finally we realize all things that come within the arena of our experience are meaningful. Every event is both actual and symbolic. The world is our story. Even our third dimensional "reality" is but a dream when viewed from higher dimensions of consciousness. We will spend forever simply waking up from the previous dream and discovering an even greater reality that awaits us. So dream on dear fellow traveler. Such is the travel to the greater mansions that God has prepared for us.

Discussion Question: Can you remember a dream that had a powerful message for you?

WALKING THE SPIRITUAL PATH 26

You may discover your path on a vision quest.

There are many ways of discovering your spiritual path. Going on a vision quest is one of these ways. On a vision quest you leave the "world" and enter a sacred space of nature to commune with nature and have revealed to you your inner nature and purpose on this planet. This revelation may come through visions, signs, symbols, animal totems, the sound of the wind, plant energies, etc.

On a vision quest you go through necessary purifications, meditate and pray and engage in watchful waiting. You surrender to the powers that are watching you.

The doctrine of correspondences explains much of what happens on a vision quest. Every occurrence on the quest is both what it is and also symbolic of something greater than that. An eagle soaring in the heavens is an eagle soaring in the heavens, but it is also more. It may be a spiritual sign of your Spirit which is preparing to soar into the heavens and be met by a heavenly messenger. It is important on a quest to look behind every common occurrence for the hidden spiritual meaning. In this way the Powers test you for alertness and openness for revelation. There are no accidental happenings on a quest for you have given yourself over to greater spiritual powers for your keeping and instruction.

In the first hours of a quest, not much may seem to happen. You are going through a gradual period of detoxification and attunement. The noisy world must leave your consciousness preparing a space for the descent of Spirit. When Spirit begins to call you may enter a state of altered consciousness more like dream time than real world time. Your sensory ratios are readjusting for reception of subtle psychic broadcasts. It is important not to get impatient or restless. All things come to those who watch and wait. We are often tested before revelation descends. Our ego is the worst enemy during this period suggesting we are wasting our time, or worse, losing our mind.

Sometimes a feeling of fear or invisible presence sweeps through our consciousness as Spirit approaches. We often feel the strange presence as ego alien. Here the temptation is to turn our heels and run from the scene. Old fears may be activated by a rustle in the leaves or the sound of an animal call. We may feel strange body sensations or have hot or cold flashes. Again the instruction is to watch and wait.

What happens next can vary greatly. You may have a vision or receive a visitation. You may experience a dramatic night dream or experience an out-of-body experience. It may be less dramatic than this. You may have a strong feeling rise into your consciousness or suddenly have a confident knowing. You may experience a strong desire to do something upon your return.

Sometimes the value of a vision quest extends for many weeks following its completion as your conscious mind debriefs the quest. The meaning of the vision quest may slowly come into focus after you have returned to the "world." No matter, it is never the same for two different people and you will never be the same after the quest. You have journeyed into the world of Spirit.

Discussion Question: Would you like to go on a vision quest?

WALKING THE SPIRITUAL PATH 27

You must escape the major traps on the path (ego, money, fame, and power).
The ego makes a wonderful servant but a poor master. It feels it is the center of your life and it seeks to collect all the goodies it can get your hands on. Ego, money, fame, and power are only a few of its obsessions. Many people spend their entire lives in pursuit of these outer trappings while ignoring soul development. Because the ego is our major vehicle for moving around in this third dimension, it should be viewed in positive terms. You won't do much without it. Like an automobile it is a useful conveyance but has no inner connection to your self. The problem arises when you feel your ego is your identity and you give in to its whims.

You are not born with an ego. You have only the capacity to develop one as a result of your experience in this dimension. Our ego develops early in life. It takes a particular shape because of our associations with family and the impacts of our early environment. It is also affected by our genetic inheritance and to a small degree by our soul radiation. Early in life we develop a sense of identity and the ego assumes it is that. After all, that is what other people are reacting to in us and we take our cues from them. Because our world is tuned in to material acquisitions, we develop a sense of worth based on how many of these acquisitions we possess. Each time the ego collects something else, it believes it is better off, perhaps even better than other people who possess less.

For those fortunate enough to come into contact with some source of spirituality, a new identity is awakened. The soul arises above the horizon of consciousness and the rays of the Spirit illuminate it. The ego is threatened by all of this. Perhaps it is not the center after all. A long battle will ensue in the person as the ego fights its displacement by soul. Only after much effort and repeated acts of will by the person, will the ego step aside and permit the soul to gain mastery of the person. The soul has no great desire to collect anything. It is a vehicle of Spirit, which possesses all and makes available that which is needful for service in this world. Money, fame, and power may be granted if they are required for world service. Since the person is no longer under the control of the ego, there is no identification with these externalities. They can no longer constitute barriers for Spirit contact and full soul function.

For most of you reading these words, the battle is on. The ego is still in center position although you have a deep yearning to live as soul. If you retain this love of soul and Spirit, it is only a question of time and struggle before you win and take your place among the world servers. You may be poor or rich. You may be powerful or unnoticed. It matters not. You are living as soul and can claim the entire universe as your home. You own nothing, yet, have everything at your command as need dictates.

Discussion Question: What traps has your ego placed in your path?

WALKING THE SPIRITUAL PATH 28

With each step on the path you experience a growing sense of identity.

Who are you? We are born not knowing. Some die without knowing. However, others discover their true identity as they grow in spiritual awareness. Each day can be a day of new revelations by the Soul. With each step on the spiritual path we should advance in knowledge and self awareness.

The line of descent is Spirit—Soul—mind—emotions—body. Our true identity is Spirit—a facet of God shining through us. It is an individualized aspect of Divinity that takes form in us. Spirit shines into Soul and Soul takes its imprint to a greater or lesser degree. Soul is a form of low density spiritual matter. Spirit is neither matter or energy. It is consciousness. Soul to a greater or lesser degree reflects Spirit, but is not initially connected directly to it. Soul then radiates into mind. This is a difficult step-down transfer. Mind has a hard time understanding Soul. Then mind steps-down into emotions. Finally emotions step-down into body. The objective is to have a body incarnation of Spirit. With the transfer from Spirit to body, heaven is born on earth and earth ascends into heaven.

Your identity is composed of all these levels. You are body, feelings, mind, Soul and Spirit. If these are in alignment you have achieved enlightenment and are a fully integrated person. This type of alignment is rare in our culture. It takes a lot of effort and often a lifetime of learning. Modern society offers lots of distractions. Most people's sense of self is simply what other people think about them; they become their social role. Since there is no Soul contact, there is nothing to offset this false perception.

Another source of clues concerning our identity consists of the situations we attract. Like attracts like. The Soul knowing the lessons that must be learned before it can perfectly reflect Spirit attracts the necessary learning situations into our lives. If we have limited or no soul contact, these circumstances will come as a total surprise to us. The Soul always works in our behalf, although it may not seem so at the time. At first the mind (ego) resists the Soul since it thinks it is boss and resents any outside intrusion that would displace its sense or primacy. Later in our walk upon the spiritual path, Soul wins over mind and mind becomes an obedient servant of Soul.

The universe streams through your sense of identity. You personalize every aspect of it. All perception is personal. Many of the energies of the universe we believe to be blind forces are part of the personhood of higher forms of created consciousness. They too are personal. Everything that involves personhood involves distinct personality and style. The universe is personal. We are in relationship with all parts of it. As we understand more about ourselves, we understand more about the universe.

Discussion Question: Have you ever sensed a larger identity overshadowing you?

WALKING THE SPIRITUAL PATH 29

With each step of the path you experience a growing identification with nature (all that is).

When you begin life you experience yourself as a separate entity. The ego fosters individuality and pits itself against an alien world. When you are nearing completion of your spiritual walk on this earth, you sense your identification with All That Is. You are not separate but instead a member of a vast interrelated family of Beings—mineral, plant, animal, human, and beyond human.

How do you get from a feeling of isolation to a certain knowledge of relationship? You achieve this sense of relatedness by expanding your ring of awareness and bringing more and more of the universe into your ring. You are it. It is you. You practice reaching out to embrace as self that which you have been calling other. As Buber might say—"You pass over to the standpoint of the other." You reduce the distance between I and Thou. You accomplish a mind merge as your essence mixes with the essence of the other and you discover that both of you are composed of the same type of spiritual substance.

The earth and all of its inhabitants are part of a common warp and woof of creation. Although humans have individual souls they are related intimately to all other souls on the planet. We are all branches on the same vine. In the same fashion we incorporate the mineral, plant, and animal orders of creation in our own bodies. We have parts of creation within us and we are part of that which lives beyond us. There is an integrity of form and function that binds all of us together. Nothing stands alone. Everything is related to everything. Change one thing and you change everything.

As one of the highest life forms upon the planet at this time, we have the responsibility of preserving and nurturing all other life forms. We are the Gardeners of the Earth. Our challenge is potentiating all other lives—helping them evolve into their fullness of Being. As each individual life form evolves, so does the mass of life forms. So there are individual and collective destinies—evolution of the parts and evolution of the planet. The whole must wait upon the development of its parts to achieve higher orders of wholeness. Evolution means growing in complexity. Complexity requires high levels of integration. Integration depends upon connecting up healthy growing parts. In that sense the part that does not do its part, holds up the whole that cannot become whole. Everything must work together.

Interlude I

As we walk the spiritual path our sense of self expands and we reach out to embrace all that surrounds us. The ego is no longer our container. It becomes the source of our navigation into new worlds waiting to link up with us.

Discussion Question: How does your organization preserve and honor nature?

WALKING THE SPIRITUAL PATH 30

Happiness is finding your right path—doing who you are.

There are many paths. Walking the spiritual way means finding the path with your name upon it. Your path must parallel your soul's purpose in this life. Happiness is doing who you are. Any old path will not do.

Many people are not treading their paths. They are unhappy trying to do who they are not, becoming who they never can be. Without soul contact, the ego is at a loss to know what it is or where to go. With no known sense of identity it is likely to pick up someone else's definition or simply succumb to cultural images of success and prestige. As a result many people are mismatched in their marriages, professions, and locales.

Soul contact is fostered through study, meditation, and prayer. Keep asking, "Who am I?" This passionate inquiry attracts the soul and in response it downflows into the mind, emotions, and body. In addition, it reconstellates reality events to facilitate your search. However, you must ask frequently and sincerely. The search for your personal identity is the golden key that unlocks the universe to your bidding. When you know your "name," all of creation responds to your requests and actions. When you know as you are known, you have allies at every point on the path. Your identity is your role in All That Is.

When your soul and your path are correctly matched you have an abundance of energy and life becomes much easier. You are not working against the universe but with it. You are not imposing your will upon things but understanding the Will that is working through them. You then become a facilitator of what is trying to happen. As a boat upon the lake, the wind of Spirit pushes you along. You provide direction. The Spirit provides motive power. You are in a cooperative relationship with all around you. The very elements can be commanded in this state of consciousness. You are them. They are you. The line of separation has been removed between you and the rest of creation.

In a sense the path finds you. If you are open and available, you attract Spirit which then leads you. If you try too hard and force your way, the universe resists your efforts and you will be worn out and frustrated. When it is right, it happens almost without effort. You feel the power of connection and know your rightful destiny is assured. You try by not trying. You work without really working. You are simply present and available to Spirit as it moves through you and the universe. You are not two, but One.

Discussion Question: What are you the happiest doing?

WALKING THE SPIRITUAL PATH 31

As we progress on the path we enter increased dominion or estate.

As we progress on the path, we gain capacity and as a result of increased capacity we are given more responsibility. Our domain or estate is increased to permit us to grow beyond our current limitations.

There must be a balance between who we are and what we are doing. If we have more capacity than opportunity to put that capacity into action we regress rather than progress. If we have more demand upon us than ability to meet that demand, we are frustrated and may well fail in our assigned tasks. Therefore a balance must be maintained between our inner and outer states. That means the external environment must be adjusted to our rate of spiritual evolution or growth.

In spiritual government there is always a balance between competence and station. People are where they are for good reasons. They are qualified to hold those positions and would be removed if they failed to maintain the required capacity. In spiritual government there is no jealousy. You do not covet a position for which you are not qualified. You would simply fail in such an assignment. You also maintain high respect for those who have a more elevated position than yours. They are there because they deserve to be there. When you have developed sufficient ability, you will be promoted into a more elevated station with its attendant responsibilities and obligations. Wouldn't it be nice if the government of this world ran on the same principles? The President of the United States would then be the most highly evolved soul in the nation. He/she would be recognized by all persons as fit to hold the highest elected office.

This means you are where you are, to learn what you need to know, and when you master the current challenges, you will be moved to a new assignment. The simple rule is—be content and do the best job you can. Try to outgrow your current job by mastering every facet of it. Serve faithfully and depend upon those who witness your dedication and excellence to move you when the time is right for your departure.

In the eyes of God there is no such thing as an unimportant job or one type of job that is "better" than another. Everything that is needful must be done. Willing hands must be found. You cannot impress God. Running the country is no more important than sweeping a floor. Each should be done in the same sense of dedicated excellence. When we overcome ego we no longer think in terms of status or prestige. We do what we are assigned to do. We do it as long as needful. We do not ask for a change of assignment. We will be moved when we are ready for the move. There is a natural humility that comes from simply understanding the hierarchy of creation. There is also a great feeling of contentment and bliss that comes with that understanding. Enjoy where you are. Enjoy what you are doing. You will not be returning to this place again. New mansions await you and it is nearly time for your journey to continue.

Discussion Question: How does your current job fail to tap your inner potentials?

As we progress on the path we have more spiritual energy.

As we continue to walk the spiritual path we will notice an increase in energy at all four levels. We have more physical stamina, our mind operates at a higher velocity, our feelings are more sensitive and encompassing, and we feel powerful surges of psychic energy emanating from the spiritual planes. We are developing into high energy beings. Our vehicles will stretch themselves trying to incorporate new levels of activation. From time to time we may experience some discomfort and intermittent problems in the vehicles as they adapt to the new requirements.

Greater energy gives us the motive power for greater accomplishments. Our impact on the world increases for either good or evil. Our personal radiations affect life forms in all dimensions throughout the universe. We become more creative and our environments begin to more perfectly reflect our thoughts and intentions. The interval between cause and effect shortens. We are immediately caught up in our errors and see the benefits of our good work just as quickly. Our evolution is accelerated. Our accountability becomes more exacting. The universe can now use us as a junction point for planetary operations. We have volunteered ourselves for such service and will be treated accordingly. The dense matter around us responds quickly to our heightened states of consciousness.

Our degree of spirituality will be tested as temptations to misuse our gifts become a possibility for the first time. We count for something and will be utilized by either the forces of light or darkness. The spiritual path is a path of service. We seek to know in order to better serve. We seek empowerment in order to help realize God's intentions on this earth. We seek not for ourselves, but for the greater good.

All energy comes from the Source. As we come closer to the Source we are energized. Modulating the use of this energy is a necessary developmental skill. We can fritter it away in worry and negative actions or we can conserve and focus it on the work to be done in our organizations and communities.

Energy flows from high potential to low potential. When we are in the presence of low potential individuals, we will feel the tug on our energy vehicles. Then, we must make the decision to either share our energy or cloak it. There are some people who function as "psychic vampires" and drain energy from all available sources in their environment. We must protect ourselves from these creatures of desperation. Other low potential people may be calling out to us for healing and wisdom. To these calls we must respond with our abundance. Spiritual discrimination is an essential skill in a high energy world server. We must help those who call and wait for those who are not yet ready.

Discussion Question: What do you do to build spiritual energy? How do you generate spiritual energy in your organization?

WALKING THE SPIRITUAL PATH 33

As we progress on the path we experience an increasing power to co-create.
We are created in the image of God. Therefore we are co-creators with Him/Her/It. We are given time, space, energy, and matter and consciousness by our Creator. What we do with them is a matter of our co-creative ability. We can co-create a heaven or hell on this earth and in fact will be permitted to do so.

It is an awesome responsibility to be a co-creator. You become responsible for what is around you. Not only are you responsible for the radiation of your energy fields—you are also responsible for your physical environment. As gardeners and caretakers of the earth we were given many mineral, animal, and plant forms. In our infancy and childhood as units of consciousness we could not have participated in their formation. We could only nurture and protect them. However, as we grew in consciousness we were expected to help them in much more fundamental ways. Unfortunately, we defaulted in our basic responsibility. We have defiled the earth and are busy killing off its life forms. For this act of arrogance we will pay a high price. We can kill, but we cannot create. Most of us cannot even co-create with any degree of facility. Yet, that is our high destiny.

As human consciousness grows in potency (the indwelling Spirit is more fully reflected in the soul) it exerts more influence over the basic elements of the universe (air, fire, earth, and water). Eventually thought becomes creative and can assemble atoms to fill out visualized thought forms. At this point of soul maturity things can be thought into existence. For a well developed person this is already true on the inner dimensions of consciousness. Your thoughts immediately manifest in subtle dream matter. Dream matter does not have the density of third dimensional matter and is easily shaped by thought. You already are a creator on inner planes. It is a good thing you do not have this ability in the third dimension or the world would be in even worse shape. Every thought would manifest in matter.

Absolute thought control is a necessity for any type of creation. Change your mind and you change your world. To a limited extent this is true in our third dimension but it takes a lot longer and since mass consciousness is consensual in this dimension it is hard to get enough clarity among the multitude to manifest anything with intent.

Interlude I

The self-inventing healthcare organization becomes a reality in the next century. A small group of organizational intuitives will achieve the clarity of thought necessary for reinventing themselves and their organization. They will decide how to manifest in the world and the world will manifest for them in the required form. Eventually this planet will attain this type of co-creative ability and will manifest the consensual mental forms of its inhabitants.

Discussion Question: Give examples of how you are a co-creator.

WALKING THE SPIRITUAL PATH 34

The further we walk the path the more ability we have to see through illusions.

At first we do not see—later we understand. Illusions are frequent guests in the unenlightened mind. Discrimination is won through hard effort and lots of living. The true and false are often intertwined like branches on a vine. If the mind is affected by the glamour of money, power, prestige and fame, it cannot see through its own glamour and unwind the vine.

When we fail to discriminate clearly we become caught in the tangle of illusion. We think we are doing the right thing when we are not. We are duped by our own nature and the natural camouflage of a fallen planet. We do not see behind false appearances and behold the hidden nature of the objects of our perception. How can we avoid this? If we maintain a clear channel from Spirit to soul to mind we will always see with truth and completeness. This is sometimes called the Buddha mind. The Buddha mind reflects the world as it is. No veils are placed between the seer and the seen.

The first challenge is to get the soul to take the impress of the Spirit. Since soul substance is very subtle it has the ability to reflect Spirit essence. However, unless the person spends much time in prayer, meditation, and inspirational study, the soul is not cultivated sufficiently for the impress to occur. Soul substance like good farm land must be prepared for the seed. If there is no soul activation, the Spirit is present but the soul cannot register this presence. The barrier is not breached and the person does not register Spirit contact. This is the condition in the majority of people.

The second challenge is to get the mind to register soul contact. The soul and the mind operate at very different "frequencies." Unless a person has trained his mind to operate in the abstract realm, contact cannot be made. The practical or pragmatic mind operates at too gross a level to catch the high frequencies of the soul. A mind tuned to philosophic frequencies is a mind attuned to spirituality.

Once the mind catches the soul frequency there will be a conflict with the ego which assumes it is the center of identity and the protector of the person. A royal battle ensues for control of the person. This is well described by Paul in the Christian scriptures. Finally, soul frequencies will gain ascendancy and the ego will retreat into the position of a servant rather than a master.

Interlude I

Once there is a straight line of descent from Spirit to soul to mind, the power of illusion is broken and the person begins to operate as Spirit in a material world. This is the goal of all those who walk the spiritual path.

Discussion Question: As a manager, in what areas are you most likely not to see clearly?

SECTION TWO: VISION

1. INTRODUCTION:
CHICKENS WITH THEIR HEADS CUT OFF

"Your old ones shall dream dreams,
and your young ones
shall see visions."

—a prophet named Joel, 400 BC

For a very, very long time, people have talked about visions. At times, visions were somehow the work of divinity. To provide a vision was to give a mechanism of warning, guidance, or comfort. The vision was usually odd enough to gain people's attention and, once understood, served as a kind of road sign or directional signal that would give some indication of how life could be lived at its best.

Today, the issue of vision is not reserved for the magical or the religious. In fact, it would be fairly strange to enter a modern workplace and not find some executive talking about the organization's vision. Many leaders in the modern workplace do not believe that full potential can be realized unless a vision is clearly articulated and the entire workplace is caught up in the direction stated in the vision.

There is an interesting common frame of reference on visions that has spanned the ages. There is general agreement that without a vision, potential and productive energy is lost, there is a vague wandering and slippage that results from lack of direction, and the power of positive morale is greatly compromised. The ancient wise men believed this; the modern organizational leader could not agree more. People—individually and organizationally—need a vision!

In the Hebrew Old Testament, there is a collection of writings called The Book of Proverbs. One unique quality of this book and its collection of wise sayings is that it is not totally a Hebrew book. The ancient Hebrew wise men sought insight and wisdom from every source. While they probably believed that the ultimate source of insight and wisdom was God, they also believed that God could speak to people in all kinds of different environments. By 1000 BC—a very long time ago—the Hebrew wise men were searching throughout the Middle East and Egypt, talking to travelers from distant lands, and learning to read any kind of ancient writings they could get their hands on—all in the name of being "smarter" about they way they lived their lives.

Thus, this Book of Proverbs is filled with examples of the very best of intelligent and intuitive insight that the ancient world had produced. There is wisdom from across the Middle East, and particularly from the rich resources of ancient Egypt. In one central section of the book, the compilers chose to include what they thought was a statement of highest insight, a statement closely aligned with our investigation in this section of our study module.

The old text reads: "Where there is no vision, the people perish." If you look deeply into the meanings of some of the key words in this old statement, there is a great deal that can be learned. First, the Hebrew word for "vision" can mean "wisdom/insight"—the ability to see depth that is beyond the surface of things; therefore, without "wisdom" and "insight" there will be "chaos"—another understanding of the word "perish."

In the modern workplace, the reality being suggested by the proverb could not be more true. Think how many times, on whatever level of the organization, when there was no wisdom or insight, no seeing beyond the surface of things. Usually, chaos was the result. It is one thing to find rationally intelligent people to come into and lead a workplace; it is quite another to find someone with wisdom, insight, and basic "common sense." Where there is an absence of "common sense," chaos will prevail.

Next, the Hebrew word for "perish" can literally be translated to mean, "throw off all constraint." In fact, the ancient words here can have the meaning, "run around totally naked, totally exposed." This was, for the ancient Hebrews, both dangerous and shameful. Without clear directions—offered in the context of meaningful disciplines, structures, and processes—an organization can become "naked" or can experience an "exposure" of some sorts that can put it in great jeopardy. We are learning quickly that "vision" is not simply a nice statement to hang on a wall in the corporate boardroom, but a catalyst for actions that are attached to plans and the processes necessary to accomplish those plans.

In East Tennessee, we have an old cliché that perfectly describes the kind of chaos which follows from a lack of vision. We learned as children that when life and work got off track—when there was no controlling center of vision, no insight and wisdom—that people would "run around like a chicken with its head cut off." For many, many modern people, that old cliché has no meaning whatsoever. But, if you were a young person growing up in the country in the middle 1900s, you often saw your mother making preparations for Sunday dinner. If a chicken was to be involved, she would go out into the back yard, grab the most suitable "fryer," and with a quick flick of her wrist, wring the chicken's neck. The body would fly off, run around for a few moments without its head, and then fall over dead. Had my mother's fried chicken not been so good, I'm not sure seeing this scene would have stimulated my appetite.

In fact, to follow the illustration, many people in business and industry have seen their supervisors and executives caught up in difficult and unclear circumstances, "running around like a chicken with its head cut off." So, vision is a strong enough, articulate and clear enough, statement of: 1.) what an organization is to do, 2.) who an organization is in terms of the kind of personality and behavior that the organization is to project, and 3.) where an organization is going so that people will be motivated, challenged, and even energized to want to do all they can to help the organization accomplish its goals and dreams. People will "get on board" with a strong vision, and they will ultimately feel that the vision is somehow their vision as well.

Finally, the old language conveys the meaning of "vision" as an authentic word. So, mixing old and new: "Where there is no authentic word, people will run around like chickens with their heads cut off." The term "authentic" is decisive. On its most basic level, authentic means that a person really means what they are saying. They are convinced. They have "bought in." What is being said is not some kind of half-truth or just nice sounding words. People have "radar screens" that sense a lack of authenticity and often are very offended by it. The leader who tries to lead without being authentic will never gain a meaningful following. You may not be able to see authenticity, but you certainly can feel it. The leader who projects real authenticity will be far more likely to get others to follow him/her than the leader who blatantly lacks the quality.

Very often authenticity means follow-through or doing what you have said that you will do. Follow-through is probably the number one test of whether we are "for real." This is where the old idea of "walking the talk" comes in; if we live what we are claiming with our words, people will notice and respond positively. If we do not live what we are claiming with our words, we will neither be taken seriously nor trusted very long. Our vision will never have "legs," especially the "legs" that have to be provided in the energies and commitments of others. Authenticity is the "magnet" which draws others into our vision and makes it their own.

So, vision is infinitely more than a "vision statement." Vision is the pulse, the heartbeat, of the organization. Something of its form may occur in words, but beyond the words, vision must be *in-formed* in the life of the leader. Only then can it be *in-formed* at the core of the organization and in the lives of the people who work to make an organization successful. To talk about vision within an organization is not just an exercise in coming up with a nice sounding set of words; rather, it is the center of defining the organization's identity and personality. It is vision that makes the organization a living, breathing "being" as opposed to a system of lifeless organizational charts, personnel requirements, and process plans.

VISIONS, GOALS, AND PLANS

On May 11, 1996, a group of seven climbers were moving up the side of Mt. Everest, the "rooftop of the world." Their efforts were the culmination of all kinds of visions, hopes, goals, and ambitions of the highest order. For centuries, climbing Everest has been a goal of countless masses of people, but in the past few decades, technological improvements, training, and a great deal that has been learned about the mountain has made it possible for people like those in this group of seven to "climb for the top" on a regular basis.

Not only had the members of this group bought the best equipment and trained literally for months for their assent, but they had employed a man named Andy Harris as a climbing coach. Harris was simply the best that money could buy—$65,000 per person. They certainly had a vision, and they were matching the power of the vision with the commitment of their energies.

One issue concerning the last segment of the climb toward the top was decisive; they had to be at the top of Everest by 2:00 p.m. in the afternoon, or they had to turn back. There was no exception. To start off the mountain any later in the day was likely to expose the climbers to deadly winds that had taken many climbers' lives in the past. In fact, this one element was so important that the climbing coach had instilled it in the minds of the climbers over and again; they had a "covenant" that at 2:00 p.m. they would turn back. The vision, you see—the powerful goal—was held in check by a plan for which there was no exception. Visions are not complete without definite plans. Plans are an intrinsic, inseparable part of any vision.

By 1:30 p.m., two of the seven climbers had made it to the top and were on their way back. At 2:00 p.m.—the "drop dead" time—the other five climbers were maybe 150 feet from the top. What would you have done? Here you are within sight of your goal, maybe the greatest goal of your life. It is so very close. Probably anyone could understand what the five climbers did and would do the same in a similar situation—they pressed on. That last 150 feet took another hour-plus to accomplish, but the goal was achieved, and the five people stood on top of the world, made the pictures that would ultimately prove their accomplishment, and then started back. They never made it. The terrible winds came—just as the plan predicted was possible—and their lives were lost.

There is a tragic, but powerful lesson that is being taught here, a lesson that has a great deal to do with "vision." On one hand, vision does involve high and lofty, top-of-the-world goals and ambitions. Goals and ambitions are inspiring, and can draw from individuals the greatest of effort. We should have goals, and these goals should have an impact on the commitment of our energies.

Yet, a part of vision is also planning. While planning may seem secondary and much less demanding of our attention, in fact, it is an integral part of the entire vision process. Therefore, a true visionary can, at one and the same time, announce powerful goals *and* give the most detailed of process plans. As the story of Mt. Everest clearly conveys, there may be more importance that needs to be placed on the planning dimension than we have typically thought.

Hamilton Jourdan gained fame in the latter part of the twentieth century as the campaign manager and then chief White House advisor of President Jimmy Carter. After Carter left office, Jourdan worked in various capacities in business and industry. A favorite activity he employed to help organizations with "visioning" was to put up two flip charts, one carrying the heading "Good News List" and the other reading "Bad News List." The flipcharts would then be used to help an organization—or some part of an organization—assess strengths and weaknesses, assets and deficits.

At the end of his exercise, Jourdan would write on the bottom of the "Good News List" in bold red letters: "Unlimited Potential Abounds!" These are all powerful words with many positive connotations. Who would not want to be part of the "good news" of unlimited potential? Surely, this is the stuff of vision. Then, Jourdan would move to give attention to the "Bad News List" and write in red again, this time asking a question: "But, Do You Have A Plan?"

We absolutely understand. It is one thing to have a vision, a great scheme enforced by abounding, unlimited potential. Yet, so many times, potential goes unrealized or is confounded by either the lack of a plan, the basic benchmarks of that plan, or the follow-through that makes certain that those benchmarks are met. We may not be thrilled by the concrete day-to-day mandates of making sure that plans and benchmarks are fulfilled, but those parts of the process must be a distinct part of the "vision" or we simply become wonderful people with wonderful ideas.

The ultimate, full picture of someone who is a "visionary" may include someone with the aura of a General Patton, standing at the crossroads of a battlefield, rallying his troops with a great deal of challenging energy being given to achieving the highest of tasks. But, this is only part of the picture. There is also the General Eisenhower-type, back in the office in London, far from the European front line, who is pouring over reports, conceiving a master plan, watching supply lines, and interpreting data from as many various sources that he can find. Without the comprehensive plans, Patton's army moves without integration and coordination. We are back to the headless chickens again with their chaos and confusion. So, "vision" must include the full merger of heroic personality *and* a conscious, strategic plan. One does not move forward without the other. One does not work very long, or with lasting success, without the other.

THE CHAMPIONSHIP TEAM

Across all of my years in management development and organizational design, years in which the whole phenomenon of leadership has been investigated and studied as closely as possible, it has been interesting to see how many organizations and leaders of organizations use athletic metaphors and examples to convey what they are trying to accomplish and the ways in which accomplishment can be assured. Maybe this is because the realm of sports commands so much attention in our society. Maybe it is because individuals who had stamina enough to be successful in athletics can translate that stamina and drive into leading businesses later in their lives.

Yet, with all of the attention to athletics that I have seen and all of the experience with athletics that I have personally had, never in my life did I ever play on a championship team. Now, don't get me wrong, I played with a lot of exceptionally talented athletes and for a few really outstanding coaches, but there was never a championship. Sometimes, in playoff systems, the teams I was on got a long ways toward the championship—but never to the undefeated end. We won big games, set our own records, and had great times, but—again—never a championship. My experience includes everything from "midget league" activities as a pre-teen to highly competitive softball leagues as an adult in my mid-thirties. We had great times, many accomplishments, but no championship.

Then, my son—who was in high school at the time—and I took on the responsibility of coaching my daughter's 11–12-year-old girls' softball team. I will never forget the first practice. Those girls made the "Bad News Bears" look like the New York Yankees. They had a tremendous time playing, but the results were unimaginable; neither the word comedy nor the word tragedy is quite adequate to describe how the team played.

Early in the season, they simply could not win. They would try so hard and occasionally come close, but in the end, they would have to go away with heads hung low and tears flowing. My son and I as coaches were always upbeat, but we wanted to win as well.

Finally, we got smart enough to figure out what to do. Our girls could stop the ball in the infield pretty well, but they could not make the long throw to first base quickly enough or accurately enough. So, we quit worrying about traditional playing strategies and stopped trying to throw runners out at first base. Instead, we focused on the relatively easy force out at second. We practiced and practiced until the girls were masters at one play in the field—getting the ball to our sure-handed second baseman. From then on, almost every opposing player could get to first base, but not beyond. We all but stopped the other teams from scoring against us. We didn't tell our "secret," and none of the other coaches seemed to look beyond traditional play to figure out what we were doing.

When we were batting, we began to understand that our traditional experiences were making us play too conservatively. Other teams could have a "Bad News Bears" dimension to them as well, especially if little girls were running bases with reckless abandon. When we got a player on base, we seldom had them stop. The girls raced around the bases as the opposing team frantically tried to throw the ball around to get them out. Sometimes they were successful; most times, they were not.

I will never forget, as long as I live, the way we made the playoffs and progressed through the various games, even against teams with coaches who had won for years and knew how to "stack" teams expertly. In fact, in the last couple of games, it wasn't even close, and we ended up the champions of the league. At the end of the season, the championship team played a benefit game against the "All Stars" from the rest of the league. Many of those girls went on to play in high school and college, but by again doing what we did best—making the force out at second and running bases—our team won.

When I think fondly about this experience, many components of "vision" were present. We wanted to win and maybe even emotionally hated to lose. But, there was much more. We were committed to having a good time, to letting those early losses go quickly into the past and never demeaning a player for mistakes or not winning. Every game, win and lose, became the occasion for learning and growing as individual players and as a team. But we clearly understood that all of the intent and positive energy in the world was not enough to be champions.

Finally, we learned what we did best, and then we worked very hard to discipline ourselves in perfecting that best. I guess that I wish I could say our philosophy of play, our vision, was tested in Hollywood-like moments when we came from behind or were down to the last out, but the fact is that once we latched on to our "vision," we were never in jeopardy of losing again. At the point that we got the "vision" right and held to the discipline of doing what we did best, everything looked and felt pretty easy. We could win and enjoy playing without all of the tensions of fear and pressure.

Now, am I saying that running a multimillion-dollar business is like a young girls' softball team? In fact, that is exactly what I am saying! Wanting to win, to be successful, to be Number 1 is fine. Who would start a season or operate a business wanting to fail or be Number 85? But, wanting something really badly or knowing exactly what it is you want is not vision. Most of the time wanting something really badly or knowing exactly what you want is pretty obvious. Obvious is not the same as vision.

Vision involves the determination of continuing to search, often beyond the "box," for what works in your unique, individual situation. Vision means capturing the unique talents of the group of players you have rather than trying to mold what you have around some pre-determined standard or ideal. Vision means never demeaning. Vision means moving beyond losses, errors, and even failures. And never forget that vision will always involve discipline and practice, working to get what you do best to be so automatic that is becomes second nature. Following this example will then allow vision to be consummated in joy and celebration, making the next challenge an opportunity on higher levels of accomplishment and solidarity. Then, work can actually become fun at times, fulfilling and joyful, with intrinsic rewards of self-realization and group-realization every bit as important as money, title, or community status.

2. VICTOR FRANKL: A PERSON OF VISION

INTRODUCTION

Throughout this entire section on vision, there has been a vital "connection" that has been emphasized between the *experience* of vision and the concrete, practical *outcomes* of that visionary experience. We have also noted that there are *external dynamics* that can contribute to a "vision" and *internal dynamics* that can contribute to a "vision." Always, we have seen that the visionary experience will result in some sort of "communication" or some sort of "insight" that rises in human consciousness to a level of recognition and consideration. Always, we have seen that human choice is a vital part of an "equation," that follows recognition and consideration, and that may or may not lead from insight/communication/consciousness to decision, choice, and action. Always, we have asserted that the *medium* of the insight/communication/consciousness is not nearly as important as the "message." So, how a person gains an "insight" is not so important; that a person chooses to act on an "insight" is decisive. There is no telling how many people may have had visionary experiences that, in retrospect, could have been world changing in their implication and provided "visionary" status for the individual, but came to nothing because of a lack of recognition, a lack of consideration, or a lack of choice.

It becomes important, therefore, to look at a concrete example of someone who had the insight/communication/consciousness, recognized it, gave it consideration, and then acted upon it. In this particular example, we also have an individual who reflected in retrospect on the events that surrounded his life and gave us a written record of that reflective consideration and the conclusions he drew from it. That person is Victor Frankl.

THE BASIC CONTEXT OF FRANKL'S LIFE

The experience of Adolph Hitler and the Holocaust for Victor Frankl was quite different from that of Martin Buber and Robert Hartman. Although Frankl was Austrian by birth (in 1905) and was one of the leading voices of European psychotherapy that came of age in the early part of the twentieth century, he was confined in concentration camps by the Nazis from 1942 until 1945; his wife died in the camps. Following the war, he not only continued his work and sustained the attention to his ideas that had become firmly rooted in

Western intellectual circles before the war, but he became a primary interpreter of the Holocaust, both from the perspective of how it had happened and how it could be transformed by individuals and the human race as a whole.

Most people think that Frankl's great writing, *Man's Search for Meaning: An Introduction to Logotherapy* (1959), was a result of this experience. In fact, Frankl says that the concept was all but complete well before the horrible war experiences and was only confirmed by what he saw in the death camps in both the lives of the prisoners and their captors. To read Frankl's accounts of the camps is startling. Had he not taken into the camps something of the insights that rise in his writings after the war, it is difficult to imagine that he could have survived. His "vision," his insight into life and its meaning led to a "vision" of life beyond the camps that sustained him in the midst of horror day after day.

Frankl saw himself as the catalyst of the "third school of Viennese psychology." The first wave, of course, had been Freud with his emphasis on the role of basic human drives—the *id*, the *ego*, and the *superego*—and the role of sexuality in the formative foundations of human experience. The *id*, for Freud, had been the basic instinct to survive and all of its manifestations. The *ego* was the potential balance of the *id* that could be found in reflective, rational intelligence. The *superego* was the force of culture and tradition that informed the *ego* and acted to harness the *id*.

Frankl affirmed that Freud's view held a great deal of objective, mechanical, instrumental insight into human action, but he contended that humans were much more complex than simply existing as almost mechanistically driven, intelligent robots who were always being driven by and contending with sexual appetites and impulses. While he admitted that we as human have certainly "come from" a place of culture, environmental precedent, and tradition, and while that certainly are ways that we are the product of genetics, for Frankl where we are going, what stimulates and motivates us in a movement to the future, is of much greater importance. Here, is a major clue to "vision." The visionary experience may have elements that rise from the past as components of possibility, but a key element in the visionary experience is the future and the possibilities/options that are out there and can be achieved. Here, the role of choice is also exemplified in a powerful light; choice can do little or nothing about the past—except choosing to let the past simply be the past—but choice can have everything to do with the future.

The second psychological wave to rise in the Viennese tradition was Alfred Adler who also was convinced that there was more to human existence than the following or the controlling of sexual drives. For Adler, human beings were often beset with a sense of inferiority—thus, the idea of an *inferiority complex*. An *inferiority complex* could be seen as a "negative vision," a diminishing of options and possibility. Adler may have been making a tremendously valid point that is confirmed in a more modern setting by the large number of persons with negative self-side balance scores on the Hartman Value Profile. Adler may have also been insightful in noting the large number of negative human actions that rose as a result of attempts to compensate for or react to the negative, inferiority complex. Hitler's actions may be a representative example of this.

A sense of inferiority might be caused by a multitude of factors—abuse, criticism, failure, lack of positive affirmation—but it could manifest itself in what Friedrich Nietzsche would later call "the will to power" in which the inferiority was thrown aside and the true self could emerge free and undeterred, ready to achieve its own actualization (Abraham Maslow) or fulfillment of being (Paul Tillich). Such "will to power" would be a "vision" of who the self could be. Clearly, there could be aberrations if overcoming this sense of inferiority was rampant and uncontrolled and sought to balance past grievances with violence and hatred—again, like Hitler. But, for most people according to Adler—and Frankl admired this conclusion—to find the *courage* to move beyond the stranglehold of the past and any sense of inferiority that might have risen from it was important, even triumphant; the task of the Adlerian therapist to *encourage* toward the good had always had great credibility for Frankl. In this sense, for our larger discussion, "courage" can be *vision* both as an original catalyst and a sustaining catalyst. In addition, there might be many roles besides the therapist that could be a source of vision for others that moved them in more positive directions.

However, Frankl had become convinced that there was an entire dimension of human existence that had not been adequately considered in either the work of Freud or Adler. The abiding desire of human beings to search for meaning in life became, for Frankl, the "window"—or the "opening"/"clearing," to use a word important to Martin Heidegger—to the deepest and most vital experiences of human existence. So, the desire to search for meaning becomes the opening to the possibility of the most important visions, and when "meaning" is achieved, visions are found. In this sense, at the initial stage of Frankl's thought, a vision can be something human beings decide to search for and not simply something that "comes to" human beings.

This search for meaning became a kind of motivating and energizing "life force" that ultimately displayed the most distinctive powers of human existence; not simply the perverse, the psychotic, power to destroy life in travesties such as the Holocaust, but the power to overcome such travesties and still be able to find—and give—joy, beauty, and even love. A reality that could move us beyond travesty and horror to the place where we become courageous agents of hope, beauty, and love would certainly qualify as a vision.

The search for meaning was ultimately a *spiritual* search, albeit without necessary reference to any cultural religion. In fact, Frankl knew a great deal about a diverse range of religions, and none by any theological or dogmatic point of reference precluded the possibility of vision, of meaning. The "search" could take place under any religious rubric or lack thereof. He had also seen distinctly religious positions become the occasion for and justification of great human violence. Religion was not the necessary precinct of vision and meaning, but "the spiritual" certainly was. Other scholars would more directly discuss it, but Frankl clearly would affirm a "tri-dimensional ontology" that saw the "nature" (the Greek *ontos*) of human life as physical/*somatic*, mental/*psychic*, and. spiritual/*noetic*. Vision, a reality that could impact and involve the physical and mental, was primarily a *spiritual/noetic* reality. No psychology of human existence was complete without attention given to the *spiritual/noetic*. In a similar sense, the options of human, organizational existence are not exhausted until the *spiritual/noetic*, the true arena of vision and meaning, are affirmed, understood, and implemented.

FRANKL'S OTHER GREAT BOOK

Certainly, Frankl's great work is *Man's Search for Meaning*, but much earlier in his life—in fact, in those moments more directly following the Holocaust, he gave a series of lectures to a small group of about a dozen people in Vienna that were published in book form in 1947 as *Der Unbewusste Gott/The Unconscious God* that explores—for me—this "opening"/"clearing"/"window" into meaning and vision in an even more profound and precise manner than the better known writing.

At first, Frankl describes *religion* as the primary, historical context of human search for meaning; for many people, if they wanted to find meaning of a vision, they would go to church or talk to a minister/rabbi/priest. From the most primitive moments of human existence, there had been evidence of religion in every culture as a reflection of the human need to gain greater insight into life's deepest questions, to find some sense of control over life's least understood eventualities, and to move beyond fear and hate to the higher experiences of peace, job, community, and love. However, the evolution of *religion* into cultural forms that lost credibility and even became destructive—Hitler's armies never lacked for chaplains—had been all too obvious across the course of human history. So, Frankl became convinced that the evolution of *religion* was not the highest plateau of the human search for meaning. There was much more. This did not mean that he launched an anti-religious zealotry or began to demean churches/mosques/synagogues. Such patterns of rejections would not have quenched his desire for vision and meaning. He simply stated that *religion*, even at its positive best, would not be enough.

At this point, decisive to our discussion, he began to talk about the *spiritual*. That which he terms *religion*, the visible, outward, cultural form of this search might be able to manifest and embrace—even advance—the *spiritual*. Usually, it simply does not—or *sadly* does not—and all too easily can even create aberrations that defy and discredit the *spiritual*. Consider the way in which there was stalwart *support* for racial injustice in the American South prior to the Civil Rights Movement that rose from Christian churches. Consider, to further the alignment with the other two Viennese schools, how often *religion* has devolved into malignant expressions that have corrupted the potential good in the sexual instinct or advanced a sense of inferiority by creating guilt in human beings that made them easier to control.

Of decisive importance for Frankl is the idea that *in addition to* any other "instincts" that human beings possess—and have to contend with on a daily basis—there is a *"spiritual instinct."* He precisely and clearly—without equivocation—states: "We now arrive at an essential revision of the previous concept of the unconscious [the positions of Freud and Adler], or more specifically, of its extent. We now have to revise its *limits* because it turns out that there is not only an instinctual unconscious but a spiritual unconscious as well (*TUG*, p. 25). Ultimately, this "spiritual unconscious"—this *spirituality*—is the core of human existence that serves as the platform/foundation for the search for meaning. Only this "spiritual unconscious" can provoke the search for meaning in its most powerful manner. This "spiritual unconscious" is the arena of vision. As Einstein said about the "sense of wonder"—that must be in some way part of this "spiritual unconscious," if we as human are blind to it, we are as good as dead; as least we are "dead" to that which can promote and drive our highest potential, our highest journey, and our highest discovery.

Then comes a critical turn in Frankl's thought. He explains that the primary manifestation of this "spiritual unconscious"—this **spirituality**, and the most regular manifestation that can be most easily followed, is a *sense of responsibility*.

Now, let's allow this decisive thought that almost serves as a "definition" of *spirituality* to sink in for a moment: (A) a basic instinct at the potentially defining core of human existence; (B) that which provokes and promotes our search for meaning; (C) that which defines us at our best—and can be seen in the teachings and examples of the greatest teachers of this planet; and, (D) that which stands in sharpest contrast to the non-human, sub-human, de-humanizing potential of individuals who leave the spiritual unnoticed or unattended to. *Spirituality*—the foundation point of vision and meaning—first manifested as *a sense of responsibility*.

Parenthetically, it can be noted that Frankl—Jewish in terms of his own religious background—has created a concept that parallels a decisive idea at the core of the Old Testament. The ancient Jewish concept of *righteousness/hesed*, that is built on as a major part of the structure of St. Paul's New Testament writings, can be understood as a three-fold process: (A) the awareness/consciousness that all human life is interconnected and interdependent; (B) the realization that I, as an individual human, can decide/choose to contribute by doing good or detract by doing evil to this connected interdependency; and, (C) actions to enhance, to make better. Thus, *spirituality* as *a sense of responsibility*, when fully consummated, can move from awareness/vision to consideration/vision to realization/vision to choice/vision to action/vision in which vision and meaning can be extended to and for others. Beyond action, there is the arena of meaning, fulfillment, satisfaction, joy, and actualization. Without action, this final arena of vision-fulfillment will be disappointed, frustrated, and denied.

THE CENTRAL ROLE OF CHOICE

At one and the same time, in the visionary experience as it is being described by Frankl, there are two movements—an inward turning and an outward turning. The visionary experience is incomplete without these two, mutually-inclusive movements. The best way to describe the movements of an authentic visionary experience is to talk of a *convergence.*

In some respects, this sense of responsibility must be inward turning as human beings are responsible to exploring their own uniqueness and its own particular manifestations of the desire for meaning. Persons have to be responsible enough to struggle and search within themselves. Here, there are clear intellectual intersections being constructed with the existential concepts of Karl Jaspers and Martin Heidegger. Jaspers emphasized the importance of self-discovery as it is manifested in terms of *deciding* what as an individual I am to be. Jaspers put forward the decisive concept of *entscheidendes Sein* which means "decided-upon Being"/"decided-upon Person." This person stands in contrast to what he called "driven Being."

A "driven Being/Person" could be motivated by base instincts like those derived from Freud's *id,* or there could be the motivation of higher drivers such as Adler's *courage* toward self-actualization. Better than either of these is to be a Person not primarily driven by any external realities, but rather driven by internal consciousness/awareness, consideration, realization, decision, and action. To be driven by one's own authentic decisions is this "decided-upon Being/Person" he so greatly admired. Here, then, is the internal dynamic of the convergence.

Heidegger then added the emphasis on this decided-upon not remaining conceptual and mental but finding concrete manifestation in the here-and-now as I actually live out the "I" that I am, that I have decided-upon. Here, then, in the external dynamic of the convergence. This is Heidegger's ultimate, "spiritual" domain of what he called *Dasein,* the Person authentically being-there, being in the midst of life. Note also that when Heidegger says the word *being/Sein,* he is not using the noun/thing of the word. He is using the verb/force form of the word. I am not a human *being* as a noun/thing. I am a human *be-ing*—a verb, a force, an action—fully immersed in and committed to the here-and-now. Only under the circumstances of this two-fold convergence of inward and outward can spirituality as a sense of responsibility find its fullest, most authentic, expression.

2. Victor Frankl: A Person of Vision

All that Heidegger would say in the highest implications of his philosophy about human authenticity and caring (*Sorgen*) connects perfectly to Frankl's thoughts on responsibility. Heidegger's life demonstrates how thinking and believing the "right things" is not enough. Even his "at-arms-length" relation to the Nazis will forever haunt his legacy. Frankl, on the other hand, stood dramatically before the Nazis' very worst and triumphed over it. Frankl's "bottom line":

Genuine religiousness [his synonym for the *spirituality* used throughout this discussion] does not have the character of driven-ness, but rather of **deciding-ness**/[choosing]. Indeed, [authentic spirituality] stands with its **deciding-ness** and falls with its driven-ness. In a word, [authentic spirituality] is either existential [the result of responsible actions taken in response to and directed toward unique circumstances] or it is not at all (*TUG*, p. 65).

This "essential convergence" that takes place in Frankl's thought is dramatically important. There is, without question, the responsibility to discover and manifest self. There is, also without question, the responsibility to care for others. The "essential convergence"—and thus authenticity—takes place when the responsibility for the achievement of the epitome of self-actualization and the responsibility for the care of others merge with one another. For Freud and Adler, there is forever polarity and contradiction between these two dimensions; for Frankl, they are ultimately one and the same and, when achieved, manifest the highest expressions of meaning, the culmination of the search.

At this point, Frankl is also very close to the dynamic continuum of human existence idealized by Robert Hartman in his "Four Self Rules": (1) Know yourself, which he identified with Plato; (2) Choose yourself, which he identified with Kierkegaard; (3) Create yourself, which he identified with Pico (*The Oration on the Dignity of Man*); and, (4) Give yourself, which he identified with the spirit of Jesus. In terms of this discussion, a partial aspect of vision/meaning takes place on the knowing level, another partial aspect on the choosing level, another partial aspect on the creating level, and a final, partial aspect on the giving level. In this way, meaning and vision keep exponentially building on each other into a fullness of meaning that is startling and wonder-full in its power and joy.

A FURTHER CLARIFICATION

Frankl provides further qualifications and explanations of the *spiritual* that are very helpful to our overall discussion. First, he is clear that *spirituality/the spiritual unconscious* will never be fully explored or explained by rational logic; it is not scientifically demonstrable, one of the most characteristic elements of authentic vision. *Spirituality* and the medium of spirituality, vision, are what he called **Urphanomen**. The prefix "Ur-" is an intriguing, cross-cultural term that has ancient etymological roots; it means *ancient, primitive, original*—the biblical father figure, Abraham, came from UR according to the ancient texts. Thus, an "ur-phenomenon" is before logic, before rationality, even before words; it cannot be explained in terms of rational constructs. It can only be experienced just as meaning and vision can only be experienced. Just as William of Ockham taught, the movement from *Urphanomen* such as visions and meaning to logical words of definition and explanation will always be a *reductionistic* process in which something vital is always left out.

However, having defeated logic and intellectual rationality is not an open invitation for Frankl to experience *spirituality/the spiritual unconscious* with mysticism or aesthetics. He is not interested, in any way, in seeing mystical reflection or meditation as the highest form of the *spiritual*. As important as mysticism and aesthetics might be in their own right—they may be means-to-an-end aspects of the spiritual unconscious—true *spirituality* is to be experienced as life grounds itself in actions of care and responsibility. The highest manifestations of the *spiritual*, the visionary, the meaning-full, are found in concrete actions of love. There is no substitute for this! In fact, he even calls on a process of "de-reflection" as a guard against human experience becoming overly stuck in an obsessive purity of reflection and meditation. The highest and finest "human existence occurs in action rather than in reflection" (*TUG*, p. 30).

Anyone who knows the work of Robert Hartman is immediately compelled by Frankl's extension of his concept of the *spiritual* to the idea of uniqueness. A primary component of responsibility, care, love, be-ing in the here-and-now is the experience of uniqueness. Uniqueness is at the core of authenticity, both as it is experienced within the individual self and as it is experienced in involvement with others.

To discover and manifest self, the highest form (not *forms*, since discovery and manifestation are mutually inclusive if vision/meaning is achieved) of self-decided care and responsibility involves finding, affirming, and be-ing unique. The highest movements of "conscience" involve intimate investigations and involvements with unique events, especially realizing that every event, person, and circumstance is unique and cannot be dealt with in terms of universal rules and laws (rational, scientific constructs). This position basically parallels Aristotle's teleological/ends-oriented ethics, Joseph Fletcher's "situation ethics," or Georg Simmels's "individual law." This is also the point of Jesus' teaching that the Sabbath was made for man, and not man for the Sabbath. Spirituality looks to find—to gain a vision—of the unique possibilities that exist in highly singular circumstances.

> The "ethical/[spiritual] instinct" is entirely different. In contrast to vital instincts [Freud and Adler], the effectiveness of the ethical instinct depends on the fact that its target is not anything general but something individual, something concrete, [something unique]. . . . Only [spiritual] consciousness is capable of adjusting the "eternal," generally agreed-upon moral law to the specific situation a concrete person is engaged in. Living one's [spiritual] conscience always means living on a highly personalized level, aware of the full concreteness of each situation (*TUG*, p. 36).

Finally, love is defined as a focus of the deepest attention—like Hartman's intrinsic valuation—on the unique possibilities inherent in another person and the potential inherent in a unique relationship with that person. This "deepest attention" is the discipline that most likely results in vision. "In love," Frankl asserts, "the self, the person, is not driven by the *id*, but the self chooses (Heidegger) the `Thou' (the unique other—Martin Buber)." To see love as a form of see-ing in which the convergence of self actualization and other affirmation is to accurately understand vision. Then, see-ing/vision leads to finding and affirming uniqueness in a way that gives love both a realizing and responding dynamic that both conveys and experiences meaning. The convergence rises. The nexus of promoting and discovering uniqueness exponentially raises the value, the worth, the meaning of life to a next, new level. In all likelihood, this "raising" is without limits and can be pursued across an entire lifetime.

VISION: ALWAYS TOWARD THE FUTURE

With this focus on uniqueness and the realization that when uniqueness is experienced that a person is very close to the engagement experienced in vision, Frankl begins to talk about the future. He has to talk about the future because the realization that comes in the vision/message/insight always will require that something be done—the outward movement of convergence. The "opening"/"clearing"/"window" that is experienced in the vision/message is always an "opening" toward the future. This is why visions all too often become stereotypically associated with something predictive about the future, how the future will be. The stereotype is close; in actuality, there is in the vision an implication for the future, a potentiality for the future, that may take place or begin to take place if the right choices are followed.

The future allows for freedom; the openness of possibility and options is freedom. The ability to respond to the vision/message with a choice is freedom. Thus, there is "freedom from" and a "freedom for." The first form, "freedom from" usually relates to conditions in the past, even conditions that have been triumphed over. Great care has to be taken in obsessively focusing on "freedom from," because the past simply cannot be relived or changed. To think that the past can be adequately compensated for is an unfulfilling ego trip that results in the huge guilt and blame. Here is the primary force of Leland Kaiser and Dan Wilford echoing repeatedly the mantra: "So what? Now what?" What has taken place in the past is a "given" that can be molded and shaped as part of a movement toward the future, but not changed. Vision leads us to the future, not to the past.

This same theme is found by Victor Paul Furnish in his *Theology and Ethics in Paul*, and note even from this title the convergence of thought (theology) and action (ethics). For Furnish, the Damascus Road "vision" of Paul did not lead him to become a theologian, spinning increasing webs of dogmatic abstraction. Instead, he was trying to provide a transition from theology to ethics before the cultural power of the theology of his day asserted itself to the destruction of the message of Jesus; of course, the message of Jesus had a stark ethical dimension and outcome with little or no theological emphasis at all.

For Furnish, Paul's vision is forever forward looking in its emphasis on "freedom for." The point of faith is not to be "free *from* sin" in whatever cultural manifestation that sin is being defined. Rather, there is freedom to stand beyond cultural definitions of all sorts—and particularly religious definitions—and experience the "freedom for" the higher *calling/vision/message/insight* of righteous living, the outward manifestation of the spiritual, the sense of responsibility. Paul's dynamic is always and forever "pressing on to the high calling" of the God/the Divine made known in the teaching/vision and example/vision of the life of Jesus. Divinity, and all of its attendant questions, is a theological issue; ethics, living toward the future in a way that will add value to life, is the compelling *vision* exhibited by Jesus.

THE POWER OF INTENT

Frankl is also very clear—and he will have to be considering the scrutiny of a modern, rational and scientific culture—that this *spiritual/spiritual unconscious* is not merely a set of nice, emotional feelings; he is not trying simply to be—as the modern indictment often expresses—"warm and fuzzy." He gives priority to Scheler's distinction between *gefuhlszustand* (a nice, emotional state that "warm and fuzzy" may adequately define) and *intentionales Gefuhl* (**intentional** feelings that consciously impact direction and movement toward the future). All of this discussion about vision and spirituality is not intent on providing *gefuhlszustand*, "warm and fuzzy" emotional feelings. Instead, we have been describing powerful intentions that rise in vision, are nurtured and sustained by continued vision, and find their dynamic power in further continued vision. We are talking about a compelling honesty that comes to grapple with and advance change in regard to real, human existence.

It is always a problem in modern civilization when conversations about the "soft side" or the "warm and fuzzy" arise. Too often, what cannot easily be appropriated by logic and reason is seen as optional and less necessary. The very opposite is the case. If the modern, demeaning language of "soft side" and "warm and fuzzy" are applied to the arena of vision, potential is debased and probably will be missed.

What is needed, therefore, for Frankl is his signature *logotherapy*. This "therapy" is designed to help human beings gain an enlightened perspective on the limits of logic, reason, and scientific inquiry. What better person to see the need to move beyond science or to see its limits that someone who has survived the technologies of Nazism and the technologies of the death camps. In logotherapy, questions of logic are limited, and to achieve the possibility of the fullest humanity, there must be an acceptable and assertive way of stretching beyond logic. We cannot do this unless logic and scientific reasoning are put in their proper perspectives. Thus, the need for logotherapy.

In logotherapy, questions of logic and reason, issues of scientific demonstrability, fall into the background. The foreground, the future, are filled with the acceptance of non-logical and non-scientific visions and messages that lead us toward ethical mandates and ethical activities. The worst advice a human being can follow is to reflect, meditate, think toward the conclusions of logic; the best advice is to decide to act, to be responsible to the individuating, singular, unique possibilities presented in living as living frees itself to look toward the future through the lens of the visions of the spiritual, the ethical, the loving. In the end, logotherapy is not traditional psychotherapy; it is, rather, **"education to responsibility,"** a powerful statement that rises out of the 1975 postscript addition that Frankl added to his early lectures (*TUG*, p. 121).

SELF-TRANSCENDENCE

In order to "activate" the possibilities of vision and the achievement of Frankl's sense of responsibility, there must be *self-transcendence*. Without self-transcendence, there cannot be healthy self-actualization; egotism and base self-serving, hyper-vested selfishness can occur that will be ultimately destructive of the human condition, of life in general. But, and this is an interesting insight that is often overlooked, there cannot be the possibility of self-transcendence unless *transcendence* itself has become a category or dimension of existence/life that is affirmed and actively embraced.

For Frankl, many—if not most—of the problems of human existence are the result of a "crippled relation to transcendence" (*TUG*, p. 70). In other words, it is not possible to talk about self-transcendence, a movement beyond where/who a person is toward the vision of where/who a person can be, unless the entire idea of transcendence, the entire modality of transcendence, is affirmed. If vision is an event of transcendence that finds its way into normative life, without some affirmation of transcendence, vision will be missed. The great theologian, Paul Tillich, understood this concept well. Tillich believed, for example, that true atheism is not the rejection of a god-concept, but the rejection and eradication of transcendence as an authentic, operative category of existence. Here, we are back to Einstein and his attention to the core of life as wonder.

A/the primary instigator, inspiration, catalyst of transcendence—and, at one and the same time, the primary catalyst for vision—is revealed in Frankl's concept of "The Unconscious God." Frankl is ready—and the Holocaust must be a prime factor in his readiness—to pronounce the "god" of the cultural traditions of the twentieth century *dead*. This "god" has at least not interfered with the destruction and disintegration, the bigotries and exclusivisms, that have spread vengefully and violently across the twentieth century. This illegitimate, pretender "god," for Frankl, has been the result of projections rightly defined by Freud that rise from human weakness more than human strength, projections that sustain and deify status quos that serve the few rather than the many, and projections that can justify the most horrific degradations of human existence. If the cultural "god" of reason and religion—in the worst senses of those words—could die, the vision of the authentically Divine might have a greater chance of manifesting itself.

Beyond the "god" of cultural religion and philosophical abstraction stands what Frankl calls "The Unconscious God." The term *unconscious* does not refer to the lack of awareness or consciousness of this "God," but the "location" of this "God." The dwelling place of this "God" is *spirituality, the spiritual unconscious, the sense of responsibility* which must forever remain immune to scientific exploration or philosophical explanation whose limits are the *conscious*. This "God" manifests as a transcendent "call"/"vision" to responsible actions of ethical engagement. Interestingly enough, this "call"/"vision" may not necessarily be experienced or responded to by someone actively involved in all of the trappings of cultural religion. It may, on the other hand, be capable of being fully embraced by someone—from the traditional perspectives of cultural religion—who is identified as being agnostic, atheist, or does not participate in the activities of the cultural religion. The key issue would be, not what a person believes or practices in terms of the traditional, cultural religion, but rather how a person responds to the transcendent vision/message of ethical responsibility. The key issue for leadership is to place highest priority on the vision/the message of the ethical, the socially responsible.

Without question, for himself, Frankl believes that this "Unconscious/Hidden God" actually exists, although concern with validating any kind of real, physical existence has no expedience for him. He is well beyond any compulsion to "prove" this "Unconscious/Hidden God," for the very mechanisms of "prove" are immediately destructive of transcendence. If you have to "prove" a vision before you act on it, you will never act and transcendence is forever hamstrung.

Transcendence can also occur, functionally and essentially, through the conscious projection of the unique self as that unique self might live on a more idealized level of ethical engagement with life. This ideal, this projection, then becomes a powerful motivating force in the potential for the ideal being accomplished. Frankl took lessons to fly small, private aircraft. Flying was a form of freedom, a form of unloosing the bounds of a rational planet, for him. He was taken by his instructor's concept of "crabbing," a word that rises out of the seemingly unsightly movements of a crab on land. If, for example, I am flying to a point directly east of my present location, and there is a powerful wind blowing from north to south, I must compensate for the wind. A direct, west to east course will leave me many miles southeast of my destination. So, I must compensate—I must "crab." I must establish an "ideal" direction to the northeast and, following this idealized point—this vision, I will have a much greater likelihood of arriving at my desired destination.

Frankl then moves from his flight instructor to the poet, Goethe: "If I take man as he is, I make him worse; if I take him as he ought to be—the vision of who he can be—I make him better." Even "crabbing" toward ethical responsibility is honorable. To provide a vision of what can be, and then to energize people toward that vision, is the essence of authentic human credibility. Robert Kennedy was famous for saying: "Some men look at the world and ask 'why?' while others look at the same realities and ask 'why not?'" Why not something better? Why not something more ethical? Why not something more humane? These are the questions of transcendence. There are the questions of vision.

NOW, A MORE SIMPLE EXPRESSION

It is altogether too easy to take Frankl's ideas and overcomplicate them. He was not beyond doing this himself. Admittedly, when conversation leads to ideas about an "Unconscious God," simplicity can go out the window. So, there is a need—and Frankl felt it himself—to reduce the possible complexities and abstractions of his thought to expressions that can be more easily followed. In this context, he began to speak to his audiences and write to his readers about what he called "The Three Cs."

The first "C" is a sense of *Call*, a pulling, magnetizing, attention-garnering sense of being addressed. This *Call* may be more intuitive than articulated; it may take a thousand different forms, but the sense of demand to respond in a responsible manner based on unique talents and abilities—based on the opportunities of "the right time"—is distinctive and difficult to escape notice if a person has any sensitivities at all.

Next, as a second "C," there is the emerging reality of a *Cause* that arrives, that presents itself, that unveils itself. The *Cause* is a unique, singular possibility that will unleash some positive potential of life that is important, that makes a difference in life moving forward in an enhanced manner. Issues such as the size or status of the *Cause* or the public attention it might attract are totally beside the point; causes are as unique as the people who will approach them. That some reality has taken on the dimension of *Cause* simply and clearly indicates the degree of engagement that is being promoted.

Finally, the third "C" is identified as *Commitment*, the ultimate level of self-giving/self-transcendence and dedication to the *Cause*, the response to the *Call*. It would now be possible to speak of at least three types or dimension of "vision": call vision, cause vision, and commitment vision. In the inward/outward convergence of the phenomenon of "vision," all of these factors are likely to distinguish themselves, and they have the chance of creating a mutual inclusiveness of synergy between themselves. When this convergence is at its optimum, the phenomenon described by Mihaly Csikszentmihaly as "FLOW" takes places. This "flow" of convergence is energizing, allowing people to stretch beyond their normal capacities to do wonder-full things.

It is difficult to assign Hartman's template of Intrinsic, Extrinsic, and Systemic to Frankl's three categories, to say—for example—that call is systemic, cause extrinsic, and commitment intrinsic. In fact, any of the three "Cs" probably involves something of all three of Hartman's elements spinning in and out of each other. At one and the same time, true convergence, true vision is likely to be systemic, extrinsic, and intrinsic.

When a person is caught up in the dynamic "flow" of these "Three Cs," a unique dialogue (or *multi*logue) begins to occur that Frankl calls "the wisdom of the heart" in which the human being accepts responsibility for fulfilling the potential inherent in a given life situation. Life is not reduced to a "search for "Self," but rather becomes a "search for meaning" that has, as a nice, ironic consequence, the achievement of authentic Selfhood as a primary by-product.

We have to learn from this *sapientia cordis*, from this wisdom of the heart, that being human means being confronted continually with situations, each of which is at once a chance and a challenge, giving us a "chance" to fulfill ourselves by meeting the "challenge" to fulfill the situation's meaning/potential. Each situation is a call, first to listen, and then to respond (*TUG*, p. 129).

NEUROGENESIS

Given Frankl's emphasis on *challenge*, it is powerfully intriguing to look at the work of individuals such as Fernando Nottebohm and Elizabeth Gould that is known as *neurogenesis*, a term reminiscent of the process philosophy of John Cobb, Charles Hartshorne, Teilhard de Chardin, and others that captured so much attention and hopefulness in the mid-1900s.

Neurogenesis was, at first, a radical departure from much of traditional brain science, but it has now become the catalyst for a great deal of the promise that is manifesting itself in stem cell research and the possibility of finding solutions to many captivating and dreadful problems of human existence such as Alzheimer's and Parkinson's diseases. *Neurogenesis* demonstrates that brains are not limited by the number of neurons that are present at or soon after birth. Instead, the brain can develop new neurons, perhaps even to the point of "repairing" structures that have become injured or genetically deficient. The implications are profound.

The neurogenesists are discovering that the brain develops new neurons *in response to challenges* that occur in real-life circumstances. The entire process of challenge causes our brains to produce neurons that help us become more adept in meeting these challenges. Now, listen to the following statement, and immediately the connection to vision and Frankl will be obvious: "She [Elizabeth Gould] found that a brain needs to `use it or lose it'—if new cells are not put to work, they will die more rapidly than *if they have a purpose*." (*The New Yorker*, July 23, 2001, p. 48). The neurogenesis research has also taken note that an adverse effect of continuous environments of stress, fear, and anxiety— evidently different than *challenge*—will diminish new neuron production. In fact, even the presence of regular physical activity and exercise is shown to facilitate new neuron production. What happens when boredom, ennui, Heidegger's *weltschmertz* (world weariness), and generally unchallenged inactivity occurs is more than obvious. The experience of vision is always a challenge. A basic character of vision is challenge, almost to the point that if a person does not experience challenge it is unlikely that vision has taken place. In a similar sense, the visionary may be, as much as anything, a person who delivers challenges. The wonderful implication is that in meeting challenges, responding to visions, that a person's capacity—even their brain capacity— stretches and grows, even to the point of being able to meet the challenge/vision that is there.

Nottelbohm, much of whose work has focused on the brains of songbirds, talks about the uniqueness of his approach, an approach fully consistent with the philosophical insights of Frankl. Note carefully how what is being said about songbirds has a clear connection with human beings. Also notice how "vision," by implication can relate to the most concrete dimensions of life:

> What kinds of things do animals do in their natural circumstances? What kinds of problems do they have? How do they solve them? Brains are not all-purpose machines. They have evolved *to deal with specific, existential problems:* How do you make it through a year with all kinds of seasons? How do you claim and defend your territory? How do you find a mate? How do you look after your offspring? How do you remember where you hid your seeds (*NY*, p. 52)?

In other words, life gives us tasks. Some tasks are glorious, and others are mundane. The point is to approach our tasks with this spirituality, this sense of responsibility. To talk about the luck, fairness, or range of difficulty (or lack thereof) of these tasks is absolutely beside the point. We have problems to solve, and we need vision. We have value judgments to make, and we need vision. We have promises to keep and miles to go before we sleep, and we need vision. Vision elevates the task to the arena to call, cause, and commitment. If the neurons of our brains can respond to *purpose-full* activities, think of the implications for the uniqueness of that nexus of cells and experiences that become the unique self in its unique time. It is the absence of purpose and *pursued vision* that creates regression and destruction of our very best potential—of who, indeed, we are.

ONLY ONE COMPLAINT

In the end, there is the active possibility of vision being pursued and happiness being achieved, both as an outcome of **Commitment** to this **Cause** as it applies to any variety of enhanced life circumstances, and as a personal reality that rises in the mist of listening to the **Call**, envisioning the **Cause**, and living with **Commitment**. Happiness, which may include both productivity and meaning, is a by-product, "something that ensues, not something to be pursued" (*TUG*, p. 85). Happiness rises from the arena of "decided upon," not "driven by." There is neither "hyper-reflection" nor "hyper-intention;" nothing hyper at all. There is rather a serendipitous, synchronistic movement within the "flow," within the convergence of *Call,* *Cause,* and *Commitment.* At one and the same time, the response to vision/this movement of the "flow," can be absolutely diligent and demanding of every strength of human character and as light, playful, and rejuvenating as the movements of children. The Dalai Lama says that the very purpose of life is to seek happiness; Victor Frankl has charted the first stages of the course.

As an afterthought, I have only one complaint with Frankl, and it is more semantics than substance. He says that, in the experience of vision/message, we are plunged into the midst of this *Call, Cause, Commitment* convergence where we encounter unique situations with our own personal uniqueness. I agree totally. We have a vision of who we are, what we can do, and what difference it can make. In these unique situations/encounters of visionary consciousness, we must choose, decide, and act; for Frankl, life becomes a matter of selectivity, discrimination, prioritization, and the struggle to find and do what is most right. He says, without equivocation, "We have to choose between what is important and what is not" (*TUG,* p. 122). Again, I agree totally.

For me, what he is talking about is *making value judgments,* weighing, assessing, evaluating. While we are *making value judgments,* we are at the doorway of vision, and the more engaged and protracted the struggle, the more powerful vision that is likely to take place. This approach, of course, is at the core of my own philosophy, the axiology of Robert Hartman, and the force of this overall presentation. Yet, Frankl has a problem with the concept of "value judgments" as he defines these terms. For him, a "value judgment" is not a singular conclusion rising from the flow of *Call, Cause, and Commitment* based on the unique person engaged in the unique encounter. Rather, he sees a "value judgment" as an exponent, an extension of the fixed, absolutistic values and beliefs of a given culture at a give time. He calls for an "abstinence from value judgments" (*TUG,* p. 123) so that an individual can be fully free to relate to personal and situational uniqueness/visions.

If "value judgment" is defined in the narrow sense advanced in the language of Frankl, I continue to agree wholeheartedly. However, I make a very close distinction between values and beliefs, that indeed are often nothing more than arbitrary cultural exponents, and the active process of value judgment that embraces every aspect of the flow of convergence that manifests itself in *Call, Cause, and Commitment.* To use Frankl's own prescriptive insights, I see value judgments in their dynamic, *verbal* force, not as fixed, objective *nouns* that can simply be "inscribed" on human life from one generation to another; there is a difference between being "inscribed" and being "inspired," and vision is never merely "inscribed" as part of some bland, cultural evolution. To me, the *process* of value judgment is precisely this "wisdom of the heart" that Frankl adorns with the highest credibility. I believe we are in total agreement here, and only need to make a minor semantic clarification. As Leland Kaiser teaches: with the body, we act; with the emotions, we feel; with the mind, we think. And, in my extension of Kaiser: with the "heart," "soul," "spirit," we *value*. Valuing is a major aspect of that which vision promotes and vision's outcome. To a large extent, when we are valuing, we are visioning.

CONCLUSION

In concluding this discussion on Frankl, it is important to emphasize over and again that he is not Immanuel Kant espousing some version of a "categorical imperative," a kind of "voice" of the universe that impinges upon humans from some outside venue that has the purpose of motivating moral behavior. Nor is he some kind of spiritualist in the more stereotypical sense of that word waiting for some "utterance" from God through some odd medium that provokes prophetic proclamation. In fact, for Frankl, the "call of conscience" is not in the form of some "transcendent command" or supersensory mandate at all. At least, the call of vision is not limited to or totally contained by the supersensory or the transcendent.

The call of vision comes most directly and most often from that arena of life where human uniqueness of talent, ability, capacity, and opportunity meet expressed human need. The call of vision is a *challenge to assume the task of higher levels of responsibility*. At some point, because of the crucial role of human realization, choice, decision, and action, the challenge will either be responded to or left wanting some response. Real, authentic commitment may have intellectual, rational, and emotional dimensions, but on that ultimate level that brings a person to put life and living on the line, the commitment involves the deepest and most intimate struggle toward actual *doing*, a struggle that is fraught with the dynamics of choice that are well beyond the clear and demonstrable dynamics of logic and reason. Meaning—the final horizon of human searching for Frankl—and then, if we are fortunate, even happiness, flows from those *actions/doings* of commitment, those decisions and choices of vision that consummate themselves in care.

Mignon Eisenberg, reflecting on the work of Frankl, makes the following, insightful expression:

We deserve to receive an answer to our questions about the meaning of Life. WRONG! It is not up to us to ask what the meaning of life is. Life Sets tasks before each person. In meeting them, we define the meaning of Our life; by our actions, we answer the questions that life puts to us.

Frankl, having triumphed over many of life's deepest miseries and evils, was fond of the insights gained in the tragic life of Friedrich Nietzsche. He admired Nietzsche's conclusion that life is being lived by most people on two levels. On one level, the major question of life is *"how?"* The "how level" is a transactional level in which life is focused on strategies that are a means to some economic or political end, ends of extrinsic, external power.

Yet, beyond this "how level," Nietzsche asserted that there was a *"why?"* Without an "adequate why" for life, a person could not live; there might be physical life, but there was not meaning. What Nietzsche understood that moved Victor Frankl, and what most modern human beings have totally misunderstood, is that this *"why?"* is not an intellectual question that can be answered with reason and logic. It is instead—and absolutely—a *spiritual* question that can only be answered by responding to the call of tasks that can inform life with care, questions of *vision* that can only be answered by living out one's uniqueness in the midst of unique situations of life with decisions and actions of responsibility. Meaning can then appear/arrive/come into be-ing as the highest *vision*, a *vision* that can continuously move us on toward higher experiences of meaning and higher engagements of responsibility. Here—at one and the same time—we do the most we can do for ourselves and the most we can do for others.

3. VISION—AN ANECDOTAL APPROACH

INTRODUCTION

Sometimes insight can be lost in concept and theory. Sometimes in our attempt to explain and understand, we simply compound complexity. There may be times when it is important to make simple, clear and direct statements. At this point, an anecdote or story may be as creditable way to convey information as any exotic theory of explanation that is available. In fact, the anecdote or story *works* with high efficiency because it gives people something they can relate to, something they can identify with in a very human way.

Wallace Stevens was one of the most important American poets of the twentieth century. Stevens' personal story is as unique, in many ways, as his writings. Across his life he was a prominently successful insurance executive for the Hartford Insurance Company in Connecticut. He did all of the work of a businessman, but still was able to create a prolific and bountiful body of poetry across the course of his life.

Stevens loved to vacation in Florida, and particularly in Key West. It was in Key West that he had a famous fight with Ernest Hemingway that he came out on the wrong side of, although he often claimed that the drunken Hemingway had "sucker punched" him. Most of the time, especially in the pre-World War II days, he would travel to Florida by car. The geography and people that he would encounter on his way South fascinated him.

This fascination with land and people peaked as he moved across the mountainous regions of East Tennessee. In the 1930s, this area would have been fairly primitive by any modern standards. Stevens felt the beauty, but he also felt a bit of intimidation; the mountains and their primitive people were full of mystery and secrets. He never experienced harm in his travels, but there were times in which he felt that events and elements of the sparsely settled mountain world might be beyond his control.

It was in this environment that he created one of his very best known poems, "Anecdote of the Jar." The poem helps us understand just how powerful and important anecdotes can be.

I placed a jar in Tennessee,
And round it was, upon a hill.

It made the slovenly wilderness
Surround that hill.

The wilderness rose up to it;
And sprawled around, no longer wild.
The jar was round upon the ground
And tall and of a port in air.

It took dominion everywhere.
The jar was gray and bare.
It did not give of bird or bush,
Like nothing else in Tennessee.

You can almost see Stevens stopping along a roadside vista in the mountains of East Tennessee. The roads in the 1930s would have been narrow, perhaps even in places unpaved. "Civilization" could easily have been far removed from his stopping point. Maybe he could have had car trouble, and suddenly he does not know where he will get help, who will come down the road next, or what it might be like to be out here in these mountains in the dark.

To help bring some sense of control—or just bring "some sense"—he picks up a jar, maybe a jar thrown from a passing car, and placed it on the side of the hill before him. The jar becomes a kind of *focal point* that gives meaning, that gives perspective. Like an artist's *focal point* that causes all of the elements painted on a canvas to form a meaningful, integrated whole, the jar seems to cause the "wilderness" to lose its chaotic randomness and yield form, structure, and meaning. The jar provides a *clarity* that is reassuring and triumphant.

Anecdotes have the same impact. An idea can be like a "wilderness," unclear and not articulated. Sometimes, even in our best attempts to explain and clarify, we can become verbose with concepts and theories. Maybe, there are times in which we simply need to "place a jar," provide an anecdote, and the difficult idea can find clarity.

It is so very easy to take a concept such as "vision" and make it even more difficult to understand. Some of the articles in this section are "heavy duty" in this regard as times. In this section, the intent is to provide a few, simple anecdotes that will basically speak for themselves without much interpretation. Once the anecdotes are read and considered, the idea of "vision" will rise to meaning, almost like the "wilderness" of Stevens' poem surrounding the hill and the jar, the *focal point*.

JOHN DEWEY'S ANSWER

John Dewey was one of the greatest philosophers of the twentieth century. Many people consider Dewey to be the preeminent American philosopher, although most people remember him as the person who created the "Dewey Decimal System," the code by which books are referenced in libraries.

Toward the end of his long life, Dewey was giving an interview to a number of newspaper writers. One man in the group was particularly cynical, and his questions began to get very negative. Dewey was not troubled by this, and seems to be almost compassionate in his answers to the man's harsh questions. At one point, referring to Dewey's philosophical writings, the man asked: "What's the good of such claptrap? Where does it lead you?"

Dewey responded quietly: "The good of it is that you climb mountains."

The questioner responded with a vengeance: "Climb mountains! And what's the use of doing that?"

In his calm, ninety-year-old voice, Dewey explained: "You climb mountains because you see other mountains to climb. You come down, climb the next mountain, and then see yet others to climb." Reassuring the questioner with a pat to his knee, Dewey concluded his answer: "When you are no longer interested in climbing mountains to see other mountains to climb, life is over."

"Vision" is as much of an event as it is an insight or a singular piece of information. "Vision" is a "happening"—at least, that is the old hippy word— that takes place *because of us* if we slow down, stop, give time to contemplation, reflection, and consideration, but that also takes place *to us, for us*, and even *in spite of us*. We may need the event of vision as much as any idea or insight that is derived because the event of vision is vitalizing, invigorating, freeing.

I once had a university professor who did not believe that roads should be built to the top of mountains. We should have to walk to the top of mountains. He even led protests against road construction that put highways across mountain tops. He believed that the magnificent view should be reserved for— and would be *heightened* in its impact on people—only if they had gone to the great effort of the climb.

I see his point. I'm not sure I agree with its intensity. But, one thing is for sure: we need "mountain top" experiences just for the sake of "mountain top" experiences. There is no telling where the experience of vision might lead us. It might not lead the next person to the same place we go. The "destination" or "outcome" may not be as important as the event of inspiration. Our problem, of course, is that mountain climbing, to use Dewey's illustration, just to see other mountains to climb does not seem to be very practical or efficient. Some people, like the newspaper reporter, may even consider it to be a waste of time.

"Vision"—in this anecdote—is an experience that happens to us, usually, only after much struggle and effort, much mountain climbing. Where "vision" leads us is not the important question. We may only be lead to climb a next mountain, ask a next question, struggle through a next issue. But, it is this very struggle toward "vision" that fills our life with meaning. We do not always have to have "answers," but we need to be forever questioning, probing, searching. Dewey is right: when we stop doing this, life is over.

OUR "WAY OF SEEING"

Another dimension of "vision" is the way that we approach issues, problems, and people. The word *attitude* is a word used in the aviation industry to describe the "angle of approach" that an airplane uses when it is landing at an airport. To have a safe landing required the right *attitude*. Too often, in our common use of the word in daily living, we see attitude as some sort of emotional quality. The whole discussion can get very complicated. Why not simply think of attitude as our "angle of approach" to life, the way we decide we are going to approach people and situations.

For example, in the movement of European conquest envisioned by Napoleon, he clearly understood the vital importance of controlling Italy. An uncontrolled Italy would make the entire southern flank of his beloved France vulnerable. He had to bring Italy into his realm of control.

The only problem: the Alps, those profound and foreboding mountains aligned geographically on the border between the two countries. The Alps were an *obstacle!* Napoleon had a choice: he could focus his attention on his *objective*—Italy—or he could focus his attention on his *obstacle*—the treacherous mountains. "Vision" in this instance becomes an *attitude,* an "angle of approach" to a situation. We remember Napoleon because he chose *objective* over *obstacle*. The world little notes or long remembers those people who surrender "vision" and stop their pursuits when *obstacles* appear on the horizon. People of "vision" focus on *objectives* and overcome *obstacles*; at least, they understand that focusing on objectives gives them a better chance at success than obsessing on obstacles.

Looking at events in the United States during the Revolutionary War can make this same point. A larger group of Hessian mercenaries who were fighting for the British were in winter quarters near present-day Trenton, New Jersey. Little in the way of battle took place in the winter due to harsh weather conditions in the northeastern part of the United States.

George Washington saw what was expected under "normal" circumstances to be the stuff of opportunity. He planned a surprise attack on the Hessians and believed that success could have a powerful impact on his troops, even give the country a reason to be optimistic about the overall war efforts. When Washington came with his troops and boats to the shore of the Delaware River across from Trenton, he found the river clogged with huge blocks of floating ice. Here, as with Napoleon, were *obstacles*.

Not only did Washington, in his "vision," believe that the obstacles could be overcome, but he also saw how they could increase his opportunity. The river was crossed, the Hessians were taken by complete surprise, and the battle—the *objective*—was achieved. What if Washington had seen the ice-filled river and turned back?

There is an old story about a New England shoe salesman whose company sent him to Africa in the late 1800s. Soon after his arrival, the salesman sent a telegram back to the owner of his business: "I want to come home. Nobody wears shoes in this part of Africa." The man returned and another salesman was sent to replace him. Days after his arrival, he also sent a telegram: "Everybody here needs shoes!"

We too often see "vision" as an event that *happens to us*, that slips up on us, that is always a matter of surprising serendipity. That may be right at times. However, the whole experience of "vision" could be multiplied exponentially in our lives if we also understood that "vision" is a result of our *attitude*, our "angle of approach." If we go looking for obstacles, "vision" will likely be absent. If we look beyond obstacles, to objectives and to opportunities, there is no telling what we may be able to accomplish.

CAPTURING OUR IMAGINATION

When I was in grammar school, every Thursday was "assembly day." For a couple of hours in the morning, grades 1–4 would meet in the gymnasium. After lunch, the process would be repeated for grades 5–8. Sometimes, we would see films. At other times we would hear speakers; usually, very boring speakers.

The students did not look forward to "assembly day;" I'm sure the teachers—getting a bit of a break from the classroom—did.

One day a man named Neil Ensminger came to speak. I knew Mr. Ensminger. He had been our neighbor before I was in school. He was the editor of the local newspaper, and—even as a kid—I recognized him as one of the most captivating speakers that I had ever heard. He had a powerful, dramatic voice, and always brought up topics that most people did not think about. Our school principal would have him speak to the students at least once a year. When I saw Mr. Ensminger on the stage as we came together for this "assembly day," I knew it would be a good day.

He began to talk about how important it was to pay attention, to notice what was going on around us. He explained that he was not talking about paying attention to a train roaring down a train track; that would be hard to miss. He was talking about paying attention to "little things" that might be very important, but that could easily escape our notice. Sometimes, he said, the "little things" may be much, much more important than the "big things" that overwhelm us with their blaring noise.

He had his own anecdote to illustrate for us what he meant. He talked about the biblical character, David, who we all knew from Sunday School, and recalled when David had led the armies of Israel against the dreaded Philistines. At one point, David is ready to attack, but he realizes that "timing" is everything in a battle, much like Washington's element of surprise at Trenton.

In the story, David asks God for help. He is told by God to hide and wait. Then, when "you hear the stirring of the wind in the top of the mulberry trees," launch the offensive and it will be successful. David did exactly this, and the battle—overcoming great odds against Israel—was won.

What captivated me was the phrase—"the stirring of the winds in the top of the mulberry tree." The way Mr. Ensminger said this is still imprinted on my mind. There have been three, long-lasting impacts from this speech. First, I forever would make a distinction in my life between the loud and the subtle, and I have really practiced trying to be attentive to that which we have to pay closer attention to in order to notice. Second, I have always been compelled as a speaker to try to be as much like Neil Ensminger as I possibly can be. My "vision" of him on that stage, captivating that audience as he did so many audiences across his life, has been my role model. And, third, I have never forgotten the power of the anecdote, the story, and have fashioned presentations across my life in terms of this example. Here, then, is "vision" played out in a multitude of ways. "Vision" almost always proliferates in its impact.

"Vision" can bore its way into our consciousness and find roots that are deep and undeniable. At least, if we are true to our vision, they will be undeniable. "Vision" at its most powerful does translate itself into the most personal question—"What am I to *do?*" Then, in responding to that question, we have the chance to find the highest meaning and the greatest authenticity.

CONCLUSION

Anecdotally, I have tried to describe—not define—"vision" in what I hope are clear and distinct terms. My description has not been exhaustive—I'm sure there are a multitude of other examples that could be used—but the intent has been to give something that can easily be grasped. There are three lessons here:

1) Vision can be the result of—figuratively and maybe even literally— climbing mountains. Vision is the result of struggle to see a little beyond what is normally seen. Sometimes it is not clear what will be seen. Sometimes it is yet another mountain to climb. But, it is in the climbing, in the struggle, in the search that life's greatest opportunity for meaning is found. Not to "climb the mountain" is not to live.

2) Vision is, partly, the result of *attitude,* our "angle of approach" to life. If we look only at obstacles, we miss objectives and opportunities.

3) Vision can be a simple turn of a phrase empowered by a visionary voice. That phrase has the power to capture our attention and change our destiny if, in our consciousness, there is the transition to the question "What must I *do?*" When we make this transition, we have "heard the stirring of the wind in the top of the mulberry trees."

In 1845, in Augusta, Georgia, a group of people came together and formed what would ultimately become the Southern Baptist Convention. My comments here are not intended to applaud the Southern Baptist Convention, or—in that instance—the support of slavery that was dividing the nation that this meeting advanced. To me, the most important activity that I identify with Augusta, Georgia, is the Masters Golf Tournament. However, on the plaque outside the building where this organizing meeting took place, there is a powerful statement that can stand on its own merit:

Here, people met who saw the invisible, who heard the inaudible, who believed the incredible, and who thought the unthinkable.

Without regard for theological or political overtones associated with the meeting that gave birth to the plaque, the words are a powerful incentive to search for and even try to be people of "vision." I wonder if there are ever times when the statement could be associated with people who lead a business. I wonder if, in the boardrooms and production facilities of organizations across the land, there are people who will see the invisible, hear the inaudible, believe the incredible, and think the unthinkable. Can the wind stir in the mulberry trees in corporate settings that have powerful impact on life in our modern society?

4. VISION: AN HISTORICAL PERSPECTIVE

> If you can imagine it,
> you can create it.
> If you can dream it,
> you can become it.
>
> —William Arthur Ward

INTRODUCTION: THE MIRROR OF LANGUAGE

Language is a wonderful mirror of the life of human beings over generations. Follow the movement of language, and you can see the diverse range of human potential unveil itself right before your eyes. Words fall into and drop out of language just like people—even whole civilizations—come and go over time. Let there be a monumental time, and language will reflect unique changes. Let there be an important person who touches the movement of civilization, and language will somehow be inevitably altered and enhanced by something that person says.

Sometimes an old word will take on an entirely new meaning. Compare, for example, the way that Edgar Alan Poe used the word *rap* in his famous poem, "The Raven," to the meaning the same word would hold for Sean ("Puff Daddy") Coombs or someone else familiar with the movements of modern music.

Sometimes a word used in one culture, even though the roots of that culture may be very close to those of another culture, have little or no meaning in another culture. The English use the word *lift* for the word *elevator* used in the United States. In a stranger sense, the word *umbrella* in New York City would be *bumpershoot* in London. Whoever is able to explain either of those strangely constructed words is a much better linguist than I will ever be.

Sometimes language is generational and can change, be handed down, or become totally lost from one generation to another. My grandparents were born in the 1870s in Upper East Tennessee. There lives were wonderfully provincial, albeit severely isolated from many of the movements of the middle part of the twentieth century in which their lives matured. I believe they liked their isolation, and a radio was the nearest intrusion of the modern world they allowed into their simple home. Both of them used the word *chick* for my *creek*. They said *aboot* for my *about*. All of this was very curious to me. I would laugh at their pronunciations, and they seemed not to mind. Grandpa sometimes used *thee* and *thou*, and I simply thought he had been reading the Bible too much. I wish now I could remember all of the other words they carried in their isolated vocabularies.

Then, there are times when a word can span the centuries, and end up being used by human beings thousands of years separated in time from each other. In all likelihood, when this phenomenon occurs, the word will not be used consistently and uniformly across time, will become clichéd in its distinctiveness, and actually lose meaning. In these kinds of circumstances, a word will have almost as many potential meanings as there are people to offer meanings. More often than not, this circumstance only allows for people getting crossways with each other over the meaning of a word, feeling the need to defend their own usage, and only confusing the situation even more.

A perfect example of this increasing "fuzziness" of language and compromising of distinct meaning can be seen with the word *vision*. This word was important in the earliest civilizations known to historical research. Almost every ancient culture—and every culture since—has used the word liberally. The word has achieved newfound status in the modern world of management theory; almost every organization has its own "vision statement." The need for "visionaries" has spanned the ages, although once a "visionary" was a distinctly religious figure, and today the desire for "visionaries" is a corporate or political goal. In the midst of all of this chaos of diverse usage, exactly what a "vision" actually is and how a "vision" might be experienced has become obscured. We now have a word that we use a great deal, but we really are not sure what all we might be meaning when we use the word.

One way of abridging confusion and regaining clarity on an important word that has gotten "fuzzy" in its usage is to carefully go back and try to understand exactly what the word meant in its original usage. Once some degree of insight has been gained in this arena, it may be possible to take the word in its modern usage and give it greater meaning. Then, when the word is used in its modern circumstances, it can have clarity, distinctiveness, and power; we can use the word and it can have credibility and authenticity because it is now connected to its own heritage and roots.

The task of this presentation will be to look carefully at the roots of the word *vision*, and try to see exactly what it meant in its earliest usages. This task will not be easy since, by the time that the formal work of etymology (the study of the history of words and language) begins, most important words have already gone through many evolutions of inconsistent and mixed usage. However, if we are particularly careful in our pursuit, profitable insight and greater precision of modern application will result. An old word can bring new light to a modern situation. We must look back the better part of 2000 years in order to gain insight into how the word *vision* can best be understood in our modern, organizational culture.

THE "LENS" FOR OUR INVESTIGATION

Most investigations will have some sort of "tool" to help in advancing the investigative process whether there is a modern scientist with an electron microscope or the Hubble telescope or a forensic anthropologist taking DNA samples. In this particular search, the "tool" or "lens" being used is the formative work of Robert S. Hartman.

Hartman believed that life was often manifested in three dimensions. A *systemic* or "S" dimension involved—for Hartman—the broadest level of abstraction, a looking at life from the proverbial 30,000 feet. The *systemic* dimension is usually fairly dispassionate and theoretical, a kind of "mental map" of general orientation. An *extrinsic* or "E" dimension involved the most concrete levels of practical and pragmatic process, the level of the most basic engagement with day-to-day life. Finally, an *intrinsic* or "I" level comprised the metaphysical, beyond the physical and rational (whether physical and rational are expressed in intelligent theory—"S"—or concrete practice—"E"), and—in most cases—related to issues that are ineffable, non-demonstrable, non-verbal, and—to use William of Ockham's wonderful designation—"First Intentional." The *intrinsic* will always involve the mysterious and that which cannot be reduced to rational constructs.

It is possible to use Hartman's "lens" to compartmentalize life in almost any context imaginable. Here are several examples that will make the point of this "lens" fairly easy to understand. Anyone reading this material can add their own examples and make the Hartman distinctions come alive even more.

Systemic	Extrinsic	Intrinsic
1. NaCl	1. Table salt	1. Lot's wife
2. Force, action and reaction	2. A baseball being hit	2. Aaron's 715 homerun
3. Rope	3. Noose	3. A lynching
4. Food	4. Desserts	4. Mom's apple pie
5. $A = L \times W$	5. A house	5. My home

Now, if Hartman's patterns are correct and if they can be applied to almost every aspect of life, it makes sense that language about some reality may find expression in systemic, extrinsic, and intrinsic forms. If this is true, then understanding any word that has found conceptual expression—the word *vision*, for example—can be advanced by using the Hartman "lens" at some point. We will attempt to see if this "lens" has application to our search for understanding the historical roots of *vision*. The reader should be prepared for some intriguing correlations.

One disclaimer should be added at this point. My expertise in terms of ancient cultures and thought forms focuses primarily on Ancient Greek and Hebrew precedents in philosophy and theology. You have to look into philosophy and theology in these ancient cultures to study the word *vision* since *vision* in its first usages was primarily a philosophical and theological term; there were no companies or business organizations using the word *vision* at that time in any way similar to its use in those contexts today. My primary linguistic expertise is also in Greek and Hebrew. Therefore, in looking at the etymological roots of the word *vision*, I will look primarily in these areas. However, in other ancient cultures where my expertise is less, I have made enough of a summary study to conclude that expertise in non-Greek and non-Hebrew cultures would likely reach conclusions similar to those I will attempt to unpack in this study.

THE ROOTS OF THE ANCIENT LANGUAGE REVEALED

(Please note: In the part of the presentation that immediately follows, the original Greek will be used when possible. Each time that a Greek word is used for the first time, it will be followed by a parenthesis that includes a transliterated English spelling of the Greek word. This process may help in pronunciation and identification. There will be times when the computer program will not allow for diacritical/accent marks, but on this elementary level there should be no problem. It can also be noted that a good deal of the research on the concept of *vision* in the ancient world is derived from a lengthy article by the scholar Wilhelm Michaelis found in Gerhard Kittel and Gerhard Friedrich, eds., *Theological Dictionary of the New Testament*, Vol. 5, pp. 315–381.)

The ancient Greeks focused on three words for our word *vision*. These were, in no special order of priority: οπτασια (optasia), οραμα (horama), and ορασισ (horasis). In general, these words related to something that a person has seen, sometimes with the actual, physical eye, but more often with the "minds-eye." When what is seen is observed with the physical eye, it is something so "out of the ordinary" and mysterious that it cannot be explained by pure reason alone. The emphasis on "pure reason alone" will be important later. Many ancient texts speak of "night visions," events that would be roughly equivalent to our dreams. "Day visions," also mentioned in ancient texts, would be unusual waking events that could not be explained by pure reason alone. These "day visions" might be the "appearance" of some semi-physical or metaphysical (beyond the physical) reality (although the use of the word *reality*, in its common form, may be troublesome here). A "day vision" could also be some insight that rises to consciousness in a non-standard way such as "thoughts" we have while showering, taking a long walk, or in the "zone" we sometimes achieve while driving.

A good example of these kinds of *visions* would be the Damascus Road experience of St. Paul (then Saul of Tarsus). The ancient texts refer to the event as an ουρανιο οπτασισ (ouranious optasis), a "heavenly vision." It is not clear, exactly, what happens to Paul on the Damascus Road. The event certainly exceeds any purely rational parameters. Normal language descriptions fall flat on their faces in terms of clear and precise explanation. These characterizations fit the event/experience of *vision* perfectly for the ancient world. The ancients could not explain them, but—at the same time—they could not deny them either.

The ancients had two other words that are important for this early part of the discussion. The word ορατοσ (horatos) meant "visible," and the word αορατοσ (aoratos) meant "invisible." This distinction, for the ancients, was roughly equivalent to our modern "rational" and "non-rational" (although I am clearly seeing "non-rational" in no way as "ir-rational;" the "non-rational" used here more precisely means "supra-rational" in the sense of "beyond the normal rational"). Thus, *vision* is a *mechanism of communication* that relates primarily to the "invisible." Please keep this decisive phrase in mind: *vision* is a *mechanism of communication* that relates primarily to the "invisible," the non-rational/supra-rational.

Vision, therefore, is not simply *what* is seen. *What* is seen (or heard) may never be completely understood in a rational manner or explained adequately. *Vision* is more *how* someone is seeing. *Vision* is a way, a means, a *mode of seeing*. *What* is seen—the supposed *vision*—is all but wholly dependent on *how* a person sees, the *mode of seeing*. Clearer insight may be derived if *vision*—the noun, the event, the experience—takes second priority to *vision-ing*—the verb, the act of seeing. In this sense, a *vision* is fully dependent on *vision-ing*, the *mode of seeing*. These odd grammatical constructions actually fit well with modern usage; for any modern, scientific optometrist, for example, *vision* would probably be defined as a "capacity" for sight. This is almost exactly what the ancients thought, except they made a critical distinction between various "capacities" for sight, and true *vision-ing* would be the result of one of those "capacities."

At this point, a highly, highly critical aspect of the overall discussion must be carefully accented. If the event/experience of *vision-ing . . . vision* is understood as a *mechanism of communication*, then that which is communicated is vastly more important than the "medium" of the communication. Our modern, practical minds become so consumed and obsessed with the "medium" of the communication that we miss the "message" of the communication. For the ancient world, unlike our modern world, the "medium" was decisively *not* the message. In our modern world, we get so "hung up" on having to have a fully rational "medium" as a necessary prerequisite for allowing a "message" to qualify as having any truth value that we often deprive ourselves of "messages"—we "hang up on" messages—that could be of utmost importance.

B. D. Napier, writing in *The Interpreter's Dictionary of the Bible* (Vol. 4, p. 791), says that the core of *vision* is always "the Word that is disclosed" and the "meaning of life" that potentially rises from this disclosure. In this sense, *vision* usually becomes an option, an invitation, a "call" to some way of seeing life, self, and others that—if acted upon—can produce dramatic change. In this sense, there may actually be a connection between *vision* and the modern expression, "out-of-the-box thinking," although I am committed to believing that "out-of-the-box thinking" is seldom *thinking* in any normal sense of that word. There may not be any literal "words-as-language" in the *vision*, but there is still communication. Sometimes "words-*not*-as-language" can be more powerful in terms of communication than "words-as-language." The key, decisive issue with *vision* is that communication takes place.

Sometimes, a *vision* may powerfully impinge upon us from outside of us in a way that we have no control over. The Damascus Road experience may be a good example of this. On the other hand, we have no real idea of how events leading up to the Damascus Road experience had "readied" St. Paul for the *vision*. At other times, the potential for *vision*—for communication—may have been there all along, and we may simply have been too busy or otherwise engaged to notice. In the famous story of Moses and the burning bush, the ancient text says that one day Moses "turned aside" to see why the bush burned but was not consumed. "Turned aside" means a very conscious decision on the part of Moses to change a typical, regular path that is being taken. In other words, he may have walked near the burning bush—the "platform" for *vision*—many, many times but made the decision to keep on with "business as usual." In any event, *vision* never appears to be a unilateral, one-sided event.

A "source of communication"—a "speaker" for want of a better word—is required, as is an "object of communication"—a listener, a see-er, a vision-er. *Vision*, as an event/experience, is always a "two-way street" that depends as much on the preparation of the listener, see-er, vision-er as it does any message source. Clearly, that "preparation" can be accidental and the *vision*, thus, highly serendipitous. Our challenge is to see that the event/experience of *vision-ing. . .vision* can also be highly intentional, something that we consciously prepared ourselves for and, under certain circumstances, expose ourselves to. Both options are intriguing, but in our Western world with its obsession on *doing,* to contemplate a kind of preparation that might enhance the chances of events/experiences of *vision-ing. . .vision* is tantalizing.

A final point before moving on: do not get caught up on giving too much emphasis to *vision* as a **mechanism of communication** based on words. The ancient Greeks precluded a great deal of Western rationalism with their use of the word λογοσ (logos). Hereclitus and Aristotle built the foundations of Western scientific rationality on the word. Γογοσ (Logos) is the rational principle that underlies all of existence and gives existence its coherent, orderly operation. All that humans have to do is to become attuned to and aligned with λογοσ, and life can be understood, managed, and—dream of all dreams—controlled. Γογοσ not only makes sense; λογοσ *is* sense, the very foundation of "Truth."

However, these same ancient Greeks understood the limits of λογοσ. Their highest word for "Truth" went well beyond scientific rationality. There was also the word αληθεια (alethia) that meant to "un-veil" or "reveal," and indicated that the highest truths were beyond rationality and demonstrable proof. The highest truth "happened," if a person was in the "way" and in a "way" where un-veiling/truth-ing could occur. This is Einstein's "sense of wonder" that is at the core of all science and humanities, a sense/mode that causes a person to be "rapt" (Einstein's word) or "wrapped" (my word) in awe. This sense/mode of existence is so decisive to Einstein that he says that failure to position oneself so that "wonder" can be experienced makes persons "as good as dead—their minds and eyes are blind."

Martin Heidegger, the great German philosopher, spoke of highest truth, αληθεια as "Das Anwesen des Anwesenden"/"The Arrival of That Which Arrives"/"The Appearance of That Which Appears." Heidegger's concept of highest truth—truth that surpasses scientific rationality—as "arrival/appearance" is exactly what the ancient Greeks meant by οπαματα (hopamata)—"appearances" or *visions*.

The fundamental key for us is to try to make sure that we make space and time for arrivals, appearances, unveilings, revelations—that we make space and time/establish the mode of living that allows for *visions*. Then, like those people surrounded by the events of Pentecost in the New Testament Book of Acts, we will be able to ask "What does it mean?" We will, then, we able to appreciate the fact that "meaning" can be housed in scientific, rational data, but that it can also be housed in that which radically transcends science and reason, can never be captured or contained absolutely by it, and that will always and forever be beyond definition. When we open ourselves to that which is beyond definition, we are exposed to the *mechanism of communication* that is *vision*.

EXPLORING THREE, DISTINCT WAYS OF SEEING

Two points are now clear, one explored to a limited extent and the other waiting to be explored. First, the event/experience of *vision-ing. . .vision* is more a matter of *how* than it is of *what*, more a matter of the "message" communicated than the "medium" of that communication. The critical issue, if *vision* is ever to be more than serendipitous accident—as important as such an event may be—is to create a posture, a positioning, a mode of existence in which *vision-ing. . .vision* can occur/can arrive/can appear/can become αληθεια.

In other words, *vision-ing. . .vision* depends upon a *way of seeing*. It is with this issue of *a way of seeing* that the ancients can be most helpful. In a second consideration as yet only introduced, matching what the ancient Greeks had to say about *seeing* with Robert Hartman's template of systemic, extrinsic, and intrinsic dimensions of existence can bring the ancient understandings into the modern world in a highly usable manner.

For the ancient Greeks, there were three, dominant *ways of seeing*. First, there was θεωρεω (theoreo) from which our modern word *theory* is derived. The modern word *theory* has, in fact, preserved a great deal of continuity of meaning with θεωρεω. To encounter life/to see/to experience with θεωρεω—theoretically—was to experience in more global, broad-brush strokes, to see the forest and not simply react to an individual tree. The great playwright, Aeschylus, used the term for observing a spectacle, an entire stage at a theatrical performance, or to have an "overview" of something like all three rings of a circus.

This usage is consistent throughout many of the writings of the ancient time. By the time Josephus wrote his histories, he used the word precisely to convey seeing that was "from a distance." At that time, the closeness of the word to the Greek word for divinity, Θεοσ (Theos), suggested that the broad, comprehensive overview of God should be described as θεωρεω. This assertion certainly makes sense; who could have any broader and more encompassing view of reality than God? God would know enough to make all *theories* exact.

Most importantly, θεωρεω was looked upon as a wholly *mental* event. It was linked with the Greek word νουσ (nous) which is the word most easily defined in modern usage as *mind* in the sense of the rational, calculative capacity of human existence. Again, as far back as Josephus, qewrew was distinctly seen as *mental*. In terms of the paradigm established by Robert Hartman, θεωρεω is systemic. Hartman consistently associated the systemic evaluative capacity as relating to larger overviews, abstract rational constructs, and "big picture" realities. To relate *theoretically* would be to relate systematically.

The second *way of seeing* for the ancient Greeks was βλεπω (blepo) which is basic, physical sight, the basic physical ability for visual experiences. The opposite of basic physical sight would be physical blindness—not spiritual or emotional blindness, anything esoteric, simply the inability to physically see. Blepw is a "function of the eye" and is associated with σομα (soma), the physical body.

Obviously, there is no diminishing of βλεπω, or no statement that physical sight is "mere" physical sight. Not to have physical sight would leave a person tragically encumbered. No one would desire physical blindness, although in the ancient myths the physically blind could often have other ways of seeing heightened; consider, for example, the place of blind Tiresias in the Greek legends. However, in terms of day-to-day, basic functioning, clear physical sight would be a practical necessity. To follow the Hartman paradigm, βλεπω is clearly extrinsic. The extrinsic relates to the altogether important domain of functioning effectively and efficiently in the physical world, being able to accomplish processes and tasks proficiently. Without βλεπω, the extrinsic would be seriously negated.

Finally, there is a third *way of seeing* for the ancient Greeks that becomes the most important arena of insight for our present discussion. The Greeks also talked about οραω (horao). Plato, in his important philosophical writing *Timeus*, made special reference to οραω as "spiritual sight." It was, at one and the same time, the "gift of the gods" and the specific "love of the philosophers"—the "lovers of wisdom." To see, οραω, was to have the capacity to *perceive*, and "perception"—as opposed to physical sight or theorizing rationality—was the "path to αληθεια," the "path to Truth." Οραω was identified as *consideration*, a word of highest importance that literally meant "with *sider*." *Sider* was an ancient, cross-cultural word for the deepest wisdom possible of human beings. *Consideration* was, therefore, the most fundamental evaluative capacity, the most fundamental judgment capacity, the most fundamental *way of seeing*.

Words such as *evaluative* and *judgment* are clearly more modern words, but they capture perfectly οραω both as a process of focused attentiveness and as an outcome. For the Greeks, οραω was associated with ψυχη (psuche), the soul. On this "soul-level," that was ultimately beyond rational definition, the Greeks were simply sure that there was a *way of seeing* that was distinctively different—and the implication cannot be missed, distinctively superior—that human beings were capable of and needed to develop and use at every opportunity. There is an old Greek saying that expresses this conclusion in a profound manner: "The eye of the soul is better than ten thousand eyes." Following the Hartman paradigm, οραω would be like the intrinsic. The intrinsic is highly personal, intimate, metaphysical. It is beyond definition and highly relational, the result of the closest involvement rather than practical process or distant theory. Hartman was sure that individuals who were regularly acquainted with the intrinsic would have the deepest insights into life, make the best leaders, and be decisive for the higher potential movements of civilization. This is Hartman's concept of "Differentiation," the capacity to *notice* that which is more subtle, that which has more to do with "depth" than with "surface."

(Please note: The word *spiritual* used above in regard to the Greek concept of "spiritual sight" should not be seen as a synonym of the word *religious*. Religion is a cultural phenomenon, more extrinsic and systemic in its impact. Religion is very much the result of human cultural processes and definitions.

The *spiritual* runs much deeper. It is possible to experience the *spiritual* outside of the cultural context of religion. Ideally, a cultural religion will also be *spiritual*, but this is not a necessary connection.

In a further, parenthetical consideration, it can be noted that the Greeks had two other important words that are related to this overall discussion. The word ειδον (eidon) is another word occasionally used for "to see" and is a rough synonym of βλεπω, although in the lack of uniformity common to language usage, it can be found at obscure times to be a synonym of οραω. In addition, the Greeks frequently used the word πνευμα (pneuma) that means "spirit" as a synonym for ψυχη, "soul." Therefore, it would be linguistically and philosophically accurate to see "spirit" and "soul" as being practically interchangeable.

Finally, note parenthetically, that in the *LXX—The Septuagint*, the Greek translation of the Hebrew Old Testament—the word ψυχη/psuche/soul—is used as the translated equivalent of the Hebrew *nephesh*, one of the most highly evolved and important words in the Hebrew language. For the most part, everything that is said about the Greek words for *soul* and *spirit* can be connected to the Hebrew *nephesh*.)

The following diagram may be helpful at this point to establish a conclusion to this section of the discussion and prepare for the next section. If a person understands the basic distinctions of this diagram, a great deal of the force of this discussion is being followed accurately. It will be helpful at this point for the reader to pause for a moment, embrace carefully the following distinctions, and let the diagram find its way into solid consciousness. Do not quickly pass over this diagram. By embracing it carefully, a kind of "lens" can actually be created that will enhance the reader's ability to develop within himself/herself the three *ways of seeing* that are being described. By embracing this diagram carefully, the reader will be able to clearly distinguish when he/she is seeing/θεωρεω, seeing/βλεπω, or seeing/οραω.

Greek Word	Way of Seeing	Related To	Hartman Parallel
θεωρεω/theoreo	theoretical, mental	νουσ/nous/mind	Systemic
βλεπω/blepo	physical sight	σομα/soma/body	Extrinsic
οραω/horao	"spiritual sight"	ψυχη/psuche/soul	Intrinsic

THE PRECISE RELATIONSHIP TO *VISION*

A careful following of the linguistic discussion in the previous section provides the essential groundwork for a creditable and convincing connection with the most important insights concerning *vision*. A conclusion can now be drawn that is impossible to miss.

First, go back and look at the key, critical words that the ancient Greeks used in reference to *vision*: οραμα (horama), ορασισ (horasis), ορατοσ (horatos), and αορατοσ (aoratos). In each of these words, even a person fully unfamiliar with the ancient Greek language can see the clear connection to the root word οραω (horao) that we have looked at closely in the previous section and defined as the intrinsic *way of seeing*.

In other words, and this is the critical conclusion, in order to experience *vision(s)*, there must be oraw; there must be an intrinsic *way of seeing*. The person who is blind to the intrinsic and only sees through the lens of the extrinsic and the systemic will not experience *vision(s)*. Here, we see the ancient injunction about having eyes to see but still be blind. So, the experience of *vision(s)* is much more dependent on the "viewing posture," the "seeing orientation" of the person desiring the experience of *vision(s)* than it is the catalyst, origin, or what Aristotle called "the Prime Mover" of the *vision(s)*. Better yet, if there is to be *communication*—the critical outcome of *vision(s)*—there must be *both* the catalyst or the origin and the "seeing orientation" of the person capable of the experience. When these two aspects coincide, there is "meeting" (what the German philosophers called *Begegnung*) and a heightened sense of relatedness or relationship (what the German philosophers called *Zwischenmenschliche* or "between-ness"). The result of this "meeting" is communication usually in the form of that which is referred to as insight, meaning, or even enlightenment. The ancient metaphors of moving out of darkness into light, moving from blindness to sight, become powerful reinforcement for these concepts.

Here, Hartman sees the movement from "Differentiation" to "Integration" in which a person is integrated with/aligned with existence on a more profound level and gains insights that cannot be had on other levels (the systemic and the extrinsic). For Hartman, it must also be realized, that his "integration" does not stop with a spectator-like observation of life (βλεπω) or some rational synthesis of life into rational constructs (θεωρεω), but consummated in an "integration" that actually solves problems, finds solutions, and makes decisions on a higher level, a level in-spired by οραω/vision.

4. *Vision: An Historical Perspective*

SO, WHO IS THE MODERN VISIONARY?

This discussion must now move out of the realm of the ancients and their formative language, and begin to ask about modern applications. Most importantly, there will now be a series of conclusions that attempt to establish *who* the modern *vision*ary—person of *vision*—actually is, and what this person does/must do in order for *vision(s)* to be an active part of his/her life.

1. In order to be a person of *vision*, there must be a highly developed appreciation for the intrinsic. As long as a person is only operative in the extrinsic and systemic dimensions, the experience of *vision* will be accidental at best and probably go unrecognized.

2. It will not be enough to simply *appreciate* the intrinsic. It must be put into conscious and strategic use. This requires specific time given to contemplation, reflection, and stillness. The noise and traffic of life must be consciously bracketed out so that the quiet and tranquil can prevail. There must be contemplation spots and contemplation moments. The intrinsic cannot be rushed, and we must be hushed. These are heady requirements that only the most stubbornly persistent person of increasing focus will achieve.

3. The *medium* of *vision(s)* is not very important and should not consume too much attention. The *message*—the communication—is vital. This message will likely take the form of some insight that had not come through traditional rational means; that is, insights that had not come through the extrinsic and the systemic.

4. There will, then, likely be some necessity for respecting the insight that has come. This respect will be important for the insight may be non-traditional or not in keeping with easy rationality. It would not, however, be appropriate to call the insight that is troublesome "counter-intuitive" since it is, in fact, highly "intuitive." Respect can be measured by the degree to which the insight is actualized in real-life practice.

5. The major task—the task that ultimately defines *vision*ary—is the ability to extend the communication, the insight, to others in a way that it can be understood and—if accepted—create a new *structure of meaning*/a new *structure of value*/a new *set of priorities* for their lives. This new *structure of meaning/structure of value* that is created as an option for people to follow with commitment and dedication is driven

by the personal power of the *vision*ary, the *vision*ary's personal conviction about his/her *vision(s)*/communication/insight, and the degree to which his/her own *structure of meaning/structure of value/value system/set of priorities* has felt the impact, and embraced/integrated/aligned with the impact, of the *vision(s)*/communication/insight. In other words, the true power of the *vision*ary is the ability to impart to others new options, new meanings, new structures of value and priority, that can, then, engage their lives; they "see" the *vision*, they "buy into" the *vision*. At the core of the experience of *vision*—both as *vision* is received and as *vision* is advanced—is the capacity to be "open" in a conscious and strategic way *and* the ability to communicate with clarity and conviction. When options are increased, and usually options that have not been seen before, *vision* is consummated, it "sows its seeds," it opens the door to the birth of new possibility.

CONCLUSION

There is the ancient maxim—probably one of the best-known statements about *vision* ever given expression—that says: "Where there is no *vision*, the people perish." In the context of this discussion, *perish* is a very relative word. In fact, without *vision*, there may not be perishing at all. In fact, on extrinsic and systemic level, there could be evidence of substantial thriving. The problem, of course—and it may be that here we find the major problem of modern civilization—is that there can be thriving on the extrinsic and systemic levels, and yet still be great emptiness and hollowness on the intrinsic level that manifests itself as a stark absence of meaning, a loss of priorities, and then even a gross narrowing of options that lead to lives of worth and value. We see these crushing realities on every side of modern life.

So, the necessity of *vision*aries is exceedingly high. There is a need for people who have active disciplines that will expose them to the possibility of *vision(s)*. There is a need, then, for these people to work tirelessly and fearlessly to *communicate* new *visions*/new options/new structures of meanings/new structures of value/new sets of priorities. Without these, we may thrive in some ways, but—inevitably—we may perish in others.

INTERLUDE II

TRANSFORMATIONAL LEADERSHIP

TRANSFORMATIONAL LEADERSHIP 1

A manager, to heal an organization, must become a transformational leader. Transformation means to change the structure of the organization, i.e., to give it a higher form.

The two major dimensions of any organization are energy and form. The transformational leader must be able to generate high mental velocities in the organization and then create new organizational forms to capture and express these energies.

Transformation is alchemy, changing base metals to gold. It is a spiritual refinement process that expands the awareness of everyone in the organization.

I am going to identify for you the qualities of a transformational leader. As I discuss each quality, I want you to examine yourself and ask, "Does this fit me?"

1. Spiritual awakening

A butterfly is not a caterpillar that has grown twice as large. Metamorphosis of the caterpillar is a change of state. Transformation requires a spiritual awakening. The manager may attain this awakening through the pursuit of various religious, philosophical, ethical, or humanistic traditions.

The manager's ability to generate transformational change in the organization is limited by his/her state of awareness. Transformation requires "big ring" thinking.

The successful hospitals of the future are not just more of the same. They are organizations that have undergone a change of state. They are led by transformational managers.

Interlude II

TRANSFORMATIONAL LEADERSHIP 2

Spiritual awakening causes the leader to resonate with higher order energy systems in the universe. Resonance always results in energy transfer. At spiritual levels we call this enspiriting. Enspiriting is an energy transfer from a higher level transmitter to a lower level receiver. This downflow of energy increases the mental velocity of the leader and results in an endowment of personal charisma.

Transformation in an organization requires the presence of high spiritual energies. The transformational leader acts as a receiver, conduit and distributor of these energies. Everyone in the organization is affected by this radiation. Soon a core group of people form in the organization and act as an amplifier and extender of the leader's energies.

A transformational leader is a necessary but not sufficient condition for the transformation of organizations. Enlightened and committed followers are just as important as enlightened leaders. The leader can point the way but cannot change an organization in spite of itself. The organization's collective will must come into alignment with the consciousness of the leader. Transformation must become a group process of enlightenment and service to humankind.

Without a spiritual basis, organizational transformation is not possible. Unlike other theories of management, transformation requires an inner change in the leader. Transformation is not something that can be learned out of a book or taught in a business school. It is a way of life and a response to a spiritual calling. It is a descent of grace. Any manager can decide to become a transformational leader and prepare herself/himself for the descent of grace. Then comes the patient period of waiting. The descent of grace cannot be commanded. It is a spiritual gift that comes from on high.

2. Inclusive perception

A transformational leader senses the hidden potentials in people, programs or organizations and then acts to release these potentials in third dimensional reality. This is a more inclusive type of perception and permits the leader to see "what could be" as well as "what is." The leader acts as a bridge between spirit and manifestation.

A transformational leader perceives in a more inclusive way. His/her vision extends to the inner depths of things. The light coming from the leader shines upon the object of inquiry and reveals its hidden pattern of being and becoming. This type of extended perception permits the leader to function as an agent of planetary evolution (continued).

TRANSFORMATIONAL LEADERSHIP 3

Inclusive perception operates in a dimension beyond words. The light of the mind reaches out with an inner illumination and reveals the inner essence of anything it touches. Everything is perceived from the inside-out. It is knowing without thinking.

Ordinary leaders are word bound. For them, thinking is silent speech. If they can't word it, they can't think it. Their thinking, therefore, is limited to the peculiarities of their language and times. Transformational leaders operating in a dimension beyond words perceive in a fashion that is relatively free of language and historical period.

We often use the word intuition (inner tuition) to describe the realm of extended perception. That word is as good as any other because what it describes is beyond words anyway. Intuition is the immediate apprehension of a thing. It is wordless insight. The perceiver later translates the insight into words in order to communicate it to others. This is a frustrating and difficult thing to do. When the mind is no longer word bound it operates at an enormous velocity. It may take months of translation effort to word, insights gleaned in seconds.

Meditation, contemplation, and reflection prepare the mind for wordless thought. Transformational leaders solve problems by not thinking about them, or perhaps we should say, by thinking about them without words.

Imagine a transformational meeting in the hospital where the staff comes together to contemplate. No words are used until after the period of contemplation when members share their insights with one another. The mental velocities generated in such a circle of silence will exhibit vortex phenomena.

Imagine a transformational physician that makes diagnoses with this type of extended perception. He/she sees with an inner mind what the external tests later verify.

Imagine a patient experiencing transformation. Healing depends upon a more inclusive type of patient perception. A patient's internal healing system can often be activated by mythological symbols or by the healing presence of a transformational healthcare professional.

Transformational leadership involves more than the management subsystem of a healthcare institution. A more inclusive consciousness must characterize everything the institution does. Transformational medicine, and transformational nursing are just as important as transformational management if you want a transformational organization.

Interlude II

TRANSFORMATIONAL LEADERSHIP 4

Changing the locus of perception

Where is your locus of perception? It seems only natural for consciousness to be wherever your body is. Most people are the center of their universes. They see everything happening around them. A more inclusive perception permits the transformational leader to change his/her locus of consciousness, "to pass over to the standpoint of the other." Seeing the world through another person's eyes creates an intense empathy with that person and an in-depth understanding of his/her world view.

A leader must understand his/her followers. Egocentric perception does not permit this kind of understanding. You see other people only in terms of yourself. Other-centric perception enables you to shed your self-interest, biases, and distortions and see the world as others see it.

Often hospital administrators are bound by ego-dominated perception and cannot see their hospitals as the hospitals are viewed by the community. The administrator acts as if his/her institution is the center of the universe, rather than just one institution in the community. A transformational leader demonstrates community leadership because he/she can take-in the nature and potential of all healthcare institutions in the community and can therefore perceive the greater good of the community which can never be viewed from the confines of just one institution.

A four-wall mentality is one of the great problems in healthcare today. When each institution pursues its self interest, the greater good of the community is not served. Collaboration will replace competition as hospitals begin to adopt transformational strategies. In a connected system, if one part loses, all parts lose. In transformational philosophy, competition is replaced by the pursuit of excellence and drive toward individuation. Each institution tries to become the best that it can become. It pursues its own individuality while supporting and being connected to the efforts of all other institutions to collectively serve the community's health. Individuation permits consumer choice. The commitment to excellence is a positive emotion and replaces the negative emotions generated by competition.

In inclusive perception, we-they, becomes us. The transformational leader perceives gestalts—wholes which are greater than the sums of the parts. Community is a whole and the health of the community is greater than the sum of the interests of all the individual healthcare providers.

TRANSFORMATIONAL LEADERSHIP 5

Developing a more inclusive perception

How can you develop a more inclusive perception? You must learn to perceive beyond the label, the word. Wordless perception is inclusive.

We learn early in life to process words and call it thought. We are a verbal culture. Wordless perception comes in the form of images or intuitive knowing. Wordless perception happens when you rest your mind on a thing and resist wording it. You allow your consciousness to envelop the object, but not label it. Your mind is held in abeyance. You meditate on the thing.

You must learn to move the locus of consciousness from inside yourself to outside your self. You let it rest lightly on the object you want to perceive. By not labeling, wording, reacting, forming judgments about, or associating to an object of perception, the mind slips into a much deeper kind of knowing.

How do you learn to do this? How do you learn to ride a bicycle? You learn by trying it until you can do it. The following three exercises will help you develop this skill.

Exercise 1

Sit in a chair and relax deeply. Look across the room at an empty chair. Move your center of consciousness from inside yourself to the empty chair. Look at yourself from the empty chair. Early practice sessions should last for no longer than 5–10 minutes.

Exercise 2

When you go to bed at night, close your eyes, relax deeply, and move your awareness through your body from your toes to your head. Sometimes it helps to tense each body part and then relax it. Then sweep your awareness from your head to your feet. Sweep back and forth several times until you have full body awareness. Now imagine a circle a foot or so around you. Allow your consciousness to fill this envelope. Now expand your consciousness to the size of your bedroom. Then fill a ring as large as your house. Then move out to your city block. Keep imagining larger and larger circles until you have trouble filling them. Hold your largest circle for about 5 minutes and then go to sleep.

Exercise 3

Lie down on your back, relax, center your consciousness in your head. Imagine it is a pendulum on a clock. Start it swinging with larger and larger arcs until it is moving several feet on each side of your body. Continue for 5–10 minutes. When you are ready to stop, slow down the arcs until your consciousness is once again centered in your head. This is a good exercise to do before you go to sleep at night.

All of these exercises loosen the focus of consciousness in your body/mind vehicle and allow you to extend it to outside objects and events. Do not rush things. It will take time to convince yourself of the reality of awareness beyond words and the ability of consciousness to assume multiple foci.

A transformational leader can shift his/her awareness from the outside appearance of a thing to its inner nature. By using this mobility of consciousness, he/she escapes the usual time/space limitations of perception. Transformation depends upon the ability of a leader to see a person, group or institution in their potential future forms.

This ability to disconnect from what is and perceive what could be, is also the basis for perception and creation of alternative realities and parallel futures (continued).

TRANSFORMATIONAL LEADERSHIP 6

Systems Orientation

The universe is a system, within a system, within a system, within a system . . .

The transformational leader is a system existing within a larger systems context (the body of the universe) and containing within his body/mind vehicle many smaller dependent systems. You are the universe for your red blood cells. You are also a cell within the body of the universe. Do you treat your body as well as you want to be treated by the universe?

The transformational leader always perceives and acts within a systems context. All things are viewed in relationship.

To transform anything, it must be viewed in its completeness, its relatedness and its connectedness to the universe. To transform anything you must understand how it is embedded in its causal network, i.e., what it supports and what supports it.

Any person, object, or event stands in relationship to everything in its past, present, and future. You may transform anything by altering these temporal relationships.

Often the easiest way to change the present of a healthcare organization is to change its future. Generating a powerful vision of the future of the organization feeds back energies that alter the way people act in the present. Their behavior begins to conform to requirements of the new vision. In psychotherapy, changes in the way a person views his past feed forward to alter the present. Changes initiated in present time feed both backwards to alter the past and forwards to alter the future.

You can transform many things by creating a point of intervention several systems levels removed from where they are manifesting. A good example would be altering a physician's practice behaviors. If you change the economic context of the physician's practice (how you reimburse care), you will change the physician's practice behaviors without ever talking to the physician. It is a great irony that you can transform many things by leaving them alone and simply changing the context in which they exist. Pay physicians to provide preventive care to their patients and they will provide preventive care. This is not so much a problem of transforming the doctor's mind as transforming the economic context in which she practices medicine.

Interlude II

By creating a positive organizational culture, we encourage individual transformation. Changing organizational context is a powerful strategy for transformation of individuals living within that context. Work redesign and TQM change organizational context, i.e., the way people relate to one another. As a result of the changing context, behaviors of individuals change. Kurt Lewin, a field theorist, developed the formula, $b = f(p.e)$. Translated this is, "behavior is a function of the transaction of personality and environment." Note that you can change behavior by simply changing the environment (e) without ever dealing directly with the person (p).

The person and his environment form a system and they influence one another in a mutual way. Change the environment and you change the person. Change the person and you change the environment. A transformational manager does both. She develops educational and "therapy" programs for individuals and restructuring programs for organizations (continued).

TRANSFORMATIONAL LEADERSHIP 7

Understanding interdependence

Because of interdependence, it is difficult to change anything in isolation. A transformational leader wanting to transform her institution must also be involved in the transformation of her community. Just as a person has a form, so does a community have a form.

Transformational leaders help communities change their forms. Community forms are always a mixture of traditions from the past and challenges of the present. Transformation focuses upon possibilities of the future.

Transformation always requires raising the consciousness of what is to be transformed, i.e., making the form more conscious. In this instance, community leaders are made more aware of community health problems and are then motivated to do something about them. The community is empowered to act in its own behalf. The seed for this type of transformation is the transformational leader. The vehicle of transformation often takes the form of a "design party", where people come together to engage in intentional design of a healthier community.

In a real sense transformation makes healthcare less distinctive—set apart. Health becomes an overarching concern for everything you do in the community. The school, church, and workplace are just as involved in health as the hospital or doctor's office. Health becomes an integrative decentralized effort. This requires healthcare professionals to power share with people coming from different sectors of the community. Rather than providing services to business and industry, healthcare institutions invite business and industry to become co-designers. Rather than face each other as adversaries at managed care negotiations, they "get married."

Transformation requires us to be open to the possibilities of the moment—to be connected to all that is. Our most powerful stance is "that we don't know." Think how powerful a design party would be if participants acknowledged "they didn't know but were willing to listen to one another and trust the process." The "transformational opening" emerges as a result of honest, prolonged and intense dialogue. The opening is a creation of the participants and their shared situation. It cannot be known beforehand. Neither will it appear if any of the participants have a "program" to spring on everyone else. Each person must come to the table as a learner and release pet solutions of the past and favorite ideological positions. Creation is always unique to the here and now (continued).

TRANSFORMATIONAL LEADERSHIP 8

Plays win-win games

A transformational leader plays win-win games. The norm for our culture is win-lose games. Competition in healthcare is a good example of the win-lose mentality. The negative egocentric energies generated in win-lose efforts are not consistent with love, nurturance, and concern for the good of all people required in transformational efforts. To this degree a transformational manager is currently counter-cultural in orientation. Another way to say it is that he/she is ahead of the times. It soon will become evident that competition is not working in healthcare. Even in the computer and automotive industries, collaboration is now evident, albeit collaboration in order to compete more effectively with the rest of the world.

Transformation is always a collaborative activity between the transformer and the one transformed. This may be between the mentor and the protégé or between the Higher Self and the ego in an individual. You can't be transformed in spite of yourself. Neither can a society. This is why regulation and competition are doomed to fail. Both try to force people to do things they don't want to do. As a result, people spend lots of time and money trying to do end runs around the system. This is the motivation for litigation. Until a person or a society reaches a certain point in moral evolution, transformation is not a possibility. Competition and regulation are necessary to protect people from themselves.

In our new century we will arrive at a point of social consciousness where transformational strategies become the norm for the planet. Win-win strategies are based on the notion of universal abundance and a realization of the seamless nature of reality. What benefits all, benefits each. The problem on the planet today is not need. It is greed. There is more than enough to go around.

High technology accelerates the contest of good and evil. A win-lose mentality eventually destroys a planet. Unless transformation takes place, planetary destruction is a certainty.

Diversity, choice, and excellence are heightened by collaboration. Win-win strategies in healthcare organizations decrease status differentials, redistribute power, increase individual accountability, and maximize team accomplishments. When the organizational energies that previously went into conflict and internal competition are channeled into transformational projects, miracles begin to occur. The twenty-first century healthcare organization is a vehicle designed to promote higher consciousness in its patients and employees. It works with the community to promote the highest level of health attainable for all residents. No longer will hospitals engage in activities that are not in the community's best interest. The hospital and the community maintain a collective win-win orientation.

Analyze your current state of consciousness. Are you engaged in any win-lose transactions (note the word game means transaction)? To that degree you are not in a transformational mode. How do you avoid being competitive? Just commit to the highest level excellence you can achieve with the help of others and you will not need to worry about being competitive.

TRANSFORMATIONAL LEADERSHIP 9

Mentors organizational members

The transformational leader is a mentor. Mentorship is an essential skill of transformational management.

Mentorship greatly facilitates transformation of individuals, organizations, and communities. The transformational leader has discovered one of the basic laws of the universe—you must always have a mentor and always be one.

A mentor looks at the protégé and sees an aspect of the Divine imprisoned in human form. It is the job of the mentor to work with the protégé to release this "imprisoned splendor."

Each member of the organization is one aspect of the "All That Is." Each member requires mentoring to nourish and incubate that hidden potential. In a sense, each person in the organization is an aspect of Divinity in disguise.

Each protégé forms a relationship with a human teacher who can penetrate the disguise and release the aspect waiting to be born. In addition, each protégé must open internal communication channels with the Spirit for direct inspiration.

This is not to be confused with the New Age doctrine, that we are all gods. Rather, it says that God is reflected in all of creation. Each created thing is one reflected aspect.

God knows himself/herself/itself through creation. The challenge facing twenty-first century humanity is to realize God's qualities in a material creation. For this to happen in healthcare organizations a mentorship program is needed.

The twenty-first century healthcare organization is a spiritual organization that transforms patients, employees, doctors, family members, and the community. It is transformational because it releases the spiritual power of its people.

In a hospital mentorship program each new employee is assigned a mentor for the first year. The job of the first year mentor is to help each new arrival become seated in the organization. At the end of the first year, employees may choose from a variety of other organizational mentors for further work. Of course, their chosen mentor must also choose them. It is a mutual effort with responsibilities, obligations and rewards on each side. Each organizational mentor has a declared area of interest and a small group of employees that he/she is responsible for.

The twenty-first century healthcare organization will have a training program for organizational members that wish to become mentors. In addition, all employees will be trained in the essential skills needed by protégés being mentored. The mentoring program is an add-on to the regular organizational tasks performed by both mentors and protégés.

A very special relationship exists between the mentor and the protégé. The mentor is more than a teacher. He/she must share some essence with the protégé. There is an exchange of subtle energies between the two people. The relationship resembles parenting or coaching. It requires a "working through" on the part of the protégé. Although exchange of knowledge is involved, it may be the least important of the exchanges. You can get knowledge from a book. You cannot get mentoring from a book. Always to some degree, there is a passing of the mantle between the mentor and the protégé. The protégé is responsible to the universe to make good use of the mentoring and in turn become a mentor for others.

A mentor can only take others to the level he/she has reached. A mentor can remove barriers in the protégé because the mentor has met and overcome the same barriers in himself/herself.

We all wait upon those teachers who are further along on the path and can help us remove the rocks that block the way. A mentor will seldom remove your rocks, but will show you how to do it. Dependency is the great problem in mentoring. The mentor must know how to help "just enough" for the protégé to get the job done. Too much help becomes a barrier of its own.

Mentorship always involves sacrifice. In addition to the time and effort expended, mentors may become engulfed in the problems of their protégés. The general rule for the protégé is "keep your nose clean." Do not make life difficult for your mentor. The mentoring relationship is always voluntary and may be terminated by either party, at any time, for any reason. On the whole, however, mentoring relationships tend to endure for many years.

If you want to become a transformational leader, become a mentor. If you want to find a mentor, do your best, and one will find you.

TRANSFORMATIONAL LEADERSHIP 10

Is a Role Model for Transformational Behaviors

Behavior speaks louder than words. The transformational leader must be able to put ideals into action and demonstrate to the organization "how to do it."

The subtle skills pass from the energy field of the mentor to receptive members of the organization. The transmission occurs as a result of "laying on the hands." Subtle skills are incubated in the students via energies set into motion by the mentor.

Transformational management cannot be taught in a conventional way in traditional business schools. It cannot be mastered by reading books or demonstrated by passing a written examination.

The transformational leader seeks to impact the organization at spiritual, mental, emotional, and physical levels. The transformational leader creates the conditions necessary for manifestation and manifestation occurs. The transformational leader is a reduction valve for potent spiritual energies and seeks to "bring them through" into the plane of manifestation with a minimum of distortion in the translation. The low density energy must be converted into a high density event. At each level of densification there is ample opportunity for distortion to occur. If the leader injects her/his personality, distortion can be severe. Successful creation requires a high degree of loving detachment. The creator must operate outside the orbit of his/her ego. The image must be perceived in its pristine clarity and then slowly densified as it drifts down into the plane of manifestation. This is a delicate alchemical operation. The lead is changed into gold. Gross material substance receives a spiritual imprint.

The role model is one who has created a suitable mind/body vehicle for energy conduction. At this subtle level of energy exchange nothing needs to be said. The teaching is the presence of the teacher and the learning is the presence of the learner. Being communes with Being.

Transformational leaders of twenty-first century healthcare organizations are qualified by consciousness, then by experience, then by credentials. The question asked of the CEO applicant is "how have you chosen to BE in the world?" Of course if the interviewer is also upon the path of transformation, no questions are asked at all. Why ask, when the answer can be perceived intuitively?

TRANSFORMATIONAL LEADERSHIP 11

Spends Quiet Time Each Day

For the well to give water, it must be continually filled from subterranean channels. For the transformational leader to emit transformational power, Source energies must flow freely into his/her life.

The Source must be contacted daily in periods of reflection, contemplation, meditation, inspirational reading, music, or art.

Spiritual energies flow freely into the attuned life of the leader. They are then given a characteristic coloration by the personality and are radiated out to nurture other life forms.

The transformational leader must escape the constant temptation to become over involved in high density reality. At the ego level the leader is tempted to give the problem situation more time and effort than it deserves. What takes months to do at the ego level may take only seconds to do at the transformational level.

The transformational leader must find his/her natural rhythm of infilling and outworking. Too much outworking and there is insufficient transformational power to get the job done. Too much infilling and the psychic energy backs up on itself with no channel for expression.

Most intrapsychic power transfusions require a quiet place and a focused attention upon the work at hand. If the mind is too keyed up it cannot relax enough for the infilling to take place. Often being in nature or visiting a power spot facilitates the transfusion.

The transformational leader maintains a constant awareness of his/her power levels. When the tank says empty, then the leader does not drive further without infilling. This may take 15 minutes or less, or on occasion may take much longer.

The trick is not to run on empty. This requires a practice of energy economy. Do not use more energy than it takes to do the job. Do not permit yourself to be in a situation that causes a sudden energy loss. If an emotional trap is looming before you, put up your energy shield. Such cloaking will prevent a catastrophic loss.

Intuitive perception does not require a lot of energy but will not take place if your energy level is too low. This makes you vulnerable to whatever happens to come along. When your perceptual field begins to shrink, be aware of it and take the measures necessary to restore your energy balance.

TRANSFORMATIONAL LEADERSHIP 12

Understands the Connectedness of Things

Nothing stands alone. Everything is connected to everything. The universe is one fabric. If you change it "in here," you change it "out there."

The transformational leader understands the law of cause and effect. All events are effects (they had causes). Your reaction to the events (effects) generates further causes of yet additional effects, and so the chain continues.

The effective leader generates new causes, produces reciprocal effects and thereby becomes a critical linkage in multiple cause effect chains.

The transformation of one person's consciousness creates a planetary hologram of possibility for the transformation of all peoples' consciousness.

Your every thought, feeling, and behavior tilts the destiny of the planet. By becoming transformed yourself, you enable the transformation of others.

A small vortex group working in a hospital creates an energy field sufficient to induce change in the entire organization.

Because of the principle of connectedness, very small things change large things. The transformational leader leverages consciousness utilizing the principle of connectedness.

Since you are connected to everything, you can communicate with everything. A universe of connections creates a universe of potential relationships. Whatever you relate to, you share energy with, and to some extent exchange consciousness.

Transformation means the realization of new connections, the induction of new energies and an exchange of consciousness with larger minds.

Since the universe is a set of relationships, the transformational leader is characterized by diversity, depth, and richness of his/her relationships. Such a leader is not hung up at the level of personality differences or narrow points of view. The leader is able to "think globally and act locally."

When everything is connected, here is there and now is then. Consciousness begins to free itself from the limitations of time and space. Travel is changing the locus of awareness. When you transform your consciousness, you transform your relationships with the world.

Interlude II

TRANSFORMATIONAL LEADERSHIP 13

Is Tolerant and Open Minded

The transformational leader understands that truth is where you find it and you will find it many places. No source is a single source.

There are many different and equally acceptable ways to understand anything. If the mind is open to new possibility, life will always be an unfolding possibility.

The great mistake is to identify with your concepts. All ideas are provisional and will always be modified by greater experience.

Anything that you know is always a limited case of a greater principle or outworking. Like moving into an infinite funnel, you voyage into the expanding infinity, always moving from the more specific to the more general.

Some managers live in small boxes. Other managers ride the spiral of light. The two managers live in parallel realities.

We cannot comprehend the All That Is. To make the infinite, finite, we create small boxes and then pretend our boxes are reality. When we tire of "playing house" we move to larger boxes. When boxes no longer give us enough room, we move to circles, and then spirals, etc. We will always need vehicles for our consciousness. When we are open minded, we can easily change vehicles. When we are closed minded, our boxes become prisons.

The transformational leader knows it is always upsetting to people to open the lids of their boxes and let some light in. Yet, that is what transformation requires. Transformation is getting people out of their boxes. This is the function of Coyote in Native American lore. Then along comes Raccoon who tries to help people live in the greater light.

Sometimes the light is too great and the time too soon. Love then dictates that we help people return to their boxes. The right thing at the wrong time is the wrong thing. Transformation is only an opportunity we provide to others. It is not a command.

To the degree that you are open minded and tolerant, you are a candidate for further transformation. When it is too much, you too will look for the comforting shadows of a familiar box.

TRANSFORMATIONAL LEADERSHIP 14

Practices Value-Based Decision Making

Transformational leadership is value-based. It places a high value on transformation, i.e., changing anything into its higher form.

The transformational leader believes in a continuous evolution of forms. By definition, any form is more advanced than it was in the past, and less advanced than it will be in the future. It is always in an intermediate stage. It is moving toward something. The something it moves toward will be more inclusive and differentiated. It will participate to a greater extent in the universe. The transformational leader attempts to accelerate the rate of natural unfoldment, i.e., to beat the rate of evolution.

Of course, any form of life may also devolve. This applies particularly to will-creatures. A theologian would call it sin. If advanced life forms make poor judgments over a period of time, a planet can become "lost" to the universe, at least for a time, perhaps forever.

Not only does a transformational manager value transformation, he/she also practices related values such as growth, unfoldment, synthesis, ecology, community, healing, system, inclusion, group, spirituality, collaboration, global, etc. Transformation is part of a value cluster.

In our new century, hospital managers will manage by transformational values. We will move slowly toward planetary values, that endorse the unfoldment of all planetary life forms. Competition will be transformed into collaboration as the interdependence of all planetary life is understood.

In the coming years, hospitals will begin moving toward their communities. Community values will become more important than institutional values. Curing values will be integrated with healing values. Prevention values will be integrated with treatment values.

Ultimately health is a spiritual value and health administration a spiritual pursuit. The patient's spirit vehicle must receive as much attention as the body vehicle.

The value of disease will be understood as a spiritual initiator. The value of death will be understood as celebration.

The healthcare administrator will face a major challenge in value education in his/her organization. In a high-tech society, most of the decisions are ethical ones. The "why" questions loom large.

In a cosmic perspective, our planet is known as a dark planet, i.e., a planet ruled by hate and aggression. It is primitive in its value structure. Religion has had a mixed effect. It has made some things better and other things worse.

Because transformation is a spiritual activity, it transcends religious differences. I believe that many religious hospitals will lead the way in transformational activities since their values are compatible with transformation—that is, if they avoid becoming mired down in doctrinal differences.

The transformational leader does not believe that ends justify means. If the means are not value consistent, they are not employed.

The big question for the transformational leader is, "what do you value?"

TRANSFORMATIONAL LEADERSHIP 15

Uses Conflict as a Creative Instrument

The transformational leader views conflict as an opportunity to achieve a higher order of resolution of the opposites. All of the created universe is upheld by polarity. The poles are always opposites. They are resolved in a higher order creation. The male and female are opposites resolved in the creation of the child. Gender at the physical level expresses itself as sexuality. It exists in all other dimensions and planes, but not as sexuality.

The swing of the opposites is used to produce stability in all lower order life forms. The forms swing one way and then the other to produce balance at the middle. You see this phenomenon in the tides of the sea and in the mood swings of an individual. You see it in the cycles of the biorhythm.

The greater the tension of the opposites, the greater the difference in electromotive potential, and the more power produced. A great deal of creativity is released in any conservative (repressed) person who later in life discovers the freedom of a more inclusive world view. It is the tension of restriction vs. freedom that generates the creative release.

With greater mastery of consciousness, the swing between the opposites is replaced by the ability to hold both poles simultaneously. Like a controlled nuclear reaction this yields a steady supply of high quality energy.

The transformational leader uses conflict to bring opposing parties together in the organization. By finding the "middle way," the energies of both parties are synthesized into new organizational creations. The secret is to balance the energies, not exhaust them by playing them against each other.

In a recent "confrontation," doctors who thought they were on the other side from the management discovered they were actually partners in an exciting new venture. If they had not been excited and mad (polarized) it would have been impossible to produce the energy release essential to the new synthesis.

Conflict is a powerful tool. When you feel the opposing energy, connect to it, harmonize it with its opposite energy, and return it in the birth of a new form. This is the power of reconciliation.

Interlude II

TRANSFORMATIONAL LEADERSHIP 16

Has a Well Developed Right Brain

The transformational leader has a well developed right brain.

Transformation requires intuitive perception and creativity. These are right brain functions. Of course, left brain function is important in implementation.

As a person or organization evolves, aesthetics plays a more important role. Increased personal or organizational sensitivity requires a higher order of artistic function. Highly evolved entities possess the beauty of symmetry and inner radiance.

Creation is not only functional, it is beautiful. Creation requires an artistic sense. For the same reason, helping a person realize her/his potential is as much a work of art as it is a work of science.

A hospital should not only be functional, it should be beautiful. In addition, it should possess consciousness altering properties. Ancient temples met all three criteria. Temples of the mind need to be constructed along similar lines.

Ritual, rite, celebration and ceremony are right brain creations. Their power is beyond the rational. This probably explains why hospitals have little activity in these areas. Most healthcare managers have been trained only on one side of the brain.

The transformational leader goes beyond the rational and invokes the power of the hidden splendor. He/she usually does this through imagery resonating deep with the psyche of the person or the collective psyche of the organization.

The twenty-first century healthcare organization is a mandala, a medicine wheel. It is an art form as well as an instrument for working in a rational world.

A child often utilizes right brain function. Many adults have forgotten how to access this kind of intelligence. In that sense, we must all become as little children. Many great spiritual leaders demonstrated this type of child-like innocence and instant knowing.

There are many good books written on exercising right brain function. If you are too far to the left, you will benefit from reading them and doing the exercises.

TRANSFORMATIONAL LEADERSHIP 17

Has Intuitive Perception

The transformational leader is intuitive. Intuition is immediate apprehension with no intermediate mental processes such as association or analysis. In intuition, you know that you know, but you do not know how you know.

Intuition is a mediated by higher centers in the brain. It should not be confused with instinct or sensing which is located in the solar plexus or feeling located near the heart.

We all have intuitive ability. It can be further developed with practice. When you "sleep" on a problem you are positioning it for possible solution. By refusing to use the analytic mind, you "turn on" intuition.

Since everything in the universe radiates its nature, you can know a thing by coming into resonance with it. Open yourself and allow its magnetic spectrum to impress your consciousness.

Intuition is a lunar brain function and depends upon your state of receptivity. This contrasts with expression which is a solar function. An intuitive speaker blends the lunar and solar aspects.

When the mind is quiet it is most open to intuitive impressions. You must learn to "rest your mind" upon things without thinking about them.

Intuition may manifest in your consciousness in the form of words or images. It may manifest at an even more subtle level, imageless thought.

To move from analysis to intuition you must "change your mind." With practice you become proficient at altering your consciousness.

Often when helping another person in his/her transformation you will receive intuitive impressions directly from the other person's higher consciousness. His/her soul views you as an ally and will impress you with information it cannot get through to its own person.

When transforming an organization you may perceive it in its future form. You touch its future thought form and know enough to help it become what it already is in future time. You have intuited its projection in future time.

If you want to be a transformational leader, you must develop your intuitive perception. The good news is, you can!

Interlude II

TRANSFORMATIONAL LEADERSHIP 18

Easily Passes Over to the Standpoint of the Other

A transformational leader passes over easily to the standpoint of other people. He/she has the ability to change the locus of consciousness from self to other. This is a special kind of "listening."

The average person is so egocentric that everything is perceived in relationship to self. The universe is seen as moving around himself/herself. A leader who has undergone the process of personal transformation has learned to move outside of the normal orbit of ego consciousness. Because, he/she is not caught up in internal noise, perception is much more acute and responds to the subtle radiations given off by other people.

Passing over to the standpoint of the other goes beyond empathy. At its most profound level it is a blending of consciousness. For a moment at least, the "two become one." For this to occur "permission" must be given by both parties involved. Without permission, intrusion would exist and this is a violation of cosmic law. However, permission may be given at a higher level (soul) of the person and not be known to his/her ego. Archetype can speak to archetype if the intention of one is to help and heal the other. In that sense, you can help another person against the will of his lower self, but not against the will of his higher self. Passing over to the standpoint of the other also permits you to know more about another person than he/she knows about himself/herself.

A transformational leader knows that All is One and One is All. We are all branches fed by the same vine. One branch can know another branch because they are connected (Christian).

When you see the world through the other person's eyes, their choices will make sense to you. If you look only through your eyes, their life will always be a puzzle. You can become a transformational leader when you learn to move outside the orbit of your ego consciousness.

TRANSFORMATIONAL LEADERSHIP 19

Opens Doors for People

A transformational leader is a mentor for other organizational members and is anxious to see everyone reach his/her full potential. Accordingly, the transformational leader uses his/her power to open doors of opportunity for those ready to move ahead in their lives and careers.

Happiness and fulfillment depend upon a match between consciousness and space. The job space should match the awareness and talent of the job holder.

A growing employee should outgrow his/her job space. Unless new challenges and opportunities are presented, stagnation is likely to set in.

Job re-design is an essential activity in all healthcare organizations. Re-design deals with both horizontal and vertical promotions.

The horizontal dimension is primarily concerned with gaining increased competence (knowledge)—knowing more about more things. The vertical dimension is primarily concerned with growth in consciousness (wisdom) and focuses upon issues of spirituality and the right exercise of power and accountability.

The vertical and horizontal dimensions intersect and form a cross. The vertical arm of the cross is spirituality. The horizontal arm is materiality. If you take the cross, transform it into a grid and place it over the organization, you can plot the spirituality vs. the materiality of a healthcare organization (you can do the same thing with a person).

Both material doors and spiritual doors should be opened for a person on the path of actualization and transcendence. A dimensional balance is required. This means that promotions in organizations should be designed to benefit individual employees as well as meet organizational needs.

The universal law of service assures that as we open doors for others, doors will be opened for us.

TRANSFORMATIONAL LEADERSHIP 20

Engages in Possibility Thinking

The transformational leader lives in a universe of infinite possibility waiting to happen. Nothing has to be the way it is. There is no one right way to do anything. For everything that is, there are an infinite number of things that could just as well be. You can always substitute one reality for another. If you do not like a reality, you do not defy it, you re-define it.

All reality is viewed as an outcome of the interaction of what is "out there" with what is "in here." The transformational leader is always a participant and can change reality by changing his/her participation. Reality is plastic and multidimensional. We can think of it as existing at various levels of density. At low density levels, mind alone structures it. At high density levels, it appears to exist independent of the way we think about it. This is not true, however. Even high-density reality changes over time if we change the way we think about it.

A highly potent consciousness can change high-density reality in the twinkling of any eye. This happens in the realm of magic, miracles, and healing.

The transformational leader understands that he/she manages reality. For every reality experienced there are many probable realities waiting to happen. It is important to be aware of these alternative realities and to consciously choose the reality you want to actualize for your organization. This is the purpose of the visionary group in the organization. By visioning, group members glimpse alternative realities.

The creative imagination of a small circle of visionaries is potent enough to create a whole spectrum of alternative realities. By sharing the vision and inviting people to elaborate the vision, they are enrolled in the process of altering the current reality in favor of a cherished alternative reality. The organization at this level of consciousness becomes self-designing and begins to reorganize its environment.

A given reality is held in place by the consciousness of the people who support it. If the people change their minds, the reality changes. This places an enormous responsibility on the leadership of the organization. Unless the leaders work from a position of expanded consciousness, the organization will suffer from suboptimal reality. What many leaders do is get caught up in the problem of adapting to an oppressive environmental reality, rather than changing it. The transformational leader, by contrast, is a magician and understands that all reality is subject to transformation.

Interlude II

TRANSFORMATIONAL LEADERSHIP 21

Has a Vision of the Future Organization

The transformational leader often utilizes a vision of possibility as catalyst for transforming individuals, organizations, and communities. The leader's vision, intuitively generated, is a probable future reality that must be acted upon by the client before it becomes an actuality.

The leader presents the vision as an opportunity for choice. The client must accept or reject the vision. The ethic of transformation requires the leader to bring the client to a free and enlightened choice regarding the future, but forbids the leader to compel a particular choice.

If the transformational leader is highly intuitive, she will see the array of alternative future realities open to the person, organization, or community. If the client is a person, the leader may also perceive which alternative future is most closely aligned with the client's well being.

The time dimension is more fluid in intuitive states of consciousness. The transformational leader uses intuition to extend her normal range of perception. By definition, the leader must be able to see "invisible" pathways leading to the future. Without this skill, "the blind lead the blind." This is a good example of the leader being qualified by consciousness. Being able to "see" has little to do with traditional credentials or previous business experience.

Since transformation is a spiritual activity, success in transformation rests upon the leader's spiritual depth. She can only take her client where she has been. She can only give the client what she has earned through her experience.

As healthcare moves in to the twenty-first century, it will be governed by collective visions of the communities it serves. We need transformational leaders who will teach the visioning process to community leaders.

As healthcare organizations leave their boxes to become spirals, we need transformational leaders who will generate the powerful organizational vortices needed to invoke the best futures imaginable. As healthcare moves into the twenty-first century we need transformational mentors to help our children envision and then create a healthy planet.

We envision in order to transform and thereby become the best we can be. The vision is our chosen destination.

TRANSFORMATIONAL LEADERSHIP 22

Frequently Experiences Synchronicity

The transformational leader frequently experiences synchronicity. Synchronicity is the tendency of related events to occur together. One event does not cause the other event. They occur together because they are related—much in the same sense as the head of a coin "causes" the tail of a coin.

The spiritual dimensions of the universe work by association. Like attracts like. What looks like coincidence is actually relationship. If you are working to accomplish the purpose and plan of the universe, the universe is working with you.

This type of spiritual association is always a source of great perplexity for linear thinkers. It is not logical. It comes and goes of its own accord. It cannot be commanded or produced on demand. Yet, it greatly adds to the efficiency and effectiveness of transformational leaders. Synchronicity can produce in minutes what hard work cannot accomplish in years.

Synchronicity is most likely to occur when you are in elevated states of consciousness. A few minutes "ascending the planes" may be the most efficient use of your time during the work day. We often accomplish in quiet meditation what is not available to us in hard thought.

The more you learn to depend upon the synchronous, the more available it becomes to you. It must be courted as a divine friend. It is a descent of grace. You must wait upon it, confident and accepting. You must thank it even when it fails to appear. Often it is working for you out of range of your perception.

Sometimes you will feel a fullness that is a forerunner of its appearance. You are pregnant and about to deliver. This is creation at its highest level and it depends upon your faith and stewardship. Synchronicity always has a gestation period which may be short or long. Rest assured—events that resonate with you are always moving toward you. They will appear when you need them.

Interlude II

TRANSFORMATIONAL LEADERSHIP 23

Assumes Responsibility for "What Is"

The transformational leader assumes responsibility for her environment. That is, she feels well placed in the environment and knows she is there to accomplish an appointed task.

We are where we are to do a job that needs to be done. When we have completed our job, the universe moves us to a new setting with new challenges.

Our space fits us. It contains the key to our development. It is an outer radiation of our consciousness. It is a womb. The most powerful spaces are often the most negative ones. We seldom learn much in a comfortable space. Mastery is gained by pushing against circumstances.

People often want to flee the very spaces they need to develop inner qualities of consciousness. Not only must the transformational leader assume responsibility for "what is," but also for "what could be." We must see the gap between the actual and ideal and then move to close the gap.

People often say, "What can I do, I can't change the CEO?" We focus on the outer interpersonal relationships rather than the inner connectivity of consciousness. Perhaps your role is to create positive thought forms that enter the stream of consciousness of the organization.

There are highly developed teachers who spend their lives creating positive thought forms to serve as vehicles for lesser developed brothers and sisters operating on lower levels of consciousness. Even in a very negative organization these powerful thought forms can exert a profoundly positive effect.

Remember you are always generating your environment. The environment is a solidification of the collective consciousness of humankind. You are part of humankind.

We need to practice developing positive thought forms. Any idea held with intensity tends to manifest on the material plane. The mentor builds a thought vehicle for his student to occupy. The mentor builds thought forms for his organization to occupy as it moves into its future.

The secret is to avoid being caught up in the negative turbulence of your organization. To transform anything you must project an image of possibility that is more potent than the thought form it currently occupies.

Easily perceives patterns or relationships

The transformational leader understands that the universe is composed of an infinite number of patterned energies. Nothing stands by itself. Everything depends upon something else and something else depends upon it. There is a vast harmony of interacting energies. The leader, therefore, looks for patterns and relationships, because he knows they exist at all levels.

Because everything is in relationship, changing one thing changes all things. The leader can change his consciousness and produce corresponding changes in the organization. The leader is always involved in a divine dance. He romances reality. Everything that happens is meaningful both as symbol and as reality. Everything means what it means in the most simple obvious way, and it also is a metaphor for deeper levels of significance.

Because of the multidimensional nature of reality, meaning exists on each of the dimensions or levels. An "accident" may be understood as a simple result of conflicting physical forces. It may also be a technique used by the soul to introduce a delay factor in a series of life events that are unfolding too fast for the person's good. Both explanations are "true" but exist at different levels of reality.

Understanding the deeper levels of meaning in any life pattern requires a meditative state where your ego is open to communication with your higher levels of consciousness. It is interesting that you must deal with reality at all levels of manifestation, i.e., you have a cast put on your arm and also meditate on the deeper level of significance of the accident.

Someday hospitals will have a special group of people who reflect upon the patterns and relationships experienced by the organization as well as meet in small vortex groups to create new patterns and relationships.

Because we are co-creators with the universe, we do not have to play only a defensive game. In addition to reacting we can act and recreate our organization's reality. If hospitals acted now to do the right things they could avoid some of the more punitive probable realities waiting to descend upon them. Like the hawk, they could fly over the swamp rather than slogging through and becoming mired in it.

Transformation goes way beyond adaptation. It changes the rules of the game. Hospitals will be forced to reform. They could instead choose to transform.

Interlude II

TRANSFORMATIONAL LEADERSHIP 25

Thrives on Chaos

The transformational leader thrives on chaos. Creation comes from the Void or primal chaos. Chaos is a precondition for creativity. Things must fall apart before they can fall together again in new and better ways.

The beginning years in our new century are years of chaos. Towers are falling. Traditions are failing. We will soon have a pile of building blocks where are proud institutions once stood. Once the energy captured by old forms is released, it is available for building new structures.

Many old systems do not have sufficient degrees of freedom to permit reformation. They are bound up in their past and unable to move into the future. They will not survive over the long term.

Destruction precedes creation. The transformational leader must often destructure a system before he can restructure it. Mental and psychic energies are tied to traditional symbols and keep pulling the organization back into its past rather than propelling it toward the future.

The manager must transform the organization's symbols, i.e., move energies grounded in the past to a modern expression. The same core ideas or values are retained but in an updated form.

What looks like chaos is actually a large pattern beyond your perception. It will eventually come into a clearer focus if you can hold it in your consciousness and wait for resolution. Generally you will feel in over your head.

In chaos dwell alternative realities and parallel futures. Chaos is the mother of manifestation and holds all potentials waiting for expression. It is the ground of Being. Since your ego wants order and structure it will always feel overwhelmed in chaos.

Your personal life too will go through chaotic periods when destructuring and restructuring are in order. Any initial freedom will eventually imprison you and you will have to break free from it. Illness, separation, sorrow, sudden opportunity, grace from heaven—all create chaos and release of bounded energy. Death too may be viewed as a period of chaos and destruction of obsolete forms pending a new birth.

TRANSFORMATIONAL LEADERSHIP 26

Often has a reverse perspective on things

The transformational leader often has a reverse perspective on things. By seeing behind appearances, the leader perceives an array of alternative realities waiting to happen. What is and what could be lurk behind the same surface manifestation.

Polarity alternates at different levels of reality. Just as a photographic negative has dark areas where there are white areas on the positive, so the level of pattern has a reverse polarity from its reflection in the dimension of form. The form is positive in relationship to its pattern.

Because of the reversibility of energies, the transformational leader knows that hate can be changed to love and fear to courage. By appropriately using his mind/body vehicle, the leader can reverse the energies of a group of people. This requires a reverse perspective and an ability to attract group energies and transform their polarity.

Energy reversal is the secret of transformation. It also explains why it is so difficult for any leader to work with an apathetic group. There is no energy to reverse. Since potential is negative to its manifestation in form, the leader must attract the negative energy by providing his vehicle as a positive channel of manifestation. If he gets caught up in the energy being manifested by the group he is positive to positive, and no transformation will occur. He must know his polarity at all times and change it as the need occurs.

Everything in the universe that can occur will occur and everything can occur in an open universe. This multidimensional nature of the universe creates alternative realities and parallel futures. The transformational leader knows that a given reality is only one of many that could just as well manifest. If he does not like a reality, the leader does not defy it, he simply redefines it. While other people react to what is, the transformational leader creates what could just as well be. His perspective is the reverse of his associates.

A powerful method of creating alternative realities is to use assumption reversal. Since assumptions structure reality, reverse assumptions create reverse realities. Perspective is a reality selector (maker).

The most important question you can ask a group is, "how do we choose to think about this?" The question creates a reality frame.

TRANSFORMATIONAL LEADERSHIP 27

Often motivates others by his presence

The transformational leader radiates an aura of joyful living with the freedom of self-determination and the wonder of journeying through an open universe. This often contrasts with the more limited view of associates. The contrast creates a ray of interest. How can this "up" person live in freedom while those around him seem to live in bondage to their life situations? Often the first contact between a protégé and a mentor is caused by this wonderment. There is a growing realization that the mentor lives in a different reality. The protégé is then highly motivated to experience that new reality.

The transformational leader radiates his nature. He emits an energy field that will resonate with any like-minded person in his proximity. The greater his energy, the greater the proximity of influence. The recipient must be open and ready to receive. Unless the "ground has been prepared" in the recipient, he will not detect and respond to the energy.

The transformational leader as mentor teaches more by his presence than by his words. That is why people like to be around him. They partake of his energy and corresponding changes begin appearing in their own lives. You must "pick up" the qualities of consciousness you desire for someone who is emitting them. No amount of study can produce this inner change. The mentor "primes your pump." Once the "baptism" occurs, you can continue to develop the energies on your own.

In all inner traditions, the mantle is passed from teacher to student. Much of this is an oral tradition. The teacher is qualified by consciousness to teach. The student is qualified by intention to learn. The student in turn becomes a teacher. This important property of true learning is often missed in modern institutions of higher education, where degrees are substituted for levels of consciousness. To graduate in any inner tradition, you must demonstrate consciousness via an initiation. There is then no doubt about your worthiness.

Remember, all of you affect every life form you contact. As a human energy system, you are a gardener of the planet. You motivate rocks, plants, animals, and people. All of creation awaits transformation. Higher consciousness always transforms lower consciousness. We serve and we are served. Big rings motivate smaller rings. It all goes together.

Discussion Questions:

How do you affect your associates?

How do you impact your organization?

TRANSFORMATIONAL LEADERSHIP 28

Has boundless energy and vitality

The transformational leader projects boundless energy and vitality. She resonates with higher order systems and pulls down energies into her body/mind vehicle. Because she is well grounded, she conducts energies to and from the body of the earth.

The transformational leader also is in alignment with her archetype. This archetype or energy hologram referred to as spirit in sacred writings is an infinite energy source that will electrify mind, emotions, and body if they are in sympathy with its expansion into earth manifestation.

Another reason for the energy and vitality of a transformational person is the absence of conflict in her psyche. The average person is conflicted and lacks integration and focus in life. Precious energy is burned up in the heat of conflict or dissipated in many uncoordinated channels of effort.

Transformation is an inner alchemical work that requires the presence of higher energies freely circulating through the mind/body and vehicle and focused upon appropriate action in the world. Appropriate action is any action in accord with the purpose and plan of the Source. The transformational leader "sources" these higher energies and brings them into manifestation in the material plane. As the energies circulate, mind, emotions, and body come into resonance with infinite spirit patterns.

A transformational manager practices "energy economy." Energy levels in the psyche are monitored at all times. When needed, energy levels can be doubled or tripled, or if desired, allowed to enter a quiescent state where kinetic energy is translated back into potential energy awaiting direction from consciousness. It is from these deep meditative states with tremendous potential energies that creation and the building of potent thought forms becomes possible.

If a manager allows herself to become "run down," the inner alchemical processes are slowed and the effectiveness of her action in the outer world is jeopardized. For this reason, transformational leaders spend the necessary meditative and reflective time needed to generate psychic energies and are very careful in the expenditure of these energies. As a result, they always are full of zest and vitality.

Discussion Question: Are you usually full of zest and vitality?

Interlude II

TRANSFORMATIONAL LEADERSHIP 29

Puts out "good vibes"

We all are surrounded by a strong "magnetic" field affecting everything that comes within its presence. We generate the field with our consciousness. Its strength and qualities are a function of the way we modulate energies sourced from inner dimensions. Our field interacts with all other fields in the universe. It affects and is affected by them. We all sense this field effect intuitively and say a person is putting out "good or bad vibes."

The transformational leader is pulling in high energies because she is attuned to overall cosmic purposes, i.e., the healing and restoration of the planet earth. These energies are not blocked or distorted by her ego, so she radiates a powerful presence that nurtures and restores all life forms. These energies manifest in her life space or work environment as synchronistic, synergetic, and serendipitous effects.

A group of transformational leaders working together blend energies and create vortex effects that can bend space, alter time and change circumstances. In the future they will form the nucleus of metanoic healthcare organizations that probe the limits of this creation space. Through mindlinking transformational leaders planet-wide will create "virtual organizations" that amplify and focus mind power on planetary restoration projects such as the cleansing of our noosphere (thought stream). Since virtual organizations do not exist in any tangible sense, they transcend the limitations of most high-density organizations. In a virtual organization, there is a natural hierarchy of consciousness. The bigger rings naturally enclose the smaller rings and all works in perfect harmony.

Global consciousness will soon be a reality. The new planetary paradigm nurtured by the twin roots of quantum physics and mythology is preparing mass consciousness for a radical mind change. WE ARE ONE SYSTEM! We are our brother's keeper.

In healthcare we will see evidence of the new paradigm with recognition of the hospital's mind field and its energic impact on patients, employees, and the community. Healing healthcare requires activation of our higher senses in order that we may perceive and direct transformational energies. All of these energies must pass through the body/mind vehicle of the healer. They must be conducted from one living system to another living system. The two systems must be tuned to one another to permit transfer. Doctors, nurses, and other care givers must be qualified by consciousness as well as possess the knowledge base needed to practice their specialty.

Managers too will be qualified by consciousness. They must create the special mental holograms that provide spiritual maps for employees to navigate as they enter new dimensions of consciousness. The organization's spiritual data banks will determine its future role and function.

Most of what managers do today will be delegated to other workers skilled in manipulating high densities. Spiritual mapping becomes the job of the CEO and executive leadership group. They must take the plasma of subtle mental substance and form it into highways for the mind and pathways for the organization. Here mental alchemy is the essential skill. This is the essence of transformation.

Discussion Question: Have you ever provided a spiritual map for another person?

Interlude II

TRANSFORMATIONAL LEADERSHIP 30

Attracts talented people to the organization

The transformational leader sounds a "note." Workers across the planet "hear" the note and are attracted to the organization. A small circle is formed. Energy builds. The organization becomes nodal. Like a beacon the organization sends its rays into all dimensions of consciousness.

Inside the organization a special space is being built that incubates new potentials. Like a womb it protects and nourishes its ideas and people. The organization becomes "magnetic" and attracts financial resources and favorable circumstances. Its vortex energies begin to reconstellate ordinary reality and move it toward an alternative reality.

People outside the organization look upon it with wonder. How does it manage to escape the common fate and set its own course? Where are all these new people coming from? Have they known each other before? What is the energy you feel when you walk down the halls?

There is the organization that everyone sees, the external form. Then, there is the organization of the mind, it is held in the consciousness of the few. These mental creators build out the energy hologram that organizes events in the material dimension. As above, so below.

The transformational leader is a mental alchemist. He knows how to bring together the essential people, in the right place, at the right time to do the appointed task. By surrounding his people with an encompassing mind field, the transformational leader enables them to do their work.

For workers in a nodal organization, work is high play and every day is an adventure in consciousness. Each person gives and grows. The small circle of transformational leaders have arrived from various corners of the earth and meet once again to accomplish their appointed tasks. A love joins them. Bonds of consciousness are so strong they cannot be broken by adversity or strife. Each person knows and is known by every member of the group. They work together on the vanguard of consciousness.

As hospitals become nodal organizations they assume spiral forms. They organize themselves as circles, within circles, within circles. Group consciousness becomes the operative mode. People act in concert with one another. Each knows and respects the abilities of the other. High levels of integration create organizational metanoia.

Gets more done in less time

The transformational leader gets more done in less time. This is partly attributable to an actual alteration in the time dimension. In more inclusive thinking (big circles), human consciousness moves through space, and therefore, time more rapidly. More is taken into account. This generates precognitive and retrocognitive effects. With more of the past and the future in view, cognition operates in a wider and more efficient field of perception. What others struggle to understand, the transformational leader takes in at a single glance.

The transformational leader is also operating in a higher energy state. This permits her to access more readily the mental and spiritual dimensions of the universe. If an answer to any problem has ever been thought by anyone, its representation flows in the thought stream and is therefore available to the transformational leader.

High energy also creates a resonance with other intelligences in the universe and may result in a kind of entrainment or resonance where the higher mind downloads into the lesser mind. This is called "overshadowing." In a word, the transformational leader gets a lot of help from other living beings. Synchronicity also plays a vital role here. The transformational leader projects a question with such intensity that the answer rushes toward her. The number of occurrences of synchronicity provides a rough measure of the degree to which you are tuned into the universe.

The transformational leader is also more aware of the cosmic purpose and plan on this planet. She is a cosmic surfer. By catching the waves, she amplifies her actions many times over. While many managers try to stop the wave, the surfer utilizes the wave to take her to a chosen destination. The leader often stops to ask, "what is the universe trying to do here?" Once she knows this, she acts in concert with the universe's intentions.

Transformational leaders also spend regular periods in meditation. Here, they charge their batteries and reduce stress levels. With more life force flowing through their mind/body vehicles, efficiency is much improved.

Lastly, the transformational leader does not engage in negative thinking or other energy reducing activities. The practice of psychic economy makes anyone more efficient. Some managers waste more energy worrying than they need to get the job done. For all of these reasons, transformational leaders get more done in less time.

TRANSFORMATIONAL LEADERSHIP 32

Organization thrives under his/her guidance

The transformational leader builds a circle around his/her group, department, or organization. It is a charmed circle. It is a circle of protection and nurturance. Within the circle each employee is encouraged to self-actualize, expand management skills, and serve humankind in new ways.

The circle is maintained by the consciousness (power) of the leader. It is an aura that deflects negative outside influences. It cannot, however, protect group members from themselves. They must still make mistakes, learn, and unfold their potentials, as must all life forms in the Cosmos. The circle creates a powerful invitation, but does not compel behavior from those who occupy it. The size and potency of the circle depends upon the power being transmitted through the leader.

Transformational leaders do not generate their own power. They are "plugged" into the Source and simply convey the power to the planet and its life forms. Being empty of ego, they do not distort the power or color it with their personalities.

Many employees need this type of "jump start" to get their own development underway. Outside the circle they are subject to too many divisive forces to maintain a steady course of development. Inside the circle they borrow the power of the leader (mentor).

Of course the transformational leader must maintain the circle in a high density organization often filled with people not yet ripe for consciousness expansion. This requires the leader to have well developed political and managerial skills. She is able to do this because she does not come from the point of ego but from the standpoint of principles and universal values. Although other power holders in the organization may not understand her, they are influenced by her and understand that something different is going on in the circle and that they had best leave it alone.

The vibratory rate of a powerful circle generates a vortex action. It separates spiritual substance by density. People ready for the circle are attracted to it. People not ready for the circle are repelled by it. Each rate of consciousness finds its own level.

The transformational leader creates a safe harbor for her people. This harbor is an organizational womb and loom.

Views problems as opportunities

The transformational leader views problems as opportunities. He is always trying to translate Spirit into matter and appreciates the difficulties in translation. The third dimension has a high density and "resists" the imprint of Spirit. However, once imprinted it tends to retain the imprint over time. Like a statute carved in stone, it maintains the sculpture even in the absence of the sculptor. This is not true of many other dimensions such as the dream dimension, where out of mind means out of existence.

The transformational leader also develops mastery by "pushing against the density" of the third dimension. Learning has a very tangible quality in this dimension. In fact, some things can only be learned here. Without resistance, muscle cannot be developed.

In fact transformational leaders often seek out problems in order to create an expansion of consciousness. They often seek what others try to avoid. Crisis is a precondition of consciousness. If things are not going well, you are probably learning something. The idea that high consciousness people have few problems is false.

Weaknesses and liabilities will surface if you are on the "fast track." They precipitate matching life events. The eager leader may have more problems than he can handle. How else can he be trained to be of world service. If the little things throw him, he will be of little service when facing the big things.

There is satisfaction in mastery. Mastery is demonstrated in difficult situations. The transformational leader does not go around causing problems, but the problems in him go around attracting situations. You are attracted to situations where you can learn. Situations are attracted to you for resolution. Always accept responsibility for what is around you. You are it and it is you. Change yourself, and you change your life situation. Reality is a dance. You are one of the partners. You start out being led in the dance. Eventually, you lead the dance. But, it is always a dance.

You are a running total of what you have experienced. All experience is gained in life spaces. A design for life space is a design for consciousness. What space are you now in?

What are you meant to learn in your current space? Why was it attracted to you? What do you need to do to resolve the current dilemma? If you know the answers, you are well on the way to your own transformation.

Interlude II

TRANSFORMATIONAL LEADERSHIP 34

Transmutes negative energy

The transformational leader knows that her body/mind vehicle is an energy machine. She knows that her vehicle is a microcosm of the macrocosm. All the energies flowing through the universe flow through her. Learning the right use of energy is a requirement for her personal transformation.

Negative energies are disordered. They have lost harmony with the pulse of the universe. As rogue energies, they tend to disorder all they touch. Yet, they are powerful and can be utilized as fuel for individual and organizational transformation.

Transformation transmutes negative energies. It is an alchemical reaction carried out in the body/mind vehicle of the transformational leader. The leader takes in the negative energy and by staying in a neutral emotional position, gives it a reverse spin. The more negative it comes in, the more positive it goes out.

Either high negative or high positive energies further transformation. Only indifference, or passivity is not reversible. It is hard to reverse the course of something that does not exist. If inertia is the condition, then, the transformational leader uses her own energy to spark a change. Because she practices psychic economy, she has a ready reserve to deploy. As the leader begins to emit energy, passive people will be activated and observers will feel the energy level in the room begin to rise. This energy is like a blood transfusion. It will nurture back to health, listless, drifting people. This may have to occur several times before the passive people are "jump started." Several transformational leaders working together can create an energy vortex that moves hundreds or thousands of people.

Of course, if the transformational leader is vulnerable and reacts to the negative energy, she cannot transmute it. She then becomes part of the problem rather than part of the solution. You learn energy balancing by falling down on your face. When you blow it, go back and see what tripped you.

Eventually you will be able to perceive the energy spectrum radiated by any person or group and will know how to proceed. Until then, use your best judgment. Of course, any person or group can reject the opportunity you offer them. In that case, hand back the cleansed energy as a gift from you to them. They are better off for having met you and may return at a point of greater readiness. Remember, in alchemy, lead is transmuted into gold. You are a spiritual alchemist. Seek out the lead and refine it in your retort of awareness.

Interlude II

TRANSFORMATIONAL LEADERSHIP 35

Removes boundaries

The transformational leader is a boundary spanner. He realizes the universe is unbounded. Boundaries are created by limited human consciousness. They can be removed only by a change of mind. A boundary is the circumference of your consciousness. Inside the ring is everything you know. Outside the ring is everything you don't know.

The future is about getting people and organizations out of small rings into bigger rings. Some folks have been living in small rings so long it distresses them when you suggest the possibility of life in a larger ring. Small rings provide security by creating a false message that your ring is the only ring in existence. People who live in small rings know little about people living in larger rings and assume all people experience the same reality.

The mindset that changes small rings into larger rings is contained in the following statements: "What you are doing is just as important as what I am doing. We are both working as parts of the same thing. If we know more about one another, we can work more closely together and we will both be better off and so will our shared project."

Any group technique which encourages small ring dwellers to find their places in a larger shared ring will bring about an expansion of consciousness. A medicine wheel is a good example of this.

Trading-in small rings for larger rings is a primary task of all transformational managers. The small rings may be hospital departments, medical subspecialties, or different organizations in the same community.

A big ring thinker needs to be well versed in quantum physics. Quantum thinking is at great variance with classical physics and the classical worldview. In the quantum world there are no separate objects contained in empty space interacting with each other in simple deterministic ways.

The transformational manager should help his organization take the "quantum leap" in consciousness. Workshops on the quantum worldview need to be conducted with an opportunity for all participants to develop cognitive skills essential in quantum operations and understandings.

As we move toward big ring thinking, healthcare will go through four evolutionary stages: (1) anarchy, (2) competition, (3) cooperation, and (4) integration. Quantum understandings are essential for entry into stages 3 and 4. If you think healthcare organizations should be engaged in zero sum competition, you cannot lead them into cooperation or integration. When you remove the false boundaries between healthcare organizations, you are leading them into Stage 3. Organizations must be in Stage 3 for some time before you can move them into Stage 4.

We all have a spiritual ring, a mental ring, an emotional ring, and a physical ring. The rings may be different sizes. For instance, your mind may be better developed than your emotions. The transformational manager needs a symmetrical development of all rings.

Expansion of the spiritual ring permits you to enter multidimensional realities. Expansion of the mental ring brings increased insight and intelligence. Expansion of the emotional ring enables you to feel the radiation given off by all things. Expansion of the physical ring gives increasing control of your physical body.

An underdeveloped ring creates a developmental liability. It represents the point of your potential fall. This liability will attract matching circumstances thereby enabling you to learn the needed lessons and expand your ring size.

It is very comforting to know you are not limited to the size of your current ring. You may expand your ring whenever you wish. Growth is always up to you. The universe does not limit your awareness. You have created your existing boundaries and you must dissolve them. As your ring expands you gain in wisdom, power, resources, and accountability. You move from victim to victor.

TRANSFORMATIONAL LEADERSHIP 36

People are "uplifted" by her counsel

The transformational leader is operating at a high velocity of consciousness. She puts out powerful vibes that expand energy fields of all life forms. This produces a "lift" effect in people around her. They feel more positive, receive an energy transfusion and find their mental horizons expanding. Like flowers seeking out the sun, employees seek out the transformational leader for her enLIGHTenment.

High energy flow also makes the transformational leader a healer. Her ordered energies tend to induce order in a patient's disordered system. This happens automatically, but even more so if the leader intends the healing transmission and is trained in therapeutic touch.

We all depend upon mentors to introduce us to the higher energies that will expand our consciousness. The mentor permits us to tap into her energy field in order that we may know what it feels like, i.e., how to get to it. This may or may not happen in the physical presence of the mentor. These energies operate at a distance as well as locally. It is hard to command what you cannot imagine and have never felt You can get a lot out of books but all advanced work is mentor to protégé. It must also happen when life circumstances permit it.

The transformational leader can also induce an "uplifting" effect by perceiving the hidden potential in the archetype of the protégé and then begin working to release it. In these cases the protégé is often required to do difficult things that will permit the eventual breakthrough.

The "uplift" feeling is celestial. It is the highest feeling a human being can experience. It is sometimes called the heavenly manna. Once perceived, no ego feelings or earthly accomplishments can match it. It produces a divine intoxication. That is one of the problems. The transformational leader may keep her head in the clouds, but her feet have to be planted firmly on the ground. There is a lot of work to be done in this dimension before we leave it for a better home. Once you have experienced mystical "uplift," you understand how slow and dark this dimension is. It feels like walking through molasses.

When an employee has been put in "touch with herself" (sensed her archetype), there is no longer a problem with motivation and job performance. From the higher altitudes her job will look different, however, she now has a sense of life direction and an appreciation for excellence in all that she does. She knows that she will qualify herself for residency in higher dimensions by her performance in this one. A poor craftsman here is not promoted to work in the beyond. Work is work, in whatever dimension, and the same standards of quality apply. Promotion depends upon mastery and performance, commensurate with ability.

TRANSFORMATIONAL LEADERSHIP 37

Is lighthearted in adversity

The transformational leader receives "bumps" in life just like everyone else. Adversity is a characteristic of life in the third dimension. The difference is, the transformational leader takes downturns as a matter of course, knowing that polarity is a requirement of third dimensional manifestation. A high requires a low. A white requires a black. Happiness cannot exist without sadness. Duality is a characteristic of material manifestation. Duality does not exist above the level of creation.

Since the transformational leader lives by the law of cause and effect, for the most part he is master of his destiny. He intentionally engages in positive actions and waits for beneficial results. However, because he is also a member of a family, social group and nation, he is often caught-up in group effects, although he did not directly generate the causes.

A transformational leader, as an act of grace, may "buy-into" the negative effects being experienced by another human being. Love is then expressed in sacrifice. He meets the effects meant for his "friend." Since All is One, we cannot separate ourselves from the life experience of our brothers and sisters. By helping them we help the All. Although there is justice in the universe, there is also love. Love is the higher law.

Imagine a healthcare organization operated on the principle of love. Each person is his "brothers' keeper." Love heals the employees. Love heals the patients. The organization becomes a fully functional family in the best sense of the word. Mentors abound. A natural hierarchy of consciousness exists. The wise lead the way. Those who stumble are lovingly placed back on their feet. The organization is fully integrated by its shared vision. Each member of the organization feels a "calling." As each employee serves she is transformed by her service. It is hard to imagine, but that is where we are going in future healthcare.

Although you will experience negative conditions in your life, if you meet them with a positive outlook, you will transcend and eventually transform the conditions themselves. Nothing is in manifestation without a support structure. By beaming in positive energy, you alter the support structure and then the manifestation. It is all about energy fields, your energy field and the energy field of the environment. It is always a dance and you always have a partner.

With the right attitude, the fires of adversity become fuel for your alchemical transformation.

TRANSFORMATIONAL LEADERSHIP 38

Knows that "this too shall pass"

Transformation is about continuous change. Nothing in the manifested universe remains constant. All is in flux. Whatever situation you are in, good or bad, this too shall pass.

The transformational leader understands that everything in manifestation is held in a matrix of balanced and interacting forces. Everything manifests in its current form as long as the precipitating balance of forces remains constant. If the balance is altered, manifestation changes.

Any event comes into manifestation because of an initial energy "charge" and will "build itself out" until the initial charge is exhausted or the matrix is impacted by new and potent energies. We might say, "things run their course" unless interrupted. The transformational leader often represents the interruption.

As healer, the transformational leader disturbs the disease producing matrix in a patient. As organizational change agent, she disturbs the disease producing matrix in the organization. There are two major variables here: (1) do you choose to intervene? and (2) how competent are you? If you choose not to intervene, things follow their natural course. If you choose to intervene and are competent enough to do so, your energy impacts and alters the matrix and manifestation changes. The patient is healed. The organization recovers. In both cases, a new balance of forces is created. You have "connected yourself" to the new matrix. Since you have "bought-in," you now have a new accountability for future outcomes. Of course, refusing to "buy-in" is also an act of accountability. In this instance you are accountable for your non-involvement.

You are changing as everything around you is changing. Everything is in mutual interaction. You are dancing the dance. You may choose your dance partners or be chosen by new dance partners. In any case, you are always part of the dance and can always change the dance. If you do nothing, things will eventually change of their own accord. If you do something, you can change them now.

The best transformation is the accelerated evolution of a person, object or thing. You as mentor help it become what it already is in potential but has not yet arrived at in expression. You shorten the path of unfoldment. You provide an opportunity for something to move into a higher form of its expression. You will only help a thing become what it is, never, what it is not.

If you are in a bad situation, "this too shall pass." If you wait long enough, natural forces of evolution will break-up the situation. On the other hand, as a transformational leader, you may elect to enter the fray and re-balance the forces. This is always your option. You are a spiritual warrior. You cannot fight every battle that comes along. Your developing powers of discrimination will tell you when to engage and when to walk away.

TRANSFORMATIONAL LEADERSHIP 39

Expands people's rings

The transformational leader is committed to expanding rings of consciousness of all life forms, thereby liberating their potentials and accelerating planetary evolution. The leader knows he is connected to all life and therefore must share its destiny. Only when a person is in the grip of his personal ego, does he think he will be saved while all else is lost. The universe is one fabric. Everything affects everything else. Help one thing and you help all things.

The leader expands other people's rings by acting as a mentor and aiding them in their growth efforts. He sees potential and understands the environment needed to trigger its unfoldment. The job space is one potent environment the transformational leader uses for employee unfoldment. Other environments outside the job are also often necessary to complete an overall development strategy.

The energy consciousness radiated by a transformational leader is a powerful "magnetic" field that stimulates dormant growth potentials in anyone ready to "listen." The field may have enough intensity to fill an auditorium or be felt throughout an entire organization. The leader nurtures by his presence. Thoughts will be carried from his mind to all minds. Teaching is done in silence. The "field effect" is the hidden dimension of a mentor. Results in the lives of his protégés can be explained in no other way.

The ring of consciousness represents the amount of the universe a person can take into awareness. It represents his known world and defines his reality. Events outside the ring cannot be perceived. The mentor may use his energy to "force the students ring." The student is usually unable to hold the expansion for long. However, once the student has witnessed the greater reality, he wants to return to it. This provides the hope and motivation for more self-work.

Consciousness rings should expand more rapidly as we age. Since experience builds upon experience, the rate of ring expansion will eventually become logarithmic. Unfortunately, in some adults the rings shrink. Consciousness is never static. If it does not progress, it regresses to an earlier stage of its development. Many adults are in arrested development. They have stopped using their minds. We have lots of "mind shrinkers" in our culture. TV often fills this role. Reading a difficult book, or accepting a tough job assignment, by comparison, expands the mind. What is the condition of your ring? Is it bigger than last year? What are you currently doing to stretch your ring?

TRANSFORMATIONAL LEADERSHIP 40

Increases your "mental velocity"

The transformational leader uses the power of ideas to transform the consciousness of her organization. These "cluster ideas" are sprinkled throughout the organization. The clusters form a matrix that attracts associated ideas from the hospital staff and before long a new organizational myth is born.

Most people's lives are built around a rather small set of core constructs (ideas). These constructs are over-elaborated and in time create a confining reality frame for the person. They form a perceptual grid that may eventually become a closed cognitive system. No transformation is possible in a closed system. The transformational leader creates an alternative set of ideas and makes them available to members of her organization. These ideas have a large expansion potential. They are alternative world views and have the power of liberating people from their imagined constraints. At first, organizational members will be fearful of letting go of old ideas. The transformational leader must support these organizational members until they develop the courage to move forward in their thinking.

As minds open to the new idea clusters, the mental velocity of employees is quickened. They suddenly become aware of unrealized potentials and new opportunities in the environment.

The transformational leader must "sense" which idea clusters are appropriate at any given stage in the evolution of her organization. The right ideas at the wrong time are the wrong ideas. Sequencing the organization's development is always a challenge and more difficult than sequencing an individual's development. The transformational leader depends upon her intuition and experience in making this vital discrimination.

Visionary transformational methods depend upon instilling new and more inclusive images in people's minds. Images are actually more creative than words. The transformational leader often discovers these new images in her inspirational reading and spiritual meditations. Often the images and ideas have been placed in the thought stream by spiritual teachers working to advance the evolution of humanity.

Once an image or idea is seeded in the consciousness, it rests there until the person is ready to utilize it. The idea or image then rises above the natural limen of consciousness with a burst of energy. This is the quantum leap.

The high mental velocity induced by the transformational leader creates a "stimulus hunger" in the followers. They seek out the leader in order to be "fed." The mental and spiritual level of the entire organization begins to rise. People who are not ready or do not want to grow become uncomfortable and will often seek out other employment. This is not bad since every person needs to be where he needs to be. If the healthcare organization begins to rapidly evolve, not everyone is ready to make the necessary changes.

Transformation is never a comfortable process. It requires a cognitive, emotional, and spiritual stretch and the learning of new habits of being and doing. Yet, that is what we are about on this planet. To refuse to transform means you will eventually be thrown out of the forward evolutionary current of the planet. You have a right to regress, but not the right to hold others back. The good news is, no one can hold you back and there are always plenty of people to help you move forward.

TRANSFORMATIONAL LEADERSHIP 41

Explores alternative realities and parallel futures

The transformational leader understands the multidimensional nature of the universe. He knows that "what is," need not be, and can be replaced by many alternative realities, each of which creates parallel futures. Reality is a participative event. The transformational leader "romances" reality and understands that as he changes his mind, he changes his reality.

Quantum physics gives a clear rationale for the existence of parallel universes and empowers us to become participant observers. Mythology enables us to use our creative imagination to spin and then occupy alternative worlds.

In time, the earth will become a "designer planet." As we escape the orbit of natural evolution, humankind assumes its role as designer, custodian, and guardian of the planet earth. We begin co-creating with the Source to recreate Eden. You can see the beginning of this movement in our global efforts to restore the physical environment. The "greening" of consciousness will pick up momentum in the next few years.

A polluted earth is one reality—the one we are currently affirming. Its future is a dead planet. A non-polluted planet is an alternative reality and one we will soon be affirming. It produces a parallel future with a living planet. In absolute terms one alternative reality is no more "real" than another. We can have either one we want. We will get what we create.

As healthcare professionals, our challenge is to empower our institutions and communities to create realities of their own choosing. This requires a paradigm shift or a radical restructuring of community consciousness. An unhealthy community is no more "real" than a healthy community. We are the creators of both. Yet, most people like to put the power outside themselves and blame the government, the devil, or someone else for all of our disease and distress.

It is time for the hospital to step out and take the lead in community-based healthcare redesign. Healthcare can only be reformed from the bottom up. It will not happen from the top down. The difference between victim and victor is consciousness. It has nothing to do with the inherent nature of the universe.

Transformation allows humankind to occupy new worlds and achieve what it can collectively imagine. We should accept no less. We need transformational leaders to make that vision a reality.

Views reality as preference, not necessity

The transformational leader knows that ultimately we manage only our preferences. Our assumptions create our strategies. Our strategies create our outcomes. We work for the outcomes we prefer. Our preferred outcomes are a statement of our values. All management is value based. The question is, "Whose values will prevail? Will we use institutional values or community values?"

In the coming few years, community values will be declared preeminent. Healthcare providers will be viewed as community servants working together for the good of the community. This will require a change of mind for some providers who have been oriented primarily toward their bottom line. This change of mind also heralds collaboration and resource sharing as the watchword of the 90s.

The reality we now face in healthcare in the United States is the reality we have created. The chickens have "come home to roost." There is no one to blame but ourselves. We are the creators of our world. Things do not need to be as they are.

Our new century is a period of empowerment. We must claim responsibility for the way things are, and more importantly assume responsibility for changing them. The federal and state government cannot bail us out. Healthcare is a local issue and must be solved locally.

The locus of control is within our healthcare organizations. We have the resources and power to transform the system. We do not yet have the will. Does the healthcare system in the United States need to bottom out, or can we begin now to make the necessary changes before the pain threshold increases?

The final test of any planet is its value system. The test comes only when the planet is capable of utilizing its technology to destroy itself. We are approaching the time of planetary initiation. In our new century, the planet earth, third from the sun, will either blink "on" or blink "off."

Our challenge is to heal the planet. The first step in planetary restoration is to heal your community. This is an exercise in transformational leadership. Will you invite the "movers" and "shakers" in your community to participate in the dialogue? We do not have time to waste.

View your competitors as allies. See disease, disability, poverty, and ignorance as the enemy. We fight not against one another, but against the powers of darkness in high places. Even now we enter the era of a politics of consciousness. Ideas must become ideals. Ideals must become the law of the land. We must elect politicians who can lead us into the new era. Values, knowledge, and power must come into balance. We will survive together or perish together. At this point in our planetary evolution there is no insulated or privileged class. We are One.

Views management as design

The transformational leader knows that managers of contemporary healthcare organizations are designers, architects of the future of their institutions.

In former times managers were maintainers. They worked within the existing structure of their organizations. In our rapidly changing age, maintenance is no longer an option. Organizations must change their forms as quickly as the environment changes. They must change more quickly, if they wish to be leaders and exert a shaping influence on their communities.

Organizational transformation requires a vision or plan for unfoldment. This vision must be generated by the employees of the organization. They must be enrolled in the visioning process. The transformational leader is the initiator and orchestrator of the visioning process. She must be able to turn people on to the process without dictating end results. If she is a visionary herself, she must not use her power or influence to override the visions of others. This is the skill of incubation. It occurs when the transformational leader creates the right "mental field" for the group. Her energy is used to stimulate and expand the consciousness of everyone in the visioning group. Often to her surprise, her personal vision may come out of the mouths of other group members who are resonating with her consciousness.

Design is the mental hologram that provides an energy matrix needed for manifestation. For rapid manifestation, the design image should attain crystal clarity. Pictures, models, drawings, or computer images help attain this clarity. The secret of creation or manifestation is non-ambiguity. A group may need to spend considerable time melding the separate images of its members. A single thought form or matrix empowered by the group is a living vortex of power that clusters the atoms needed for manifestation. If this degree of power cannot be achieved, then the group must depend upon the synchronicity of external events to provide an indirect path of manifestation.

Design is a full-brained activity. The right brain generates the image. The left brain implements the image. These separate brain functions may be contained within the mind of the transformational leader or may be distributed among various group members.

The transformational leader may dip into the thought stream to seize images as they "float by" or she may generate images herself, sourced from her reading, study and life experiences. It takes some skill to determine where the images originate. However, it makes little difference. A good image is a good image.

TRANSFORMATIONAL LEADERSHIP 44

Easily senses the moods, emotions and intentions of others

The transformational leader has developed a high degree of capacity to "listen." He does this by putting all self concerns out of mind and by tuning in to the moods, emotions, and intentions of another person. He becomes a receptive medium that can be impressed by the energy field of any other life form.

Everything radiates its nature. The energy emission is simply a part of its indwelling energy and is therefore identical in all respects to it. It may be read by any consciousness attuned to it. A human being puts out a very strong field, more so, than a mineral, plant, or animal.

The energy is easiest to read when the transformational leader is in the personal presence of the other person, but may also be read at a distance through the leader's extension of consciousness. The leader may simply read the person's energy or seek to modify it through his own countertransmission. If the leader is operating at a potent level of consciousness, he can temporarily override a weaker field. Of course, this should only be done if the other person is seeking help and has given consent to the energy transfusion. This is essentially what happens in healing. The healer is operating in a high energy state and can convey powerful healing thoughts that are incorporated into the energy field of the patient. The same type of relationship takes place between a mentor and his protégé.

As with any type of transfusion, the healer needs to transmit "untainted energy." If the healer is caught up in any type of negativity, it is transmitted to the patient. Also, if the healer has not escaped the orbit of his own ego, his reading of another person will be distorted. Often what the immature healer sees in the other person is simply a reflection of his own unresolved problems. In this case, the blind lead the blind.

Since transformation requires the conduction of spiritual energies, the leader must practice some regular type of spiritual discipline. He cannot transmit what he cannot conduct. This is the difference between leaders who talk about metanoia and those who perform miracles.

Learn to listen to a person's words and then sense their corresponding energy transmission. If the energy is not there, the person is all words. Powerful teachers often teach best in silence. They say nothing but project a potent teaching energy that creates appropriate thought forms in the minds of their students. A skilled teacher may be teaching verbally on one level and mentally on several other levels. Each student hears at his own level. If students compare notes, they will discover they were taught different things.

Gives inspirational presentations

When a transformational leader gives a presentation, it consists of more than just words. A subtle energy is encoded into the words and the message is transmitted simultaneously on as many levels of consciousness as embodied by the leader. This permits a wide range of hearers to decode the energies at their individual levels of understanding. Each hears a different message.

When a leader's words are not a representation of her consciousness, they sound hollow and unconvincing. Her energy does not correlate with her words. It is difficult for an audience to gain anything from this kind of transmission.

The energies transmitted by the leader are part of her essence. They come from her psychic energy stream and can transfuse anyone operating at a lower energy level. Because she loses energy in the transfusion, she must have a good connection with the Source for ready replenishment.

The effectiveness of a transformational leader's communication depends more on her energy level than her words. If something very important is at stake she will go "into the wilderness" to build energy through communion with God and nature. This is the basis of the vision quest. When her energy is at the right level, she will communicate her message and her words will be fiery darts that strike at the heart of the problem and move it toward resolution.

Energy potency is at the heart of all religious magic. There is nothing magic in the words. They are only containers for the magician's energy.

Psychic energy is accumulated through right living, meditation, and avoidance of energy "sinks" that drain away potency. When the empowered magician speaks, all nature listens and responds.

When you listen to a speaker you can determine the extent of her connection with the Source (God). A high energy transformational speaker gives you enough energy to accomplish feats you could never do unaided. You actually borrow her energy for a time and can rechannel it for your own healing and actualization. The mentor provides this type of energy for her protégé.

It is important for you to constantly monitor your level of psychic energy (life force). When it falls below a critical level, do not attempt a critical communication until you have restored your potency. Avoid things that pull your energy down. Notice what builds your energy. When you approach an energy sink (person or situation), put up your energy shield to avoid loss. This type of "cloaking" is necessary to protect yourself from psychic vampires. Some negative people will "suck" the energy out of you. They feed off unwary souls.

The next time you are going over the draft of a speech you are going to give, choose the right words, but remember the outcome of your communication will depend more upon your "energy state" when you make the presentation than upon your words.

Words spoken with extreme energy potency are creative. They begin immediately to move their associated internal images toward manifestation on the material plane. Words spoken with low potency dissipate quickly on the mental plane and never become manifest. High potency words permit co-creation with the Source.

As you gain energy, you are a greater force for good or evil in the universe and your accountability increases. At some point, you are recruited by either the forces of light or darkness on this planet. When your energy mastery "turns the bell on upstairs," you must count for one side or the other. It is up to you. You may be transformed into either an angel or a demon. You will sway crowds for either good or evil. Powerful forces are ready to respond to your words. By your words, you are blessed. By your words, you are cursed. And the same is true of those who listen to you.

Releases the power in a group

Future healthcare organizations are managed by groups. All organizational employees are group members. Teams make important organizational decisions, implement needed solutions, and hold themselves accountable for desired outcomes.

In the future triangular organizations become circular organizations. The power of groups replaces the power of single individuals directing organizations. The transformational manager becomes a first among equals. He is recognized by all group members as the most developed member of the group. He exhibits the most inclusive orbit of consciousness. Yet, he never uses this status to override the group's collective will. He serves as the focal point of group consciousness and the appointed channel for its expression. Yet, he always remains a servant leader. He does not take the group where it refuses to go.

This new organizational form requires managers skilled in group development. Traditional managers have been trained to act as solo players rather than players in concert with others. By contrast, transformational managers must be trained to orchestrate the consciousness of groups and release their collective powers.

The transformational manager must evolve a group structure that permits full actualization of each group member. This requires an appreciation for group diversity, a tolerance for individual styles of expression, and a recognition of each member's consciousness and potential.

With time and know how, a collection of individuals is forged into a group. With further development the group evolves into a small circle, the most potent form of power known in divine magic. Members of small circles think as one mind and generate vortex power. Vortex power reconstellates reality events. Thus, the destiny of future organizations hinges upon the potency of its groups rather than the exigencies of its environment.

Group members are carefully selected and matched to one another and to the task to be accomplished. Energy must flow through the circle without disruption. Any member has the potential to negate the circle, hence each member is held responsible for the circle's integrity. As the circle's collective consciousness grows, members learn to "read" one another and can tell immediately if there is a problem with one of the members. In a well functioning circle, the subtle is visible and the unmanifest is perceived. Of course to operate at this level, group members have to be free of ego and its associated psychological problems. Although this is quite a severe requirement for contemporary health groups, it will be achieved before the end of this century.

Our new century is evolving a mental and spiritual paradigm focused upon inner realities. Management is increasingly viewed as an inner activity reflected into the outer world. Current preoccupation with the material and the outer is even now beginning to yield to perception of the spiritual and the inner.

When transformational managers learn to release the power of organizational groups, we will have taken a giant step toward our realization of planetary consciousness.

Is a natural mythmaker

The transformational leader lives in two worlds, the world of consensual reality and the world of myth. He sees everything as both real and symbolic of something else. He sees everything in its material dimension and also in its corresponding spiritual matrix. This makes him a natural mythmaker.

Mythmaking occurs when we confer meaning on something. The job of the healthcare manager is to confer meaning on employees, patients, families, and visitors. Any job has both its "real" aspect and its mythic aspect. A janitor who mops the floors may also be a healer. Living in two worlds means patients will feel the janitor's healing energy and also benefit from cleaner floors.

The transformational leader creates a sense of the spiritual, the numinous in the institution. Healing architecture, murals, statues, rituals, celebrations, music, plants, trees, flowers, skylights, etc. create an ambiance that makes mythic identification easier for his associates. Since the transformational leader also follows some spiritual path, he radiates a consciousness energy that affects all life forms.

The transformational leader also helps others find their own personal meaning. He does this by making many opportunities available to members of his staff. Outside speakers, theme weeks, a videotape library, a book discussion club, renewal retreats, etc. set the appropriate tone. Many messages must be given that the hospital is not primarily a business, although it is operated in a businesslike manner. Mission, value and vision are stressed. Employees are rewarded and promoted as they contribute to the elaboration of the institutional myth. A founder's room traces the roots of the institution. Important celebrations help employees remember the institution's honorable past. If possible, the institution ties its symbols to the history of the land and may incorporate in its architectural forms, aboriginal religious motifs.

Once the transformational leader "sounds the note," high consciousness people will begin appearing at the door seeking association and employment. They have heard the sound and have come to build a new center, a nodal place, where the "spirit of the age" will manifest. Before long, a seed group will form and the transformation of the hospital is assured.

The mythic lifts us out of the ordinary and transforms the most menial tasks into loving service for the Source and ministry to all humankind.

Interlude II

TRANSFORMATIONAL LEADERSHIP 48

Plants many "seeds" in a conversation

The conversations of a transformational leader occur on many levels. He uses words on one level, but his consciousness is projecting meanings on multiple levels. His listeners "tune-in" on the level they are ready to hear.

The level just above the one you ordinarily function on will be "seeded" in the transformational leader's conversations. These seeds are thought forms you take into your magnetic field. They circulate in your psychic atmosphere. They are like time capsules. They remain in a quiescent state until they are triggered by resonating life events or by the natural progress of your unfoldment. When their time arrives, they "drop" into awareness ready to serve you in your expanded consciousness. The leader must place seed thoughts into his followers well in advance of their need or they will not be available at the appointed time.

If you are very aware of your stream of consciousness, you will recognize that a seed thought is not of your origin. Most often you simply accept it as one of your own that has "dropped in out of the blue."

Seed thoughts may also come from meditation, spiritual guardians or books. Often, a book comes into your life at just the right time and contains the material you will need in the future.

Magic can be printed in "plain English" and be safe from profane minds because its real meaning is concealed in seed thoughts that only come into awareness when the reader has reached a certain level of consciousness. Until then, the reading material sounds like nonsense. This type of concealment is most obvious in alchemical texts.

Some seed thoughts can only be "quickened" when the individual has performed certain rituals or dances that unlock their meaning. Other seed thoughts wait upon the right environment to trigger them.

When you want help, you can hold your question in mind and then meditate upon it. Resonating seed thoughts will be attracted to your conscious mind. If you can reach a "high state" in your meditation you can often give birth to a seed thought in advance of the time of its natural descent. The trick is to be able to hold on to it as you descend through the lower layers of consciousness. Like a dream, the seed thought is fragile. Even when you give birth to it, you may not understand it in its full meaning. In time, you will. It is always fun to go "fishing." You also need to recognize and seek out your richest sources of seed thoughts.

TRANSFORMATIONAL LEADERSHIP 49

Awakens the organization

Every organization from time-to-time needs a wake-up call. The transformational leader serves as the messenger for this awakening. The great danger for people and organizations is to lapse into unconsciousness, to become over conditioned by the environment and day-to-day operations. The possible, shrinks as minds narrow their focus and become captured by self-imposed boundaries.

The transformational leader spends time each day expanding consciousness. She enters the Void of infinite possibility. She contacts transforming cosmic energies and is swept up in the great currents of creation as they flow from the Source. When she returns from her daily trip of inspiration, she brings back heavenly manna. She is able to feed those who have not yet learned to use their wings.

The wake-up call make take the form of a new vision that can be shared with other people in the organization. It may take the form of a shadow or warning of imminent danger. It may come as a reminder of things past or an omen of things to come.

When the transformational leader travels through other dimensions of consciousness, space-time boundaries are loosened. Like an eagle soaring in the heavens, she experiences a more encompassing perspective that upon her return she shares with her earthbound associates. When they toil in mud up to their ears, she tells of a path that lies ahead and will soon become visible to low-cast eyes. She is an inspiration and a harbinger of hope. Because she can see, others will trust and finally learn to see.

Our eternal journey is a series of wake-ups. We know we have been dreaming when we wake up. What happens when you wake up from being awake? Ahh, then you know you have been sleeping once again. Each wake-up makes current reality a dream when compared to the larger realm that you have now entered.

Transformation requires the perception of a new and larger reality that is available to you. The transformational leader is a broker of these alternative realities. She can help any organization perceive its larger potential being. More than that, she creates a desire among organizational members for transformation and the collective will to achieve it.

The price of being a transformational leader is creative discontent. She knows what is and what could just as well be. Never again will she rest content. Once the voice of the muse is heard, she will always follow that phantom sound throughout all eternity.

All human progress is dependent upon wake-up calls. The calls must come from those who have seen a better land and who through their love of humankind are willing to sacrifice security and stasis for the risk and challenge of a beckoning frontier.

TRANSFORMATIONAL LEADERSHIP 50

Liberates the potential in any form

Any form is the expression of an unlimited archetype resting in the mind of the universe. The archetype must be progressively invoked in order to unfold its successive stages of manifestation. The invocation is performed by one who loves the archetype and can sound its depths through sympathetic identification. Love calls forth manifestation. The archetype slumbers like Sleeping Beauty until it hears the voice of its lover. It then reveals its hidden face and descends to the material plane for manifestation.

The transformational leader is a spiritual scientist who knows that forms are a condensation of subtle energies which in turn reflect aspects of archetypal consciousness. Co-creation is the invocation of the archetype. The leader and the archetype "communicate" until a bridge of trust is formed which becomes the pathway of release for the form. The expansion of the form is made possible through the love of the leader who reaches for the archetype as the archetype reaches for the leader. It is a co-creative process.

Without great love the leader cannot reach the archetypal plane of consciousness. Since all forms are unique, the leader attempts to release the imprisoned beauty behind the limited form. The form may be a person, object, event, organization, program or anything in manifested existence. It is always a dim reflection of is source, the archetype.

If the leader accepts the limitations of a present form, he cannot release its future potential. For this reason, the archetypal leader has dual vision. He always sees forms both as they are and as they will be. His vision of the possible is the pathway of release and discovery for the form. For this reason forms love him. They see in him the liberator of their captivity.

A form is captured by the density of its heavy matter. The transformational leader is a conduit for subtle energies. He "shakes the form" and frees it from encrustation. If the form is a person or organization, this can be a painful process. In this sense the transformational leader is a Divine agitator. He must stir up the sediment at the bottom of the pond to create the possibility for new life. At first forms resist this invasion of their security and fixity. They fear the transformational leader yet are fascinated by the potentials they feel wafting through their souls.

Transformation means death of the old and birth of the new. It means expansion into larger Being. In the long run it is the inevitable destiny of all created forms. In the short run, it is fraught with trouble and anxiety for any form. The transformational leader may love, comfort, and nurture the person or the organization, but he cannot transform them until they open themselves to the descent of new energies and possibilities.

A form cannot expand "before its time." Reformation is a process of maturation. A premature awakening can be a setback for any form. The wise transformational leader senses readiness. He may accelerate the timing to some degree, but is always limited by the elasticity of the form. Often he must simply wait until growth has done its work with that form.

The reason healing is so appropriate in the hospital is that disease, pain and distress often loosen the fetters of a patient's old life and fixed habits. What a tragedy if doctors and nurses view disease only as pathology. Disease may be an important part of the pruning process needed by the patient to create room for new growth.

The next time you encounter any form, ask yourself, "What is it waiting to become and how can I best help it?" In time you will become a gardener of forms.

Interlude II

TRANSFORMATIONAL LEADERSHIP 51

Views the organization as an art form

The transformational leader blends art and science in his style of leadership. He knows that aesthetics is an important part of transformation. For this reason, the transformational leader views healing healthcare organizations as art forms existing simultaneously in physical, mental and spiritual dimensions.

Aesthetics exerts a profound effect on the consciousness of people occupying a physical space. A building is a "conversation in stone." It carries an imprint of the consciousness of its builders and it will imprint the awareness of its residents. Characteristics of the physical environment are reflected in reciprocal mental structures. It is for this reason that sensitive people can often recover the history of an ancient building by simply entering it in a meditative state. Buildings speak to those who will listen and affect even those who cannot hear. Buildings heal and buildings cause disease. A physical architect is also an architect of the mind.

Aesthetics of the mental environment requires that the transformational leader project harmonious thought forms to fill the organization's mind space. Thoughts of beauty, love, healing, and nurturance are harmonious forms on their own plane of existence. They also affect our plane of third dimensional reality. A healing healthcare organization would do well to empower its "high consciousness people" to spend time generating harmonious mind fields. A hospital with the right mental aesthetics becomes a metanoic organization that creates healing miracles for its patients.

Every organization has a unique mind field that is its "fingerprint." You can feel the dissonance in some organizations as easily as you can feel the harmony in other organizations. Without a matching mental architecture, the potency of a building's physical architecture is reduced.

Aesthetics of the spiritual environment requires the transformational leader to be a lightning rod attracting and distributing spiritual power throughout the organization. Future healthcare organizations will represent a natural hierarchy of consciousness. The leader and his small circle will form a spiritual vortex that will be further amplified by all of the employees in the organization. This may be hard for you to visualize, but remember, the community hospital, by the middle of this century is a subtle organization and most of the healing and curing interventions take place at the quantum level.

At the quantum level, disease is a disharmony, a lack of aesthetics. Disease is healed by restoring harmony. The universe at the quantum level is a complex art form. When you encounter it, you begin to understand more about the Artist. It the final analysis, design in all dimensions is about values and aesthetics.

Interlude II

TRANSFORMATIONAL LEADERSHIP 52

Encourages lifework planning in the organization

The transformational leader appreciates all of the employees who work for the organization. She knows they have chosen to spend part of their lives with her and the institution. Because of this decision, the transformational leader views herself in a trust relationship with her people. Time spent in the organization is precious. Time wasted can never be recovered.

Time spent on the job should advance the life purposes of the employees as well as perform tasks essential to the work of the organization. For this reason, the transformational leader encourages each employee to formulate a lifework plan, suitable to his/her stage of unfoldment and interests.

Lifework planning sessions are held at regular intervals and all employees are encouraged to attend. A certificate is awarded at the completion of the course. In addition, a copy of the plan is filed with the human development counselor.

To the degree possible, and according to the specifications of their lifework plans, the hospital will make opportunities available to their employees. This may take the form of educational support, coaching, attendance at special meetings, or psychological counseling. Each employee is also encouraged to select an organizational mentor who will assist with formulation, revision and implementation of the lifework plan.

Regular classes are also held for employees who have completed their own lifework plans and wish to obtain further training to order to become organizational mentors. Again, a certificate is awarded at the completion of the mentoring course. In addition, several special self-development sessions are held throughout the year for the group of mentors, since they do most of their mentoring work on their own time and deserve special recognition and reward.

The human resource is the most valuable resource any healthcare institution possesses. It should be carefully cultivated. The investment will pay off in the special atmosphere created by happy and self-fulfilling employees. It takes a few dollars to put this kind of program into action. Transformation is not cheap. However, not doing it, is too great a cost for any healthcare organization to pay.

Every person in the universe has a "divine right" to become who they are. If they work for us, it is our "divine responsibility" to help them fulfill their hidden potentials. A lifework planning program is one of the best ways an organization can meet its cosmic responsibility.

TRANSFORMATIONAL LEADERSHIP 53

Uses metaphors to escape cognitive limits

The transformational leader often uses metaphors to link small ring thinking with big ring thinking. The metaphor is a bridging device that enables a person to make an intuitive leap from one ring size to another.

Outside your ring of consciousness is a nimbus. The nimbus represents the area of your next ring expansion. Although you are not yet conscious within the nimbus, a well chosen metaphor may enable you to "intuit" what lies within it. In a sense, your intuition gives you a preview of the new reality. Even a glimpse of the next ring accelerates your consciousness and shortens the gestation time required for you to be "reborn" into the next ring. If today you can catch a little bit of what lies in the nimbus, tomorrow you will be able to get more. Eventually, you will make the leap into the larger ring.

Note that the nimbus is a metaphor itself. The nimbus around the moon often foretells a storm. In our lives, the storms make the nimbus apparent. We, like the moon, only reflect the light of the source. Once you think about the nimbus surrounding your ring of consciousness, you begin to look for it. You become sensitive to minimal cues. You only need a slight nudge to move into the area of the nimbus. You wait for the spoken or written metaphor that will supply the needed push. It often comes from a spiritual teacher who veils the truth in a simple example you can grasp.

The transformational leader is always handicapped by her inability to explain what is unknown to others. Obviously words will not do, since words depend upon a body of shared experience and there is none between different ring sizes. The ring the transformational leader is moving in is not yet within the reality of the followers. Furthermore it cannot be explained. The best that can be hoped for is a parable, analogy, or metaphor that will give the follower an opportunity to make a cognitive leap and thereby gain a glimpse of a new reality.

At a more prosaic level, metaphors can be utilized to help people change mindsets. For instance, the metaphor of hospital as a cathedral produces a very different train of images than the metaphor of hospital as automotive repair shop. Metaphors determine: (1) the kind of questions you ask, (2) the type of answers you accept, (3) the vocabulary you use, (4) behaviors you use to treat patients, (5) the responses patients give in return, (5) areas of legitimate clinical research, (6) interfaces with other health professionals, and perhaps,

(7) whether or not the patient recovers from his illness. Metaphors are no small matter. They can lead to revolutionary paradigm changes.

Interlude II

TRANSFORMATIONAL LEADERSHIP 54

Manifests unconditional love

The transformational leader manifests unconditional love toward all creation. She knows she is part of the All and does not exist independently of it. The whole universe is part of her body and in her body is the whole universe. The love of others is love of self, and love of self is love of God and others. All are branches on the same Vine.

In addition to this generalized attitude of love, the transformational leader is able to perceive the perfect archetype or pattern that resides behind manifestation. She sees another person both as an imperfect ego and as a perfect archetype trying to manifest. The person many not be manifesting in a lovely way, but his archetype blazes forth in Divine glory. By bypassing the ego and touching the archetype, she touches an aspect of Divinity waiting to reflect into personhood. At the spiritual level, archetype meets archetype as she meets the other person. This enables the transformational leader to serve as a bridge to the becoming of others. She perceives the perfect pattern and in love reaches out to touch it. Even though the ego of the other person may not understand the contact, his archetype does and reaches in turn toward the transformational leader.

Because the transformational leader can see the enfolded perfection in all forms, she is a servant of creation. It is her duty and calling to be a planetary guide. Even the earth (Gaia) senses the radiation of her presence. As with St. Francis, the animals come to honor her incarnated light. Even plant forms manifest a phototropic response to a planetary sun that is shining through her onto them.

Love is the great force that will structure and animate future healthcare organizations. Love recognizes the natural hierarchy of consciousness and follows the greater lights while serving the lesser lights. Obedience is natural when you understand your place in the order of things. Love unfolds the lesser into the greater. There is a place for everything and love helps everything find its place. Love makes no demands, it only shows the way.

Transformational leadership accelerates the evolution of the organization and the planet. It takes everything a quantum leap into the future. Not every organization or person is yet ready for that kind of travel. Yet, I see many encouraging signs.

A new drama is about to begin. The play has been written. The stage crew has arrived. The actors are in the wings. The audience will soon come. Where are you? Where is your organization?

TRANSFORMATIONAL LEADERSHIP 55

Views reality as something we create

The transformational leader lives in a participative reality. Reality is not an external thing that exists as some outside force. In full accordance with quantum theory, the transformational leader is always a part of the dance and changes reality as a result of his presence and participation.

Reality is definitional and can often be redefined to take different forms. The transformational leader does not defy an undesirable reality. If he does not like it, he simply redefines it. The ability to redefine reality depends upon the transformational leader's access to the universe's subtle dimensions and powers. If he does not have enough potency, he may not be able to change an undesirable reality that is in fact changeable by a person with higher powers. Also, a reality that involves the lives of other people must be changed with caution. Some reality situations are karmic and therefore not within the leader's domain to change. Thus, although there are exceptions to the general rule, reality is mutable and takes the form given it by consciousness.

The destiny (reality) of a healthcare organization depends upon the consciousness of the people who manage it. Although outside forces (reimbursement, etc.) play a role, they never determine the organization's destiny.

In transformational management, managers are reality makers. In traditional schools of management, managers are taught to manage within the constraints of conventional reality. In transformational management, managers are taught to manage beyond the constraints of conventional reality and to in fact create new realties. This is a more powerful practice of management and places the manager in the position of co-creator of new worlds.

Only transformational management will rehabilitate the planet or reshape its healthcare systems. The old paradigm that created our planetary problems cannot solve them. A mature planet is the creation of its inhabitants. It will take the form they give it.

The first domain of the transformational manager is changing the reality of his self. He must acquire power over his own body/mind vehicle before he can be trusted to manage other people's circles. In the schemata of eternal progression, every person is given a size of domain that matches his power of consciousness. As he grows, his domain grows. Everything stays in balance. Although this is the way the cosmic hierarchy operates, it is not the way we do things in our society. The most capable person is not always the one that runs the hospital. Suppose tomorrow, because of the Andromeda Effect (to pick a name at random), your CEO was the most qualified person on the planet to run your organization. Would you have your present CEO?

In the latter part of this century we will select our CEOs by consciousness. I can't wait, can you?

TRANSFORMATIONAL LEADERSHIP 56

Honors the right of people to make choices

The transformational leader honors the right of people to make choices. Free will is regarded as a sacred gift given to humankind in order that men and women may learn through making both good and bad choices and reaping the consequences thereof.

Because choice making is sacred, the transformational leader respects the choice making of all employees. However, the other side of choice making is accountability. The leader holds himself and all others accountable for choices made. If an employee consistently makes poor choices endangering other employees or the good of the organization, cosmic law may require the transformational leader because of his position of entrusted authority in the organization to act as an agent of karmic justice bringing discipline or termination to the employee.

Choice making is a special application of the law of cause and effect. By our choices we are blessed and by our choices we are cursed. The same law applies to all creatures in the Cosmos and to the Source Itself.

A choice initiates a sequence of events. It sets in motion a purpose (cause), a result (effect), and a balance factor. The purpose is the motive, the result is the law of return for that motive, and the balance factor is what the initiator must repay in order to regain equilibrium with the Cosmos.

Your evolution depends upon the kind of choices you make. Good choices bring positive effects. Positive effects alter your body/mind vehicle and accelerate your rate of evolution.

At the spiritual level, you learn to recognize good vs. bad choices. Bad choices are usually due to defects in your ego obstructing the light of your higher self. If you change your focus of attention from your ego to your higher self, you will perceive the stirrings of the Spirit as it moves within you to guide your choices.

Often employees do not perceive the connection between the choices they have made in the past and their present life circumstances. When this occurs, the transformational leader acts as a guide or mentor and educates the employee about the operation of Cosmic law. Without this understanding the employee will never be able to master her destiny through right living. Of course, the employee must be "ripe" for this kind of counsel. Transformational leaders sense this ripeness and do not proceed to give counsel unless it is present.

To do so violates the right of any employee to choose ignorance over enlightenment.

Because the transformational leader honors the right of any person to make bad choices, and because the leader himself has made bad choices in his own past, he exercises loving tolerance, understanding and support toward people making poor choices and the inevitable consequences they will suffer as a result of those choices. The transformational leader knows that we all learn either the easy way or the hard way. It is always up to us to choose which way we will learn.

TRANSFORMATIONAL LEADERSHIP 57

Celebrates life in all its richness

For the transformational leader, life is a celebration. The Cosmos is a song of the spheres. The atoms sing with celestial music. The universe in all its richness is a gift of love made available by the Source for human growth and enjoyment.

The transformational leader experiences the joy of being a co-creator with the Divine. The leader experiences a fullness within himself that cries out for expression. He has the privilege in his own life of making the unmanifest, manifest. He has the ability to perceive the unmanifest in all that surrounds him. As he perceives the potentials in the unmanifest, he thrills to a sea of infinite sound as it dashes against the shoreline of material expression.

The transformational leader is a world server. He is a conscious agent of human evolution on a prison planet. He sees what is, but always sees also, what could just as well be. He knows that in all disorder is the potential of order waiting to be evoked. In primal chaos is the first ray of a new creation. For that reason the transformational leader is not caught up in the disorder around him. Because of inner vision he has a sure compass in the most troubled waters.

The transformational leader knows the breakthrough in planetary consciousness will first be evident in the field of healthcare. Health is the lowest common denominator in any society. When the medical profession's concern with curing is transformed into a concern with healing, societal transformation is not far off. A healthy body, a healthy organization, a healthy society, a healthy planet, all of these are stages in the unfolding epic of planetary transformation.

Ritual, celebration, and ceremony are mythic expressions of well-being. The universe is a plenum, and you are a child of the universe. You are part of All That Is. Such richness cannot be conceived of by the human mind. Yet it is true. Today we have an economics of scarcity. With a growth in consciousness we will have an economics of abundance. Imagine, the management of abundance! Today we manage disease. Soon we will manage health.

Poverty and disease are symptoms of misalignment with the universe. The Spirit knows neither. In God's house are many mansions. We can occupy these mansions as soon as we are qualified by consciousness to do so. The transformational manager seeks to produce better alignment on all levels, hence celebrates life in all its richness.

TRANSFORMATIONAL LEADERSHIP 58

Has an uncanny ability to predict the future

A transformational leader has an expanded ring of consciousness. Expansion of consciousness changes the leader's relationship to the coordinates of time and space. It spans more of both. This means the leader's consciousness reaches forward and backward in time and also reaches out from here to there. Extension in future time brings a measure of precognition. Extension in space brings the capacity for remote viewing. The higher the consciousness, the more free it is of third dimensional time and space limitations.

Another reason the transformational leader has an uncanny ability to predict the future is that she can sense events in the plane of formation before they descend into the plane of manifestation. She reads the blueprint before it is built out with high density matter in this dimension. Everything that exists in this dimension has its blueprint in another dimension. Eventually doctors will be able to diagnose and treat diseases in the plane of formation before they materialize in the plane of manifestation. The plane of formation is more subtle than subatomic particles, so it has not yet been discovered by mainline science.

A third reason the transformational leader can predict the future is that she can tap the thought stream and perceive what people are thinking about. Creative thoughts in the thought stream will later manifest in the works of their creators or in the works of other individuals who have access to the stream. Things "hang in the air" for a considerable length of time before they are "fished out" and translated into reality. The thought stream is like a movie of what is likely to happen.

A fourth reason for the predictive capacity of a transformational leader is her ability to understand the Cosmic law of cause and effect (sowing and reaping). If she knows the major causes that have been set in motion by a nation, she knows the major effects that will surely follow. Timing is difficult, since the effects are adjusted by many other variables. It is easier to specify the effect than predict exactly when it will occur.

A fifth reason the transformational leader may be able to predict the future is that she is often a self-fulfilling prophet. She makes a prediction and then goes and fulfills it. This is the best kind of prediction or futurism. It happens when the leader and her organization have achieved enough integration and resulting potency to impact the environment in a purposeful way. In its most potent form, it is magic. It is always an exercise of will. With advancing evolution a person, organization or nation lives in a more predictable reality.

Avoids the negativities of the environment

The transformational leader rises above the negativities of his environment. He is in tune with the fires of the Universe and seeks to impart a healing, nurturing presence upon all creation. Because he senses the energies streaming from situations, people, animals, plants, rocks, etc., he easily avoids entrapment in negative eddies or energy pools.

Most people have not learned to insulate themselves from their environment. They take into themselves the energies that surround them and become like their life situations. The transformational leader always regulates his energy exchanges with the environment. Because he is an alchemist, he can transmute negative energies into positive energies as long as these energies are in his immediate presence. Of course, when he leaves the situation, the energies often regress to their former state.

The energy field of the transformational leader is positively polarized so it tends to repel negative energies. Because there is nothing in him that responds to hate, fear, anger, jealousy, frustration, envy, malice, depression etc., negative energies simply bounce off his energy shield.

Since people have a right to channel negative energies, the transformational leader has no right to deny them their choices. For that reason he engages in transmutation on a selective basis, usually in response to some soul that is trying to extricate itself from the bog of despair. The transformational leader is authorized by the Cosmos to heal only when healing is actively sought by some person or group. He is not permitted to reverse the destiny of an institution or group of people in spite of themselves.

Hospitals will become healing institutions when a majority of their employees are healed. Healing is a function of Being, not doing. A hospital that wants to heal its patients must help its employees claim their Being. This requires an intensive educational, transformational effort. It means changing the energy matrix of the institution. When the hospital becomes a transformational place, it engages in spiritual alchemy and transmutes negative patient energies into positive patient energies. Of course, this requires the consent of the patients. Some patients do not want to be healed or at least they do not want to go through the personal transformation that healing requires. For this reason, most hospitals will designate special units where healing takes place and designate other patient units where curing is the only objective. A hospital must fit its interventions to the consciousness of its patients, just as a mentor must fit his teaching to the consciousness of his students. People and institutions become ripe for transformation in their own time. Intervention before ripeness is folly and may be an invasion of people's right of free choice.

One of the hardest assignments is to be a transformational leader in an institution not yet ripe for transformation. The leader may choose to do what little he can to prepare the soil or he may choose to depart for greener pastures. The question is always, "Where will your efforts contribute most to the purpose and plan of the Cosmos?" You are not required to work where there are no people who can respond to your Spirit. The work that is not yet timely for you to do will be done by another when the time is right.

Views circumstances as a teacher

Transformation is a growth process. The sources of growth are both inner and outer experiences. The inner experiences come from spiritual realms and are apprehended through your spiritual consciousness. The outer experiences are gained by your ego as it reacts to external life circumstances. Some lessons can be gained through direct spiritual insights not mediated by contact with the material dimension. Other things you must learn through your work in the external world.

Any deficiencies in your ego or society's ego will attract corresponding adverse circumstances that are actually veiled opportunities for "working through" unresolved issues. Some life circumstances you attract because of personal ego deficiencies and other life circumstances you attract because you are a member of a society with collective ego problems. Most of the current problems in American healthcare would disappear overnight with a changed societal consciousness. Lacking that, we must all learn together, the hard way, by slogging through seemingly insurmountable problems until we "catch on" that we are the problem. The problems are inside us, not outside us. At that point a change of consciousness occurs, then a change in our actions and then the problems simply melt away. They are "written out of the script." This simple dynamic also applies to any of your personal problems. When you "catch on" the problem disappears. It has served its purpose in your personal transformation.

Therefore, you should view all life circumstances as your teachers. Always ask, "What can I learn from this circumstance? What elements in my nature have attracted this opportunity? What actions must I master to put this thing behind me as a lesson learned?"

Some life circumstances will be hard for you. They will take a disagreeable form. This is necessary to get you to focus your full attention on them and begin dealing with your own unresolved issues. These are the very issues that are blocking your further transformation and they must be cleared away before you can progress further on your pathway of transformation.

If you look carefully, you will discover that external circumstances are actually a projection of your own unresolved issues. They are a mirror image of your soul. Your life circumstances are a dramatization arranged by the universe to get your involvement. In a sense, all of our work in the material dimension is really self work. This is true until we have reached mastery in third dimensional materiality. Then, we will discover our work in other dimensions.

The transformational manager, then, realizes that all her life circumstances are both real in their own right and also symbolic of her unresolved inner tensions. By engaging in "right action" and solving the external problems, she also solves her inner problems.

The problems in healthcare today are created by the mass consciousness of our society. As managers we are often immersed in this consciousness. Therefore, we are actors in a national dramatization generated by faulty thinking. We have earned our parts in this national theater and must play them to the best of our ability. The end of the play is always open for change. It can be rewritten at any point.

The transformational manager discovers the world is a stage for the play of consciousness and simply reflects whoever occupies the stage. It is a simple radiation of the collective consciousness of the cast. In some cases the transformational manager can share insights with other cast members, alter consciousness, and change the play. In other cases this is not possible. The other cast members are not ripe for such insights. Then, the transformational manager must enter the play, confront the circumstances, work them through with the cast. In the end, this causes the necessary transformation of cast consciousness and creates a better ending for the play.

Does not "put people down"

The transformational leader is always looking for the best in everyone. For this reason, she does not put people down. Since the transformational leader is a mentor, she looks for signs of growth potential in everyone she meets. Although the leader holds her followers accountable for their job performance, and demands appropriate interpersonal behavior, she does not elevate her ego by reducing the ego of others.

As a result, the transformational leader creates an organizational climate that is enthusiastic, innovative, and upbeat. Employees are turned on by what they are doing. Because of good organization/person fit, employees accomplish personal goals by accomplishing the goals of the organization.

By focusing on what is "right" in an employee, the transformational leader gains enough trust and good feeling from the employee that she can then focus on areas of needed improvement. Each employee is viewed as a mix of strengths and weaknesses. It is the job of the leader to further develop the employee's strengths and help him/her overcome any weaknesses.

The orientation of the transformational leader is on the person and the job. Although the leader cannot act both as a psychotherapist and a manager for each employee, she gives appropriate guidance and makes a referral if more in-depth work is needed.

If the healthcare organization is viewed as a womb for employee, patient, physician, family, and community transformation, all interpersonal interactions have to be conducted in this light. That means the employee is first and foremost a person with a need to succeed and grow. The job is a vehicle for this growth. As the employee achieves a higher degree of personal and professional excellence, better job performance is evident.

Some employees have been conditioned to believe that "a job is a job." These employees expect no job enrichment and usually experience none. They lead lives of "quiet desperation." It will take time and demonstrated caring to change this culture of mediocrity. Since actions speak louder than words, the transformational leader must set the example for the "new view." It takes time to put employee suspicions to rest.

If employees are not healed, they cannot heal patients. Transformation must spread through all levels of the organization for the hospital to become a healing place.

TRANSFORMATIONAL LEADERSHIP 62

Is not tied to the past

The transformational leader managing in our material world is always oriented to the future although he may have excellent access to times past and present. Since he is living in this dimension, he is subject to the forward arrow of time. When he is operating in other dimensions, he experiences and moves in different rhythms of space and time. All dimensions of creation have coordinates of time, space, and condition. Only above the level of creation do these not exist.

Although not tied to the past, the transformational leader knows that all things now in existence have their roots in the past. He knows the present by understanding the past and is able to alter the present thereby changing the future. Since the arrow of time moves only one direction, he goes with the flow of time but is always engaged in future making.

Transformation itself takes place in time. It occurs in stages and the unfoldment of each stage is preceded by a period of ripeness. The leader can often hasten ripeness through consciousness-raising activities sponsored in the organization. Yet, there are limits to how fast an organization or a person can change. Patience is an important attribute for any anyone involved in personal or organizational transformation.

Cause and effect is one of the most important manifestations of cosmic law in our dimension. Its operation requires time. Cause precedes effect. By mastering the causes you generate, you begin to master future effects and therefore, time. By generating no causes in this dimension, you move beyond time in this dimension.

The transformational leader knows the most important way to change the present is to change the future. Therefore, he uses visioning to help both individuals and organizations escape the limitations of their present time and conditions. Creation is always dependent upon the present generation of images which are then fulfilled in future time. The transformational leader by definition is a visionary.

Although the transformational leader "escapes his past by creating his future, he will help individuals or organizations return to their pasts if they are "stuck" there. Sometimes organizations cannot escape their traditions or people cannot escape their traumatic pasts. In this case, the transformational leader who is a time traveler returns to the past to perform a rescue operation.

The past still exists as a vibratory hologram. The leader by entering this hologram with the person or organization helps them "relive and alter the record." Only the record in personal or organizational consciousness can be altered. The cosmic record of the past is inviolate.

Fear can return a person or organization to its past. Here the leader, who must be fearless, enters to "change the record" and release the organization or personality.

Since the transformational leader has no fear of his past, he is not bound by it. Fear prohibits transformation and often locks both people and organizations into past time. However there is a solution. The grace of an abundant future permits escape from the past.

TRANSFORMATIONAL LEADERSHIP 63

Is part of a transformational network

Transformational leaders do not work alone. They network with other world servers sharing a common vision of humanity restored, on a garden planet. Although they may not enjoy many soul mates in their organizations, transformational leaders are part of a global network of light committed to transformation of humankind.

Organizations, communities, nations, and planets are not changed by a population majority. They are transformed by committed minorities who generate a transformational energy vortex fed by small circles of people loving, trusting, and sharing with one another.

Each soul radiates its own unique tone. However, it is also part of a family of like souls. Like attracts like. We are drawn by invisible chords to other people who share our mission and consciousness.

The Internet is an instrument of global consciousness. It is only in its infancy. Its future is uncertain. It will only become what we make it. Yet, it provides a force for pushing the edges of the envelope. Some of the concepts we discuss here would not be appreciated or understood in many healthcare organizations. It can be lonely when you have no one with whom to share ideas. This is the advantage of an electronic network. It doesn't matter where you live or work. When you enter cyberspace you are a member of an extended family.

In your own organization, you also need to form a network of a few people who constitute a small circle and create a personal foundation for organizational transformation. You need to amplify your personal efforts. One of the most important features of a vortex is its ability to amplify small signals to large magnitudes. You can't do it by yourself. The universe is designed as a sharing place. There are more powerful networking methods than the Internet, but at this point in our collective evolution, the Internet provides a needed bridge for realizing the enormous potentials of nonlocal mind.

As you contribute to the Internet, you create a connection to nonlocal mind. Reading Internet material passively confers a benefit, but it does not create a vital energic connection to group mind. To do this you must draw upon yourself and your connection to All That Is. As you compose your responses, try to "draw down" ideas. Feel them enter your consciousness from their own realm. Become a living connection. You are a cell in a planetary brain. Working with other cells, you can do much to foster the growth of healing healthcare in your institution.

TRANSFORMATIONAL LEADERSHIP 64

Escapes long-term habit patterns

The transformational leader refuses to become a victim of long established habit patterns. She does this by entering high energy states. In these states she overrides existing mental forms and creates new energy pathways.

Any energy channeled by the mind creates a mental form as its conduit (function creates form). Over time the form becomes rigid and resists any change in energy circulation. Only by transcending ordinary mental functioning, is it possible for the transformational leader to alter her obsolete thought forms. In deep meditation states she can tap this energy and direct its flow into the personality.

Studies of the brain will reveal "branching" where new energies flowing into the cerebral cortex create new nerve pathways.

We are victims of the past until we throw off the old forms and move forward. The old thought forms are not bad. They brought us to where we are today. They served as developmental links in our pathway of eternal progression. However, once they have served their function, they impede further progress. As a snake sheds its skin, so we must shed the old form in order to grow a new one.

A thought form exists on the mental plane. It is reflected into the physical plane as a habit or habitual tendency of behavior. We often identify with our thought forms as part of ourselves. Just as we must not identify with our shoes, we must not identify with our thought forms. Both are useful tools but not part of our essential nature.

Early life experiences often creates thought forms that are pre-verbal. We feel these forms but cannot put them into words or touch them with our reasoning. Often they are coded into our muscles. One of the values of therapeutic massage is its ability to loosen the physical manifestations of hidden thought forms. A good massage may cause us to relive early traumatic events. The reliving often brings the event to consciousness where it may be processed by words and discharged. Release may occur in meditation when the body shakes as high spiritual energies dissolve old crystallizations and create new energy pathways.

Ask yourself, "Which of my long-term habits are holding me back? When did I acquire them? What purpose did they once serve? Do I still need them today? Can I enter deep meditation states and generate the energy needed to transform these old vessels?"

Accelerates the evolution of all he/she touches

The transformational leader knows that everything in the universe is in process. Enfolded within it is a blueprint for unfoldment. The transformational leader hears the "nothing crying out to become something" and responds to the call by providing nurturance, encouragement, energy, and opportunities for greater manifestation. We might say the archetype of the leader contacts the archetype of all he/she touches and communes with its Being.

Although potentials to develop are contained within the archetype, its actual expression is determined by its ongoing interaction with all that is. The archetype does not predestine. It is an initial individualized expression of the Divine Creative Nature with a potential to grow through its interaction with other archetypes. Its potentials are released through the loving ministry of higher life forms (mentors). Thus the law of service obtains throughout the universe—higher life forms release the potential in lower life forms. The Divine Creative Nature has left lots of room for surprise and innovation.

We are created in the image of the Source and therefore are co-creators in the universe. This means we can do endless variations on the theme of any archetype we encounter. Although we cannot change the Divine emanation itself (the core archetype), we can give it endless qualities of development and manifestation. Of course this assumes the archetype is available to us through the "permission" of its holder. Man can cooperate with minerals, plants, and animals to release their hidden splendor. Devas (spiritual entities) can be enlisted in this effort. This has been demonstrated many times at Findhorn. At the human level we can accelerate the evolution of each other. We in turn are assisted by Devas or angels. The entire creation is meant to be interactive and transformational. Even minerals can be accelerated in their evolution by loving contact with humans. This is one of the secrets of alchemy—the conversion of base metals to gold.

Not only beings (plants, animals, humans, Devas, etc.) are subject to the law of progression (evolution), so are ideas. In their own plane (the mental plane) ideas are entities (egregors) and have a life of their own. When the transformational leader creates a thought (like the future of his organization), his thought takes shape on the mental plane (becomes an egregor) and attracts mental substance. The idea is attached to him by an umbilical cord. It will feed off his energy. It will also attract like ideas in the mental plane and will grow of its own accord. Since it is attached to its creator (the leader), via a psychic umbilical cord it will feed back to him its own growth and "independent" ideas. He feeds the egregor and is fed by it. If this child of thought is generated by a vortex group, it has multiple parents and will feed and be fed by all of them. Multiple parenting often occurs on the Internet where the cords of thought attach to the many contributors. Simply reading the Internet will not result in this kind of attachment, since there is little or no creative energy flowing from the reader. However, when you begin to create ideas, the attachment is made.

View yourself as an accelerator of evolution, of everything you meet. You can nurture and help unfold the hidden potential that awaits your recognition.

Resources seem attracted to him/her

Resources gravitate to the transformational leader. He assumes that "everything is always here" and indeed it is. Ideas are subtle energy. Matter is dense energy. Dense energy always pursues subtle energy. Density is the only difference between ideas and objects in our manifested universe. "Densify" an idea and you have an object. The manifested universe is simply a network of energies of varying densities.

The manifestation of resources (money, people, equipment, enabling legislation, buildings, etc.) follows the general laws of creation in third dimensional reality. Since the manifested universe exists at different levels, you may create from different levels (spiritual, mental, or physical).

When you create from the spiritual level you generate a clear mental hologram of what you wish to manifest at the physical level. By an act of will you then invoke the image and call it into being. The image and the call attract spiritual entities and energies required for manifestation. As a child of the Cosmos, you have co-creative power and work with the Source accomplishing its purpose and plan on the earth. We usually call this kind of manifestation a miracle. The law of spiritual manifestation requires (1) that you possess enough mental control to produce a pure thought form or hologram and (2) that you have no ego attachment to the creation. Spiritual manifestation must be ego free. You are calling upon spiritual powers to benefit humankind. This is spiritual alchemy. Manifestation may be nearly instantaneous. There is little or no karma since you have no attachment to the creation.

If you wish to manifest a resource for personal benefit, you are expected to work for it like anyone else does by using methods of the mental plane or physical plane.

In mental manifestation you create a clear vision of what you want to create and then activate the image with strong personal desire. The activated image is a thought form that goes out from you to attract needed circumstances and events. Because of the law of synchronicity, resources rush toward the thought form as it rushes toward them. When they meet the thought form is "built out." In mental creation you also act upon your own image and become a self-fulfilling prophet. Your actions in turn precipitate more actions and a network of interacting causes and effects results. Because your vision is a "child of your desire," you are attached to it with a psychic umbilical cord and therefore are connected to all karmic consequences of your creation. Manifestation will occur according to the confluence of time, space, and condition. It has to be sequenced in the physical plane, unlike a spiritual creation which descends from the spiritual plane. Depending upon your potency and the nature of your creation, it will manifest soon or later.

In physical creation, you utilize physical labor to achieve your desire. You may work for money and exchange it for the labors or materials of your creation or you use direct labor to achieve the object of your desire as a sculptor works a stone.

The general law of cause and effect requires that you labor for all that you desire. In the universal plan there is no "ill gotten gain." You work and enjoy the fruit of your labor. This universal law is suspended only when you work to achieve no personal benefit.

Easily integrates the spiritual and the material

The transformational leader lives in an integrated world where spiritual, mental, emotional and material energies are simply different manifestations of the one great Divine energy. All the world is sacred and every action taken in it is a spiritual action. The material is in the service of the spiritual and provides a high density channel for its manifestation.

Patients are viewed as multidimensional beings. The physical body is a manifestation point for emotional, mental and spiritual energies. The spiritual body of the patient is the most powerful leverage point for therapeutic intervention and if activated can heal disease by removing its genesis. In spiritual healing, the disease simply disappears. Doctors are often confused by their examination of the patient. It is as if the disease was never there. In mental healing, the mental body is activated and the brain produces a variety of chemicals that facilitate rapid recovery from the disease. In emotional healing, the brain acts the same way as in mental healing plus the emotional body receives powerful healing energies through therapeutic touch and the love emitted by healers. Presently most of our interventions in the hospital are at the physical level. This can be effective in many cases. Unfortunately it can also simply cause the underlying problem (disordered energy vortex) to manifest at a new site or in a new way. A disease is often the symbolic manifestation of a hidden conflict. It is a message from deeper layers of the Self and if frustrated by physical medicine will simply choose a new and perhaps more virulent form of expression. If we simply cure patients (physical) and do not heal them (spiritual, mental and emotional) we run this risk of energy displacement and continued physical manifestation of the underlying disease process.

In the integrated world view, all employees of the hospital are also viewed as spiritual beings manifesting in physical bodies. The transformational leader working at emotional, mental and spiritual levels generates a spectrum of energies essential to the evolution of each employee, and therefore, the total organization. At the spiritual level the transformational leader pulls down high vibratory energies and creates a special atmosphere in the organization. One can "feel" the presence of the Spirit in the halls of the institution. This is also seen in the aura of the organization. At the mental level the transformational leader creates powerful thought forms manifesting on the physical plane as insight, breakthrough, innovation, bliss, and discovery.

At the emotional level the transformational leader empowers the organization through love, nurturance, and caring. Love energy releases the hidden potentials in all created forms. Love is what helps patients unfold. It makes the hospital visit a growth experience.

At the physical level the transformational leader uses shapes, sounds, colors, lights, and texture to create powerful physical environments resonating symbolically with spiritual, mental, and emotional energies. Architecture is a Divine science that creates suitable physical vehicles for manifestation of the subtle energies of the Cosmos. Buildings can heal employees and patients at the physical level by invoking these subtle energies and radiating them through space. Buildings can initiate people into higher consciousness. This is the realm of sacred architecture, a physical science taught in the perennial wisdom.

Exerts considerable control over his body/mind vehicle

The transformational leader is at home in many vehicles on many planes of consciousness. His dream body is well developed for travel on the astral plane. His spiritual body is fitted for travel on the spiritual plane. His mental body is developed for travel on the mental plane. His physical body is utilized for travel on the physical plane. The transformational leader knows that if he has a defective vehicle or an underdeveloped one, he will not be able to do his work on that particular plane of consciousness. For this reason the transformational leader perfects each of his vehicles for greater utility and service.

The transformational leader utilizes his movement on other planes of consciousness to accomplish transformation on this plane. He brings through spiritual, astral, or mental energies to impact physical forms and transform them into higher expressions.

Consciousness always requires a vehicle for its expression. The vehicle must be built out in the density of the plane of its expression. Its materials and operation follow the laws of the plane it is operating on. You know this from your dream body. You can do many things on the dream (astral) plane that you cannot do on the physical plane. Laws of movement, light, gravity, space and time are all different.

When you change planes, you change vehicles. If you have control of your dream body, you are a lucid dreamer and can move about on the dream plane at will. The same is true on all other planes including this one.

By helping people have healthy physical bodies, we enable them to move about on this plane with freedom and grace. By teaching them to exert more control over their bodies, they have even greater freedom and capacity. When patients are in our hospitals we should be teaching them to better understand and operate their physical vehicles. Basic training in relaxation and visualization are two valuable skills that should be taught to all patients.

When consciousness is extended to another dimension of consciousness it begins to build a vehicle on that plane. It is born to that plane much as a baby is born on this one. At first the infant body does not work well and the person has very little awareness in that body. With time and experience and careful parenting, the body begins to unfold its inherent potential. The person at some point wakes up in the body and has a sense of self awareness. We have the potential to be born on many different planes of consciousness and to build out our vehicles on these planes.

TRANSFORMATIONAL LEADERSHIP 69

Views organizational life as an adventure

The transformational leader views life as a cosmic adventure. This includes her life and work in the organization. In the transformational perspective, the purpose of life is to gain experience, to increase ring size, to encounter new possibilities and achieve increased mastery through loving service to all of God's creation.

Because life is an adventure, it is meant to be enjoyed, whether in rain or in sun. What we declare a curse often ends as a blessing and what we think is a blessing may prove to be a sorrow. From our limited perspective it is wise to withhold final judgments and simply get on with the task of living, serving and loving.

Certain lessons can only be learned in great adversity. Compassion, for example, is gained through suffering. There is no other way to attain this quality of consciousness. If you refuse the experience of suffering you are giving up all cosmic assignments which require compassion for their successful completion.

Your assignments in the universe are determined by your consciousness which in turn is a result of your experience. By experience, you qualify yourself for greater assignments and more inclusive consciousness, and so you grow.

Wherever you are, whatever you are doing, accept it as your rightful assignment for this time. Master its difficulty and grow in consciousness. At some future time, people will marvel at your capability and will wonder how you attained it. You will know. You purchased it with your experience.

Begin each new day knowing it adds one more day to your eternal progression in consciousness. This may be the day when you break through to a new level of Being. This is a day of adventure. You are the central character in an unfolding dramatization on the planet earth. The memory of today will be added to your eternal record. Live it well and with joy!

Creaturehood is a blessing beyond compare. Thank the Source and seek to explore the further bounties of creation. There are many worlds yet to explore, and within these worlds new roles to perform. You are involved in the living of infinity and your current role is part of it. It matters not whether you are here or there. Since you are here, why not be here with your might? Soon you will be there and will have passed beyond this point of experience. Savor and enjoy, you will pass this way but once. Each day is unique and offers a one-of-a-kind experience. What will be your experience today?

Practices the "inner game" of management

As we progress in our new century, the practice of management becomes more subtle. Management is a shared "mind field" generated by organizational stakeholders (employees, etc.). Subtle qualities of consciousness come into prominence. The CEO should be the person with the most inclusive consciousness and the greatest love and concern for all sentient beings in the world. The power of the CEO is the power of his consciousness which transforms everyone coming within the energy field of the organization. As the energy field radiates from the organization its transforming influence is felt in the community, nation, and world. Many organizations and people linked together across the planet in shared awareness create planetary consciousness. With the achievement of planetary consciousness, the world takes its place as a designer planet within its constellation.

The skills that constitute the inner game include but are not limited to intuition, telepathy, remote viewing, dimensional travel, parallel realities, aura reading, thought form construction, magic, alchemy, revelation, prayer, meditation, inner teachers, mentoring, healing, miracles, inspired teaching, psychometry, futurism, genetic consciousness, morphic resonance, transformational leadership, divine science, and mythology. A casual glance will reveal that few of these are listed or looked for in the curriculum vitae of current CEOs applying for jobs in contemporary hospitals. The reason is obvious. In the current paradigm, management is viewed as an outer game. By the end of this century we will train and select managers on their demonstrated skills in the inner game. Two types of managers will emerge, those most skilled in dealing with cosmic energies and those most skilled in building forms to contain and express these energies. Inspirational leaders working with skilled form builders constitute the future management team.

As management becomes more subtle, organizational structures also become more flexible and ephemeral. The old solid pyramidal form is replaced by a "plasma form." The virtual organization appears which is an organization of the mind and has no solid form at all. This is made possible at first by the Internet spanning the globe. At a later point the Internet will be largely replaced by telepathic linking. At some critical point, the whole earth will reform itself based on the collective hologram of humankind created by its unified mind field. The spiritual dimension of management will be uppermost.

Interlude II

The material will simply reflect the spiritual. The inner game will be the outer game. All things will be in harmony and we will be ready to link up with yet higher order systems waiting for our graduation from materiality.

Builds a pool of ideas

The transformational leader understands that ideas form the basis for all reality construction. We literally think things into existence. Ideas create thought forms which in turn constellate material events.

The leader builds a pool of ideas in the organization. He provides intellectual stimulation and encourages everyone to think, intuit, feel, sense, read, study, and travel. The transformational leader knows the organization itself is simply a materialized thought form and can change its form as quickly as it can change its collective consciousness.

Every organization has a mind field (collection of thought forms) which is unique to that organization. It draws from the background consciousness (thought stream) of the planet, but reflects most clearly the consciousness of organizational members. The mind field is usually turbid and confused. It lacks coherence and clarity. However, if enough people in the organization are thinking the same thoughts or sharing the same visions, the mind field clarifies and begins to take on the character of an independent entity (egregor) operating in its own right. We say the organization has a character and a life of its own.

Powerful ceremonies or rituals can create a temporary egregor which under certain conditions can be perceived by sensitive people. However, the temporary egregor dissipates unless it receives constant energy input from human sources. Daily temple rituals have this purpose. They create constant energy input and therefore a constant "presence."

The pool of ideas circulates through the psyches of all organizational members. It stimulates thinking even in people who are not mental types. The intellectual tone of the organization improves over time.

A transformational leader decides which "seed thoughts" are most needed in the organization at a particular time and then arranges to put these thoughts into circulation. He may generate the thoughts himself or may bring in outside resource people to assist in the effort. The question always is, "What ideas does this organization most need at this time?"

External consultants are often brought into the organization because of their ability to project very clear thought forms, thereby creating energy matrices. The matrices are fed by organizational members and they feed the same organizational members that feed them. Over time, the matrices (egregors) can attain enough potency to create metanoic events. The organization becomes a power in its own right and empowers everyone who enters it.

Creates images of possibility

For the transformational leader creating images of possibility is a most enjoyable activity since it brings his mind into contact with God's mind. They meet on the mental plane where an infinite number of idea possibilities are stored, awaiting reception by created beings throughout the many universes.

By an act of invocation, the transformational leader stimulates Divine mind and downloads possibilities within the scope of his consciousness and interest at the time of invocation. The ideas come in the form of fleeting images and apprehensions. Until they are processed by the transformational leader's mind, they are not ideas as we define the term. Of course the act of processing alters the image as it takes upon itself some of the individual characteristics of the perceiver. In other words it is translated, not just perceived. The same idea possibility often has a better translation (purer form) on other inhabited planets.

Idea invocation from the mental plane is not to be confused with fishing the thought stream surrounding our earth. The thought stream consists of all those ideas generated by life forms upon this earth, past and present (and to some extent future). Many ideas can be gleaned here, but they come from created minds, not the Uncreated Mind.

All ideas in the mind of God seek expression throughout all worlds in all times. They slowly descend from higher planes into the mental plane. Although nascent ideas can be contacted in the spiritual planes, it takes a more highly developed consciousness to reach them. Most of us have our hands full trying to navigate the mental plane.

Once an image of possibility has been invoked by the transformational leader it is cloaked with his mental substance and becomes a thought form. By projecting desire into the thought form, the leader activates it. From this point on, the thought form is an entity with a life of its own, although it remains connected by an emotional chord to the leader. It is a child of his mind and draws upon his energies to continue manifestation. This is similar to a man and woman giving birth to a child. The child is an idea potential (archetype) in the mind of God until it is invoked by conception and given a body by its parents. In time the child will have an identity of its own, but will always remain connected by an emotional bond with its parents.

At the transformational level, management is co-creation with the Source. The mind of God creates the first matrix. By invoking this matrix, we become co-creators with our Source.

Transformational management is spiritual practice. It becomes possible when any healthcare organization discovers the spiritual dimension of management and medicine.

Forms a consciousness-raising seed group

Change seldom comes about because of majorities. Committed minorities are usually found to be the critical factor. The transformational leader forms a consciousness-raising seed group in the organization. This group generates thought forms that are picked up by other people in the organization and further amplified. Finally a synergistic thought form generated by the seed group and amplified by many employees gains enough power to become a turning point for the organization.

The transformational leader develops people in the organization that are ripe for transformation. He also recruits new people into the organization that respond to his "call" and are anxious to become part of a nodal organization on the leading edge of change.

Consciousness raising depends upon: (1) the presence of high vibratory energies channeled by a leader and (2) a group of followers anxious to utilize the energies to expand their awareness. The energies impact their body/mind vehicles and through resonance induce sympathetic responses. Like creates like.

All accelerations in consciousness are induced in this fashion. Accelerations come not just by reading a book or even doing exercises. They come in their most potent form from a living source that is already radiating high velocity spiritual and mental energies. This is why all wisdom schools have living teachers. It is the teacher who reaches the high states, conducts the power downward through lower states of consciousness and distributes it to the followers. The small circle of followers in turn become teachers to other receptive followers and further distribute the energies. Consciousness begets consciousness.

The level of consciousness attainable in any healthcare organization is determined by presence of the person with the most inclusive perception. This person may or may not be a member of the senior management team. Since most hospitals are not currently aware of the subtle dimension of management, many of the most talented members of the organization are not identified as such. In the future this will not be the case. Organizational position will be determined by inclusiveness of perception. Until that time comes, small seed groups will meet on an informal basis. However, the products of their shared consciousness will still impact the organization and often lead it in the correct ways "in spite of itself." Many times it is the advisor to the throne who holds the keys to the kingdom. Find those who think as you do. Form a consciousness-raising seed group. Project a powerful vision of the future. Generate the thought forms that will carry the organization forward.

Generates energy and excitement

The transformational leader generates energy and excitement in the organization. She has an optimistic disposition and is skilled at reframing negatives into positives. Because she operates at high energy potentials she overshadows lower energy people in the organization and actually accelerates their rate of mental development.

Energy flows easily from high potential to low potential sources. For this reason, workers enjoy being around transformational leaders. Their batteries are charged through proximity effects. Of course this would draw down the leader's energy level, except she is wise enough to continually renew her energy pool by drawing directly upon the Source.

When operating at high energy levels, the transformational leader attracts other energies, resources, and entities freely circulating through deep space. They seek out the source of high radiation and then add their contributions to it. Like attracts like. As above, so below. Thus, the organization becomes metanoic and rises above ordinary earth force and circumstance. As it attains a higher energy state, the organization begins to transform its people and its environment. Patients experience healing. Physicians and nurses work as team members. Visitors remark about the serene healing atmosphere of the hospital. Workers come from afar to join the effort. Energy vortices begin to appear. Higher levels of integration are now in evidence. Less "work" is going in, more "value" is coming out. The organization as a system is feeding from cosmic energy reservoirs that will eventually enable it to generate alternative realities and parallel futures. Resources appear from nowhere. The unusual becomes usual. The hospital is honored in the court of public opinion. A new energy foundation is being created that will transform the organization into a multidimensional spiritual thought form that travels easily in other worlds.

The high energies of the transformational leader are modulated by her personality. Depending upon personality type, they will take different forms. This is true throughout the universe. All individualized entities have distinct personalities. Some will appeal to you and some won't. The secret is to never permit personality to get in the way of relationship. If your development is arrested at the level of the ego, you will have a problem with this. You will then be tested on the point of personality. With further growth, you will learn to cherish diversity.

Begin today to create energy and excitement in your organization. Energy feeds upon itself. Start the vortex and you will be caught up in it.

Stimulates the right brain

Everything that can happen will happen, in some time, at some place. Why not here? Why not now?

The transformational leader lives in a realm of probable realities. What is and what could be exist side-by-side. By an act of consciousness, the leader can exit one reality and enter another.

Parallel realities exist in their own time/space quadrants. They are waiting to happen but must be triggered by an act of the leader's imagination. Imagination is invocation and calls forth the possible. Many of the parallel realities were created ages ago through the mentation of other beings. Some are being created even now.

Although the basic structure of a parallel reality exists, as it is—it can also be modified through the thought process of the one who invokes it. Just as our current reality is modified by the acts of humankind, so alternative realities can be modified by those occupying them.

The transformational leader knows that right brain visualization is essential to altering current reality or entering parallel realities. He therefore does all he can to stimulate right brain functioning in the organization. He stresses creativity, innovation, visualization, futuring, and visioning. Current reality is viewed as no more real than a parallel reality that could just as well exist.

When organizations assume a vortex shape, a small group of people will assume responsibility for shaping the future reality of the organization. They will use group imagination to scan the spectrum of available realities. They will activate the matrix of a chosen parallel reality and then begin reshaping it to fit their value ideals. The same thing will happen on a planetary basis when the earth becomes a designer planet.

Advanced planets occupy realities of their own choosing. They can visit parallel realities, check them out, and if they see something they like, return to reshape their current reality.

For years, the Planet Earth has simply reacted to whatever was happening and adapted to it. This produced a low common denominator of life quality. In the future, humankind will assume responsibility for all that happens. In a real sense, the universe will recognize the shared visualization of the planet.

Interlude II

Destiny is choice. Choice is destiny. Parallel realities can be fitted on in the same manner as a chosen piece of clothing. Humanity will make the big breakthrough mid-century. In the meantime, we still think healthcare problems are outside us and we react and adapt to them as a given. It has not yet occurred to us that we are their inventors, and that a change of our collective mind is all that is needed to change our shared reality.

SECTION THREE:
TRUST

1. INTRODUCTION

To begin this discussion, I want to bring together three stories—which are actually reflections on real events—that focus attention on the meaning of trust. Trust can be a really elusive idea, but we do not need to get too abstract in our discussion of it. Instead, we need to arrive at an understanding that has real, concrete application to our daily lives.

The first story involves an event from World War II. Elements of the United States Army 101st Airborne Division under the command of General Anthony McAuliff had pushed their way, in order to stop the German advances of the Battle of the Bulge, far beyond Allied lines to the town of Bastogne where they found themselves surrounded. During the harsh cold of winter approaching Christmas in 1944, the American troops faced the best forces Germany had left. If Bastogne, an important crossroads, could be overwhelmed, the German armies would have many strategic advantages. In response to a German call to surrender, McAuliff wrote the now-famous response, "Nuts!" The Americans held the city until they were almost miraculously liberated, and McAuliff and his men became heroes.

After the war was over, McAuliff was asked how he could have made his response under such great opposition. Was he simply filled with battlefield bravado, or did he know something the Germans did not know? It was neither. In fact, for McAuliff, what he had done was not that big of a deal and certainly not "heroic." For him, it was simply a matter of trust. He trusted Eisenhower, Bradley, Patton, and the other generals of the American Army. Then, when he was asked to clarify exactly what he meant by trust, McAuliff had an important answer: "I knew," he replied, "that everyone in the chain of command above me was out there, somewhere, doing everything within their power to relieve my position. I knew they were giving the best energy they had to help us. All we had to do was our part, and they would get there as quickly as was humanly possible."

McAuliff's words were, in essence, repeated by three American astronauts when their Apollo moon rocket was struck by lightening on takeoff and they drifted without much hope of safe return in dark, empty space. Their safe return required innovation and creativity beyond anything that had ever happened in the U.S. space program. The slightest wrong turn or inadequate decision, and these astronauts would have died. After their return, the astronauts did not act like heroes either; instead, they were just doing a job. What gave them confidence was that they trusted that everyone in NASA was doing his/her job, bringing to bear every possible insight and intelligence on their situation. In retrospect, the astronauts were amazed at how calm they had remained; the high level of trust had generated, not simply empty hope, but a real sense of confidence that all would work successfully.

A more recent, powerful story involved Air Force Captain Scott O'Gready. As his jet fighter patrolled over the Bosnian-Croatian battlefield during that explosive, horrific war, it was struck by a surface-to-air missile. The plane disintegrated in a ball of flame around O'Gready, and he miraculously parachuted into an enemy-controlled war zone. For days he lived off the land with enemy soldiers walking so close to him in their search that he could have reached out and touched them. But, O'Gready prevailed, was able to make radio contact with a fellow pilot who was out looking for him, and was rescued. His story was the same: he had great trust in his friends, his commanders, and his country as a whole. He knew everyone was out there doing all that they could, working, praying, planning, and ready to come to his help at the slightest indication that he was still alive.

Trust is a reality generated between people when there is a need for being able to depend on someone else. There is no way that we can take care of every reality of our lives by ourselves, so we have to be able to trust others. When you get on an airplane and fly 30,000 feet above the ground at 500 mph, think about the network of people you are trusting: pilots, mechanics, aircraft builders, air-traffic controllers. When you go to a restaurant and have a meal, think of the trust involved in food selection, storage, and preparation. The list goes on endlessly. We are continuously caught up in a nexus of trust relationships that crisscross our lives like a delicate spider's web.

But, trust is much more than simply hope that people will do as they are supposed to do. Trust is a more highly-developed belief in people (or another person) that manifests itself as confidence, a kind of confidence which gives us comfort rather than fear, worry, and anxiety. In fact, sometimes trust can be so strong that it will drive away fear, worry, and anxiety, thus allowing us to focus all of our energies on helping ourselves as much as we possibly can. A reliable relationship of trust is one of the greatest gifts that people can share with each other. To know beyond doubt that you can trust another person is a unique dimension of relationship that usually individuals have with only a very few, select people of their acquaintance.

1. Introduction

DYNAMICS OF TRUST

1. *Trust is earned over time.* Seldom is trust simply bestowed. It is, almost without exception, the result of real precedents, real actions. I have come to think that I can trust the person I am married to. After many years of life together, I absolutely know that she is a person who will always act in my best interests, the best interests of our children, and the best interests of our family as a whole. I totally trust her.

There may be other people that I think I can trust, but—in every instance— that is because of specific events when I have observed them in action. If their actions have been well-intended, intelligent, caring actions, the ability to trust is increased. If they are inconsistent, do not know what they are talking about, or sometimes do not invest their actions with care, it is very difficult to trust them about anything of much importance.

I can set out to gain trust with other people. This will not happen overnight; rather, it will be the result of perhaps years of consistency, hard work, and good decisions. For some people, however, especially if they have been victimized by breeches of trust, to gain their trust may be almost impossible.

2. *Trust and general morality*—Across the ages, human existence has produced general ideas of what is moral and what is immoral. While there are certainly times when "rules" and "laws" have to be modified to meet the demands of specific situations, the general rules of human conduct, respect, and decency that have been established are predominantly helpful and have good outcomes in mind. When individuals "play fast and loose" with these general principles of moral conduct, it becomes very difficult to trust them with major decisions or major responsibilities. If I would "let my guard down" on issues of basic moral conduct, how can I be trusted to perform important tasks or be consistent in my decision-making when difficult circumstances arise?

3. *When trust is broken*—It would probably be unrealistic to think that there would not be times when trust will be broken. I am not talking about major breeches in morality, for which it may never be possible to achieve the old status quo of the way things were. We may be able to forgive, but we probably never forget because something of a "crack" in the trust relationship hangs back there in the recesses of our mind forever.

I am talking about those breeches in trust when we have not followed through, kept commitments adequately, or performed at the level of expectation required. How can we come back from these kinds of events? The first step is honesty. When we have been less than our best, either intentionally or inadvertently (perhaps not paying adequate attention to what we are doing), or when we have let someone down, we will likely have the opportunity to explain ourselves. We are at a critical point in this "moment of truth." We have the chance to immediately determine whether the path to restructuring a relationship of trust will be enhanced or further encumbered. Honesty, even as it may hurt, is the key. If we choose to be less than honest, the chances of trust being reestablished all but evaporate. The relationship to telling the whole truth and trust is one of the most intricate relationships of human existence.

4. *Trust and processes*—In most of our interactions with other human beings in the modern world we live in, there is not direct contact. Instead, we made contact with others through the products and processes that we create or take part in delivering. Think for a few minutes about all that you do that does not bring you into direct contact with another person, but that has a real impact or influence on the life of another person.

I may be a pharmacist who is responsible for compounding medications. My job requires a tremendous amount of attention to detail and precise accuracy. I may never actually see the person who takes the medicine I have created; I may not even know the person's name. Yet, what I do will have a direct impact on this person's life. There is a specific relationship of trust that we will share because of my work, the product I create, and the processes I am responsible for. To be involved in a trust relationship means that we personalize our actions and the processes we are a part of. To personalize actions means simply to realize that our actions will touch the lives of another person—a real, live, breathing person. We do not live and act in neutral vacuums, but in a what Martin Luther King, Jr. called a "network of humanity." An old piece of poetry explains that no person is an island, but that everyone is part of a larger continent—a part of a larger humanity—in which actions and processes have implications and consequences and in which our lives inevitably and invariably touch each other. To be motivated by these realizations, to care how our actions and processes touch others, is to recognize that we are bound together by trust.

I once knew a pilot who flew for Delta Airlines for over thirty years. A few times I flew on flights when he was sitting in the captain's seat. He was a study in trust. He was out and around the airplane for fifteen or twenty minutes before it took off, looking at the mechanical workings, peering into the engine with a flashlight, talking to the ground crew, even watching the way luggage was loaded. The mechanics and the baggage handlers seemed to know him personally as they talked back and forth. You got the idea that this plane was *his* plane and that he took careful pride in every aspect of its operation.

In a while, when the passengers got onto the plane, he stood at the door and greeted them, always taking a bit more time for children, old people, and anyone who might be exhibiting any fears about flying. On the airplane intercom, he was always advising passengers of any changes or explaining any odd noises or turbulence that the plane was flying into. I especially liked the way he would tell you where you were and point out any important sights on the ground. At the end of the flight, he was standing at the front again, wishing you well for the remainder of your travel. You can imagine his reputation, the way his fellow employees and employer thought of him, and the safety record he maintained over the years.

One time, near the end of his career, we sat together at a social function. He was talking a lot about his life as a pilot. I asked why he felt that he did such a good job. His answer was immediate, clearly something he had thought about often: "I see those people waiting to get on my plane, and I talk to them as they are boarding. I always make it a point to do this. As I look back into the cabin at the people I will be flying today, I do not think about them as just passengers. Some of my colleagues use the word 'cattle.' I think of my mother and father, my wife, and my children. Those passengers are someone's parents, spouses, or children. They count for someone, so I make them count for me." Now, that's the kind of person I want flying me through the air. There is a relationship of trust. He may never know their names, what they do, or where they are from, but they count. They count, not like a number, but like a unique person with a life that is attached to others.

It is important, especially in our work, to give real consideration to how our lives touch others through the products we create or the processes we are part of. The exterminator who sprays our house is meticulous to a fault about his chemicals. I trust him. The physician who gives me my checkups takes precious time to address my worries and tell me what he is doing as he makes his examination. The business where I get my oil changed in my car has an aggressive waste disposal program. In these situations, and many more, trust is a critical issue. This "network of humanity" is beautiful and profound; it is also delicate and fragile. Life depends on the exercise of trust.

5. *Avoiding the Clandestine*—Most organizations have the potential for becoming awash with clandestine, behind-the-scenes politics. It becomes

altogether too easy, at times, to "play games" and be manipulative in achieving vested interests or gaining some sort of personal advantage. Often, such backdoor maneuvering can destroy the trust dimension of an organization and jeopardize every agenda for advancement that an organization has. Once trust is made vulnerable and the clandestine, backdoor maneuvering begins, the internal stability of an organization is ruptured.

Where trust prevails, there is an atmosphere in which people, as adults, bring issues "to the top of the table" where they can be discussed, modified, refined, integrated until some sort of consensus, middle ground, or more conclusive decision can be made. If the atmosphere is right, all kinds of discussion and dissent can prevail until a decision is made; then, the group decision becomes the decision of the individuals in the group. When everything is "on the table," difference of opinion and belief can be vented, but trust can be preserved.

I encountered a situation a few years ago in which a board chairman of an organization was best friends with a couple of contractors who wanted to build a new office park for the organization. The organizational CEO had already conducted a thorough study which indicated that such a building project would not be in the best interests of the organization or the general community; he had said "no" to the project. But if the CEO could be moved out, a circumstance that the board chairman could manipulate, then a new person could be forced to "see the light" that would be favorable to the board chairman's contractor friends.

The board chair began to work behind the scenes to find some way to discredit the CEO, or at least to make his work so difficult that he might want to leave. The board chair broke trust with the organization, even with the larger community. The problem, and this can often be the case, was that he was so "connected" and so personally "slick" that it was all but impossible to override his undermining strategies. Suddenly, people who had easy relationships with each other felt a strong awkwardness with one another. The efficiency and effectiveness of general communication was eroded. Critical decision-making ground to a halt all because someone broke trust and started using deceiving, behind-the-scenes tactics to gain their own personal advantage. This series of events took place in the mid-1990s; the organization has not recovered from it to this day. There is still a loss of leadership balance, still a sense of vulnerability, and still a lack of ease with open communication. Breaking trust carries a huge price tag.

CONCLUSION

In 1998, Michael Annison and Dan Wilford wrote a book with a title that captures the essence of our present discussion—*Trust Matters*. So often, we take the trust dimension of relationships and organizations for granted, and do not take careful pains to make absolutely sure that trust is being realized on the highest levels possible. Think about the care that must be taken to create the infrastructure of a great skyscraper. You may never see the foundation plates or the steel rigging hidden behind walls, but if these essential elements are not constructed with care, the entire building is subject to collapse. In a similar sense, trust is the support structure of organizations and individual relationships. There is no substitute for trust. Annison and Wilford write: "Trust matters because, like water, it is essential for our well-being, and like water, we take it for granted until it begins to slip away."

In the end, the entire issue of trust raises some of the most personal of questions. I must have a very clear understanding of whom I can trust based on past experiences and real-life precedents that I can depend upon without question. I must also have a clear understanding of what personal qualities I possess that make me trustworthy to others. On some of these personal qualities, I may be very strong and consistent; on others, I may need to focus attention for improvement. If I am a leader in an organization, I must work especially hard in promoting trust as an essential ingredient in a successful work environment, making certain that my own actions never jeopardize the trust dimension. At the end of the day, there are some dimensions of life that are only marginally important, that do not matter as much. There are other realities that are of decisive importance. Annison and Wilford are absolutely correct in their assessment—trust matters!

2. THE VITAL ROLE OF TRUST IN MODERN ORGANIZATIONS

TWO WORKPLACE MODELS

A *transactional model* dominates organizational settings when functional means and economic outcomes take precedence over human ends and personal outcomes. In every respect, functional means and economic outcomes are important—very important—but when they take on highest priority, the workplace becomes a *transactional* environment. In fact, human ends and personal outcomes probably do not occur with high plausibility without functional means and economic outcomes, so the agendas relating to functionality and economics have to be respected and carefully managed. The problem occurs when the functional and economic triumph, and the human and personal are given secondary emphasis.

There are numerous examples of the *transactional model* that can be described. I taught in a state community college for over twenty years. Early in that experience, deep meaning was derived from helping students who, more times than not, were the first of their families to attend college. Great attention was given to treating each student as a unique individual, trying to understand how success might be most readily achieved, and doing class scheduling in a way that would allow for jobs and personal life commitments.

About five years into my teaching experience, all of this changed. Suddenly, our funding formula from the state was changed, and our existence as an institute depended on FTEs (Full Time Equivalents), and we had to live with the severe mandate to get as many students into as many classes as possible. Our entire counseling processes changed, and we became almost like pushy salespeople. Little concern was directed at how many hours a student could reasonably handle or if their classes "fit" with the rest of their lives. There is no telling how many times we set students up for frustration and even failure.

The relationship with the students became a *transaction*. The students had value for us, not as human beings we could really help, but as numbers. The more numbers we could put into the classes, the more state funds we would receive. The powerful mandate became, "Just keep them in your classes through the fourteenth day!" Fourteen days into the term, the magical FTE count would occur, and—for many leaders in the organization—what happened to students after that date made little difference.

Eventually, we took the *transaction* one step further. We became very sensitive to failing students or giving them low grades. Bad grades could translate into a factor of discouragement, and the students might not return for the next term. Again, the entire focus was on FTE. These strategies had a direct impact on quality of education, the challenge students could be given, and artificial grade inflation. For many of us who were trying to be competent professionals, the *transactional model* was devastating to our ideas, turned us into scheming rule-benders who did everything we could to fight the system we were part of. We may, at times, have been heroic and actually helped students, but little of it felt very good.

In a similar sense, I have one hospital that I used to call on that believes it has been very inventive about bringing to the attention of its employees what the hospital leadership feels is most important. When employees come into the hospital either to begin their workday or after lunch or breaks, they must run their name badges through a slot that feeds their information into a computer. It is possible to know exactly when an employee is in the work area, how long they have been on break, or if they leave early or come in late. The machine is a punitive influence. The machine also has a screen—many employees believe with a camera that ensures that no one slides another person's name badge—that conveys special information. It might tell, for example, about special meetings that are taking place on a given day, or important visitors—Joint Commission—that are in the hospital.

Most importantly, the screen reads out its own FTE numbers regarding patient census, year-to-date census, and how far behind or above budget that the organization is operating on this particular date. The screen could describe important employee milestones—anniversaries, birthdays, etc.—but it is never used in this way. Many workers feel that the machine is invasive, treats them like children, and suggests the wrong set of priorities from the moment they enter the workplace. *Transaction* rules in this work environment.

A final example of the *transactional model* relates to a project I did a few years ago with physicians who are involved with a major healthcare system in Tennessee. The point of the project was to improve physician-system interactions, to gain a greater sense of the physician's needs, and basically convey to physicians that they were important. All of these initiatives were well-meaning and well-received.

I was stunned by the way in which my interviews became almost counseling sessions time after time. These highly-professional doctors needed to "vent" so much about certain stressors of their work, that I found myself having to be an agent of sympathy and encouragement more than a kind of system "good will ambassador."

I began to keep track of "data" regarding my interviews. Over the course of three months, I spent one to two hours with two hundred physicians representing almost every healthcare specialty. Of this group, 160 were between the ages of forty-five and fifty-five; in other words, at what you would expect to be the core of their careers and their most productive years. Of these 160 mid-career caregivers, fully 80 percent talked to me about one, common factor. They talked about how, if they could figure out how to get their finances in good shape, they would end their careers and find something else to do!

This experience was amazing. The amount of dissatisfaction and pure angst was written into the worry lines on their faces and the near depression in their voices. They talked about how they no longer could take time to really care and give the attention needed and deserved to their patients. They knew those critical numbers that measured how many patients had to be seen in a day in order to pay for the overhead of their practices and the staff necessary to support their work. They talked about offices that were compared to assembly lines. They talked about not knowing anything about the personal side of the people they treated; they were "walking illnesses" or "walking maladies." This was absolutely *not* why they had given so much of their lives to the study of medicine. They talked about the endless array of papers and forms demanded by government and insurance companies. Everything had become a *transaction.*

When human ends and personal/interpersonal concerns take priority, the result is a *relational model*. Fortunately, examples of this model can also be noted. One of my major clients across the years has been the Memorial Hermann Healthcare System in Houston that has become one of the most important not-for-profit healthcare systems in the nation.

The medical facilities of the system are supported by a central Executive Office Building in the southeast area of Houston that houses all of the primary system offices—finance, human resources, all computer operations, etc.—and is the workplace of over a thousand employees. It is highly unlikely that these employees will ever see a sick or injured person, and—by the very nature of their work—transactional issues dominate their workdays.

However, if you walk up and down the hallways of this complex, multi-level building, you cannot walk twenty feet without passing an enlarged photograph mounted on the walls of the hallways. There must be literally hundreds of these photographs throughout the building. Each picture features some caregivers extending skill and compassion to a person in need. There are pictures of pediatric nurses working with premature babies, exercise therapists working with senior citizens who have broken a bone, and flight doctors and nurses working with the pilots and technicians of Memorial Hermann's "Lifeflight" program.

There is huge intent and purpose in the placement of these pictures. No one working in this Executive Office Building can lose sight of the fact that their highly transactional work actually has a human, highly personal end and outcome. Continuously, system employees are reminded that the work they do with numbers, money, and computers makes it possible for more direct caregivers to help sick people. In fact, it is made clear to these people that the direct caregiver is limited in what can be done at their end of the healthcare system if they do not do an excellent job at their end of the healthcare system. Memorial Hermann actively promotes the idea that their system is highly *integrated*, with every person playing a vital role in the entire program of care provided by the larger system.

A second example of the *relational model* rose in the context of Memorial Hermann. In 2002, a new CEO came to the healthcare system, a man by the name of Dan Wolterman. Wolterman replaced almost a legend in healthcare in the United States, Dan Wilford. Wilford set a high standard that emphasized human ends and personal outcomes. System employees wondered what kind of administration the new CEO would initiate.

In his first movements within Memorial Hermann, Wolterman took up an exhaustive schedule of meetings with employees across the Houston area at all times of the day and night. He wanted to put a human face on a name, and also leave no doubt about what kind of agendas he would place priority on. In a major statement that was echoed all over Houston, Wolterman gave great emphasis to saying: "I will not make a single decision as CEO of Memorial Hermann without understanding how that decision impacts the patient at the bedside." Wolterman has also insisted on keeping in place all of the employee benefit and development programs that have become a vital part of the identity of Memorial Hermann. When the person at the top of the corporate ladder advances this kind of passionate agenda, the *relational model* has its best chance of success.

I would also like to finally say in offering these contrasting examples that the *relational model* in not limited to not-for-profit arenas. A very different client, U.S. Xpress Enterprises, one of the largest trucking lines in the United States, is a for-profit, market-traded company of the highest order. It has an energetic board, high-expectation stockholders, and a strong accountability to be profitable. When you walk through the work areas of the company, it is buzzing with business deals, negotiations, the realization of how tough the competition in this industry is. The leadership of U.S. Xpress has to have its "head" totally alert to the *transactional*.

However, the atmosphere that has been created in this company is one of the most humane environments I have ever seen. There is a rich sense of diversity, and an absence of "glass ceilings" that deprive people of opportunity. There is especially an atmosphere that rewards and recognizes young adults and their creative insights. The company is literally being remolded by people in their mid-twenties and early thirties. "Human capital" is acknowledged from the high-tech screens that constantly keep the vision and mission of the company, along with work anniversaries, birthdays, and special employee events, before the workforce on a continual basis to the encouragement to become involved in community volunteer efforts that help improve the lives of less fortunate people. Cubicles have glass walls so that people do not feel isolated. Every floor has an exterior patio/observation deck where people can go and be outside for a while. The basic architecture of the interior of the building makes you feel as if the outdoors have somehow flowed into the indoors.

People seem to have a naturalness of interaction with each other that I am not used to in most workplaces. People actually seem to smile and laugh more. All of this is within a business that is part of an industry that often is "dog eat dog." There is plenty of *transactional*, and there must be, but the *relational* is not lost.

These examples are meant to create an introductory contrast between two, distinct models that can be chosen and implemented. In the organizations noted above, the *transactional* and the *relational* are in a nice balance with each other with at least a visible edge to the *relational* that is part of the "pride of leadership" of the people in the top executive chairs of these organizations.

They believe that the *relational* is the "smart" way to run an organization, the best way to run an organization, and the "right thing to do." It should also be noted that these organizations are highly profitable and very secure on the *transactional* level. They have become the "employers of choice" for their industries in the communities they are part of. Even when "harder times" have come—as they do and will—the *relational* has not been the first "head" to go on the chopping block. These companies are run by skilled, tough business persons who see the *relational* as the essential, and who are convinced that when the *relational* is sustained that the *transactional* has its best chance for success.

PHILOSOPHICAL PRECEDENTS

What can be seen through the lens of actually, organizational circumstances can also be seen—in a somewhat broader context—in important, philosophical precedents. Anecdotes are descriptive; philosophical precedents can be wrapped around a wider range of situations. At the end of the day, the anecdotal and philosophical can greatly reinforce each other.

The first, philosophical precedent comes from the ancient Greek philosopher, Aristotle. Aristotle focused a great deal of attention on the *causes* that acted as catalysts for events. He described two forms of causation. The first is *necessary causation* and relates to realities that are vital and indispensable. A *necessary cause* would be something so important that it becomes a valuable end-in-itself. The air that we breathe would be a *necessary cause* for our existence as human beings.

For Aristotle, there is also *sufficient causation*. A *sufficient cause* relates to realities that are desired in a secondary manner, to what are typically called "wants" as opposed to real "needs." Usually, *sufficient causes* are on the level of means-to-an-end, not ends-in-themselves. The air that we breathe is necessary, while a filet mignon to eat would be a desired, *sufficient cause* for our existence.

Substantial problems can be created in life when we experience what Aristotle called "cause confusion," a reality that takes place when *necessary causes*/"needs" are confused with *sufficient causes*/"wants." When this confusion occurs, the meaning of life is threatened, undermined, and even destroyed. In common language, "cause confusion" is usually manifested in a confusion of priorities or a confusion in values clarification. Without any question, "cause confusion" occurs when the *transactional model* overwhelms the *relational model*. This is especially true when everything gets reduced to a dollar sign and economics triumphs.

A second, philosophical precedent is found in the work of the modern thinker, Ayn Rand. Rand's philosophy is brutally honest, and—whether our idealism likes it or not—may be more correct in its assessment of the modern world than we would ever like. Rand sees herself as a powerful pragmatist, and simply wants people to awaken to the real world and quit living inadequately in an imagined, idealized one. Aristotle, with his necessary causation, is stupid. We should grow up and become thoroughly modern people. "Meaning" is an immature, child's toy.

In her philosophy, there are basically two types of people who have value: those who consume what we produce, and those who produce what we want to consume. Everyone else is "worthless" or worth less.

For example, imagine again that as a kind of "second job" I build hang gliders, those bird-like flying devices that are popular in the ridges and mountains of East Tennessee. I become aware, from a passing conversation, that Mary Smith thinks hang gliding is stupid, something that she would never try under any circumstances in her life. Because she is not a potential consumer of what I produce, she has no value for me. Then, I find out that John Jones is somewhat adventurous and is considering taking up hang gliding. Suddenly, he has a degree of value and worth for me since he may be in the market to buy what I am selling. Finally, Tom Wilson comes on the scene, a seasoned hang gliding enthusiast who has decided to invest $5,000 in the latest model glider available. I can create that for Tom, so he suddenly takes on the highest value. He is a potential buyer. I may court him, invite him to my home for dinner, put him on my Christmas card line. He has value and worth because he represents a really big sale!

Move the conversation in another direction. I could say that I love grain-raised, premium midwestern beefsteaks, the kind of steaks that very few grocery stores would ever have. I find out that Mary Smith has a small cart that she sets up downtown on the weekends to sell food to tourists visiting our town. She only has cheap hamburgers and hot dogs. No premium steaks. Mary has no value or worth to me. She is not producing something I want to consume.

Tom Wilson, however, works at a small grocery store that carries specialty items, and occasionally is able to get premium meat. Tom suddenly takes on a new importance to me. I will curry favor with him, and maybe he will reward that with a nice steak on occasion. But then there is Tom Wilson. His brother lives in Omaha, works for one of the most exclusive meat processors in the country, and sends Tom a box of his finest steaks on a monthly basis. I'm telling my kids to get to know Tom's kids. I'm telling my wife to invite Tom's wife to the club for dinner. I'll treat Tom as if he has the highest value. He has something I want.

The dialogue at this point, honestly, starts getting pretty disgusting to me. I do not want to believe Ayn Rand. I do not want to think that she is right about this, and that this is really the way that most people live their lives. This is purely *transactional* to me and deeply effaces the *relational*. For Ayn Rand, we need to grow up, get ourselves a network of production/consumption, create some marketable commodity or service, and negotiate. Any idealism that suggests that a human being is valuable in and of himself/herself is only likely to put us at deep disadvantage.

The choice seems to be between Aristotle and his clarification of *necessary causes* that should get our greatest attention, and Ayn Rand's concept of value that is assigned only if the network of production and consumption works to our favor. It might be interesting to have an honest dialogue about how people actually see the world in which they live; not what they might like to see, but what they actually experience on most days.

AN IMPORTANT DISCLAIMER

But, before we get too hard on ourselves, maybe believing that in actuality Ayn Rand is more right than Aristotle, let's clearly understand that we are not bad people. We simply find ways to take "the path of least resistance." We think it is easier to build lives based on *transactions* than on *relationships*. Maybe, it is, because relationships depend upon *trust*, and *trust*—though extolled and idealized on every hand—may be one of the most difficult realities to actually achieve that there is. Therefore, people will opt for the *transactional* because the *relational* is so difficult. *Trust* may be easily talked about, but it is actually a complex reality that requires the greatest determination and discipline.

THE CHALLENGE: DEFINING TRUST

At this point, the attempt will be made to move beyond pleasant clichés and platitudes, and come to grips with what *trust* actually involves. Instead of defining *trust*, I want to say that *trust* is a "condition" that rises under certain circumstances. It is a "by-product" of certain circumstances. When certain "conditions" prevail, *trust* becomes an operative, causative reality in life. Our task is to understand these "conditions" and try to create them so that *trust* has a chance to prevail and exert its optimum influence. If *trust* rises, the base for the *relational* is provided, and people actually have a chance of moving beyond the *transactional*. Without *trust*—the *transactional* is more likely, and the *relational* is very hard to achieve.

In what will follow, seven "conditions" that contribute to *trust* in a positive manner will be described and explained. The list noted here is not exhaustive, but should be able to convey the idea that *trust* is this special "by-product" that results from "conditions" that competent leaders and creditable organizations can work to produce.

1. Trust is the condition that rises from the realization that someone is behind the scenes working on my behalf and holding my best interests as a major priority.

Dr. Robert Demos is a retired Chattanooga physician who my wife and I came to know in the 1970s. Dr. Demos was my wife's gynecologist. We had had one child and hoped to have a second. Unfortunately, my wife had severe endometriosis, and the odds of a second pregnancy given the degree of her problems were very slim. Dr. Demos had already endeared himself to us with all of the compassionate care he had given my wife.

Finally, with one pregnancy after another being thwarted, the decision was made to perform a delicate and demanding surgery to remove enough of the endometriosis that a pregnancy might be successful. On the day of the surgery, my wife was taken to the operating room, and Dr. Demos came by to speak to my father-in-law and me. He explained that the odds were short that he would be successful, but that he would do everything within his power to complete a surgical procedure that would work. It should take a couple of hours, and he would have his nurse keep us posted.

Two hours passed with no word, and then Dr. Demos' nurse came to the room. She reported that the surgery was more complicated that first thought, but that Dr. Demos still felt optimistic. He should be another hour or so.

Two more hours passed, and the nurse was back in the room with about the same information. More complications, but still optimism.

Finally, after more than five hours, Dr. Demos came to the room. He was an older man, but he looked more beaten and drained that I had ever seen him. He was absolutely exhausted. With a unique smile on his face, he said to me:

"Phyllis is fine. I have never worked so hard, but I think we got it all." Now—and his smile increased—he told me, "If you will do your part, I believe everything will work." Indeed, it did. In a little over nine months, by wife gave birth to a beautiful baby girl—exactly what we had dreamed of having—the first girl born on my side of the family in over seventy years.

My father-in-law had become incredulous, on the day of the surgery, at how I had remained calm and collected. With his beloved daughter in the operating room that long, he was anything but calm. A little while after Dr. Demos left the room with his good news, he asked me how I had remained under such control.

My answer was quiet simple, but very real: I *trusted* Bob Demos. I knew he was in that surgery suite taking care of my wife like she was his own daughter. I knew he would leave no possibility for success untried. I knew he had our very best interests at the forefront of his priorities. We were in the best of hands. My *trust* in Dr. Demos took care of my fears. Every time I look into the face of my daughter, now a wonderful young woman, I feel the most powerful sense of gratitude for this great physician *and* trusted friend.

I have heard other people describe *trust* in similar terms. Soldiers on battlefields often talk about the fact that, indeed, they believed in their cause or had a great deal of dedication to their country and its flag. However, in the chaos of battle, the primary motivation for efforts that were often heroic was the other members of their platoon or company who were counting on them. I have shared a similar experience with fellow players on athletic teams. The bonds with these people have sustained themselves across a lifetime because we have been in our own kind of "trenches" together where we had nothing more important to depend upon than the *trust* we had for each other.

2. Trust is the condition that rises from authentic conversation.

Conversation, dialogue—all forms of communication—can either be authentic or inauthentic. Since communication and language are such vital factors of our lives together as human beings, the choice between authentic and inauthentic conversation is absolutely, incredibility decisive. *Trust*, on any significantly operative manner, cannot exist in the midst of inauthentic conversation.

Authentic conversation is inhibited by lies, half-truths, and any form of deception. Denial and conflict avoidance are also inhibiting factors. In fact, once someone, some organization, or some service or product of an organization has acted toward us with lies, half-truths, and deception, it is all but impossible to ever construct a whole relationship based on full *trust* again.

Authentic conversation is also inhibited by our inability to ask for help, admit that we do not understand, that we are "in over our heads," or that we are afraid. This particular "inhibition" is often characteristic of very strong people and people in places of high leadership. We can become convinced that to ask for help is a sign of weakness or an admission of some sort of lack of competence.

I struggle with this sort of inauthentic conversation almost daily. Something will be troubling me, and my wife is particularly sensitive to these kinds of realities. She will ask me, "What's the matter?" My tendency is to say, "Nothing." I can almost be accusative back toward her, as if I am wondering why in the world she would ask such a question. In a while, she will say again, "Now, I know something is the matter. Tell me." I am likely to respond, a bit more seriously: "I said, nothing is the matter." She tends to not let things like this rest, so at a later moment she will speak with her own strength, "Now, I know something is the matter. What is it?" When I approach the point of saying, "Nothing dammit!," it is abundantly clear that she was right all along. I will usually seek her help, and the situation is almost always better. Why I did not seek help to begin with is often a mystery that I find almost impossible to understand. Strong people can greatly diminish authentic conversation and *trust* because they fear needing help, being weak or afraid, or not wanting to admit some inadequacy.

3. Trust is the condition that rises from a belief in forgiveness and the importance of "second chances."

Only in a perfect world is trust not broken at one point or another. Clearly, there are some instances of broken trust that are too great to be healed. However, there may be countless other instances of broken trust that do have to be the end of the matter. For this to occur, there has to be a strong commitment and belief to the possibility of new beginnings. New beginnings will be advanced more quickly if forgiveness is part of a person's approach to life.

Forgiveness is a work more commonly experienced in a religious setting, but it should not be limited to that setting. Forgiveness can also be initiated in multiple ways that increase the option of its coming into play. The offending party can ask for forgiveness. The offended party can offer it. A third-person mediator can suggest it to both parties as a plausibility. Forgiving does not have to mean forgetting. It only has to mean a willingness to functionally let the past be past and move toward the future with a determination to make the new agenda work. In this determination toward the future, old wounds can be healed.

4. Trust is the condition that rises from facing adversity together.

The Center for Creative Leadership has done substantial research on how human beings learn. About 15 percent of our learning comes from formal education. Having been a college professor, I hate to see this, but in my heart I know it is true. Close to 20 percent of our learning comes from on-the-job training. How true this is as well. People constantly graduate from college, get a first job, and then immediately enter a training program that is designed to teach people how to perform the tasks they have been hired for. Then, approximately 25 percent of learning comes from mentors, role models, and real-life examples. Most people's experiences will confirm this finding. How often teachers as individual people have had a larger impact on us than any content taught by that teacher.

The remaining 40 percent, the largest impact on learning of any of the various sources, comes from adversity. In facing difficulty, we tend to gain strength. The experiences found in adversity constitute some of the most life-changing experiences we have. Then, to face these experiences of adversity with someone else tends of create a bond of trust that is profoundly substantial. It is no accident that Stephen Ambrose—and then Steven Spielberg and Tom Hanks—named their World War II epic "Band of *Brothers.*"

5. Trust is a condition that rises when we open ourselves to intimacy, struggle, and hurt.

I recently talked with a young woman who has gone through a set of life experiences that has left her with a great deal of wisdom. First, she was raised in a particularly harsh and hard environment by parents who were both alcoholics and had times in which they were abusive of their children. Perhaps, as a consequence of this, she married late in her teens in an attempt to escape her home environment. Getting married at this early age and under these less-than-ideal circumstances led to other negative situations, disappointment, more abuse, and a divorce. She had hoped to have children, but even developed a conditioned that her doctors told her would prevent her from ever becoming pregnant.

After a decade of being single and finally achieving some degree of success and self-affirmation through work, she married. This marriage was pretty successful, although she says that she never "opened" herself to her husband in an unguarded way for fear of getting hurt again. Surprisingly, in her late thirties, she became pregnant and had a little girl. Her background was so negative that she even felt a coolness to this child. The kind of hurt she had experienced ran very deep.

Then, when the young girl was nine years old, a powerful change took place. She realized that her coolness and detachment could have an impact on her child that was similar to the negative experience she had encountered herself. She became determined to open herself fully to her child. To be ready for hurt if that came. To accept pain in order to experience the highest of pleasure. In other words, she decided to take down barriers and begin to trust. In this process, the intimacy, affection, and even love that she had for her husband reached higher levels. Now, she was able to trust him as well. Finally, the relationships she had at work began to take on a different significance as she began to trust people—imperfect, fallible, capable-of-disappointing, and capable-of-hurting people. Work has taken on a new joy that she had not expected or experience before. Finally, the entire way she feels about herself as an individual has improved.

I am convinced that this story, in one form or another, is repeated in many dimensions of people's daily lives. To trust puts us on a different level of intensity with people. That intensity can be negative at times, but it can also be highly positive. If we live in a way that avoids the negative—that is, if we refuse to go out on the limb of trust—we will not experience the highly positive. Cool detachment—often the opposite of trust—may protect us from hurt, the intricacies of intimacy, or the risks of loving, but the cost of such "protection" may be extremely high.

6. Trust is the condition that rises from the foundation of the strengths found in family and community.

It is critical to preserve as much balance between life and work as possible. This balance is often jeopardized by the high demands of a workplace, but when this balance is ruptured there will be significant, negative implications for the quality of effort and concentration that a person brings to work performance.

2. *The Vital Role of Trust in Modern Organizations*

The issue of work/life balance is not only a personal matter, it must also be a matter of concern and strategy for those leading the work environment. In general, strong work skills, attitudes, and commitments will either be enhanced or diminished by the foundation and strength provided by a person having a strong support structure of family and community.

7. Trust is the condition that rises from the foundation of high standards of personal morality.

When there are lapses in personal morality, often even small lapses, trust is diminished. Once someone "bends the rules" of basic morality, a question mark is placed in the mind of almost everyone aware of this "bending." When will the next lapse occur? Will the lapse occur in a circumstance relating to some agenda or priority important to me or for which I have some accountability? A "balance" is broken that is difficult to rebuild.

By way of review, it is interesting how all of these seven items work in concert with each other in many relationships to create a nexus of trust in which the various elements of trust reinforce each other. When trust rises from all—or most—of these seven areas, the trust factor becomes almost palpable. High trust is a powerful catalyst for the enhancement of organizational success.

CONCLUSION

The problems and challenges facing organizations at the advent of the twenty-first century are so demanding and so complex that they will not be met unilaterally by any one part of an organization working by itself. This principle can be within an individual organization where people develop relationships based on trust, or it can be within an industry even where competition in high. Respecting the phenomenon of trust will raise the quality of life and its potential on every side.

Yet, if we cannot get beyond the *transactional models* of organizational existence and return to our roots in the *relational*, our lives will only become harder. And, if someone is saying/thinking, "What is being written here is right, *but* we cannot afford it," then sufficient causation, cause confusion, and the *transactional* have already triumphed. That which is necessary—the air that we breathe—that which is vital is lost.

In fact, we cannot afford *NOT* to extend every effort to reclaim, sustain, and advance the *relational*. It is not a "child's toy" that is at stake. In the balances is the meaning and joy of this one life that we have to live.

There is an interesting story about a Texas Ranger who is sitting in his patrol car along an Interstate Highway looking for speeders. It is the middle of the night, the Interstate is not very busy, and he is drifting in and out of sleep. Suddenly, a car goes roaring by a nearly a hundred miles an hour. His radar gun begins to blare. He fires up his car's engine, turns on his siren and lights, and begins a hot pursuit of the speeding driver.

Strangely enough, the speeder does not stop. In fact, he increases his speed, and soon the two cars are racing across the Texas night at over 135 miles per hour. Then, just as quickly as the speeder had raced away, he pulls over and stops. There is no explanation. Maybe he has run out of gas. Maybe he has decided he is in enough trouble as it is.

The Ranger approaches the car and begins to speak to the speeder. Did the man realize how fast he was going? The very nonchalant answer is a simple yes. Did the man have any idea how much trouble he was in? Again, a totally bland answer comes back—no, he did not. The policeman can't believe the cool detachment the speeder is having to his problem, so he asks for an explanation.

The speeder has an explanation that is totally plausible to him. He tells the Ranger: "Two weeks ago, my wife ran off with a Texas Ranger. I thought you were bringing her back!" Then, the speeder adds—and what leadership development consultant could resist this concluding statement?—"I can no longer live in the past. I must move toward the future as quickly as possible."

In organizations—in life in general—we have a foundational choice that we must make. We probably make it every day in one way or another. Our choice: will be move in the direction of the *transactional*, or will we move in the direction of the *relational*? The *transactional* will ultimately fail. The *relational*, with its foundation on *trust*, will sustain us.

3. TRUST AND THE SHADOW

THE CRITICAL MATTER OF TRUST

You move into the interior of a modern jet airplane preparing to fly cross-country from one location to another. The fully loaded plane weighed many, many tons. It will fly above 35,000 feet at a speed of well over five hundred miles per hour. You are literally hurtling through space at the mercy of a collection of people you do not know. How tired are the pilots? Did an air traffic controller just come to work with a severe headache and suddenly realize that he left his glasses at home? Did a mechanic get ordered to work through dinner, and he already is loosing focus because of diabetes? Did the variety of people responsible for making sure the gas tank is full really remember exactly what the training officer said about reading the gauges?

Suddenly, you understand how much *trust* is a defining factor in the successful completion of your flight. My illustration is nothing more than an indicative paradigm of the interdependent world we have created. Martin Luther King, Jr. talked about a fragile web of interconnections that unite us all. He was exactly right.

A fundamental problem with trust is that we actually know very little about the people we are trusting. We see only surface realities, all the while knowing that most people are driven by issues—realities—deeply enclosed beneath that surface. If my brother were flying the plane, and if another brother were working as the mechanic, and if my brother-in-law with all of his precision of detail were in the air traffic control tower or checking gas gauges, I would find it easier to trust. I know these people, at least to a larger extent than most, from the "inside out." As for these others that I am describing, I see only surfaces, and I am dependent on an entire range of other unknown individuals who have checked their work, cleared them for such sensitive duty, and somehow validated that they are able to do their jobs.

These beneath-the-surface realities, Carl Jung called "shadows." At times, shadows are the unrealized parts of our potential as human beings, and the unrealized might under certain circumstances be very good; under other circumstances they could be very bad. The "shadows" that exist beneath the surface of which people are may be more determinative about outcomes than any surface matter. Only as we better articulate and better understand shadows will we be able to determine if trust is well founded.

Our story goes even deeper. Not only can we talk about the shadows of others and the degree of trust that is possible, we can also talk about our own shadows that are at the core of our individual uniqueness and the degree to which we can trust ourselves. How can I trust myself, much less others, if I do not have some degree of consciousness and realization concerning my own shadows?

So, the work of Carl Jung is decisive. Jung pursues the concept of shadow more than any other modern thinker. Looking through the lens of his decisive insights, it is possible to have a deeper insight into those regions of human existence that are often more hidden and undeclared, more unexamined and unresolved. In understanding that we are beyond the surface of outward manifestations, we will be able to trust ourselves better, have a better grasp of our own potential for positive or negative decisions and actions, and—in the end—create the ground for the full establishment of our own authenticity.

A FIRST INSIGHT INTO JUNG

In the early pantheon of voices that have directed the movement that has become modern psychology, Carl Gustav Jung (1875–1961) is considered to be a parent figure. Born in Switzerland, Jung was the son of a Protestant clergyman. While he earned a medical degree in 1902, Jung was fascinated with a broad range of interests that moved from biology to archeology. Following in the wake of Sigmund Freud, and at one point almost filling the role of Freud's self-appointed heir, Jung created approaches to human self-understanding that exhibited a concreteness and practical application that sometimes were not present in the complex but often absolutistic expressions of Freud. After reading Jung, even the most passive observer will quickly understand how so much of popular psychology depends on, at least, some interpretation of his general categories—even the prominent Myers-Briggs Type Inventory used in a wide variety of public settings to gain insight into human personality attempts to be Jungian at base. Whether Carl Jung had all the right answers is really beside the point; he probably did not, and he always insisted that he was initiating a conversation for consideration rather than handing down psychological encyclicals of "truth." The fact remains that Jung asked a lot of the right questions, and we are still caught up in the explanations and conversations he started. Several of these conversations have direct application to leadership in the corporate arena.

In the presentation that will follow, a general format is being established which will make the presentation easier to follow and key discussions initiated by Jung easier to grasp. The attempt here is to start a conversation, not to give an introductory course in modern psychology. Readers must use their own experiences and insights to extend this conversation into their particular lives or their specific work environments. The interpretations and applications are my own. For some Jungian specialists, the interpretations will be helpful additions; for others, they may not go deeply enough into Jung's own complexities. In no instance, I believe, would the interpretations be considered inaccurate or misleading. With each dominant Jungian idea, the following process will be found:

1. The Basic Concept
2. Interpretation and Questions/Problems/Issues
3. Practical Application

Also keep in mind that this presentation is not attempting to be an exhaustive analysis of Jungian psychology. The emphasis here is on critical ideas and their application to concrete realities of people's lives, particularly in work environments. The most desired outcome of the presentation is that persons in places of leadership in work environments would gain helpful insights into how they are leading, the impact of that leadership on others, and—perhaps of most importance—the impact of that way of leading on their own personal lives. So much of the expectation of modern organizational existence is destructive to the lives of people in places of leadership. Sometimes that destructiveness is passed on to workers and/or taken home to family. The whole equation of potential destruction is heightened when it is recognized that this phenomenon of powerful and excessive expectation is often more internally, self-imposed than it is imposed by the external demands of an environment.

THE PERSONA
THE BASIC CONCEPT

"Attitude" is important to Jung. Our attitudes become a kind of approach by which we enter into the world—our relationships, our work, and our perception of self. Attitude is likely a mirror of who we are internally, or at least a measure of the peace/accommodation/detente we have made with our world and our own selves as we live in the world. Attitude probably reflects with a high degree of accuracy a great deal of—at least the public side of—our personal value system. (A value system is different from a belief system; beliefs are held mentally within our rationality, while values are lived out in the decisions we make and actions we take based on those decisions. There may be a high correspondence between our belief systems and our value systems, but the two realities can also be in high conflict with each other.) To describe attitude in terms of "outlook"—"Oh, we really love Jane's attitude; she is so positive and upbeat" or "Come on, John, get rid of that downtrodden, negative attitude"—is too shallow and, like so much of Jungian interpretation, fails to see the depth of what he can tell us. Ultimately, a cheery or surly "outlook" only scratches the surface of the kind of values/attitudes which drive the way intelligence and emotion are implemented in the world in which we live.

Attitude certainly is dynamic, and clearly it evolves over time, adapts to conditions and circumstances, and is—to some, real extent—the by-product of the cultures and civilizations we are part of on global, national, regional, local, and family levels. Attitudes/values are made more complex by issues of race, ethnic background, gender, and physical/intellectual/emotional uniqueness. Without question, there may be really significant dimensions of attitude/values that come into place—even powerfully so—without very much self-awareness or self-consciousness. Most cultures tend to believe that they are protecting themselves by encouraging a lack of doubt, questioning, or investigation. On the other hand, there can be high levels of attitude/values development that is the result of education, conscious self-awareness, and intentional decision-making. There may be strong cultural forces which inhibit this process and even penalize it, but a self-conscious development of who someone is as a unique individual can still happen. The modern existentialists called this "authenticity."

Jung believed that there would almost always be a collision with the expectations of culture that would result in people hiding or repressing major aspects of who they were on a base, natural level. He had in mind something like Freud's id, those natural tendencies for aggressiveness, lustfulness, dominion, and self-gratification that were part of our animalistic origins. These tendencies may have provided for personal survival, but they might not always be in the "best interests" of civilization. At best, they might be allowable for the few, but organized civilization could not tolerate them for the many.

Therefore, for Jung, people—on a dynamic continuum that ranged from "are given" to "consciously develop"—have/create/are a persona. The persona is the self that we present to the society/societies which we are a part of. It is the self which we "wear" out into the world almost like we wear the clothes which we have selected—or which culture has deemed fashionable and appropriate—to wear for some occasion which demonstrates that we are culturally correct, deserving of being included, and " a part" of what is going on around us. If you think about the time and energy spent in making sure we are correct and appropriate in terms of clothing, you get some idea of the energy given to presenting the correct persona.

The persona is the role we play. Shakespeare then becomes very much on target when he describes human beings as actors on a stage engaged in a play. The line about being "full of sound and fury, signifying nothing" may intimidate us a bit in our most honest moments of reflection or personal angst and self-doubt, but we muster up the courage to play on. The "show"—as our cultures have ingrained into the very marrow of our bones—must go on!

The persona becomes a "mask" which people wear. The term itself actually comes from the word for the masks worn in ancient stage productions to convey the role that an actor was portraying. The mask—or "role identity"—can become so strong, of course, that the real person's unique face/character/personality/being fully embraces the impression made by the mask to the point that what is real and what is unreal can no longer be distinguished from each other. When this happens, there will be a tendency to defend and drive away any challenge to the mask-person; to accept challenges to the mask might convey a lack of authenticity too profound to tolerate. It can be easier to wear the mask and defend it than it is to question it and open it to investigation. Of course, there are both individual and corporate/cultural/organization masks; more often than not these collective masks only serve to more powerfully reinforce and defend each other.

INTERPRETATION AND QUESTIONS/PROBLEMS/ISSUES

Without question, all that Jung says about the persona has a great ring of truth about it for most people. We know that we wear the "mask," we see it in the lives of others, we learn its dynamics very early in the socialization process, and it is easily manifested in the lives of all kinds of corporate entities from families to businesses to even nations. Most of the time, the existence of these persona-masks does not make a great deal of difference, especially in a more democratically open society. Of course, I present a persona that is crafted to make my access and interaction with circumstances easier and more fluid, more to my advantage at least in my perceptions. No big deal most of the time; it is all simply part of the normal movements of life. We can't go around analyzing our navels all the time. Even mask environments can function pretty smoothly, efficiently, and even with some degree of meaning and satisfaction much of the time.

Unless I desire to be some sort of rebel, to make some sort of "statement," to be "different" for the sake of being different—and we probably all do something of this at some time or another, even if it is simply when we are "fed up" with some element of the status quo—and create an "anti-persona," I can become very adept at putting on the right "face" for the right situation thus proving that I am civilized or should be granted entree. In fact, even an "anti-persona" could be precisely the acceptable persona for a subculture; as the 1960s musician, John Hartford, sang so poignantly: "What's the difference being different if its difference nowadays that looks the same." An anti-mask that could assert authenticity can easily become inauthentic. Most of us move in and our of so many subcultures that it takes a great deal of effort just to keep track of what mask needs to be worn when. For many of us who are at mid-life, there are old pictures of tie-dyes, peace necklaces, long hair, and ragged jeans. How "Man In the Gray-Flannel Suit" we weren't. Yet, how perfectly in keeping with our own culture we assuredly and assertively were!

The real problem occurs when we lose sight and control of this persona dynamic that we play in and out of. As long as we are clearly aware of what is a consciously created and manifested persona that fills a legitimate and creditable purpose—for example, the easier flow of basic day-to-day existence—there is likely to be little problem. Once our role identity overwhelms, effaces, and destroys unique self-identity, huge problems begin to occur. If the real self is lost, real relationships are impossible. A haunting level of the fake, the phony, the pseudo triumphs. On some level, we probably know this—although not necessarily in terms of rational knowledge—and a reservoir of self-conflict, even depression, begins to slip up on us.

When the persona triumphs, we become all but incapable of being honest with ourselves and, by necessary implication, with other people. Self-deception and unreasonable levels of self-justification prevail. Real introspection and reflective examination face an almost insurmountable firewall of individual and cultural defense mechanisms. Self-truth, relational truths, and even the pragmatic truths by which we operate the processes of our life and work get lost in a chaotic vagueness. Less than adequate decisions are made, mediocrity rises, words like excellence and quality become mindless, empty clichés, and no one is really talking—they are afraid to come out from behind their masks, they are using all kinds of personal energy to defend mask-turfs. This is Scott Peck's "pseudo community" of political correctness and polite nicety that achieves self-absorption but drains itself of any real power.

PRACTICAL APPLICATION

Go back to the point above about the way in which our ability to deal adequately with pragmatic, process issues can be compromised when we lose sight of self-truths and relational truths. How is it possible, for example, to have a strong family if there is a lack of honest communication between a mother and father? How is it possible, by extension, to have a high level of honest communication with a mate if a person is individually in a state of self-delusion or not having honest, internal communication within the self? All of these varying levels and kinds of—for want of a better word—truth are inextricable interfaced and overlapping with each other.

In this regard, it is highly important that individuals be engaged in a high level of self-dialogue about persona-masks that have been created and are being worn. Lines of demarcation must be clearly drawn between what legitimately does not matter all that much and what, by contrast, may matter a great deal. And, since it is so easy for the lines between matter/not matter to be blurred, outside perspectives are often invaluable.

There must be consciously devoted time for reflection and introspection. The whole concept of Jungian persona-masks must be explained and actively contemplated. Levels of self-honesty can be advanced and evaluated by significant others, creditable pieces of self-growth and development writings, and by competent counselors. It is also indispensable in the workplace to have associates who are willing to say, "The King doesn't have his clothes on." To have an atmosphere in which this kind of statement can be made without fear of retribution or reprisal is highly unusual. However, without this kind of atmosphere there is an added dimension of vulnerability that holds an entire enterprise in jeopardy. Am I trying to say that everyone needs to be in counseling, especially if they are in an important role of leadership in organization? Not exactly. But, I am absolutely saying that all of us need someone who can play the counselor role, someone who can be absolutely honest with us about our persona-masks dynamics. On a practical level, these conversations need to be a regular part of our lives—as important, surely, as taking care of our property and vehicles, planning our meals or vacations, or—again—deciding what we are going to wear to the various functions that populate our existence.

On an organizational, corporate level, there are all kinds of conversations, meetings on every hand—strategic planning, process refinement, visioning, personnel reorganization, fiscal integrity; the list goes on and on. Yet, what concrete, specific attention and time are corporate groups giving to introspection and reflection about organizational persona-masks? Do we ever talk about the masks that we wear with each other that debilitate and destroy real conversation? Do we ever talk about the degree to which the communities we are establishing are real or pseudo? Do we ever constructively agree and covenant with each other that open, heartfelt conversations can occur with threat of punitive reaction? Even if we talk about these issues, what is the track record of the organization like in regard to those voices that have spoken out in honest disagreement? In general, if there is no high toleration for honest, open conversation, there will be evidence, not in the way the organization "talks," but in the way it "walks"—there will be a lot of conflict avoidance, instances of passive-aggressive behavior, people refusing to speak-up, and great vacuums of quietness and acquiescence around the board table or in the critical decision-making arena. Honest voices of disagreement have probably already been filtered out, placed in lesser roles, frustrated away by having never been listened to, or summarily dismissed because they were not "team players." If there is no atmosphere of healthy tension and conflict—if everyone is struggling to keep their persona-mask safely in place, an invariable negative is being directly played to the bottom line of every objective of the organization. Even if the organization survives with its persona-masks in place, it will be mediocre in its accomplishment and less than satisfying in its ability to create a place for meaningful work. Most mediocre organizations have failed to make peace with the entire persona-mask dynamic; as long as this "out of sync" remains, the potential power of the organization is compromised. Morale, motivation, and commitment in such a situation will be little more than decorative window dressing.

EXTRAVERT/INTROVERT
THE BASIC CONCEPT

The ideas of Extravert and Introvert, largely because of the broad influence of the popular psychology produced in the United States in the mid to late twentieth century and the highly accessible Myers-Briggs Type Inventory, are the components of Jungian thought that have made their way into the general mainstream of modern thought. It would not be accurate to say that most of these mainstream presentations have missed Jung's points, but it may very well be that popular understandings are dangerous shallow. This shallowness of understanding can, in itself, contribute to the complexity of negatives that are possible in individual and corporate assessment.

On the surface level, the terms have come to be identified with a whole set of too-easily-assigned caricatures and stereotypes. An Extravert is seen as someone who is socially aggressive, unintimidated by social events, upbeat and outgoing in human interactions. The Extravert is a pat-'em-on-the-back, never-met-a-stranger, life-of-the-party social butterfly who could talk to Presidents and sell the proverbial refrigerator to an Eskimo. The Extravert is usually "well liked," to use a hauntingly prophetic phrase from Arthur Miller's *The Death of a Salesman* and, given the social dispositions of modern Western society, highly desirable.

The caricatures that surround the Introvert create a severe counterpoint. The Introvert can be conceived as a near social cripple, certainly a non-engaged and intimidated "wallflower." The Introvert is shy, reticent, and even backward. The movements of Introverts are usually awkward and downcast in social situations. Almost without question, parents of children who develop tendencies of Introverts would want to intervene with some sort of counseling or therapy so that their child might stand the chance of being "well liked;" who knows, some important popularity contest, job opening, or large paycheck might depend on it!

In the end, there is constructed in most shallow approaches to these concepts of Jung a deafening either/or. A person is typecast and will forever be bound by the categorizations of the stereotypes. Not only is this approach patently unfair to people, but also to Jung. I have seen people, after profiling has been brought to their workplace, wearing colored discs on their name tags indicating if they are "blue," "red" or whatever people with personality traits deeply encoded in their genetic psyche and now designating code colors that will reveal the truth of who they are. Such approaches are not psychology; they are human-limiting nonsense.

In dealing with the two concepts, it should always be kept in mind that Jung himself felt that every person had both tendencies, albeit in the way a unique person is raised in culture, one may dominate. In a healthy, whole Self, there is a conscious alignment of the two tendencies, and both are used self-consciously as various situations arise. To the extent that Jung may have seen these tendencies as having an innate character, I would differ with his approach, denying that either is "in-born." It is not necessary in any way, at this point, to enter a conversation of innate/not-innate; I am simply highly moved by the arguments put forth from John Locke to the existentialists that humans are born with no innates which would undermine the whole concept of human freedom of will. In fact, I am convinced that Jung was a precursor for a great deal of existentialism's emphasis on an authenticity of human living that is predicated more on choices and decisions than on either innate, in-born necessity or the indelible impressions of some Freud-advanced, powerful experience of early childhood.

INTERPRETATION AND QUESTIONS/PROBLEMS/ISSUES

There are two major problems with the shallow, simplistic rendering of Jung. First, from a personal perspective, I can report that across twenty years of dealing professionally with the Myers-Briggs (which I believe can serve to create credible discussions), I have always tested out to be an extremely strong Introvert; not quiet off the "I" scale, but close to its extreme parameter. The Inventory is very correct—if—you follow the easy stereotypes noted above and look at me at certain kinds of social functions. You might have trouble, however, looking at me—even finding me—since I am likely to be uncomfortably over in the corner with the wallflower group. Certain kinds of social settings make me irrationally uncomfortable and, more often than not, I have tended to avoid them. I am being somewhat facetious, of course, since I can go out—especially if my non-introvert wife is along as a buffer—and have a basically good time.

What is strange about all this is that I make my living—and have across three decades—in the most Extravert of professions. Constantly, I am involved in group activities from small scale to very large. Ironically, I have developed at least some reputation for having skills in teambuilding, organizational development, and corporate communication. My point: the shallow stereotypes may have very little to do with reality, or be any kind of reliable predictor of what a person may be able to do in response to the requirements of performance on some job. Johnny Carson, the affable and highly-engaged talk show host, one of the most outgoing persons on the planet, was probably as introverted and private as a human being could be. The shallow, stereotyped interpretation simply does not suffice.

In a more important, second qualification of the shallow insights into Jung, Extravert and Introvert have very little to do with shyness or social adroitness. For Jung, they clearly indicate responses to problem-solving situations. In this regard, the categories have a great deal to do with axiology or value theory, the ideas advanced by Robert S. Hartman that the core movements of human existence occur when people evaluate, weigh, make assessment—when humans make value judgments, decisions, solve problems, and move toward action based on these judgments.

Jung believed that human beings respond to the powerful influence of certain archetypes (more below) that act as dominant role models for behavior. While there are numerous archetypes that can be discussed in a comprehensive investigation of Jung, I am particularly compelled by the models focused upon in the work of John Maurer, Gary Koyen, and Becca O'Connor (The Warrior and the Monk: The Journey to Wise Leadership and Market Dominance, Merdian Consulting Group, 1999). In their advancing of modern leadership theory, they at least give an intellectual "nod" toward Jung by mentioning the distinctions between "The Warrior" and "The Monk." The Warrior, in most respects, is the archetypal Extravert. When a problem occurs, the initial tendency is to aggressively attack it; not exactly "shoot first and ask questions later," but almost. The Warrior is confident, strident, unrelenting. The downside of the Warrior mentality is, of course, that there may be insufficient "looking" before there is "leaping." This take-no-prisoners attitude/value orientation may leave clean-up, after-the-fact realities that are costly, but if there are mistakes, they will be aggressive mistakes. There is a high amount of energy around the Warrior that is magnetic and even charismatic; there usually is a waiting line for students, disciples, and followers that the Warrior tends to find very gratifying. To say, with Socrates/Plato, that "the unexamined life is not worth living" is hardly part of the Warrior's marching orders.

The Monk, by contrast, becomes the archetypal Introvert, but—again—issues of problem-solving approach and not social engagement dominate in a correct reading of Jung. The Monk tends to stop and reflect, to withdraw into that which is removed and quiet. Our word consideration comes from two ancient words—con and sider—that carry the respective meanings of "with" and "wisdom." Wisdom is more than rational logic; once again, we are at the point of Hartman's higher order property of human existence, the capacity to make value judgments. The Monk is the expert at sider. The Monk values reflective "time out" in which the appearance of insight has a chance to occur.

Some people may be distinctly Warriors and could profit from the counterpoint of the Monk's perspective; others may be distinctly Monks and in need of the Warrior's capacity to immediately react. Most work groups could profit from a mixture of both types, although there are likely to be times of conflict between the groups; they do, after all, approach problems from a different perspective. Most people are probably some combination of the two types or have both capacities. It might simply be important to make sure that conscious time is given to being able to move in either/both directions as they are appropriate to particular circumstances. It is also important to keep in mind that Jung's ultimate ambition for human beings was the achieving of a self-actualization ("individuation") of wholeness in which a balance of extravert and introvert was achieved; to the extent that these realities are out of balance, wholeness is compromised. The goal for Jung would never be becoming an Introvert or Extravert, or would it be ceasing to be introverted or extraverted. The goal would rather be finding a clear understanding of tendencies and then working out a desired balance in the "Individuation," actualization, or uniqueness of the person's own self. For further consideration, there is an almost endless list of "opposites" which have been discussed across the history of civilization which correspond to Jung's extravert/introvert dichotomy. Consider the following:

Extravert	Introvert
1. The Apollonian tendency for rules and order advanced in Greek thought and in the work of Nietzsche.	1. The Dionysian tendency for nonstructure and play.
2. The Second Intentionality or "abstractive cognition" concepts of William of Ockham.	2. Second Intentionality or "intuitive cognition."

Extravert	Introvert
3. The entire left brain, masculine set of concepts popular in contemporary psychological stereotypes.	3. The right brain, feminine emphasis.
4. Kant's *a posteriori*, experiential thinking.	4. The *a priori*, nonexperiential arena of experience.
5. Jung's animus/male tendency.	5. Jung's anima/female tendency.
6. In my (see below) alternate way of looking at the Myers-Briggs Type Inventory, the "S"/Sensing and "T"/Thinking dimensions. The "J" Judgment dimension of the MBTI may best fit here.	6. In my (see below) alternate MBTI concept, the "N"/Intuition and "F"/Feeling dimensions are found here. The "P"/Perception dimension of the MBTI may best fit here.
7. The "Yang" of ancient Chinese philosophy.	7. The "Yin."
8. The Warrior archetype.	8. The Monk archetype.
9. Modern.	9. Primitive (Jung's archaic man).
10. Instinct.	10. Consciousness.
11. The "morning of our lives"/ achievement.	11. The "afternoon of our lives"/wisdom.
12. Thinking in equations.	12. Thinking in symbols.

PRACTICAL APPLICATION

We may not talk easily of archetypes, a central Jungian concept we will explore in greater detail below, but we certainly understand the power of role models. For many of us, there are parents, coaches, teachers, ministers, even old drill sergeants who have had a prominent impact on our lives. We try to imitate and emulate them, mirror their strengths, even master their walk, the tilt of their head, or their speech patterns. We have been influenced by an array of movie characters and sports figures. Whether it is real, individual figures, some composite of admirable attributes, or a mentally constructed ideal, we find high motivation in the examples of role models.

This process of being motivated by role models is generally a pretty tame and generally positive process. However, it should never be allowed to become unexamined or taken for granted. Its impact could become negative. For example, the Warrior model could gain absolute, unquestioned priority and leave little or no room to appreciate the positive implications of the Monk model. This is typically what happens in most organizational settings. The aggressive, take-charge, decisive Warrior is highly valued. The Monk is almost wimpish by comparison.

Organizations and leaders of organizations who only take a kind of John Wayne approach to management and see leadership as a mythic, heroic General Patton storming across Europe on a crusade against Nazis may have more mistakes than successes as an outcome, especially if that aggressive charging is not moderated by reflection, contemplation, and examination. The belief that there is no time for the reflective dynamics is an accident waiting for a place to happen. There must always be conscious time for the Monk to find his place, and the more complex the process or high level the leadership position, the more contemplation time that is required. Any truly effective strategic planning process will need Warriors, but will also make sure that there is real space—not just randomized, left-over space—for the Monk. Every strategic planning process should consciously incorporate "Monk" agendas as a structural necessity alongside of every "Warrior" agenda. Every planning and implementation team should have Warrior representation and Monk representation that work in full parity with each other in a context that is fully respective of both positions. There is great necessity, for want of better terms, to make sure that a masculine/extravert and feminine/introvert perspective is consciously incorporated into decision-making. Without both, decision-making will be one dimensional and lack for proportionality. Keeping in mind, however, that simply because someone is female, for example, in gender does not mean that Jung's "feminine"/introvert perspective will be advanced; to be male in gender is, likewise, no guarantee of the "masculine"/extravert perspective. Jung is not trying to create or advance stereotypes, but to create an ability to see through and move beyond stereotypes. The key is to move beyond stereotypes to an understanding or uniqueness and the experience of wholeness in which there is balance in an "equation" between all that is implied by extravert and all that is implied by introvert.

Such balance, understanding of uniqueness, and experience of wholeness does not just happen by accident; it certainly does not happen by executive mandate either. Jung taught the concept of the temenos, a ancient Greek term that means sacred, protected space or private place. One of the deepest needs of human beings is to create and have readily available a private, personal space. The operative "center/base/essence" of the unique person is only protected and given the chance for highest actualization when there is a temenos. Yet, for most Warriors there is seldom any uncluttered space or uninfringed-upon time; if anything, the work requirements only increase, the work day only lengthens, the time away all but disappears, the to-do lists, voice mails, and e-mails become a tangled web of backlogged gridlock. It is the Monk who understands the vital necessity of temenos, and it is no conventional piety that speaks of a "sacred space;" the deepest recesses of our core humanity cry out for temenos. The executive leader who does not have the highest, active respect for temenos is compromising the health and well-being, not only of personal self, family relationships, and organizational responsibility, but the very depth of human uniqueness conveyed in that singular conception referred to as soul. Often, if the soul of the leader is compromised and at risk, the soul of the organization (and all the other significant relationships) is in jeopardy. Soul is understood as that dimension or quality of human existence that can assign value, yearn for meaning, or experience wholeness.

In essence, these are "spiritual" concerns, defined in terms of the depth of human existence and not in terms of conventional, institutional religious dogma and doctrine. If this approach to the spiritual, the sacred—the temenos—cannot be respected and actual private space created and used, the odds against organizational credibility, integrity, character, and meaning are very strong. This discussion of a "spiritual" domain or dynamic that go beyond conventional religious dogma and doctrine would not be inconsistent with Jung. He clearly believed that there were—in his language—"transcendent" domains and dynamics that defied logic and logic's conventional language, but realities that were a factual part of life. This "spiritual"—for want of a better word—or "transcendent"—for want of a better word—may be more of a felt reality than logically demonstrable reality, but it is an absolute reality all the same. There is no "business" approach or "business" domains and dynamics that can, with genuine credibility and authentic insight into life, simply dismiss this particular kind of approach to the "spiritual."

What does all of this mean? If we want to be successful leaders, should we head for the nearest church? Should we fully embrace the rituals and rites, the dogmas and doctrines of conventional religion, and then we will automatically become good leaders, good business men and women? Not necessarily. In fact, for better and for worse, conventional religion can have its own problems, both individually and institutionally, achieving this "spiritual." No invitation is being given here to demean or disdain conventional religion; that is another story. Clearly, however, there is an invitation not to bracket out what may have been at the core of the most authentic, conventional religion; as the old cliché goes, not to throw the baby out with the bath water, even if a lot of the bath water is pretty dirty indeed. A healthy exploration of this "spiritual/transcendent" may create options and insights that have been obscured, even by that medium—the church—which was supposed to make such options and insights clear and viable. To explore this "spiritual/transcendent" is to explore human existence and human interaction on deeper levels.

This exploration cannot, in turn, keep from helping advance our pursuit of Self, our understanding of Others, and enhancing any capacity we might have to live meaningful lives, have satisfying and fulfilling experiences, and even become better leaders capable of making the kinds of impacts on life that promote that which is better and more valuable. Who knows, this exploration might even have viability for our pursuit of what Rudolf Otto called "Holy Other." Leadership is, therefore, empowered to act as a means to a greater end; it ceases to be an end in itself designed only as a mechanical mechanism to achieve a high level of self-aggrandizement and self-gratification measured by dollar marks. Careful here: this is no diatribe against dollar marks that create no negative unless they become an end in themselves. Even the dimension of "Soul"—for want of a better word—may be experienced, the dimension for Jung in which human beings experience both their own uniqueness and the unique connectedness that they have to other unique human beings and the whole of the created universe.

The singer/song writer, Steve Earle, writes a ballad entitled "Ben McCulloch" that describes the destructive strategies of a Confederate general from Texas that led to the deaths of many of his soldiers. The ballad, sung from the perspective of a deserting, yet-surviving soldier talks about the soldier signing up with his brother to fight for McCulloch in the midst of a great deal of fanfare and bravado. This all changes in the first major battle where the brother is killed. In the midst of a condemnation of the General, the ballad declares in muted and somber tones: "He took the lives of many and the souls of many more." There are some who have died; they are gone. There are others who remain, alive in a technical sense, but who have lost their souls, a depth of self/uniqueness/self-realization/Jung's "Individuation" and wholeness that sustains living on any qualitative level. One is reminded of the biblical injunction (Matthew 10:28) to fear that which can kill both the body and the soul. In the Greek language that is used here, the word kill means a special level of obliteration that is more than simply physical death.

The point is that organizations and organizational leaders can create environments, processes, and approaches to human beings that can effectively "kill their souls." People become disposed of and disenfranchised from the highest sources of power and potential that would allow for excellence of production and meaningfulness of work. These two realities are joint necessities which must both be available for either to be available at its best. To promote and protect the soul of the organization, the souls of the workers of the organization is the highest calling of leadership. To miss this high calling is to guarantee mediocrity and emptiness.

THE UNCONSCIOUS
THE BASIC CONCEPT

To first speak of "The Unconscious," there must be a touching base with traditional interpretations. Most of the history of psychology, following from the strong influence of Freud, has held to this traditional interpretation. Jung makes room for the traditional and pays adequate homage to Freud in doing so. His ideas about the "personal unconscious" give adequate agreement with the traditional interpretations of the Unconscious that will be explained below. What will become critical is to see how he radically moved beyond traditional understanding, even to the point of breaking with Freud. It is this movement beyond that gives so much of Jungian thought its own uniqueness and provides concrete applications that are indispensable to the modern world. We must see both how Jung agrees with and then departs from traditional views of the Unconscious in order to gain great insight into his teachings and, more importantly, into our own selves.

A common facet of early psychological dogma, a concept that turns up in one form or another in the ideas of numerous thinkers, is the belief in some sort of Unconscious. The Unconscious is generally conceived as a collective repository of all that does not fit within the culturally correct persona, all those natural instincts and tendencies which have been repressed, and that "side" of individual and group existence which is too negative/bad/dark to even be admitted to. The Unconscious asserts itself, according to many of the standard psychological teachings, in dreams, or may even manifest itself in some uncontrolled "explosion" in which the "inside" that has been pushed down and held back leaps out of it subterranean depths in usually some kind of aberrant and aggressive manner. So, everyone is carrying around some kind of subterranean—or better yet, sub psychic—monster of sorts that threatens to surface at the most untimely moment with destructive force. A great deal of psychotherapy, therefore, must be devoted to analyzing, understanding, and defusing the power of this Unconscious. There can also be a Collective Unconscious that threatens all of a society or humanity as a whole. This Collective Unconscious is both the sum total of all personal, individual Unconsciousness and a kind of preexistent, negative "given" that is much a part of human life—even before the actual physical onset of that life—as the old concepts of "original sin" conveys in its distinctly religious orientation. These are ideas primarily initiated by Freud, with the Unconscious becoming a reckless, infantile "Id"/"Libido" on the loose, so to speak, seeking destructive and sexual self-gratification.

The Unconscious becomes like a great, concealed, omnipotent and omnipresent "Secret" that is there against the backdrop of life, powerful and threatening in its potential impact, that no one really wants to talk about. A kind of almost universe denial or avoidance quickly is put in place when thoughts or discussions about the Unconscious take place—if you refuse to talk about it, perhaps it will go away or perhaps it really does not exist after all.

My father used to tell my younger brother and me stories about a "Booger Man" who lived under the ground. With each story, some awful feature of this "Booger Man" man was added—his nasty breath, his infected skin, his scaly, bloody feet, his broken teeth. Clearly, these were graphic extensions of potential human maladies, but my brother and I were yet to learn of Bultman's process of "demythologizing." The "Booger Man" lived right under a field that my brother and I had to cross regularly, so "His" presence was constantly nearby. We might cross that field together, both thinking about "What/Who" right under our feet, but neither of us ever brought it up. We walked very carefully and softly, shallow breathed, and wide eyed, always with the greatest sense of relief when he were in the yard with the field behind us. God help you if you had to cross the field by yourself or—worse yet—by yourself at night. In fact, you absolutely depended on God to help you. Your mother's precinct seemed to be God, and her bedtime Bible stories, especially those in which God helped young children overcome great odds, filled your mind as you crossed that field; you prayed every step of the way—after all, it was the God of a good and loving God which kept the "Booger Man" at bay.

As psychology, in the new edges of a scientific mentality which was finding their way into the nineteenth century, began to move beyond religious and mythic explanations, ideas about a "Booger Man" went away—along with a great deal of talk about witches, devils, ghosts, and demons. With a real fanfare, implying that a more sophisticated way of relating to life had evolved in which childish assumptions had been transcended, now it became possible to talk about "The Unconscious." In most respects, only the language had changed; the effective difference between psychology's "The Unconscious" and my father's "Booger Man" were nil.

Why my father told these stories is not clear. If you read the writings of Bruno Bettleheim, you quickly understand that he was part of a time-honored tradition that went back to the beginnings of civilization and was richly populated by personalities as diverse as the Brothers Grimm and their fairy tales of big bad wolves or Washington Irving and his headless horseman of Sleepy Hollow. Maybe my father thought his stories constituted a kind of rite/right of passage that would make us stronger for facing a world in which there were real challenges and obstacles to overcome. Maybe he was "whistling in the dark," covering his own deep-seated fears as he laughed before our quaking in fear. Maybe he was simply doing with us/for us what his father had done with/for him. The fact that my mother had a readily available counterpoint with her Bible stories and—almost of equal value—that motivational piece "The Little Engine That Could"—distinctly a role model archetype that has held with great power across the ages of my own life— clearly plays into Jung's insights about a male animus and female anima (see below) which are part of the building blocks of human self-understanding. Jung would also not have been surprised that my father's "Booger Man" was dark and black, a representation of fairly typical racial and ethic stereotypes that have always played a distinct part in the bag of fears and unmerited conclusions that have attached themselves to this "Underbelly Consciousness."

While it may be more the precinct of the academic psychologist or historian of psychology, keep in mind that there was a distinct difference between Jung and Freud concerning the "Unconscious." Freud gave emphasis to the infantile, the sexual, the aggressively beastly of the human "id" that was always at the edge of being out of control. His unconscious was altogether negative. For Jung, this "Unconscious"—a set of semi-remembered/half-forgotten ideas and experiences which were so weak in their day-to-day impact that it could be difficult to bring them into full awareness—could just as easily be positive. We could be "religious" or "spiritual" beings motivated by that which is moral and good, as easily as sexual animals that every force of rationality and culture must suppress. Just as we could get negative stimuli from the Unconscious, we can also get positive stimuli. Therefore, instead of always being negated or avoided (or clearly held under control by our rationality or our societal customs and laws—Freud's ego and superego—the Unconscious can be embraced, explored, and looked upon as a repository of that about us that is filled with positive potential. Dreams, for Jung as will be seen, can become cues/clues to advance our lives in a fully positive direction.

In a final, academic regard, Jung also talked about the distinction between a "Personal Unconscious" and the "Collective Unconscious." His distinctions have profound implications. The "Personal Unconscious" relates to historical events that have occurred in my personal life which are weak in terms of being readily available to memory, but what may assert themselves at odd and random times. Note carefully: the primary causative factor is history, not some in-born, innate tendency or reckless Libido. I sometimes have agitated dreams about being late for some event. I hate to be late and, in real life, can get in a "state" when interference to getting somewhere on time takes place. My father was that way. Nothing of genetics here, but the real memories of him being in the car ready to go, sounding the horn, and then becoming very angry with any transgressions. Without question, I carry something of this around in my own, personal unconscious. In a similar sense, I easily cry at movies in which there is some kind of death or separation, especially when a child loses a parent; that my own mother died when I was thirteen, without question, creates this "personal unconscious" element which I think of seldom in a conscious way, but which can randomly impact my life.

The "Collective Unconscious" would involve similar experiences taken to an exponentially higher level and involving much of human kind; on a negative side, for example, the fear of the dark—on a positive side, the value of individual, self-concept. Jung felt this latter consciousness was somehow or somewhat innate in a qualified sense; I have difficulty with the traditional, hard line and arbitrary idea of innate as I have said throughout, but Jung means much more than what the traditional original sin or original graces concepts have advanced. "Collective Unconscious" is a concept that arose for Jung out of his contact with a wide diversity of different people from across the planet, people of differing cultures, socio-economic backgrounds, and degrees of education.

INTERPRETATION AND QUESTIONS/PROBLEMS/ISSUES

Historically, it is fairly easy to trace the causative roots of this concept of the Unconscious. Ancient, primitive civilizations believed in an underworld that was the repository of chaos and turmoil, the abode of devils and demons, a reality right beneath the surface of life much like my father's "Booger Man." This underworld could release its powers without notice, and life was constantly in peril and danger. Paul, the famed New Testament writer, captured this whole mentality perfectly when he expounded that we "struggle with principalities, powers, rules of the darkness of the world." The entire darkness/light dynamic is a power relic of this mythic past that still finds its way into multiple dimensions of our modern lives.

If we had lived in a primitive world subject to a volcanic eruption, for example, or had we seen a calm sea turn into a ravaging typhoon or hurricane, we might have easily come to the same kinds of conclusions. When people actually dug into the earth, finally exploring its depths with scientific precision, the chaotic, demonic underworld as a physical reality went away. Perhaps, it was simply too easy of a transition to demythologize the physical world, dispense with an archaic Underworld concept, and "transfer" (for Jung, a technical term which describes our ability to "project"—see below—thoughts, impressions, and feelings from one domain/dynamic/dimension to another) all of its baggage to a psychic underworld, "The Unconscious," which carried something of the same psychological impact as the old Underworld. Whether human civilization had really advanced by making this transition/transference is highly open to question; we simply, and only slightly, changed the wording on the contract.

It is also possible to go beyond the arena of the history of mythology and talk about "The Unconscious" in regard to sociology. Without question, there has been an undercurrent, a presence, of that which is evil and malevolent constantly beneath the surface, around the corner, part of the backdrop, of human civilization. Watch *The Godfather* movies or HBO's *The Sopranos*, read about the horrors of the Inquisition or the reigns of terror common in ancient and medieval civilizations that accompanied political and religious transitions, or sense the dark side that shows itself in modern expressions from

Star Wars' archetypal and mythic Darth Vader to the all-too-real modern expressions of evil in *Natural Born Killers* or *The Talented Mr. Ripley*.

Sociologically, it is probably also possible to look no further than our own family "skeletons" which, consistent with all the old images and traditions, are firmly held in our "family closets" and talked about, if at all, in whispers and guarded secrets. Just don't use the euphemism of "skeletons in the closet" in earshot of children when it is nearing their bedtime. They will not understand the sociological implications or metaphorical language; they will simply stay awake all night, eyes fixed intently on the nearest closest, interpreting any night sounds as those skeletons coming to life—preparing to come after them.

Maybe it is past time to stop talking about "The Underworld," "The Unconscious," even "Skeletons in the Closet." Maybe we have actually reached a level of sophistication that will enable us to see that under ground there is more ground, more dirt, that this Unconscious is a psychological remnant and extension of old history and old myth, that evil is a real part of life borne of malevolent or absent nurturing more than some demonic nature, the result of bad choices rather than some bad karma, original sin, or primordial evil power. The old concept of "the Devil made me do it" is simply a lame relinquishing of accountability, a classic "cop out" which destroys personal accountability, personal credibility and integrity.

Maybe it is time, and the best of Jung at least paved the way for this, to start talking about our capacities to evaluate, to make sound value judgments, to create value systems that manifests themselves in productive and enhancing attitudes, behaviors, and actions. If we exchanged the energy we use following this path of mythic, religious, psychological history for energy devoted to sound observation and examination, sound synthesis of what this observation and examination have given us, and sound decisions leading to sound actions based on this synthesis, we would confront life much more realistically, find a true base for all of our idealism, and solve real problems that touch the lives of real people. The likelihood, in this process, of achieving meaningful work, meaningful relationships, and personal meaning/satisfaction/peace is greatly enhanced.

I am left with a kind of uncertain lack of closure when I hear Jung describing this "Unconscious" as an "instinctual pattern of behavior and perception." The idea of a controlling instinct sounds too much like a pre-existing innate about which human beings can do nothing. If this connotation prevails, the idea of human freedom of will/choice is demeaned. If there are pre-existing, predetermining innates/instincts, the conversation is essentially back to the point of conventional "original sin" concepts; there is little or no room left for personal authenticity. I feel much more comfortable with John Locke's *tabula rasa*/blank table theory which allows for no innate predispositions or predetermined behavioral and perceptual realities.

But, keep in mind, that Jung is clearly making a positive "nod" in the direction of the Freudian applications that he will not totally discount, any more than he will totally apply to humanity in general. When he leans toward innates, instincts, or in-borns, he is only admitting to a fraction of the "Personal Unconscious" which has many historical determinants unique to particular individuals. The Unconscious, both in its personal and collective dimensions, is much, much more than this. It is in this "much, much more" than Jung departs from Freud, gives us a fuller picture of the potential of the Unconscious, and opens the door for using the Unconscious for positive benefit.

PRACTICAL APPLICATION

Since we live in language and the connotations of that language have so much impact on our emotional engagement with life, perhaps we need to be very careful about the words we choose to use in describing the negatives of life that, indeed, are very present. Maybe we could let go of our historical fascination— passed down to us in the language of the ages—with "The Underground" or "The Unconscious." Could we simply attest to the fact that there is a negative "Underbelly" to life—a usable, convenient term which may not abound with such emotion? This "underbelly"—let's use a small case "u" to take away some of the personal potential of the word—is the result of bad value judgment, inadequacy of evaluation, too hastily weighing out the options and possibilities that are available. These bad value judgments are the distinct result of poor nurturing, inadequate training and experience, insufficient education, or intellectual or emotional weakness. Genetics or disease may play a role in these inadequacies at exceptional moments, but for the most part they are the result of poor judgment and poor choices.

Jung is, however, absolutely correct is bringing focus to the realities of denial and avoidance. The only way denial and avoidance can be conquered is to recognize their reality and actively make sure that conversations occur which seek them out, bring them to the light—to use the old language, name them, recognizing that the demons and devils in the old explanations who were named ran away and troubled you no more. We have to be able as individuals to admit to our strong capacities to avoid and deny. "To thine own self, be true" should not signal high moments of guarding self-interest, but should convey the utter necessity of self honesty—"To thine own self, be truth-full!"

We should not kid ourselves—"regress," to use another Jungian term, to childish and child-like assumptions and strategies. To be strategically and consciously self honest is impossible to achieve all of the time even for the most authentic person. This is why it becomes so vital to have a relationship with some significant other who loves and cares for us enough that they will bring levels of truth that puncture and let the air out of our schemes of denial and avoidance. How unfortunate when someone loves us enough to give us honesty that we can respond with anger, belligerence, and sometimes even violence—all manifestations of denial and avoidance taken to far extremes.

In a corporate setting, to create an atmosphere in which honesty can prevail is essential, albeit astoundingly uncommon. Without the honesty of confession, the higher activities of understanding/explanation, education toward improvement, and true transformation are fundamentally impossible to achieve. We are back to Peck's pseudo-community that has no real power, or at least dramatically compromises the real power it could have. It is amazing sometimes to see the powerful anger that can rise in a person in executive power who is challenged. Once confronted by that kind of anger, especially in a public setting, it is a rare person who will bring honesty back to the table. Instead there is a kind of screw-you, fall-on-your-own-face mentality that eradicates any semblance of "team."

I once knew of an executive who hired a college fraternity brother for a position of importance in his company equivalent to a executive vice-president. He paid the man accordingly and, in fact, placed him in an office adjacent to his own. These events did not take place as an extension of some "good ole boy" system but rather as a distinct strategy. While the college fraternity brother had no real training in the man's specific business, he did have the talent/skill/ability/gumption to be uncompromisingly honest. As an extension of the distinct strategy, the executive fully realized that he and his old friend would have disagreements, conflict, sharp words. There might even be times when he would want to fire him. So, he gave the man a lifetime contract that could not be rescinded. Obviously, there is a great degree of trust that is being exhibited here, but—again—the executive was smart enough to understand the need for uncompromised honesty that the entire process was put in place and adhered to rigorously as the result of mature insight and conscious strategy.

Do any of us have the ability to recognize when we are practicing avoidance or in denial? Probably not. Are any of us likely to be fully honest with ourselves all of the time? Probably not. So, what strategies do we put in place to protect ourselves and what is important to us? Somewhere there must be strategies that will carefully maintain some conduit to questions, objections, doubts, and expressions of honest disagreement. If we do not consciously do this, we will be right back to some combination of either, "The Devil made me do it" or, "If it is the will of God, it will happen"—both of which are tantamount to an abrogation of personal accountability and personal responsibility. We will head for the excusing cover of old explanations, and the capacity for real individual and group value judgment will be squandered.

In addition, there is high importance to the practical applications of the "Collective Unconscious" concept. If all human beings, regardless of those external distinctions which have so typically separated us from each other, have an underpinning of experiences, feelings, needs, and psychic realities which are generally the same, then to treat people differently in terms of external realities of sex, race, ethic divergence, or socio-economics becomes patently absurd. In Jung's concept of the "Collective Unconscious," there is his highest ethical mandate; a demand to treat all people with a parity of justice and—at least at times—an equality of love. The practical application of these concepts for a basic, organizational ethic and standard of daily operation is abundantly clear. Exceptions to this mandate will destroy the "soul" of an organization just as readily as it will destroy the "soul" of an individual who does not practice a personal mandate borne of the reality of the great "sameness" of humanity that exists in our world.

THE SHADOW
THE BASIC CONCEPT

The nationally-known healthcare futurist and able philosopher, Leland Kaiser, has a captivating presentation in which he describes what I would call a "hierarchy of life." At the top of Kaiser's hierarchy is—for want of a better word, but to honor the word that has established itself in human civilization on this planet—God. God is conceived as the creative power of the universe, the ultimate source of goodness, and the standard for the highest potential of love. Kaiser is not hung up on words, so he has high respect for the "god-words" that have appeared in other cultures and believes that the words are all pointing mechanisms that convey attention toward that "Holy Other"—for want of better words again—which is the absolute point of reference that all the god-language intersects with. I feel that Kaiser would probably be satisfied enough with the terminology growing out of Robert Hartman's axiology that this "God" is "The Value of All Values."

Kaiser, of course, also has a human dimension in his hierarchy. Here there is the mind, the physical body, and the emotions of the living human being. While Kaiser can talk about these three dynamics almost as "levels" that have proximity to each other in some descending degree of importance—mind, emotion, body—in fact, they constitute an integrative nexus that operate in varying degrees of collaboration and synthesis with each other.

It has always been intriguing to me in listening to Kaiser to see that he has distinct "above the human being" dimensions to his hierarchy, but no "below the human being" dimensions. I have not asked him, so I could be putting words in his mouth, but it would appear that the sub-human, the non-human, the sub-god, ungodly possibilities that exist in life are not the result of some "below the human being" powers. The "below the human" appears to be fully encased in the human capacity to choose the positive potentials that exist in situations or to choose negative potentials. If there is evil that takes place, it will be the result of human choice.

I am most intrigued, however, by the dimension that Kaiser describes as existing between God and human beings. This middle ground is the arena of "spirit" and "soul." If there is ever connectedness between God and human beings, it will occur in this middle ground. "Spirit"—and this next phrase is critical—is, in Kaiser's explanation, a reflection of God, much in the same sense that a crystal-clear, smooth and still mountain lake can give a perfect reflection of forests and mountains beyond it in the distance. This reflection, this "spirit" is abroad in life—careful here, the language available to us is being stretched and at least a hint of old language is creeping back in around the edges of our conversation—and can be experienced, "picked up on" as it were, by that unique capacity for "reception" and "encounter" (the Jewish philosopher and theology Martin Buber's *Begegnung*/"encounter-meeting" might be an instructive concept to follow here) which Kaiser identifies as the human "soul," a higher-order capacity for human beings than rationality or emotionality. For me, since valuing, value judgment, and evaluation are a higher order property of human beings, then "soul" is an axiological arena, the arena of valuing and ultimately the values which drive human attitudes, behaviors, and actions. The coalescence of Jung's psychology, Kaiser's spiritual philosophy, Hartman's axiology, and my own syntheses creates a fluid flow of thought running in and out of each other like a powerful mountain river.

This second dimension in Kaiser's hierarchy is a dynamic interchange; that accessible "part" of God, although a reflection is not a physical "part," meets, runs into, encounters the highest order activity/capacity/sensitivity of human beings—"Soul." There is conversation and dialogue within this encounter/interchange that is beyond normal word language. It is very real all the same. As the medieval philosopher, William of Ockham, taught, words—even beautiful poetic expressions—are always a reduced form of reality; absolute reality is always more than and beyond words. Kaiser's middle ground is devoid of reductionistic speech. It is not a logically demonstrable reality, but a felt reality. Our problem in western civilization is that we struggle to give credence to felt realities and only feel comfortable with demonstrable, logical realities. Yet, even the most basic realities—the love we feel for mates or children—immediately demonstrate beyond question that which defies words is representative of our highest and most profound realities. Jung would completely agree with this assessment of language, conveying in numerous writings how language was always only marginally efficient in conveying the depth of the psychic arenas he was attempting to explore.

Kaiser's ideal is to talk about an "alignment" or "atonement"/"at-one-ment"—perhaps an "in-tune-ment"—which can exist between all of the dimensions from God to real actions pursued by real people. When this alignment occurs, there is the existential sense of "orientation" described by the philosopher of religion Mercea Eliade (*The Sacred and the Profane*) which is the antithesis of that "disorientation" or ennui or dis-ease which produces the highest levels of fear, angst, and internal self-conflict and lack of direction— that ultimately undermines the foundation upon which interpersonal relations can be built and promotes sickness and a pervasive lack of well-being.

What does all of this have to do with Jung's "Shadow"? In fact, a great deal. "The Shadow" is the reflection of the negative elements which make up at least a very real part of what once might have been called "The Unconscious"/"The Underworld." We might never be able to fully see, for Jung, "The Unconscious," but we can feel/encounter/experience its reflection, its "Shadow." This "Shadow" can exist in individuals; it can also exists for corporate entities, groups, nations, even all of humanity. "The Shadow" for all of humanity (or any grouped part of it) would be some expression of, primarily, the "Personal Unconscious" but also to some extent of the "Collective

Unconscious." It might even be possible to talk of this "Shadow" as a kind of "Anti-Reflection" or "Anti-Soul/Spirit" just to make sure that all of its negative connotations are maintained.

For Jung, "The Shadow" is the most available, outward manifestation of the negative elements of "The Unconscious," exposing or reflecting—for want of better words—childish fantasies, natural impulses, and inferior motivations humans are capable of, the "hidden" that has been pushed down and yet might be very close to some untimely spark which would make it explode. Yet, he clearly puts forward the juxtaposition that everyone has a "Shadow," and the only way to keep from casting a shadow would be to have no substance at all.

For Freud, there would be little than an individual could do about this "Shadow." It would be there as a constant companion, ready to trample good judgment given even the slightest hint of openness. Jung objected. For him, this "Shadow" could be exposed in conversation, understood to some extent, and triumphed over. The point for Jung would be to honestly admit its existence and come to grip with its implication; a "Shadow" exposed was a "Shadow" diminished in power. He describes a process that begins with confession—abject confrontation with negatives that exist, moves through some dimension of understanding and explanation, manifests itself to a larger organization through education, and triumphs in transformation, dramatic, lasting change.

INTERPRETATION AND PROBLEMS/QUESTIONS/ISSUES

It might appear to be somewhat surprising that the intent of the section above on "The Unconscious" was to create a means to move beyond this "Unconscious" as some sort of negative, personal reality loose in the world, to find a way of reconfiguring language about negatives in life that was not so dependent on ancient history and myth. Ultimately, in Jung's new way of understanding "The Unconscious," those dimensions which held positive potential for growth toward understanding uniqueness/"Individuation" and achieving "wholeness" could be given attention. In fact, he finds a way to even allow ancient history, myth, and mysticism to become avenues for bringing greater distinctiveness to the understanding of "The Unconscious."

Beyond this, Jung—and I have never been fully convinced that even he was fully aware of the implications of what he was saying—talked about "The Shadow" in a way that totally moves beyond anthropomorphic personalizing of negative realities in life to the point that they take on an almost personal identity capable of interacting with human persons. In doing so, he opened a way for us to be able to use the category "Shadow" to have meaningful discussion about very real dynamics of human existence.

Without the slightest equivocation, Jung says that "the shadow is a moral problem" (*The Shadow*, Collected Works 9ii, par 14). No longer a beastly monster foaming in a real or psychic underworld beside my father's "Booger Man;" now a moral problem. For me, of course, a value problem. His fuller statement:

> The shadow is a moral problem. . . . No one can become conscious of the shadow without considerable moral effort [considerable value effort]. To become conscious of it involves recognizing the dark aspects of the personality as present and real. Experience shows that there are certain features which offer the most obstinate resistance to moral [value] control and prove almost impossible to influence. These resistances are usually bound up with projections [more about this below], which are not recognized as such, and their recognition is a moral achievement [a value achievement] beyond the ordinary.

These are powerful words that have high application to the most modern of our life circumstances. No longer are we in the world of cosmic ghosts and goblins; now, we are talking about very real, dark aspects of human character. Without question, many of these are deeply ingrained and obstinate in their resistance. The control that can be achieved over them is not a mystical, magical power exerted by shamans and gurus but rather a moral control that begins in conscious recognition. Jung is very sure that such honest recognition, honest conversation, honest confrontation—at least a beginning point—of these "dark aspects" is a moral achievement.

Now, we are giving consideration (recall con-sider, "with wisdom") to a set of realities that I can absolutely relate to with clarity. There are "dark aspects" to almost any dimension of our lives from the most private and personal to the most all-encompassing of our common humanity. These "dark aspects" present themselves as moral/value problems. The solving of these problems is greatly inhibited by denial, avoidance, and transference. The solving of these problems is greatly inhibited by unrecognized and misunderstood projections (more below). For most of us, if there has ever been success—even the beginnings of success—in triumphing over these dark aspect moral problems, there has had to be the honest moment of recognition. Often this moment has come not just as a result of our own self honestly, but because of the caring courage of someone else that was honest with us in a way that we may not have been able to be honest with ourselves. In this sense, the moment of recognition is—without question—a moment of moral achievement beyond the ordinary. Our problem: there are not enough of these moments. The inadequacy of our "recognition" dis-ables us in situations which cry out for high levels of "en-able-ing" and "im-powering."

Finally, with compelling insight, Jung reminds us that perhaps the greatest enemy of the realization and recognition of the dark aspect moral problems is the persona, the "Mask." Remember the persona, that mask of cultural nicety that we spend so much time and effort getting ready before we wear it out into public. Part of that persona insists that nice people do not have dark side, do not have moral problems to resolve, do not have any troubles. To admit to any dark sides would be to lower the mask a bit too far. To talk about or seek help for dark side moral problems would perhaps be a sign of weakness or confession that you were not a good person. In much of our modern culture, such admissions and confessions would not be "manly" and a whole set of new obstacles are put in place. So, we refuse to seek help—real, strong people solve their own problems. Recognition and realization never occur, and the moral problems seem only to grow and become even more resistant.

PRACTICAL APPLICATION

I may not need to worry too much about Underworld monsters or a psychic Unconscious filled only with that which is negative and destructive. My organization may not need to call in security agents to protect ourselves against the ravages of these cosmic foes. Yet, I better give close attention to my dark side moral problems or those of my organization. I had better be conversant about "Shadows," those distinct moral problems that reflect and refract themselves throughout human existence with the power of incisive laser beams. My movements of denial, avoidance, and transference move these realities into a realm of, at least, "sub-consciousness" where they avoid Jung's moral control, and thus place me in jeopardy.

Jung is helpful is additional ways. He illustrates the way in which everyone has shadows, dark aspects, moral problems. In ancient mythology, only the Devil had no shadow; the Devil was beyond the benefit of light. We are not devils, we are human beings with our own unique mixtures of light and darkness, the dynamic of contrast that creates shadows. Yet, the involvement of light conveys that there is always an arena of positive possibility, growth and development, maturity—enlightenment. Admitting that we are all in this life together with our dupe's mixture of light and darkness might make it somehow easier to move toward the moral achievement of recognition and honest discussion/confrontation.

And, of most significance, Jung clearly understands that this dynamic of "Shadow" can be created by both negative weaknesses and positive strengths. Just as the Unconscious can harbor positives, so "Shadow" can involve positives. This singular point cannot be made strongly enough; here is the key for this whole discussion in many respects and especially for the conclusion that is being built toward. Let Jung speak for himself:

> It has been believed that the human shadow was the source of all evil. It can not be ascertained on closer investigation that the shadow does not consist only of morally reprehensible tendencies, but also displays a number of good qualities, such as normal instincts, appropriate reactions, realistic insights, creative impulses, etc. (*Conclusion*, CW 9ii, par 423).

The key question: how can "good qualities" contribute to the "Shadow" and thus become dark aspect moral problems? The answer: when good qualities are taken to an extreme, they can become negative in their implication and impact. In some sense, our greatest strengths have the potential—if taken to the extreme—to become real weaknesses. There is a distinct need for Jung's moral control and recognition/realization as much in regard to our strengths as in regard to our weaknesses. For most of humanity, in fact, reprehensible weakness is not the real problem; most of us have an operative level of decency and moral intent that is beyond reprehensible weakness. However, we become the very people who are capable of taking strengths to an extreme that they create their own moral problems.

A simple example: I love to run. A long run on a beautiful day adds to my life in immeasurable ways. Running becomes my sanity in a way, and sometimes when I am really struggling for insight and articulation, a long run—with its "runner's high"—can give me ideas and insights that seem impossible to achieve in a cloistered office. In addition, running is good for my health; when I am really on my running discipline, I have no weight problems, little susceptibility to colds, few headaches, and gain a real sense of beneficent well-being.

However, across thirty years of this discipline of sorts, I have never failed to let the process get away from me. I begin to challenge myself to run greater distances at faster speeds. I start competing more with my fellow runners in the community "races" that are frequently staged where I live. Just to finish in the top ten in my age group and gain mention in the local newspaper becomes more important, in some ways, that all the benefits of the exercise. I start seeing myself as a much younger man than I actually am. I have Olympic-caliber dreams. I start envisioning a level of accomplishment that is unrealistic, but I am driven toward it all the same.

And, what inevitably and invariably happens—I hurt myself! A hurt tendon, a pulled muscle, a stress fracture. The running stops. There is disappointment and self-blame. "I know better than this. How can anyone be so stupid?!" You see, I have taken something that is very good, filled with benefits of every variety, a true strength, and I have turned it into something that is indeed, for me, very negative. There has been bad judgment, inefficient valuation, an erroneous and damaging projection of inadequate archetypes (more below), and I have to stop running. My fine and wonderful strength has its own potential "Shadow," and I have assembled a set of inadequate judgments that have allowed that "Shadow" to assert itself.

Business, organizational, and institutional settings can become involved in similar dynamics. The most common form has to do with work ethic; the whole idea of "ethic" brings us again close to the area of moral and value judgment. To have a strong work ethic in our modern society is a distinct value and highly desired by most people in the workplace. Too often, work is seen as an entitlement and not as an opportunity; the degree of actual effort and committed determination can be lacking. So, to find someone who will really put forth effort is highly appealing, especially in a time in which downsizing and reorganization has used as a standard tactic organizational arrangements designed to get more work out of fewer people.

Add to this contemporary dynamic a particular set of realities that heighten the intensity of "work ethic," and it becomes possible to see how real—as opposed to mythic—"Shadows" are created. For many so-called "Baby Boomers," children of the post–World War II era, who are in the late core of their working careers, the issue of "work ethic" is most dominant. They have contributed to the establishment of an American and world economy unsurpassed. They have created a level of affluence in the United States that would have been beyond the imagination of their parents. They have created educational institutions that have educated a generation of people that have succeeded in putting people on the moon, overcoming horrific diseases, and established communication and media technologies that will probably be greater in their implication than Gutenberg's printing press. They know about "work ethic."

Their parents were part of a generation devastated by "The Great Depression" of the early part of the twentieth century. Driven into the minds of the "Baby Boomers" was never, never to experience the dregs of economic disaster like the Depression ever again. The Boomers were taught, with pathos, that to be successful, you had to be sure to work harder than the next person. The post-Depression mentality concerning work took the pervasive concept of "The Protestant Work Ethic" on which the United States was founded to a new echelon of intensity. While it is clearly metaphorical, to start talking about a powerful, "Collective Unconscious," even an Underworld monster begins to almost make sense. The Protestant Work Ethic and The Great Depression created powerful undercurrents that have, absolutely, had an amazing impact on many people who have risen to places of high, corporate leadership in the United States today. Add to all this that raging immigration into the work force of women, minorities, and people consciously migrating to the United States to achieve "the American Dream" for themselves, and the competition of hard work has only been dramatically heightened.

So, we get a lot done. We have soaring stock markets, productivity trends, numbers of people employed, and the Gross National Product—surely the measure of our credibility and character as a people—only continues to establish new standards of achievement. The rest of the world wants to be just like us. Literally, there are people in what used to be called the Third World who really believe our streets—not a mythic heaven—are paved with gold. Now, some of these Boomers are saying, not altogether facetiously, that if God really wanted to bless them, He would allow them to be reincarnated as their own children. We know about work ethic; it's part of the moral fiber of our existence.

We also know about the individual, family, and organizational disasters that have come as a result of the "Shadow-side" of this work ethic. In fact, most of the disasters have not been organizational; it is amazing how a person can literally work himself/herself to death for an organization, no longer be present, and the name on the door be replaced with the greatest of ease. We have become a disposable culture when it comes to workers who work themselves to death as well.

The real disasters have been personal and family-related. The heavy toll taken on personal health and well-being, and the chronic toll taken on relationships with mates and children in the name of "doing a good job" are inestimable. Too often, people really learn of these "work ethic costs" after it is too late and health or relationships are damaged in a way that cannot be remediated. The old idea of no one being on a deathbed and desiring one more day at the office is probably instructive.

In concluding this section on practical application, what has been said here—in one way or another—is a part of the conversation of the modern workplace. People recognize and express feelings about the pain they see, complaint about how things could be better, or talk about how these issues really do need to be addressed at some point. The point simply never comes. It is not enough to "feel the pain" of people who have taken their work ethic too the extreme. It is not enough to have a compassionate sidebar conversation about knowing how people are being pressed and pressing themselves toward breaking points. It is not enough to keep making all those relationship promises about how there is going to be more time very soon, how you will be home early today, how you will take a long weekend off and do something with the family very soon.

The whole issue of work ethic, both positive and negative, must be a central conversation on the leadership level of organizations. The problem or potential problems must be monitored on an ongoing basis. Above all, this must be an area of honest conversation. Just like any, obviously negative "Shadow" would be carefully guarded and policed, so must those positive "Shadows" which can be taken to destructive extremes. There simply must be consciously pursued strategies that act as a vigilant counterpoint to the excesses of work ethic. Let us get our work done and do it as well as it can be done, but let us not destroy life in the process. We must take these ideas seriously. We cannot let them wait. In most workplaces, now is the time! In fact, in most environments, it is past time!

ARCHETYPAL PROJECTIONS: THE FINAL HORIZON OF INSIGHT
THE BASIC CONCEPT

Jung perceptively describes what I would call "stages of development" which take place, to one degree or another, in the life experiences of most human beings. While he tends to suggests that there is a consistent pattern to this "development," my thought is that he is describing a fairly common experience, but an experience that is not an arbitrary necessity or the same for all people. By "stages," he is describing an unfolding, evolving pattern of "projections" which build—one on another—and have a distinct impact on the evolution of self-identity. The "projections" can become what Jung sees as archetypes, compelling and powerful model/patterns which constitute the frameworks/ideal options in which the self finds directed parameters of growth and development.

That Jung talks so vividly about development and evolution indicates that he strongly believes that human beings can grow, and that they are not simply the victims of genetic and cultural dispositions. It is possible to consciously grow beyond even the Freudian influences of realities such as the id, libido, and superego. It is also possible to grow beyond negative experience of childhood. For Jung, there are early stages of consciousness of the world and ego development, the "morning of our lives" in which consciousness is expanded as we encounter and deal with problems and challenges, and the "afternoon of our lives" when we live by choices informed by wisdom and perspective. The ideal would be for elements of this "afternoon" wisdom to come chronologically earlier in our lives so that we can come to the point of self-consciously determining projections and archetypes that will be most productive and meaningful for the Individuation, uniqueness, and self-realization of our own existence.

For example, in the historical uniqueness of my own upbringing—for better and for worse—because of the influence of my two older brothers, older youth who took on a kind of heroic status in my community, coaches, television, and the type of person my unique culture liked/affirmed/blessed, the powerful model/pattern—the archetype—that my life until about twenty years of age was dramatically influenced by might be called "The Great Athlete." It was all I wanted to do, all that I dreamed about, the parameter that most drove the direction in which my life was going. In my instance, that "Great Athlete" was a football player; had I been being raised in Russia, it might have been a hockey player or in Argentina, a soccer player. The parameter/ideal/archetype was the result of a large number or interacting influences particular to my culture, my community, and my family. That I ended up being successful in athletics was highly fortunate for me in the sense that I found a great deal of affirmation from the sources that had created the archetype. I have often wondered about the frustration, lack of fulfillment, and struggle to find identity that would have been experienced by someone raised in the same environment that was not successful. The archetype could have also become very destructive if I reached a point, for example, in which I could not continue to be "The Great Athlete" and did not make appropriate adjustments or modify the model or replace it with some other archetype. Or, there could have become a time in which I wanted to pursue some stronger model, and my old community or family cultures might have wanted to hold me in the old model which they more easily identified with or felt was more important to aspire to than a new model. Great conflict, misunderstanding, and pain could be the result.

This pain and conflict may have been felt more by others in my community than by me, especially if I had "made my peace" with the movements beyond the old persona that had actually been given to me more than consciously chosen by me. Of course, on a very immature and unsophisticated—teenager—level, I had chosen in keeping with the highly desirable, positive reinforcement of the community, but in the beginning stages of what I hope could be called "authenticity" that can begin to develop in late teens and early twenties—especially in the context of strong educational experiences—that old persona was beginning to be seen for what it actually was. It had worked efficiently enough, even been fun, but now it was time to move on—the "when I was a child, I responded as a child, but when I became an adult, I put away childish ways" cliché. Do not get me wrong: I still am very nostalgic about that time, recall the successes with real joy, and greatly enjoy football to this day. That I did not, however, become "Jim Taylor"—the great Green Bay Packers fullback who was my primary role model and archetype—never was a problem. My mother would dress me up on Sunday morning, stick a Bible under my arm, and send me off to church with the description, "He's my little preacher." I heard that statement repeatedly; even had it echoed by three aunts. Lots of kids were brought up in the church like I was, but few of them "felt" as if they should be a minister by their late teens like I did. The power of my mother's projection—the archetype she laid down and the persona she advanced for me—were powerful. That she died when I was thirteen only made the power of the archetype grow. In no way, did she mean harm; she was dealing with a cultural archetype of her own that had, for her, nothing but positive connotations.

By the time I was part way into college, a teacher/professor image had begun to dominate, along with a more authentic understanding of the dynamics that had surrounded my mother, our community, and me. To not be a minister in the fullest sense of that vocational type was—just like being a professional football player—moved beyond without much pain. On the other hand, there were still people in my community who wanted to see me in that role/persona, feared that somehow I was not doing the "will of God," and wondered at what kind of inner conflict I must have been feeling. It may be of interest that I have continued to do some work in relationship to churches, but—for me—because I see potential for good and opportunity to make the society better, not of which have much to do with what my mother wanted me to become vocationally. In fact, I think that she would, even more, have wanted me to fulfill images of being a good husband and father than any of these vocational images anyway.

In some individuals, the power of these projections may be immense; in others, they may be hardly noticed. When the projections are positive, healthy, and productive, they may stand in consciously visible and affirmed ways in the forefront of an individual's thinking/feeling/evaluative processes; when they are negative, unhealthy, or hurtful in some way, they are pushed down into that part of our conscious thinking/feeling/evaluative processes that is less-than-readily-available.

To use Jung's terms and those common to a great deal of psychology, the negative projections are repressed into the Unconscious where they are capable of influencing a person in very negative ways until they are more reasonably sorted out. I have no problem with this description, just as long as the "Unconscious" does not become some sort of personalized monster-being. Focus most closely on the unfolding and developing nature of the projections, and it becomes possible to introduce dynamics of development that are easily applicable to most individual's past histories.

I have always felt particularly close to the ideas of classic existentialism as it parallels Jung in some of its key concepts. An individual may have an "essence," a central "hub" from which the various aspects of self-manifestation take place. I am a father, a husband, a teacher, a neighbor, a citizen, a brother, a son, etc., etc. Yet, at the "hub" of all of these manifestations is a core "me," Self, the "essence" my being. However, this "essence" is not something that I am born with, some innate essence over which I have no control. In reality, my early stages of being do involve "essences" which are given to me by family, community, and culture—Jung's persona. I am not very introspective about this "essence," and probably do not ever realize initially that it is being given. However, when I begin to have an introspective and reflective existence that is more my own than given, I can begin to choose who I am, construct my own "essence," identity, Self. The existential maxim of "existence precedes existence" can then apply to the authentic essence that I begin to build. Clearly, there is always an interplay between authentic essence and given essence which never ends, but to the degree that my "essence" is primary and for the most part my own, I transcend given persona, cultural archetypes, and the combination of "Unconscious"/"Shadow." In authentic existence, there is always the sustaining of the distinction between persona and person. The person can be authentic; the persona can only be authentic when it is a fully chosen extension of the person/the Self. When this happens—and it definitely can—Jung talks about the experience of a sense of "wholeness," an alignment/atonement between persona and person.

First Archetypal Projection—The initial movement of archetypal configuration begins immediately after birth in the parental relationships of the family of origin. The initial male experiences with the father create the animus, the generic male archetype. The initial female experiences with the mother create the anima, the generic female archetype. There is likely a correspondence between the x and y chromosomes of the human genetic structure. There is no underbelly of innate, personal Unconscious except in the metaphorical sense.

The impact of the anima and animus can move in a number of potential directions. There may be both male and female dimensions of personality that develop, although I feel strongly that characteristics and tendencies develop that are labeled "male" or "female" by cultural stereotypes and caricatures. The anima experienced by a male may have some impact on the mate choice that occurs in adulthood, either in the choice of characteristics that were conceived as positive or the avoidance of characteristics that were conceived as negative. The animus experienced by a female may have a similar impact on the choice of a mate later in life. This process does not have to be unconscious, but can be highly conscious in the interception and personal examination that humans are capable of. Only for the non-introspective and non-examining person of less intellectual and cultural sophistication would these archetypes be part of an unconscious, undeveloped, unacknowledged self-awareness. Animus—in our more male-dominated culture—may have some impact on how God as "Heavenly Father" is conceived; a positive father experience may generate a more easily appropriated God concept, while a negative father experience may create resistance to God concepts.

3. *Trust and the Shadow*

Second Archetypal Projection—A next level of archetypes begin to accumulate as lived experiences are gained with other individuals in the process of becoming older. There may be older siblings (I recall at about four years of age, my brothers shaving off my eyebrows with a razor so I could be like this older brother who was greatly admired), people we become aware of in our communities, heroes from athletics or the movies, personalities we encounter on television. There may be particular role models—Roy Rogers, Luke Skywalker, Zorro, Batman, Annie Oakley, Charlie's Angels, Wonder Woman—or composite models constituted by assembled strengths and virtues that have been experienced or logically induced. Ancient civilizations projected perfected human attributes onto the cosmic universe and came up with a pantheon of deities; we take similar attributes and create archetypal role models.

Such projections are not necessarily harmful. They may represent goals and ambitions that are worthy and elicit positive growth and development. However, if the particular role model does not live up to his or her image/ideal, the ensuing disappointment can be devastating. Again, there is no "Unconscious" substrata at work here, only the relatively simply process of becoming attentive to something that is admirable or desirable and wanting to emulate that. Certainly, some of these emulations are sophomoric, even asinine, but—given the larger movements of human existence—they are probably fairly normal.

Third Archetypal Projection—A third level of archetypes usually appear and correspond to more adult levels of maturity and sophistication. On this third level there is a greater awareness of what an archetype is, how it comes to be an element of influence in our existence, and the potential interaction we have with the archetype. By this time there may have been psychology courses which, in great detail, explore archetypes, persona, the Unconscious, Shadows—a full gamut of introspective cues and prompts. This is the level where the multiplicity of Jung-like examples come to play a more dominant role in our lives. There are all kinds of examples: The Suffering Servant (based on the prophet Isaiah's concept that has been liberally applied to Jesus), the Wounded Savior, the Servant Teacher, the Great Athlete, the Wise Old Man, the Monk, the Warrior, the Lover, the Southern Gentleman (perhaps the result of too many Rhett Butler/Gone With The Wind exposures), the "Cool Dude," the Perfect Father, the Perfect Mother, the Perfect Mate—the list of these configured role models is potentially endless.

These archetypes are much more sophisticated and potentially powerful than an adolescent infatuation with some movie star or sports hero. Most people can readily see and clearly understand the role these kinds of archetypes have taken in life. There may even be times in which we are able to say: "Yes, I am aware of that archetype. I have a distinct realization of where it has come from. I recognize its impact on my life. All of this is fine. If that influence helps me realize the virtues and strengths exemplified by the archetype, I am likely to be a better person."

Fourth Archetypal Projection—So far, we have seen archetypes which influence gender identities, biases, and decisions, archetypes which give human beings preliminary models for behavior which often translate into goals and ambitions, and sophisticated archetypes which channel identity, self-consciousness, and the person—not persona—that a human being is capable of becoming. We have admitted that there are times when the power and interplay of these archetypes may exist beneath the level of operative consciousness, but we have also advanced the idea that there are other times in which a person—not a persona—can understand the historical and causative presence of these archetypes, sort them out in ways that are meaningful, and have a thoroughly authentic life as a whole Self.

The fourth archetypal projection that follows at this point is not a necessity, but it certainly has become a likelihood for many people. At least, if not a likelihood, it certainly happens with a large number of people, especially when a large number of archetypes such as the competitive "Great Athlete" or aggressive "Warrior" are present as part of the backdrop of people's lives. The fourth projection may be more present for men than women, although with the advent of the supposed liberation movements of the last generation, women in business settings often come to deal with the same competitive, aggressive models.

In the fourth archetypal projection, Jung creates a distinctly important term: inflation. We are capable of taking all of our composite collection of archetypes and role models and construct them into an idealized image of what a person ought to become/ought to amount to. The "inflation" occurs in the exponentiation effect that the combined archetypes and role models have on each other. A super being is conceptualized in a powerful manner. In the mind's inflating, a perfect being is configured.

There may have been times that this composite configuration inflated to the level of the super and the perfect filled out a personal or cultural view of

God. In some respects, this may continue to happen in many people's lives. However, leaving the super and the perfect to God has not always been/does not have to be the end point. In fact, in an age in which the theological often recedes into the background to be replaced by the egocentric, human, personal individuality, that these composite configurations are passed onto an understanding of God is not of much more than passing significance; not all that many people are spending a great deal of time focusing on God.

What happens is that the composite configuration of archetypes and role models is inflated exponentially and transferred to human beings as a personal barometer of credibility and integrity. This transfer can be "aimed" at others as a set of expectations, but is most powerfully aimed at the personal self as a form of self-expectation. The expectation becomes that I must be the superman, the superdad, the super boss, the super employee; that I must be perfect—all things to all people.

INTERPRETATION AND PROBLEMS/QUESTIONS/ISSUES

I am not very concerned about the initial series of three projections. If we are self-conscious and introspective about these, their potential for being helpful can be as prominent as their potential for being negative. The entire process seems fairly normal and generally difficult to prohibit. In fact, there might not be a strong reason to worry about prohibiting the process. Of course, a strong self-consciousness of the process is important; the interplay of unacknowledged and non-conscious archetypes could easily produce personal negatives.

On the other hand, I am tremendously concerned about the fourth project in which an unrealistic image of the Self as "super" and "perfect"—an inflated view of realistic possibility—finds dominance. This projection often occurs with very talented, competent, and hard-working people who, in fact, achieve a great deal that is far beyond the mediocre and ordinary. Yet, it is these very people who seem utterly compelled to push their personal envelope of potential and energy well beyond normal and highly acceptable competence and talent. They push themselves into patterns of self-abuse—in the name of excellence—that destroy health, eradicate a sense of well-being, and cripple relationships. How easy it is to take the mandate to do a successful, competent job and inflate that mandate toward a demand to be super, perfect, all things to all people. A mistake is never allowed. A day off is never allowed. Letting something go that will, indeed, easily wait is never allowed. A deep breath is never allowed.

All to often, these are the same people who implicitly make their pattern of living/not-really-living the standard that others are expected to follow. For Jung, the "Shadow" can triumph; what could have been altogether positive if it had been held in rational moderation and common sense has become altogether negative in its impact on fellow workers and—by extension—their families. Ironically, there is little satisfaction in this inflation process since satisfaction is overwhelmed by a pervasive frustration over not getting everything done, not accomplishing every task, not being mistake free, and not making everyone happy. To somehow find liberation and emancipation from this inflated super person archetype is to be free at last, to be free to be a real person, and to be free to pursue with creativity and imagination unfettered by the frustrations of not being perfect.

Again, these images of the super boss, super manager, super executive have been predominantly male oriented. Not anymore. The Super Woman myth/persona is extremely prominent in the modern workplace. In fact, sometimes it can achieve it own exponentiation. A woman can feel that she has to be successful for the entire female gender. She can also feel that she has to do everything at work perfectly, and then go home and be a perfect mother, perfect wife, perfect homemaker. The load is overwhelming and ultimately destructive.

One more step: when workplaces are populated by this Super Person concept, it becomes very easy to transfer the idea of super people to the idea of a super organization that can—within its area of specialization—be all things to all people. In this process of extreme diversification, organizations can lose sight of the "core business" that made them successful to begin with, the "core business" that they were truly expert in advancing, and a "core business" that, in fact, deserved and demanded a precise, strong focus if it was to be as good as it could be. When the attention to the core is lost, compelling and satisfying identity can also be lost with motivation and morale quickly following in the wake of the loss.

When the Acme Car Company, the makers of wonderful quality automobiles, begins to make razor blades, operate vacation resorts, and grow tomatoes in greenhouses, they may forget how to make really good cars, their leadership may be subdivided in its focus, and money problems which rise in one area may handicap the ability to operate competently in every area. When

XYZ Hospital starts using the terms "comprehensive" or "integrative," forming insurance companies, buying physician practices, and building nursing homes, neighborhood clinics, and retirement villages, great care must be taken. There is the possibility that basic patient care—the very reality that gave the institution its credibility and reputation—can get lost in the process and, if expertise in the other "product lines" is inadequate, the very economic base on which patient-care opportunities rest can be jeopardized. There is no guarantee that either of these scenarios will happen, but it is as difficult for an organization to be all things to all people as it is for an individual to pursue this impossible task. The Don Quixote of the modern age is not jousting at windmills; he is creating a comprehensive, integrative system of work that takes care of everything for everyone, accepting a level of accountability that tries to be almost messianic and Olympian in its implication. The inflated, fourth projection only laughs back at these honest movements of question and lack of comfort: "The difficult requires an hour; the impossible may take until noon!" The competitive, aggressive "Warrior/Great Athlete" can prevail. The highest levels of diversified success may not be impossible, but great care must be observed with each Superman bite that is taken—it might be bigger than we can chew.

PRACTICAL APPLICATION

Please, please do not get me wrong. I am not trying to demean or criticize what Acme Automobile or XYZ Hospital is trying to do. It may even be honorable to attempt to be all things to all people. It may even be possible to pull it off, although most people and organizations do not. The key is to realistically count the costs of a potential endeavor before it reaches some critical mass, point of no return. The archetypes of modern management theory—"The Entrepreneur" and "The Risk Taker"—simply sometimes defeat common sense realism. There is no invitation to mediocrity here, no invitation to stay comfortably in boxes of unimaginative dullness. There is only an invitation to count costs, and particularly human costs.

In like manner, I have no desire whatsoever to be cynical about the person attempting to grow and develop, to "be all that you can be." Such goals are always admirable, without question. To move toward the "super" and the "perfect" can be honorable ambition and not necessarily hubris/pride of the sort that almost invariably precedes falls. In all honesty, however, this potentially obsessive-compulsive forward movement can also be the result of unexamined archetypes that become the moral-problem "Shadow" of Jung's most sophisticated interpretations. Again, the issue is to count the costs, particularly the human costs. Only in this "counting" can the shadowy moral problem be addressed.

Especially, I must be dramatically aware of the impact of my pursuit of the "super" and the "perfect" on the lives of my fellow workers and their families. We are ultimately accountable for trying new agendas and processes, not resting on past laurels, and pushing the envelope of new opportunity and success; we are also accountable for the human costs that accrue along the way. There is an extremely delicate balance between following the organizational archetypes prominent at the end of the twentieth century and preserving the sanctity of human life—both that of ourselves and others. If the organizational archetype becomes "The Spiritual/Value-Based Leader," the maintenance and nurturing of this balance will command first and absolute attention, will always command a careful looking before we leap, and will command a first duty to persons and not to some potentially-destructive, organizational persona. When the quality of human life is compromised and sold off in the attempt to accomplish a Superman or Super Organization persona, the price is too high. When a would-be Superman or would-be Super Organization does not carefully understand the whole persona/archetype concept and honestly pursue the exposure of its own potential "Shadow"—bring it to "The Light"—Jung's moral problem surfaces, and human chaos will prevail.

Please, please understand that I am not accusing those people who pursue Superman agendas as being criminal in their intent or callously unfeeling in their humanity. In most instances, the very opposite is the case. They are usually people of highest character and the greatest desire to serve, make a difference, and do something exemplary in life. Their "inflation" of goals and ambitions—usually for their organizations and professions than for themselves personally—are usually motivated by an authentic desire to improve the quality of life for others. They are often even personally sacrificial to the utmost degree in pursuing these goals, dreams, and sometimes glorious ends. There is nothing "demonic" here; in fact, the pursuit may be conducted within the context of that which is felt to be absolutely "godly." Yet, the impact of cultural persona and cultural archetypes—even religiously-inspired archetypes—can resist honest examination; the most positive agendas can generate the most negative consequences. Look at the Crusades, the Inquisition, the desire to convert American and African natives. That people are absolutely and acutely well-meaning, does not mean that the outcomes pursued by their enthusiasm and devotion will be productive of truly human existence. The call is simply for great, great care to be taken in the processes we pursue.

Healthcare futurist Leland Kaiser, writing in the February 28, 2000, edition of *Modern Healthcare*, writes about the industry he knows so well: "The question is, how much of your life do you want to sacrifice to stay afloat in this industry? Is it worth the price of your soul?" Kaiser talks about 70–80 hour work weeks becoming standard, estrangement from family, and managers with stress-related illnesses. People are counting the days until the "golden parachute" of employee contracts can be deployed. And Kaiser emphasizes that he is not talking about social or vocational "losers," but the best and brightest in the industry.

Jung would completely understand. It is the Self/the Soul that is lost as homage is ultimately given to the persona and cultural archetypes laid down by the dictates of the post-Depression, obsessive work ethic that determines self-worth by the degree of "soul" that is owed to the company store. That health and personal well-being can go on without adequate attention, that relationships can continue without loving maintenance, that more and more ways can be found to cram more and more hours of labor into a day—these realities boggle the mind and leave fellow workers standing in the hallways anxiously contemplating how long it will take for some acuteness of breakdown to occur.

A WELL-MEANING ASIDE:
THE MYERS-BRIGGS TYPE INVENTORY

The whole concept of "types" of individually unique human beings was advanced by Jung without any equivocation. He felt, however, that across the course of civilization—both formally and informally—that many, various "typologies" had come into existence to help human beings understand each other. Many of these more primitive typologies had worked, for Jung from the outside to the inside, the external to the internal. A big, strong man would have more courage than a small, muscularly weaker woman. He used the example of phrenology in which knots on the skull would determine disposition, characters, even vocation. He noted those early typologies in which people were defined in terms of the signs of the Zodiac or the ancient Greek formulations of phlegmatic, sanguine, choleric, and melancholic. The ancient Hindus taught that personality could be dominated and directed by shakras, regions of the physical body that could influence behavioral outcomes. The lists of such "typologies" is endless across culture and underscores, once again, the credibility of Jung's concept of the "Collective Unconscious."

However, when Jung decided to talk about "types," consistent with his overall approach to psychology and life in general, he desired a "sturdy empiricism" when possible that could reduce complexity and provide simplicity of explanation and understanding. For him, different "types" rose in response to the way that different people dealt with obstacles and problems when they occurred. He used the example of a person approaching a stream where there is no bridge. Here is the obstacle/problem, and "every individual has his accustomed way of meeting decisions and of dealing with difficulties." One person may jump just for the fun of it. Another may simply assess the situation and feel there is no other alternative. Another may be met with a sense of challenge and be provoked to meet challenges in whatever form they present themselves. Yet another may not want to go to any extra effort and walk away. A fifth person, again following Jung's simple example, may decide that there is nothing on the other side worth jumping for.

In this rather simple context, Jung pulled together what we can call for now what appear to be three dichotomies that indicate how a person has become predisposed in his evolving experience and existence to deal with obstacles/problems. First, there are the basic categories of Extravert and Introvert—noted in what will follow as "E" and "I." (I am not aware that Jung used the letter symbols, but they are logical enough.) Then, Jung taught that there was a "fourfold classification" of cognitive processes that he identified as sensation ("S"), thinking ("T"), feeling ("F"), and intuition ("N"—as opposed to "I" which has already been used with Introvert).

Here is what is very important: Jung saw these dimensions of human existence as complimentary, overlapping, and evolving from one to the next. They were not seen as opposites, nor were they seen as fixed determinants that were not open to change. Therefore, sensation could discern through the sense that which is; thinking could allow for basic meaning in regard to the relation of entities presented to the sense to each other and to the context which they inhabited; feeling could assign levels of value; and, intuition could at least give cues/clues to a higher order of potential realization or manifestation. All would be important in an ascending order, but none possible without the others. He did not see these cognitive capacities as drives or needs; he rather talked decisively of "value intensities" that ultimately allowed for fuller "pictures" of that which is. In addition to the S, T, F, and N, the overlay of the Extravert/Introvert could convey the reality of what he called the "two depths" which human beings are continuously caught up in, the external which is viewed by looking outwardly and the internal which is viewed by looking inwardly. To find a balance of most views, plus an evolving ascendancy of the four cognitive processes would be the surest track toward a holistic encounter with existence. Finally, Jung did talk about a how "each of these functions [S, T, F, N] varies according to the general attitude [E and I], and thus produces eight variables [types]." To follow the symbolic references that are being used, these Jungian types would thus be: EST, ESF, ENT, ENF, IST, ISF, INT, INF. I have no awareness of whether Jung personally ever used these kinds of labels. How he would have arrived at these labels, or some semblance of them, is also not abundantly clear. My guess is that he would have come to the different characterizations by conversation and observation.

In the United States, these insights of Jung were picked up and developed in a much more specific manner in the late-1950s and early-1960s by Isabel Myers and Katherine Briggs. They created the Myers-Briggs Type Inventory (MBTI) as a personality inventory to help individuals and groups of individuals understand themselves more readily. The MBTI has received highly successful marketing and has proven itself to be the most accessible and easily used of the psychological/personality inventories that have been developed in the past half century.

To describe this aside as "well meaning" is my way of saying that I hold the MBTI in sufficiently high regard. I have no need to diminish its impact or disdain its intent. I have seen the MBTI create valuable dialogue and conversation for both individuals and groups; I frequently use the Myers-Briggs materials in concert with The Hartman Value Profile. Profiling instruments are not crystal balls or magic wands. Their value comes from the conversations that they establish. In this regard, the MBTI has substantial value for me. The comments that I will now offer are intended to build on—and possibly enhance—what the MBTI has accomplished.

First, in the spirit of Jung himself, the MBTI is designed to simplify and have concrete application. It does this. However, I wonder if there has not been some oversimplification that needs to be addressed. For example, there is little indication of the evolving, growing, overlapping nature of the types seen in Jung. For the MBTI, a person is—to me—"typecast" into one of sixteen types. There is more of a tendency to see a person as what he/she is, and this is what he/she will be. Period. More discussion needs to be given to evolving and growing.

Second, the MBTI tends to chart differences and extremes of the dichotomies it assesses. A person, for example, may be an extreme or moderate Introvert or heavy into Intuition/"N" as opposed to Sensing/"S." This charting must be seen only as a diagnostic beginning point. The goal is for balance and a coalescing wholeness in which extremes are mediated. Little discussion of the MBTI moves in this direction of insight.

Third, Myers and Briggs introduced the additional dichotomies of Judgment/"J" and Perception/"P" which they clearly state is not directly found in Jung but implied in his work. I am not sure of this and am not clear that the "J" and "P" categories add depth to what Jung has said. There is the movement to sixteen types now made possible by the four sets of variables. Where a person falls into these types is determined by a multi-item, word association instrument; this seems adequate enough, and the emphasis on work association is certainly in keeping with Jung's practices. In general, a stronger "J" type will show concern with the outcome of information—conclusions, assessments, decision-making, closure; the stronger "P" type will show concern with the input/incoming of information and may be more readily involved with curiosity, seeing divergent possibility and potential, and less need for closure and finalization. In the end, the "J" and "P," like the MBTI in general do not stand in contradiction of Jung or take away from the substance of his work. Millions of people may know little of the psychological theories of Jung, but they may have been significantly helped by the MBTI.

Fourth, there is a need to make the interpretations truer to the approach and insights of Jung. As they presently exist, the interpretations make a general application that can be used in making personal assessments and an organizational application that can be profitably used to help build more self-conscious teams of workers. However, nothing of what Jung talked about in terms of cross-cultural allusions, historical precedents, and references from interdisciplinary academic disciplines is even mentioned. In my experience with The Spiritual Leadership Institute of the Memorial Hermann Healthcare System in Houston, it has become clear that the expansion of leadership theory into more complex areas of growth, development, and exploration is both highly desirable and altogether useful. As the Institute presses beyond conventions of management development theory, participant response is extremely positive with many individuals regularly reporting in their evaluations of the Institute that it is the best leadership development programming that they have been exposed to. The insights of the MBTI would be advanced in a positive manner if a further nexus of references beyond conventional personality profiling responses could be provided.

Fifth, with the overwhelming emphasis that Jung made on the form of the circle as opposed to the form of the square, the MBTI constructions would be more appealing to me if they did not take the form of the sixteen-box/type squares. Some kind of concentric-circle matrix might better convey the individuation-wholeness-balance spectrums presently conveyed in line diagrams. Modern, computerized graphics could improve on the overall presentation of the profile's findings.

Here is what I would consider an enhancement of the insights of the MBTI, again considered in terms of some sort of circle diagrams rather than lines and squares. First, I would conceive results in terms of three, integrative "levels." The first level would be devoted to the basic categories of Extravert and Introvert. A fuller definition of all that Jung conveyed in "E" and "I" would be offered. More detail would be offered which conveys that "E" and "I" are complimentary and vary in their manifestations based on situational contexts. Suggestions would be made about processes and activities that might bring the "E" and "I" into a healthier balance.

A second level would then move to examine the four cognitive interactions specifically advanced by Jung; this is the Sensing, Thinking, Feeling, and Intuitive. Notice that I do not find Jung seeing these interactions as dichotomies—Sensing vs. Intuitive, Thinking vs. Feeling—and thus creating the entire dynamic of either-or, good-bad, better-worse. I see him as asserting four stages that evolve out of each other and establish increasing levels of sophistication of consciousness in his "value intensities." He clearly talks about the movement from "S" to "T" to "F" to "N." These are different dimensions of valuation that build on each other. The MBTI could successfully be structured to demonstrate the relative strengths that a person has in these four areas and, again, suggestions could be made to strengthen weaker areas or articulate the problems that occur when any of the four areas may dominate the others. (In understanding group dynamics, it certainly would be possible to attain a more self-conscious balance and perspective by establishing a balance of the Extravert and Introvert approaches, creating decision-making formats using all of the four interactions, and even establishing who might have "experience" in Perception and Judgment types of exposure to the world in general.

A third level could also be included by giving separate consideration to the "J" and "P" indicators. Without question, regardless of how much Jung may have described these tendencies directly, there are persons who exhibit valuing capacities more given over to conclusions, decisions, and closure (the "J") and other persons whose valuing capacities are more given over to exploration, openness, and divergence of possibility and potential.

In the end, I find important information on all three levels. I simply believe it is better to segment out the three levels rather than to overly integrate them. The great difference with the existing MBTI would be the middle level in which the four cognitive interactions/value intensities are seen as stages. The more arbitrary "type casting" of the present sixteen blocks of the MBTI is diminished, and the Jungian understanding of human beings as dynamic, adaptable, changing individuals capable of evolving toward wholeness, self-realization/actualization, and unique Individuation is more clearly conveyed. Consider the follow diagram:

Intuition

Feeling>^

Thinking>^

Sensing>^

CONCLUSION

In 1933, Jung wrote as essay entitled "Modern Man in Search of a Soul" that is one of the most assessable pieces that he ever created. The essay may be almost three-quarters of a century old now and the idea of "modern" transcended many times over, but it is as applicable today—perhaps even more so—as it was when Jung first composed it. Jung envisions a unique personality who is in search of Soul/Self. Most people will simply not become involved with this "search" because their lives are so caught up in fulfilling the "herd" expectations (from Nietzsche) passed down to them by their cultural circumstances. In fact, for Jung, previous generations may not have been able to so consciously pursue this process of Soul/Self discovery because the advent of psychology had not taken place for them. Psychology was at least allowing for a new medium of exploration as opposed to the old mediums of search primarily advanced and defined by traditional religion. A truly modern person would explore existence in a personal, even remote, manner in which religion is replaced by all that may be involved in a deeper level of what might be called—for want of a better word—spirituality. In some respects, spirituality may be the "soul" aspect of the "Collective Unconscious."

The modern person in search of Soul/Self will have an astoundingly high awareness/consciousness of his "present;" that is, there will be a highly developed sense of the very ideas Jung is trying to teach, ideas about the authentic Self that stands beyond persona and archetypes, approaches that understand the dynamics of persona, archetypes, Shadow, and Unconscious. This modern person "stands upon a peak, or at the very edge of the world, the abyss of the future before him." This is not a threatening or fearful stance, but rather a moment of optimum challenge in which—with full consciousness of the dynamics of life explained by Jung—the future can be created by conscious design and Self/Soul affirming choices. To stand at this "peak" is, at one and the same time, the epitome of opportunity and the epitome of accountability—the Self/Soul is at stake!

This modern person will be—to use Jung's terms—"solitary" in the sense that the edges of Self/Soul pursuit can be singular, non-establishment, and even lonely. There is also a need to be "unhistorical" in the sense that cultural precedents do not dominate in ways that drive life by "norms" from the past or "expectations" coming from the future. Past and future are not demeaned or eliminated, but real present-tense experiences are hallowed and guarded; what difference would it make to keep all the rules/norms handed down from the past and meet all the expectations/requirements of the future if the present is squandered in the process? There is little Self/Soul in "keeping up with the Jones', meshing life with the images created by modern advertising to sell their products, or giving all of life's energies to fulfilling the persona/archetype dynamics current at any transitory moment in cultural history. There is also little Self/Soul in a reactionary being different for the sake of being different. Only in the exploration and expression of authentic uniqueness and personal interaction borne of that uniqueness can authentic Self/Soul be experienced.

For most people, all of this means a radical reevaluation of the impact that work makes on people's lives and the degree of commitment that people make, and are expected to make, to work. The most powerful persona/archetypes are handed down, in our time, not by church, state, or educational environments, but by work environments. By making transformations and having conversations like the ones stimulated by this presentation in the workplace, there may be a greater chance of having an impact on human life—in the present, "modern" age—than through the traditional mechanisms of church, politics, or education. Transform the "Soul" of the workplace at the beginning of the twenty-first century, and you will transform the "Soul" of the culture.

Read Jung's essay closely and it appears that he is conceiving of three stages of human evolution that have taken place in the modern age. Perhaps "modern age" begins with the advances of the late Middle Ages when basic survival did not have to be the compelling motivation of human existence. When there is at least enough "civilization" to see survival as a kind of likely entitlement, human energy can be spent in other pursuits. His first stage becomes the medieval pursuit for metaphysical certainty, the time in which the majority of human intellectual energy was spent pursuing/proving the existence of God with the newly enthroned rationality of the emerging scientific worldview.

A second stage takes place when the pursuit of God in terms of rational metaphysics—and the power of the "Divine" probably deteriorates markedly with rationality, science, and industrial productivity—is replaced by the pursuit of material security. This pursuit still defines the basic operating parameters of modern, western life. The line between "wants" and "needs" is forever becoming more escalated. What is required to "be financially secure" is forever being redefined upwards. The amount of work and intensity of work to secure enough financial, material security and positive societal identity becomes more and more with each passing year. Thus, we arrive at the destructiveness of the modern workplace. Yet, to do away with the modern workplace or to walk away from the modern workplace are not Jung's options; in fact, the best opportunity for achieving a "third stage" will be accomplished by people "who are sound and proficient in the best sense—people who have achieved as much as others and a little more." The modern workplace must, rather, be transformed.

A third stage is, at least, assumed in the essay. This stage is neither metaphysics or economics. There is a need to ask "spiritual" questions or "moral" questions for Jung, for it is ultimately the "spiritual" and the "moral" which is lost in the obsession with cultural security defined by the things and the "Image"—the triumph of persona/archetype—of material-compulsive societies. These are the "Value" questions or axiological questions at the core of the work of Robert S. Hartman, the "value intensities"—a powerful phrase—which replace drives and needs.

It is abundantly clear that the pursuit here is not of "Underbelly Monsters" of a primordial "Unconscious" nor of an infantile sexuality that rises from some fantasy world of repressed Ids. The "spiritual/moral/value" questions arise when there is a serious, honest pursuit of the recovery of human uniqueness, wholeness, the Self, the Soul, when there are conscious strategies to make this recovery concrete. These strategies of pursuit, it must be kept in mind, will stretch conventional Western science and rationality, leaving a wide open door to explore the depths of human pursuits of meaning that are ancient, culturally diverse, and sensitive to the insights of the arts and humanities as much as the sciences. That there is a way to have economic, business success and still sustain a healthy Self/Soul uniqueness is the challenge of this modern age. That most businesses and business leaders are not consciously pursuing these spiritual/moral/value questions makes this modern age a profoundly dangerous environment in which to try to live. The profound and massive hurt, the painful dysfunctions and tragedies taking place daily as a consequence of workplace demands gone totally beyond any reason must become catalysts for change before it is too late for too many. We must name our "Shadows," especially those reflections of our best Selves taken to their destructive extremes. We must create concrete strategies that will curtail and manage the acutely negative implications of these "Shadows," or we will become lost in our own darkness. The ultimate questions are moral questions/value questions; our very "Spirit," our "Souls" are in the balance, and we—the most "modern" of human beings—have the very capacities needed to take on these changes and bring them to triumphant reality.

Finally, we must reassert the vital concepts of "The Monk" and "The Warrior." We must not see these as polar opposites incapable of meeting on both individual and group levels. Instead, we must understand that personal and corporate alignment, reconciliation, integration, wholeness, and "at-one-ment" cannot occur unless both are fully and consciously brought together. Timing is everything. As the ancient writer of the Old Testament book of Ecclesiastes insightfully conveyed: "For everything there is a season, and a time for every matter under heaven." There must be time for "The Warrior" with all of the aggressive responsiveness that is required to complete tasks, take risks, be proactive, be entrepreneurial. There must be time for "The Monk" with all of the reflective insight and retreat that is required to weigh, evaluate, value, and make decisive value judgments about how our grand rationality and exquisite emotion, our technical processes and material abundance will be used to actualize the options, capacities, and dreams of our organizational and personal lives in a difficult balance that becomes a beautiful dance.

While it has not been a major focus of this particular discussion, there must also be time, both individually and corporately, for dreaming. Dreams are for Jung a powerful source of information and stimulation, of insight and direction, which can be profitably pursued. In his powerful book, *Apology for Wonder*, Sam Keen described four of his own "types" of persons: Homo Faber, the human as worker; Homo Fabricatus, the human reduced to an extension of work, the cog in the machine; Homo Tempestivus, the human consummately sensitive to the kind of "timing" noted above; and, Homo Admirans, the human as dreamer. The first two types are representative of the negative directions implicit in modern organizational society; the second two represent the higher potential still inherent in human life. The respect and regard which people hold for dreams and a conscious pursuit of dreams do not gain sufficient attention. That the most profitable dreaming may occur when we are rationally "stuck" for Jung is of great meaning since becoming "stuck" personally, relationally, and organizationally is an increasingly prevalent reality of modern life.

Jung's conclusion to his essay in 1933 is as pregnant with meaning today as it was then—perhaps even more so:

> The living spirit grows and even outgrows its earlier forms of expression; it freely chooses the persons in whom it lives and who proclaim it. This living spirit is eternally renewed and pursues its goal in manifold and inconceivable ways throughout the history of mankind. Measured against it, the names and forms which men have given it mean little enough; they are only changing leaves and blossoms on the stem of the eternal tree.

One is left wondering what this "goal of spirit" is, for individuals, interpersonal relationships, organizations, and communities. Perhaps, this "goal of spirit" is the ultimate search of soul/self for meaning. Perhaps, the specific meanings that are found and goals that are achieved are as varied as the unique individuals, relationships, organizations, and communities that will pursue them. Perhaps, there are other meanings and goals that touch and even have the potential of transforming the "collective." "Wholeness"—in every potential dimension—is an unequivocal part of the "goal of spirit" and a reward and blessing for that goal being given priority and attention. The balance and equilibrium—grace—that is manifested when consciousness expands toward perspective and wisdom is also clearly part of the entire continuum of experiences which this "goal of spirit" enchants with and magnetically draws us toward—if we are alert, alive, awakened to the movements of this spirit.

Earlier in this book, I relayed a story that has additional meaning in the context of this discussion. This is in regard to Mr. Neal Ensminger, the editor of our local newspaper, a man of deepest wisdom and charisma, who came to our grammar school every year as an assembly speaker. In visiting the story of David again, the most powerful story for me that he told, David was looking for some sort of guidance from God that might give him a competitive advantage. He is told: "When you hear the stirring in the tops of the mulberry tree, then stir yourself. . . ." David, evidently, was sensitive to this "stirring," stirred himself, and led the Hebrews to an unlikely victory.

What I have recalled over more than four decades is the image that Neal Ensminger provided and profoundly enhanced by his capacity to create something of the "tone" of that moment in the story that he made come alive. Somehow, I believed then and have continued to believe that there are "stirrings" which are going in and out of our existence continuously. If we could be more sensitive to what all ever this is, this "stirring," something would be recognized/revealed/found that would—as Frost wrote—make all the difference in: our personal lives, our sacred relationships, our organizations, and our communities. There is even the thought that if it were possible to align my own self—"stir" myself in the Davidic image—with this greater "stirring" that life would take on a higher, deeper meaning, self-realization could be achieved, and some special dimension of wholeness/sense of uniqueness/Jung's "Individuation" could be achieved. Herein, there might even be the realization of "calling" and "destiny," of balance and equilibrium, of blessing, reward, and life as gift. The critical need is to "hear the stirring." Here is the beginning of the search for Soul and Self.

When this "search" moves in positive directions, the phenomenon of trust is extended into almost every human relationship. We can trust ourselves more, and trust those around us more. The confident flow of our movement and our movement with others becomes more of a "dance" in which we trust what we are able to do and what our partners might do.

4. TRUST AND TELLING THE TRUTH

At the central core of the entire phenomenon of trust is telling the truth. Truth is the fulcrum upon which trust usually moves. To become haphazard with truth is to put the very potential of trust at risk. Any consideration of trust must give prominence to the role of telling the truth. The very finest and most successful leaders look upon telling the truth as an essential expectation for working with them and being part of their organizations. Only the weakest of leaders—and here, the word may cease to even fit at all—play avoidance games with half-truths and want their staffs to be more expert in political correctness than honesty. When truth is not the goal, it is likely that denial and corporate gamesmanship is triumphing in an organization.

There used to be an old cliché: "Statistics do not lie." Most people today would, however, doubt this old saying in a moment. We live in a time when we are used to statistics being manipulated to serve almost anyone's immediate needs. One presidential candidate uses statistics to demonstrate the terrible condition of the economy, clearly the fault of his opponent's party; another candidate uses the same statistics to talk about "recovery" of an economy that is actually healthier than at any time in the history of the country—especially those times when his opponent's party has been in power. When we are unable to trust the objective factuality of basic number, what can we trust? Yet, we know better—probably children know better; people "cook" numbers every day to make whatever point is expedient.

It is seldom clear who is telling the truth and who is lying. The concept of "the whole truth and nothing but the truth so help me God" seems like a maxim left over from some ancient civilization that no longer exists. When we are the least bit cynical, we are sure that no such civilization really ever existed. How unusual it would be to ever have any reality or situation about which we really felt that we had the "whole truth." It is no wonder that trust is so difficult to achieve. Again, even children seem to understand that guilt or innocence in a prominent trial is more dependent on who gets the smartest lawyer who can "tilt" a jury than any supposed "facts" of a case.

In the past few years, major national media publications such as *Time Magazine* and *U.S. News and World Report* have studied the phenomenon of truth-telling. No one knows exactly what to do about the problem, but the conclusion seems clear that this is a core ethical matter that has much more than passing implications for the quality of life in the United States that has been so prized in the history of our country. What kind of models of behavior are we creating when Presidents lie about inappropriate involvement with staff or why they have led a country into war? What kind of models of behavior are we creating when Little League coaches alter birth certificates to gain unfair advantage over opponents, or church bishops lie to cover the horrible excesses of parish priests?

The following research findings will probably not surprise or startle many people. Unfortunately, that this is the case holds its own interesting implications:

- In response to the question, "Have you been less than completely honest on tax returns?" approximately 25% of the population of the United States answered, "Yes." Leading this group in terms of age was the age group 60 and above. One wonders if this group was simply being more honest about their dishonesty.

- An average of 88% of the population surveyed admitted to lying "once in a while" to family members, and 80% said they lied to bosses and work colleagues. Does this mean that people will lie to family more easily than to business associates? Most of these lies were not seen as "lies of expedience"—lies that seemed to make little difference such as "Oh yes, I think that new hair style looks good on you"—but "lies of deception"—lies that were intended to cover up larger moral lapses.

- Approximately 18% admitted to having padded expense accounts, and 33% said that calling in sick when they were not sick was typical behavior on their part. These kinds of lies were often excused and justified because of the harshness of the way company policies were enforced.

- In an NBC television network poll, 61% of high school students admitted cheating on tests; 31% of college students did the same. For most, the process was a "game," not a necessity for passing a test. Speaking of games, the NCAA, college sport's governing agency, keeps a constant vigil on cheating as it relates to student athlete grading processes. At any given time, 20% of the major university sports programs are under some sort of NCAA investigation or inquiry. Coaches are usually on the horns of a dilemma: run a "clean" program and lose games and your job, or run a "dirty" program and keep your fans satisfied with championships.

- Both 31% of college graduates and high school graduates said that lying on resumes was a normal practice. They felt it was necessary to do this in order to keep up with other people they assumed would be lying on their resumes. (By contrast, I know a company president who will check all resumes diligently. The moment a lie is found, a person is immediately fired, asked to clean out the desk, and is escorted from the company property. All of this is very public in this company, and serves notice that lying is never acceptable. This president believes that if a person lies on a resume, they will lie on other issues relating to his company. If he "looks the other way" on this issue, he will create a climate that lessens the trust needed for people to do business with each other.)

- In a *Time Magazine* poll, 75% of the surveyed population felt that the federal government was less honest today than it was a decade ago. During the presidency of George H. W. Bush, 71% of the population felt his "no more taxes" pledge was a lie when he made it; and 63% did not believe his statements about the Iran-Contra affair. For Bill Clinton, 40% felt that he had lied about his draft record, over 50% about his supposed sexual liaisons, and 68% about whether he had smoked marijuana without inhaling. By the time the Monica Lewinsky rumors began to circulate, lack of belief and trust in the president ran at nearly 100%. With George W. Bush, 80% of the population—including many who voted for him—felt that he had been "less than honest" about his past activities involving drugs and alcohol and about his "service" in the National Guards. Bob Woodward's book, *Plan of Attack*, clearly substantiates that within days of the terrible events of 9/11 that Bush was finding an opportunity to begin the creation of a war plan against Saddam Hussein without regard for being able to substantiate a connection between Iraq and the attackers on that fateful day in 1991.

In *Time Magazine's* cover issue on lying, that appeared in October of 1992, attention was paid to the administration of Jimmy Carter. As he had taken office, Carter was adamant about being an ethical, above-board leader as president. Truth-telling would be a hallmark expectation of his staff and subordinates. Carter promised: "I'll never lie to the American people." By most measures, Carter kept his word. Yet, the Carter administration has been generally characterized as one of the most ineffectual presidencies in many years. Was Jimmy Carter "too good" and "too moral" to be president? Do our rogue-like presidents who can play fast and loose with the truth make for better operatives in a "real" world?

Winston Churchill once said: "Truth is so precious that she should be attended by a bodyguard of lies." Clearly, Churchill's statement came in a time of war, and most people would probably agree that in desperate situations leaders are more than justified in lying. In a similar sense, lying might even be heroic as in the wartime incident where a Dutch family hides the valiant Anne Frank and her family. We would even *hope* that people would be inventive enough to lie to Nazis and their like if human lives are at stake. How sad it is that, in our time, a great deal of skepticism has even been directed at the Anne Frank story, with suggestions that her father—who survived the war—may have "created" a story that he knew would have high impact on a post-war generation.

Yet, when you begin to make truth relative too easily, and then depend on the "moral authority" of leaders, there can be great problems. In the early 1960s, the administration of Lyndon Johnson wanted to become more greatly involved in South Vietnam. The United States Congress would not give a declaration of war without some blatant act of provocation. Some kind of "incident"—it still is not clear exactly what—took place in the Gulf of Tonkin that allowed Johnson and his advisors to claim that the United States had been attacked. Vietnam proceeded to become a mud hole of lies and half-truths, and the trust of an entire generation of Americans from their governmental leaders suffered serious disruption.

In a similar sense, when Ronald Reagan was president, there was an attack on Libya and the terrorist leader Muammar Kaddafi. Certain concessions were demanded of Kaddafi, but no response was forthcoming. The Reagan administration let information slip out that a second, more severe, attack was coming. Kaddafi caved in and concessions were made. In truth, no second attack was even being considered seriously. In the face of these events, one of the most respected journalists in recent U.S. history, Bernard Kalb, who was serving as Reagan's chief press secretary, resigned. He could not tolerate any breech of truth with the American public. Others would argue that Reagan's "lie" was a much saner and more humane strategy than a second bomb attack with its likelihood of "collateral damage" to innocent civilians. Others then added that no real truth was deserved by Kaddafi, whose terrorist actions were much more terrible than any "mere" lying. Who owed the evil Kaddafi truth? If lying can disrupt and diminish the actions of terrorists, after the horrific attacks on New York City and the Pentagon, most people would probably see truth existing on a very secondary tier of importance. The American public sees credibility in "dis-information" campaigns if terrorists are thwarted in their activities, but they do not want this kind of campaign expertise so easily floating over into domestic issues that relate to their own lives.

Following the "logic" of the argument that "bending truth" can, at times, be easily justified, *Time Magazine* featured an article by the noted historian, Garry Wills, on Abraham Lincoln; interestingly enough, Wills entitled the article "Dishonest Abe." He demonstrated that there would have been no way for Lincoln to have attained the greatness that he attained and lead the United States through the Civil War had he not had a tremendous ability to "bend truth." Wills showed how "America's most revered politician in history dismembered truth, waffled, told racist stories, and consorted with corrupt politicians—all in his noble effort to free slaves and save the Union."

The conclusion of Wills' article is intriguing: "It is time to rescue the good name of politics, not by renouncing the dubious means that politicians have always used, but by coming up with ends that make means worth using."

In other words, if the ends are worthy enough, then the means that are used to accomplish those ends will be concluded to hold a similar worth. This is a slippery slope. Wills is trying to say that our real problem is the establishing of such worthy "ends" that bending truth to accomplish those ends would be easily justified. Since when, however, have people seen politics so enamored of "worthy ends" of such high magnitude?

The issue of truth is, therefore, raised to a new, next level: do we have enough trust in our leaders in government—or business in the aftermath of Enron, Tyco, and many others—to allow them the prerogative of lying to us without accountability? In a court of law, a witness who has a track record of lying is seldom given sufficient credibility to impact a decision; yet, in leadership, we seem to recognize lying as a mechanism that can be used with whatever frequency is needed—just as long as someone is convinced that the ultimate outcome can be seen—or explained in a way—that it holds some barest quantity of possible nobility or political efficiency. Do we simply create a pressure on leaders to say whatever seems necessary, and then construct elaborate and expensive, additional mechanisms that ensure that they do not get exposed and caught?

Looking at all of these precedents, and the many others that could easily be added from individual life experiences, there is certainly no clear formula for when truth-telling is the only legitimate and authentic course of action, or for when truth-telling can be set aside for some greater end. The only "formula" that I can see is the assurance given and taught by my mother that a lie that is told will spawn twenty other lies that attempt to cover it up. Maybe there is no way to always have the "right answers," the "truth-full answers," or the "trust-worthy" answers. Maybe the most ethical activity that any of us is capable of is the personal struggle to be authentic. At least, if truth is stretched, bent, or even consciously compromised, it should be only after the most authentic struggle that we can mount in our lives. It may be that this struggle over the truth is what ultimately gives our final decisions, whatever they might be, credibility and authenticity. Such an assumption requires the height of human responsibility, a reality that can never be easily accomplished or assumed. What we more normally see is feigned and faked struggle when, in fact, a person or leadership group knew exactly what they wanted to do and were going to do, no matter what.

For every example from the world of politics—and it may be that it is all too simple to create discussion about politicians and lying—there must be hundreds and thousands of similar circumstances that appear in daily, work environments. It might be interesting to keep some sort of log on events in which truth-telling held some sort of priority in a normal work setting and how these situations were handled. What kind of "portrait" of leadership in the United States would such a log unveil?

For example, a leading California physician recently reported dealing with a patient who wanted to stop using a number of high-powered sleeping medications. One option at the doctor's disposal was a placebo—a "sugar pill"—that would probably have the same effect as the other medications but without the actual chemical interactions. This particular physician could not, however, tell the patient that the placebo had no medicinal value. He would have to lie.

This particular doctor's equally respected partner had no such reservations. Give the placebo. The patient didn't need to know. The lie was "for his own good." It was basically a fact, this second doctor felt, that about 31% of all medications work on the basis of a placebo effect anyway. Yet, the first doctor told the truth. He could not accept the full accountability of "playing God" with the lives of patients in a way that he could so easily use the justification "for their own good." Start this process, and it will only become increasingly more easy to use. The patient could do counseling and behavior modification. To get beyond the dependency on the sleeping pills might be a long process, but it would be an honest process. Saving time, making a more "efficient" decision to simply save effort was not an option. What would you have done? Why? Better yet, what would you have wanted a doctor, in a similar situation, to do with you? Would you say okay to the sleeping medication situation, but not want the same strategy used with other conditions or events? But, then, who gets to draw the line? Raise the ante one more step: how do you put into perspective the opinion of patients who "don't want to know the truth" about their condition if that "truth" is fraught with the possibility of negative outcomes?

On the other hand, in an article that appeared in *The Washington Post* by Blain Harden on May 2, 1982, there is the report about a six-year-old boy whose left leg had to be amputated. For a while after his surgery, the boy insisted to everyone that his leg was under his bed. His doctor believed that the boy needed to think this about his leg in order to cope with his overall situation. Without any hesitation, the doctor agreed with the boy about where the leg was located. In order—in this opinion—to be a good doctor, he had to be a good liar.

Most people, either individually, as a part of a family, or in the work groups within which they vocationally are involved, must work out in conscious detail what will constitute a lie. This process becomes a specific "need to know" list of the highest order. It may be important for people to consciously go through a person, family, or group process of determining what would be considered a lie in various situations that might come up in the future of their lives. It is, at least, better to get a clear understanding of what needs to take place in a certain relationship or situation *before the fact*. In a business or professional setting, it would be possible for managers to talk with employees about standards of truth-telling in particular work environments. In this way, employees have a clear and precise idea of what is expected and demanded *and* what the implications and consequences will be when these expectations are not met. When people do not respond to these expectations, the reality of consequences need to be followed with great care, or the entire force of the seriousness related to truth-telling will be undercut.

4. Trust and Telling the Truth

In every instance, once "standards" are established in regard to certain, specific situations, these expected and required modes of behavior cannot be treated in a cavalier fashion. They must be exacting and specific, and they must be exacting for all involved, not with one set of expectations for one level of an organization and other set of expectations for another level. Common standards of moral decency must also be respected. It is, for example, difficult to ask employees not to steal or cheat on time and money issues when their supervisor gets away with pressuring someone for sexual favors. Again, these are the very issues that need to be discussed openly and precisely in organizational environments. Without clear understandings and basic, conscious principles of operation, trust and ethics are thrown open to luck and chance. In fact, a lack of clarity on operational principles will all but encourage abuse.

We all have to be able to articulate for ourselves and bring into conversation with others our own "lines" that we draw in regard to truth-telling. Such conversation can then, with others, becomes a basis for dialogue, expectation, and some range of meaningful consensus that can become a guide for group behavior. We actually need to go through this kind of process. Only then will truth-telling move toward some clarity of expression, and trust become a more well-grounded reality of our lives. Since we talk incessantly about every other issue related to life and work, why not have specific conversations devoted to the issue of truth-telling? We should never assume that truth-telling is a matter that will "take care of itself."

For me, I have decided that a lie takes place when there is malicious intent, a conscious desire to deceive in order to advance one's own agendas and purposes without consideration for others or without some considerable and evident degree or viable, redeeming value. Real lying consciously hurts and diminishes an ability to think about options. Real lying short circuits a person's (or a group's) ability to struggle with hard decisions, make well-informed and difficult choices, and have the personal credibility of knowing that easy shortcuts were not made in dealing with realities that usually have some impact on the lives of others. When lying subverts real dialogue and the right to make one's own ideas known, it becomes most dangerous. There are no checks and balances.

In addition, lying—for me—relates closely to certain kinds of situations. If someone asks me for an absolutely honest opinion about something, I will give exactly that to the best of my ability. I may ask first if they are sure what they are asking for is what they want. If this person does not, then, like or agree with what I have to say, they bear the brunt of responsibility; they should not have asked for absolute honesty. On the other hand, I take no joy in the old cliché about "the truth hurting:" my suspicion is that too many people hide behind this old maxim, and use it as an opportunity to give vent to that which is little more than mean-spiritedness.

If I am employed by an organization that has specifically informed me that honesty is part of their behavioral expectations, then I will try to be as absolutely honest as possible. If anything punitive comes as a result of my honesty, then I will intently hold them accountable for the situation they have created. Organizations cannot insist on honesty and then punish people when it occurs. Let such negative behavior happen once, and truth and trust will almost immediately go underground with the most severely negative implications.

U.S. News and World Report once created an article on lying that I agree with very much. Three types of unacceptable lies are articulated as "lies of expediency and cowardice":

- Lies that give the liar an advantage that he/she would not otherwise have, such as inflating credentials to get a job or lying about a colleague to give yourself unfair advantage in some way.
- Lies that allow the evasion of responsibility such as placing unfair blame on others or letting subordinates take full punishment in a way that avoids the complicity of superiors.
- Lies that manipulate others to the direct advantage of the liar and disadvantage of other persons involved.

A great deal of decision-making occurs on the basis of models of behavior and personal precedents we see in the lives of others. The problem of lying is that there are not enough models or precedents to absolutely fit every situation and every variable that might make up a situation. There is no way to know what next situation may present itself, and there may not be a model or precedent to fit. In addition, there may not be sufficient time to find dialogue and discussion that will refine decisions with precision. A person can have a set of basic absolutes, but in the next moment an overwhelming situation may occur that requires the absolutes to be set aside. In some situations, *not* to set aside the absolutes could be to create a situation that is less than human.

Is it possible that being an honest person or caring person—even a loving person—is not as simple as just "telling the truth?" The story of Pinocchio or the legend of George Washington and the cherry tree are wonderful fables. They make being an honest person seem fairly simple. The anecdotes surrounding the life of the fourth century BC philosopher, Diogenes of Sinope, are probably more accurate. Diogenes was said to have wandered the streets of ancient Athens with a lantern day and night looking for an honest person. It is reported that his search was never successful. Were there no honest people, only people of malicious intent and vested interest? Or, was life simply so complex and chaotic, that real honesty was all but impossible to achieve if people were to survive and live comfortably with others? Who knows. But, one reality is for sure: authentic honesty and truth-telling, the foundation of trust, is extremely difficult to achieve consistently over time and requires the greatest of diligence and effort.

So, in the end, purity of truth and a perfection of trust may forever escape us. However, the struggle toward truth and honesty can be a compelling and demanding goal for people intent on the highest authenticity. When we struggle in individual situations to be true to this goal, we give credibility to our lives and the decisions we make. When we make lying all too easy, authenticity is diminished, sometimes irrevocably.

When truth is upheld as a primary core of our existence, trust has a chance of becoming operative as a special kind of "glue" that holds our lives together. To engage each other in discussions about truth, honesty, and trust creates a kind of "refiner's fire" that tempers and sharpens the chance we have to be more and more honest, more and more truthful, and—in the end—more and more trustworthy.

5. TRUST AND THE COMMITMENT TO FAMILIES

It may seem a bit strange, in a section of articles that focus on trust, to include reflections on the institute of the family. What might be the connection to insights designed to discuss issues primarily relating to business and professional leadership concerns? In fact, to leave out comments concerning the family would be a real mistake. Issues of trust as they relate to the care and sustenance of the family must be at the core of any discussions relating to leadership in the larger arena of work. If the family is not given consideration and attention, how is it possible for a leader to be seen as a person of good judgment, appropriate prioritizing, or basic good sense? How can we trust a leader to make good decisions about business if that leader is not making adequate decisions about his/her own family dynamics? To create some sort of separation of work responsibility and family responsibility is to create a false dichotomy, an unrealistic and inappropriate approach to life that makes any decision-making process suspect. To forget about family or put family in some second-order rank of priority is to make higher levels of trust all but impossible.

Human beings create institutions that—supposedly—help those human beings to retain and improve upon their humanity. Governments provide laws, at their best, that allow for fairness and justice within the general population and that protect that general population from threatening forms of extreme behavior. Churches add a moral tone and establish religious ideals that— again, at their best—provide models for exemplary human behavior. Schools provide the education necessary—if moral teachings ever become part of the evolving conversation—for achieving options that are only possible with some degree of intellectual and rational sophistication. Yet, for human beings to become fully formed in terms of potential, these created institutions usually are not enough. Even at their very best, there is a component of reinforcement and personal solidarity that is lacking, a component that these social "connections" cannot fully provide.

Beyond these various social institutions is the institution of the family, an extended group of significant others that nurtures, emotionally reinforces, defends, protects, and teaches. In human civilization, the family has been the most important institution for conveying the deepest human experiences and human values. Where families have been strong, a context has been established for qualitative growth and enhancement. There has been the stability that becomes the foundation of self-esteem and self-confidence. Almost without exception, where there are people who experience individual emotional health and a sense of personal well-being, there has been the influence of a strong family.

If there has been one, major change in American civilization in the past two generations, it has been the role and status of the family. There is no question that there has been a literally drastic decline in the place and role of the family in American society. A lot of this change has had to do with an increase in mobility that has found family members spread out from shore to shore to shore and border to border—even beyond borders is not all that unusual. There has also been an emphasis on radical individualism that has made something of an ideal out of the rugged individual who is out "doing his/her own thing." The demands of a materialistic society that judges people in terms of the things they have, and that has spending and acquiring habits that can only be supported by more and more emphasis on work, sees to take its first and strongest toll on the family. The family is assumed to be there—always patiently waiting for attention and nurture—and when this assumption is followed, it is often with devastating and destructive implications.

Across the history of civilization on this planet, an extended family living in close geographic proximity has been the norm for communal existence. It is only in the post-World War II period in the United States that this circumstance has changed. The present structure (or, de-structure) of American society is a rank exception. There is no way to predict how this exception will play itself out. If crime statistics, divorce rates, abuse and addiction, depression and suicide are any indications, a civilization in which the extended family has been essentially lost does not exactly have a comforting future.

Some social critics insist that the problem is young people and young adults. They want to get away from home and get "on their own" as soon as possible. They see older people as obstacles that stand in the way. They are interested in older people moving on to retirement so that there will be more room for them to have upward mobility. They simply do not have time for the previous generation. There is little sense of gratitude for the efforts and even sacrifices that have provided comfortable upbringings, good educations, and starts in life not fraught with struggle.

Others argue that the problem is on the older adult end of the spectrum. In past generations, older adults were more dependent on their children, had practically no mobility after about age sixty, and thus were available to maintain a more stable home environment for children and grandchildren. Now, older adults are fully mobile in most instances well into their seventies if not beyond. They are continually involved in "retirement" activities that have them out "doing their own thing." The often-observed bumper sticker on the back of huge mobile homes and recreational vehicles—"I'm spending my grandchildren's inheritance!"—is not all that exceptional.

So, families disconnect, and in that disconnection both older and younger elements must seek surrogates—day-care workers and retirement center employees—to do the work that was once shared in the family. The "safety net" that an extended family once represented has almost ceased to exist. The pressures and stresses on young adult couples who live at great distances from any extended family, and especially the pressures on single women heads of household, is tremendous.

However, as difficult as all of these dynamics might be, the major problem confronting American families today has to do with the amazing demands placed on individuals by their work environments and assumed by individuals because of their response to their work environments. More times than not, employees—including executives—are put into a position of deep conflict: either they choose to give priority to their family at the risk of losing the opportunity for advancement and higher pay, or they choose to give priority to their work and create a situation of neglect as far as family responsibilities are concerned.

Yes, work environments may provide health and dental insurance—all kind of "benefits"—or elaborate recreational centers, but when it comes to the matter of time, very little if any initiative is provided to allow for time and attention to family matters. Many employees report that even in those situations in which family leave days, personal leave days, or reimbursable comp time is available "on the books," that employers react negatively to employees that take this time, time that in fact is fairly due them and has been earned.

Many men—and now women—come to make a compromise. They say: "I can't be with my child or mate, but by working the kind of hours that I do, I can provide them with a good income, and they can have some of the extras that they might not otherwise have." Unfortunately, if you look at interviews that have been done with numerous children and teenagers, they will convey unequivocally that they would rather have the parent's time than all of the perks that the parent's money can buy. Is anyone listening to what these children are saying?

There are major questions of ethics and trust on both sides of this issue. Employers must reflect carefully on the ethics of the demands that are being placed on employees that draw them away from their families. Are many employers thinking about this dimension at all? Are there discussions going on in work arenas concerning the family impact of work assignments and expectations? When John Doe is asked to be in Topeka on Friday and then stay over so that he can be in Santa Fe first thing Monday morning, is anyone considering that an entire weekend has been lost for John and his children, John and his mate? Do any employers keep concrete track of the amount of work being taken home, and then insist that home be for family and not an extension of the office?

On the other side, it may also be important for working individuals to consider the ethics of neglect. Is all the time away from family necessary? Is it possible to call a halt, to initiate conversations with supervisors and executives concerning the impact work demands are making on family? Are there times when the amount of demand work requires might become the object of a family discussion? Could an entire family decide that lines of limitation should be drawn? Should children, for example, have some say in the amount of time that parents are away from them in work-engaged activities?

Sometimes, these questions are simply a matter of the lifestyle that a person or family chooses. I know a talented young man who is making some decisions about what his college major will be and the vocational directions he will take. He is talented enough and intelligent enough that he could pretty much do whatever he wants to do.

Part of the time, this young man is considering medical school and becoming a physician. This profession would allow him tremendous economic freedom and options available only to those who are the most affluent in our society. The young man is very much aware of all that is out there to be had in the world, of all that he could provide for a family. He is also aware of the tremendous commitment of time involved in most medical practices, a lifestyle that gives up a great deal of personal existence in exchange for superior economic rewards. He has friends whose fathers are doctors; in most instances, their family life is all but nonexistent.

At other times, this young man talks about being a teacher and a coach. He loves to be around young people, and very much likes the variety of people and experiences that teaching would allow. He also likes the idea of a month off at Christmas and three months off every summer. He knows that this profession would allow him a tremendous amount of time with children and his mate.

But, he also knows that in our society teachers do not make money commensurate with the role they play in people's lives. This is unfair, certainly, but still a fact. On a teacher's salary, he would never be able to have many of the "finer things" in life. He might also have to end up comparing himself and what he might have to friends and acquaintances that have a lot more for themselves and can give a lot more to their families.

Decisions like this one are extremely difficult. It is almost impossible to have life both ways, to have plenty of money and still have a strong family life. It is almost impossible to gain something without having to give something else up. The place of the family is always in the balances.

The ancient Chinese sage, Confucius, embraced very little of what we would recognize today as religion. He was not involved with institutional religious practices, did not write holy books, and did not spend his time in prayer and meditation. He felt that the deep, emotional commitments that people often give to gods or religious institutions should be given to the family. The family should have the highest priority of human existence. He taught as his highest virtue, *Hsiao*, family loyalty.

For Confucius, the family was the key element in human existence. Where families were strong, individuals within those families were people of self-confidence, self-worth, integrity, and the strength of courage. Where families were weak, people tended to be disoriented, alienated, and dysfunctional. This principle of *Hsiao* was especially extended to older people who were seen as being repositories of wisdom—particularly that wisdom gained only from experience. Civilizations that did not care for old people and hold them in places of esteem were vulnerable to any manner of threats and inadequacies. Based on what is taking place in the American family today, Confucius would be frightened about America's future.

Business and work were important to the wise old teacher, but business and work always had to be in a place of at least second priority. If work became the highest priority, it typically did so at the loss of the most important human concerns. To put business first required pushing the human into the background. When this occurred, the world of business and work could—and likely would—

become too easily corrupted and the possibility of moral lapses less checked. It is almost as if, in his teachings, that a high emphasis on family values and family priority allowed for a humanizing element to remain present in the world of work. (Stop for a moment. Please go back and contemplate these last three sentences. Contemplate the key idea here that a strong family existence is a prime catalyst for humanizing activities in the world as a whole.)

And, a careful distinction must be made between verbal priorities and actual priorities. In other words, it is not unusual in the modern work arena to find people who will say that their family is of highest priority, perhaps second only to God. However, simply verbalizing these priorities does not make them *actual* priorities. Actual priority is judged in terms of what we do, not what we say. Put a clock on time that is given to family and mate, especially time when energy is still strong, and immediately you will know what the actual priorities are.

In an attempt to become politically correct, many people have turned the concept of "family values" into just another social cliché or a platform from which to shout their own personal biases. The real issue is not to define or trumpet "family values," but rather to place the family as the high point of priority. This high point of priority would be right up there on the same level of significance as the individual self, perhaps even more so. It certainly would be on a higher level of significance than work.

Emphasis placed on family experience is of *intrinsic value*. Realities of intrinsic value exude the height of the interpersonal, exist beyond words of explanation, and plumb the depths of the relational potential of human existence. On the other hand, while work experiences can and should have an intrinsic potential, they are more prominently of *extrinsic value*, manifesting measurable and rationally discernible process, procedure, and practices. To place work before family is to create a situation of dis-value, a situation in which an intrinsic value is reduced to or replaced by an extrinsic value. Such reductions undercut the core "soul" of human existence.

When issues of material and financial gain come to the forefront in work-related issues, the extrinsic can become even more pronounced. Every reality is measured first and foremost in economic terms. This is not to say that there is not some intrinsic element in being paid money and having money to spend to promote intrinsic experiences. However, in many instances, even when the money is used to "make a better life" for the family, the time spent making that money is usually in a more extrinsic than intrinsic environment. The intrinsic is usually lessened when more time is given to the extrinsic. This may not be too much of a price to pay and may be carefully controlled. It can also very easily get out of control, and too much of the intrinsic can be compromised while achievements in the extrinsic are taking place. An extremely careful balance of intrinsic and extrinsic must be maintained, or a great deal of personal and family unhappiness can be the result.

The real question is what degree of ethical responsibility employers have to provide opportunity for positive, intrinsic, fulfilling family experiences. Should employers be concerned about—and be actively involved in—helping their employees have good family lives? Are there agendas employers can pursue that would heighten the possibility of intrinsic family existence? A company picnic every Fourth of July weekend or a company Christmas party only plays lip service to the needs that are really there in most families. At the very minimum, the following options should be examined and appropriate action established if *ethics* is to prevail:

- A concrete policy statement concerning the priority that the employer places on the family. A specific statement of behavioral expectations concerning family prioritization. Concrete examples of how these expectations can be carried out.
- Discussions among leadership, from executives to line supervisors, concerning the kinds of examples that they need to establish as a leadership group for the general employees to observe as it applies to the priority they place on family.
- In-service training for all employees at least twice a year that discusses family value issues.
- The availability of referral to family counselors, and some degree of financial support for these services.
- "Family leave" given for designated family situations. This leave should have no bearing on other types of leave or vacation time. This leave should not be solely for death. It should as easily be for a special ball game or special award recognition, even to help with a school field trip. Of decisive importance: this time should never be given begrudgingly.
- Specific in-service training for line supervisors that will better equip them to be sensitive to and deal with personal and family-related issues.

5. *Trust and the Commitment to Families*

These options may seem to be ambitious. In fact, they may not be ambitious enough if an organization really wants to get beyond the lip service stage of paying tribute to the "family value" section on its vision/mission statement, a section that is almost always present in most organizational documents. In the end, these options will probably not be all that expensive to install. In fact, numerous studies have indicated that such privileges are seldom abused, create whole new patterns of respect and morale among employees, and probably contribute to higher loyalty and productivity. This type of emphasis, beyond building good will, is likely to pay for itself many times over.

If the kind of options suggested above are not embraced, employers stand a strong chance of creating situations of conflict—internal, personal conflict among their employees that will generate the most negative of reactions. I am not describing workplace anarchy, strikes, or job actions here; rather, I am giving emphasis to those most negative feelings that occur at the core of our being when someone puts us in conflict with ourselves about issues of deep importance. An employee may want to do a super job, advance in a chosen profession, and make more money. That same employee may also want very much to be a good parent and a good mate. If these desires rise in conflict with each other, an employee's work efficiency will probably drop and, even more importantly, a highly negative attitude will develop toward that person or company that is responsible for placing the person in the situation of conflict. At one and the same time, families can be hurt by neglect, and companies can be disdained as the culprit in the process—no one wins!

Family issues must be addressed if ethics plays any part in an organization's existence. These issues are of utmost importance to the life of our civilization. And, civilization is not a faceless abstraction. On the level of real people with real faces and real names, when family issues are not addressed, there is a disruption of trust on the most fundamental levels, and employers and the organizations they represent are seen as not being trustworthy and ethical. When this deep type of trust and ethics is abridged, meaningful and productive work will suffer. The sense of "community" that is the ultimate power of the work environment will be squandered and lost.

At the end of the day, the question of who you are able to trust will always be a compelling question. Transposed to the workplace, whether you can trust the people you are working for and who are in primary places of decisions will always be critical. To a real extent, those organizations and leaders of organizations who place authentic emphasis on families and make decisions that enhance family existence are people to be trusted. When trust is established around the priority given to families, that trust can support the deepest levels of loyalty and commitment to an organization and personal loyalty to those who stand in leadership positions.

INTERLUDE III

TRANSFORMATIONAL LEADERSHIP— CONTINUED

TRANSFORMATIONAL LEADERSHIP 76

Orchestrates the consciousness of a group

The transformational leader orchestrates the consciousness of the group. He knows the management team should span the full spectrum of density of consciousness. He needs very right brain people, very left brain people and everyone in between.

Destiny is consciousness. With an orchestrated group the widest possible resonance with the cosmos is possible. Numerous opportunities that would be lost with a narrow spectrum of group consciousness are picked up by a wide spectrum group.

Ideally the diversity of the team mirrors the diversity of the universe. The organization is a microcosm that reflects the macrocosm. Universal energies flow through various team members, who conduct the energy, step it down, and make it available to all members of the group.

In our new century healthcare organizations take a more subtle form. Increasing focus is upon the inner nature of patients and caregivers. The "collective energy field" (aura) generated by caregivers in the organization gives the organization a distinct personality and competency. Some hospitals will routinely experience "miracle cures" with their patients and others hospitals will not.

Advanced psychotronic technologies of the future can only be operated by individuals with the requisite type of consciousness. Consciousness and hardware interface. Unlike today's machines which anyone can plug into a wall socket and operate, tomorrow's technologies must be plugged into the right type of consciousness in order to produce the desired outcomes. A good low-tech example of machine/consciousness relationships is dowsing. Anyone can hold a dowsing rod. Only a dowser can operate the rod to locate water or minerals. In psychotronics the consciousness of the person interacts with electronic or photonic devices to create outcomes beyond the capability of the hardware itself.

Interlude III

Another example of recruiting people by consciousness will be the formation of a group of "intuitives" in the hospital who employ their consciousness skills to solve problems defying rational analysis. Our new century will be characterized by rapid, unexpected and often catastrophic changes. Rational problem solving skills are of little use in this type of environment. "Sensing" becomes one of the most valuable management skills. Many children now being born into our society possess this sensing skill. We will re-design our elementary and secondary schools to cultivate the natural talents of these exceptional children. They are arriving on the world scene just in time.

Of course, healing is another example of a consciousness skill. In tomorrow's healthcare organizations, healers will work side-by-side with technical people to achieve integrated patient care interventions.

Remember the two recruiting questions for any job applicant in the future: (1) Who are you (consciousness)? And (2) What do you do (skills)?

Shakes up personal constructs

The transformational leader knows that many people become victimized by their own stale constructs (thought forms). Any beliefs held unchanged for a long period of time lose their benefit and vitality. The vitalizing energy departs from the thought forms and leaves behind empty containers. Higher level energies cannot enter and activate the dead forms. In fact, the forms resist any new energy configurations. As a result, the person is surrounded by a sheath insulating him from evolutionary changes in his environment. The dead forms surround him creating an alternate reality which is like a continuous tape replaying past scenes. You often witness the dance of dead forms in older people who are returning to the past and reliving old events in a vain effort to extract any meaning that may still remain in them.

Mental substance is plastic and assumes the form given to it by the occupying energy. It is naturally resilient and reforms itself as the individual enters new life experiences and calls upon higher order energies. However, if a form is occupied for too long a time by the same energies, like a rubber band, it loses its elasticity and becomes rigid. At that point, the person stops growing and simply relives the past.

The higher self (Spirit) knows this situation and arranges for a crisis to disrupt the old thought forms. The life crisis shakes up the person and destroys old life patterns. It is a crisis of reorientation and creates chaos in the person's life. Chaos in turn breaks up the old forms and permits them to be reabsorbed into the stream of mental substance where they dissolve and become available to humankind for the construction of new thought forms.

The transformational leader understands the need for renewal and shakes up the constructs of his followers. He does this in a kind and loving, but firm manner. However, he does not engage only in deconstruction, he also helps his followers reconstruct their lives and build new thought forms appropriate to their continued journey on the path.

Of course, there must be agreement at some level on the part of the follower for this deconstruction to take place. If the follower is not ready, he simple feels a repulsion for the leader and avoids any personal contact that might threaten his old familiar world view.

Transformation cannot take place without shaking up old personal constructs. Transform means to change the form—in this case, the old thought forms. Often the transformational experience provided by the leader takes the form of a rapid expansion of existing thought forms. Sometimes, however, expansion will not do the job and destruction of the old thought forms is necessary. In either event, fear is evoked in the follower. He must let go of old fears in order to embrace new possibilities. He must trust the transformational process. He must enter the void (dark night of the soul) in order to emerge as a new creation.

Manifests creative dissatisfaction

The transformational leader exists in a state of creative dissatisfaction. She senses the tension between the actual and the ideal. It is this tension that empowers her transformational urges and gestates her leadership.

If you are happy where you are, you will remain there until you become restive and desire to move on. If you accept the actual as the possible, no forward motion is possible. You have overadapted to what is, and have no vision of what could just as well be.

This means the transformational leader perceives the archetype inherent in all things vs. the manifested stage of development. She hears potential crying out for birth into materiality. She can therefore act as a midwife. She senses the distance between latent and the manifest and closes the gap through an act of radical leadership.

If you can access potential, you always long to materialize it. You therefore exist in a state of tension. Tension is necessary for creation. Creation is an outworking of the inner workings of the Creator. The tension between the potential and the manifest motivates the Creator to continue the process of creation throughout all eternity. As co-creators we partake of this same nature and exist in the same state of tension as the Creator.

Creative dissatisfaction is not frustration. Frustration is a blocked emotion. Creative dissatisfaction is an opening into pure possibility. The transformational leader knows it is only a matter of time and opportunity until all the potentials of creation are realized. The leader volunteers her person as a channel for this realization.

Transformational leadership is joy. The leader's previous failures create a deep wisdom and a wide tolerance. She provides loving nurturance to all who struggle as she remembers her past struggles and the loving attention of her previous teachers.

Creative dissatisfaction leads to patience, understanding, and a deep respect for timing. A certain ripeness must exist before any thing can transform itself into its next higher stage. Ripeness is a result of struggle and experience for all sentient life forms. It cannot be hurried.

A good leader maintains a depth of being that holds a place for the follower's struggles. She knows what it is to be lost. She has been there. She serves as a beacon for those who are lost in their upward journey. She knows there is a destination for every seeker. She beckons but never pushes. She accepts what is, but always encourages what can be. She lives in the wonderful tension of creation.

Initiates organizational renewal

The transformational leader is committed to renewal, reformation, regeneration, and transformation. She always perceives the distance between the ideal and actual and seeks to close the gap.

Renewal depends upon touching back to the taproot and drawing from the tradition as well as touching into the future and drawing upon images of possibility. We are strengthened by remembering what we have been and by imaging what we can be.

Renewal is an antidote to obsolescence. Everything runs a given course and then begins to deteriorate. Unless renewal takes place, death is inevitable. Renewal extends possible life by adapting to changing environmental conditions through altered internal structure or by changing the environment itself in order to better fit the existing internal structure. In slow environmental change, either strategy will work. In catastrophic change, both strategies are problematical. Too much internal change may break the integrity of the organization. Also, it may not be possible to impact a violently changing environment. In general, however, renewal is both possible and desirable.

Because the universe is in a constant state of change, to avoid obsolescence, organizations must modify themselves as quickly as the environment changes. To exert leadership, they must change themselves more quickly than the environment shifts. Visioning assists in this effort by helping organizations think in future time. Future images stimulate renewal. Future images feedback and alter the present.

We must think in terms of personal, organizational, and community renewal. They are interdependent. Renewal at any level stimulates renewal at all levels. The transformational leader understands this and engages in renewal programs at all levels.

Renewal makes everything new again. It is a rebirth. However, it is not a return to the condition at birth. It takes place on the next higher turn of the spiral of transformation.

In our sector of the universe, there is birth, death, and transformation. Rebirth avoids death at least temporarily, but it is always in the service of transformation. Death is usually necessary to break the bonds of habit and rigidity (in persons and organizations). If rebirth takes place, these bonds are broken within and do not require the releasing power of death. However, rebirth itself is a type of internal death and reorganization that may be as profound as external death. You see this death to the old and rebirth to the new in a religious conversion experience.

Creates a tension between the present and the future

The transformational leader must be firmly seated in the present at the same time his vision is anchored in the future. The tension between the two time periods generates a unique energy that propels him forward.

Transformation requires a very firm grip on reality. The leader must be concrete and practical. At the same time, transformation requires high abstraction and the ability to enter visionary states. These two mental states seem to be opposites but when viewed from the next higher order of abstraction it is apparent they are two sides of the same coin and give birth to a transitional form that exists between the two, thereby allowing one reality to meld or transform into the other.

Because the transformational leader has learned not to become over-identified with any mental state, he can easily move among them all. Like putting on and off clothes, he puts on and off, the present and the future.

Most people identify Self with the mental state they occupy at the moment. The transformational leader knows the difference between Self and the mental state he is employing. He is not identified with any of his mental states and therefore can change any of them by simply changing his focus of attention.

Managers who are too locked into present difficulties cannot perceive future possibilities. They think the world has to be the way it currently appears. The transformational leader recognizes the current cast of reality but also perceives the availability of parallel realities in present time and alternative realities in future time. A good example of this multidimensional mind is Tesla, who anchored a thread of his consciousness in current reality, but kept most of his consciousness in future reality. He outlined devices he saw in the future that scientists have still not managed to build in the present. He also had such a concrete grasp of current reality that he would do the experiments in his head, put the results in a sealed envelope, and then check the results with his lab assistants when they performed the actual experiments at a later time.

The ability to think in future time is critical for today's healthcare managers. As the present breaks down, the future is pregnant with possibility. The trick is to manage the breakdown without breaking down and to lead the organization into an abundant future reality.

Interlude III

Look always for the tension between what is and what could be and ride the energy current into the future.

Constantly scans the environment

The transformational leader is alert to alterations in her environment. Frequent scanning is necessary to identify new forms, first detected through visioning, now manifesting in the material dimension.

As an intuitive, the transformational leader accesses the thought stream and senses the changing currents. She observes thought forms descending from spiritual, mental and emotional planes. These forms flow into receptive channels (people and organizations) for manifestation. Just where they will "pop up" is often a surprise even for the transformational leader.

Scanning provides an early warning system indicating when the time of manifestation is near. A good example are the number of healing healthcare images now circulating in the planetary thought stream. With this type of image pressure, rapid physical manifestation is assured. However, the birthplace of the new thought forms, and the unique shape they will take can only be known through environmental scanning.

Since the transformational leader is in "the creation business," she is always interested in the impact of materiality on spiritual, mental, and emotional substance. High density matter in the third dimension (3D) always distorts subtle thought forms and compromises them in order to fit the circumstances of their emergence in time, space and condition (major vectors of 3D). A sculptor suffers this same frustration as she takes the picture in her head and tries to make it leap forth from the stone.

Scanning can take many forms. Networking and use of the Internet represent two of the best. Breakthroughs occur in very small circles. The reason is simple. Circles amplify energy and create a strong attraction for ungrounded thought forms circulating in the thought stream. One of the challenges facing materialistic science is creating "conditions suitable for manifestation" if they wish to replicate breakthroughs achieved by pioneers working in small groups. A healer working in a patient care setting can demonstrate successful outcomes not repeatable in a controlled laboratory environment. A few people working in an Internet group can create a "small circle effect" and pull down stuff from the noosphere (thought stream) that none of those participating in the circle could produce by themselves.

Once a scan reveals the birth of a new form, it is important for pioneer workers to "visit" the site and "lock in" the new energies. Like a newborn infant, the emerging thought form requires careful nurturance until it achieves the status of independent entity and is able to grow on its own.

Is a member of a small circle

The transformational leader is often a member of one or more small circles devoted to personal, professional, organizational, community, or planetary transformation. These small circles are responsible for many of the innovations in healthcare taking place in our country.

Small circles develop a "vortex effect" where very intense energies are generated and circulate throughout the group. This "cones of power" attracts energies from higher dimensions, accelerates evolution of individual members, and often produces magical outcomes (metanoia).

The small circle has long been recognized as a powerful type of spiritual and social organization, whether it takes the form of a prayer circle or a medicine wheel.

In a small circle it is possible to orchestrate the consciousness of the membership. Members are carefully chosen for their talents and compatibility with one another. Usually a trial period precedes acceptance by the group. Often a single veto is sufficient to exclude a potential member. Small circles will not function unless there is a high degree of harmony among everyone present.

When the circle forms, some type of warm-up exercise is used for attunement. Members feel the energy as it begins to circulate. If anyone is blocking the energy, it will become immediately apparent to all members of the group. The circle tries to maintain a stable membership and a consistent vibratory tone. If a member is "off key" for one reason or another, the member will volunteer or be asked to step outside the circle rather than disrupt its finely tuned operation.

Most healthcare administrators have never been members of transformational groups. Task forces, committees, governing boards, and medical staffs are usually collections of individuals rather than groups. It takes time and practice to achieve "a unity of the diversity."

Most management groups concentrate on defined work tasks rather than release of their inherent transformative potential. For this reason group work in our healthcare organizations is seldom inspirational or metanoic. As a simple rule of thumb, if you come out of a management group meeting with no more then you took in, the group output is not transformational.

Interlude III

Most small circles consist of face-to-face contact. However, it is sometimes possible to achieve small circle effects in an online group on an interactive website. Small circles may also be formed through telepathic linkages.

TRANSFORMATIONAL LEADERSHIP 83

Encourages the organization to take necessary risks

The transformational leader knows that personal, organizational, professional, community, or planetary transformation is not without risk. Nothing ventured, nothing gained. The process of unfoldment takes us down pathways and sometimes into byways. We may wander around in byways for months or years until we find our way onto the pathway once again. Nothing is ever lost in our many side explorations. We learn from each encounter and come away richer for the experience gained. Often a short term loss becomes a long term gain. We may fail to recognize a blessing until many years after we have participated in the event. As we come closer to the Source, we bless our past and realize the role it played on our present and the preparation it gave us for our future.

Consciousness leads us into experiences, gives meaning to our experiences, and is a running total of our experiences. All consciousness is gained in spaces. A design for space is a design for consciousness. We master the challenges of our spaces and in this way gain mastery as individual units of consciousness. We are tested all along the way. What appears as a risk is often an initiation. If we pass the initiation, we continue forward on the path. If we fail the initiation, we turn into a byway, where we gather our resources and prepare ourselves again for the next attempt.

Eventually we outgrow what a space (environment) can teach. We are then ready for a new space. The transition between spaces means letting go of the old in order to embrace the new. This is always a risk. What if the new is not as good? What if I cannot make it? What if I lose the old security and meanings? There are no assurances as you move forward on the path other than the realization that you are part of All That Is. What you may lose in one part of your Self, you will gain in another part of your Self.

The same is true of your organization. The price of potentiation is continuous unfoldment. Every organization at the archetypal level consists of infinite potentials manifesting in parallel realities. Some of these potentials will manifest in our 3D reality if your organization is willing to continually risk itself in perpetual renewal. By attempting to hold on to your secure past or present, you lose them. By giving them away, you realize a higher form of their expression in your future.

Interlude III

As managers in a high change world, we must use our visions as the bridge between present and future. The greater the clarity of our vision, the less the risk we face in our passage.

To hold on to the old is to die. To grasp the new is to be continually renewed. The dragon that must be slain is the Fear of Change. It is a fire-breathing monster that guards the door of the Cave of Infinite Possibilities. When most people face the dragon they turn sadly away and return to the Village of Security, locked in times past. The transformational leader wielding the sword of discernment defeats the dragon and continues on his/her journey.

Is a skillful communicator

The universe is information. The story of our evolving universe is written everywhere for those who have eyes to see. Everything in the Cosmos radiates its own nature. Whatever we can come into relationship with, we can know. The size of our circle is our only limitation. If we can bring a thing within our circle (frequencies), we can absorb its nature into our own nature (we ingest its frequencies and are therefore altered to a degree by them).

The transformational leader is a natural communicator. He accesses information, packages it into knowledge, and disseminates it to those ready to hear. The leader knows that knowledge expands awareness. He knows which knowledge the learner is prepared to assimilate, and how to bring the knowledge within the codes of intellect of his hearer. Because the transformational leader is a multidimensional Being, he is a multidimensional communicator. The same message is coded on all energy bands that are sourced by the leader. The listener can "pick up" the message on any of those bands within the range of his attunement.

At the highest level of communication, the transformational leader transmits images direct from his mind to the mind of the listener. These images are then translated into words by the listener, unless the listener has direct access to the images (is telepathic). Image communication has greater accuracy than any other form of communication and has the advantage of allowing people with different languages to employ a metalanguage.

If a transformational leader is speaking, and a recording is being made, some people will remember hearing things they later cannot find on the tape recording. Their brain produced the words in response to the leader's images and intentions. This is the true ability to "speak and hear in tongues."

Teaching is communication. The transformational leader is a powerful teacher, who teaches by precept, word and example. He is teaching his essence, not something he read in a book. The words of a true teacher "ring true." The mental velocity of the student is accelerated as his consciousness is impacted by the patterned energies flowing from the teacher. This high impact teaching "seeds" the student's consciousness for later maturity of the ideas when the student is ripe for harvest. The student often feels the energy, but cannot yet process the ideas. The ideas will rest in the student's consciousness until the wake-up call comes from his Higher Self.

Interlude III

A healthcare organization is limited by its consciousness. Its consciousness is limited by its knowledge. The transformational leader communicates essential knowledge needed to expand organizational awareness. Organizations of the future are primarily organizations of the mind. They are virtual organizations.

Has a high tolerance for stress

The transformational leader has a high tolerance for stress. She regularly utilizes stress reduction techniques such as relaxation, visualization, and meditation. She also participates in the redesign of the workplace to remove unnecessary stressors.

Poorly designed organizations react to change with stress. Well designed organizations welcome change and feed on the excitement of infinite possibility. What manifests as stress in a poorly designed organization, manifests as creative potential in a well designed organization.

It is not the stimulus as much as the stimulus context that creates negative stress. With the right orientation, negative stressors become positive stimuli and promote organizational unfoldment and growth of employee consciousness.

As the transformational leader knows, the practice of loving detachment also minimizes her stress. The transformational leader is "centered" and does not lose her sense of perspective. She avoids being "pulled into" job crises or entanglements and the many apparent threats of the external environment. She operates in an eternal frame of reference. She sees life events as "passing mirages" on the screen. She knows that everything is happening in its own time and is following the universal laws of change. Nothing in her world is fixed. Therefore she does not over-identify with the affairs of the moment or the threats of the future. She is committed to do her best for others wherever she is. She leaves the results up to the universe. She works from principle, not from panic. She is grateful for the gift of manifestation in the third dimension and lives to the best of her ability in good or bad circumstances. She has learned that her "worries" seldom happen. Most of the bad things that do come her way, come as total surprises. Therefore, she accepts "what is" and always tries to transform it into "what it can become."

The transformational leader appreciates the value of creative tension. She understands the law of polarity. For a positive to exist, there must also exist a negative. To live in this world, she must partake of both poles of manifestation. With the right orientation to life, even negatives become positives in the experience of the transformational leader. She has mastered the skill of transmutation and amplification of psychic energies. She transmutes the negatives into positives and amplifies the positives into even greater positives.

Interlude III

All the energies of the universe flow through the human being. Through right relationships, the transformational leader can utilize these energies for desired manifestation. She can balance imbalanced energies and create energy where very little exists.

The right use of energy makes anyone a leader. It is one of the hardest skills to master. Many people are dominated by the energies that flow through them rather than master those energies for creative use.

Honors the tension between Spirit and form

The transformational leader respects the tension between Spirit and form and indeed utilizes this tension to generate high levels of creativity. Spirit is always trying to become form and form is always trying to become Spirit. Transformation is the link between the two states. The transformational leader invokes Spirit after creating expanded organizational forms to contain it. Existing Spirit-filled organizational forms are then further expanded and thereby invoke even higher levels of Spirit. The transformational leader must thus be able to both invoke Spirit and build forms to contain it.

A healthcare organization always maintains some kind of balance between Spirit and form. It may at one extreme become nearly pure Spirit and discharge energy much like a volcano with no useful work done, or it may become rigid and form-bound and lose Spirit. Ideally it rests somewhere between the two extremes.

As the organization evolves, it can attract and hold higher levels of Spirit. Since higher levels of Spirit are less dense, the new forms must be more ephemeral. Employees have adapted to gross levels of form and have to be encouraged to stretch their consciousness to contain more subtle forms. Ultimately the leader is limited by the extent of organizational consciousness expansion. Therefore, the leader must be an organizational teacher and mentor as well as a leader.

As the planet completes its own evolutionary destiny, it depends upon the highest embodiment of Spirit on the planet, which is humanity. Humanity and the planet must work together to enter the next octave of development. When the planet evokes higher levels of Spirit, planetary matter is also transformed into a more subtle state. It may undergo this alchemical transformation of matter in a peaceful or very turbulent manner. If humankind refuses to open to the new spiritual potentials, the planet reacts with all types of natural disasters. It will achieve its new alignment with or without its current huge human population.

The present emphasis on preserving the natural environment is an outworking of this new Spirit/matter alignment. It will result in a "rebirthing of the planet." We are moving toward designer planet status. We will either become guardians of the planet or we will lose it.

Interlude III

Since transformation is inherently a spiritual process, the transformational leader is a spiritual person. In healthcare we are witnessing the birth of spiritual economics and community well-being.

Now is the time for bold initiatives. We have a narrow window of creative possibility. If we act now, we can avoid the more severe economic and social disruptions scheduled to arrive on the horizon.

Has begun the search for the whole

Transformation requires sensing an implicit whole or greater pattern of which you are a part. A finite series of partial expressions or forms moves toward an infinite archetype. Your current life expression is one of these limited finite forms. You are on an infinite journey into greater connection and wholeness.

Intuitive perception reveals the archetypes themselves as part of an integrated eternal pattern in the mind of God. Creation is a reflection of Deity in high density form. Since Deity is integrated, creation is also one fabric.

For individuality to develop, separation of consciousness units was a prime necessity. There can be no sense of self without a sense of the other, or not self. The apparent separation of selves is a short-term strategy of the Divine to develop many voices that in the end will discover their essential oneness and unite in a single anthem of creation.

Until this underlying unity is discovered, each separate unit follows the path of egotism. The desire to ascend and acquire, although an illusion, is a necessary growth stage on the path of individuation. The ego trap, although a necessary stage in development, at a later point on the path becomes a barrier to transformation since it cuts the unit off from its underlying Source or Origin.

The transformational leader has escaped the trap of the ego. He senses his connection to all that is. With this desire to become aware of his origin and destiny, he moves into the next stage of personal transformation. This stage focuses upon his dependence upon and contribution to the Whole. Through the long voyage into eternity, individuality is never lost. You will never blend into the Whole. You are a reflection of an individualized aspect of Divinity (Spirit) and you will always remain so. However, evolution of consciousness gives you a simultaneous awareness of your connection to the Whole as well as your individualized role and function within the Whole.

Just as individuals evolve, so do societies. The transformational leader is a globalist and perceives the unique role of his country as well as its participation in the global community. As a healthcare administrator, the transformational leader also understands the contribution of his particular hospital and its participation in the local community and planning region.

Only by understanding mutual interdependence can each part fully individualize and yet contribute to the whole. Transformation must be by part and also by whole. In an integrated healthcare delivery system this is a design goal. It is a win-win situation. There are no losers. What damages one part, eventually damages the whole. What benefits the whole benefits each part. The whole is held back by its most tardy part. For that reason, transformation is always for both the parts and the sum of the parts.

Has undergone personal transformation

You don't learn transformational leadership as you might learn any other subject in a business school. You BECOME a transformational leader. Of course, with the appropriate effort and experience you can improve upon any natural leadership skills. However, transformational leaders at some point in their evolution have undergone personal transformative experiences. They then build upon these initiations.

Usually "a mentor puts the cloak of transformation upon your shoulders" for the first time. His/her energy courses through your Being, your consciousness is accelerated and you experience a breakthrough in Being. The mentor may be human or non-human, living in this dimension or residing in an angelic dimension. The mentor gives you a toehold. The climb is always your climb.

Everyone is born to be transformed (subject to their free will choice). However, a certain spiritual maturity is necessary before it can occur. Until this point of maturity is reached, the process of transformation will not reach completion. An immature soul has insufficient vibrational intensity to hold the experience.

Often a crisis (illness, etc.) precedes transformation. This is why it is so important for healthcare professionals to be healers. Disease is the doorway of transformation for many patients. Disease may burn-off past sins, interrupt the course of a descending life, or force necessary accountability. A spiritual diagnosis will reveal any of these dynamics. Until the caregiver has an integrated physical, emotional, mental and spiritual diagnosis for the patient, he/she is working in the dark. Any physical problem will also be reflected in the other energy bands and may indeed be generated in one or more of them. In this case, the body is simply an indicator and physical intervention alone will not be successful.

It is impossible to divorce transformation from health. Transformation is high-level wellness. As we enter higher energy states the atomic structure of the body is modified. It takes upon itself "lighter substance" which is immune to many of the forms of disease attracted to "denser substance." For example, the dream body does not experience any physical diseases but may be afflicted by astral maladies. As higher levels of perfection of form are achieved, the disease states become more subtle, as do their interventions. A defect in the spiritual body requires a very different level of intervention than a disease in the physical body.

Walks a guided path

The transformational leader is in tune with the universe. He understands his relationship to All That Is and has agreed to play his part in the unfoldment of the earth's destiny. For this reason, he walks a guided path.

To walk a guided path requires constant communication with the indwelling Spirit. It means never forgetting who you are and what you are here to do. It requires a kind of constant meditation and openness to the promptings of the inner voice of conscience and consciousness.

The transformational leader mediates Spirit and matter. He is a translator, and interpreter of the vision. For that reason, he must also have both feet on the ground and be in tune with the realities of his third dimensional environment.

A guided path is only a spiritual indicator. It never removes free choice and the need for the leader's carefully acquired discernment. To be true to the vision is a constant challenge. The little ego often occludes the vision and the leader may for a time may feel disconnected from his Source.

A guided path is always a path of reform, for it leads upward and onward and escapes the limitations of present circumstances. For that reason the transformational leader is always a reformer. He must understand the spiritual forces that maintain form and the spiritual forces needed to change form. His main tool is his access to an inner spirituality.

The spiritual dimension is only now coming into view over the horizon. We have reached the zenith of materiality and are now on the return course of spirituality. Our concern with reaching out to the community and adopting communitarian values provides ample evidence of a change of heart. Our path of healthcare in America has taken a decided turn for the better. We are not there yet, but we are in motion.

The path is always a reflection of the inner consciousness of the leader and his vow of service. The inner light of the Spirit shines upon it and it takes the leader into his chosen dimension of service.

We walk the path of our own making. At first we walk unconsciously, for at the highest levels, our soul often makes agreements with the indwelling Spirit that are unknown to our conscious ego. We feel a sense of "destiny," but do not at this point see clearly. We are led and things seem to happen. We walk in faith. Later we will walk in knowledge. In both cases, we are walking a guided path, but at different levels of spiritual maturity.

Views his vision as a special calling

The transformational leader enjoys a special sense of calling. His life is not accidental. Events do not happen in a random way. He walks a guided path. This sense of destiny is often a gradual unfoldment in his life. At first he only knows he is different in some way from other people. Later he understands this difference as a precondition for the type of leader he will become.

The "call" may come early or late in life. The call is always an invitation from the universe. The person receiving the call must "will" to accept it. He can pass the call by if he wishes. Another pattern is seen in the person who "volunteers" to be of service to the universe and after a time of testing is graced by a descent of the call. As he responds to this descending call, the qualities of transformation begin to appear in his life and in his leadership.

With sufficient determination, anyone can become a transformational leader. Some are born with the call, some receive the call later in life, and others volunteer their services and are graced with a call. The end result is the same. Everyone has the opportunity to participate. No one is left out. Which type of transformational leader are you?

Receiving the call and faithfully following it are two different things. To become a living incarnation of transformation requires a special lifestyle that puts spiritual things first and avoids the pitfalls of materialism. Transformational leaders are likely to be promoted and rewarded by the organizations in which they labor. It is easy for them to get caught up in the "success game" and forget their special reason for being in the world.

At this point the living process of transformation stops in their lives and they unfold no further. They may be able to maintain their gains or they may regress to earlier states of Being.

Transformation is a process. It must continue to unfold in a person's life or he becomes arrested in an early phase. There are many people in leadership positions who have "retired." They developed to a certain level, became distracted and continued no further. They can still help others attain to their level but not beyond it.

Since transformation is an inner process, the leader must always be open for creativity and change in his own life. For this he must have a light hold upon security and reputation. Transformation always requires risking and letting go of the known for the unknown. You can't play it safe and be a transformational leader. The price of transformation is to venture forth boldly in search of the Grail. It is not an effort for the fainthearted.

Is an organizational mythmaker

The transformational leader is a mythmaker. She creates a story of the organization, its beginnings, journey, and grand destination. She involves the whole organization as she spins the myth. Every person is invited to participate in the spinning. Every person contributes personal vitality to the creation of the egregor (organizational entity). This entity when it becomes strong enough attracts resources, people, and opportunities. It becomes a magnetic node that can reconstellate reality events and create states of metanoia (miracles). The egregor develops a personality and creates a sense of presence in the organization. It is a mental creature and impacts the consciousness of all people who enter the institution.

The highest level of system is meaning. To create meaning is to create a myth. The myth answers the question of "why." An effective organizational myth resonates with the personal symbol systems of all the employees, patients, physicians, and visitors. By encountering the organization, personal lives are fulfilled and given meaning.

A mythic organization is a womb. It is a web of spiritual, mental, emotional, and physical strands. It creates a total environment and like a womb it gestates new life. The mythic organization is like a coat of many colors. It provides a spectrum of color and sound that is the composite of the energy fields of all of its people. However, the composite is not a blend. Like the coat of many colors it places the colors side by side. Each color is distinct. This permits each employee to draw upon the color they need most to fill in their energy spectrum. Each employee contributes the color of her strength and draws upon the color of her weakness. In this way the womb nourishes a great variety of people and actually creates a higher state of differentiation in each one.

The mythic organization accelerates the evolution of all people who come within its energic field. Like power points on the earth, the mythic hospital generates a vortex. The vortex possesses a healing potential. Patients improve because of the vortex effect. Eventually hospitals will be rated on the power of their fields. People will seek out high-potential hospitals in the same way they seek out natural healing spots on the earth such as Lourdes.

Any myth generates spiritual energy. It tunes the person to his/her spiritual center. The transformational leader is a mythmaker and possesses the potential to invoke the mythic dimension in others. However, one caution is in order. When the mythic dimension is activated, the Shadow is also activated. This means a mythic organization polarizes people. Like a fertilizer spread on the field, both the wheat and the weeds grow. Therefore, a mythic organization must be prepared to deal with the best as well as the worst in its people. Some employees will get worse before they can get better. A mythic hospital understands this and encourages the healing process in all people.

Sees the big picture

The transformational leader is not caught up in the details of the moment. He always keeps one eye focused on the big picture and does not over identify with the exigencies of the moment. This permits him to view the parts, the whole, and the whole that is greater than the sum of the parts.

The transformational leader is "spanning consciousness." He is aware of more than one series of events. This is a type of figure/ground consciousness that sees the event in the foreground and the context in the background.

Seeing the big picture is an outcome of multidimensional consciousness. It requires an expansion of both time and space perception. Expanded time perception views a thing as it is now, as it will look in the future, and as it has looked in the past. Expanded space perception sees an event in multiple spaces, i.e., physical, astral, mental, and spiritual or in parallel realities.

The same event always fills multiple spaces. We are accustomed to viewing most objects only in physical space. In astral space an object is a feeling event and much less dense. In spiritual space it is an archetype. In mental space it is an idea. Change anything in one space and you change it in all spaces. Change it in one time and you change it in all times. In theological terms, every change on earth causes a change in heaven. Every change in heaven creates a change on earth.

Many healthcare managers get caught up in the rush of events and forget what it is they are supposed to be doing. If a manager gets too "busy" he will lose all of his effectiveness.

As time speeds up and space shrinks (twenty-first century), it is necessary to develop fractal perception (see patterns). Most of our societal and environmental problems cannot be fixed at the level they are generated. It is easy to get overwhelmed by the sheer number and intensity of events (fire fighting).

Sometimes the manager must withdraw from the hustle and bustle and ground himself before moving forward. What is going on here? What is it I am supposed to be doing? We must learn to practice psychic economy or we will be worn out trying to keep track of all the events swirling around us.

In time, the human race will develop some new sensory organs for doing this. We are rapidly evolving out of our five sensory modes into a multiple sensory mode.

TRANSFORMATIONAL LEADERSHIP 93

Becomes a channel for the outworking of the vision

The transformational leader bridges the gap between vision and reality. He becomes the channel for the outworking of the vision. This means he must learn to work in high density matter of the third dimension (3D). Such a work requires the acquisition of political and managerial skills. Many visionaries find this distasteful and would rather bask in the more subtle dimensions where the mind is directly creative. Transformation in our 3D takes place in high density matter so the transformational leader cannot avoid getting his "hands dirty." Generally he also generates "karma" in the process and must meet the effects of his own causes. This is a sacrifice strategy of the spiritual leader and is necessary to improve well being upon the earth. Ghandi is a good example of personal sacrifice in the pursuit of vision implementation.

By serving as a channel between the spiritual and the physical, the transformational leader is always surrounded by spiritual energies seeking manifestation through him. He is a gateway on the spiritual plane focusing those energies into physical manifestation. This rush of energy can create an overstimulation or congestion. The leader must learn how to avoid this strain by controlling the access of spiritual energies to his mind/body vehicle.

Maintaining a balance between the spiritual and the physical is one of the most important challenges we have in healthcare today. The hospital administrator must attract spiritual energy and then give it suitable expression in the "real world" of healthcare delivery. The danger is over involvement on either side of the implementation equation. The leader can get lost in the realm of spirit or mired in the density of matter. Transformational leadership is walking the razor's edge.

Implementing spirit requires a submission to its guiding impulses. Because spirit operates in another dimension, it is not impeded by the contradictions and inconsistencies of this dimension. Things are always clear in spirit. They only become murky as you try to translate them into our everyday world. Getting fidelity into the translation is the big challenge. As you know from your dreams, something can make perfect sense in your dream but when you remember it upon waking, it often seems ludicrous. Since the universe is made up of reflecting layers (Kabbalah) the problem of translation is faced every time you move from one layer to another. After you have moved through ten layers, the final product of your visioning does not look much like the source of your inspiration. Yet, this is precisely the challenge of transformation. We must contact the spiritual archetype at the highest level of existence and translate it into materiality at the lowest level of existence. This is why we are here. This is what we must do.

Interlude III

TRANSFORMATIONAL LEADERSHIP 94

Registers subtle changes in the environment

The transformational leader is very tuned in to his environment. Subtle changes that others might miss, he notices. The environment is constantly mirroring back alterations in his consciousness. In that sense, the environment functions as an early warning system. The leader may notice omens of change in his external environment before he picks up the same changes in his internal awareness.

There is always a mirroring back and forth between an organism and the environment. Balance must obtain or the organism cannot thrive. Sometimes this means the organism must adapt and sometimes it means the environment will change. It is a simple question of potency. If the leader's consciousness is stronger than the environment, the environment will mirror his mind and assume the reflecting form.

You have perhaps noticed a person enter a room and feel the atmosphere in the room change. The new arrival is changing the energy balance of the life-forms present in that space. This may create either a positive or negative effect.

In a small circle, energies circulate and create a powerful vortex (columnar wave). In a rain dance, psychic energies can become potent enough to change the weather. The same energies may be directed by group consciousness to either heal or destroy other life forms.

If there is a good fit between a person and his space, each is reinforced. The transformational leader seeks to build resonant organizational spaces that amplify his mental efforts. A bad fit does just the opposite and retards the leader's efforts.

Space is not empty. It is an energy form and is always structured by the many energies passing through it. These energies may be latent or manifest. In any space there is always more latent energy than manifested energy. The reason is simple. Most of the universe is not yet in expression and simply "inists" (as opposed to exists) as a high energy potential. By tapping these latent potentials the transformational leader is nurtured by "empty" space.

At the level of light coding, a space is structured by all the energies that have passed through it. These energy prints tell the story of the energies themselves. Every space carries a total memory of its transient energies. If these energies are replayed, the original scenes repeat themselves. Have you ever entered a space and quietly set about recovering its past history? Even organizational spaces retain this type of memory. A visit to power spots and old sacred sites will demonstrate this type of place memory.

Be alert to your environment!

TRANSFORMATIONAL LEADERSHIP 95

Manifests a growing power over the environment

As the transformational leader continues to unfold she begins to manifest a growing power over her environment. There is increasing resonance between her intentions and environmental responses. Consciousness and environment seem to be in step. Both are responding to some type of higher purpose and plan materializing in the observable universe.

Because the universe is composed of interacting energy systems, entrainment is always a possibility. Higher intensity energies entrain lower intensity energies. The environment always mirrors high potency consciousness. If necessary, the environment reconfigures itself to serve as a more suitable vehicle for expression of the higher energies. Indian rainmakers understood this relationship very well.

There is no such thing as inanimate matter. All matter is alive and is an embodiment of Spirit. All matter has consciousness at its level of expression. All matter can enter into a "conversation" with Spirit. St. Francis demonstrated his ability to converse with the animals. Christ conversed with the water and other natural elements.

One of the signs of unfoldment of transformational leaders is increasing synchronicity in their lives. Just the right books, just the right people, just the right circumstances appear in their lives as needed. Happy coincidences become the norm, not the exception. The environment begins to sing their song.

Being in nature is one way of developing rapport with the environment. Conversing with the plants, animals, streams and rocks develops the ability to see, hear, feel, and talk in new ways. All of nature will converse with you if you love it and take the time to develop the relationship.

The transformational leader must escape the tyranny of her own thought forms and the thought forms of her organization. She must open herself to the internal dynamics and possibilities of other living systems that co-inhabit her universe. She must establishment a kinship with all other living entities. Then, the environment becomes an extension of her personhood and reacts to her commands as her body would. It is her body in extension.

The environment of a planet is the radiation of its consciousness. In the planetary aura is the story of its interacting life forms. In every rock is the living history of its journey. In every rock is a conversation ready to happen. It all depends upon you as a conversational partner. Do you like to commune with rocks?

TRANSFORMATIONAL LEADERSHIP 96

Experiences elevated emotional states

Since transformation is a spiritual process, the transformational leader often encounters and conducts intense spiritual energies. He experiences these as elevated emotional and mental states. At the spiritual level this produces ecstasy. Ecstasy is a temporary separation of consciousness from the material plane and its mundane concerns.

When the physical mind/body vehicle contacts high vibratory energies, there is an acceleration of functions, a lightness, a buoyancy that is a peak experience in Maslow's terms. The leader tries to maintain this state as long as possible. In ecstasy, things usually difficult to understand become crystal clear. The mind races ahead of itself. Insights stream in that may take months to decode and translate into words. The leader has touched another dimension and "tasted" the energies that dwell there. Since the leader is a bridge between the transcendental and the material, he must translate the ineffable into the slightly more than ordinary. This is a daunting and lonesome task. To be a transformational leader you must stand slightly apart and yet be one with your peers. Your feet must be on the ground and your head in the clouds. This is a difficult yet necessary posture.

Elevated emotional states create the energy and enthusiasm needed to continue the battle in the mundane world. It may be in deep meditation or prayer that you are lifted outside yourself. It may occur during a vision quest in nature. It may suddenly appear in your drumming or the singing of a mantrum. Suddenly the mind breaks through the clouds and you behold the bright Sun (Son) shining on all of creation. Each leader must find his own path to transcendence. In the realm of the Spirit there is a unique pathway for each individual seeker. I will not travel your pathway, or you mine. We are fellow travelers, traveling parallel paths. We seek the same destination, each in his own way.

The transformational leader must be careful lest he become trapped in "sticky materialism." It is a challenge to work in this, the densest of all dimensions, upon a dark planet. Without frequent trips to the eternal fount, we would all fail. Redeeming the planet is our work and it requires the energies of other dimensions streaming through you.

We are conscious agents of transformation. The family, the organization, the community are our "playing fields" where divine energies dance upon human forms. Indeed, as a transformational leader, you are a member of a cosmic conspiracy, joined to rebirth the planet earth and permit it once again to join the Federation of Unfallen Worlds.

Experiences decreasing satisfaction from old rewards

The energies experienced in transformation, change forever a person's reward system. Ego satisfactions cannot compare with the sweet, uplifting and lingering presence of a transcendental spiritual contact. Money, sex, power, pride, position, reputation—all fade in comparison. For that reason, transformational leaders gradually evolve beyond the orbit of the ego and thereby are able to enter new dimensions of experience.

To function in the third dimension, money, food, clothing, housing, transportation, etc., are necessary. The transformational leader must utilize them as well as anybody else. However, the transformational leader views material resources in an appropriate context and does not overvalue them. It is easy to get stuck in the material dimension. Since transformational leaders have well developed ego capabilities, they can if they wish, do very well in the material dimension. It is easy for any capable human being to rationalize spending valuable time and effort collecting resources not needed for her/his work in this world.

In the higher dimensions, material resources are not present. Here, the consciousness of the leader supplies everything required. The more expanded the consciousness, the more freedom the leader has available to go wherever she wishes. The transformational leader soon learns that strong attachments to the material plane inhibit movement on the spiritual planes. To become encumbered with high density matter is to fail passage through subtle dimensional gateways.

It is important to understand there is often a time gap between the old and the new. Some transformational leaders are now escaping the orbits of ego but have not yet developed suitable vehicles for moving through subtle dimensions. It is easy in the intervening interval to wonder whether or not letting go of the "old self" was a good idea. As with the practice of meditation, patience and tireless effort are the keys here. The new must be born within you. It is not an instant transformation of the old.

Maslow understood this evolution of consciousness. You work through the lower levels before you attain the higher levels. It is important to remember that matter is frozen spirit, or spirit at a lower rate of vibration. It is not bad. Ego is not bad. It is a limited vehicle. It will take you certain places, but will keep you out of others. As long as ego takes you where you want to go, you are not likely to set it aside. When, however, you have tasted the heavenly manna of a transcendental experience, there is no going back to the old food troughs. They have served their purpose and you are ready to move on.

Also, remember to be charitable concerning others. They are often ego bound for a good reason and must grow out of it. You should not try to hurry them along before their time.

TRANSFORMATIONAL LEADERSHIP 98

Has a deep concern for social betterment

The transformational leader has a deep concern for social betterment. He is a conscious agent of evolution and plays his role in the progressive unfoldment of humankind.

Transformation is a process that affects all things in the universe. Constant change is a cosmic law. Everything is always moving toward its eternal destiny. This includes planets. The transformational leader is part of a planet's drama of unfoldment. When a critical percentage of a planet's population is ripe for transformation, transformation occurs. It is the job of the leader to participate in this expansion of planetary consciousness.

Without social betterment, improvement in the health of a population is not possible. Health is a social outcome and only occurs when lots of other things, such as sanitation, nutrition, lifestyle, education, income, housing, recreation, etc. are in order. To create healthy Americans, America must be re-designed. As I have indicated before, this is the major agenda item for our new century.

To a large extent, social betterment is a spiritual issue. When we become our brother's keeper, we will begin redistributing societal resources from the have's to the have not's. The good of the many will take precedence over the good of the few. At this point in our world it is hard to conceive of such disinterested brotherhood (and sisterhood). However, after we have suffered the tribulations of our current excesses, it will become more feasible.

Hospitals are beginning to title themselves. Many volunteers are working to take services out to those in need. The healthy communities movement is well underway. The problem of crime is getting attention in the highest circles in Washington. Many mayors are acting to reclaim their cities. We are talking about reinventing government. Large business corporations are serving as catalysts for global rehabilitation. Good things are happening and are an omen of better things to come. We are not there yet, but we are on the way.

As people become transformed, they in turn transform their environment. Deep ecology is an indication of spiritual renewal. Healthcare institutions can play a lead role in the rebuilding of society. The best place to begin is the place you work and live. The battle will be won, community by community. Leadership must come from the grass roots level. Empower yourself to become a channel for the outworking of societal transformation.

Has a systems perspective

The universe is a system, within a system, within a system, within a system. All systems share common properties. The transformational leader understands his place within the systems hierarchy of the universe. He knows all systems are interrelated. If the transformational leader alters system functioning at his level, the reverberations produced will extend to all systems levels above and all systems levels below. Change earth and you change heaven. Change heaven and you change earth.

Transformation is systems evolution. Systems evolve through identifiable stages as they expand into their infinite unfoldment. The transformational leader accelerates systems evolution. He does this by imparting his energy to the system, thereby "kicking it to its next highest level."

Energy always flows from a high potential source to a low potential source. You see this energy flow in the guru/chela relationship. The guru operates at a higher energy level than the chela (advanced student) so he can transmit energy to the chela. The chela in turn operates at a higher level than the neophyte (beginning student), so can transfer energy to the neophyte. The neophyte operates at a higher level than the casual follower so can transmit energy to the follower, etc. The energy hierarchy of the universe operates in this fashion all the way up to the Source and all the way down to the most elementary particle. Little lives always depend upon greater lives, just as the cells of your body depend upon you.

Because of the systems nature of the universe, you are always in relationship with All That Is. You can never be isolated or alone. You can converse with suprasystems above your level or you can converse with subsystems below your level. Everything depends upon everything. Everything is important and has its part to play in the whole. Love binds all the parts of the universe together.

Usually people are aware only of their system level. Intelligence (energy) coming from other levels is rejected or simply does not rise above the limen of consciousness. The transformational leader, however, can change his point of attention and become aware of events occurring at supra and subsystem levels. This permits him to anticipate effects that will appear at his system level before they arrive. He sees the energy descending or ascending. Here we can think of the metaphor of Jacob's ladder. Imagine you are a step in the ladder and can observe the angels (powers) ascending and descending. A systems orientation is a great comfort. It permits you to see all things in relationship.

Recognizes patterns in the making

The transformational leader recognizes patterns in the making.

She has this ability because she "looks at things afar off." By rising above the material dimension she is able to perceive the constellating matrix of events moving toward manifestation in the material dimension.

Everything that manifests in third dimensional reality, or is about to manifest, has its origin in an energy matrix residing in a more subtle neighboring dimension. Science will soon reveal this subtle matrix that even now has been detected through Kirlian photography. The matrix is composed of subatomic matter.

Eventually, medical technology will bring us highly sensitive atomic scanners able to see the precursors of a disease years before it manifests in the cells of the physical body. The disordered energy matrix will then be reordered thus avoiding the later disease. Of course, the patient also has a role to play in his continuing recovery. He will have to learn to think in new ways to prevent the re-formation of new matrices similar to the old ones that were reordered.

What is true of the human body is also true of the body of the planet. The matrix of coming events is reflected in the subtle ethers. The etheric images are high probability matrices formed as a result of the collective thinking of humankind. Unless reversed or significantly weakened they will manifest in third dimensional reality as quickly as the earth's time/space/condition continuum permits their third dimensional manifestation. The images are as it were "hanging in the air" waiting for a chance to enter the wings of the world stage. Prophets of all ages have possessed the ability to read these ethers and predict coming events. Of course, a shift in the thinking of humankind can and often does change the matrices, so a margin of error always exists in human predictions. Only God can predict with absolute certainty.

Recognizing patterns in the making is one of the first indications a higher consciousness is breaking through in the transformational leader. She is seeing behind real events and detecting the subtle swirls and vortices of incipient manifestation. By reading what is "on the wall," she can anticipate coming events and prepare for them.

In some cases, the leader may attempt to generate counter vortices to prevent the current ones from moving any closer to the point of manifestation.

Interlude III

Once a matrix has attracted third dimensional matter it is too late to stop manifestation although the course of the manifestation can often be altered. A partial rather than a complete manifestation may then occur.

A good spiritual leader knows there is always a relationship between the mass of thought forms produced by her organization and real world events that will happen to her organization. Sometimes she can avoid negative probabilistic futures and sometimes she cannot. Often the leader must have the combined energies of a small seed group to reinforce her own efforts. The destiny of the entire organization may rest with this small group. Just as a "mother yeast" is the secret of the brew, so the yeast of the small group may be the point of genesis for the organization's success in the world.

Feels the rhythm of the lifespace

The transformational leader is tuned in to his environment and therefore feels the rhythm of his lifespace. All things in the universe are related and work as an integrated whole. For this to occur, a rhythm is required to produce the proper spacing and relationship of the many to the One.

Creation unfolds in time, space, and condition. In the unmanifest these three qualifiers do not exist. In the manifest they are a necessity. Since things must occur in sequence, the leader tunes in to the multitudinous streams of cause and effect. He senses the probabilities of future events and is able to create synchronicities for manifestation.

If the leader's timing is off (the day begins all wrong), he will quickly insert a quiet interval to change the sequencing of events and get back in stride with a better rhythm. In this way, bad does not become worse, but changes to better. It is amazing how many people get off to a bad start and continue on the same downward path all day long.

The transformational leader can also sense possibility waiting to happen, i.e., a seed condition on the spiritual plane waiting for an opportunity to manifest on the physical plane. He can then create physical circumstances that permit the manifestation to occur. To do this leader must stay tuned in to the spiritual at all times and avoid being overwhelmed by the flow of physical events.

Nature has a natural rhythm and if the leader can escape the turmoil of human-made confusion, he can tune in to nature and use its rhythm to readjust his own psychic functioning. This rhythmic property makes nature a great healer. Much disease is created by social and organizational discord.

Because of its rhythm, nature gives warning of impending world changes. These are read by the animals, but often missed by humans. The wind and water teach for those who have ears to hear. Every tree is a prophecy for the reader of signs. The power of nature can be summoned by the lover of nature.

Watch for natural cycles. Study synchronicity. Generate causes and wait upon their effects. In this way you will learn lessons that cannot be taught in books. Every life space is humming with intelligence, with memories of things past and prophecies of things yet to come. Do not stand apart and observe. Enter and become.

TRANSFORMATIONAL LEADERSHIP 102A

Tickles the Void and gives form to the formless

The transformational leader feels equally at home in the formed and the formless. Through deep meditation he ascends the planes of consciousness to enter the realms of limited light where he "tickles the Void" in an effort to give form to the formless. This is an act of invocation and an act of co-creation.

The Void is an outreach of the mind of God and consists of all those things God has deemed ready for entrance into the worlds of creation. The Void is the background of creation. It lies far beyond mind, thought and image, but is within the realm of Spirit. No created being can go beyond the Void. Beyond the Void is the Godhead.

In the Void is infinite possibility waiting to happen ("inistence"). It must be contacted at a very subtle level of consciousness and allowed to impress the spirit of the visionary leader. When he perceives it, he gently begins bringing the impression down through the lower layers of consciousness. Once it reaches the level of concrete mind, it is within the realm of third dimensional reality (existence). As a result of the descent, the mental image is now only a distant reflection of the impress of the Void (looking through a glass darkly). In addition it is distorted both by its densification as well as the distorting mind of the visionary.

One of the secrets of co-creation is to be a clear transmission channel for the descending images. When the transformational leader escapes the orbit of his ego, he attains great clarity in his ability to respond to impressions of the Void. He will still distort the light somewhat and as a result is likely to be frustrated with his creation. The density of the third dimension always distorts the light coming from higher dimensions.

Many transformational leaders cannot reach the level of awareness needed to enter the Void. Rather they enter the thought stream that circulates around the planet. By attuning their mind, they attract desired images from the thought stream and bring those through into manifestation.

The future potentials of the planet are already circulating in the thought stream waiting for cosmic fishermen. These Images are placed in the thought stream by "explorers of the Void" who move potentials from the Void into lower dimensional levels. These workers do not condense the images further than the abstract level of the mental plane. The images will remain there until a lower density mind can contact them.

The transformational leader with appropriate training and experience will be able to first enter the thought stream and later, perhaps, the Void.

TRANSFORMATIONAL LEADERSHIP 102B (continued)

The transformational leader in deep meditation approaches the boundary of the Void (background of Being). He then invokes the Void and it gives birth to new forms. The forms that before inisted, now are born into existence. He moves them from potentiality to actuality.

When the transformational leader approaches the Void, he does so in deep expectation. He is searching for a particular category of possible forms. Because he knows what he is looking for, he resonates with isomorphic potentials "floating" in the Void. His thought forms approach the rare density of the Void and stimulate resident potentials that are similar enough in kind, to react to his stimulation. Since the Void contains all potential being, it cannot respond to general requests. It contains all potential things and no particular thing—all at once. You have to know what you are looking for to find anything. The more specific your invocation, the better are your chances of getting a response.

Many heath care leaders are limited to operating in the manifest world. The transformational leader can also work in the unmanifest. The unmanifest world is just as real as third dimensional (3D) reality. It simply is much less dense or tangible. For someone operating in 3D reality, the emotional planes, the mental planes and the spiritual planes are not visible (they are unmanifest). Of course when you are operating in those planes they become manifest since your consciousness is operating at the same density as everything else in that plane. The difference with the Void is that nothing in it is ever manifest, even when you are operating close to its density.

It is from the Void that all forms are born, whatever their plane of manifestation. If you passed the boundary of the Void and actually entered it, you would cease to exist. You invoke the Void by entering its boundary condition, not by entering it in its fullness.

The Void is the wellspring of creation and appears to us to be in a timeless, spaceless condition. The closest words we can use to describe it are the "broodings of God." It is the realm of pre-creation. It, however, can respond to created beings who approach it in a state of "readiness."

For the beginner, the thought stream is often confused with the Void. Actually the two have almost nothing in common. The thought stream consists only of third dimensional thoughts circulating around the earth. Many of these thoughts have not yet manifested in the world. However, entering the thought stream can be an exciting event. Innovators can tap the thought stream and bring into our world "new" things. All of these "new things" are old things from the point of view of the Void.

Observing the thought stream caused Solomon to declare "there is nothing new under the sun." Most of the thoughts in the thought stream have been placed there many times, by many people, in many places. By contrast, potentials residing in the Void have been not been witnessed by anyone until they are born the first time.

TRANSFORMATIONAL LEADERSHIP 103

Is the guardian of the spirit of the organization

The transformational leader is the protector of the spirit of the organization. The spirit of the organization is built up over many years of organizational functioning. It is the subtle body of the organization and the source of the organization's nature and characteristics. It exists on the inner dimensions and is fed by the beliefs, emotions, and spiritual energies of the employees. Employees feed the spirit and are nourished by it.

Many organizations have a languishing spirit. It starves for want of nourishment. If employees focus only on the material transactions of the organization, they do not build spirit. Spirit is fed by emotions, focused beliefs, and high spiritual purposes. The transformational leader uses ritual, rite, ceremony, and celebration to feed the spirit of the organization.

The original spirit of the organization was created by its first founders. Later generations of employees may know little about the founders or their aspirations. As a result they typically wander far from what the founders intended. This is why it is good to have a Founders Room in the organization where employees can re-connect with the original spirit of the organization. By contacting that spirit, they become energized and "catch on fire."

Just as people can be born again, so can organizations. The taproot of the organization is always in its historical past. However, the spirit of the organization lives also in its present and future on the subtle planes. Through study of the organization's past, the investigator's consciousness is attuned to spirit and spirit downflows through the investigator. You may have looked at old photographs or toured some of the original buildings of a hospital and heard spirit calling to you to become a present incarnation of its energy. It is important to never remove all of the old buildings or relics in a modernization program. When this is done, the link to the past is often broken. Spirit no longer has the "old body" for incarnation. Items from the past serve as contact vehicles. They should be carefully preserved. This is probably one of the sources of appeal for family heirlooms and antiques.

The spirit of the organization will continue to grow and develop as it is fed. It grows as the organization grows and the organization grows as spirit grows. Spirit has crossover ability, which means it gains energy from the spirits of other similar organizations, in this or other times. For instance, the hospital spirit could gain considerably from contact with the spirit of the old dream temples. Seldom, however, is such contact attempted.

TRANSFORMATIONAL LEADERSHIP 104

His power is synergic and metaphoric rather than egoic

There are three main types of power on this earth. Egoic power is power over others (law of the jungle). Synergic power is releasing the power in others (Ghandi). Metaphoric power is the power of the symbol (the Christian cross). The most powerful power is metaphoric. The power of the symbol activates tremendous energies in the universe. Like above, so below is a principle of the perennial wisdom. A symbol in lower dimensions of the universe releases the power of its source in higher dimensions.

The transformational leader employs both synergic and metaphoric power, but primarily metaphoric power. The leader through organizational myths connects with the psychic energy and personal mythology of the employees. The transformational leader is an experienced mythmaker. Through stories, personal deeds, ritual, ceremony, and celebration, the leader creates a living myth in the organization. Employees gain renewed personal identity through their personal participation in the mythic activities of the organization.

The missing element in most healthcare organizations is the spiritual dimension of mythmaking. If hospitals see themselves as business organizations rather than healing temples, they are not able to mobilize metaphoric power. The whole emphasis on quality improvement will fail unless this mythic element is energized. Who wants to work under the demanding constraints of quality improvement unless there is a transcendent purpose to justify all this effort?

A symbol channels spiritual energy as well as mental and emotional energy. It lifts up the organization and all the people in it. Spiritual energy has the capacity to reconstellate reality (bend the usual rules) and permits the organization to experience metanoia (unexplainable results). Therefore the ultimate edge any organization has is the heightened consciousness of its people.

A surprise coming in outcome analysis is the discovery of better outcomes experienced in high consciousness organizations. High consciousness hospitals can heal patients as well as cure them. A left-brained analyst will be puzzled by these unexpected results and will be unable to account for them even if he observes the staff in action. Just as quantum mechanics discovered the subtle subatomic particles that make up the universe, so will transformational management discover the subtle energies at work in healing and potentiation of patients. At that point, hospitals will begin recruiting staff by consciousness as well as by credentials, experience, and recommendations. The unseen organization (spiritual matrix) will become more important than the seen organization (gross third dimensional form). Future schools of business will have course work in philosophy, theology, metaphysics, spiritual practice, and mentoring. Our new century will see the movement of management into the subtle dimensions of our universe.

Maintains poise and bearing

The transformational leader is able to maintain poise and bearing because she is grounded in this dimension while maintaining perspective through her perception in other dimensions.

Meaning depends upon circle size. Poise and bearing relate to meaning. If you can make sense out of your life events, you can maintain tranquillity even in highly unstable environments.

The transformational leader builds an inner space of tranquillity. This is a sacred space and cannot be entered by external agents of confusion. The sacred space is an inner temple. It is constructed of spiritual matter and is a safe sanctuary. Ceremony, ritual and prayer create this safe harbor. It can be entered at will. The circle is closed upon your entry and not reopened until you exit. It is a safe refuge in the storms of life.

The transformational leader also practices self-remembering. She is never totally caught up in the external events of her life. She participates in these events, but has no loss of memory as to who she is and why she is there. She is able to span consciousness. She maintains the roles of both observer and participant. You might think this would make her less effective. In fact, it makes her more effective. Effectiveness is determined by her resonance with higher order systems. When she is tuned in to higher dimensions, she achieves great efficiencies in this lower dimension. Her spiritual thoughts are rapidly converted into material expression.

When you lose your poise and bearing, take note. This is an area that needs some work. It indicates unfinished business in the evolution of your psyche. Something has penetrated your protective energy field. It has penetrated because of a local turbulence triggered by the aversive stimulus.

Sometimes people misinterpret poise and bearing as insensitivity or callousness. They expect observers to be caught up in their own melodramas. You cannot help anyone if you become entangled in their problems. You must perceive with a clear mind and open heart. Your perception becomes clouded if you are snagged by their difficulties. Know your weaknesses and stay clear of people who trigger them in you. Until you overcome your difficulty, you are a hazard to yourself and to them. Sometimes mentors are pulled down and engulfed by the problems of their protégés. This is an unwise mentor who failed to respect her limits. Know your limits and live within them.

He has confronted his Shadow and incorporated it

Everyone carries a Shadow, which consists of all the unacceptable parts of himself that are repressed or denied and projected upon others. For a transformational leader, the Shadow is a real problem. It warps, twists, and distorts the Light that shines through him. Since the transformational leader is in a position of power, such distortions are passed from him onto others and in the end his Shadow distorts the organization.

Therefore the leader must confront his Shadow, permit it to enter his consciousness, redeem and reform it, and integrate it into himself. Since the Shadow has energic properties, when it is reintegrated into Self, it empowers the personality and converts Shadow energy into personality power in service of the Light.

The Shadow is always lurking behind stage. It often reveals itself in the dreams and fantasies of its host. If it gains enough power it may invade the personality and obsess its owner. The more it is denied, the more power it develops.

Because of the power of the opposites, the more Light there is in a person, the greater the potential of the Shadow to obscure that light. The further up one progresses on the ladder of evolution, the further down they can fall. We see this in mythical stories of the fall of high beings that are cast out of heaven.

The Shadow feeds upon fear. Therefore you must not permit yourself to fear it. The Shadow is not an alien being external to yourself. It is you, a part of you separated from your main self. As the denied part, it seeks re-entry. But it must be entry on your terms. It must be redeemed and rehabilitated by your soul's Light.

Often your Shadow has a rather infantile nature. Much of it was formed by bad childhood experiences. Feelings of guilt, and low self-esteem were internalized often at preverbal levels. Only the Light of your love can melt down the Shadow. You accept it like a prodigal child that has returned home.

In Hitler you see the power of a Shadow to reap devastation upon the world. Leaders carrying this fatal defect destroy many others and eventually themselves. There is no limit to the degradation they can visit upon the world. For the Shadow has no Light, and therefore no conscience.

Interlude III

In most people the Shadow is weak and mild in its negative aspects. In a few people it is strong. One of the requirements of leadership should be an examination of the Shadow and an assessment of its potential. With enough power and ego inflation, even a weak Shadow can become a terror. This is why transformational leaders carry a heavy responsibility to know themselves—both their light and dark sides.

With sufficient soul evolution, the Shadow is redeemed. The power of God can remove all traces of it. For the Christian this is the work of the Holy Spirit. Until that point is reached there is always the possibility of a fall.

Transformational leaders always proceed with great care and humility. They have witnessed the fall of some of their brethren who now work on the side of the dark forces.

He protects the organization from his own weaknesses

The transformational leader is self aware. He knows his weaknesses, admits them to others, and strives to overcome them, as he is able. Because he is self aware, he avoids distorting his relationships with other people and with the organization.

Since the organizational leader wields power, it is imperative he use his power in accountable ways. If he does not do so, he will create dis-ease wherever he goes.

An organization with a neurotic leader becomes neurotic. The inconstancies of the leader are magnified many times over in the reactions and actions of other managers. The disturbed leader creates a field of dissonance which magnifies the troubles of everyone he contacts. Negative energies warp his body/mind space and produce interpersonal and transpersonal disasters.

The more powerful the leader is, the greater the distortions he produces. We sometimes refer to these leaders as masters of darkness. Their influence can contaminate a nation or an entire planet. Weak people are immediately drawn into the orbit of such leaders and seem to experience soul loss as they are overrun by the dark powers. Like a moth drawn to the flame, their life is eventually extinguished.

Of course, such exaggerations of negative power go well beyond what we see in hospital CEOs. However, the differences are a matter of degree, not kind. All of us are subject to the same pathologies, only to varying degrees.

Effective prevention of such problems requires a high degree of self honesty coupled with good mentors and a loving group of friends, quick to identify such tendencies and press for their recognition and correction. We must all hold up the light to each another to avoid stumbling on the path.

If the leader has great weaknesses but acts in good faith to come to terms with them, he will seek out the counsel of those who can help. The light then reaches him through other lives. If he responds positively to admonition, he is walking the path of transformation.

The usual human reaction is to avoid corrective admonition and bask instead in the flattering and false light of the little ego. Organizational power becomes a personal tool used to gratify self and attain self glorification. The way is then prepared for a great fall. However, heaven is still open after the fall, if the leader repents of his evil deeds and seeks to provide recompense to those he has injured.

He is free from negative addictions

Transformational leadership requires a concentration of power in the body/mind vehicle of the leader. Negative addictions drain off power. Without power reserves, the leader cannot empower his mental creations with an act of will. Magic requires high psychic energy. Worry, envy, anger, jealousy, depression, drugs, excessive sexuality, etc., are negative addictions and are therefore power sinks. By contrast, meditation is a positive addiction and builds power reserves.

Thought forms produced by the transformational leader are energy matrices. They are mental frameworks but have no power until they are energized by astral, mental or spiritual energies. Often people unwittingly energize negative thought forms, which then take the forms of obsessions or compulsions and thereby acquire quasi-independent status. They afflict the person and through a psychic cord attach themselves and become a permanent drain on the energies of their creator. Therefore, negative addictions not only produce undesirable thought forms. They also energize these thought forms by drawing upon the energies of their creator.

Astral or emotional energies are the most common power sources drawn upon by thought forms. For this reason the transformational leader keeps his emotions in check. Mental energies are the next most common source. Worry or confusion produce a cloud of negative energy that obscures the Light coming from the Source. Spiritual energies may come either from sources of Light or Darkness. They create thought forms in the spiritual dimension. Often they take the form of entities and can confuse the leader who cannot tell his own mental creations from entities that exist in their own right.

Often new agers become lost in the crowd of their own thought forms. They think they are communicating with a deva when in fact they are communicating with a thought form of their own creation. Most of the channeling works are of this character. If you examine the material carefully, it is a mishmash from the channeler's own mind. Communications coming from an independent entity of spiritual origin are almost impossible to word. The thoughts are not coded in earth language. The best that can be given are metaphors and stories that try to make up for the deficiencies in our language. Channeling rapidly becomes a negative addiction.

The transformational leader conserves his energy and uses it with great economy. Breakthroughs in consciousness require high energy focus.

Views the universe as a super abundance that knows no scarcity

The transformational leader lives in a universe of super abundance. He knows that scarcity is a phenomenon of limited consciousness and has nothing to do with the amount of resources in the universe. The universe is a plenum with an outrageous supply of everything that can be desired and many things that cannot as yet even be imagined. Limited consciousness is consciousness out of relationship with All That Is. It is caused by an excessive focus upon self, greed, jealousy, envy, aggression, lack of love, etc.

The level of consciousness on a planet determines its level of supply. Planets with limited consciousness experience severe shortages, deterioration and high levels of toxicity and pollution. They "run down" and eventually become dead planets. Planets with abundant consciousness are Gardens of Eden where there is no lack of any kind. On these garden planets each unit of consciousness is interested in the good of all things. The planet "runs up" and takes its place in the government of the universe.

The earth is a learning planet and is approaching the time of initiation. At this point in its history, the earth is mainly characterized by limited consciousness, hence the many environmental, economic, social, political and religious problems. However, there is a tremendous opportunity for all of us to "turn it around" and move our earth toward its destiny as a planet of light.

The transformational leader plays a pivotal role in planetary transformation. He helps people understand the critical relationship between the inner environment and the outer environment. He models abundant consciousness and helps others achieve heightened perception and functioning. He helps his organization and community change its collective mindset.

A good example of transformational work is the "healthier communities" movement in the United States. Every community already has sufficient resources to meet its healthcare needs if it changes its collective mind. With a changed mind, resource allocation patterns are changed and suddenly there is enough to go around. With the old mind, the community experienced scarcity. With the new mind, the community experiences abundance.

The new paradigm demonstrated in healthier communities can become the gateway program for total habitat redesign. Transformational leadership is the key. The consciousness of abundance must be taught by transformational mentors to community members that have reached the appropriate degree of spiritual maturity. It is now happening across the United States.

Believes that personal and organizational resources are a matter of relationship to "all that is."

The transformational leader sees things in perspective. He knows the universe is a system, within a system, within a system. Therefore his knowledge of context enables him to understand the relationship between what he is doing and "all that is." He understands how his undertaking affects the big picture and how the big picture affects his undertaking. Utilizing whole system thinking he is able to tap resource bases many steps removed from his project and also to use his project to increase those resource bases.

Until a manager can engage in whole system thinking, he sees everything in isolation. He views his person as separate and his organization as independent. He is unable to reach out and "touch" the larger universe. Transformation is a process of coming into relationship with new centers of power inside the self and outside the self. Isolation gives way to relationship and everything is seen as connected to and affecting everything else.

Overcoming self ego, family ego, institutional ego, community ego, national ego, and world ego—such is the work of transformation. The ego is a necessary step in the journey into transcendence. It provides the separation necessary to develop individuality. However, at a later stage in evolution the ego must be transcended in order that the person may rejoin the ground of being or "all that is."

In healthcare we will see this same evolutionary sequence from: (1) organizations in isolation, to (2) organizations as part of integrated delivery networks to (3) community as organization. Later evolutionary stages will take us to (4) nation as community, and finally (5) world as community.

American healthcare is currently moving now from stage one to stage two. Competition is still doing its necessary work. Creating healthier communities is the horizon of stage three where collaboration will replace competition as the motivating force for development. Stages four and five will not occur for many years.

The transformational leader is a pivot point for this evolutionary sequencing in healthcare. He now pushes organizational boundaries outwards from institutional ego to community ego. Later, he will push from community ego to national ego, etc.

Interlude III

To be effective the transformational leader must always be operating one circle of expansion larger than the status quo consciousness. If he operates more than one circle size larger, he can lose his relevance to status quo consciousness. He must always function as a bridge between adjacent rings. Of course, at a personal level he may be much more expanded than this, however, at an organizational level he must work within the consensus consciousness to be truly effective and transformational.

Attracts energy, money, and people

The transformational leader is a magnetic center attracting energy, money, and people. He projects a highly focused beam of consciousness into the universe. His personal energy acts like a chaos attractor for unattached resonant energies, events, resources, and individuals which respond to his transmission and stream toward him.

Reality is a transformational dance. It is highly interactive. The universe is an interlocking energy grid. Any energy you emit becomes caught up in the dance. Matching partners come forth to help you complete your dance. You lead. They follow.

It takes a clear, focused mind, powerful imagery, and an act of will to project a beam of consciousness into the Void. Less than this will not work. This explains why many non-transformational managers lack the ability to manifest their desires. The universe cannot reply to a confused signal. Like attracts like.

Any process of transformation whether personal, organizational, or community based requires an admixture of existing and new elements. The new elements must be recruited from the universal supply. The supply exists in the ground of Being (Void). The supply of elements is infinite, but the elements are held in place by strong or weak energy bonds. The transformational leader generates enough power to become an attractor, releasing some of these bonds, thereby causing a stream of new elements to rush into his field of transformation. He becomes a creative node in the ever changing fabric of the universe. He has emitted a soundless sound that is heard throughout the universe. The right people begin appearing on the doorstep, often unsure of what brought them to this place. Necessary resources arrive by phone and mail. The energy level in the field of transformation increases manyfold. The process of transformation is underway.

The motto of the transformational leader is, "everything is always here." Apparent lack is never a supply problem. It is always a consciousness problem. The difference between scarcity and abundance is creativity. Transformation is creativity (creating).

It appears we have a lack of healthcare resources (listen to the debates about reform). This is not the case. We only lack consciousness. Resources are infinite. When our healthcare leaders become transformational leaders, resources will abound. The leaders will then be limited only by their collective imagination. Transformation depends upon conception. You cannot have what you cannot imagine.

Is in tune with the natural rhythms of the planet

The transformational leader is in tune with the natural rhythms of the planet. Everything in nature has a rhythm, an inbreathing and an outbreathing. By harmonizing with planetary rhythm, the leader is able to feel the ebb and flow of planetary energies. There are daily rhythms, weekly rhythms, monthly rhythms, yearly rhythms, seasonal rhythms, rhythms caused by the sunspots, rhythms caused by the passage of the earth through galactic space, etc. Since the human body/mind vehicle is a microcosm of the macrocosm, fluctuations in these universal energy fields impact human life and create corresponding energy flows in the human body.

The reverse is also true, humans can generate powerful energies that impact the universe and alter its functioning. There is only one interconnected body, the universe, and everything in it affects everything else. The rituals at Stonehenge altered the weather, affected crop fertility, and created changes in the movement of heavenly bodies.

Wherever you are standing, that is your point of power. You are a radiant body constantly broadcasting your messages to the worlds.

Mantra, meditation, vision quests, lucid dreaming, and various other psychotechnologies are all strategies for altering personal energy patterns. They are tuning exercises.

To the degree possible, rhythms of nature should be built into patient spaces. Rhythm gives a feeling of security and belonging. It is tangible evidence of the cosmic dance and permits you to know your next steps. Since a rhythm by definition is a repeating pattern, it both confirms your past being and gives you assurance of your continuance.

Rhythm is detected at a cellular level. By listening to your body you connect. You feel the energy inrush and outrush. You become a part of sentient nature.

As the planet moves through high energy belts in outer space it is refreshed and renewed. Much of management is coming into relationship with the natural rhythms of the environment. Many modern healthcare organizations violate this simple way of being in the world. They impose false schedules on living rhythms. The result is confusion.

Just as we now predict the weather, we will one day predict fluctuations in planetary energies that will be affecting people and organizations for the next day, week, month, etc. There are good times to start organizational projects and there are bad times. Because we are multidimensional creatures living in a multidimensional universe, we can be aware of the fluctuating energy patterns around us while we go about our daily duties. When the power is available, we tap into it. Rather than finding our work tiring, we find it refreshing.

Has learned to escape the orbit of his own ego

One of the first challenges for the transformational leader is to escape the orbit of his own ego. The ego likes to think of itself as residing at the center of the universe. Everything revolves around it. This encourages the ego to think it is on center stage and in control of its environment.

Ideas of centrality and control actually imprison the ego in its own shadow. Life then becomes shadow boxing. The ego has generated a false boundary line that captures consciousness and prevents its outward expansion.

To escape the ego, the consciousness must be projected beyond the limits of the body. Reality is where your attention is fixed. Change the focus of your attention and you change your reality. Magic is often defined as the ability, at will, to change the focus of consciousness. The new focus may center at different points in third dimensional space (awareness at a distance) or in other dimensions altogether (alternative realities). Scientists tell us they can demonstrate mathematically the existence of at least ten dimensions in hyperspace. Since we live typically in only three, there are many other places to go. The ego by its very structure is confined to three dimensions. Live in the ego and you live in a universe of only three dimensions.

Experience gained in other dimensions does not translate well into the ego realm. We say the experience is ineffable. If you could translate the experience perfectly as an ego, you would change dimensions immediately, thereby negating the whole point. The best you can do is use metaphors and thought experiments to convey to other ego-bound consciousness what lies beyond three dimensions.

The fourth dimension is a time/space continuum. In it you travel to other times and other spaces. Space travel then becomes a change in dimension, not a change in distance. For the transformational leader this is a big advantage. He has access to the realm of probable futures and the spaces which hold the matrix of third dimensional reality. This permits the leader to direct his organization toward probable futures and arrive there before the natural time of manifestation, thus becoming a prototype or future state existing in the present. Knowing probable futures permits an acceleration through time. You unfold faster and so does your organization and your community.

Transformation by its very nature is hyperdimensional. You certainly have to learn to work in our "solid world" of three dimensions. However, you should not stop there. Your archetype (essence, seed, spirit, soul, Higher Self, energy hologram, etc.) does not reside in the third dimension. It simply reflects into it. Since the universe is self-reflexive by nature, a connection of sorts is possible between the ego and the archetype. In higher dimensions that connection is greatly increased. We say connectivity is greater and therefore the downflow is increased and the ego slowly expands into its higher energy octave which looks like it is disappearing, but is simply moving into a higher matrix of being.

Eventually healthcare managers will operate in hyperspace. However, they cannot do this until they adopt spiritual values and stop playing silly ego games in the marketplace.

Moves the organization beyond its centrism

The transformational leader sees the big picture and therefore is able to move the organization beyond its centrism. Organizational centrism is like ego centrism. It focuses attention on too small a circle while ignoring the larger context.

Transformation is only possible by relating to something larger than the self or the organization. Our universe is a universe of relationships. Centrism ignores interdependency and interlinking. Although the larger world still affects the smaller self, the influence is not recognized.

Since the universe is a ring, within a ring, within a ring, within a ring—one can relate to rings smaller than the one currently occupied or rings larger than the ring of current residence. In both cases, a better perspective results and an ability to understand the mutual influences that always move in all directions.

Smaller rings depend upon you in the same way that you depend upon larger rings. You serve and you are served. You are the agent of transformation for smaller rings. Larger rings are the agent for your transformation. Egocentrism or organizational centrism denies this critical mutuality and isolates the little self.

Systems thinking, systems analysis, and systems design help organizational members understand this network of mutuality. Systems thinking should be taught to all employees in our healthcare institutions.

Once you perceive your self or organization as an address on the net, you have a new sense of security and well being. If the current address proves undesirable for any reason, you can relocate in many different directions.

Collaboration and interagency cooperation flow naturally from the new world view. Out of it grows an integrated community health system built upon a "win-win" mentality. In a net there are no losers, only interdependent players. Whole communities will eventually be transformed by the new paradigm and will become self-sufficient, healthier communities.

The big view at first seems idealistic. Later it appears too confining. It all depends upon your vantage point in the net. Transformation takes place from your current address and takes you to your new location.

TRANSFORMATIONAL LEADERSHIP 115

Pulls levers not available to the linear mind

The transformational leader is able to move freely in the right brain function and is therefore able to view reality in a way not available to the left brain linear mind.

Everything that is, exists at various levels of density. As an object, a thing has its highest density expression. As an energy pattern it exists at a lower density. The right brain can perceive the energy pattern and alter it, therefore changing the object in its high density expression.

In the future, physicians will work directly with the energy body. Changes wrought in this subtle network will then result in changes in the gross physical body. Evidence of impending disease is obvious in the energy bodies long before it appears in the physical body. Much of disease could be eliminated with this type of early detection followed by changes in lifestyle, which would in turn "heal" the energy body.

The same thing is true of organizations. They exist in a solid state. They also exist as emotional, mental and spiritual thought forms. The transformational leader can perceive them at all levels. Trying to change an organization in its highest density state is often an exercise in futility. It requires too much force over too long a time. However, interventions aimed at more subtle organizational states can be effective in a remarkably short length of time.

To deal at subtle organizational levels, the leader must be a working mythologist familiar with spiritual technologies. Celebration, rite, ritual and ceremony are potent organizational change methodologies. Organizational thought forms respond almost immediately to symbolic energies. When employees are caught up in myth and ritual, high psychic energies are released and then express through appropriate organizational channels. This is an alchemy of the mind that changes lead into gold.

Our current emphasis on the business aspects of hospitals, formation of integrated delivery networks, downsizing, competition, etc., destroys the mythic and results in organizational confusion and disarray. Employees are confused and caught up in the negative swirls. They respond in kind with anger, depression, and disease. In this kind of organization the energy fields are weak and misaligned.

The transformational leader understands the need to maintain focused, strong, and inviting spiritual, mental, and emotional thought forms. With these high energies present, the magnetic fields in hospitals are so strong that the more mundane aspects of management are easily accomplished by the employees.

The mandate for the future is the change from a vertical to a virtual organization which in turn is driven by its mythology. Virtuality is a powerful lever available to the transformational manager. What is accomplished on the symbolic level easily generalizes downward to the high density physical level.

TRANSFORMATIONAL LEADERSHIP 116

His mind is radically open to new ideas

The mind of the transformational leader is radically open to new ideas. He understands that his assumptions create his current reality and with a change of assumption, he would experience a change of reality. He knows that imagination is a cherished body sense that permits him to push against his ring of ignorance and explore alternative realities and parallel futures.

The sense of the possible creates a limitation. By making the seemingly impossible, possible, the limitation is removed. Thinking, not the universe, is the constraint. The transformational leader also knows that much of his thinking is word dependent. If he cannot word it, he cannot think it. Learning new vocabularies becomes a path to exploring new realities. There are many exotic vocabularies in science and mysticism and behind each of them lies a corresponding reality open only to those who speak the language.

The transformational leader also knows his thinking is culture dependent. For this reason, he is a student of history, archaeology, and anthropology. To escape the hypnosis of his culture is a major challenge. If a culture says something is not real, it is hard to go against the cultural stream and discover it to be real.

Every culture defines its reality from the infinite possibilities that exist in the Void. No two cultures do this in the same way. For instance, if you are an Australian bushman, you move in the dream time. It is your reality. If you are a typical American in our technological age, not only do you not enter the dream time, you cannot even conceive of its possibility. Yet, your reality and the reality of the bushman are equally real.

Because the mind of the transformational leader is open to many realities, he must decide how much time to spend in each. In a sense, he can experience an identity conflict induced by competing realities. The majority of people will not experience the burden of this joy. Consensual reality is all they know. If fact, the average person shys away from anything that even remotely suggests a challenge to "common sense thinking." They live in one world and do not even suspect the existence of many worlds. To travel in many worlds requires multidimensional awareness and the ability to hold mutually contradictory constructs with ease and an appreciation for their differences. The "many worlds" experience of the universe yields the insight that they are all right, and that none of them are right. Everything in the universe exists in many ways and is never fully revealed in any single way. The transformational leader bridges the gap between the current consensual reality and a future reality waiting for manifestation. The leader lives in two worlds and can make them meet in the circle of his being.

TRANSFORMATIONAL LEADERSHIP 117

Does not limit his mental horizons by thought or belief

The transformational leader does not limit his mental horizons by thought or belief. Often a thought or belief limits the leader by denying vast realms of possibility. In that sense a thought or belief may represent an artificial limitation. What the believer thinks is impossible is in fact impossible for him as long as he thinks it is impossible. History is full of such artificial limitations.

Much of religion has been overturned by science challenging limited assumptions of its doctrines. The doctrines were doctrines of men, not doctrines of God. We often limit God by our presumptions. Every time we do, we end up embarrassed.

The transformational leader may have a very active faith and yet remain open to revision of his faith as greater light streams into his consciousness. The universe is very large and resists our efforts to hem it in by our limited assumptions. Truth is progressive. By that I mean, you progress in your understanding. If you hold the same world view year after year, it is a sign you are not growing in your comprehension of the universe.

It is hard for people to shed old beliefs and habits. The old always gives a sense of security even if it is wrong. The transformational leader does not throw out the baby with the bath water. Some beliefs and values prove themselves over and over again. They are grounded in the sacred scriptures and even more obvious with increased life experience. The leader does not change for the sake of change.

Ask yourself, "Do I hold any thoughts or beliefs from my past that are preventing me from entering a more abundant future? Am I willing to challenge any of my assumptions about the world?"

The reversal of long held assumptions about medical care, hospitals, and doctors may be the most important thing the transformational leader can help his board or medical staff accomplish. The most dangerous assumptions are those that are unconscious. You accept them as common sense. The world is just that way. This is a type of naive perception. Many people do not even know they have a mindset. They assume the way they think it is, is the way it is. This is never true. It is always much more than you think it is. The leader, then, moves in a rather hazardous territory as he challenges long held thoughts and beliefs.

People's sense of security is usually in the past. The transformational leader has to help these people find a security in the future. This often involves developing new expanded thoughts and beliefs better adapted to our changing world.

An open mind permits an open reality. A closed mind creates a closed reality.

Interlude III

TRANSFORMATIONAL LEADERSHIP 118

Pursues truth wherever it may lead

The transformational leader is not a captive of any inherited or learned belief system. He feels free to pursue truth wherever it may lead. Any belief system is viewed as an approximation of the truth, a vehicle that will take him the next step in his eternal journey of progression. However, the leader is loyal to the system he now lives in and will remain with it until something better comes into view. He is not a nihilist. He simply understands the Cosmos is too big to be captured by any one conceptualization, no matter how grand. The transformational leader tries to increase his circle size through continuous expansion of his insight and practice. He is eager for new and transcendent experiences.

The transformational leader tries to convey this same continuous learning mindset to his organization. He labors to build a learning organization, open to new possibilities as they appear on spiritual and mental horizons. A learning organization escapes the orbit of its past as it journeys into the future. Although the transformational leader is an innovator and keen observer of the times, he is not easily caught up in the latest fads and fashions. More attuned to the infinite, he is less likely to be swept up in the forms of mass consciousness.

The transformational leader pursues truth. He does this through study, meditation, and communication with others on the path. Not content to simply plod along in mass consciousness, the leader must frequently escape the pack and sit alone upon the mountaintop. For that reason, transformational leaders often experience periods of loneliness. They hear the sound of a different drummer. Yet, their responsibilities in their organizations require a constant focus on current reality. The dissonance between these two rhythms is a constant source of frustration. But transformation requires this dissonance. The leader is the bridge between two worlds. He must be involved in both at the same time and feel the tug of each on the other. The body/mind vehicle of the transformational leader is a chemical retort. His is the job of spiritual alchemy. He will bridge the actual and the ideal. He will transform lead into gold. Then the gold must be refined into an even finer gold.

The work of transformation is hard but offers a joy all of its own. The destiny of planets is closely linked to the consciousness of their highest life forms. Planets move through stages of evolution just as people do. Agents of transformation participate in the unfoldment of planets. Consciousness builds upon itself. Any individual or organizational benefit quickly becomes a planetary benefit. Therefore a transformational leader works both for time and for eternity.

TRANSFORMATIONAL LEADERSHIP 119

Nothing is viewed as impossible

For the transformational leader nothing is viewed as impossible. Everything that can happen (in the universe), will happen, at some time, in some place. Why not here? Why not now? In other words all combinations and permutations occur sometime, somewhere in the universe. In fact, the atoms have a type of intelligence that impels them to try out new combinations. This is the source of alternative realities and parallel universes. Matter has an inborn desire to combine, and recombine in all forms, in all places, and at all times. For this reason at any particular time, in any specific place, there are parallel realities that may be entered by simply changing the focus of awareness. Reality is where your attention is fixed. A change of attention is a change of reality. Just as cyberspace creates computer-generated worlds ready for exploration, so in the mental and emotional planes (dimensions) are worlds ready for exploration.

In another sense, to have simply thought of something, means that it exists. It exists as a thought form. All you need to do is add density to it and it exists in the material plane. The ultimate limit you face is simply your imagination. If you can imagine it, it exists. Therefore nothing is impossible. The only limitation is your ability to conceive of a possibility. That is why science fiction is so important and why it acts as a stimulus to scientific development.

Many thoughts that enter your head come from the thought stream. They simply flow through your consciousness. Because you are not attentive, you fail to recognize you did not generate them. You accept them as your own. Each of these thoughts exists and has its own life. However, it is possible, although not likely, for you to think of something for the first time. In that event you would create it. Mental substance is plastic and takes the forms we give it. Think an original thought and it exists in mental substance. At that point it enters the thought stream and can be accessed by any mind tuned to its frequency. Perhaps another person accessing the thought will add density to it and cause it to appear as a real object on the material plane. You gave the idea birth in mental substance. Another person gives its birth in the third dimension.

The transformational leader is skilled in helping people think thoughts that were previously "impossible" for them. In this way he makes the thoughts possible and invites the people to take the new thoughts, add density to them and birth them on the material plane. In this way the transformational leader is a mentor to the healthcare organization. She pushes back the limits of possibility. A good leader challenges the impossible and makes it possible. Thoughts are subtler on the emotional plane than the physical plane. They are subtler on the mental plane than the emotional plane. They are most subtle and difficult to reach on the spiritual plane. To reach spiritual thoughts, deep meditation is necessary. When the spiritual dimension is reached, a limitless realm is entered. Truly, it is a wonder to be a child of an infinite universe.

Interlude III

TRANSFORMATIONAL LEADERSHIP 120

He knows that anything that can happen, will happen

The transformational leader views the universe as infinite possibility waiting to happen. What does it wait upon? It waits upon you to volunteer yourself as a channel of manifestation, to become a conduit for third dimensional realization.

The universe is a living demonstration of outrageous creativity (the mind of God displayed in high density matter) where anything that can happen, will happen, in some place, at some time—why not here?—why not now? This leads to the doctrine of emergence. If everything is trying to happen, why not just enable the thing of your preference to happen through its emergence as a natural phenomenon? The phenomenon of emergent leadership is at marked variance with the prevailing idea of leaders who "make" things happen whether they want to happen or not. The latter kind of leadership is violent. It wrests things out of context and is always followed by a backlash as the natural order of the universe seeks to restore equilibrium. Emergent leadership, by contrast is gentle and ecological. There is no backlash, since the leader merely "bends the twig in order to help the tree grow in a direction that will avoid its future obstruction." The leader is thus a friend of nature. He is an agent of potentiation that assists nature in its natural patterns of unfoldment. The transformational leader is open to the possibilities of the moment and moves in a simple and natural way to achieve preferred possibilities. He practices co-evolution and views nature as an ally, not something to be vanquished.

The transformational leader lives in a big universe. Like the iceberg, it is mostly out of normal view. What is visible is existence. What is invisible is "inistence." The leader seeks to make the "inistent," existent. This requires archetypal vision or sensing. What is the larger pattern here? What is trying to happen? How can I assist the natural process of evolutionary unfoldment?

Transformational leadership is spiritual leadership. It is accomplished through meditation, study and reflection. It requires the unfoldment of spiritual senses, each having their correlates in physical reality. Spiritual seeing, hearing, smelling, tasting, and touching correlate with but greatly extend the range of the physical senses. In addition there are senses that have no correlation in physical reality, but are unique to their own spiritual dimension. In this sense, the transformational leader is a dweller in two worlds, the world of the manifest and the world of the unmanifest. He passes easily from one realm to the other and is a bearer of gifts to both.

TRANSFORMATIONAL LEADERSHIP 121

He views reality as preference, not necessity

The transformational leader lives in a world of probable realities. For him, reality is a preference, not a necessity. In the best tradition of postmodernism, the transformational leader knows that social reality is a human invention. It is what people say it is—no more, no less.

As a student of history, the transformational leader studies past cultures. Each of these historical cultures lived in a different reality, with different religious, political, and economic systems. Each felt their reality was the true and only possible reality. As far as we know none of the cultures consciously invented their worlds. It was usually given to them by the "gods" and passed down to succeeding generations. In that sense, reality was unconscious and not a matter of choice. All that is now changed as we prepare to enter a new millennium. Our future realities will be a matter of collective choice. We are the first generation to engage in conscious world building. We will imagine and then reinvent our world.

An invented reality doesn't need to be a mere figment of the human imagination, although it could be that as we see in the virtual worlds of cyberspace. An invented reality can draw upon larger superordinate systems existing in the universe. Reaching out to God or the Source to determine macro level patterns in the universe and then reflecting these patterns into our 3D reality is a perfectly acceptable methodology. In fact, it is probably the method of choice if we wish our reality to be in sync with other superordinate realities in the universe. We can invent heaven or hell on this earth and use archetypal patterns for our creative efforts.

In our new century, America will become the pattern maker for created realities. For the first time, mass consciousness will achieve the potency to engage in co-creation. Other nations will model our success. Transformational politics is even now appearing on the American horizon. Most of the current problems in our society are unsolvable given the current reality frame. They cannot be "fixed," but many of them can be designed-out. The healthier communities effort is an important national initiative to redesign human habitats and generate health. Hospitals and other healthcare organizations must rise to this important historical occasion. This is our window of opportunity to use healthcare as the gateway to total societal redesign, beginning at the neighborhood level.

Because different people need different environments in order to unfold their inner potentials, an array of designer realities must be created. The environment is then viewed as a training space, an artificial womb, to be used for a time and then discarded as the person needs a larger reality for a further expansion of consciousness.

What an exciting time to be in healthcare!

TRANSFORMATIONAL LEADERSHIP 122

He knows that nothing has to be the way it is

The transformational leader knows that all reality is tentative, provisional, and consensual. Nothing has to be the way it is. It could just as well be some other way. Reality is held in place by a mindset. A change of mind is a change of reality. For each reality in manifestation, there are many other probable realities waiting to manifest. They wait in the wings, so to speak, until they are invoked by a change of mind.

The transformational leader thus lives in a reality of his own choosing. He tunes in to what is and what could just as well be and then makes choices. This often produces a frustration, as the leader realizes that the ideal is just a thought away, yet, people choose to remain within their own self-imposed limitations. The tension between what is and what could be is a burden all transformational leaders carry.

Because nothing has to be the way it is, the transformational leader always scans for the array of things wanting to happen. The universe is always trying to happen in all possible ways. If the leader can arrange (stage) the environment properly, things trying to happen, will happen. They will emerge as naturally as a flower opens to the sun.

The transformational leader opens himself to the possibilities of the moment and acts upon the inherent potentials of that moment. This requires a special frame of mind in the leader. He must not override the potentials of the moment with any preconceived notions or plans. To have a sense of direction, yet be open to infinite potential, is the balancing act required of all transformational leaders. This is often apparent in the way the leader "listens" to his environment. He is very sensitive to small potentials existing in any human situation. He will often incubate metanoia with such an attitude. The miracle may only happen once, because that was the time and place of the opening.

Because the universe is dynamic there are always windows opening and closing. The reality mix is like a collage of intersecting possibilities. The leader like an artist must choose from the palette what will appear on the canvass of reality. In that sense, reality is always an art form. It is what the artist calls forth from the possibilities in the canvass and the possibilities in the color palette.

You happen to reality as much as reality happens to you. Reality is always a conversation, a transaction between you as the observer and the observed. It is always open to radical redefinition unless you accept it simply for what it appears to be. Think of yourself as an artist. Think of your situation as the canvass. What are you going to call forth?

TRANSFORMATIONAL LEADERSHIP 123

He can substitute one reality for another

One of the great powers of transformational leadership is the ability to substitute one reality for another. Any given reality is seen as tentative, provisional, and consensual. It is not enduring and can be changed by an act of redefinition by the leader.

We should live in a world of our own choosing. We are the designers. Reality is what we design. Rather than adapt to the level of crime, disease, ignorance, and poverty in a society, we should transform the society. This is sometimes called co-evolution and simply refers to the fact that a potent person, organization, or community can re-design the environment.

Goals of the healthier communities movement include habitat redesign, generation of health, reduction of crime, better education, and economic development. An attempt is made not just to enlarge the emergency room, but to decrease the need for it. Much of the use of the ER is lifestyle related and therefore preventable.

We are moving toward "designer planet status" and will eventually become the builders of a new era of health and longevity. We do this, not by adapting to disease, but by generating health.

The substitution of reality becomes possible when we discover reality is a social invention (postmodernism) and is what we say it is. Earlier cultures thought their realities were the only way things could be. They accepted the inevitability of a reality. In America, we are coming to realize that reality is not inevitable. It is an invention. It may be either unconscious or conscious, but it is invented. Since it is invented, it can be re-invented. How encouraging to discover that most of our societal problems can be designed out—not designed out in a "Big Brother" fashion, but by attunement to the same Spirit that pervades all realities.

The building blocks of consciousness, time, space, matter, and energy are provided to humankind by the Source. What we do with these is a matter of our own concern. We can assemble heaven or hell from the same parts. As we become conscious designers, we will discover we have all that we need planet-wide to live lives of abundance and joy. We will soon live longer and better. We will eventually colonize outer space.

It is an exciting time to be in healthcare. Healthcare is the gateway to total societal redesign. Let us reach out to our communities and begin designing a new reality, a new reality for a new century.

TRANSFORMATIONAL LEADERSHIP 124

He often reverses organizational reality

What is reality? Why is the reverse not also possible? A thing and its opposite may both be true. Reality does not have to be any particular way. The transformational leader is tuned in to the possibilities of the moment. He understands that alternative realities always exist, waiting to be invoked. Reality is what we say it is. Reality is a social invention, the creation of our collective mind. This is another way of saying that reality is made up as we go along. It is a story we write.

Most people accept the legitimacy of the current reality. They suppose it to be true and valid. Their job is to adapt to it and do as well as they can in the process. We see this currently in healthcare. The "in-thing" is specialty hospitals, geographic concentration, competition, mergers and acquisitions, etc. Few people ask, "Is this the kind of reality we want to create?" We could end up inventing a new healthcare system everyone dislikes. Yet, I see little evidence that providers are taking responsibility for our newest healthcare creations. Most providers just get in line and follow the leader without asking where the journey is taking them. Another way of saying this is that our society is not yet conscious of itself and its ability to self-create its reality. In terms of social reality, we are the rule makers. It is what we say it is.

I see this same phenomenon at the personal level. People accept their life situations without asking about the necessity or desirability of those situations. Why do they adapt to negative environments when they could just as well co-create positive behavioral settings? The answer to the dilemma at both the societal and personal levels is the same. It is a question of consciousness. At lower levels of consciousness, you must adapt to what is. At higher levels of consciousness, you have the option to co-create what could just as well be.

Utilizing the visioning process, the board, medical staff, and management can co-create the destiny of the hospital. Co-creation means the outcome of the vision is a vector of the combined forces of the hospital group and the larger environment. We never create in a vacuum. We have the ability to rearrange time, space, energy, and matter. We do not create them. We may obey the laws of the land at the same time we are re-inventing them. We may submit to the accreditation process at the same time we are in the process of re-inventing it. We may practice allopathic medicine at he same time we are setting up complementary and alternative medicine clinics. We may work with managed care at the same time we are seeking a better payment alternative. The rule is simple. Take responsibility for what is—own it—and then, transform it.

TRANSFORMATIONAL LEADERSHIP 125

He sees ahead in time and knows what the organization can become

The transformational leader is less bound by time than his peers. He lives suspended between the present and the future and can therefore see into the future. What he sees are probabilistic realities competing for manifestation. He sees the most probable future for his organization but also less probable futures that may, in fact, be more desirable.

The current rush of events often catches up his organization and pushes it along its current course. The job of the transformational leader is to help the organization take a "time out" to consider the most probable versus the most desirable future. By taking the right action the organization can change its probable future into its preferred future. This often means pushing against the tide of events and thereby establishing an island in the current. At this point, things will get rather chaotic until the organization moves into a new pattern of equilibrium with its environment.

Any organization exists as an idea in the mind of the universe. This idea exists outside the limitations of time, space, and condition. It is a pure idea (in the Platonic sense) and therefore is capable of infinite extension in time and throughout space. The infinite extension of the idea creates the capacity for organizational potentiation. Potentiation means the organization slowly becomes what it already is but has not yet arrived at. It unfolds in time. The implicate becomes explicate. To perceive this potential destiny, the transformational leader must move beyond his current limitations of time and space (third dimension). He does this in deep meditative states where his consciousness soars unfettered by the limitations of the third dimension. The answer to his organization's potential exists in the fourth, fifth, and sixth dimensions. Here, swirling patterns of pure possibility exist, waiting to take shape in the lower dimensions.

By invoking its potential in higher dimensions, the organization moves beyond the orbit of evolutionary necessity. It escapes cultural conditioning and transcends many environmental limitations faced by its peer organizations. It moves into a state of metanoia where the improbable becomes the possible. This same set of dynamics exists for people operating in the third dimension. The potentiation of people and the potentiation of organizations are related. To become a transformational organization, you must transform its managers. In this sense, personal development is a precondition for organizational development. You can't have one without the other. Living entirely in the present is an evolutionary dead-end as our investor-owned chains are discovering.

Living in the future is the pathway for evolutionary progression of the not-for-profit hospitals in the United States. However, this high destiny is not assured. It depends upon the presence of transformational leaders.

Interlude III

TRANSFORMATIONAL LEADERSHIP 126

Forces or accelerates the evolution of the organization

The transformational leader forces or accelerates the evolution of his organization. He understands that any organization has an infinite potential to unfold as an idea in time. The organization's natural rate of unfoldment normally depends upon the rate of change in its immediate environment. However, it also has a potential to "fast track" and demonstrate in a few years what would ordinarily take decades to achieve.

To invoke the future form of their organization, selected organizational members must meet in quiet reflection and seek to resonate with the spiritual currents that hold the organization in material manifestation. Utilizing their sacred imagination, organizational members can touch the subtle patterns beginning to coalesce prior to manifestation. These subtle currents naturally descend slowly into manifestation on the material plane. However, they can be drawn down into materiality much faster if they are attracted by the powers of group imagination. When organizational members first attempt this exercise, they may think they are making the images up in their own minds. Later they realize the collective group mind is reaching out to attract existing subtle patterns already residing in spiritual dimensions.

It takes lots of practice to know whether the origin of a thought is inside or outside your head. The reason is simple. You must attune the inner mind to attract what is in the outer mind. They are very similar stimuli and easily mistaken for one another. When you experience morphic resonance for the first time, you will swear you generated the idea, when in fact you simply became a channel for it.

The transformational leader must exercise caution in his attempts at accelerated evolution. If he moves too quickly, the existing organizational forms will shatter. If he moves too slowly the forms will rigidify. Every organizational form has an inherent elasticity, which must be respected. Like the ego of a person, the form cannot be "hurried" beyond a certain rate of expansion. However, the transformational leader can improve the "fitness" of the organization for transformation. He can teach classes in personal and organizational evolution. He can coach individuals. He can utilize site visits, visiting consultants and literature reviews to great advantage. All depends upon readiness.

Many healthcare organizations have no personal development or group development programs in existence. Accordingly there is little personal or group capacity for change. In these instances, it may take several years of preparation before accelerated evolution is possible.

Does not push the organization beyond its limits

Any given form in the universe has only so much elasticity. Push it beyond this point and it implodes or explodes. An organization is no exception to this general rule. The transformational leader senses the limits of elasticity of her organization and works within these parameters until she can expand the organization's ring. This requires a delicate sense of balance. If the leader does not push hard enough, she loses valuable evolutionary time. If she pushes too hard, she is likely to set back considerably the course of the organization.

Elasticity may vary by organizational level. The board may be more elastic than the CEO but less elastic than the medical staff. Since these levels all must be satisfied, the transformational leader often works differently within each level, but hopes there will be some transference from one level to another.

Elasticity of the organization is often related to the amount of change in its environment. If the environment has been stable for a long period of time, the organization tends to be more rigid than it would be in a more dynamic space. One of the major functions of chaos is to break down rigidities and calcifications. This is precisely what is happening in healthcare today. The environment is changing rapidly and challenging all organizational forms. Some organizations are being stretched beyond their limits. Confusion often reigns in these organizations. They may simply fail or sell.

An effective transformational leader will attempt to get key organizational members away from the institution on continuing education trips and site visits. This helps expand the rings of these organizational members. When they return from the visit they are more open to new ideas and experiences. We are the result of our experiences. If we have led a sheltered life, we have very little concept of the possible.

Of course meditation and spiritual experiences also open the mind and make it more elastic. When boundaries of inner space expand, boundaries of external space also become larger. The outer reflects the inner.

The ring of consciousness is often called "the ring pass not." It represents the boundary of your awareness as well as the perceived boundary of your external environment. It is what you push against in order to grow. The boundary gives you definition but also limits your knowledge and expression. What is a boundary for one person may be an open gateway for another individual. Just as people are limited by the size of their rings, so are organizations. It is always a matter of elasticity.

Interlude III

TRANSFORMATIONAL LEADERSHIP 128

View problems as opportunities

The transformational leader understands that all growth occurs by pushing against a resistance. If there is no resistance in the environment, the organism cannot develop any competence or mastery. The organism must define itself against a background of resisting forces. It pushes and grows in the process. It learns to incorporate its environment and expands its circle of competence to include ever more of the environment.

This same law applies to human beings. Accordingly, the transformational manager views all problems as opportunities. The organization grows as it solves first small and then larger problems of integration and differentiation. Problem solving creates a higher degree of inner capacity. The brain is channelized through experience. Problems create a high degree of attention focus and therefore better channelization. In addition, problems cause the organism to explore its environment and discover new resources and allies. Thus, problem solving causes both inner growth and a better understanding of the larger universe.

Often the transformational leader is surrounded by people who are problem avoiders. They dislike change and resist new routines. The leader must teach these people the creative process and enable them to relish change and its attendant opportunities. The ability to embrace chaos and relish change is a function of the degree of personal security and comfort. Insecure people have a tough time getting through their own inner turbulence. For this reason, the transformational leader schedules personal growth courses in the hospital. As employees are able to expand their own rings of consciousness they are able to tolerate higher degrees of disorder in the environment. With greater inner comfort, employees learn to seek out change and become creative problem solvers.

We are entering a high change era in healthcare. More than ever before, transformational leaders must train their organizations to use creative imagination to pattern chaos into cosmos. In the next few years a window of opportunity opens for the transformation of American society. Healthcare must be the gateway for this societal transformation. Management becomes design and at its highest level, management is creation. At first problems assume a negative form. Later they assume a positive form as challenges to organizational creativity. Then there are approach behaviors rather than avoidance activities among members of the board, medical staff and management. The hospital becomes a leader in the creation of healthier communities. It becomes a guiding force in habitat redesign.

TRANSFORMATIONAL LEADERSHIP 129

He is value directed

The transformational leader is value directed. He attempts to realize the right, the good and the true. To his values, the leader adds knowledge and power thus realizing the three dimensions of transformational leadership. It is useful to think of these three dimensions as three sides of a management triangle. By bringing these three dimensions—values, knowledge and power—into perfect balance, the leader is able to create in the material plane.

Values are affections of the heart. They are mental, emotional and spiritual in nature. They form the basis for discrimination and conscience. Values may be inferred from a person's behavior. We act upon our values. They create a feeling of goodness and security in us as we relate to the universe. Love is the primary value in the universe. From this root value other values radiate in many directions.

Many of the problems we are currently experiencing in American healthcare can be traced to faulty values, i.e., values not based on compassion and love. When a healthcare provider believes making a profit is more important than helping children in the community without basic health services, we have a value problem. When people do not love their own bodies and care for them, this faulty value will manifest as lifestyle violations. When we do not love and value the earth we have environmental health problems. When we do not love the people living in other countries, we have war, etc.

The evolution of consciousness is always in the direction of adopting more inclusive values. Love of the self evolves into love of others and finally love of the All. A hospital is at first concerned only with its own patients. With expansion of consciousness, it becomes concerned with the health of all people who live in the community. A hospital is first an institution with walls. Later it evolves into an institution without walls.

The budget provides the best documentation for what a hospital values. It is therefore the primary ethical document in the institution. Resource allocation is an ethical act based upon values, whether it is a household budget or an institutional budget that is being considered. Observing what percentage of the budget is spent on prevention tells the story of the institution's values regarding disease prevention vs. disease treatment.

Transformational Leadership—Continued

A transformational leader values transformation above all things. He believes that spiritual development is the ultimate purpose for both people and institutions on this planet.

Interlude III

TRANSFORMATIONAL LEADERSHIP 130

Is both a culture builder and a culture changer

The transformational leader is both a culture builder and a culture changer. He seeks to reinforce the good in existing organizational structures, but also seeks to go beyond these limiting forms to higher energy expressions. Therefore, the transformational leader is an agent of both culture maintenance and culture change.

The transformational leader knows that all future progress builds upon present structures. Each evolutionary step creates the foundation for succeeding steps. Deterioration of an existing form is always bad. It causes a setback in the progression of unfoldment. By keeping his attention focused upon both the present and the future, the transformational leader is able to orchestrate the evolutionary unfoldment of any energy form, be that a person, organization, or community.

An energy form is any form that embodies Spirit. Forms both express and limit Spirit. A form can hold only a finite amount of Spirit. If more Spirit were to flow through the form, it would destroy it. Typically, forms expand to the limits of their structural capacity in an attempt to express greater and greater amounts of Spirit. At some point the expansion limits of the form are attained. Now, Spirit can descend in no greater magnitude until it can induce a transformation of the form. The form must undergo metamorphosis in order to attract and express yet higher levels of Spirit.

Since Spirit resides above the Line of Creation it is not limited by time, space, or condition. When it incarnates below the Line of Creation it is limited by all three. Because of this difference in dimensionality of entities above and below the Line of Creation, Infinite Spirit impulses (verb) an infinite progression of forms below the Line of Creation as it seeks to manifest itself in the third dimension. The transformational leader can feel the impulses (noun) of Spirit and can also sense the limitations of form. This gives the transformational leader an ability to facilitate "reductions of the Spirit" and expansions of embodying forms. Hence, the transformational leader is like an electric transformer with different voltages on different sides of its coils. Mentoring is a type of transformational leadership. It depends upon the ability of the mentor to match the descent of Spirit with the ascent of the protégé's form nature.

The function of chaos is to break up old limiting forms and prepare the way for metamorphosis and the resulting embodiment of higher levels of Spirit. The transformational leader views chaos as an ally. He embraces chaos as a long lost friend that enables the transformation of high density forms. Future years are just such a period in American healthcare. They will permit the transformation of our healthcare industry.

Interlude III

TRANSFORMATIONAL LEADERSHIP 131

Recruits organizational members by consciousness

The transformational leader recognizes people on the basis of their consciousness or internal properties. He is able to recruit them to positions they can fill because they are qualified to perform the required tasks. Although the transformational leader takes into account credentials, experience, and references, he really selects people on the basis of their consciousness.

To do this the transformational leader must be able to perceive consciousness in another person. He may sense it, see it, hear it, feel it, or intuit it. The perceptual modality chosen depends upon which spiritual channels are open in the leader.

As we move into our new century, a greater number of people will manifest extrasensory perception. This will cause a shift in our concept of leadership and followership. In an ideal society, those who serve are the best qualified to serve in a particular capacity. There can be little doubt about that since internal qualities are immediately obvious to anyone who cares to look. Politics and deception no longer play a role in political or organizational advancement. Of course, this heightened perceptual ability will not be fully developed until the end of our century but it will begin to emerge in the next few years.

Organizations in general assume a more spiritual form as we move into the future. Gross matter is replaced by subtle matter, better able to reflect and carry emotional, mental, and spiritual messages. In the progress of history, aristocracy gives way to meritocracy which in turn gives way to a spiritual hierarchy where occupational position is always earned and is appropriate.

However, transformational leaders even now can apply this principle in the formation of management teams. It is necessary to have some type of consciousness taxonomy and the required perceptiveness to employ it. The Myers-Briggs is an early attempt to use this method of recruitment by consciousness. Of course, this inventory does not require any extrasensory capacity. The Hartman value profile is another excellent instrument.

On a good management team you need a sensor, feeler, thinker and intuiter. You need a balance of right and left brain function. You need a balance of introversion and extroversion. You can then orchestrate the consciousness of the team or load it in a particular direction depending upon the tasks you want to accomplish.

In hospital-based leadership training programs it is important to help participants identify their "consciousness type" and then develop the ability to identify the "consciousness type" of other team members. Of course, you do not want to just typecast individuals. You have to know what the next steps will be after the initial classification.

Growth and change are not only possible, but desirable. However, this growth can best take place if team members understand types of consciousness and how to build extrasensory capabilities upon each type.

TRANSFORMATIONAL LEADERSHIP 132

Seeks a diversity of skills on the management team

The transformational leader seeks diversity in everything he does. This applies especially to members of the management team. Diversity assures the team can address a wide range of issues and bring a high level of creativity to problem solution.

The challenge of diversity is unified action. The more heterogeneous a group, the more difficult it is to manage. Cherishing diversity is a value that must be learned by team members. Cherishing differences goes beyond tolerance. It is an attitude that comes about when team members understand that diversity and interdependence are prime variables in creation. Diversity is Divine.

When you understand the System of which you are a part, you perceive the Divine intention in diversity. You are related to all that is in its infinite range of manifestation and splendor.

The orchestration of diversity requires a knowledge of how the pieces fit together. How do you relate team members that manifest intuition, feeling, thinking and sensing? How do you integrate right and left brain function? Knowing how the pieces fit together requires a transcendent view. The transformational leader must rise above the fray at least long enough to perceive emergent solutions that are waiting to happen.

The human body is a marvel of diversity and unity. A human community is a marvel of diversity but not unity. We have not yet learned to build human communities that emulate the connectedness of biological systems. As Kevin Kelley points out in "Out of Control" we will soon witness the rise of a neobiological civilization where human systems will be patterned upon biological models. This suggests a new role for physicians who are "experts" in a biological model (the human body), but are seldom involved in the design of healthier communities. Physicians must learn to think of the community as a body with all its necessary parts and connections. A new role for physicians will be community organization and development.

A great problem with some of our integrated healthcare organizations is their tendency to reduce diversity in the name of standardization. I believe standardization is a fetish of small minds. Indeed, if necessary, the integrated delivery organization should subsidize diversity in order to match its array of services with the natural diversity of the human community it serves.

Does not take credit for the success of his vision

The transformational leader has escaped the orbit of his ego and does not seek credit for his accomplishments. Furthermore, he realizes that his success depends upon the contributions of many people working together. All is one. The one cannot exist without the other. All work together for the good of the whole. The leader is quick to give recognition to the contributions of others, but slow to accept recognition for himself. This attitude comes not from a sense of false modesty, but from a deep realization of how dependent any transformational leader is upon the people around him.

For a vision to succeed it must be held in common by the group of people who will implement it. The leader does not bestow the vision upon others, rather he works with others to generate the vision as a product of group intention and visualization. The vision must reach deep into the psyche of all those who will invoke its possibility. Each group member contributes his experience and energy to the vision. The vision draws upon all of them and in turn feeds all of them. The vision is a vast energy reservoir, a collective thought form that will have a life of its own. The idea has become an entity upon its own plane of existence. It will seek its own realization through any existing channels. An open channel on the other side of the world can attract the vision and embody it. In this manner the vision can spawn multiple realizations in many parts of the world. The vision is not the property of the group that generated it. Like children of parents, the vision develops a life of its own. On the reverse side of this equation, you can become the willing manifestation of a vision generated by another group at another time. The secret is to attune yourself to the possibility waiting to happen. Through meditation and reflection you can create an open consciousness that will birth visions seeking incarnation.

The success of a vision depends not only upon its potency but upon its cultural fit. A vision may be before its time or after its time. If the vision is not attracted into material manifestation it remains in waiting until receptive conditions are created sometime, somewhere. A transformational leader may thus attract a vision generated centuries before in another period of history. The vision will be received in a moment of inspiration. The exact form it takes will be modified by the consciousness of its recipient. Therefore the same vision may assume different forms depending upon the mental conditions of the recipients.

Interlude III

A group attuned to a vision will receive more than a single individual since the diversity of group members will attract diverse elements of the vision. This is why it is desirable to orchestrate the consciousness of the visioning group in such a way that all types are represented. A balanced and diverse visioning group gives birth to the full incarnational breadth of the vision.

Escapes the crowd to renew her energies

It is in the quiet that energies of the soul are renewed. The transformational leader knows she must escape the roar of the crowd and go into the desert or into the mountains to find repose and let her Spirit soar to heavenly realms.

When this is not possible, meditation in the home or office will serve the same purpose, although less completely. Nature supplies many vibrant energies not found in human made environments. The trees, birds, plants, wind, sun, and rain are filled with life-restoring energies that buoy up the soul and enable it to transcend the immediate environment and ascend into higher dimensions of consciousness.

An important lesson any transformational leader must learn is orchestration of psychic energy, using no more than required for the task at hand. Orchestration of energy is both an energy conservation and an energy focusing technique. Many people use a cannon to attack their problems when a pea shooter would work. They exhaust their daily energy supply before completing their daily tasks.

Sleep provides an important highway into superconscious realms. From lucid dreaming to ascent into higher dimensions, psychic energy is required. If you are too tired when you go to bed at night, the required energy is not present. Watching TV before going to bed is probably the worst thing you can do. It fills the mind with an array of confused thought forms and also creates a psychic energy leakage. Inspirational reading, meditation, or soothing music is a great prelude to a night of "traveling."

You should monitor your energy level throughout the day. When you find it running low, do whatever is necessary to rebuild the supply. A brisk walk, meditation, or set of affirmations may do the trick. Microsleep provides some of the same energy building potential.

Remain vigilant to any work situations or people that act as energy drains or "sinks." Avoid these if possible. If not, then build up your energy levels before encountering them. No one has a "right" to drain your energy. Learning to build your energy shield can be quite helpful.

Of course, worry, envy, anger or any other negative emotions should be avoided to the degree possible. These emotions act like a short circuit in your psychic energy system. Love, hope, peace, and compassion have just the opposite effect. The main thing is to be aware of all energy exchanges. You are an energy machine operating in an energy universe.

He knows how to enter the thought stream

The transformational leader perceives a thought stream surrounding our planet. It is a running river of the collective thoughts of humankind. In it are thoughts at all stages of development. The transformational leader in a meditative state can tap into this steam. He can draw from it and add to it.

The thought stream is a major reservoir of creativity. Inventors often access it unconsciously. This explains how simultaneous inventions occur. Different people in different places on the planet are feeding off of the same root thoughts.

Discrete thoughts can be picked from the stream or thoughts can be combined in new and novel ways. What cannot be accessed from the stream are thoughts that do not exist in it. Therefore at any given time the evolutionary potential of the planet can be determined from the potentials of the thoughts that circulate in the stream. The stream is a byproduct of mind. Although the brain is the instrument of thought for humans it is not necessary for mind. Mind is nonlocal. Brain is local.

There are special types of individuals who spend their time "seeding" the stream. These are conscious agents of evolution who create possibilities other minds can access and further develop. Once a mind has generated a thought, it enters the stream. It is already a "thing." It exists and has density in its own realm. Of course it may exist only as an infant thought and may require the work of many minds before it reaches maturity and descends into manifestation in the third dimension.

Future healthcare organizations will appoint a group of visionaries who regularly access the stream to assure the organization's pathway on the leading edge of evolutionary possibility. This is beginning to occur in this century as we begin to escape the materialistic stranglehold on our healthcare system and begin to adopt a more spiritual orientation. Before long, visionaries from various healthcare institutions will be mind-linked and will constitute a very special group. They will seed the stream by forming a group mind (morphogenetic field) that takes them beyond the thought possibilities of any single group member.

If these ideas seem a little farfetched to you, be assured they will occur as we begin to create virtual organizations and move into cyberspace.

Interlude III

The current chaos we are experiencing is a signal of a rapid evolutionary change occurring on our planet. Ten years from now we will live in a very different world. It will be more a world of mind and less a world of matter. Actually, it would be more accurate to say matter will become more spiritualized.

She is often a lucid dreamer

The transformational leader is often a lucid dreamer. The reason is quite simple. The dreamband where lucid dreaming occurs must be passed through on the way to other dimensions of consciousness. In a sense, we go to sleep and wake up again each time we change dimensions of consciousness. So from waking, we go to sleeping. From sleeping we go to dreaming. From dreaming we go to the borderland between dimensions where out-of-body experiences occur, etc. The secret is to maintain continuity of consciousness as we move from state to state.

In the lucid dream state, you are aware that you are dreaming as you are dreaming. You may attain lucidity in an ordinary dream or you may move directly into the lucid state when falling asleep.

In the lucid state you will feel a great excitement, buoyancy, clarity of mind, and freedom from the body. You can make a mental command to be a particular place or do a particular thing and it will manifest immediately. The best command to make when attaining lucidity is "take me to where I need to go, to learn what I most need to know." Immediately, you will find yourself in some type of learning situation, probably a class.

From my explorations in the lucid state, I have determined there is not a direct correlation between what you experience "there" and what is going on in third dimensional reality. Does this mean that you are only exploring your own mental ideas and not the world as it exists? I suspect you are in two worlds at the same time with a mixing of the experiences of both. It takes practice to separate out the various elements and make sense of them.

For the transformational leader, lucid dreaming provides an opportunity to explore the preferable and probable futures by living in them. It also releases tremendous creativity since in the lucid state you have access to everything that has ever occupied your consciousness as well as the collective awareness of humankind (the thought stream). From the lucid state it is possible to enter higher states of awareness. In a sense, lucid dreaming is the gateway to higher dimensions of consciousness.

The future healthcare administrator possesses multidimensional consciousness. She is able to work both in the realms of matter and the higher realms of mind. Multidimensionality is a natural occurrence as creativity is sought and the mind becomes more intuitive in its operation. In higher dimensions of awareness, time and space become more plastic. The healthcare administrator is able to preview the future and explore alternative futures. In addition she is able to access knowledge not available to her conscious mind. Remember, spirituality is wed with materiality in higher levels of management.

He can enter the silence through meditation

The transformational leader is an experienced meditator. He can enter the silence, wherever he is, and whatever he is doing. By learning to span consciousness, part of his awareness is always centered in the inner temple while the remainder of his consciousness is focused upon the task at hand.

Transformational activity is by definition spiritual and beyond the confines of the small ego. All the inner dimensions of consciousness are reached through meditation. The ego provides such a strong stimulus that it overrides inner awareness. Thus it is necessary to suspend the ego in order to tune in to subtle inner stimuli.

At first the transformational leader must be in an altered state of consciousness to reach the inner dimensions. Later, he develops a dual awareness with one set of stimuli in the figure and another set of stumuli running in the ground. He can easily shift back and forth from figure to ground.

The silence is not really silent. It is the soundless sound. It represents the full presence of many potentials waiting to happen. The Void may be experienced as a very low hum or Aum. You feel something like that hum if you are around the giant turbines in a dam or standing below a great waterfall.

The silence is the sound of creation. It is pregnant with life trying to be born. It is the great womb of creation. The transformational leader creates from this place as he touches archetypes descending from higher dimensions. If the leader can tune into these possibilities, they spark across his consciousness and take form in his imagination. He has access to the highest forms to which he attunes himself. Higher forms beyond his reach will require a more developed consciousness for capture. Like attracts like in this arena as in all others. As the transformational leader becomes more inclusive in this awareness, he can attract more subtle forms. Once the archetype is captured, it simply reflects into the leader's awareness. It may be simply a fleeting image. As the leader holds the reflection in his awareness, he adds density to it and becomes a channel for its birth in the high density world of the third dimension.

Entering the silence, being inspired, and then giving expression to the inspiration constitutes the subtle rhythm of creation. It is like breathing. The in-breath is inspiration and the out-breath is expiration (work in the real world). This rhythm, once learned, can be attained whenever desired.

Interlude III

TRANSFORMATIONAL LEADERSHIP 138

He sounds a note that others can hear and follow

The transformational leader radiates his consciousness such that anyone in his vicinity is impacted. He "sounds the note." Those who are ready to "hear" respond and follow.

Consciousness begets consciousness. Radiation stimulates a resonant response. Energy flows from one vehicle to the other. This is the value of any spiritual teacher. He creates an energy that can jump-start other vehicles that have reached a sufficient degree of maturity and readiness.

It is by first leaning on the teacher that the student gains the strength to try his own wings. Once the student feels the energy, i.e., "hears the note," he is able to generate the same type of energy in his own vehicle.

The transformational leader leads by inspiration. He creates a mood and tone and range of possibilities for the group. The CEO bears this sacred responsibility and should be the most highly evolved consciousness in the institution. Since the leader's ego is not connected to the status of his consciousness, there is no pride or false status involved.

The rule has always been, "when you learn to swim, you can swim with the swimmers." Until then you must observe and practice. Since currently the spiritual senses of most people are underdeveloped they cannot easily discriminate between swimmers and non-swimmers. As a result, CEOs may not be the most spiritually evolved members of their organizations. All of this will change in our new century when a person's state of consciousness will be perceived by your inner eye as surely as your outer eyes now detect certain frequencies of physical light.

In a well designed institution each member functions according to his capacity. Each member is a mentor and is mentored. All students learn from teachers who have developed the requisite capacities. There is no jealousy for a greater position than you can comfortably occupy with your current consciousness. A rise in rank and responsibility is conditional upon a rise in capacity and consciousness. Everyone knows why you are in your current position and what may be expected of you.

The "note" is heard with the inner ear and causes immediate response and attraction. Pay heed and listen. Someone is now playing your music or soon will be. And remember whether you try to or not, you are always sounding the note for other people who will respond and seek you out.

He taps knowledge beyond reason and intellect

The transformational leader taps knowledge beyond reason and intellect. He uses intuition, draws upon the collective consciousness of humankind and functions in the many dimensions of the superconscious or spiritual universe.

Of course the transformational leader uses reason and intellect. He also plays close attention to his instincts and feelings. The universe is a multidimensional communicating entity. The leader can tap into many sources of information and guidance.

As the paranormal powers of the leader unfold, he becomes precognitive. He can think in future time and enter the realm of probable futures. The realm of probable futures represent the most likely future events being triggered by the current flow of events. Every current action leads to an array of probable future events waiting to be selected by further actions of human consciousness. These probable futures exist as images in higher bands of consciousness. No particular image has to happen, but some are much closer to manifestation than others. At some point the pressure to manifest becomes so strong that it is nearly impossible for it not to do so. Thus a good prophet is seldom wrong.

Because the transformational leader can see alternative futures he is in the position of being able to help some futures along rather than others. The leader would like to function as a self-fulfilling prophet by selecting more desirable futures and then working to make them manifest. Of course, probable futures are the work of the whole of humankind, so the leader can only do so much to make a desired future happen. This is the reason the leader often works with a small seed group. The group can generate more energy than the leader working as a solo agent.

In future healthcare, these high consciousness seed groups will become the most important part of healthcare organizations and the communities they serve. By the middle of our new century the mass of humankind will understand they are the creators of their society and their world. Reality will be viewed as a social invention. The earth will move toward the status of a designer planet. A great deal of disease, poverty, crime and ignorance will be designed out of society. Healthcare will be largely habitat design and its most important product will be human potentiation.

The right side of the brain will receive more emphasis as transformational leaders learn to orchestrate the consciousness of their organizations and stimulate them to imagine and then create preferred futures. Rationality will still be an important management activity but it will be balanced by intuition and higher brain functions.

He has escaped cultural determinism

The transformational leader has escaped cultural determination. He is no longer hypnotized by the prevailing social theories and norms. The leader understands that every culture makes up stories and creates interpretations about life and how people should live it. Reality is a social invention. Different societies invent different realities and pretend they are true. Most individuals simply adapt to the prevailing social ideas and ideals without giving it a second thought. They believe that is simply the way the world is.

Many practices and norms in a materialistic society such as the United States are not favorable to the inner life or the development of spiritual capacities. It is easy to get caught up in the storm of modernism. The transformational leader avoids this plight by carefully examining what is out there in the mass media. He will accept some things and reject other things. For this reason the transformational leader avoids attempted manipulation and mind control by those agencies that benefit from the multitude's mindless assumptions of materialism, capitalism, and urbanism. The transformational leader is not a terrorist or militant political organizer. He understands maya for what it is and silently goes his way. For this reason he will not stand out in a crowd. Most friends and associates know little about the leader's inner life or citizenship in multiple worlds.

The transformational leader will become a primary architect of life in our new century. Since he knows reality is a design project and may take any form we give it, the transformational leader is in a prime position to help create a self-designing, self-sufficient, healthier society. Transformational leaders working in healthcare will assist in the development of the two major future dimensions of healthcare which are human potentiation and habitat redesign. At first these ideas will seem strange to the populace. Within 50 years they will be the accepted reality. Canada and the United States will become the first nations in the recorded history of the Planet Earth to achieve self-conscious design capacity. Eventually, the earth will achieve designer planet status.

TRANSFORMATIONAL LEADERSHIP 141

He knows that nothing has to be the way it is

The transformational leader knows that nothing has to be the way it is. It could just as well be some other way. For every reality that is in place, there are many others waiting in the wings. By a simple act of invocation, the transformational leader can substitute one reality for another.

The substitutability of reality is a form of empowerment. Don't defy reality, redefine it! The universe is always trying to be all possible ways. By creating an opening, a reality that is trying to emerge, can emerge. This empowers the leader to scan available realities and select one that seems to fit the present need.

The leader can change reality for himself only, or he can convince other people to join him in the effort. Powerful seed groups can create consensual realities they all enjoy together.

In the third dimension (3D) a reality is a mind state plus the clustering of matter and events around that state. Because of the density of the 3D it takes time for this condensation to occur. In some other dimensions, a change in conceptualization results in an immediate change of reality. This is true in the dream band, for instance. Think another reality and you are immediately standing in it. Because of the inertia of the 3D, you must maintain the structuring mindset as well as aid in its implementation in heavy matter. Although this seems like a limitation, in fact, it is a blessing. Once you have a creation it has enough density to endure even when you are not thinking about it. This is not true in the mental plane. There the rule is, out of mind, out of existence. This is why it is difficult to maintain a mental creation or ever visit the same place twice. Things change too quickly. They are ephemeral.

As we move into our new century, actualization will follow more quickly upon the heels of visualization. We are moving into a zone of more subtle densities as the earth continues its migration through space. It is essential that we learn now to hold the mind in concentration and to create powerful group thought forms.

Every healthcare organization needs to form a seed group with the express charge of creating its preferable future. This group will project a unified thought form that forms the matrix for the attraction of isomorphic matter and events. The future becomes a group design project. The gross levels of our current healthcare management will give way to subtle levels where mind and imagination reign supreme. The virtual organization is first and foremost a creation of the mind.

Note: This is the end of the series in transformational leadership. I hope you enjoyed it. Better yet, I desire you to take your place as a transformational leader in the field of healthcare. Truly, the future will be as great as we can imagine and create out of the abundance of our universe. Godspeed, fellow traveler!

SECTION FOUR: SPIRITUALITY

1. INTRODUCTION: SPIRITUALITY AND BUSINESS?

"Because the sage never thinks,
he never ruins anything."
—Lao-Tzu

"We are being destroyed by our knowledge,
which has made us drunk with power.
And we shall not be saved without wisdom."
—Will Durant

Why should people in business, industry, and professional organizations talk about spirituality? The whole concept of "should" is beside the point; the fact is that people in business and industry—workplace professionals on every level—are talking about spirituality! The number of seminars, conferences, books, and other materials on the subject of spirituality in the workplace is not surprising; it is astounding! There may be many answers: the voids and vacuums increasingly apparent at the core of what Wayne Oates call "workaholism;" the devastation of the personal lives of people who have successfully navigated the sometimes treacherous waters of corporate politics and attained corporate power that is devoid of sufficient or lasting meaning; a desire to find new wrinkles in leadership theory that will promote greater motivation, productivity, teamwork, or—if a business person is particularly creative—meaningfulness of work (although meaningfulness-of-work discussions are often justified as a means to better retention and lowering of very expensive attrition).

At any rate, the discussions about spirituality are there—right in the middle of the executive boardroom, alongside of the managers and production workers on the assembly line. Unfortunately, much of this talk about spirituality stands on a weak base of opinion, misunderstanding, and poor intellectual precedent. Sometimes, the conclusion is reached that spirituality in the workplace means setting aside a time for prayer, Bible study, and meditation or simply replicating religious-like events learned from peripheral church/synagogue/mosque experiences during one's youth. As is too often the case, theological predispositions begin to slim and start raising the expectation that to work in a particular setting as a spiritual person means to embrace the personal belief systems and theological conclusions of a particular, dominant community or even of some key executive or leader in the work setting. Spirituality then becomes the basis for debate, diatribe, and division, with as many people being excluded as they are included. "Included" makes spirituality another exclusivistic club, whose membership is dependent on beliefs, concepts, creeds, and dogmas; decisions and actions of human care and community responsibility quickly get lost, and the possibility of true meaning is compromised and lost once again.

So, this chapter seeks to define spirituality in some greater detail and with every attempt to promote clarity. There will be terms, names, and ideas here that will be new to those engaged in a steady diet of management and organizational development books. In some respects, the chapter will be a primer on spirituality. The only blatant aspect of the chapter's purpose is to give a base, an underpinning that is not dependent on any religious perspective and is not "pushing" any particular belief system. In the end, this chapter yearns for a careful hearing, but it is not trying to "preach." In the end, the reader is being asked to come to his/her own conclusions, to be accountable for "making up" his/her own mind. The input the reader is about to receive is not necessarily traditional or conventional, so there is much that will be found here that is likely to be new. There is little dogma or doctrine here, but hopefully, there is a great abundance of good sense.

Much of this chapter is like a mosaic with small pieces fitted together with careful intent to create a larger whole which makes some lasting impression. But, move slowly here. Even if you have a fairly active religious involvement of some sort, much of this material will likely still be new. In the end, my total intent in creating this mosaic is as straightforward as I know how to make it: if we are going to talk about spirituality, let's try to make sure that our talk is grounded in the very best information that is available, and—above all—information that is presented in a way that leads to community and conversation, and not to division and confusion.

BEGINNING WITH THE CONCLUSION

Standard operating procedure for writing an article or a chapter in a book dictates that there be an introduction— a section that develops and explains an idea—and a conclusion. Here, we will disrupt that standard order and start at the end: offer a conclusion that advances itself with simplicity, and then move in the direction of explanation and understanding. In this way, there will be a greater clarity about where the leading ideas are moving. In fact, if the reader finds it necessary, there will be the ability to move to a concluding concept without having to delve into the detail of the explanations. With something of a disclaimer now in mind, we will begin—at the end.

In the initial sessions of the Spiritual Leadership Institute, which is based in Houston, participants came to know Professor Chandra Joshi. Professor Joshi is from Bombay and brings to the Institute insights from the traditions of Hinduism. Even more, Professor Joshi manifests those characteristics many people would identify with a wise man or guru, so it has been very beneficial for our mostly western audience to be exposed to him. His personal carriage, demeanor—presence is probably the best word— creates an ambiance that clearly communicates a special experience of spirituality.

Professor Joshi took the opportunity to sit through all of the initial sessions, develop a rapport with the participants, and then gave a final meditation at the conclusion of the session. He had undergone and processed the Institute experience, thus being able to create a kind of "last word"/synthesis that would send participants on their way back to their work and regular life responsibilities.

Professor Joshi was intimately in touch with the elements of struggle that the sessions had given the participants. Joshi smiled as he talked about the often-difficult and new concepts and the way in which participants had distinctly been "stretched" to at least find a dimension of openness to a wide range of new ideas. Struggle is important to Joshi, as he feels it is the open door to insight and the depth—for want of a better word—which spirituality is. He believes that in any learning experience that stretches people toward that which is new that a powerful dynamic is taking place, creating an experience well beyond the ordinary status quo of most participants' lives. He explains:

You are the Guru and the Disciple.
The duality is within you.
The sense of inquiry and devotion is the discipleship.
The intensity toward the divine in the Guru.

Yet, Professor Joshi related to the Institute audience with a distinct turning toward compassion. He wanted the participants to go away with some clarity about spirituality that they could grasp. So, he began to use the metaphor of the mountain. The Institute had been an acute part of a journey that can capture significant dimensions of a person's life and can evolve across a lifetime. The Institute's pursuit of spirituality was like climbing a mountain.

For American westerners, raised in their rationalistic and competitive culture, there are powerful realities that would present themselves if a mountain were being climbed. For example, you would have to have demonstrable information about the mountain: how high it is, what are the best routes to the top, its name, the type of rock that might be encountered in a climb, and on and on. There would, of course, be the need to get to the top— nothing less would be acceptable—and even to get to the top ahead of everyone else. By comparison, any discussion of spirituality would have to end in definition, explanation, demonstrability— naming, putting into words. In addition, there would have to be some sort of "topping out" and "arriving," or the entire process would leave something to be desired.

For Joshi, of course, the "mountain" of spirituality would never be reduced to demonstrability and logical explanation; it would never be named and put into words, nor would there ever be a "getting to the top" in a way that would provide an ultimate, absolute, comprehensive overview and defining perspective. There would forever be more "mountain" to be climbed, more paths of journey to be explored, more unique vistas to be unveiled. Naming, putting into words, definitions—all of these mental constructs of rational thinking— become non-essential.

I was reminded of the poetic expressions of the American poet, Charles Wright, whose work has won the Pulitzer Prize and the National Book Award, and who teaches at the University of Virginia:

The world is a language we never quite
understand,
But think we catch the drift of.
Speaking in ignorance
And joy, we answer
What wasn't asked, by someone we
 don't know, in strange tongues.

Similarly, Francis Fergusson writes in *The Idea of a Theater*:

.... reasoned concepts never quite fit, and he is troubled, even in his rationalizing, by sensuous images of undecipherable significance; by

1. Introduction: Spirituality and Business?

sympathetic awareness of other persons; by a vague desire for light and freedom of another order; and by memories of his unregenerate state when his soul, in the innocence of childhood and with an animal-like unity of thought and feeling, moved simply "toward what delights it."

Yet—and here was his powerful, primary point— somewhere along the way of the "climb" and the struggle, there would be an insight that would "dawn" on the struggling climber. For those who might know of the work of Martin Heidegger, this is the point of Heidegger's clearing along the forest path where light breaks in and startles with the new awareness it provides, the point of Heidegger's "Das Anwesen des Anwesendens"—the "arrival of that which arrives," the point of the Greek concept of "Truth" as alethia, that which "un-veils" itself. This "dawning" is serendipity and enlightenment is the highest senses of these words.

Then, with clarity and power, Professor Joshi focused the intensity of his own personal uniqueness. The audience did not move. There was that silence and stillness in the room that would make a pin-drop resound and echo. That which "dawns" is that this "mountain"—this profound metaphor for spirituality—is the mountain of caring. In the end, spirituality is caring. Not just love, although love is present (or present-ing or a present), for love can too easily be purely or primarily conceptual, but caring, actions, deeds, involvements, or choices are consummated in deeds of compassion, transformation, and redemption.

His meditation was perfect. As participants, we might never reach a "top" where absolute explanation and perspective came into view, but we could care. In that caring, the phenomenon of the spiritual could be both advanced and experienced. The highest expression of leadership could be advanced in terms of care— care for workers, care for personal relationships, care for quality of workmanship and excellence of execution of plans and strategies, even care of self in the midst of all of the demands that confront persons in the workplace. Care as an event, a moment, a timeless and priceless expression of kairos (intrinsic time/spiritual time) in the midst of chronos (mechanic/clock time) could be achieved.

Suddenly, Professor Joshi had taken the participants to the bottom line essence of the great religions and the great religious teachers at their best. The ultimate "test" of faith was always—again, at its best—not an issue of theology, dogma, or church politics; rather, the ultimate "test" was always caring. From this perspective, the words of Jesus—simply epitomizing the words of all the greatest teachers—echoes with deep meaning: "whatever you have done unto the least of one of these, my brothers, you have done to me"; "greater love has no person than that he would lay down his life for his neighbor"; "what does it profit a person to gain the world materially and lose his soul"; "I have given you an example, now go and do as I have done"; and, "...love your neighbor as you love yourself." Jesus' "Parable of the Good Samaritan" is the epitomizing moment; if most of us only had this parable as the religious/spiritual teaching of all of life, we would have enough to work on modeling and replicating for the rest of our lives.

The book of I John at the end of the New Testament advances the same witness and—again—simply captures in one tradition what the best of all of the great traditions and teachers taught: "Everyone who loves is born of God and knows God. He who does not love, does not know God, for God is love"; "we know that we have passed from death to life because we love our neighbors"; "whoever see his brother in need and shuts up his heart from him, how does the love of God abide in him?"; "let us love not in word or in tongue, but in deed and in truth." Paul captured all of this intent and emphasis with his bold conclusion to the theological and ecclesiastically intricate letter to the church at Rome when he proclaimed: ".... the greatest of these is charity." Even the apocalyptic book, Revelation, concludes its judgment scene with an emphasis on divine judgment being based on deeds of care, compassion, and love.

For many years I have had—and treasured—a lithograph that a group of Iranian students gave me following a comparative religion class that they had attended. Drawn and lettered in beautiful calligraphy by an artist named Jeff Streiff, there are five children of varying skin colors, cultural dress, and religious posture. One is meditating, three are bowing in various forms of prayer, and one stands with hands reaching toward the heavens. Faces capture the serenity and innocence of childhood. Filling spaces near the children, under the heading "Golden Rule," are the following statements:

Buddhism—"Hurt not others in ways that you yourself would find hurtful."
Judaism—"What is hateful to you, do not to your fellow man. That is the entire law; all else is commentary."
Christianity—"You must love your neighbor as yourself."
Islam—"No one of you is a believer until he desires for his brother that which is desires for himself."

1. *Introduction: Spirituality and Business?*

Baha'i—"Blessed is he who prefers his brother before himself."

And, in these statements, only the surface of the great religions—at their best—and the great religious teachers are put forward. This is the core, the "mountain of caring." That the artist coupled the words with images of children is profound. Children know this truth and have little trouble living by it; as we become adults, we somehow lose our way. We create dogmas, theologies, and institutions—a structure for division and even violence that pushes care into a distant wilderness of concern and meaning which strips it of power and vitality. This distance from caring always is the destructive antithesis of the spiritual, although this distance is often the very defining stuff of religions as they stalk the trench lines of what they are against. Charles Wright, again, from a poem entitled "Portrait of the Artist with Li Po":

The distance between the dead and the living is more than a heartbeat and a breath

How much there is the possibility of being technically alive as a homo-sapien— with heartbeat and breath fully intact— but being very much dead in terms of soul and spirit. Where there is life without caring, there is death; perhaps, since potential still fully exists, this is a death much worse than the simple end of physical heartbeats and breath.

The philosopher Martin Heidegger has had more to say in terms of formal, philosophical writings about care that any modern thinker of note. Although not many people are very conversant with Heidegger's ideas because of their intellectual complexity, the concept of care is at the core of his thinking and must be—at least marginally— understood, or care too easily is reduced to the shallow point of jargon and platitude. By looking at Heidegger, the immediate understanding is at hand that care is not simply a nicety or an obvious "be good to everyone" conclusion to an explanation of spirituality that can be dismissed, as convenience might demand, without much feeling of consequence. Religions, for example, can advance a Heideggerian form of care and be spiritual; religions without this core of care are devoid of meaning, legitimacy, and authenticity.

To say that Heidegger's writings are absolutely daunting and forever imposing is the height of understatement; what James Joyce's *Ulysses* is to literature, Heidegger's magnus opus, *Being and Time*, is to philosophy. Yet, couched in the midst of the great work is an old fable that may be seen as the pulsing heartbeat of some of his most important ideas. In this old fable, at least as ancient as the Roman Empire, care is personified in a unique manner. The meaning Heidegger attaches to the fable must—to me at least—be part of the core of what it means to be a human being and a spiritual person. Here, also, there are powerful implications for understanding what a spiritual leader must wear as a mandate for action. The fable conveys almost a creation narrative tone:

> Once when Care was crossing a river, she saw some clay; she thoughtfully took up a piece and began to shape it. While she was meditating on what she had made, Jupiter came by. Care asked him to give it spirit, and this he gladly granted. But when she wanted her name to be bestowed upon it, he forbade this, and demanded that it be given his name instead. While Care and Jupiter were disputing, Earth arose and desired that her own name be conferred on the creature, since she had furnished it with part of her body. They asked Saturn to be their arbiter, and he made the following decision, which seemed a just one: "Since you, Jupiter, have given its spirit, you shall receive that spirit at its death; and since you, Earth, have given its body, you shall receive its body. But since Care first shaped this creature, she shall possess it as long as it lives. And because there is now a dispute among you as to its name, let it be called homo, for it was made out of humus (Earth)."

Here, care is caricatured as a power which thoughtfully, meditatively, devotedly gives shape to that which is a power that nurtures and develops possibility, a power which is committed across life to giving form in terms of a projected hope of what can come and finding an absolute commitment to helping "what can come" find reality, even a reality which will continue to evolve, be sustained, and be nurtured toward yet more sophisticated levels and dimensions. As long as there is life, the role of care becomes paramount; without care playing its role, there is not life—only heartbeat and breath. Without care, there is ailing, Mahaleka (Hebrew), Nyon Mong (Tibet), Klesha (Sanskrit)—that which afflicts from within, destroys peace of mind, brings about disturbances within, and defeats the harmony that is at the core of community; without care, there is dis-ease.

1. Introduction: Spirituality and Business?

So, we are immediately beyond care as simply a clichéd, nice and gentle kindness— although there is nothing wrong with kindness, as it would certainly always be a character of care. Care becomes a continuous, ongoing power that shapes, molds, nurtures, encourages, and moves toward futures defined by hope and projections of what can be. It is interesting that care is personified as female in the fable, for the sustaining, nurturing, loving, shaping work of a mother, for example, may be a powerful metaphor for defining exactly what the work of care is like in its real, temporal manifestations. This concept is more than radical, especially if you were to say that the role model for a spiritual leader or spiritual executive is a good mother. That concept certainly goes against what Heidegger might call the "normal" mental constructs of modern society, but the work of care is constantly in *Being and Time* the setting aside of "normal" limiting boxes of status quo conceptuality, and the creating of "clearings" in wooded forests and "turns" along mountain paths where new light of potentiality and meaning breaks in to define life on new levels of beauty and power. The truly spiritual person of care is the guardian and trustee—a steward—of these clearings and turns where "truth" breaks in (aletheia); then, as guardian and trustee, the truly spiritual person of care is "used of the clearing" to impart what is unveiled to others.

To at least touch base with Heidegger's philosophical language, he says that human beings live in a real world; we have existence that he calls "being-in-the-world." This existence can very likely be inauthentic, hollow, devoid of real meaning. This inauthenticity typically takes place when people try to live life in terms of societal norms, the expectations of others, surrendering their uniqueness to the designs of others, and often defining self in terms of material accumulation. That such inauthenticity is typical is also tragic, the embodiment of Nietzsche's "herd mentality." There is the possibility for all— though this possibility is only achieved by a few—that authentic existence can be achieved, and that individuals can live out of the context of an understanding and realization of uniqueness where self is created, designed, lived out in choices that rise from that understood uniqueness. Heidegger also knew that authenticity is continuously advancing and receding—a reality that has to be recaptured, reclaimed, and redeemed at every turn of life. The opposite of this care—what Heidegger calls its "deficient modes"— would take the form of neglect, renouncing, leaving undone, taking a rest (in the sense of not "pressing on to the high calling" of life/living at its best). Ultimately, spiritual selfhood is a living beyond these deficits and achieving an ongoing "way of being/mode of existence."

> The struggle for proper selfhood puts the individual at odds with its normal world in which it has its possible roles and identities set for it. To be a proper/authentic and self-authenticating self, an individual must take cues for living from unique being, not from standards of community normalcy (Scott, *The Question of Ethics*).

"Being-in-the-world" authentically is not simply a physical reality (heartbeat and breath/the clay of the fable), nor is it only a mental reality/an intellectual concept, nor is it an elusively defined spiritual reality. For Heidegger it is a nexus of "all of the above" that manifests itself almost aesthetically as a "felt reality"/experiential reality/existential reality/intrinsic/first intensional reality which is referred to as Dasein. In the end, Dasein is life/living/existence beyond definition and explanation. To define it or explain it would be to reduce it to something less. Dasein is simply the profoundly conscious reality Being-there (Being, the German *sein* and There, the German *da*). If I am truly alive in the real, present tense of life, engaged and experiencing the world that I am a part of through the lens of my own, conscious uniqueness, I am experiencing Dasein; in a sense, I am Dasein. Within Dasein, I can "hear the call of conscience" which Heidegger sees as the call of Care (the German Sorgen) and concern (Besorgen).

Then, Heidegger makes this powerful, fundamentally central statement: "Being-in-the-world is essentially care—care is the 'being' of Dasein." Care is the core of it all, especially as "it all" is defined in terms of life at its best, continually straining forward toward new and better shapes of continuous reclaiming, renewing, and redeeming.

Yes, Heidegger would agree that care manifests itself in deeds of kindness, beneficence, and—in his terms—solicitude. This is caring and concern in their traditional sense. There is nothing wrong with this traditional sense; it is simply not enough, does not go far enough. He has no problem saying that "Being-in-the-world" needs to be "Being-alongside the ready-to-hand" which means being for real people with real needs in real communities. Mother Teresa working with lepers in the slums of India and Jimmy Carter building Habitat for Humanity houses are easy role model paradigms for care as "Being-alongside the ready-to-hand." This dimension of care should never be demeaned or allowed to drift toward cliché and jargon; true care of this dimension is always necessary and always a distinct part of truly authentic existence. For Heidegger, this authentic "Being-in-the-world" is called indwelling; the similarity to the Christian "incarnation," Hindu "avatar," or Buddhist "bodhisattva" is intriguing.

Yet, the forever necessary emphasis on care as shaping, molding, nurturing toward the future, defining and creating future in the process, must always be included and lead the way in any understanding of care. One is back to the fable and—if the fable is too ancient—the metaphor of the good mother. Heidegger calls this future impetus of care, empowered by the projections of hope, "Being-ahead-of-itself." The core characteristic of spirituality is "Being-ahead" which manifests itself as renewing, redeeming, shaping, nurturing, and molding toward that which is better. This is self-actualization in a way, but it is always more than self-actualization; it is actualization/realization of others, of community, of nature—of existence itself. By implication, spirituality is continuously the "Being-ahead" which shapes and molds life; the mandate to spiritual leaders is abundantly obvious and overwhelmingly challenging. Involving oneself in the meeting of that challenge brings the highest vitality and meaning to life.

Care, for Heidegger is a "primordial structural totality." With this statement, he is—again—trying to prevent care from being reduced to merely a benevolent attitude, a conceptual claim, or some action in some situation. True care occurs as a "totality" when theory and practice, conceptual idea and action, word and deed are absolutely merged with a devotedness that defies being torn apart. To attempt to bring new life to cliché, in authentic care, our "walk" and our "talk" is at one with itself; there is alignment and atonement. To be in care, in spirituality— to again follow the fable— is to proceed with shaping, not with obsessive rationality or reckless emotion, but with thoughtfulness, pausing along the way, meditation, and devotedness. Such movements are not often the role models of modern executive leadership, family and community leadership, or religious and governmental leadership; because of this, spiritual leadership is a rare commodity. Ironically, the voids and vacuums created by "normal" leadership may precisely be that which is provoking at least an interest in spiritual leadership.

The conclusion to the conclusion is now fairly simple to construct, although—after moving through Heidegger—it is clear that this simplicity is actually the axiomatic centerpiece of a very complex dynamic that is supremely difficult to achieve in reality. Simply constructed, spirituality is caring. For Heidegger, there must be the movement out of the normal, herd mentality to the manifestation of uniqueness in authentic existence. This process does not occur "once and for all," but becomes a way of being, a mode of existence that is continually being renewed. There is always a movement forward and a movement backward, an advancing/retreating/need for reclaiming that which is lost. The poet, Stanley Kunitz, at age 90 reflected:

> Years ago I came to the realization that the most poignant of all lyric tensions stems from the awareness that we are living and dying at once. To embrace such knowledge and yet to remain compassionate and whole—that is the consummation of the endeavor of art.

At the epitome of authenticity is not simply or exclusively self-fulfillment or self-actualization, but a devoted commitment to thoughtful, meditative shaping toward that which can be "ahead" in a better way. To return to Robert Hartman, there must be the movement (to follow Hartman's "Four Self Rules") beyond Plato self-knowledge, beyond Kierkegaard's self-choice, beyond Pico's self-creating, to Jesus' self-giving. Giving— as care—is, indeed, understood in terms of what some call random acts of kindness or even great strategies and commitments to benevolence. Giving—as care—must also, above and beyond, be this commitment to shaping, molding, nurturing, and sustaining toward this renewing, reclaiming, redeeming "ahead." The defining mandate of the authentic spiritual leader is the way-of-life/mode-of-being commitment to the kind of care-giving which is presented here as a working definition for "the spiritual."

To paraphrase the powerful voice of Stanley Kunitz, taking what he has had to say about poetry and applying it to spirituality:

> Spirituality would be easy if our heads weren't so full of the day's clatter. The task is to get through to the other side, where we can hear the deep rhythms that connect us with the stars and the tides.

The moment a leader in the modern world of business and commerce begins to savor this thought, become curiously drawn to find its meaning— even be troubled and disturbed by it a bit—the horizon of spiritual leadership has shown itself. Nothing will ever be the same, nothing will ever seem "right" until that horizon is pursued.

A DETAIL OF EXPLANATION: INTRODUCTION

Having already offered a "conclusion" and having built a strong identity between spirituality and caring, expanded the concept of caring beyond trite cliché, and explained caring as the epitome of authentic existence, attention can now be given to a more fully developed set of details on the concept of spirituality. Visually, this larger explanation can be seen as a pyramid of ideas that builds from a base of basic concepts to a pinnacle of restatements of critical religious understandings. The goal is for these restatements to create plausibility that will intrigue and draw the attention of people regardless of conventionality of belief or lack thereof. In the end, there will be a fairly expansive restatement of conventional meanings so that a real vitality of possibility will be available for understanding spirituality and undergirding the work of individuals and of persons compelled by the idea of spiritual leadership.

Hermes—or Mercury—was understood in the ancient mythologies to be the messenger of the gods. Thus, hermeneutics—generally translated as "interpretation"— involves the process of delivering messages. While we seldom use this word, the phenomenon of delivering messages is one of the most important realities of civilized life. Think about all of the messages that you came in contact with today: everything from the digital beeping of cell phones, pagers, and answering machines to billboards along the roadside. Especially in a so-called "information society," the priority placed on delivering messages— and doing this with consummate precision— is profound.

Hermeneutics is probably both an art and a science. As a process, it clearly embodies the realization that messages are always embodied in contexts, and there is a pressing need to understand as much about the context as possible in order to be successful in communicating the message. The primary stress for hermeneutics is that the context in which messages are being delivered is always and forever changing. Therefore, messages must be updated, renewed, transformed—re-stated—for each new generation. If they are not, the messages will turn into jargon and clichés; they will be "full of sound and fury, signifying nothing;" they may lull people into a peacefulness of familiarity, but they will lose their potential for meaningful power. People may say, "tell me the old, old story," but in all likelihood that "old, old story" is being tuned out, putting people to sleep, or doing little more than becoming the occasion for drifting off into sleep. Watch the expression on most parishioners' faces in the midst of most Sunday morning sermons, and all honesty will have to admit that very little communication is occurring, that very little power of expression or listening is really taking place.

So, there is the greatest need—especially when the arena of concern has been attended to across generations by "old, old stories"—to find new mechanisms of expression, new words which may excite and capture attention, and more vital approaches which may stimulate contemplation and reflection. Hermeneutics has become highly prominent as a stated concern of religious studies and religious proclamation in the past century as sensitive scholars have strained to find ways to allow truths and meanings that are of highest value to find an audience in the context of a new and modern world. In some respects, the basic emphasis of a great deal of this particular writing has been hermeneutical—theology and dogmatic philosophy have been re-stated in terms of axiology and an emphasis on values; religion has been re-stated with an emphasis on the "spiritual;" the primary arena of positive change in society has been re-stated, not in terms of church ecclesiology or politics, but in terms of attention to the workplace as a primary fulcrum upon which so much of modern life turns.

If this explanation of hermeneutics is too academically complex, a couple of anecdotal illustrations might give broader meaning. I can recall, for example, a teacher early in high school determining that we young teenagers were ready for the sophistication of Homer. *The Odyssey* and *The Iliad* became standard reading assignments. Most of us, languishing in a life devoted mainly to sports and dating, were overwhelmed. What we might later come to appreciate and even understand was oblique, dense, and basically non-communicative. We probably, by implication, developed a negative image of the ancient Greeks and wondered if people really even talked like Homer wrote.

While studying for a mid-term examination, I recall suddenly remembering a stash of old comic books that had belonged to an older brother. There were the standards that had garnered my attention, but I also remembered what were called "Classic Comics" that had been of little interest. They were about old books, old themes, "stuff" that had not interested me—but at least something about Greeks and Romans. Sure enough, digging through the action hero comics that usually got my attention, there they were—"Classic Comics"—"Helen of Troy," "Jason and the Argonauts," and "The Odyssey." In the comic book version, a format and context for delivering a message that I clearly understood, the old story came alive. I followed the plot, and came to recognize the characters—I "aced" the test.

What the classic comics writers had done was hermeneutical; they had re-stated an old story in a new method, with new images, and new words. They had not diminished the story, although my English teacher—had he known—might disagree; they had made it come alive. Twenty years later, teaching literature and the humanities myself, I would use the old comics to make the Odyssey come alive to my own students.

Modern teachers and students will not need a stash of old comic books. Thanks two a couple of very creative Hollywood artists, the Coen brothers, a next hermeneutical step has been taken. The movie *Oh Brother, Where Art Thou?* is *The Odyssey* all over again. This time, Odysseus/Ulysses is George Clooney as an escapee from a Mississippi chain gang. There are inviting "sirens" and John Goodman, who became famous for his role in the sitcom *Roseanne* makes a powerful Cyclops monster. Throw in a few politicians, some church choirs, and even a bizarre KKK rally, and—at least for people who have grown up in the South—there is an unforgettable and funny story. That it is a movie gives a new hermeneutical method that will be particularly acceptable to this modern generation, but the "message" is the same, the same powerful tale of an adventurer facing great odds who is triumphant in the end—the Odyssey.

Now, understanding hermeneutics becomes easy. First, there was the "Old West" of Tom Mix, Roy Rogers, and Gene Autry. Then, there was the more complex and sophisticated "Old West" of *Bonanza* and the family dynamics of the Cartwrights at the Ponderosa. Then, there was the almost "modern" treatment of that same "Old West" seen through the eyes of Larry McMurtry's *Lonesome Dove* or E. L. Doctorow's *Welcome To Hard Times.* With each step along the way, the "message" had changed very little, but the "medium," the delivery mechanism of that message, had continued to transform itself. In some respects, there is not a great distance from Odysseus/Ulysses to the characters captured in John Wayne movies to Luke Skywalker and Han Solo in *Star Wars*—there have simply been hermeneutical transformations to capture the attention of new audiences all along the way.

In a similar sense, there was *I Love Lucy, The Dick Van Dyke Show, The Honeymooners,* and *Donna Reed.* Then, for a next generation, there was *All in the Family.* Today, the next new generation has now moved beyond *Roseanne* and *Thirtysomething* to become attuned to the thoroughly modern themes of *Ally McBeal, Will and Grace, Friends,* and *The Real World;* the process will forever continue. In terms of hermeneutics, there are still groups of people—now perhaps straining the concept of "family" for some—trying to make sense of self, sense of others, and sense of the worlds in which they live. One can only imagine the hermeneutical transformations that might come in the next decade, but whoever captures that transformation and articulates it most clearly will gain significant attention and make a decided impact on people's lives. Again, we may derive some nostalgic comfort from the pratfalls and chaos of Lucy and Ricky Ricardo or the bullish tenderness of Ralph Cramden, but these characters are relics in a way that no longer help us define our own lives in a meaningful way. Surely, those realities that relate to religion and the spiritual do not have value as only relics that provide nostalgic comfort. If—or when—that is the case, it will be no wonder that modern generations will look for others avenues of plausible answer and direction for the deep questions of their lives. It is no longer enough to "Tell me the old, old story of unseen things above . . . .," to "Sing them over again to me, wonderful words of life. . . ." All of this is very nice, very comforting, very nostalgic, but by the time we have gotten through the first verse, a whole generation has moved on. We can demand that they come back to where we were, but there is no vitality in that demand and—in all honesty—not much real conviction.

As the great teacher clearly understood in his own hermeneutic of not coming to destroy the old way, but to "fulfill" it—to raise it to a new level of meaning—it is impossible to put new wine in old wine skins. That lesson cannot be lost on us if we ever really want to communicate with power. So, we talk about axiology instead of theology, we talk about values rather than dogma, we talk about spirituality instead of religion, and we talk about workplaces instead of churches or politics. Above all, we affirm that "talking" is never the end of the matter anyway, but that only when we come to the place of "walking" our "talk," living our spirituality, do we really come to an authentic and meaningful consummation of our values, of who we are. It is the "old, old story," but it is also "new wine."

FIRST LEVEL CONSIDERATIONS: CULTURAL RELIGION VS. SPIRITUALITY

A few years ago, I had the opportunity to work over several weeks with a missionary couple that was serving in Colombia. As we moved in and out of the several conferences we were doing, there was a great deal of time for conversation. I was intrigued and overwhelmed by what I learned about their work and the environment in which they were living.

First, I learned that Colombia is the most "Christian" nation in the western world. In terms of the baptismal records and other church documents, there are almost 95 percent of the people who are aligned with the Christian church, primary the Roman Catholic faith. The churches are filled on the high holy days, and the cities and towns of Colombia grind all but to a halt on the wide range of holidays that have religious implication. Religion is everywhere at the center of traditional Colombian life.

However, there is also a profound disjunction. Crime, including the most violent sorts, is a daily occurrence. Their home area of Medellin is the center of drug trafficking for most of the western hemisphere. Human life has all but no value. These missionaries were working with young teenagers to try to prevent their early engagement with gangs and a lifestyle that threatens life expectancy in a cruel and inhumane manner. All too often, by the time a young person is at mid-adolescence, there is either a horrible destiny already in place, tremendous pressure to enter the drug culture, or death.

How would it be possible for such a disjunction to exist? How could there be, on the one hand, the most "religious" environment in the western hemisphere and, on the other, the most destructive, dangerous, and demeaning culture perhaps in the entire world? The missionaries were uncompromising in their response to these questions. There was, indeed, religion—plenty of religion—but the religion that existed was cultural religion. Religion had become an extension, an adjunct, and a traditional by-product of the culture. People were religious by osmosis; their parents had been religious, or they simply had involvement because it was the accepted thing to do. Religion was on the surface, but had no meaningful depth.

These missionaries lived in a guarded, gated community with razor-sharp concertina wire on the top of the high, concrete wall that surrounded their neighborhood. In the years they had been in Colombia, they had not traveled into the legendarily beautiful countryside. It was too dangerous. To go into the countryside was an open invitation for mayhem and the victimization of crime.

In the week before their return on furlough to the United States, the wife had experienced a carjacking at knifepoint—on a main city street in broad daylight. Yet, here was life in an absolutely, on paper, Christian nation.

What is so disconcerting about the Colombian experience is the potential for the same kind of activity being realized in the United States. The rise of violent crime and drug traffic has been astounding over the past decade. Try to watch the movie *Traffic* without icy chills of prophetic realization running through your veins. And, there is a causal connection to also be made. There is a great deal of cultural religion in the United States. People go through religious motions without real conviction or meaning. There is a great deal of the right talk without the authenticity of connection to real actions of care and compassion. Names on church roles and high, per capita numbers on census surveys about belief in some kind of divinity do not prevent the hollowness and emptiness of spiritual meaning that is the catalyst for genuine belief.

So, in this discouraging and frightening context—albeit an honestly described context—what is to be done? Where is the better answer? It clearly is not in the arena of mental agreement with dogmatic concept or rote participation in traditional religious ceremonies. Rather, there is the pressing need to create some kind of spiritual experience that has personal legitimacy and credibility.

In the work we have done at the Spiritual Leadership Institute, there is the conviction that leadership is not empowered by osmosis or cultural traditions. Leadership is one of the results of the impact and ownership of something that is highly personal, struggled for, and arrived at only with the deepest personal journey. We have tried to take individuals "out of the box" of the constraints and definitions of cultural religion and tried to give encouragement—even permission—to search and struggle for that which is personally meaningful. An end result has been the meaningfulness of many participants beginning to move beyond "religion" to something that is "spiritual" in authenticity and power. A real outcome of this process has also been a growing of self-respect about one's own beliefs and one's own self, a growing respect of others and what they have come to, and a breaking down of the partitions of division that have separated people from people—often even in the "name of God." This sense of respect and affirmation of the power of affirmed diversity has high implications for building a more meaningful workplace to which people can choose to devote time, energy, and devotion. Stronger individuals build stronger organizations, which, in turn, build stronger communities. The authenticity of a hybrid religion is at the core of this entire continuum of realities.

What takes place in Colombia is, at least, a warning. That experience is not good enough and will never work for reasonably thinking people. Religion as a cultural tradition will become a cultural relic. Spirituality can become the process and experience which transforms personal and then community self-understanding. Spirituality can thus become the essence of the be-ing that raises living to new levels of meaning, fulfillment, and joy. Cultural religion will finally only disappoint.

Most people have heard of Galileo and Copernicus. These two great thinkers made a simple "revision" in the way most people had seen the universe. With the discovery of the telescope, both men quickly realized that the old Ptolemaic theory of the universe, which placed the earth at the center, was absolutely wrong. Both Galileo and Copernicus got in a great deal of trouble for their "heliocentric"/sun-centered view of our solar system, an idea that children now learn very early in their educational processes. Why did they get in trouble? The church had advanced the Ptolemaic view as being scriptural and inspired by God; their "geocentric" view was dogma and doctrine, the fixed line of the church's proclamation. The church defended the Ptolemaic view in the face of all the new "science" that was being advanced; if the church could be wrong about the universe, what all else might it be wrong about? Authority would not be challenged, and Galileo was so threatened and punished that he recanted what he had discovered and what he knew was true.

Few people, however, have heard of Giordano Bruno. Bruno was a priest and highly articulate writer. He kept abreast of the latest cultural events and was well versed in the discoveries of Galileo and Copernicus. But Bruno also understood the theological implication and was honest enough—or brazen enough—to explore those implications openly. If the universe was infinite, which was the exact opposite of the finite, closed universe of Ptolemy and church dogma, where was the place of God? In the Ptolemaic/church view, God was just "up there" and "out there" a bit, watching over all that was taking place on the earth. Yet, when the telescopes looked "up there" and "out there" a bit, there was no evidence of any heaven, any place of God.

Bruno concluded that it was meaningless to talk about the spatial location of God. God was in no place that could be scientifically demonstrated, and the most powerful telescopes that would ever be created would ever "see" God. The church hated this idea and hunted Bruno down like a hideous criminal. He was tortured and punished for seven years, but would not surrender his truth. Finally, this pious and decent man was burned at the stake. His writings remained on the Index, the church's list of forbidden books, until after World War II.

Bruno believed that the most appropriate and accurate way to talk about a "location" for God was to describe a personal locus or personal location. Most reliably, God existed within the existence of human beings—whether you wanted to say within the "heart" or within the "soul" or whatever was beside the point. That God might have spatial location somewhere else was also beside the point because it could not be demonstrated or proved scientifically. The personal locus within human existence was altogether valid and dramatic, but that was not good enough for the church.

The force—the "pulse"—that is identified by some people with the word God ultimately resounds within a personal locus. The God—if you choose to use that particular word—who ultimately exists for me resounds (a better word than resides) in my personal locus and no one else exactly experience this phenomenon as I do. A personal locus is not transferable, so I cannot in the end "know" the same God that my mother knew, nor can I give that which is within my personal locus to my children. I must find and define this reality for myself. We must finally experience all of this for ourselves and find the affirmation of the reality of the experience within ourselves. Of course, a mutuality of dialogue can be of benefit just like mutuality of dialogue can be helpful in most dimensions of our lives. That dialogue must manifest a powerful respect for the experience that rises within the personal locus of others. The dialogue can never be allowed to be reduced to who is right and who is wrong. Religion has such contests—or wars—but spirituality does not.

SECOND LEVEL CONSIDERATIONS: WILLIAM OF OCKHAM

Across the course of Western civilization, many philosophers have gained more recognition than William of Ockham. Almost lost in the early middle ages, Ockham certainly is not seen to inhabit the same terrain as an Aristotle, Descartes, or Aquinas. This judgment is, at the very minimum, short sighted, for Ockham had insights that are critical for understanding existence and gaining a deeper appreciation of life in general. At first sight, he is known for "Ockham's razor," a philosophical concept that emphasized simplicity. Why,

1. *Introduction: Spirituality and Business?*

Ockham questioned, was it better to explain some reality with many, many variables when a few variables would suffice? Simpler was infinitely better.

He was responding to a time in the history of thinking when almost everything had become too complex and complicated. Explanations on top of explanations proliferated and, while they did, meaning got more and more removed from normal people living normal lives. Philosophy, religion, theology—once the prize of the intellectual arts—became inconsequential and mundane for the masses. So, Ockham wanted to restate a great deal of thinking with simplicity and with a basic sense that real people could relate to meaningfully. The concepts he developed still have a powerful implication for modern life today.

Ockham believed that the world we experience is a real world. We experience this world through the senses, and these sense experiences are real—pure, distinct, simple. Yet, our definition of "reality" and of what our "senses" are capable of are both limited. Because of these limitations, we tend to only experience part of all that is possible to experience in life.

Formally, Ockham said we have two types of experiences—"experiences of first in-tension-ality" and "experiences of second in-tension-ality." This sounds very complicated, so let me explain with the help of a fairly easy illustration. I love the subdivision where we live in East Tennessee. From the front, it is all pretty normal with streets, houses, and well-manicured lawns. But, in the back of our house, especially when the trees are lush with leaves, you would think you lived deep in the Smokey Mountains; you can't even see another house. The lot our home is built on, like many lots where we live, drops off from the front to the back. The deck on the back of our house is almost twenty feet off the ground. When you walk out on the deck, you almost feel like you are walking into the top of an arbor of trees. It is beautiful! I love being on that deck when the trees are full of leaves.

Given this context, the rest of my explanation will be easy to understand. Sometimes while we have lived at this house, especially when I was still teaching and our children were young, I was the first one up. I would walk out onto the deck. I can assure you that I was not sentient or rational, just almost non-consciously—in terms of rationality—walking out on the deck. I called this my "meeting with the morning." Sometimes I was totally quiet; sometimes I might "aaah," "oooh," "brrr," or simply sigh deeply—my responses to the morning. My experiences, at this moment, were pre-verbal, non-verbal, simply experience as experience—for Martin Heidegger, simply "being there."

Ockham believed this experience was the first experience, the primal experience, a dimension of reality that was absolutely authentic and creditable. Our cat, stretching awake from her spot on the recliner's cushion, having her own "meeting with the morning," may have been having her own first in-tension al experience.

In a while, my wife would come downstairs. Her concerns—still absolutely authentic and creditable—were different from mine. She had to help children get dressed for school, so she would ask me "What is it like outside?" Sometimes, I would tell her, "aaah, oooh, brrr," or I would simply sigh deeply. She tolerates me at these moments, but this is not what she was wanting. Clearly, knowing what she wanted, sometimes I would say something like: "It is thirty-six degrees, with a cold front moving in from the west; the wind is sixteen miles per hour, and the dew point is 2.6." Her typical response was something like: "How can a reasonably intelligent person be such a smart aleck this early in the morning!"

You see, my wife wanted me to take my first in-tension al experience and put it into words (mental constructs, rational statements). Such statements would be more helpful, in a practical manner, than my emotive expressions, but never would my words absolutely capture the reality experienced in my "meeting with the morning." For Ockham, second in-tension ality or second intension experiences are experiences contained in rationality, mental constructs, put into words. They have credibility and necessity, but they do not inscribe or explain reality in its totality. There is more, much more, but if we only allow for that which can be expressed in words or housed in mental concepts, we cut ourselves off from extensive ranges of reality that are so often missed.

So, Ockham wanted to convince people to use rationality, to create all kinds of mental constructs, and develop precise language of detail and expression. However, he also wanted to absolutely affirm reality that could never be confined and captured in words. Simply, there was word reality and non-word reality. Both have absolute credibility.

I believe that a significant number of readers will have their own personal examples that will confirm the truth of what Ockham observed. My brother once watched a space shuttle roar from its launch pad into space. The experience meant even more to him because he is a pilot. He can put into words many of the basic details of what he saw, but somewhere in his descriptions he simply stops talking, tears come into his eyes, and he shrugs. That shrug coveys more of the experience of the space shuttle launch he experienced than any words he could use. I recall seeing my son throw a touchdown pass to win a close game against an important rival in the final seconds of the game. Tacklers were hanging all over him, and he threw a perfect pass forty yards to one of his friends. The friend's father and I were hugging each other on the sidelines, jumping up and down, crying like really weird adults. It was first in-tension al. I saw my daughter born and held her in my hands moments afterwards. I recall saying, "Hello, pretty girl. How are you? I'm your Daddy." Tears were streaming. First in-tension ality.

Why is all that Ockham says crucial to our discussion of spirituality? Because, at its core, that which is being referred to with the word spiritual is first and foremost a first in-tension al reality. The whole process of approaching the experience that is being termed spiritual is not capable of being sorted out, resolved, explained, and made sense of with words. When it is put into words—anytime first in-tension ality is put into words—a reductionistic process takes place in which the first in-tension al experience is reduced to something less than it actually is. It is made less, inferior, a "shadow of its actual self."

Our lives are not open to that which we are terming spiritual unless we allow for that which is first in-tension al. All that Ockham was saying is that the first in-tension al is also real; in fact, it may be "more real" than that reality which is inscribed and captured in definitions, explanations, the words of philosophy and theology. All that we do with words is of deep meaning, simply not the deepest meaning. Unless we can come to grips with this understanding, accept and affirm it, the likelihood of formative experiences of that which we are calling spiritual is not very great; it may not be even possible at all. There may be hints of the spiritual that occur by accident and serendipity, but without Ockham's insight and claiming his insight as distinct and absolute fact, there is probably little chance that the first in-tension al will become an actively meaningful part of life. Without this active meaning, life is delimited—reduced, never as full as it might otherwise be.

SECOND LEVEL CONSIDERATIONS: MARTIN BUBER

By the 1930s, Martin Buber was a force to be reckoned with in Western Europe. He believed that Jewish identity was being lost in the movements of European nationalism. Traditions, even the Hebrew language, were being lost. Buber worried that a new generation of "integrated Jews" would rise who did not know the old ways, and thus would lose their identity. This loss of identity could be an easy prelude to a weakness capable of allowing all Jewish people to be victimized out of existence. He worked tirelessly to focus attention for Jews and what it meant to be Jewish; people without an identity may cease to be people.

Of course, with the rise of Nazism, Buber rushed to fight against the dehumanization and destruction of what would become the Holocaust. He became a hunted man and barely escaped to Israel with his life. But—but!—in Israel, he began to make radical statements. He would not hate the German people. The soldiers of the Third Reich, for the most part, were victims as much as the Jews. They were, ultimately, just people. They had to be seen as people first; issues of nationality, ethic background, and all the rest, were secondary and—in a humane society—had to remain secondary. When Israel began to move to establish itself as an independent state, Buber advanced the causes of the Yihud movement, a political position in which Arabs and Jews would form a joint state. People were people, and any divisions that artificially drove them apart would be ultimately destructive. Of course, the exclusivistic Zionists—not the Yihud—won the day, and Buber's prophecy about a destructive future came true—is still true.

He ultimately left Israel and came to the United States. He taught for years at the University of Chicago. His writing, especially *I/Thou and Moses*, has established him as one of the greatest theologians of the twentieth century.

In 1960, William Hamilton and Thomas Altizer—theologians at the Candler School of Theology of Emory University—wrote a book entitled *Radical Theology and the Death of God*. The public media attached itself to the idea of "The Death of God," and a firestorm of mostly inaccurate, but powerful conversations rose around the book. Buber, of course, was asked what he thought about this "death" of God. His response was profound.

Buber said that it was incredible to talk about God's death, a reality that could never be proved or disproved. He knew that the title of the book had little to do with the book's content. But, he was convinced that we do live in a time of "the eclipse of God." In an eclipse, a reality—the sun, for example—does not cease to exist; there is no "death." Instead, our view of the reality—as when the moon passes between the earth and the sun—is obscured. For Buber, very distinctively, we do live in a time in which our "view" of divinity is obscured.

1. Introduction: Spirituality and Business?

This obscuring, this "eclipse of God," is the direct result of the "eclipse of the personal" that has taken place in our modern/post-modern society. This "personal" has gotten pushed to the periphery primarily by the rampant materialism of the modern age. People—interpersonal relationships, the Self—are given a lesser priority in the rush to compile and consume things. When things dominate, when the personal is lost, the chance of having meaningful relationships is demeaned and diminished, the chance of meaningful self-awareness is all but impossible, meaningful experiences with the beautiful don't happen, and developing a relationship with "God" is off the charts of viability.

Therefore, if there is a chance to reclaim the experience of divinity, there will first have to be a reclaiming of the "personal." This statement is easy to make, but the task of actually reclaiming the "personal" is daunting, requires the greatest discipline, and will result only in a process of absolute, focused conscious effort. Business/work is a powerful interference because of the way that devotion is demanded that competes with the "personal" and almost forces it toward secondary significance. A value-based or "spiritual" workplace, or leadership in such an organization, is challenged to be successful in all the ways that success is measured but also maintain an environment in which the "personal" can be sustained. If the "personal" is lost—or compromised, the possibility of the spiritual doesn't happen. At least, the possibility of the spiritual does not happen in a way that has a power than can sustain itself and provide decisive meanings for people's lives.

SECOND LEVEL CONSIDERATIONS: VICTOR FRANKL

(Please note: This short section on Victor Frankl is repeated in this volume from the section on "Vision." However, the two pieces are not exactly the same. The Frankl remarks in the "Vision" piece are a revision, expansion, and somewhat differently-emphasized writing that the one found here. I have included both for two reasons. First, a reader may not see both. Second, both—in their own versions—are critical to the sections where they are included. In regard to Hartman, he felt that the work of Frankl and Maslow were important touchstones for this own work. Clearly, if you have read the section on Frankl under "Vision," you can quickly scan these next few pages.)

The experience of Adolph Hitler and the Holocaust for Victor Frankl was quite different from that of Martin Buber and Robert Hartman. Although Frankl was Austrian by birth (1905) and was a leading voice of European psychotherapy, he was imprisoned by the Nazis from 1942–1945; his wife died in the concentration camps. Most people think that Frankl's great writing, *Man's Search for Meaning: An Introduction to Logotherapy* (1959), was the result of this experience. In fact, Frankl says that the concept was all but complete well before the horrible war experiences and was only confirmed by what he saw in the death camps. To read Frankl's account of the camps is startling; had he not taken into the camps something of the essence that rises in his thought after the war, it is difficult to imagine that he could have survived.

Frankl saw himself as the forbearer of the "third school of Viennese psychology." First, there was Freud with his emphasis on the role of basic drives, the id, ego, and superego, and the role of sexuality in the formative underpinnings of human existence. Frankl would affirm that Freud's view held a great deal of objective, mechanical, instrumental insight into human action, but that humans were much more complex than simply existing a almost mechanistically driven manifestations of sexual impulse. While we have all "come from" a place of culture, precedent, and tradition, and while we have all been something of a product of genetics, for Frankl where we are going, what stimulates and motivates us in a movement to the future is of much greater importance.

Next, there was Alfred Adler who was also convinced that there was more to human existence than Freud's seminal drives. For Adler, human beings were often beset with a sense of inferiority—thus, the idea of an inferiority complex. This inferiority might be caused by a multitude of factors, but it manifested itself in a Nietzsche-like "will to power" in which the inferiority was thrown aside and the true self could emerge free and undeterred, ready to achieve its own actualization (Maslow) and fulfillment of being (Tillich). Clearly, there could be many aberrations that could rise if overcoming this sense of inferiority ran rampant and uncontrolled; Hitler may be a good example of this. But, for most people—and Frankl admired this conclusion—to find the courage to move beyond the strangleholds of inferiority was always important, and the task of the therapist to encourage had all kinds of credibility.

However, Frankl had become convinced that there was an entire dimension of human existence that had not been adequately considered in either the work of Freud or Adler. The abiding desire of human beings to search for meaning in life became, for Frankl, the "window"—the opening as it were—to the depth of human existence. This search for meaning became a kind of motivating and energizing "life force" which ultimately displayed the most distinctive powers of human existence; not simply the perverse, the psychotic, power to destroy life in travesties such as the Holocaust, but the power to overcome such travesties and still be able to find—and give—joy, beauty, and even love. The search for meaning was ultimately a spiritual search, albeit without necessary reference to any cultural religion. Often scholars will talk of a "tri-dimensional ontology," seeing the "nature"(the Greek *ontos*) of human beings as physical/somatic, mental/psychic, and spiritual/poetic.

Certainly, Frankl's great work is *Man's Search for Meaning*, but much earlier in his life—in fact, in those moments more directly following the Holocaust—he gave a series of lectures to a small group of about a dozen people in Vienna which was published in book form in 1947 as *Der Unbewusste Gott/The Unconscious God* that explores this "opening," this "window" into human existence in—for me—an even more profound and precise manner than the magnus opus.

At first, Frankl describes religion as the primary, historical conduit of human search for meaning. From the most primitive moments of human existence, there has been evidence of religion in every culture as a reflection of the human need to gain greater insight into life's deepest questions, to find some sense of control over life's least understood eventualities, and to move beyond fear and hate to the higher experiences of peace, joy, community, and love. However, the evolution of religion into cultural forms, which lost credibility and even became destructive—Hitler's armies never lacked for chaplains—was all too obvious. Yet, Frankl was convinced that the evolution of religion was not the highest plateau of the human search for meaning; there was much more.

At this point, decisive for our discussion, he begins to talk about the spiritual. That which he terms religion, the visible, outward, cultural form of this search might be able to manifest and embrace—even advance—the spiritual; usually, it simply does not—or sadly does not—and all too easily creates aberrations that defy and discredit the spiritual. Consider, to find alignment with the other two Viennese schools, how often religion has de-volved into expression of the sexual instinct or those defense mechanisms that are reactions against some sort of felt, cultural or personal senses of inferiority.

Of decisive importance for Frankl is the idea that in addition to any other "instincts" that human beings may legitimately have—and have to contend with on a daily basis—there is a "spiritual instinct." He clearly states: "We now arrive at an essential revision of the previous concept of the unconscious (i.e., the positions of Freud and Adler), or more specifically, of its extent. We now have to revise its limits because it turns out that there is not only an instinctual unconscious, but a spiritual unconscious as well" (*TUG*, p. 25). Ultimately, this "spiritual unconscious"—this spirituality—is the core of human existence that provokes human search for meaning.

The primary manifestation of this "spiritual unconscious"—our critical concept of spirituality—is a sense of responsibility. Let's allow this decisive thought to sink in for a moment: a basic instinct at the defining core of human existence, that which provokes and motivates our search for meaning, that which defines us at our best, perhaps the pervasive content of the greatest teachers of civilization on this planet, that which stands in sharpest contrast to the un-human, the sub-human, the de-humanizing—spirituality as a sense of responsibility.

In some respects, this sense of responsibility in inward turning is the human need to be responsible to one's own uniqueness. Here, there are clear intellectual intersections being constructed with the existential concepts of Karl Jaspers and Martin Heidegger. Jaspers emphasized the importance of self discovery manifested in terms of deciding what as an individual I am to be (entscheidendes Sein—decided-upon Be-ing as opposed to driven Being); Heidegger added the emphasis of this decision not remaining conceptual and mental but finding concrete manifestation in the here-and-now as I actually live out the I that I am. This is Heidegger's ultimate, "spiritual" domain of Dasein; authentic "be-ing/Sein"—note the verb force of "be-ing" as opposed to the noun force of "being" (I am not a human being as a noun, a thing, but a human be-ing as a verb, a force, an action)— fully immersed in and committed to the here-and-now/Da. Take note of all that has been said above regarding Heidegger and care/sorgen, and the connection to Frankl's thoughts on responsibility are abundantly clear. Frankl's bottom line:

> Genuine religiousness [that which is defined as spirituality throughout this discussion] does not have the character of driven-ness, but rather of deciding-ness. Indeed, [authentic spirituality] stands with its deciding-ness and falls with its driven-ness. In a word, [authentic spirituality] is either existential [—the result of responsible actions taken in response to unique circumstances —] or not at all (*TUG*, p. 65).

1. Introduction: Spirituality and Business?

Also notice that there is an essential "convergence" that is taking place in Frankl's thought. There is, without question, the responsibility to discover and manifest self. There is, also without question, the responsibility to care for others. The essential convergence takes place when the responsibility for the epitome of self-manifestation and the responsibility for the care of others merge. For Freud and Adler, there is forever polarity and contradiction between these two dimensions; for Frankl they are ultimately one and the same and, when achieved, manifest the highest expressions of meaning, the culmination of the search. As will be manifest throughout, Robert Hartman's concept of the "Five Self Rules" explores the precise gamut of meaning conveyed by Frankl.

Frankl provides further qualifications and explanations of this spiritual, which are very helpful for our overall discussion. First, he is clear that spirituality/the spiritual unconscious will never be fully explored or explained by rational logic; it is not scientifically demonstrable. Spirituality is an "Urphanomen." The prefix "Ur-" is an intriguing, cross-cultural term that has ancient etymological roots; it means ancient, primeval, original—Abraham came from Ur according to the ancient texts. Thus, an "ur-phenomenon" is before logic, before rationality, even before words; it cannot be explained or reduced to logical constructs. Here, the overall discussion returns to Ockham.

However, having defeated logic and intellectual rationality is not an invitation for Frankl to experience spirituality/the spiritual unconscious with mysticism or to see mystical reflection or meditation as the highest form of this "spiritual." As important as aesthetics is—and he sees aesthetic experience as a component of the spiritual unconscious— true spirituality is to be lived in concrete actions of care and responsibility. The highest expression of the spiritual is found in concrete actions of love. There is no substitute for this! In fact, he even calls on a process of "de-reflection" as a guard against human experience becoming overly stuck in a purity of reflection and meditation. The highest and finest "human existence exists in action rather than reflection" (*TUG*, p. 30).

Anyone who knows the work of Robert Hartman is immediately compelled by Frankl's extension of his concept of the spiritual to the idea of uniqueness. A primary component of responsibility, care, love, be-ing in the here-and-now is the experience of uniqueness. To discover and manifest self, the highest form (not forms, as discovery and manifestation are mutually inclusive if meaning is achieved) of self-directed care and responsibility involves finding, affirming, and be-ing unique. The highest movements of "conscience" involve intimate investigations and involvements with unique events, especially realizing that every event, person, and circumstance is unique and cannot be dealt with in terms of universal rules and laws. (This is Aristotle's teleological/ends-oriented ethics, Joseph Fletcher's "situation ethics," or Georg Simmel's "individual law; it is also Jesus' concept of the Sabbath being made for man and not man for the Sabbath.) Ethical conscience looks to find the unique possibilities that exist in highly singular circumstances.

> The "ethical instinct" is entirely different. In contrast to vital instincts [Freud and Adler], the effectiveness of the ethical instinct depends on the fact that its target is not anything general but something individual, something concrete. . . . Only conscience is capable of adjusting the "eternal," generally agreed-upon moral law to the specific situation a concrete person is engaged in. Living one's conscience always means living a highly personalized level, aware of the full concreteness of each situation (*TUG*, p. 36).

Finally, love is defined as a focus of deepest attention—Hartman's intrinsic valuation—on the unique possibilities inherent in another person and the potential inherent in a unique relationship with that person. "In love," Frankl asserts, "the self is not driven by the id, but the self chooses (Heidegger) the 'Thou'" (Buber's German *du*, the informal second person, the address used between lovers). To see love as a form of see-ing, find-ing, affirm-ing uniqueness gives love both a responding to and a causative, creating power which both conveys and experiences meaning. The nexus of promoted and discovered uniqueness exponentially raises the value, the worth, the meaning of life—of live-ing—to a next, higher level.

With this focus on uniqueness, there is the additional element of a movement that is always to the future and potentiality is always a future dynamic. The "freedom to be" is ultimately a "what to" freedom, not a "what from" freedom which focuses on the individual self triumphing over something in the past; such "what for" freedom usually is frustrating since the past cannot be relived or changed. To think that the past can be adequately compensated for is an unfulfilling ego trip that results in the most damning of obsessive-compulsive behavior. Here is the primary force of Leland Kaiser and Dan Wilford echoing repeatedly the mantra: "So what? Now what?" What has taken place in the past is a "given" which can be molded and shaped—potentiated—toward the future.

Victor Paul Furnish in his "Theology and Ethics in Paul" finds this same theme. For Furnish, Paul was not trying to be a theologian, spinning increasing webs of dogmatic abstraction. Instead, he was trying to provide a transition from theology to ethics before the cultural power of theology—which Paul knew well as a "Pharisee of Pharisees"—asserted itself to the destruction of the message of Jesus; of course, the message of Jesus had a stark ethical dimension with little or no theological emphasis at all. Furnish's Paul message emphasizes "freedom for" as opposed to "freedom from." The point of faith is not to be free from "sin," in whatever cultural definitions might prevail at any given time, but to be free for the higher calling of righteous living. Righteousness is understood as a dynamic which moves in two, concurrent motions: first, an awareness that all of life is interconnected; and, second, living out of that awareness which is designed to enhance that interconnectedness. Paul's dynamic is always and forever "pressing on to the high calling" of the God/the Divine made known in the teachings and example of Jesus. Divinity, and all of its attendant questions, is a theological issue; ethics, living toward the future in a way that will add value to life, is the Jesus issue.

Frankl is also very clear—and a statement of this kind of clarity is likely to be needed when his concepts face a more scientific culture—that this spirituality/spiritual unconscious is not merely a set of nice, emotional feelings; he is not trying simply be—as the modern indictment often expresses—"warm and fuzzy." He gives priority to Scheler's distinction between Gefuhlszustand (an "emotional state" through which "warm and fuzzy" may be conveyed) and in-tension al Gefuhl (in-tension al feelings which are consciously directed and experienced). We are not talking here about feelings of goodwill, but rather a movement beyond the normative ways of talking about human consciousness to a less limited field of inquiry which honesty comes to grapple with the authentic depths of human existence.

Therefore, Frankl's signature logotherapy—a complex term that he was bullish about leaving unamended—has great meaning: there is a primitive, previous, first-in-tension al/in-tension al Logos which is beyond any rational, scientific, demonstrable logic. All of the logic of even the most modern science hardly touches the Logos, the Urphanomen, the "irreducible (to logical and rational, mental constructs) phenomenon" in human existence—in the existence of the universe—which is spiritual. (Both Heraclitus' Logos concept and the

Logos emphasis in the Prologue to the Gospel of John can be instructive at this point. In John, this Logos that is "made flesh" and represents the fullness of the presence of God is not a mental concept but the concrete, ethical example of Jesus' life. Questions of divinity, and other theological questions, are beside the point; questions of ethical mandate prevail. In the end, to echo Job: all of the brilliance of man does not skirt the edges of the wisdom of God. The worst advice a human being can follow is to reflect, meditate, and think toward the conclusion of logic; the best advice is to decide to act, to be responsible to the individuating, singular, unique possibilities presented in living, especially in those engagements characterized by the responses of the spiritual, ethical instinct/conscience and love. In the end, logotherapy is not traditional psychotherapy; it is, rather, "education to responsibility," a statement that rises out of the 1975 postscript addendum which Frankl added to his early lectures (*TUG*, p. 121).

In order to "activate" the schemata for the concrete living of Frankl's philosophy there must be self-transcendence. Without self-transcendence there cannot be healthy self-actualization; egotism and basic self-serving, hyper-vested selfishness will occur that will be ultimately destructive of the human condition, of life in general. But, there cannot be the possibility of self-transcendence unless transcendence itself has become a category of existence that can be affirmed and actively embraced. For Frankl, many if not most of the problems of human existence are the result of a "crippled relation to transcendence" (*TUG*, p. 70). As Paul Tillich clearly understood, true atheism is not the rejection of a god-concept, but the rejection and eradication of transcendence as an authentic, operative category of existence. For Einstein, the experience of awe and wonder—legitimate and fundamental forms of transcendence—is at the core of all of life, but a person who is blind to this transcendence is "as good as dead, their minds and eyes are closed."

Fortunately, the experience of transcendence—of "that which" is beyond humans and not the result of humans (as in Freud's projection theories). There is almost a "smorgasbord" of possibilities here, and there is no necessary competition between the various "entrees;" all can be filling, depending on individual preference, and all are likely to be complementary and can achieve similar ends. The achieved ends, the successful nurturing and sustaining of living—to follow the metaphor—is the reality to be accomplished in the future which is of most importance.

1. Introduction: Spirituality and Business?

One instigator, inspiration, provocateur of transcendence is revealed—"hinted at" may be a better term—is found in Frankl's leading concept of "The Unconscious God." He is probably working out of the comfort zone of his own belief system at this point and the culture in which he was raised. Yet, his concept is anything but conventional. The "God" of cultural religion and all of its destructiveness and disintegration may be thankfully dead; of course, this "God"—still fueling bigotries and exclusivisms across the planet—is anything but dead. Yet, if this illegitimate, pretender "God" who is clearly the result of processes of projection explained accurately by Freud could cease to exist, and human being—life in general—would absolutely not be devoid of divinity. In fact, if the cultural "God" could die, the authentically Divine might have a greater chance of manifesting itself.

Beyond the "God" of cultural creation and philosophical abstraction stands what Frankl calls—for want of better words—"The Unconscious God." The dwelling place of this God is the spiritual unconscious, which must forever remain immune to scientific exploration or philosophical explanation. This God manifests itself as a transcendent "call" to responsible actions of ethical engagement. Interestingly enough, this "call" may not necessarily be experienced or responded to by someone actively involved in all of the accoutrements of cultural religion; it may, on the other hand, be fully embraced by someone—from the perspective of cultural religion—who is identified as being agnostic or even atheist. (For the atheist who lives in response to the transcendent call to ethical engagement, the Unconscious God has simply not become conscious as yet, or the barricades and obstacles of conventional, cultural religion may still be too strong to allow for a comfortable embracing of the Unconscious God as a conscious reality). Without question, Frankl believes that this "Unconscious/Hidden God" actually exists, although concern with validating any kind of real, physical existence has no expedience.

Transcendence can also occur, functionally and essentially, through the conscious projection of the unique self-living on a more idealized level of ethical engagement with life; this ideal then becomes a powerful motivating force in that ideal level being accomplished. Frankl took lessons to fly small, private airplanes. He was taken by his instructor's concept of "crabbing." If, for example, I am flying to a point directly east of my present location, and there is a powerful wind blowing from north to south, I must compensate for the wind. A direct, west to east course will leave me many miles to the southeast of my destination if the wind is strong enough. So, I must compensate—I must "crab." I must establish an "ideal" direction to the northeast, and, following this "idealized" point, I will have a much greater likelihood of arriving at my desired destination. Frankl then moves from his flight instructor to Goethe: "If I take man as he is, I make him worse; if I take him as he ought to be, I make him better." For some, this expression of transcendence may be too "humanistic," devoid of any God-concept. Frankl is concerned with the outcome of ethical actions, and the result can very authentically be the same.

Not to be overly simplistic or pedantic, the ontological reference point of Frankl's transcendence—be it an Unconscious/Hidden God or a projected ideal that rises out of my own uniqueness—is of little or no consequence. Instead, attention can be given to what I would call "The Three Cs" of Frankl's presentation. Again, apologies for simplicity. First, there is a sense of Call, a pulling, magnetizing, attention-garnering sense of being addressed. This Call may be more intuitive than articulated; it may take a thousand different forms, but the sense of demand to respond in a responsible manner based on unique talents and abilities is fairly distinctive.

Next, there is the emerging reality of a Cause, a singular outcome that will unleash some positive potential of life that is important, that makes a difference in life moving forward in an enhanced manner. Issues such as the size of the Cause or the public attention it might garner are totally beside the point; causes are as unique as the people who will approach them. That some reality has taken on the dimension of Cause simply and clearly indicates the degree of engagement that is being promoted. Finally, there is the phenomenon of Commitment, the ultimate level of self-giving, dedication to the Cause, and response to the Call.

When a person is caught up in the dynamic of these "Three Cs," a unique dialogue begins to occur which Frankl calls "the wisdom of the heart" in which the human being accepts responsibility for fulfilling the meaning inherent in a given life situation. Life is not reduced to a "search for Self," but rather a "search for meaning" which has, as a consequence, the achievement of authentic Selfhood as a primary by-product. He says:

> We have to learn from this sapientia cordis, from this wisdom of the heart, that being human means being confronted continually with situations, each of which is at once a chance and a challenge, giving us a "chance" to fulfill ourselves by meeting the "challenge" to fulfill its meaning. Each situation is a call, first to listen, and then to respond (*TUG*, p. 129).

1. Introduction: Spirituality and Business?

Given Frankl's emphasis on challenge, it is powerfully intriguing to look at the work of individuals such as Fernando Nottebohm and Elizabeth Gould known as neurogenesis, a term reminiscent of the process philosophy of John Cobb, Charles Hartshorne, Teilhard de Chardin, and others that captured so much attention and hopefulness in the mid-1900s. Neurogenesis was, at first, a radical departure from much of traditional brain science, but it has now become the catalyst for a great deal of the promise that is manifesting itself in stem cell research and the possibility of finding solutions to many captivating and dreadful problems of human existence such as Alzheimer's and Parkinson's diseases. Neurogenesis demonstrates that brains are not limited by the number of neurons that are present at or soon after birth. Instead, the brain can develop new neurons, perhaps even to the point of "repairing" structures that have become injured or genetically deficient. The implications are profound.

The neurogeneticists are discovering that the brain develops new neurons in response to challenges that occur in very real-life circumstances. The entire process of challenge causes our brains to produce neurons that help us become more adept in meeting these challenges. Now, listen to the following statement, and in your mind's eye you can almost see that contemplative smile of Frankl creeping across his face as important realization takes place: "She found that a brain needs to 'use it or lose it'—if new cells are not put to work, they will die more rapidly than if they have a purpose." (*The New Yorker*, July 23, 2001, p. 48). The neurogenetic research has also taken note that an adverse effect of continuous environments of stress, fear, and anxiety— evidently different than challenge— will diminish new neuron production. In fact, even the presence of regular physical activity and exercise is shown to facilitate new neuron production. What happens when boredom, ennui, Heidegger's *weltschmertz* (world weariness), and generally unchallenging inactivity occurs is more than obvious.

Nottelbohm, much of whose work has focused on the brains of songbirds, talks about the uniqueness of his approach, an approach fully consistent with the philosophical insights of Frankl:

What kinds of things do animals do in their natural circumstances? What kinds of problems do they have? How do they solve them? Brains are not all-purpose machines. They have evolved to deal with specific existential problems: How do you make it through a year with all kinds of seasons? How do you claim and defend your territory? How do you find a mate? How do you look after your offspring? How do you remember where you hid your seeds? (*NY*, p. 52)

So, life gives us tasks. To talk about the luck, fairness, or range of difficulty (or lack thereof) of these tasks is absolutely beside the point. We have problems to solve, value judgments to make; we have promises to keep and miles to go before we sleep. If the neurons of our brains can respond to purpose-full activities, think of the implications for the uniqueness of that nexus of cells and experiences which become the unique self in its unique time. It is the absence of purpose and pursued vision that creates regression and destruction of our very best potential, of whom, indeed, we are.

In the end, there is the active possibility for happiness, both as an outcome of commitment to this Cause as it applies to any variety of enhanced life circumstances and as a personal reality that rises in the midst of listening to the Call, envisioning the Cause, and living with Commitment. Happiness is a by-product, "something that ensues, not something to be pursued" (*TUG*, p. 85). There is neither "hyper-reflection" nor "hyper-in-tension " about these matters, but rather a serendipitous, synchronistic movement within the "flow" (again, the reference here is to the complexities of Csikszentmihalyi's concepts and not a laissez-faire "going with the flow" mentality) of call, cause, and commitment. At one and the same time, this movement within the flow can be absolutely diligent and demanding of every strength of human character and also as light, playful, and rejuvenating as the movements of children (see Sam Keen's concept of paidia/child's play in *An Apology for Wonder*). The Dalai Lama says that the very purpose of life is to seek happiness; Victor Frankl has charted the course.

As an afterthought, I have only one complaint with Frankl, and it is more semantical than substantive. He says that we are plunged into the midst of this Call, Cause, and Commitment dynamic where we encounter unique situations with our own personal uniqueness. I agree totally. In these unique encounters, we—existentially—must choose, decide, and act; for Frankl, life becomes a matter of selectivity, discrimination, and prioritization. He says, without equivocation, "we have to choose between what is important and what is not" (*TUG*, p. 122). Again, I agree totally.

For me, what he is talking about is making value judgments, weighing, assessing, evaluating. This, of course, is at the core of my own philosophy, the axiology of Robert Hartman, and the force of this overall presentation. Yet,

1. Introduction: Spirituality and Business?

Frankl has a problem with the concept of "value judgments" as he defines these terms. For him, a "value judgment" is not a singular conclusion rising from the flow of Call, Cause, and Commitment based on the unique person engaged in the unique encounter, but rather he sees a "value judgment" as an exponent, an extension of the fixed, absolutistic values/beliefs of a given culture at a given time. He calls for an "abstinence from value judgments" (*TUG*, p. 123) so that an individual can be fully free to relate to personal and situational uniqueness.

If "value judgment" is defined in the narrow sense advanced in the language of Frankl, I continue to agree wholeheartedly. However, I make a very close distinction between values and beliefs, which often are nothing more than arbitrary cultural exponents, and the active process of value judgment. To use Frankl's own prescriptive insights, I see value judgments in their dynamic, verbal force, not as fixed, objective nouns that can simply be "inscribed" on human life. To me, the process of value judgment is precisely this "wisdom of the heart" which Frankl described. I believe we are in total agreement here, and only need to make a semantic clarification. As Leland Kaiser teaches: with the body, we act; with the emotions, we feel; with the mind, we think; and, [this is my extension of Kaiser's thought] with the "heart," the "soul," the "spirit," we value.

I wonder what Frankl would think of the profound implications of the proclamation of the ancient prophet, Jeremiah:

Behold, the days are coming, says the Lord, when I will make a new covenant with my people. . . . I will put my law within them, and I will write it upon their hearts. . . . No longer shall each man teach his neighbor and each his brother, saying "Know the Lord," for they shall all know me, from the least of them to the greatest. . . ." (Jeremiah 31:31ff).

In concluding this discussion on Frankl, it is important to emphasize over and again that he is not Immanuel Kant espousing some version of a "categorical imperative," a kind of "voice" of the universe that impinges upon human from some outside venue that motivates moral behavior. Nor is he a spiritualist in the more stereotypical sense of that word waiting for some "utterance" from God that provokes prophetic proclamation. In fact, for Frankl, the call of conscience is not in the form of some "transcendence order" or supersensory mandate at all. The call comes directly from that arena of life where human uniqueness of talent, ability, capacity, and opportunity meets expressed need. The call is a challenge to a higher level of responsibility. At some point, the challenge will be responded to with commitment and action, or it will be left wanting a response. Real, authentic commitment may have intellectual, rational dimensions, but on that ultimate level that brings a person to put life and living on the line, the commitment is existential—fraught with the dynamics of choice behold the clear and demonstrable dynamics of logic and reason. Meaning, and then—if we are fortunate—even happiness, flows from those actions of commitment, those decisions and choices to care. Mignon Eisenberg gives this expression:

> We deserve receiving an answer to our questions about the meaning of life. WRONG. It is not up to us to ask what the meaning of life is. Life sets tasks before each person. In meeting them, we define the meaning of our life; by our actions we answer the questions that life puts to us.

Clearly, Frankl was fond of many of the insights gained in the tragic life of Friedrich Nietzsche. He saw Nietzsche observing life being lived by most people on two levels. On one level, the major question was "how?". The "how level" focused on the strategies used to move from one moment of life to the next, often with the motivation of creating strategies that would produce wealth, fame, or physical pleasure; Kierkegaard's Don Juan in "Either/Or." Yet, beyond this "how level" for Nietzsche was a more dominant and existentially essential question, "why?" Without an "adequate why," a person could not live; there might be physical life, but there was not meaning. What Nietzsche understood that moved Frankl, and what most Westerners especially have totally misunderstood, is that this "why?" of adequate meaning was not an intellectual question that could be answered with reason and logic. It was rather—and absolutely—an existential question—that could only be answered by living out of one's uniqueness in the midst of the unique situations presented by life with decisions and actions of responsibility and care. Meaning would then appear/arrive/come into be-ing, not as an intellectual construct, but as an existential, spiritual phenomenon manifested in the midst of an exponential nexus of uniqueness.

SECOND LEVEL CONSIDERATIONS: ALIENATION

An encompassing sense of alienation is the fundamental result of both an inability to affirm and experience first in-tension ality and the eclipse of the

1. Introduction: Spirituality and Business?

personal. The best explanation of alienation that I have ever experienced comes from the cultural anthropologist and philosopher of religion Mircea Eliade in his book, *The Sacred and the Profane*. For Eliade, human beings are deeply affirmed in their humanity on its highest levels by a sense of orientation, a sense that they somehow "fit," or even as the old hippies used to say, a sense of "having it all together." We certainly know what it is like to be "at loose ends," so we also know what it is like to have our tangled, frazzled ends "all together." I recall a country music singer intoning in a song that I know no more about than its resilient refrain: "My life is like a jigsaw puzzle, and none of the pieces fit." On the other hand, we also know what it is like for the "pieces" of our lives to be falling into place, sometimes even with the joy, exhilaration, and power of Mihaly Csikszentmihalyi's "flow." This is orientation, and it is a wonderful, highly desirable, and highly sought-after experience.

Eliade used the provocative example of ancient clan/tribal groups who had some sort of totem or "sacred pole." Usually, there were elements of the totem that recalled great events, great leaders, or deities unique to the tribe that gave it identity. The totem was always protected and in the guarded possession of tribal rulers and priests, much like the care that was devoted to the famed Ark of the Covenant of the ancient Hebrews. As the tribal clan traveled, the totem—the sacred pole—went before it, usually perceived as the connecting point of the direction and will of the divinity. When the clan camped, the sacred pole stood in the midst of the camp as a point of reference and security not unlike the way that church steeples are present in communities in the United States or flags are present with military groups. The sacred pole/totem plays an overwhelmingly significant role—it was the point of orientation. As long as there was orientation, there was security, identity, a sense of place, and a reference point that connected the present to both the past and the future.

The greatest tragedy was signaled if the sacred pole/totem ever was taken away. In the Old Testament, the ancient Hebrews are in psychological, sociological, and spiritual ruin when the Ark of the Covenant is captured by the powerful Philistines of Goliath fame. In a sense, they are also in axiological ruin as the object of greatest value which carried a myriad of references to their highest values as a people is stolen. Suddenly, their value as a people—even the value of their supposedly all-powerful God—is in a kind of value limbo. Orientation is lost and alienation on every level of their being as a people is compromised; vulnerability rises with devastating power.

In a similar sense, it is possible to read Civil War narratives that recall the abject devotion that is given to a unit's colors. The flag of a unit became its "sacred pole," carrying with it the identity of home, the glory of past battles, and the pride and personality of every soldier in the group. It was an honor to carry the colors, the colors led the unit into battle, and if one color bearer fell in conflict, immediately the flag was taken by someone else and pressed into the front of the battle. Even to let the flag touch the ground was infamy. Clearly, there was the practical advantage of having a point of reference for the movement of troops on a battlefield, but far beyond this practical dimension was the powerful personal statement that the colors conveyed. To have the colors captured or—even worse—to have to surrender them to an enemy was the rankest disaster. Orientation was surrendered, and a sense of devastating alienation followed in its wake.

In a sense, orientation is the same as wholeness, integration, alignment, "at-one-ment." If spirituality is talked about experientially, at the core of that experience is something of orientation and thus of meaning, satisfaction, wellness/well-being, and peace. When this orientation/wholeness is broken, the antithesis of experiential spirituality is manifested as alienation. If "salvation" is defined in terms of wholeness, then the opposite of salvation— "lostness"—probably has a great deal of accuracy if a person is "lost" from self, from others, even from that which is identified as the divine.

Across the course of human attempts to articulate life in some meaningful way, the concept of alienation has shown up in a number of expressions. In every case—either individually or in some kind of combination, the loss of orientation is a noteworthy consistency. The language of articulation has changed from one cultural context to another, but the reality being pointed toward or grasped at with the language has sustained itself across the centuries. And, if there is any thought that these concepts of alienation and orientation do not apply to organizationally secular environments, a large misunderstanding is being advanced. People absolutely experience dimensions of personal alienation that will impact work. They also experience varieties of alienation in the workplace that diminish morality, dedication, and motivation. Every implication of this discussion of spirituality and alienation can find manifestation in the workplace in numerous, direct ways. Spiritual leadership will consciously create strategies designed to diminish alienation and promote orientation. More productive and more meaningful work will always be the result, and productive work and meaningful work are forever and absolutely mutually inclusive; to treat them as options, either/or, or exclusive domains of the work experience is at the causative core of alienation on the most basic level of organizational existence.

The historical discussion of alienation can go back at least as far as Augustine. For the ancient Roman scholar, alienation was articulated in terms of sin. In spite of the ideas of Carl Menninger, to talk about "sin" seems only to be appropriate in a much more primitive world than our own. To talk biblically about sin as "falling short of the glory of God" may, in fact, sound like cliché and jargon that will not be listened to seriously for very long by people in our modern world. However, when the ancient prophet, Isaiah, calls out in his temple vision (Isaiah 6:1ff) "woe is me for I am undone," one is back to the core of the above discussion with many modern people being able to easily identify with feelings of "un-done-ness." A hermeneutics of "sin" would probably bring conversations right into the middle of modern existence.

Compared to Augustine, the discussions of Freud are altogether more modern. His discussions of internal dynamics of human existence that are not necessarily in harmony with external dynamics have been paid compelling attention by an entire generation of modern readers. The interplay of subconscious/unconscious and conscious aspects of the human personality make a great deal of sense to the experiences of many people. But, the basic issues of orientation and alienation remain. There is still the need to find alignment between these "arenas/domains/modes" of human living. As long as there is disparity and lack of balance with, for example, ego, id, and superego, there is massive dis-orientation, out-of-control behavior, and lack of clarity in self-understanding. The words may have changed from Augustine, but the "felt realities," the experiential outcomes are probably very much the same. The spectrum that rules from alienation to orientation remains the nexus of human existence. That Freud adds the superego, thus extending orientation and alienation to incorporate social existence beyond the exclusive, singular individual does add a fuller, more accurate and comprehensive set of variables to the entire experience. Without question, the reality of other people and their impact on my existence will contribute to any experience of alienation or orientation that I may experience.

The discussion finds new levels of sophistication in the work of Victor Frankl and Emil Durkeim. Frankl sees alienation as a consequence of human beings' experience divorce from meaning. Frankl's search for meaning as the primary activity of truly human beings is ultimately a search that will be consummated when orientation is achieved. Durkheim is a bit more concrete in talking about the role that traditions play in orientation. Traditions create an intimacy with personal and community history that undergirds personal identity. In a throw-away, disposal culture in which potential tradition evaporates before it can find concrete expression, talk about tradition seems like a relic from prehistoric times. In personal, family, and organizational life, when conscious strategies create and honor traditions, the possibility of orientation and meaning are promoted in a positive manner.

Karl Marx made the application to work environments even more specific. What Marx had to say, absent the academic frills of philosophy, theology, or psychology has power and pertinence. The problem with most work for Marx was that it promoted alienation, not only of the worker from other workers and the organizational hierarchy, but from his/her own self. Alienation occurs when labor is meaningless, when work is empty. The problem with so much modern labor is not long hours or inadequacy of pay, but emptiness of meaning. Read Studs Terkel's powerful *Working*, and you will see the accuracy of Marx's insights in a modern dress that has become business-as-usual in our modern world. When the human spirit is unengaged by work and work makes up the majority of how we expend energy in our lives, alienation will invariably follow. Spiritual leadership will find a mandate in Marx, which causes meaningfulness of labor to be a powerful priority in evaluating the health and well-being of the workplace.

Martin Luther King, Jr. provides yet an even more contemporary addition to the kind of alienation that manifests itself in modern life. His concept of "estrangement" plumbs the depths of the alienation that rises when people-as-people, with accidents of birth that are not even skin deep, are unnaturally separated from each other by artificial barriers of color, gender, ethnicity, or socio-economics. For King, when people who belong together as people are segregated for artificial and inauthentic reasons, a platform of alienation will prevail at the core of societal existence that will compound exponentially every other form of alienation that is possible. It becomes difficult to make advances in personal dimensions of alienation when stark levels of societal existence prevail in a society.

At the core of all these discussions, synthesizing all of them in an insightful manner, is the work of Robert Hartman. For Hartman, alienation would take place when there is value dysfunction, an absence of clear value judgments in regard to the general world, to others, and to the self. Axiological health and well-being would involve appropriate valuations, appropriate prioritizing, or—at least—a struggle to find propriety of valuing and weighing which moves beyond intellectuality to wisdom (the Hebrew *hokmah*, the Greek *sophia*) and—for want of better words—"good sense." Hartman searched for an "organization of goodness" which could easily be an "orientation of goodness" that resulted in realities fulfilling their highest capacity, their highest potential, the height of what is comprehensively experienced in a reality's in-tension-ality, extensionality, and ententionality (more about this four-fold dynamic below). For Hartman, value is ultimately manifested in care, and the discussion circles back to Heidegger's sorgen/besorgen. What is valued is cared for and is taken care of. Here is an "axiological axiom:" there is a direct relationship between valuing and taking care of. Taking care of must ultimately be consummated in concrete actions; it is never enough to intend to take care of or conceptually see the benefits of taking care of. Where care is paramount—in its many and varied dimensions, orientation is advanced and alienation beaten back. Care must become the factor of judgment, the factor of valuation at the core of every action, thus making those actions axiologically authentic and legitimate. The concrete strategies that "give legs" to care—that organize care—represent the advance of valuing, of goodness, on the highest levels. This is the task and mandate of spiritual leadership. A spiritual "felt reality" of meaning and fullness along with actions that eradicate the eclipse of the personal will be the concrete outcome.

FIRST FINAL CONCLUSION

When we think of ancient Greece, we think of a land populated by rich traditions of literature and philosophy; from Homer to Socrates, Plato, and Aristotle, some of the most powerful pursuits of human self-understanding are encountered in Greece by at least 2500 years ago. But, while Socrates and Plato are seen as the father figures, there was a great deal of important philosophy taking place before these men came on the scene. In fact, if we had more of those known as "Presocratics," their insights might have rivaled the best of the known masters.

Heraclitus is a primary example. All that we have of this man are hints, guesses, secondary references, and a few fragmentary writings. On the basis of this small amount of information, however, we find indispensable wisdom; if we had the entire corpus of his work, it might have transcended Socrates and Plato. As it is, we know that he was born in Ephesus in the middle of the sixth century BC. He was a younger contemporary of Pythagoras, and his Logos concept has resonance with Pythagoras' concept of the "harmony of the spheres." He was caught up in a debate with Parmenides about the nature of existence, and thus is identified as an ontologist. Parmenides, in a sense was the status quo, traditional voice, and Heraclitus was capable of the more expansive, out-of-the-box creativity of insight.

I am convinced that it is possible to find four "worlds" in the thought of Heraclitus. As these four worlds are articulated, a message as modern as the morning newspaper is revealed. Admittedly, there is distinct reinterpretation that is hermeneutically taking place here, but the core of Heraclitus' thought seems to make the conclusions about the four "worlds" justifiable.

The first "world" is the physical world that is at hand, the world that meets human beings in terms of physical proximity. The old biblical line might say that this is the "world" in which we "live and move and have our being." This at-hand world is characterized by the word *Becoming*, is constantly changing and rearranging itself, and therefore is devoid of predictability in any absolute sense. Heraclitus is probably best known for his statement "you never step in the same river twice," which captures the flux that life is. His illustration is appropriate. Approach any body of water, step in and out, in and out, and you have never been able to step literally in the same body of water. Its molecules have rearranged themselves between steps, new water has come in, water has evaporated out, even fish swimming around have redistributed the river's water in different and varying ways. Life is much like this, never standing still long enough to be "captured" in any stable and final form.

These thoughts by Heraclitus were very disturbing to many of his contemporaries. It sounded as if life was chaos to him, and chaos was seen as the encroachment of some sort of primeval, negative force that could overwhelm life in a destructive manner. While he did not buy into thoughts of primeval forces, he was adamant about his chaos concept. Yearn as we might for order, predictability, and structure, in the end, chaos was more characteristic of at-hand reality. This first "world" was difficult to live in, but at least he felt he was making a realistic assessment of it.

Beyond this first "world," Heraclitus conceived of a second "world." This world had a pattern and unity that existed behind/beneath/beyond the at-hand world. This pattern and unity provided balance and stability, constancy and solidity. In the end, the pattern and unity were assured by what we might more easily understand as "Divinity," although Heraclitus tried not to use the term in order to stretch human consideration beyond the traditional connotations generally aligned with the term Divinity. While this second "world" was not capable of being seen by human beings, it was all there nonetheless. Thus, there was "eternality" to life that was totally capable of harmonizing all potential opposites and apparent contradictions in its grasp.

This second-world concept is not all that different, in some respects, from a great deal of contemporary, traditional faith with its emphasis on the ultimate power of God. Heraclitus would never have sung, "He's got the whole world in His hands," but that same sort of stability that is evoked in the song is essentially at the core of his second world.

A third "world" concept begins to reveal the uniqueness of Heraclitus' timeless contribution. We exist in both chaos and eternality, but we also exist in language and in words. In fact, when he calls his ultimate principle of life "The Logos," he is saying that ultimate dimensions of existence are rational and logic, at least capable of being put into words and thereby given control and definition. It is language that bridges the gaps between the at-hand world and the eternal world, and when we are able to find coincidence between the at-hand world and the eternal world through words, we exert some degree of control, predictability, and stability. In the evolution of this third "world," we move in the modern age from the Enlightenment and Age of Reason to the Industrial Revolution to the Technological Society to the Information Age. Without question, what we have done in terms of language and logic has revealed many of the rational principles with which the eternal world has been formed and come into existence. Even when elements of this rational world have threatened to devastate life—for example, the creation of nuclear weapons—we have used information and communication/dialogue—other forms of language and logic—to keep these potentially devastating elements from running rampant.

Even the old metaphor of stepping in the same river twice can find application in this third world. We bring some dynamic of control to the literally ever-changing river by naming the river, by plotting its location with rational constructs (another form of naming), and defining (another form of naming) its characteristics so precisely that it could be no other river in any other place than this particular river. Once we have named the river, other myriad changes seem almost peripheral. Ironically, while we have appeared to exert more control with our logic/reason/words than previous cultures could ever have imagined, we have also created something that is the most artificial, un-real, and divorced from reality.

With our words, we have created simply a mental construct, the most minimal of concreteness. All that we do with words is important and decisive; no one would want to go back to the implications of an illiterate society. Yet, there is a problem which rises when we fail to see that what is done with words/language/logic is not the absolute and ultimate level of life. Let's use words and do all that we can with words, but we should be carefully clear that we must not stop at this point no matter how successful and productive our "word-ing" allows us to be.

Most discussions of Heraclitus stop at this point and exult in the power of his insights. However, there is much more; in fact, if we stop at the Logos Principle, we may have not gone the essential distance of his thought. There is, now, a fourth "world." Heraclitus points to this final and truly ultimate "world" when he talked about "the boundaries of the soul." Notice very, very carefully that we are now in a "world" that is absolutely beyond language, beyond words, and beyond reason. If this "world" is ever put into words, it is reduced and diminished into non-reality in the process. Like the Taoist phrase that "the Tao that is named is not the true Tao," so the fourth "world" that is defined, explained—named—is not the fourth world at all; it is not even close! The fourth "world"—to use the words of Robert Hartman—is a purely intrinsic, non-denumerable infinity of reality. It cannot be measured—"you would not find out . . . traveling along any path, for its measure is so deep."

Very quickly, questions will not likely be raised about explaining this fourth world; clearly, that is impossible. Rather, questions will be raised about how this fourth world can be experienced. Experience is ultimately superior and consummately more complete than explanation. In most instances, the entire phenomenon of value is finally a matter of actions and experience as opposed to explanation and concept. Again, the ultimate test of value is care, and conceptual care or care limited to words does not even come close to rivaling care in action and deed. So, the "boundaries"—the "horizons"—of the soul must be experienced.

In our post-Cartesian world, we have determined that when there is a problem, it can be solved by education; if there is almost any sort of need, throw education at it! The traditional role of teachers coming at impressionable times in our lives has emotionally conditioned us to see education as the most important arena of wise answers. The dialogue and conversation which takes place between teachers and students resulting in some piece of information being "poured" from a full teacher's mind into an empty student mind is still a dominant pattern of how people come to learn.

Yet, Rousseau living in the immediate aftermath of Descartes' emphasis on thinking as the highest accomplishment of human existence moved in a distinctly different direction. For Rousseau, especially in his *Emile*, it was experience which took priority over traditional, formal education as the mechanism—not just of mental, intellectual, mind-centered reality—but of learning how to live, what to value, and how to make productive and meaningful judgments of maturity.

For Rousseau, the most fundamental values of life were in-formed, not in conceptual intellectualization, but by engagement in a real, experiential world. Fundamental values rise from an experienced world, not exclusively from within the cloistered walls and artificiality of classrooms. Compare the way we learned in antiseptic classrooms to the vitality of the all-too-infrequent "field trips." We do not need to just talk about this fourth "world." We do not need to obsessively pursue definitions and explanations. We need to experience the fourth world; it has to be experienced because we have already established that it is beyond words. But, how can all of this experience begin?

Perhaps, the clue to the "boundaries of the soul" was there all along, right in front of our eyes at the core of Heraclitus. The clue was back at the river, the stepping into the river, and the contemplative reflection of felt insight that rose from it. Our problem: we are too busy to take time—as a conscious strategy of our existence as human beings—to step in many rivers. We take little time for the contemplative reflection sparked by stepping in the river. So, we move through the at-hand world, hoping that there is an eternal-pattern world, and we exert amazing energy with language and logic to gain some semblance of what we convince ourselves is control, and the ultimate "world" is not even touched. Maybe somewhere in these thoughts there is a pointing toward that reality edged up on in the words, "He makes me lie down in green pastures, He leads me beside still waters, He restores my soul." Yet, we know next to nothing about lying down in green pastures or being led beside still waters. We probably did as children or young lovers, but we have forgotten and it has been so long.

SECOND FINAL CONCLUSION

Sometimes in our modern cultures we fail to respect anything that is not sparkling new. Henry Ford's supposed comment that "History is bunk" can too easily become the mentality of a technological society, and that which is ancient is relegated to distant edges of our concerns. Such an approach can be unfortunate. There are vitally important lessons to be learned from ancient civilizations and, once these lessons are learned, there is usually amazement that people so old could speak with voices that still have modern application. At the end of this text, there is an intriguing insight that helps bring this discussion to closure.

In ancient cultures, the phenomenon of signs played a prominent role. The Greeks, for example, spoke of *semia*, signs which were "pointing devices" designed to make life more manageable. Such *semia* were basically logical, clear and distinct, and not unlike the signs which populate our lives today. A hexagonal STOP sign, the EXIT sign that stands over a door in a building, or the NO SMOKING sign lighted in airplanes are all examples of *semia*. In a similar sense, the signage that allows us to move along roadways or through the interiors of architectural structures is a prime example of *semia*. Again, the key point is the connection to a logical rationality that helps us live our lives in a directed, purposeful manner.

Sometimes *semia* can also have an emotional overlay. Think about, for example, a flag or a religious symbol like the cross. The *semia* have distinct logical and rational meaning, but there is more; emotional content is added to rational meaning due to past history and cultural associations that have become a part of these particular signs.

Semia proliferate in our culture. The old, counter-culture song that rang out "signs, signs, everywhere a sign" is absolutely right, but we do not seem to be troubled by this except when billboards along roadways interfere with natural beauty. We probably even like *semia* when we are in places that do not have total familiarity to us. *Semia* give us a clear expectation of what we are to do. Can you image trying to negotiate a large city, for example, without signage?

Yet, the ancients would have quickly asserted that to reduce life to a system of *semia*, to ever believe that life could be conveyed totally and absolutely in logical rationality, would be negative, inaccurate, and would have the end affect of diminishing the richness of potential implicit in life.

Beyond *semia* there was *thauma* or "wonders." Wonders were conceived as higher order directional pointers. Wonders were ultimately non-rational, but this does not mean that they are ir-rational; perhaps the term supra-rational has greater credibility. That there is the non-rational dimension is likely to mean that there will be a non-comfortable dimension, but life lived totally within rational comfort zones seems patently artificial from the onset.

Thauma/wonders are achieved when we wander. We likely need to be in environments where there are few or no directional arrows or signs. There is a likelihood that we might think of such environments as wilderness, but could we not as easily see them as "wander-lands" or "wonder-lands." Our problem: we give little attention to strategies that consciously incorporate "wandering" into our lives. How intriguing—and instructive—that some of the greatest "teachers" of modern civilization were wanderers: Wordsworth, Van Gogh, Thoreau, Goethe, Rousseau, Beethoven. I am particularly intrigued by the later stages of the life of Friedrich Nietzsche when some of his most remarkable writings were accomplished. He moved to Turin in Northern Italy and walked usually three times on extended "hikes" along the rivers and through the mountains every day. It should also not be lost on us when we consider the "wandering" that Jesus, Socrates, and Buddha accomplished some of their most important teachings while they were wandering through their own countrysides.

My wife's grandmother was a true original, a beautiful woman who brought a charm to life that is still unforgettable. She loved beautiful places and beautiful things—a sunset, a mountain vista, light shining through homemade jellies, her own quilts, or the changing leaves in the fall. When my wife and I were first married, we took great delight in driving her grandparents through the hills of East Tennessee along back roads that they had known in their youth. Sometimes her grandmother would see something that totally captured her attention. She had a striking phrase that she saved for such occasions. With a twinkle in her eyes, hardly dimmed by age at all, she would say: "It's a wonder-ment. It's a wonder-ment." I have no idea where the word came from. My bet is that it is very old. The question that is provoked in me: when is the last time that I experienced a "wonder-ment"? How often are "wonder-ments" a part of my life? Would it be possible to construct conscious strategies that guaranteed that the opportunity for "wonder-ments" were a regular part of our lives?

What the experience of wandering/wondering/wonder-ment points in the direction of is not the major question. Experiences of wonder should not first be seen as a means to an end, but rather as an end in themselves. What is "pointed out" will be unique to every person and every individual situation. The efficacy, truth-value of the experience in and of itself—the existential, experiential moment—is of first importance. What is "pointed out" is a next dimension of wandering/wondering, and it may not be most important to know where all of this might lead.

The ancients had yet one more level/dimension that they were interested in describing. Beyond the phenomenon of thauma, as an ultimate degree of potential for human experience, is musterion—mystery. Mystery is ultimately ineffable, a non-denumerable infinity of possibility. Well beyond language and explanation, like thauma, the mysterious is the consummate of experiences. Musterion is the ultimate "pointer," directional indicator. It is never proven, yet seldom capable of being doubted. Often musterion is experienced in the height of relatedness or connectedness like that found in the most intimate of interpersonal relationships or with contact in nature. This is the level of "knowing" which is described in the ancient texts as the highest form of intimacy and, for Leland Kaiser, the "knowledge" which only "spirit" and "soul" are capable of.

The best interpretation of musterion rises in the context of Zen Buddhism. Zen believes that there is a "height" or "depth" or "breadth" of experiences that moves beyond normal, day-to-day awareness; we might call it a Zen "whole." This sense of "wholeness" can be achieved in basic, conscious steps. The first step makes the entire process all but impossible for most Westerners. Zen's higher consciousness experiences are first dependent on stillness. Yet, in western culture, there is almost a hyper activity of movement that never stops; it is almost out of character with the culture to be still. How interesting that the ancient Psalmist in the Old Testament understood the path to God to be contingent on stillness: "Be still and know that God is God."

Beyond stillness, there is the experience of being able to distinguish between "whatness" and "thatness." Whatness has to do with roles and expectations usually derived from the general culture that persons live in. Thatness has to do with experienced uniqueness that stands beyond any roles. I can define the whatness of my spouse—her age, height, weight, hair color—but her thatness is beyond definition and can only be experienced in proximity to her uniqueness.

There is a wonderfully engaging story of a young married couple that deals with the wife's desire to know exactly why the new husband loves her. The young boy is undeterred in his attempt to give expression to his love; he loves her ability to cook, how clean she keeps herself and their house, and—straining beyond answers that are not working—the fact that she is such a good driver for a woman. With his third answer, she breaks down in tears. He doesn't know what to do, and in utter frustration, he begs for some explanation of her emotions. Finally, she explains: "You have told me that you love me for what I am. I want you to love me that I am." She wanted a response to her thatness, not her whatness.

When thatness is capable of being experienced/affirmed, Zen talks about the achievement of *satori*. In most western explanations, *satori* is seen as the epitome of the Zen experience. Usually, *satori* is defined as "enlightenment," but western "enlightenment" is almost always understood in terms of rational insight. For example, I might sit in an advanced math class for weeks hearing about axioms, formulae, or equations, only to be totally lost. Then, one day there is a kind of "aha" experience in which the pieces start making sense. I see the connections. I figure out what all of the symbols mean. In a sense, I have achieved "enlightenment;" the processes make sense.

For Zen, however, *satori* does not mean rational "figuring out" at all. In fact, *satori* enlightenment conveys the insight that the ultimate levels of life are not rational at all. The highest levels of enlightenment have nothing much at all to do with rationality. *Satori* asserts that there is yet another dimension beyond the rational, beyond any enlightenment; there is *Mu* and—of course—the Zen *Mu* is musterion/mystery. *Mu* is like the ocean. It can never be explored in its entirety, even across generations of human beings intent on doing so. It can never be grasped and held, contained or controlled. Sometimes, the best we can do is go down to the edge of it and play in its shallows near the shore.

Our major, human questions may need to be: When do we become engaged with or encounter the mysterious? What cues about the mysterious do we receive in our normal, daily lives? What do experiences of the mysterious point us in the direction of? Following the mysterious, what have we found?

Albert Einstein—and who could be more representative of a voice of reason or rationality? —toward the end of his life made one of those summative, once-in-a-lifetime statements that often define the insights of a lifetime. He talked about some reality that was at the essential core of both all of the arts and all of the sciences. For Einstein, that reality was a sense of the mysterious. All begins in mystery. Then, Einstein adds: to those who cannot sense this mysterious, there is little opportunity for living at its best. Without a sense of the mysterious, for the great master, people were as good as dead, their eyes and minds were blind.

We live in a world of signs, *semia*. In most respects, we have mastered this world and improve on that mastery with each passing day. Yet, we must understand that in our mastery of signs, rational pointers, and logical indicators, that we have only skimmed the surface of existence. How much we must learn of thauma and then of musterion? The arena of spirituality is the arena of wonders and mystery. Without eyes and minds open to wonders and mystery, spiritual experiences will occur only by accident and insufficient serendipity.

THIRD FINAL CONCLUSION

This last conclusion will, of course, be a concluding attempt to tie a number of these ideas that we have been exploring together in a concise manner. Since we have looked at a broad spectrum of issues, to pull all of this together is no small task. In addition, I am interested in giving a kind of template for consideration that can be used not only for this discussion but also for a wide variety of other life situations. I would ask you to "pull your thinking caps on a bit tighter" at this point as, at least on the surface, the ideas captured here are somewhat more complex. In fact, I hope that there is a great deal of "good sense" here that will be fairly easily embraced and become part of the "good sense" with which you conduct your own life.

I am most interested in describing four, complimentary "movements" of our engagements with life that can build on each other in both a productive and meaningful manner. There are plenty of implications here for the synthesis of philosophical and theological concepts and concrete work experience. My goal, especially in the "fourth movement," is to bring the force of all that has been said about spirituality squarely into the world of real, lived human life and that world as it involves work environments.

In describing a "first movement" of human engagement with the world, I would emphasize the word "in-tension." At this point, I am going all the way back to what was said earlier about William of Ockham and his thoughts about how the human engagement with life begins with what we called the "felt reality" of a stirring, "internal tension" (thus, in-tension). We are also on the ground of the ancient Hebrew conception about how "righteousness" begins with realization. At times, this in-tension can be totally and completely without words, pre-verbal, and then it is likely that it will move toward some form of articulation and verbalization.

1. Introduction: Spirituality and Business?

A "second movement" would rise out of the understanding that as important as in-tension is and as curious as we can be about it, that it is not complete. Non-completion is not meant to demean in-tension, and moments of in-tension should definitely be respected and even pursued, but to stop at in-tension will not bring about meaningful and productive consummation in real life. Therefore, it is important to conceive of a next "movement" in which the experience of in-tension gathers force with the addition of in-tension. This "second movement" is built around the normative understanding of intent, where intent is seen as the gathering force of will and conviction which will give internal power to that which has come to the point of feeling and articulation. This intent is likely to start off of a less powerful level and can move to a more powerful level. Without the building of intent, it is likely that in-tension will get lost.

Intent is honorable and can even be dramatic when it is expressed with strength. However, even the strongest intent can fall well short of activity. If all that we do is to generate great energy of intent, we have not really done a great deal. We may, in fact, create grounds for disappointment, loss of credibility, integrity, and trust because there is no follow-through. A "third movement" is required, and many people fail to advance to this "movement." A great deal is lost at the table of possibility when in-tension is the stopping point of our journeys through life.

The "third movement" is thought of in terms of extension. While this is a bit contrived, I am thinking of a "tension" that finds external expression in a real and concrete manner. That this expression is still going to be primarily conceptual; it is more "tension." That it is finding real concreteness, the prefix "ex-" is creditable. What I am conceiving here is that moment when there is a movement beyond intent to actual strategizing and planning. When in-tension and intent result in real, concrete strategies and plans, there is extension.

I am reminded of the work of Hamilton Jourdan, the South Georgian whose family had established the communal living experience known a Koinonia Farms. Jourdan came to prominence as the Chief of Staff for Jimmy Carter's White House. Since that time, he has been active as a consultant, planner, and writer of important impact. Sometimes Hamilton Jourdan will be working with a group analyzing its assets and deficits, its strengths and weaknesses. He will create a flip chart under the heading of "Good News List" on which assets will be listed. A similar flip chart will carry the heading "Bad News List." After taking a group through an interesting and productive experience with the two lists, he concludes the exercise. At the bottom of the "Good News List," he writes in bold lettering: Unlimited Potential Abounds. This is a powerful, positive statement in which every word has remarkable connotations that everyone will like. Then, at the bottom of the "Bad News List," in equally bold lettering, he writes: But . . . do you have a plan?"

His point is well taken. All of the most abounding potential that could ever be experienced is usually contingent on a plan. Without a clear plan and strategy, all of the "vision" in the world is left wanting. Clearly, the plan/strategy will not get the task accomplished, but without a clear plan most tasks never get done very well.

The final "movement" is, of course, Extension, in which all that has been felt and found rudimentary articulation, all that has built up a force of intent, all that has been planned and strategized moves toward consummation is real actions. That activity can be divided into these "movements" may be particularly helpful in keeping track of all that is going on in life or a workplace. We can usually pinpoint exactly where we are on an issue in regard to this four-fold mapping process. Such mapping is very helpful in actualizing potential.

Beyond these "movements," there is also the need for debriefing and evaluating of all that has taken place. This can be a process in which mistakes are studied. Even more, it needs to be a process in which all that has gone well and succeeded can be closely investigated. You will have a much higher batting average by studying what you did correctly when you hit the ball and "programming" this into your mind-eye-body connections than you will grieving or being frustrated about strike-outs.

All of this detail of conclusion—which in fact makes a great deal of good sense—can be finally expressed in what Robert Hartman called his "Four Self Rules." Here, then, is the final conclusion for the entire discussion.

The first "Self Rule" is *Know Yourself*. Hartman associates this with Socrates/Plato and the basic examination of those individual properties that make an individual unique. There is no contest with other people at this point, that kind of contest borne of inane cultural priorities, but rather a genuine and honest assessment of personal uniqueness. There is something of in-tension and discovery here that works its way toward articulation.

Beyond this, there is a need to *Choose Yourself*. Here, Hartman is feeling close to the work of the Danish existentialist, Søren Kierkegaard. In Kierkegaard's thought, the movement toward authenticity and the initial possibility of the expression of human uniqueness takes place when we affirm and assert, "I am the one I am!" In other words, when in-tension and self-knowledge gathers force through intent, through choosing that the "I am" that I have discovered is the "I am" that I will be determined to become, the possibility of real, authentic existence is accelerated.

The third "Self Rule" involves moving beyond intent to the point of actual creation and expression. Like an artist, I may come to the conclusion that here is where my particular talents lie, and I may also determine with great intent that this is what I will do/become/be. I still have to put brush to canvas. In other words, there is the need to *Create Yourself*. The association is with the Italian Renaissance thinker Giovanni Pico della Mirandola. Pico wrote a powerful guide for life during the height of the Renaissance entitled Oration on the Dignity of Man. By emphasizing dignity, as opposed to something like Luther's conclusion that humans were sinful creatures deserving damnation or Montaigne's conclusion that humans were inept buffoons, Pico believed that human beings were capable of great dignity—his word for authenticity—if they would become involved in actions of self creation. It was never enough, although it was often the extent of human expression, to experience self, evolve some intent about self, make plans about self, but never see those plans move toward actual creation.

Finally, Hartman—with three of his "Self-Rules" filling the continuum that I have described as moving from in-tension to extension—added a fourth maxim, *Give Yourself*. His final associate is with Jesus and takes self-creation in the specific direction of concrete actions of respect, care, and love. Love becomes synonymous with the highest level of intrinsic experience and intrinsic valuation, especially as this valuation is manifested in mutual inclusivity of intrinsic valuation of self, world, and others. Love becomes synonymous with that kind of care (Heidegger's *sorgen* and *besorgen*) that "shapes" life in directions—again—which is both productive and meaningful.

I would even add a fifth "Self Rule"—with passion. The association here is with the German philosopher, Friedrich Nietzsche. Nietzsche believed that what the world lacked, more than anything else was passion—living with spirit. Spirituality finds its highest expression when it is passionately lived! Where there is no passion, no living with spirit, the world creeps toward mediocrity and hollowness. Both productivity and meaning—those two, inseparable, spiritual partners—are compromised and lost.

2. HIGHER CALLINGS AND SPIRITUALITY

In John Updike's *Seek My Face*, a younger woman is talking to an older woman—an artist—about a young man the younger woman is considering marrying. The young man is nice enough but fairly one dimensional in his interests and opinions. He is not all that interested in art, one of the young woman's life passions. The older woman is concerned about the boy's close-mindedness, wondering if it might not signal a distance that could make a relationship vulnerable.

The older woman—the artist—believes that the boy's openness to the world of art, to the joy and wonder that can be experienced there, will represent a kind of "test" as to whether he is the right one for her new younger friend. The older woman explains: "You tell that young man of yours to *open himself up* when he goes with you to a gallery. If he can't see the fun of it, he may not be the right one for you" (p. 254, italics mine).

The work of art hanging in the gallery becomes a paradigm for existence in general. The work of art (and/or the artist through the work of art) *speaks* or "intends." A conservative, close-minded stubbornness of opinion and diminishing of possibility becomes a major obstacle and stumbling block to the potential contained in the work of art—contained in life—and the experience of the gallery—the experience of living. There is a vital need to practice *openness*, to *make oneself available* to the possibility inherent in a situation.

Life is, and always will be, a journey, but that journey is a connected string of individual moments. If we do not have real, authentic moments, then the journey is a mental concept, a history devoid of happening. The difference between authenticity and mental concept is the conscious act, strategy, and discipline of *openness* to present-tense, real moments. Life, then, can become "momentous" rather than dull, caricatured, and absent of surprise.

The young boy is representative of an entire way of life that is increasingly empty, a life that has traded real moments for goals, objectives, and plans. Updike's older woman/teacher/mentor/artist says that what the boy is experiencing "... was part of the old way, the way mapped by religion, to see yourself on a path, within a journey...." (p. 71). Her name is, notably, "Hope," and she hopes for her young friend "an unaccountable present tense, an unframed *now*" that will become the basis for an authentic path and journey. If "religion" maps out path and journey without real moments, creating thinking instead of living and conceptualizing instead of experiencing, then would "spirituality" map out an ever-expanding and ever-enriched string of real moments which establish a path—even destiny—and, in retrospect, can be reflected upon as having been a journey? Within authenticity, there is an attending to, a making available to, a listening to that which speaks, that which calls out. And, how intriguing, that Updike's mentor suggests that this "calling"/"speaking" is manifested in a way that "imposes duties."

Sometimes there are biblical texts that remain confusing and perplexing over long periods of time, but—almost like a rough place on a tooth that you can't keep your tongue away from—you keep returning to them over and again in search of meaning. One such text for me is found in the Book of Judges with its battle scenes depicting conflict between infant Israel and its neighboring array of enemies and invaders. The Gideon sequence of stories was particularly revealing. In this early period of Israel's history as a fledgling nation, there was little or no standing army as we know it today. An invasion would occur or begin to be threatened, and a *call* would go out for people to fight. From these volunteers, an "army" would be put together—soldiers would be *chosen*. However, there is a key, middle ingredient: before the *call* could be brought to closure with a *choice*, there had to be the phenomenon of individuals *availing* themselves, making themselves *available*. The entire dynamic depended upon *making available*; without the conscious openness of *availability*, the process of *calling* being consummated in *choice* was null and void. The human role is accentuated; the nation—or, by extension, the divinity—could call and choose, but only the human could create *availability*. The human choice to be *available* was as important, in most respects, as the divine choice to call and choose.

Of passing interest, it can also be noted that at the core of the words *avail* and *availability* is an old etymological root, which, in one application, is close to the modern word *valor*, and in another application is close to the word *value*. In the ancient Greek, *to avail* carried connotations of strength and power. So, to choose to make oneself available carries the force of an action of valor, which holds great value and worth, an action that manifests itself in strength and power.

Just as the young man in the Updike novel needs to choose to *open himself* and make himself *available* to the experience of the art gallery, the intent of the artist and the art, so the issue of being *called* in some "higher calling" or of being *chosen* is always contingent on an active willingness and conscious decision to make oneself *available* to the experience of the dynamic of *calling-choosing*. To be <u>*open to the intent*</u> that impinges itself upon us, often in the form of Updike's emphasis on "duty," is the key to personal authenticity, the reality of care (to follow Heidegger), and the possibility of the transformation of existence in a positive manner.

At this point, I will move beyond the previous discussion to examine four ways in which "higher callings" may manifest themselves. Precedents from both the Old and New Testaments will then be used as leading examples of each type of "higher calling." There is no hierarchy of "types" here; one may relate to a reader's own experiences more than another, but each may have its own viability. All four intimately depend on making oneself *available*, being <u>*open to the intent*</u> that impinges itself upon us as "duty."

Type 1—Sometimes "higher callings" are part of a larger destiny that is somehow working its way out in life.

There is a visual image implicit in the terminology "working its way out" that is important here. I am thinking of a splinter that has lodged itself in a finger. The splinter is evident; it can be felt and its imprint even seen right beneath the surface of the skin. It may also be painful in some way. Over time, it will come to the surface and present itself. It will "work itself out." There may be times when "something" is planted deep within us that is always there, perhaps painfully, that tries to surface itself, that eventually surfaces itself, that "works its way out."

The visual image may, for some readers, demean and lessen the concept of "destiny," but the ease with which this word is sometimes used and the easy assumptions that are built around it bother me at times. I almost want to make a distinction between a "hard destiny" concept in which a deity in some eternal plan of creation has determined that a person will have certain outcomes in life, and a "soft destiny" concept in which any number of diverse variables may come to have powerful bearing and influence on the direction that a life may possibly take. In most instances, I personally feel more comfortable with a "soft" concept than a "hard" concept because the "hard" concept may too easily diminish the role of human choice and self-determination.

In the Old Testament, there is the engaging story of the young boy, Samuel, who is being mentored by the great, early prophet-priest of Israel, Eli. Samuel is a novitiate, a young man in the first steps of a religious vocation. In the story, one night he is engaged in his evening prayers and feels—for want of a better word—the "presence" of divinity impinging upon his life; that is, God is "speaking" to him or "calling" him. The young boy does not know what to do with this experience and repeatedly comes to Eli for direction. Finally, after a number of trips back to get the prophet-priest's advice, Samuel is instructed to respond to the "voice" he is encountering by saying, "Speak Lord, your servant is listening." In making this statement, Samuel opens himself to a role of service that will take him into a life of profound influence on the history of Israel. Perhaps with the exception of Abraham and Moses, he becomes the greatest figure of leadership in Israel before there are great kings.

What takes place in this "higher calling" to a unique role of duty may be understood as the working out of some sort of destiny. Samuel's mother had been barren and had promised God, if she could have a child, she would give this child to religious vocation. She had given birth and delivered her child up to Eli to be raised in God's service. A kind of "destiny" was, therefore, created. What elements of this "destiny" were "hard" or "soft," using the distinctions noted above is beyond absolute clarity. However, in the end, there was a dominating influence that came to bear on Samuel that had powerful impact. This impact—"destiny"—cannot be denied, but neither can the role of the boy as he opens himself and makes himself available. The fact is that a dominating influence had come to bear on his life that had powerful impact. A "divine splinter" was working its way to the surface; a "destiny" was— somehow—working itself out in his life

In regard to this first type of "higher calling," I think of my great teacher and mentor, Robert Hartman. Hartman was born in Germany in 1913. He recalls, vividly, being taken as a child into downtown Berlin to watch the parades that sent young men off to World War I. There was the highest of festivity with bands playing, crowds cheering, and flags blowing in the winds. What great joy had accompanied these boys and young men patriotically marching off to another form of "higher calling."

Yet, Hartman recalled, how his own father went off to that war and was all but absent from his life for the better part of half a decade. Then, when his Uncle—who had become his male role model—was called up for enlistment, Hartman had found him crying in the deepest fear in his room, alone and utterly convinced that he would die. Within short weeks of his marching off in glory to war, the Uncle was back—in a coffin.

For Hartman, these events marked out a "destiny" in his life. Even before he could rationally articulate it, he sensed that life had two dimensions. On the surface, life could present itself in one way; beneath that surface, it could be quite different. He felt driven, compelled, *called* to live a life that explored ways in which this "beneath the surface" could be better clarified and understood. Eventually, he would face off against Adolph Hitler at a time in Germany in which Hitler had become the nation's darling. Eventually, he would give up a lucrative career with Walt Disney to write and teach about this "beneath the surface." Eventually, he would create an instrument—The Hartman Value Profile—that powerfully brings human realities to the surface. Eventually, he would be nominated for the Nobel Prize for his life's work. The repeated eventualities were the markings of destiny, commenced long ago in the inarticulate sensitivities of a young boy and manifested in adult ways that Hartman would have had little trouble identifying as something of the "will of God."

Hartman was a man who constantly—as a strategic discipline and ambition—was opening himself and making himself available to life. This constant strategy, which resulted in a life of great accomplishment and great joy, was the hallmark of his existence as a human being. As a consequence, there was a gracefulness and equilibrium to his life that was palpable. Perhaps, accomplishment and joy—in spite of hardships and challenges that are bound to occur—is the result of living with an openness and availability to life, an openness and availability to the intent of duty. My guess is that individuals such as Samuel and Jesus experienced and conveyed in their living this same sort of accomplishment and joy, this same sort of response to the intent of duty.

What *all* contributes to that which can be termed "destiny" may not be as important as embracing and living in the midst of the "destiny" (whether "hard" or "soft" stops being very important) that is continuously unveiling itself. Could it be that somewhere in the roots of language that making oneself *a-vail-able* comes close to the phenomenon of opening oneself to that which is *un-veil-ing* itself in the midst of our living? Does human "be-ing-as-availability" enable (or "in-able") those kinds of "unveilings" that have the most dramatic impacts in life? At the very minimum, it is our "be-ing-as-availability" that allows the entire dynamic of "destiny"—however it is specifically articulated—to become operative in life. [Please note: I am using the spelling "human be-ing" as opposed to "human being" in order to see human existence ("be-ing") as an active verb rather than human existence ("being") as a passive, objective noun.]

Type 2—Sometimes "higher callings" are part of a momentary event, sometimes startling in its impact, that moves us from "getting close" to "finding our way."

The visual image that I have in mind to illustrate this type of "higher calling" goes back a number of years. I was in New York City making a presentation, but staying at a Marriott hotel at the Meadowlands complex in New Jersey. I had really nice directions and, following the close of the meeting I was attending, I drove over to the Meadowlands. Dusk turned to dark quite quickly that evening, and directions that seemed obvious were not as obvious anymore.

I was stymied. I could clearly see the bright, red Marriott sign in the distance, not a mile away. I was right next to Giants Stadium, a landmark that was familiar to me. Yet, in all of my driving around for nearly an hour, I could not find my way. Eventually, like most men, I "broke down" and asked a person in a car near me for directions. It was all very simple to the person I asked. There was a roadway obscured by where I was standing. All that I needed to do was follow the road I was on all of the way to the back of the stadium, take a somewhat less than obvious turn rather than follow the main, circling road, and I would go straight to the hotel.

The man was exactly right. I had to drop my tendency for the obvious a bit, but the somewhat sunken roadway took me straight to my destination. As I saw the correct path leading precisely to my destination, I felt both relief and the joy and accomplishment I described earlier. I had been moved from "getting close" to "finding my way." "Getting close," at one and the same time was both rewarding and frustrating. I had found my way to a certain extent, but the journey was not complete. "Getting close" was okay, after a fashion, but not enough.

Sometimes in regard to "higher callings," we can be in the arena, but not in our own, unique seat; where we fit, but not exactly. All kinds of events may have prepared the ground for "getting close" to arrive at "finding our way," but the serendipitous breakthrough may not have taken place as yet. In the moment of "higher calling," we find closure. Better yet, we find "commencement," the kind of event in which a successfully achieved and enlightened plateau becomes the jumping off point for a next horizon of possibility and opportunity. "Getting close" awaits that moment of "higher calling" in which "finding our way" takes on a definitive and definite character that previously was not experienced. [Please note that the emphasis on the word *way* is at the core of spiritual insight that transcends any, particular religious expression. I am also thinking in terms of the Eastern concept of the *Tao*.]

The Old Testament book of *Numbers*, an ancient text, introduces the character of Balaam. He is known, in the traditions of Israel that have evolved since that time, as a "false" prophet. It would be more accurate to say "typical" prophet. There were hundreds of these kinds of operatives in the ancient cultures. Balaam made a living delivering prayers and curses for hire. If a king, for example, wanted approval and support for some action, he could call in a prophetic figure, let the man go through his religious gyrations, and then watch him invariably come back to the king, his advisors, and—most especially—the general population with "answered prayers" that usually involved permitting the king to do exactly what the king wanted to do all the time. If the prophetic figure were charismatic enough and respected by the masses, he could have more impact than any, modern media campaign in turning the people's heads in the direction of the king's wishes. Balaam had such power. He was in such demand that before Balak, the king of Moab, launched an attack on Israel, he first sent for Balaam to pronounce a curse against the Hebrews.

It is highly interesting, in the story, that God moves to intervene in the actions of Balaam. Had the man been of no real power, a total ruse, the thought might be why would God bother. In addition, the name Balaam is directly related to the Middle Eastern deity, Baal, a powerful war-like god who claimed followers across the width and breadth of the ancient biblical world. Ironically, however, Numbers 24:13 suggests that Balaam really knows that any, true power that he has is ultimately derived from "the Lord" (a primary term used for the God of Israel).

In other words, in spite of the way that Balaam makes his living and has established his reputation—perhaps, for convenience sake, even taken the name associated with the foreign god, he—somehow—is within the arena of a greater truth. He is "close," but not precisely "on the right way." None of this disqualifies him, in the story, from God working with him to close that distance of "closeness." How interesting that God would not simply destroy Balaam, but would continue to work with this agent of another religion and, at least, inauthentic user of religion who is advancing his own agendas and vested interests.

Balaam, to his credit, is at least honest enough with himself to keep some kind of openness to the dynamic energies that are surrounding his life in the political and religious intricacy described in the story. Finally, there is an absolutely strange moment of "higher calling" in which an animal and an angel communicate with Balaam. The story certainly gets the reader's attention and, evidently, got the attention of Balaam as well. He will not curse Israel and serve the wishes of the Moabite king. He moves from "close" to "finding his way."

The king, in the story, is incensed with Balaam, but too afraid to harm him. He basically tells him just to go on back home. Before he leaves, there is no curse against Moab given, but rather an oracle concerning the destruction that will be found for Moab when it attacks Israel. Then, the ancient text simply says: "Then Balaam rose and went back to his place." Nothing of consequence of the life of Balaam is encountered in the textual traditions again.

The point of this type of "higher calling" is perfectly illustrated by the Balaam story. Here was a man, on first sight, diametrically opposed to the God of Israel. But, on closer inspection, he was at least in an "arena of closeness." He was open enough to respect and then to listen. This was enough for him to be of some usefulness to some duty, even if "duty" simply means to do no harm.

Balaam does not become a great "convert" or saint. He never finds an identity of being "God's man." Yet, there may be times when "higher calling" does not have to mean sainthood. "Higher calling" can also simply mean coming "close" enough to find an honest "way" of doing no harm. In a singular moment, a man who is within an arena of "closeness" finds his way. At times, this may be enough.

Type 3—Sometimes "higher callings" occur when someone is "imprinted by a rush."

I know a young woman who was passionate to the hilt about dancing. When she was a little girl, she constantly dressed like a dancer and was given almost every kind of dance class imaginable. She loved this activity with all of her heart; it was never something that her parents ever forced off on her. By the time she was in junior high school, she was really very accomplished. My wife and I attended a program at which she received a standing ovation for her performance. You could see the "rush" of emotion and affirmation, the "rush" of confirmation that seems to rise from the core of her whole being. To dance was her "essence," for want of a better word, and the "rush" she experienced validated this.

She progressed in her studies and talent throughout high school and on into college, but then an "issue" presented itself that challenged every dream she had had. There was little "practical" about her dream. She was really good, but not "world class." She might star in college performances, but she became convinced by "experts" and well-meaning friends that the odds of ever being in a national company were extremely slim. It became more "sensible" for her to switch to a business degree and do something "more productive." Even with the pledge of support and encouragement of her parents to "stick it out," she became convinced that it was time for her to "grow up."

To make a long story short, she finished a business degree with honors and began to work as a drug representative. She excelled at this, also, and made a significant amount of money for young women in her early twenties. But, she was extremely unhappy, even beginning to experience a real degree of depression. She was not being true to herself in some fundamental way. Dancing, the "rush" of activity in this area had so "imprinted" itself on her life that her "higher calling" simply would not go away.

Today, this young woman—now nearly thirty—has established a very happy and successful life. She is not working in a national dance company, but dance has again become her life. She has her own successful studio, and exceptional young men and women are thriving under her gifted teaching. She dances every day, and her skills have even allowed her to participate in regional performances of some note. The depression is totally gone, although the monies being earned are not nearly as much. You, again, see the "rush" as she talks about her students, hears audiences applaud their efforts, and even as she occasionally takes her own bows on stage. There is a sense of wholeness that was lost for a while, but that the "imprint" of "higher calling" refused to let disappear. To listen to that "higher calling" allowed the "rush" of meaning and self-value to return.

The Old Testament tells the story of a prophet named Elijah. He was a stalwart man who faced the egotistical and immoral reign of a diabolical ruler named Ahaz and his consort, Jezebel. He was forever the target of their ire, and plots continuously arose to discredit and destroy Elijah. At one point in the story, a "contest" is arranged between the prophets of Baal and solitary Elijah.

In the story, the materials for a bonfire are gathered, and the prophets are called upon to implore their divinity to bring down fire and light the pile of accumulated rubbish. The Baal prophets go through all kinds of rites and rituals, prayers and incantations, but there is no fire. Finally, these prophets flagellate and cut themselves with knives to show the sincerity of their requests, but still no fire. Elijah, in the "rush" of the certainty of his faith, takes center stage by asking that water be brought in such volume that the bonfire materials are drenched. Elijah, then, humbly bows and prays to God; no circus antics or loud outcries. All is deathly quiet. Suddenly, fire comes down and the material roars with a flame that consumes everything that is near. Elijah has triumphed and the "rush" of spiritual celebration fills him.

The "rush" continues. There has been no rain in Israel for many, many months; there is destructive drought. Now, in his "rush," Elijah confidently prays for rain. Some measure of time passes and no rain appears. People begin to doubt, but not Elijah in his "rush." He sends a servant to look from a high pinnacle toward the distant horizon, and the servant comes back reporting that a small fragment of cloud can be seen in the distance. Elijah tells the people that they better start moving toward safety; a rainstorm of magnificent size is about to powerfully assert itself. The rain comes in torrents, and the day is Elijah's.

The story begins to change, perhaps in a very unexpected manner. Maybe the adrenaline of Elijah's "rush" leaves him exhausted. Maybe the ancient storyteller is simply trying to give a paradigm of the "ups and downs" that all life is capable of experiencing. Nonetheless, Elijah loses his way. He begins to fear for his life, thinking that Ahaz and especially Jezebel will kill him immediately for the embarrassment he has caused them. He runs and hides. In a consummate moment of depression, he even asks God to take his life.

But, the "imprint" of the "rush" that claimed him as a "higher calling" reasserts itself. He comes back to himself.

Type 4—Sometimes "higher callings" are simply part of a very logical and reasonable process in which need and talent meet in opportunity.

Not every "higher calling" has to involve deeply religious sensitivities or the presence of angelic proclamations; talking donkeys would always be an exceptional event. To have a "Damascus Road Experience" is not a precondition for authentic "higher callings." To get to Balaam's point of doing no harm might be a real accomplishment in many people's lives. Being "open" to the intent of life, the intent of duty, does not have to necessarily involve what could be identified as religious vocation. There are times in which the gifts, talents, skills, abilities, capacities, or training that an individual has received or accumulated in the normal course of life can simply meet with some sort of presented need. When talent and need meet, there is opportunity. To respond to that opportunity, allowing talent to meet needs, may be as fundamental of a form of "higher calling" as either of the previously noted types. In fact, this type may be the most available type of "higher calling" that most people experience. In fact, to respond on this very logical and reasonable level may be a first step toward experiencing other types of "higher callings" and being able to respond to them.

The visual images of "9/11" still provoke most of our memories with scenes that will be imprinted on our minds forever. To say that "needs" were present in every violent setting of that fateful day would be the highest of understatement; "needs" were obvious on every side. Clearly, there are also all kinds of "talent" that is present from the police and fire personnel who entered the World Trade Center buildings to the passengers who fought the terrorists in that last plane heading toward Washington, DC. The presence of "need" matched with "talent" created "opportunity." The phenomenon of "duty" rises on every side.

The critical moment comes when decisions are made to respond to those varieties of "opportunities" that presented themselves. The decisions to help, even sacrificially, represented an openness to the intent of life and a hearing of "higher callings" that is beyond profound. The image of those fire and police personnel climbing up into the Trade Center towers while those who worked there were making their way to safety epitomizes the response to "higher callings" that human life is capable of achieving.

CONCLUSION

One point that rises from this discussion is that life is alive with "higher callings" that surround us constantly. These "higher callings" can come in very different forms, some of which are more complex and intricate, and others that are fairly reasonable and logical. No form of "higher calling" is better than any other. That some people experience one form and other people other forms does not make one person any better or any more godly than another.

A common pattern has been established here which unites the four types of "higher callings." First, there is some sort of *stimulus*. This may be: (A) a soft or hard destiny that is making its impact felt in life, (B) some momentous event that moves a person from "closeness" to "finding way," (C) some "rush" of authenticity that forever imprints itself on a person, or (D) an extension of reasonable logic where talent and need meet in opportunity. Second, there is some sort of *response* to this stimulus that builds on a growing and compelling sense of duty. Third, there is some sort of action meant to outwardly impact needs that are present.

However, all four elements of this pattern must be contextualized within the frame of a conscious *openness* to the intent of life and the power of duty. Without *openness* and *availability*, done of the activities of response are likely to occur.

If we are genuinely interested in experiencing "higher callings," we must be genuinely interested in pursuing and promoting disciplines and strategies of openness so that the intent of life can speak itself into our lives. When disciplines of openness are intact, "higher callings" of one type or another—or, perhaps of all three—become plausible if not even likely. Our task is to practice openness, to listen to the intent of life and duty that stir in the branches of our trees. Our task is to create a life that, by discipline and practice, manifests the corresponding intent that rises from within our own, unique "be-ing" and says, "Speak, Lord, your servant is listening."

APPENDIX

1. THE SPIRITUAL LEADERSHIP INSTITUTE

The Spiritual Leadership Institute (SLI) has an array of programs designed to introduce the concepts of spiritual leadership for all levels of an organization in both short-term and long-term exposures.

Pathways To Spiritual Leadership is a program directed at organizational leadership on the mid-manager level and above. The program involves three sessions over a six-to-nine-month period of time and includes instruction and group learning experiences. This program is regularly offered in Houston, Texas, and has drawn participants from across the United States. The primary outcome of this program is personal growth and development, enhancement of leadership skills, and insights into how stronger organizations can be created on the principles of spiritual leadership.

Journey and Discovery is an all-inclusive, two-day program designed to give an introductory experience into spiritual leadership to any participant. The program is primarily designed as a self-growth and development process, and all of the activities of the program are appropriate for individuals below the mid-management level. This program has gotten exceptional reviews and evaluations from participants on the most basic levels of organizational work hierarchies. This program is also regularly offered in Houston, TX.

Awakenings is a one or two-day program that is designed to be used as an initial exposure to organizations. We can work to customize programming and faculty to meet the needs of individual organizations or groups of organizations in a specific location. This program has a great deal of flexibility in both content and price. It is an excellent program for on-site management and leadership development programs, executive retreats, or organizational board activities.

Each year, there is an **Annual Conference** that focuses around a special topic relating to spiritual leadership. The presenters for this meeting are a combination of SLI faculty along with guest speakers that represent the ability to apply spirituality in the business world. This meeting is a time of renewal, reinvigoration, and sustaining of friendships gained during the Institute's meetings along with offering an opportunity for interested individuals and organizations to participate in the SLI experience.

Appendix

All of our programs have been designed to achieve a wide variety of continuing education requirements. Nurses, physicians, healthcare administrators, social workers, counselors, ministers, and others are able to use our programs to fulfill these requirements. SLI supports and cooperates with any group in helping to provide validation for such credits. The programs of the Institute are particularly good at meeting the "ethics" requirements associated with many professional groups.

. . . .

The Institute also has an array of **products**—books, videos, audio disks, and DVD presentations—from faculty and other sources that can be used in both individual and group settings.

. . . .

The Institute's **web site** has a diverse range of articles and announcements that is of continual interest. The web address is: **www.spirit4greatness.com**. For further information on any of the Institute's activities, please contact SLI at 281-240-2121.

Please keep in mind that our programming is spirituality as a common core that unites all people. In this sense, all of our programs are non-sectarian and non-denominational. Our intent is to create meaningful, challenging, and informative conversation and consideration. SLI's purpose is not to change someone's mind, but to open the mind to new perspectives on the challenges we all face in life.

2. LEADERSHIP INSTRUMENTS

The Institute is strongly committed to the goal of creating a dialogue about issues relating to spirituality. Many of these dialogues are, of course, conceptual and theoretical. However, of highest significance, SLI is also committed to exploring and demonstrating the practical application of spiritual leadership. If what we are talking about cannot be *applied* in the most concrete life settings, we would only see ourselves as advocates of interesting and provocative ideas. This would not be enough. Participants do not complete the Institute's programs without a strong emphasis on application.

A major example of applications is our use of measurement instruments. We believe that this spirituality that we are talking about is *measurable* in very important and distinctive ways. To this end, SLI is able to offer expertise in the use of two important instruments. The Hartman Value Profile, and the Spiritual Tendencies Inventory. Additional material on these tools can be found on the SLI web site: www.spirit4greatness.com.

The Hartman Value Profile is the more sophisticated of the two instruments and has a validated history that goes back almost forty years. The concept behind this instrument is that all work has two underlying components—skill set competency and good judgment. Most organizations have gained an ability to measure skill set competency. The Hartman Value Profile allows for the measuring of good judgment. Good judgment, which involves much more than rational thinking or emotional balance, is seen by the Institute as a spiritual quality.

The Hartman Value Profile has four specific applications: enhanced selection and hiring (which can significantly reduce turnover and attrition), a monitor and guide for succession planning and enhanced "bench strength," team building/work unit enhancement, and individual growth and development.

The Spiritual Tendencies Inventory, though newer and more simplistic than the Hartman Value Profile, gives a significant detail of personal information that can be vital to helping individuals understand the strengths and obstacles present in their lives. This information is looked upon as being particularly helpful if a person is facing a situation of malady, stress, injury, illness, or incapacitation. This instrument, and the Hartman Value Profile, have even been used to help physicians better understand the patients they are dealing with.

In a recent MSNBC poll, 63 percent of the American public expressed the desire to have physicians who would be more open to and conversant about their spirituality. Physicians did not object to doing this, but felt that they had no way of doing this in a more scientific manner. Both instruments fulfill this need—again—in a non-sectarian or religiously biased manner.

We also have a **Peer Evaluation Instrument** that is specifically designed to provide a peer assessment based on values, behavior, attitudes, and performance. This instrument allows for the accumulation of information that can lead to important personal growth and performance enhancement.

In many instances, it is interest in these instruments—and especially the workforce selection and Team enhancement issues explored by the Hartman Value Profile—that gives the Institute its first contact with a person or organization. After experiencing these concrete applications of spirituality and values, it often leads an organization to further involvement in the Spiritual Leadership Institute's programs.

3. SELF-STUDY PROGRAM

This text is specifically designed to be used as part of a self-study program that will enhance learning and sustain meaningful recollection of basic ideas and insights. An extensive set of videotapes or audio CDs are available on each of the four key topics—Ethics, Trust, Vision and Spirituality. Interviews between Stephen Byrum, Ph.D. and various members of the primary faculty were conducted on each topic. Effort was consciously made to create conversations that are extension of the text and that did not simply repeat ideas from the text.

In this material the reader will then have the chance to see (or hear) these faculty members reflect in a more informal and immediate manner. In general, most people will listen to the specific section, read the related text section, and—for reinforcement and affirmation—watch/listen to the tape material a second time.

The interviews can be purchased from the Spiritual Leadership Institute. They will be accompanied by a "Self-Study Workbook" that goes so far as to have guided questions and exercises that the participant can complete. These workbook exercises will advance self-discovery and reinforce the ideas in the text. In our regular programs, we include this written text, and encourage participants to get the tapes, read the text, and do the exercises as suggested by the workbook. By doing this, learning is greatly enhanced in a way that makes the ideas experienced in the Institute sessions a true part of a person's consciousness and general fund of knowledge.